GMAT

GRADUATE MANAGEMENT ADMISSION TEST

ARCO PROFESSIONAL CAREER EXAMINATION SERIES

GMAT
GRADUATE MANAGEMENT ADMISSION TEST

ARCO EDITORIAL BOARD

ARCO PUBLISHING, INC.
NEW YORK

Third Edition, Fourth Printing, 1981

Published by Arco Publishing, Inc.
219 Park Avenue South, New York, N.Y. 10003

Copyright © 1980 by Arco Publishing, Inc.

Prior editions copyright © 1977, 1976 by Arco Publishing, Inc.

Library of Congress Cataloging in Publication Data

Arco Publishing, Inc., New York.
  Graduate management admission test.

  1. Management—Examinations, questions, etc.
2. Management—Study and teaching (Graduate)
I. Title.

HD30.4.A68   1979   658.4'0076   79-1214
ISBN 0-668-04917-0 (Library Edition)
ISBN 0-668-04914-6 (Paper Edition)

Printed in the United States of America

CONTENTS

GMAT
GRADUATE MANAGEMENT ADMISSION TEST

TYPICAL FORMAT OF THREE RECENT GMAT EXAMINATIONS

The following are representative of only three recent examinations. Since the Educational Testing Service frequently varies the format of the Graduate Management Admission Test, you must be prepared for all of the question-types presented in this book.

Section	Number of Questions	Time Allowed (in minutes)
Section I: Reading Comprehension (3 passages)	25	30
Section II: Problem Solving	30	40
Section III: Business Judgment		20
Data Evaluation	16	
Data Application	4	
Section IV: Data Sufficiency	30	30
Section V: English Usage	25	15
Section VI: Business Judgment		20
Data Evaluation	15	
Data Application	5	
Section VII: Data Sufficiency	33	25
Total:	183	180

Section	Number of Questions	Time Allowed (in minutes)
Section I: Reading Comprehension (3 passages)	25	30
Section II: Problem Solving	30	40
Section III: Business Judgment		20
Data Evaluation	10	
Data Application	10	
Section IV: Data Sufficiency	30	30
Section V: Verbal Abilities		15
Antonyms	13	
Sentence Completions	12	
Section VI: Business Judgment		20
Data Evaluation	10	
Data Application	10	
Section VII: Reading Comprehension (2 passages)	35	25
Total:	185	180

Section	Number of Questions	Time Allowed (in minutes)
Section I: Reading Comprehension (3 passages)	25	30
Section II: Problem Solving	30	40
Section III: Business Judgment		20
Data Evaluation	10	
Data Application	10	
Section IV: Data Sufficiency	30	30
Section V: English Usage	25	15
Section VI: Business Judgment		20
Data Evaluation	10	
Data Application	10	
Section VII: Validity of Conclusion (4 passages)	37	25
Total:	187	180

Part One

Preliminary Information and Advice

GMAT BACKGROUND INFORMATION

ORIGIN AND PURPOSE

The initiative that led to the development of GMAT came from officials of prominent graduate business schools who shared the belief that a single, uniform test, made available several times a year on a national and international scale, would help to ensure the fairness and effectiveness of their admissions procedures. Representatives of these schools in consultation with the Educational Testing Service agreed on certain important mental abilities which they judged to be essential to success in the study of business at the graduate level and also on types of test material which would satisfactorily measure those abilities. On the basis of these decisions the first forms of the test were designed. Subsequently the test has been revised and improved as the result of careful experimentation with other types of test material.

Used correctly, your "self-tutor" will show you what to expect and will give you a speedy brush-up on the subjects peculiar to your exam. Some of these are subjects not taught in schools at all. Even if your study time is very limited, you should:

- Become familiar with the type of examination you will meet.
- Improve your general examination-taking skill.
- Improve your skill in analyzing and answering questions involving reasoning, judgment, comparison, and evaluation.
- Improve your speed and skill in reading and understanding what you read—an important part of your ability to learn and an important part of most tests.
- Prepare yourself in the particular fields which measure your learning.

This book will tell you exactly what to study by presenting in full every type of question you will get on the actual test. You'll do better merely by familiarizing yourself with them.

This book will help you find your weaknesses and find them fast. Once you know where you're weak you can get right to work (before the test) and concentrate your efforts on those soft spots. This is the kind of selective study which yields maximum test results for every hour spent.

This book will give you the *feel* of the exam. Almost all our sample and practice questions are taken from actual previous exams. Since previous exams are not always available for inspection by the public, these sample test questions are quite important for you. The day you take your exam you'll see how closely this book follows the format of the real test.

This book will give you confidence *now*, while you are preparing for the test. It will build your self-confidence as you proceed. It will beat those dreaded before-test jitters that have hurt so many other test-takers.

There are other things which you should know and which various sections of this book will help you learn. Most important, not only for this examination but for all the examinations to come in your life, is learning how to take a test and how to prepare for it.

HOW TO PREPARE
FOR THE TEST

The Graduate Management Admission Test measures abilities and skills that are developed over a long period of time. It is not designed to test specific knowledge in specialized academic subjects. Normal undergraduate training, therefore, should provide sufficient general knowledge to deal adequately with the test questions which, basically, require you to think clearly and systematically.

Cramming or specialized study for the test is not recommended. The best preparation is careful and continuous study throughout your undergraduate years.

On the other hand, some familiarity with the types of questions on the test should be helpful. For this reason, we advise you to use this book in the following way:

1. Take the Diagnostic Test.
2. Determine your areas of weakness.
3. Answer the practice questions in these weak areas.
4. Take the First Practice Examination.
5. Again determine existing weaknesses.
6. Again remedy those weaknesses by answering practice questions.
7. Proceed in the same manner with the rest of the Practice Examinations.

APPLYING FOR THE TEST *

Sometime during the month before you are to take the test, Educational Testing Service will send you a ticket of admission bearing the date of the test and the exact address of the center to which you should report for assignment to a testing room. You will not be admitted to the test center without your ticket of admission. If you should lose your ticket, write or wire the ETS Princeton office immediately for special authorization to take the test. ETS cannot guarantee last-minute authorization, but will make every effort to help you.

Stapled to the ticket of admission you receive from ETS will be a mailing label giving you information about what time to report for the test, what kind of pencils you should bring, and other important details. This form also bears *your examination number*—the number that identifies all your papers and records at ETS.

It is *extremely important* that you take this form, as well as your ticket of admission, with you to the test center, because you will have to copy your examination number onto your answer sheet before you take the test. If you do not have your examination number, or do not copy it correctly, there may well be considerable delay in identifying your test score and reporting it promptly.

RULES OF CONDUCT FOR THE TEST

So that all candidates may be tested under equally favorable conditions, standard procedures and regulations are observed at every test center. The arrangements supervisors are asked to make, and the regulations examinees are required to observe, are uniform.

Supervisors are asked to arrange for testing rooms free from noise or disturbance. All visitors will be excluded.

If possible, each testing room should have a clock plainly visible to all candidates. Candidates should bring watches.

All tests at all centers will be given strictly according to the same schedule. No candidate will be permitted to continue any test beyond the time limit allowed for that test.

Candidates should bring with them three or four sharpened No. 2 pencils or a mechanical pencil with soft lead, and an eraser. *No pencils or erasers will be furnished at the center*.

Candidates will not be permitted to bring books or papers of any kind (including scratch paper) into the examination room and are strongly urged not to bring them to the examination center at all. Similarly, the use of dictionaries, calculators, protractors, compasses, rulers, or stencils is not permitted. If a candidate is found to have such material with him in the room during the test, he will not be allowed to continue the test. Scratchwork may be done in the margins of the test books.

Candidates wishing to leave the room during a rest period or while the test is in progress should secure permission from the supervisor.

A candidate who gives or receives assistance during the progress of the test will be required to leave the examination room and will not be permitted to return. His test book and answer sheet will be taken from him to be returned to ETS with a note of explanation, and the facts will be made known to the business schools he has named to receive a score report.

All test books and answer sheets must be turned in at the close of the examination. No test materials, documents, or memos of any sort are to be taken from the room. Disregard of this rule will be considered as serious an offense as cheating.

HOW TO TAKE THE TEST

Perhaps the most important point to remember when you take the test is to be sure to read carefully the directions for each section. If you skip over these instructions too hastily, you may miss a main idea and thus lose credit for an entire section.

Although the test stresses accuracy more than speed, it is important for you to use your time as economically as possible. Work steadily and as rapidly as you

*For GMAT information and registration, write to: Graduate Management Admission Test, Educational Testing Service, Box 966, Princeton, New Jersey 08541

can without becoming careless. Take the questions in order, but do not waste time in pondering over questions which contain extremely difficult or unfamiliar material. If you complete a section of the test before time is called, it is wise to go back and reconsider any questions about which you were not certain.

NO "PASSING" OR "FAILING" GRADE

The test is so designed that the average person taking it will answer correctly only about two-thirds of the questions. No one is expected to get a perfect score, and there is no established "passing" or "failing" grade. Your score compares your performance with that of all other candidates taking the test, and the report to the business school shows how far you stand above or below the "average" score for all candidates. The business school considers your total record of college work, references, recommendations, and interviews, as well as your test score, in determining your admission. Each business school will use the test score as it sees fit for this purpose.

SHOULD YOU GUESS?

Many candidates wonder whether or not to guess the answers to questions about which they are not certain. In this test a percentage of the wrong answers will be subtracted from the number of right answers as a correction for haphazard guessing. It is improbable, therefore, that mere guessing will improve your score significantly; it may even lower your score, and it does take time. If, however, you are not sure of the correct answer but have some knowledge of the question and are able to eliminate one or more of the answer choices as wrong, your chance of getting the right answer is improved, and it will be to your advantage to answer such a question.

HOW IMPORTANT ARE THE TEST SCORES?

Since the test scores provide valuable information about fitness for the study of business, many business schools give preference to applicants who have rela-tively high scores. It should be emphasized, however, that no business school admits students solely on the basis of test scores. Consideration is always given to other sources of information about applicants, such as undergraduate record, application forms, the results of interviews, letters of recommendation, and so forth.

Many business schools look for a high standard of performance on the test in making scholarship awards.

Admissions officers often find the test scores useful in discussing with applicants the advisability of attempting the study of business. The test scores may also prove helpful in counseling and guidance work with admitted students.

HOW THE TEST BENEFITS BUSINESS SCHOOLS AND CANDIDATES

The test scores have two very important characteristics: (1) They are a dependable measure of certain mental abilities which have been found to be important in the study of business. (2) The scores are based on the same standard for all candidates, regardless of when they take the test. This uniformity of standards differentiates the scores from undergraduate averages, the meaning of which varies markedly depending on the grading standards of the institution from which they come. By virtue of these two characteristics the test scores provide business schools with a means of increasing the accuracy of comparisons made among applicants. Thus the use of the test scores as a criterion for admission can help a business school to select from among its applicants those who are most likely to do well in their studies.

From the applicant's point of view, the use of the test scores makes it more likely that his abilities will be fairly evaluated. Thus an applicant with only a moderately high undergraduate record from a college with high grading standards is not so likely to lose out when compared with an applicant having a high record from a college where grading standards are relatively low.

Some people look with suspicion on the test, viewing it as an obstacle intended to make it more difficult for them to reach a desired goal. This is understandable among business school applicants who have been rejected partly on the basis of test scores or among candidates for the test who fear that this might happen. However, such an attitude toward the test is based on a misinterpretation of its purpose and function. Properly used, it can bring about a large saving in time, money and energy both for the business school and for the applicant who may not be adequately equipped to pursue profitably the study of business. It is much better that an applicant be forewarned of probable difficulty in a business school he has applied to than to struggle through his first year only to fail at the end of it.

WHAT THE TEST MEASURES

As with any test, the scores on this test can be best understood by thinking of the purpose for which the scores are used. Many faulty interpretations of test scores can be traced to a misunderstanding of the job the test is supposed to do. The test was designed primarily to predict success in graduate business schools. The test has been judged successful in performing its job because it has been found that the higher a student scores, the better are his chances of succeeding in business school. The name Graduate Management Admission Test was chosen to describe this primary function of the test.

It may help to clarify this question of purpose if we consider for a moment the kinds of information that cannot be expected from the test scores. First of all, the Graduate Management Admission Test (GMAT) is not an intelligence test. Although many of the items in the test are similar to those that are used in intelligence tests, it would be particularly unfortunate to interpret any of your scores as an I. Q. The test does not have as its aim the classification of students into categories of intelligence, nor has any formal evidence been collected to determine whether the test could be used successfully for such a purpose. No doubt, the abilities and aptitudes generally thought of as making up general intelligence are related to success in business school and are also related to scores on the Graduate Management Admission Test (GMAT), but this does not justify interpreting the scores as I. Q.'s.

A second unfortunate misinterpretation would be to think of the test scores as an indication of probable success on a job. No formal evidence has been collected relating scores on this test to job success in the fields of business, much less in other fields. Again, it seems safe to assume that there is *some* relationship between test scores and success in business—since

the test does predict success in business school and since we have every reason to believe that success in business school is related to success in business—but the extent of the relationship is unknown.

Having considered what the scores do *not* tell us, let us now return to what they do tell us. It was mentioned earlier that it has been found that, in general, the higher a student's score the better his chances of succeeding in business school. ETS has established this relationship between test scores and success in business school by experimental studies. A number of business schools throughout the country required their applicants to take the test. The test scores of accepted students were kept on file until grades were available for these same students. Then grades and test scores were compared to determine whether the scores could be used effectively to sort out the better business students from the poorer students. This kind of analysis is known as a validity study.

The validity studies of the test demonstrated that it effectively predicts which students are most likely to do well at business school. The correlation between test scores and grades is not perfect; we cannot be *certain* that an applicant will or will not perform well. The scores must be interpreted in terms of the probability of an applicant's success. That is, when a school receives an applicant's score, it is possible to state the odds that he will successfully complete his course work at that business school. The higher the score the more favorable the odds.

HOW THE SCORES ARE INTERPRETED

There are many reasons why we cannot expect a test to provide perfect predictions of performance in graduate business schools. The most obvious is that it is impossible for a test to measure all of the factors that are instrumental in determining whether an individual student will be successful. We do not know all of these factors; and among those that we do know at present there are some that are not amenable to testing of the kind done in the present program.

Because the business schools are well aware that the test does not measure all of the relevant characteristics, they use the test as a source of only one kind of information in a large pool of information about each applicant. The evidence indicates that undergraduate record is, on the average, at least as good a predictor as the test scores and most schools give it as much weight as the scores. Indeed, an admissions officer may on occasion discount mediocre test scores when they are counter-balanced by good college grades from an institution in which he has confidence. Information as to your interest in business, your willingness to apply yourself, and your character, as obtained from your application, interviews, and letters of recommendation is also included in the pool of information. In general, letters of recommendation and interviews are given the least weight in the pool of information but they could be the deciding factors in a choice between two applicants whose test scores and undergraduate records and averages are quite similar.

ETS does not set a passing or failing score on the test. Each school evaluates the scores in its own way. Of course, a total score of 700 would be considered high at any school and a score of 300 would be low, but there is a wide range of scores around 500 which cannot be considered high or low in any absolute sense. Different schools judge the scores by different standards and what may be considered a mediocre score at one school may be considered quite satisfactory at another.

In a few cases, there may be special circumstances which the admissions officer will want to keep in mind when considering a test score. He may, for example, give weight to special conditions, such as illness at the time of taking the test, which may have handicapped a candidate.

Obviously you cannot expect to be told your chances of succeeding at every business school in the country. One important practical implication does follow, however, from this discussion. You should apply to several schools. It is an unfortunate mistake to give up when a business school turns you down because your score is too low. The school that turns you down may have had an unusually large number of applicants, or it may place more weight on the score than do other schools. It is a common occurrence for students rejected by some schools to be accepted by others. Your undergraduate advisor may be very helpful in this connection. Possibly on the basis of his experience he may be able to suggest schools to which it would be most suitable for you to apply.

EVALUATING THE SCORES

The score scales for the Graduate Management Admission Test were established during the first two years of the test's existence. A reference or standardization group of examinees was chosen and the numbers 200 through 800 were assigned to their papers in accordance with the total raw scores they had received and in such a way that 500 was the average total score and about two-thirds of the group received scores between 400 and 600.

With your scores, you will receive a memorandum describing the score system and giving distributions of the scores for a large group of applicants. The distributions of scores, which give the percentages of candidates whose scores fall below each of several selected scores, will enable you to determine your standing among all applicants who have taken the test over a number of years. If your scores are very high in this group your chances of being accepted are quite good, whereas if your scores are very low you are less likely to be accepted although the exact degree of likelihood will vary depending on the schools to which you apply.

When you compare your scores with the distributions or if you should compare scores with your friends, there is one point you should remember: scores on the Graduate Management Admission Test, and in fact scores on any test, are not perfectly reliable. You should think of your score as representing a small range of scores within which your true score lies. In other words, if your score total is 500, it would be appropriate to say that your true score lies somewhere between 470 and 530. Thought of in this way, your score of 500 is not really different from scores of 515 and 490 obtained by two of your friends.

EFFECTIVE TEST TAKING

FOLLOW DIRECTIONS CAREFULLY

It's an obvious rule, but more people fail for breaching it than for any other cause. By actual count there are over a hundred types of directions given on tests. You'll familiarize yourself with all of them in the course of this book. And you'll also learn not to let your guard down in reading them, listening to them, and following them. Right now, before you plunge in, we want to be sure that you have nothing to fear from the answer sheet and the way in which you must mark it, or from the most important question forms and the ways in which they are to be answered.

HOW TO ANSWER QUESTIONS

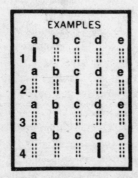

Make only ONE mark for each answer. Additional and stray marks may be counted as mistakes. In making corrections, erase errors COMPLETELY.

Each pencil mark must be heavy and black. Light marks should be retraced with the special pencil.

Each mark must be in the space provided for the question you are answering. Fill in the entire answer space.

All stray pencil marks on the paper, clearly not intended as answers, must be completely erased.

Each question must have only one answer indicated. If multiple answers occur, all extraneous marks should be thoroughly erased. Otherwise, the machine will give you *no* credit for your correct answer.

MULTIPLE CHOICE METHODS

As the GMAT utilizes a multiple choice format, we have outlined below some methods for approaching multiple choice questions which we feel are the most effective.

You know, of course, that these questions offer you four or five possible answers, that your job is to select *only* the *best* answer, and that even the incorrect answers are frequently *partly* correct. These partly true choices are inserted to force you to think . . . and prove that you know the right answer. Here are eight steps that should help you arrive at the correct answer.

1. Read the item closely to see what the examiner is after. Reread it if necessary.
2. Mentally reject answers that are clearly wrong.
3. Suspect as being wrong any of the choices which contain broad statements hinging on "cue" words like

absolute	*inordinately*
absolutely	*irrefutable*
all	*inviolable*
always	*never*
axiomatic	*only*
categorical	*peculiarly*
completely	*positive*
doubtless	*quite*
entirely	*self-evident*
extravagantly	*sole*
forever	*totally*
immeasurably	*unchallenged*
inalienable	*unchangeable*
incontestable	*undeniable*
incontrovertible	*undoubtedly*
indefinitely	*unequivocal*
indisputable	*unexceptionable*

indubitable   unimpeachable
inevitable   unqualified
inexorable   unquestionable
infallible   wholly
infinite   without exception
inflexible

If you're unsure of the meanings of any of these words, look them up in your dictionary.

4. A well-constructed multiple choice item will avoid obviously incorrect choices. The good examiner will try to write a cluster of answers, all of which are plausible. Use the clue words to help yourself pick the *most* correct answer.

5. In the case of items where you are doubtful of the answer, you might be able to bring to bear the information you have gained from previous study. This knowledge might be sufficient to indicate that some of the suggested answers are not so plausible. Eliminate such answers from further consideration.

6. Then concentrate on the remaining suggested answers. The more you eliminate in this way, the better your chances of getting the item right.

7. If the item is in the form of an incomplete statement, it sometimes helps to try to complete the statement before you look at the suggested answers. Then see whether the way you have completed the statement corresponds with any of the answers provided. If one is found, it is likely to be the correct one.

8. Use your head! Make shrewd inferences. Sometimes with a little thought, and the information that you have, you can reason out the answer. We're suggesting a method of intelligent guessing in which you can become quite expert with a little practice. It's a useful method that may help you with some debatable answers.

Multiple-Choice Methods

1. Leather is considered the best material for shoes chiefly because
   (A) it is waterproof
   (B) it is quite durable
   (C) it is easily procurable
   (D) it is flexible and durable
   (E) it can easily be manufactured in various styles

Here we see that every one of the answer statements is plausible: leather is waterproof if treated properly; it is relatively durable; it is relatively easily procurable; it bends and is shaped easily, and is, again, durable; it constantly appears in various styles of shoes and boots.

However, we must examine the question with an eye toward identifying the key phrase, which is: *best for shoes chiefly.*

Now we can see that (A) is incorrect because leather is probably not the *best* material for shoes, simply because it is waterproof. There are far better waterproof materials available, such as plastics and rubber. In fact, leather must be treated to make it waterproof. So by analyzing the key phrase of the question we can eliminate (A).

(B) seems plausible. Leather is durable, and durability is a good quality in shoes. But the word *quite* makes it a broad statement. And we become suspicious. The original meaning of *quite* is completely, wholly, entirely. Since such is the case we must reject this choice because leather is *not completely* durable. It does wear out.

(C) Leather is comparatively easy to procure; but would that make it *best* for shoes? And would that be the *chief* reason why it is used for making shoes? Although the statement in itself is quite true, it does not fit the key phrase of the question and we must, reluctantly, eliminate it.

(D) is a double-barreled statement. One part, the durability, has been suggested in (B) above. Leather is also quite flexible, so both parts of the statement would seem to fit the question.

(E) It is true that leather can be manufactured in various styles, but so can many other materials. Again, going back to the key phrase, this could be considered one, but not the *chief* reason why it is *best* for shoes.

So, by carefully analyzing the *key* phrase of the question we have narrowed our choices down to (D). Although we rejected (B) we did recognize that durability is a good quality in shoes, but only one of several. Since flexibility is also a good quality, we have no hesitation in choosing (D) as the correct answer.

The same question, by slightly altering the answer choices, can also call for a *negative* response. Here, even more so, the identification of the key phrase becomes vital in finding the correct answer. Suppose the question and its responses were worded thus:

2. Leather is considered the best material for shoes chiefly because

(A) it is waterproof
(B) it is easily colored
(C) it is easily procurable
(D) it can easily be manufactured in various styles
(E) none of these

We can see that the prior partially correct answer (B) has now been changed, and the doubly correct answer eliminated. Instead we have a new response possibility (E), "none of these."

We have analyzed three of the choices previously and have seen the reason why none of them is the *chief* reason why leather is considered the *best* material for shoes. The two new elements are (B) "easily colored," and (E) "none of these."

If you think about it, leather *can* be easily colored and often is, but this would not be the chief reason why it is considered *best*. Many other materials are just as easily dyed. So we must come to the conclusion that *none* of the choices is *completely* correct—none fits the key phrase. Therefore, the question calls for a negative response (E).

We have now seen how important it is to identify the key phrase. Equally, or perhaps even more important, is the identifying and analyzing of the key *word*—the qualifying word—in a question. This is usually, though not always, an adjective or adverb. Some of the key words to watch for are: *most, best, least, highest, lowest, always, never, sometimes, most likely, greatest, smallest, tallest, average, easiest, most nearly, maximum, minimum, chiefly, mainly, only, but* and *or*. Identifying these key words is usually half the battle in understanding and, consequently, answering all types of exam questions.

REPHRASING THE QUESTION

It is obvious, then, that by carefully analyzing a question, by identifying the key phrase and its key words, you can usually find the correct answer by logical deduction and, often, by elimination. One other way of examining, or "dissecting," a question is to restate or rephrase it with each of the suggested answer choices integrated into the question.

For example, we can take the same question and rephrase it.

(A) The chief reason why leather is considered the best material for shoes is that it is waterproof.
or

(A) Because it is waterproof, leather is considered the best material for shoes.
or

(A) Chiefly because it is waterproof, leather is considered the best material for shoes.

It will be seen from the above three new versions of the original statement and answer that the question has become less obscure because it has been, so to speak, illuminated from different angles. It becomes quite obvious also in this rephrasing that the statement (A) is incorrect, although the *original* phrasing of the question left some doubt.

The rules for understanding and analyzing the key phrase and key words in a question, and the way to identify the *one* correct answer by means of intelligent analysis of the important question-answer elements, are basic to the solution of all the problems you will face on your test.

In fact, perhaps the *main* reason for failing an examination is failure to *understand the question*. In many cases, examinees *do* know the answer to a particular problem, but they cannot answer correctly because they do not understand it.

Part Two

Diagnostic Examination

DIAGNOSTIC EXAMINATION FOR THE GMAT

The ARCO Diagnostic Exam is designed to test your ability to answer all types of questions found in recently administered versions of the GMAT. While the actual GMAT will contain only six or seven of the nine different question-types found in this exam, there is no way of knowing which types of questions with which you will be tested. The Diagnostic Examination is intended to help you discover where your strengths and weaknesses lie.

Take this examination as if you were taking the real test. Follow all instructions and time yourself accordingly. Remember to mark all your answers on the Answer Sheet which is similar to the one you will find on the actual examination. After completing the test, check your answers with those provided in the Answer Key following the last section. Explanatory Answers are also provided.

Determine your score and evaluate your performance by referring to the Unofficial Percentile Ranking Table and the Diagnostic Table found after the Explanatory Answers. For extra help with each question-type, consult Part Four of this book, the Review of Subject Areas and Question Types for the GMAT. These will allow you to concentrate on those areas in which your scores on the Diagnostic Exam indicate you need the most work.

ANALYSIS AND TIMETABLE: DIAGNOSTIC EXAMINATION

Subject Tested	Time Allowed
READING COMPREHENSION	20 minutes
PROBLEM SOLVING	35 minutes
PRACTICAL BUSINESS JUDGMENT	20 minutes
DATA INTERPRETATION	15 minutes
DATA SUFFICIENCY	20 minutes
READING RECALL	30 minutes
ENGLISH USAGE	15 minutes
VERBAL ABILITIES	15 minutes
VALIDITY OF CONCLUSION	30 minutes

ANSWER SHEET
DIAGNOSTIC EXAMINATION
SECTION I: READING COMPREHENSION

1 Ⓐ Ⓑ Ⓒ Ⓓ Ⓔ   4 Ⓐ Ⓑ Ⓒ Ⓓ Ⓔ   7 Ⓐ Ⓑ Ⓒ Ⓓ Ⓔ   10 Ⓐ Ⓑ Ⓒ Ⓓ Ⓔ   13 Ⓐ Ⓑ Ⓒ Ⓓ Ⓔ   16 Ⓐ Ⓑ Ⓒ Ⓓ Ⓔ

2 Ⓐ Ⓑ Ⓒ Ⓓ Ⓔ   5 Ⓐ Ⓑ Ⓒ Ⓓ Ⓔ   8 Ⓐ Ⓑ Ⓒ Ⓓ Ⓔ   11 Ⓐ Ⓑ Ⓒ Ⓓ Ⓔ   14 Ⓐ Ⓑ Ⓒ Ⓓ Ⓔ   17 Ⓐ Ⓑ Ⓒ Ⓓ Ⓔ

3 Ⓐ Ⓑ Ⓒ Ⓓ Ⓔ   6 Ⓐ Ⓑ Ⓒ Ⓓ Ⓔ   9 Ⓐ Ⓑ Ⓒ Ⓓ Ⓔ   12 Ⓐ Ⓑ Ⓒ Ⓓ Ⓔ   15 Ⓐ Ⓑ Ⓒ Ⓓ Ⓔ   18 Ⓐ Ⓑ Ⓒ Ⓓ Ⓔ

SECTION II: PROBLEM SOLVING

1 Ⓐ Ⓑ Ⓒ Ⓓ Ⓔ   6 Ⓐ Ⓑ Ⓒ Ⓓ Ⓔ   11 Ⓐ Ⓑ Ⓒ Ⓓ Ⓔ   16 Ⓐ Ⓑ Ⓒ Ⓓ Ⓔ   21 Ⓐ Ⓑ Ⓒ Ⓓ Ⓔ

2 Ⓐ Ⓑ Ⓒ Ⓓ Ⓔ   7 Ⓐ Ⓑ Ⓒ Ⓓ Ⓔ   12 Ⓐ Ⓑ Ⓒ Ⓓ Ⓔ   17 Ⓐ Ⓑ Ⓒ Ⓓ Ⓔ   22 Ⓐ Ⓑ Ⓒ Ⓓ Ⓔ

3 Ⓐ Ⓑ Ⓒ Ⓓ Ⓔ   8 Ⓐ Ⓑ Ⓒ Ⓓ Ⓔ   13 Ⓐ Ⓑ Ⓒ Ⓓ Ⓔ   18 Ⓐ Ⓑ Ⓒ Ⓓ Ⓔ   23 Ⓐ Ⓑ Ⓒ Ⓓ Ⓔ

4 Ⓐ Ⓑ Ⓒ Ⓓ Ⓔ   9 Ⓐ Ⓑ Ⓒ Ⓓ Ⓔ   14 Ⓐ Ⓑ Ⓒ Ⓓ Ⓔ   19 Ⓐ Ⓑ Ⓒ Ⓓ Ⓔ   24 Ⓐ Ⓑ Ⓒ Ⓓ Ⓔ

5 Ⓐ Ⓑ Ⓒ Ⓓ Ⓔ   10 Ⓐ Ⓑ Ⓒ Ⓓ Ⓔ   15 Ⓐ Ⓑ Ⓒ Ⓓ Ⓔ   20 Ⓐ Ⓑ Ⓒ Ⓓ Ⓔ   25 Ⓐ Ⓑ Ⓒ Ⓓ Ⓔ

SECTION III: PRACTICAL BUSINESS JUDGMENT

1 Ⓐ Ⓑ Ⓒ Ⓓ Ⓔ   5 Ⓐ Ⓑ Ⓒ Ⓓ Ⓔ   9 Ⓐ Ⓑ Ⓒ Ⓓ Ⓔ   13 Ⓐ Ⓑ Ⓒ Ⓓ Ⓔ   17 Ⓐ Ⓑ Ⓒ Ⓓ Ⓔ

2 Ⓐ Ⓑ Ⓒ Ⓓ Ⓔ   6 Ⓐ Ⓑ Ⓒ Ⓓ Ⓔ   10 Ⓐ Ⓑ Ⓒ Ⓓ Ⓔ   14 Ⓐ Ⓑ Ⓒ Ⓓ Ⓔ   18 Ⓐ Ⓑ Ⓒ Ⓓ Ⓔ

3 Ⓐ Ⓑ Ⓒ Ⓓ Ⓔ   7 Ⓐ Ⓑ Ⓒ Ⓓ Ⓔ   11 Ⓐ Ⓑ Ⓒ Ⓓ Ⓔ   15 Ⓐ Ⓑ Ⓒ Ⓓ Ⓔ   19 Ⓐ Ⓑ Ⓒ Ⓓ Ⓔ

4 Ⓐ Ⓑ Ⓒ Ⓓ Ⓔ   8 Ⓐ Ⓑ Ⓒ Ⓓ Ⓔ   12 Ⓐ Ⓑ Ⓒ Ⓓ Ⓔ   16 Ⓐ Ⓑ Ⓒ Ⓓ Ⓔ   20 Ⓐ Ⓑ Ⓒ Ⓓ Ⓔ

SECTION IV: DATA INTERPRETATION

1 Ⓐ Ⓑ Ⓒ Ⓓ Ⓔ   4 Ⓐ Ⓑ Ⓒ Ⓓ Ⓔ   7 Ⓐ Ⓑ Ⓒ Ⓓ Ⓔ   10 Ⓐ Ⓑ Ⓒ Ⓓ Ⓔ   13 Ⓐ Ⓑ Ⓒ Ⓓ Ⓔ

2 Ⓐ Ⓑ Ⓒ Ⓓ Ⓔ   5 Ⓐ Ⓑ Ⓒ Ⓓ Ⓔ   8 Ⓐ Ⓑ Ⓒ Ⓓ Ⓔ   11 Ⓐ Ⓑ Ⓒ Ⓓ Ⓔ   14 Ⓐ Ⓑ Ⓒ Ⓓ Ⓔ

3 Ⓐ Ⓑ Ⓒ Ⓓ Ⓔ   6 Ⓐ Ⓑ Ⓒ Ⓓ Ⓔ   9 Ⓐ Ⓑ Ⓒ Ⓓ Ⓔ   12 Ⓐ Ⓑ Ⓒ Ⓓ Ⓔ   15 Ⓐ Ⓑ Ⓒ Ⓓ Ⓔ

SECTION V: DATA SUFFICIENCY

1 Ⓐ Ⓑ Ⓒ Ⓓ Ⓔ   5 Ⓐ Ⓑ Ⓒ Ⓓ Ⓔ   9 Ⓐ Ⓑ Ⓒ Ⓓ Ⓔ   13 Ⓐ Ⓑ Ⓒ Ⓓ Ⓔ

2 Ⓐ Ⓑ Ⓒ Ⓓ Ⓔ   6 Ⓐ Ⓑ Ⓒ Ⓓ Ⓔ   10 Ⓐ Ⓑ Ⓒ Ⓓ Ⓔ   14 Ⓐ Ⓑ Ⓒ Ⓓ Ⓔ

3 Ⓐ Ⓑ Ⓒ Ⓓ Ⓔ   7 Ⓐ Ⓑ Ⓒ Ⓓ Ⓔ   11 Ⓐ Ⓑ Ⓒ Ⓓ Ⓔ   15 Ⓐ Ⓑ Ⓒ Ⓓ Ⓔ

4 Ⓐ Ⓑ Ⓒ Ⓓ Ⓔ   8 Ⓐ Ⓑ Ⓒ Ⓓ Ⓔ   12 Ⓐ Ⓑ Ⓒ Ⓓ Ⓔ   16 Ⓐ Ⓑ Ⓒ Ⓓ Ⓔ

SECTION VI: READING RECALL

1 Ⓐ Ⓑ Ⓒ Ⓓ Ⓔ 6 Ⓐ Ⓑ Ⓒ Ⓓ Ⓔ 11 Ⓐ Ⓑ Ⓒ Ⓓ Ⓔ 15 Ⓐ Ⓑ Ⓒ Ⓓ Ⓔ 19 Ⓐ Ⓑ Ⓒ Ⓓ Ⓔ 23 Ⓐ Ⓑ Ⓒ Ⓓ Ⓔ
2 Ⓐ Ⓑ Ⓒ Ⓓ Ⓔ 7 Ⓐ Ⓑ Ⓒ Ⓓ Ⓔ 12 Ⓐ Ⓑ Ⓒ Ⓓ Ⓔ 16 Ⓐ Ⓑ Ⓒ Ⓓ Ⓔ 20 Ⓐ Ⓑ Ⓒ Ⓓ Ⓔ 24 Ⓐ Ⓑ Ⓒ Ⓓ Ⓔ
3 Ⓐ Ⓑ Ⓒ Ⓓ Ⓔ 8 Ⓐ Ⓑ Ⓒ Ⓓ Ⓔ 13 Ⓐ Ⓑ Ⓒ Ⓓ Ⓔ 17 Ⓐ Ⓑ Ⓒ Ⓓ Ⓔ 21 Ⓐ Ⓑ Ⓒ Ⓓ Ⓔ 25 Ⓐ Ⓑ Ⓒ Ⓓ Ⓔ
4 Ⓐ Ⓑ Ⓒ Ⓓ Ⓔ 9 Ⓐ Ⓑ Ⓒ Ⓓ Ⓔ 14 Ⓐ Ⓑ Ⓒ Ⓓ Ⓔ 18 Ⓐ Ⓑ Ⓒ Ⓓ Ⓔ 22 Ⓐ Ⓑ Ⓒ Ⓓ Ⓔ 26 Ⓐ Ⓑ Ⓒ Ⓓ Ⓔ
5 Ⓐ Ⓑ Ⓒ Ⓓ Ⓔ 10 Ⓐ Ⓑ Ⓒ Ⓓ Ⓔ

SECTION VII: ENGLISH USAGE

1 Ⓐ Ⓑ Ⓒ Ⓓ Ⓔ 6 Ⓐ Ⓑ Ⓒ Ⓓ Ⓔ 11 Ⓐ Ⓑ Ⓒ Ⓓ Ⓔ 16 Ⓐ Ⓑ Ⓒ Ⓓ Ⓔ 21 Ⓐ Ⓑ Ⓒ Ⓓ Ⓔ
2 Ⓐ Ⓑ Ⓒ Ⓓ Ⓔ 7 Ⓐ Ⓑ Ⓒ Ⓓ Ⓔ 12 Ⓐ Ⓑ Ⓒ Ⓓ Ⓔ 17 Ⓐ Ⓑ Ⓒ Ⓓ Ⓔ 22 Ⓐ Ⓑ Ⓒ Ⓓ Ⓔ
3 Ⓐ Ⓑ Ⓒ Ⓓ Ⓔ 8 Ⓐ Ⓑ Ⓒ Ⓓ Ⓔ 13 Ⓐ Ⓑ Ⓒ Ⓓ Ⓔ 18 Ⓐ Ⓑ Ⓒ Ⓓ Ⓔ 23 Ⓐ Ⓑ Ⓒ Ⓓ Ⓔ
4 Ⓐ Ⓑ Ⓒ Ⓓ Ⓔ 9 Ⓐ Ⓑ Ⓒ Ⓓ Ⓔ 14 Ⓐ Ⓑ Ⓒ Ⓓ Ⓔ 19 Ⓐ Ⓑ Ⓒ Ⓓ Ⓔ 24 Ⓐ Ⓑ Ⓒ Ⓓ Ⓔ
5 Ⓐ Ⓑ Ⓒ Ⓓ Ⓔ 10 Ⓐ Ⓑ Ⓒ Ⓓ Ⓔ 15 Ⓐ Ⓑ Ⓒ Ⓓ Ⓔ 20 Ⓐ Ⓑ Ⓒ Ⓓ Ⓔ 25 Ⓐ Ⓑ Ⓒ Ⓓ Ⓔ

SECTION VIII: VERBAL ABILITIES

1 Ⓐ Ⓑ Ⓒ Ⓓ Ⓔ 6 Ⓐ Ⓑ Ⓒ Ⓓ Ⓔ 11 Ⓐ Ⓑ Ⓒ Ⓓ Ⓔ 16 Ⓐ Ⓑ Ⓒ Ⓓ Ⓔ 21 Ⓐ Ⓑ Ⓒ Ⓓ Ⓔ
2 Ⓐ Ⓑ Ⓒ Ⓓ Ⓔ 7 Ⓐ Ⓑ Ⓒ Ⓓ Ⓔ 12 Ⓐ Ⓑ Ⓒ Ⓓ Ⓔ 17 Ⓐ Ⓑ Ⓒ Ⓓ Ⓔ 22 Ⓐ Ⓑ Ⓒ Ⓓ Ⓔ
3 Ⓐ Ⓑ Ⓒ Ⓓ Ⓔ 8 Ⓐ Ⓑ Ⓒ Ⓓ Ⓔ 13 Ⓐ Ⓑ Ⓒ Ⓓ Ⓔ 18 Ⓐ Ⓑ Ⓒ Ⓓ Ⓔ 23 Ⓐ Ⓑ Ⓒ Ⓓ Ⓔ
4 Ⓐ Ⓑ Ⓒ Ⓓ Ⓔ 9 Ⓐ Ⓑ Ⓒ Ⓓ Ⓔ 14 Ⓐ Ⓑ Ⓒ Ⓓ Ⓔ 19 Ⓐ Ⓑ Ⓒ Ⓓ Ⓔ 24 Ⓐ Ⓑ Ⓒ Ⓓ Ⓔ
5 Ⓐ Ⓑ Ⓒ Ⓓ Ⓔ 10 Ⓐ Ⓑ Ⓒ Ⓓ Ⓔ 15 Ⓐ Ⓑ Ⓒ Ⓓ Ⓔ 20 Ⓐ Ⓑ Ⓒ Ⓓ Ⓔ 25 Ⓐ Ⓑ Ⓒ Ⓓ Ⓔ

SECTION IX: VALIDITY OF CONCLUSION

1 Ⓐ Ⓑ Ⓒ Ⓓ Ⓔ 8 Ⓐ Ⓑ Ⓒ Ⓓ Ⓔ 15 Ⓐ Ⓑ Ⓒ Ⓓ Ⓔ 22 Ⓐ Ⓑ Ⓒ Ⓓ Ⓔ 29 Ⓐ Ⓑ Ⓒ Ⓓ Ⓔ 36 Ⓐ Ⓑ Ⓒ Ⓓ Ⓔ
2 Ⓐ Ⓑ Ⓒ Ⓓ Ⓔ 9 Ⓐ Ⓑ Ⓒ Ⓓ Ⓔ 16 Ⓐ Ⓑ Ⓒ Ⓓ Ⓔ 23 Ⓐ Ⓑ Ⓒ Ⓓ Ⓔ 30 Ⓐ Ⓑ Ⓒ Ⓓ Ⓔ 37 Ⓐ Ⓑ Ⓒ Ⓓ Ⓔ
3 Ⓐ Ⓑ Ⓒ Ⓓ Ⓔ 10 Ⓐ Ⓑ Ⓒ Ⓓ Ⓔ 17 Ⓐ Ⓑ Ⓒ Ⓓ Ⓔ 24 Ⓐ Ⓑ Ⓒ Ⓓ Ⓔ 31 Ⓐ Ⓑ Ⓒ Ⓓ Ⓔ 38 Ⓐ Ⓑ Ⓒ Ⓓ Ⓔ
4 Ⓐ Ⓑ Ⓒ Ⓓ Ⓔ 11 Ⓐ Ⓑ Ⓒ Ⓓ Ⓔ 18 Ⓐ Ⓑ Ⓒ Ⓓ Ⓔ 25 Ⓐ Ⓑ Ⓒ Ⓓ Ⓔ 32 Ⓐ Ⓑ Ⓒ Ⓓ Ⓔ 39 Ⓐ Ⓑ Ⓒ Ⓓ Ⓔ
5 Ⓐ Ⓑ Ⓒ Ⓓ Ⓔ 12 Ⓐ Ⓑ Ⓒ Ⓓ Ⓔ 19 Ⓐ Ⓑ Ⓒ Ⓓ Ⓔ 26 Ⓐ Ⓑ Ⓒ Ⓓ Ⓔ 33 Ⓐ Ⓑ Ⓒ Ⓓ Ⓔ
6 Ⓐ Ⓑ Ⓒ Ⓓ Ⓔ 13 Ⓐ Ⓑ Ⓒ Ⓓ Ⓔ 20 Ⓐ Ⓑ Ⓒ Ⓓ Ⓔ 27 Ⓐ Ⓑ Ⓒ Ⓓ Ⓔ 34 Ⓐ Ⓑ Ⓒ Ⓓ Ⓔ
7 Ⓐ Ⓑ Ⓒ Ⓓ Ⓔ 14 Ⓐ Ⓑ Ⓒ Ⓓ Ⓔ 21 Ⓐ Ⓑ Ⓒ Ⓓ Ⓔ 28 Ⓐ Ⓑ Ⓒ Ⓓ Ⓔ 35 Ⓐ Ⓑ Ⓒ Ⓓ Ⓔ

SECTION I: READING COMPREHENSION

20 Minutes
18 Questions

DIRECTIONS: Below each of the following passages, you will find questions or incomplete statements about the passage. Each statement or question is followed by five lettered words or expressions. Select the word or expression that most satisfactorily completes each statement or answers each question in accordance with the meaning of the passage.

Shams and delusions are esteemed for soundest truths, while reality is fabulous. If men would steadily observe realities only, and not allow themselves to be deluded, life, to compare it with such things as we know, would be like a fairy tale and the Arabian Nights' entertainments. If we respected only what is inevitable and has a right to be, music and poetry would resound along the streets. When we are unhurried and wise, we perceive that only great and worthy things have any permanent and absolute existence—that petty fears and petty pleasures are but the shadow of the reality. This is always exhilarating and sublime. By closing the eyes and slumbering, and consenting to be deceived by shows, men establish and confirm their daily life of routine and habit everywhere, which still is built on purely illusory foundations. Children, who play life, discern its true law and relations more clearly than men, who fail to live it worthily, but who think that they are wiser by experience; that is, by failure. I have read in a Hindu book that "there was a king's son who, being expelled in infancy from his native city, was brought up by a forester, and, growing up to maturity in that state, imagined himself to belong to the barbarous race with which he lived. One of his father's ministers having discovered him, revealed to him what he was, and the misconception of his character was removed, and he knew himself to be a prince. "So soul," continues the Hindu philosopher, "from the circumstances in which it is placed, mistakes its own character, until the truth is revealed to it by some holy teacher, and then it knows itself to be *Brahme*." We think that that *is* which *appears* to be. If a man should give us an account of the realities he beheld, we should not recognize the place in his description. Look at a meeting-house, or a court-house, or a jail, or a shop, or a dwelling-house, and say what that thing really is before a true gaze, and they would all go to pieces in your account of them. Men esteem truth remote, in the outskirts of the system, behind the farthest star, before Adam and after the last man. In eternity there is indeed something true and sublime. But all these times and places and occasions are now and here. God himself culminates in the present moment, and will never be more divine in the lapse of all ages. And we are enabled to apprehend at all what is sublime and noble only by the perpetual instilling and drenching of the reality that surrounds us. The universe constantly and obediently answers to our conceptions; whether we travel fast or slow, the track is laid for us. Let us spend our lives in conceiving then. The poet or the artist never yet had so fair and noble a design but some of his posterity at least could accomplish it.

1. The writer's attitude toward the arts is one of

(A) indifference
(B) suspicion
(C) admiration
(D) repulsion
(E) flippancy

2. The author believes that a child

(A) should practice what the Hindus preach
(B) frequently faces vital problems better than grownups do
(C) prefers to be a barbarian than to be a prince
(D) hardly ever knows his true origin
(E) is incapable of appreciating the arts

19

3. The passage implies that human beings

   (A) cannot distinguish the true from the untrue
   (B) are immoral if they are lazy
   (C) should be bold and fearless
   (D) believe in fairy tales
   (E) have progressed culturally throughout history

4. The word ''fabulous'' in the second line means

   (A) wonderful
   (B) delicious
   (C) birdlike
   (D) incomprehensible
   (E) nonexistent

5. The author is primarily concerned with urging the reader to

   (A) meditate on the meaninglessness of the present
   (B) look to the future for enlightenment
   (C) appraise the present for its true value
   (D) honor the wisdom of past ages
   (E) spend more time in leisure activities

6. The passage is primarily concerned with problems of

   (A) history and economics
   (B) society and population
   (C) biology and physics
   (D) theology and philosophy
   (E) music and art

Suppose you go into a fruiterer's shop, wanting an apple—you take up one, and, on biting it, you find it is sour; you look at it, and see that it is hard and green. You take up another one, and that too is hard, green, and sour. The shopman offers you a third; but, before biting it, you examine it, and find that it is hard and green, and you immediately say that you will not have it, as it must be sour, like those that you have already tried.

Nothing can be more simple than that, you think; but if you will take the trouble to analyse and trace out into its logical elements what has been done by the mind, you will be greatly surprised. In the first place you have performed the operation of induction. You found that, in two experiences, hardness and greenness in apples went together with sourness. It was so in the first case, and it was confirmed by the second. True, it is a very small basis, but still it is enough to make an induction from; you generalise the facts, and you expect to find sourness in apples where you get hardness and greenness. You found upon that a general law, that all hard and green apples are sour; and that, so far as it goes, is a perfect induction. Well, having got your natural law in this way, when you are offered another apple which you find is hard and green, you say, ''All hard and green apples are sour; this apple is hard and green, therefore this apple is sour.'' That train of reasoning is what logicians call a syllogism, and has all its various parts and terms—its major premiss, its minor premiss, and its conclusion. And, by the help of further reasoning, which, if drawn out, would have to be exhibited in two or three other syllogisms, you arrive at your final determination, ''I will not have that apple.'' So that, you see, you have, in the first place, established a law by induction, and upon that you have founded a deduction, and reasoned out the special particular case. Well now, suppose, having got your conclusion of the law, that at some times afterwards, you are discussing the qualities of apple with a friend; you will say to him, ''It is a very curious thing, but I find that all hard and green apples are sour!'' Your friend says to you, ''But how do you know that?'' You at once reply, ''Oh, because I have tried them over and over again, and have always found them to be so.'' Well, if we were talking science instead of common sense, we should call that an experimental verification. And, if still opposed, you go further, and say, ''I have heard from the people in Somersetshire and Devonshire, where a large number of apples are grown, that they have observed the same thing. It is also found to be the case in Normandy, and in North America. In short, I find it to be the universal experience of mankind wherever attention has been directed to the subject.'' Whereupon, your friend, unless he is a very unreasonable man, agrees with you, and is convinced that you are quite right in the conclusion you have drawn. He believes, although perhaps he does not know he believes it, that the more extensive verifications have been made, and results of the same kind arrived at—that the more varied the conditions under which the same results are attained, the more certain is the ultimate conclusion, and he disputes the question no further. He sees that the experiment has been tried under all sorts of conditions, as to time, place, and people, with the same result; and he says with you, therefore, that the law you have laid down must be a good one, and he must believe it.

7. The writer is probably

   (A) French
   (B) English
   (C) American
   (D) Italian
   (E) none of the above

8. "All men are mortal;
   Socrates was a man;
   Socrates was mortal."
   The foregoing represents reasoning that is

   (A) verification
   (B) inductive
   (C) syllogistic
   (D) experimental
   (E) developmental

9. Apples are used

   (A) in order to convince the reader that fruit has
       no intellect
   (B) as an analogy
   (C) to give color to the story
   (D) for sarcasm
   (E) to compare various types of persons

10. The word "premiss" as it appears is more commonly spelled

    (A) promise
    (B) permit
    (C) premit
    (D) premise
    (E) in none of the above ways

11. The author has the approach of

    (A) a scientist
    (B) an artist
    (C) a novelist
    (D) an economist
    (E) a businessman

12. The term "natural law" as it appears in the text refers to

    (A) common sense
    (B) the "honor system"
    (C) the result of an induction
    (D) the order of nature
    (E) a scientific discovery

It is not easy to write a familiar style. Many people mistake a familiar for a vulgar style, and suppose that to write without affectation is to write at random. On the contrary, there is nothing that requires more precision, and, if I may so say, purity of expression, than the style of which I speak. It utterly rejects not only all unmeaning pomp, but all low, cant phrases, and loose, unconnected slipshod allusions. It is not to take the first word that offers, but the best word in common use; it is not to throw words together in any combinations we please, but to follow and avail ourselves of the true idiom of the language. To write a genuine familiar or truly English style is to write as anyone would speak in common conversation who had a thorough command and choice of words, or who could discourse with ease, force, and perspicuity, setting aside all pedantic and oratorical flourishes. Or, to give another illustration, to write naturally is the same thing in regard to common conversation as to read naturally is in regard to common speech. It does not follow that it is an easy thing to give the true accent and inflection to the words you utter, because you do not attempt to rise above the level of ordinary life and colloquial speaking. You do not assume, indeed, the solemnity of the pulpit, or the tone of stage declamation; neither are you at liberty to gabble on at a venture, without emphasis or discretion, or to resort to vulgar dialect or clownish pronunciation. You must steer a middle course. You are tied down to a given appropriate articulation, which is determined by the habitual associations between sense and sound, and which you can only hit by entering into the author's meaning, as you must find the proper words and style to express yourself by fixing your thoughts on the subject you have to write about. Anyone may mouth out a passage with a theatrical cadence, or get upon stilts to tell his thoughts; but to write or speak with propriety and simplicity is a more difficult task. Thus it is easy to affect a pompous style, to use a word twice as big as the thing you want to express; it is not so easy to pitch upon the very word that exactly fits it. Out of eight or ten words equally common, equally intelligible, with nearly equal pretensions, it is a matter of some nicety and discrimination to pick out the very one the preferableness of which is scarcely perceptible, but decisive.

13. According to the passage,

    (A) one should be permitted to speak in any way
        one wishes to

(B) getting on stilts should aid one in speaking more effectively

(C) it is easier to write pompously than simply

(D) the preacher is a model of good speech

(E) a grammatical background is not necessary for good writing

14. If we were to break this selection up into two paragraphs, the second paragraph would best start with

(A) "It is not to take the first word . . ."
(B) "To write a genuine familiar . . ."
(C) "It does not follow that . . ."
(D) "You do not assume . . ."
(E) "Or, to give another illustration . . ."

15. When the writer says, "You must steer a middle course," he means that

(A) you should speak neither too loudly nor too softly

(B) you should speak neither too formally nor too colloquially

(C) you should write as well as speak

(D) you should not come to any definite conclusion about what is proper or not proper in speech

(E) you should write neither too fast nor too slowly

16. By "cant phrases" is meant

(A) a type of language which is peculiar to a particular class

(B) a sing-song type of speech

(C) expressions which consistently indicate refusal to do another's bidding

(D) obscene language

(E) obsolete expressions

17. The author mentions all of the following as important to good speech EXCEPT:

(A) A good command of English vocabulary

(B) The careful selection of words used

(C) The use of allusions and metaphors

(D) Straightforward and precise delivery

(E) The placing of emphasis on important words and phrases

18. The author

(A) is critical of the person who converses in a manner which is easy to understand

(B) implies that foreigners do not speak well

(C) feels that there is no relationship between the sound of a word and its meaning

(D) criticizes pomposity of style more so than vulgarity of style

(E) urges us to speak like the actor or the preacher

Stop

END OF SECTION I. IF YOU HAVE ANY TIME LEFT, GO OVER YOUR WORK IN THIS SECTION ONLY. DO NOT WORK IN ANY OTHER SECTION OF THE TEST. WHEN YOUR TIME IS UP, GO ON TO THE NEXT SECTION.

SECTION II: PROBLEM SOLVING

35 Minutes
25 Questions

DIRECTIONS: For each of the following questions, select the choice which best answers the question or completes the statement.

1. In two hours, the minute hand of a clock rotates through an angle of

   (A) 60°
   (B) 90°
   (C) 180°
   (D) 360°
   (E) 720°

2. Which of the following fractions is less than one-third?

   (A) $^{22}/_{63}$
   (B) $^{4}/_{11}$
   (C) $^{15}/_{46}$
   (D) $^{33}/_{98}$
   (E) $^{102}/_{303}$

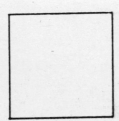

3. The length of each side of the square above is $\frac{2x}{3} + 1$. The perimeter of the square is

   (A) $\dfrac{8x + 4}{3}$

   (B) $\dfrac{8x + 12}{3}$

   (C) $\dfrac{2x}{3} + 4$

   (D) $\dfrac{2x}{3} + 16$

   (E) $\dfrac{4x}{3} + 2$

4. An individual intelligence test is administered to John A when he is 10 years 8 months old. His recorded M.A. (mental age) is 160 months. What I.Q. should be recorded?

   (A) 80
   (B) 125
   (C) 128
   (D) 148
   (E) 160

5. When it is noon at prime meridian on the equator, what time is it at 75° north latitude on this meridian?

   (A) 12 noon
   (B) 3 P.M.
   (C) 5 P.M.
   (D) 7 A.M.
   (E) Midnight

Questions 6–9 are to be answered with reference to the following diagram:

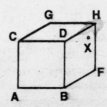

23

The diagram shows a cube. Each corner has been identified by a letter. Corner E is not shown, but its location is the one corner not shown in the diagram. The cube has a 1″ side.

6. The distance from A to D is

   (A) 1 inch
   (B) 2 inches
   (C) $\sqrt{2}$ inches
   (D) $\sqrt{3}$ inches
   (E) $\dfrac{1}{\sqrt{2}}$ inches

7. There is a dot X on the BDHF face of the cube. If we let the cube rotate 180° in a clockwise direction on an axis running through A and H, the

   (A) cube will be standing on corner C
   (B) dot X will appear in the plane where face ABCD is now shown
   (C) dot X will be in the plane where face CDGH is now shown
   (D) cube will return to its position as shown in the diagram
   (E) corner C will appear in the place where corner F is now shown

8. The distance from A to X is

   (A) more than 2 inches
   (B) less than 1 inch
   (C) between 1 and $\sqrt{3}$ inches
   (D) between $\sqrt{3}$ and 2 inches
   (E) exactly $\sqrt{3}$ inches

9. If the cube is successively rotated 180° on axes going through the center of faces ABCD and EFGH, faces AECG and BFDH, and faces CDGH and ABEF, where will the face containing point X be?

   (A) Where face BDHF was at the start of the operation
   (B) Where face AECG was at the start of the operation
   (C) Where face EFGH was at the start of the operation
   (D) Where face ABEF was at the start of the operation
   (E) Where face ABCD was at the start of the operation

10. A carpenter needs four boards, each 2 feet, 9 inches long. If wood is sold only by the foot, how many feet must he buy?

    (A) 9
    (B) 10
    (C) 11
    (D) 12
    (E) 13

11. CMXLIX in Roman numerals is the equivalent of

    (A) 449
    (B) 949
    (C) 969
    (D) 1149
    (E) 1169

Questions 12–16 are to be answered with reference to the following paragraph:

Five geometric figures have been drawn: An isosceles triangle with base equal to its altitude = a, a square with side = a, a circle with a radius = a, a regular hexagon with each side = a, and a semi-circle with a diameter = a. (The figures are not drawn to scale. All the questions assume the stated dimensions.)

12. Which figure has the greatest area?

    (A) △
    (B) □
    (C) ○
    (D) ○
    (E) ◠

13. Which figure has the shortest perimeter?

    (A) □
    (B) △
    (C) ○
    (D) ○
    (E) ◠

14. Which of the following statements is true?

    (A) ○ can be inscribed inside □
    (B) □ can be inscribed inside △
    (C) ○ can be inscribed inside □
    (D) ○ can be inscribed inside ○
    (E) △ can be inscribed inside ◠

15. Which of these statements is true? The area of

  (A) △ is just ¹/₆ the area of ○
  (B) △ is just ½ the area of □
  (C) □ is just ½ the area of ○
  (D) ○ is just ¾ the area of ○
  (E) ◠ is just ½ the area of ○

16. The ratio of the areas of ◠ and ○ is

  (A) 1:8
  (B) 1:6
  (C) 1:4
  (D) 1:2
  (E) 1:1

17. A motorist travels 120 miles to his destination at the average speed of 60 miles per hour and returns to the starting point at the average speed of 40 miles per hour. His average speed for the entire trip is

  (A) 53 miles per hour
  (B) 50 miles per hour
  (C) 48 miles per hour
  (D) 45 miles per hour
  (E) 52 miles per hour

18. A snapshot measures 2½ inches by 1⅞ inches. It is to be enlarged so that the longer dimension will be 4 inches. The length of the enlarged shorter dimension will be

  (A) 2½ inches
  (B) 3 inches
  (C) 3⅜ inches
  (D) 2⅝ inches
  (E) none of these

19. From a piece of tin in the shape of a square 6 inches on a side, the largest possible circle is cut out. Of the following, the ratio of the area of the circle to the area of the original square is closest in value to

  (A) ⁴/₅
  (B) ⅔
  (C) ³/₅
  (D) ½
  (E) ¾

20. The approximate distance, s, in feet that an object falls in t seconds when dropped from a height is obtained by use of the formula s = 16 t². In 8

seconds the object will fall

  (A) 15,384 feet
  (B) 1,024 feet
  (C) 256 feet
  (D) 2,048 feet
  (E) none of these

21. In the figure, AB = BC and angles BAD and BCD are right angles. Which one of the following conclusions may be drawn?

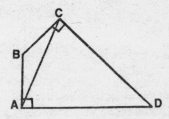

  (A) angle BCA = angle CAD
  (B) angle B is greater than angle D
  (C) AC = CD
  (D) AD = CD
  (E) BC is shorter than CD.

Questions 22–25 are to be answered with reference to the following explanatory paragraph:

  Suppose in the place of a number system a symbol system were instituted which had digits □, ∧, Z, ⋝, ▷, 5, ⅃, ⵠ, ⵝ and ⊖ corresponding respectively to the digits 0, 1, 2, 3, 4, 5, 6, 7, 8 and 9. The digit □ is used in the same fashion as the 0 in the decimal system, e.g., ∧ □ = 10.

22. Which is equal to 10²?

  (A) ∧ □ □
  (B) ⅃ ▷
  (C) ∧ □ ∧
  (D) 5 ⋝
  (E) ⵝ □ ∧

23. What is the sum of ▷ + ⅃ + ⋝ ?

  (A) Z ∧
  (B) ∧ ⋝
  (C) ⋝ ▷
  (D) ∧ ⅃
  (E) ∧ ∧

24. Which of the following indicates three-quarters of an inch?

    (A) $\dfrac{5}{\wedge\,\square}$ inches

    (B) $\dfrac{\partial}{\times}$ inches

    (C) $\dfrac{\curlyvee}{\wedge\,\square}$ inches

    (D) $\dfrac{\curlyvee}{\wedge\,\square\,\square}$ inches

    (E) $\dfrac{\partial\,5}{\square\,\square}$ inches

25. What is the value of

$$\wedge Z\,\partial - \triangleright\,\curlyvee \;+\; \frac{\wedge\,\square}{Z}\;?$$

    (A) $\triangleright\,\partial$

    (B) $5\,\curlyvee$

    (C) $\times\,\triangleright$

    (D) $\curlyvee\,\square$

    (E) $\ominus\,Z$

Stop

END OF SECTION II. IF YOU HAVE ANY TIME LEFT, GO OVER YOUR WORK IN THIS SECTION ONLY. DO NOT WORK IN ANY OTHER SECTION OF THE TEST. WHEN YOUR TIME IS UP, GO ON TO THE NEXT SECTION.

SECTION III: PRACTICAL BUSINESS JUDGMENT

20 Minutes
20 Questions

DIRECTIONS: This section consists of a reading selection which details a business situation followed by two sets of questions, data evaluation and data application. In the first set, data evaluation, you will be asked to classify certain of the facts presented in the passage on the basis of their importance. The second set, data application, will test your grasp of specific details of the situation.

Wingfleet, Inc., is the fourth largest aircraft manufacturer in the world. Last year, the company's sales revenues were slightly under two billion dollars. Wingfleet, an old company in terms of aviation history, started production in 1921, struggled through the depression, and entered World War II a medium-sized company. Thousands of fighters and bombers rolled out of Wingfleet factories. It gained a worldwide reputation for well-designed and well-constructed military aircraft and continued to grow until the late 1960s. It now employs over 100,000 people in many plants throughout the U.S. The suppliers of Wingfleet employ another 75,000 workers. In short, Wingfleet is a solid supporter of the nation's economy.

John Franco, chairman of the Board of Directors of Wingfleet, carefully studies a lengthy proposal by an executive committee, consisting of three board members and three vice-presidents, recommending that the company bid on a new military-transport plane, the 2L-1000. This will be the largest and one of the fastest transport planes in the world. It will take at least six years to design, test, and bring into full production the 115 planes to be built for the government. The project will provide jobs for 25,000 Wingfleet workers, plus 20,000 jobs for Wingfleet suppliers.

Nearly 90 percent of Wingfleet's business is with the U.S. government. Therefore the aircraft manufacturer's sales revenue is dependent on the federal budget. During times of national emergency (such as the cold war, the Vietnam and Korean conflicts), Wingfleet does very well. But lately Congress has cut defense expenditures, and these cuts have greatly reduced Wingfleet earnings. In 1966, for example, Wingfleet showed a profit of 51 million dollars. But last year, the company lost 33 million.

Thus it would be advantageous for Wingfleet to enter the commercial aircraft field to diversify its sources of revenue, and, paradoxically, this is one of the reasons why the executive committee recommends going all out to get the 2L-1000 contract. The huge transport, with slight alteration in design, will make an excellent commercial passenger plane, the committee claims.

In this connection, a preliminary survey of major airlines showed that nine domestic and foreign airlines indicated their willingness to order 201 of these commercial planes. Furthermore, should Wingfleet get the government contract, these airlines would order the planes and place immediate and substantial down payments.

Wingfleet has a tentative, but exclusive, contract with the Ponzol Company, one of Europe's leading engine manufacturers, to design and produce the plane's engines. This contract depends, of course, on whether Wingfleet decides to bid on the military contract and gets it. The fact that Ponzol engines will power the 2L-1000 should make the Pentagon regard the Wingfleet bid favorably.

John Franco ponders the possible problems that might arise should Wingfleet take on this enormous project. In order to get the contract against vigorous competition, Wingfleet must make the lowest bid, which is estimated at 1.7 billion dollars if everything goes perfectly. Therefore, the executive committee suggests a bid of 2 billion dollars. But John Franco is aware, after 33 years with the company, that it is rare when actual development costs do not exceed estimates. He realizes that two or three major structural problems would quickly eat up the estimated gross profit.

On the other hand, he figures, costs over bid might not be disastrous. It is possible to renegotiate a government contract when cost overruns occur. Wingfleet has done this many times. In fact, cost overruns average 50 percent over accepted bids, and these have usually been made up by the government. However, John Franco wonders if Congress in its present anti-military spending mood would approve an appropriation to make up the difference.

Franco is also uneasy about the Ponzol Company. He has no doubt about the quality of Ponzol engines, but the foreign firm is nationalized. Its profits have been almost nonexistent for the past few years, and governments, he has discovered, are far less patient with losses than capitalist shareholders. Suppose the European government that owns Ponzol decides to liquidate the engine company in the middle of the 2L-1000 contract? He shudders at the thought.

Even though the airlines put down substantial payments for the 201 civilian planes, this money will not solve Wingfleet's poor cash position. The company must depend on 25 banks to advance half a billion dollars for the 2L-1000 project, and this will add substantially to Wingfleet's overall debt.

Finally, Wingfleet has tried to enter the commercial airplane field three times without success. The failures could not be blamed on inefficiency or lack of knowledge of the market, because careful surveys preceded each attempt. Yet each time Wingfleet guessed incorrectly. Could this happen again?

Despite his many misgivings, John Franco decides to recommend to the full Board of Directors that Wingfleet make a 2-billion-dollar bid for the 2L-1000 contract.

(C) if the element is a MINOR FACTOR in making the decision; that is, a secondary consideration in determining the decision.

(D) if the element is a MAJOR ASSUMPTION made in deliberating; that is, a supposition or projection made by the decision maker before weighing the variables.

(E) if the element is an UNIMPORTANT ISSUE in getting to the point; that is, a factor that is insignificant or not immediately relevant to the situation.

1. Entrance into the commercial aircraft market.

2. Possible cost overruns of 2L-1000.

3. A projected six years to produce the 2L-1000.

4. The ability of the 2L-1000 to be modified to a commercial plane.

5. The possible liquidation of Ponzol.

6. Ninety percent of Wingfleet's business has been with the United States government.

7. Down payments by airlines.

8. The willingness of airlines to order 201 planes.

9. Diversification of market.

10. Government anti-military spending mood.

DATA EVALUATION

DIRECTIONS: Based on your analysis of the business situation, classify each of the following elements in one of five categories. Mark:

(A) if the element is a MAJOR OBJECTIVE in making the decision; that is, the outcome or result sought by the decision maker.

(B) if the element is a MAJOR FACTOR in arriving at the decision; that is, a consideration explicitly mentioned in the passage that is basic in determining the decision.

DATA APPLICATION

DIRECTIONS: Based on your understanding of the business situation, answer the following questions testing your comprehension of the information supplied in the passage. For each question, select the choice which best answers the question or completes the statement.

11. Most of Wingfleet's income is derived from sales to

    (A) foreign governments
    (B) the U.S. government
    (C) domestic airlines
    (D) manufacturing companies
    (E) private agencies

12. According to the passage, Wingfleet's earnings are erratic because of

    (A) poor management
    (B) cost overruns
    (C) the vagaries of the federal budget
    (D) attempts to enter the commercial aircraft field
    (E) high bank debt

13. One of the advantages of the 2L-1000 contract for Wingfleet would be that

    (A) the contract will lead to other government contracts
    (B) Congress doesn't particularly care what the cost will be
    (C) the contract will keep Wingfleet from going bankrupt
    (D) the military plane can also be sold to foreign governments
    (E) a change of design can change the military plane to a commercial one

14. A preliminary survey of major airlines shows that they

    (A) see no advantage in purchasing a commercial counterpart of 2L-1000
    (B) will purchase 201 planes of the 2L-1000 type with substantial down payments
    (C) will consider purchasing passenger planes after the 2L-1000 is produced
    (D) have no funds to buy new planes
    (E) are willing to lend money to Wingfleet to manufacture the 2L-1000

15. Regarding the 2L-1000 contract, the Wingfleet executive committee suggests that it

    (A) make a bid for the 2L-1000 contract
    (B) postpone a decision until there is further study of the project
    (C) turn down the contract
    (D) make a low bid to secure the contract
    (E) try to sell more of the commercial counterpart of the 2L-1000

16. John Franco considers the problem with cost overruns to be that

    (A) Congress has frowned on paying these costs in the past
    (B) the loss would have to be sustained by Wingfleet
    (C) in its present mood Congress might not approve these extra costs
    (D) the government has little experience with overruns since they happen so infrequently
    (E) they would indicate that Wingfleet is very inefficient

17. One reason that the Pentagon might favor Wingfleet is that

    (A) Wingfleet has an excellent reputation in manufacturing commercial planes
    (B) the national economy might be thrown into chaos if Wingfleet does not get the contract
    (C) so many banks are willing to back Wingfleet
    (D) Wingfleet has already built a plane very similar to the 2L-1000
    (E) Ponzol engines will be used

18. Which of the following is a major concern of John Franco's regarding the 2L-1000 project?

    (A) Wingfleet does not have the technical ability to produce such a plane as the 2L-1000
    (B) The Wingfleet bid might be too high
    (C) Wingfleet's suppliers in the U.S. might become bankrupt before the project is finished
    (D) Ponzol might be liquidated
    (E) A commercial counterpart of the 2L-1000 might be impractical

19. Which of the following best describes Wingfleet's financial situation in its consideration of the 2L-1000 contract?

    (A) Wingfleet will have to depend on many banks to produce the 2L-1000
    (B) Wingfleet's cash position is excellent because of recent high profits
    (C) Wingfleet can finance the 2L-1000 on its own
    (D) Wingfleet has little bank credit
    (E) The down payments from the commercial airlines will provide enough cash to Wingfleet to see it through the 2L-1000 contract

20. Which of the following best describes Wingfleet's past experiences in aircraft manufacturing?

(A) Wingfleet has had little luck in entering the commercial aircraft industry.
(B) Wingfleet was most successful in the commercial aircraft field, but gave this market up.
(C) The company avoided military plane production.
(D) The manufacturer has shown consistent losses on government aircraft contracts.
(E) Wingfleet saw no reason to produce commercial aircraft.

Stop

END OF SECTION III. IF YOU HAVE ANY TIME LEFT, GO OVER YOUR WORK IN THIS SECTION ONLY. DO NOT WORK IN ANY OTHER SECTION OF THE TEST. WHEN YOUR TIME IS UP, GO ON TO THE NEXT SECTION.

SECTION IV: DATA INTERPRETATION

15 Minutes
15 Questions

DIRECTIONS: The following questions are to test your ability to read and interpret graphs and tables. Answer each question based on your reading of the graphs or tables provided.

Questions 1–5 refer to the bar graph below. Use appropriate readings to get your answers.

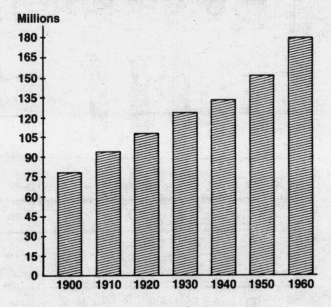

POPULATION - USA - 1900 to 1960

Millions

1. What is the percent increase in population from 1900 to 1960 (approx.)?

   (A) 100
   (B) 110
   (C) 115
   (D) 120
   (E) 135

2. In how many years after 1900 did the population double?

   (A) 20
   (B) 30
   (C) 40
   (D) 50
   (E) 60

3. The largest increase in population was in the decade ending in the year

   (A) 1960
   (B) 1950
   (C) 1940
   (D) 1930
   (E) 1920

4. The smallest increase in population was in the decade ending in the year

   (A) 1960
   (B) 1950
   (C) 1940
   (D) 1930
   (E) 1920

5. The ratio of the population in 1960 to that in 1950 is (approx.)

   (A) 8:5
   (B) 6:5
   (C) 3:2
   (D) 5:3
   (E) 10:7

31

Questions 6–9 refer to the chart below.

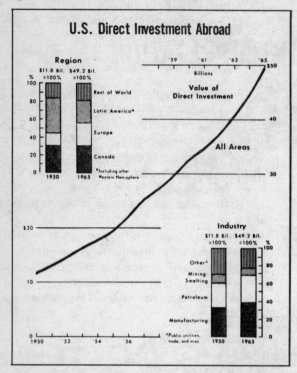

6. The United States direct investments in Europe increased by how many percent between 1950 and 1965?

   (A) 100%
   (B) 400%
   (C) 550%
   (D) 595%
   (E) 1000%

7. The 1950 and 1965 ratio of direct investment abroad in petroleum was approximately

   (A) 1:5
   (B) 1:4
   (C) 1:3
   (D) 1:2
   (E) 1:1

8. How much money did the United States invest in Canada's manufacturing industry in 1965?

   (A) $5.8 billion
   (B) $5.9 billion
   (C) $6.0 billion
   (D) $6.1 billion
   (E) cannot be determined from the given information

9. Which of the following statements is true?

(A) It is possible that Latin America received all the U.S. investment in manufacturing in 1965.
(B) Canada received about the same amount of investment in 1965 as in 1950.
(C) More money was being invested in Latin America in 1965 than in 1950.
(D) The "rest of the world" received $1 billion in investments from the U.S. in 1950.
(E) U.S. investments abroad in manufacturing exceeded $10 billion in 1954.

Questions 10–15 refer to the graph below.

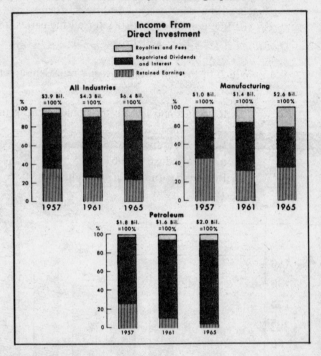

10. The manufacturing and petroleum industries accounted for what percent of income from direct investment in all industries in 1961?

    (A) 40%
    (B) 50%
    (C) 60%
    (D) 70%
    (E) cannot be determined from the given information

11. In 1957, how much was classified as "Retained Earnings" in the combined Petroleum and Manufacturing industries?

    (A) $400 million
    (B) $450 million
    (C) $520 million

(D) $630 million

(E) $900 million

12. The greatest percent increase of income was seen in

 (A) the manufacturing industry between 1957 and 1961

 (B) the manufacturing industry between 1961 and 1965

 (C) the petroleum industry between 1957 and 1961

 (D) the petroleum industry between 1961 and 1965

 (E) the combined statistics for all industries between 1957 and 1965

13. Which of the following does *not* represent an *increase?*

 (A) Royalties and fees in the manufacturing industry, 1961–1965

 (B) Repatriated dividends and interest in the petroleum industry, 1961–1965

 (C) Retained earnings in all industries, 1957–1961

(D) Royalties and fees in the petroleum industry, 1957–1961

(E) Repatriated dividends and interest in all industries, 1957–1965

14. Which represents the greatest amount?

 (A) Retained earnings in all industries in 1957

 (B) Total income from direct investment in manufacturing in 1957

 (C) Total retained earnings in the petroleum industry for all three years

 (D) Repatriated dividends and interest from manufacturing in 1965

 (E) Royalties and fees for all industries in 1965

15. How many degrees of a "pie" chart would be occupied by the manufacturing industry if the whole pie were to represent income from direct investment in 1961 for all industries?

 (A) 96°

 (B) 107°

 (C) 117°

 (D) 124°

 (E) 145°

Stop

END OF SECTION IV. IF YOU HAVE ANY TIME LEFT, GO OVER YOUR WORK IN THIS SECTION ONLY. DO NOT WORK IN ANY OTHER SECTION OF THE TEST. WHEN YOUR TIME IS UP, GO ON TO THE NEXT SECTION.

SECTION V: DATA SUFFICIENCY

20 Minutes
16 Questions

DIRECTIONS: Each question below is followed by two numbered facts. You are to determine whether the data given in the statements is sufficient for answering the question. Use the data given, plus your knowledge of math and everyday facts, to choose between the five possible answers. Mark

(A) if statement 1 alone is sufficient to answer the question, but statement 2 alone is not sufficient.
(B) if statement 2 alone is sufficient to answer the question, but statement 1 alone is not sufficient.
(C) if both statements together are needed to answer the question, but neither statement alone is sufficient.
(D) if either statement by itself is sufficient to answer the question asked.
(E) if not enough facts are given to answer the question.

1. Exactly how many inches long is the length of a certain rectangle?

   (1) If it were six inches longer it would be exactly 3 feet.
   (2) If it were six inches less it would be exactly 2 feet.

2. How much did the salesman earn from the sale of 3 cars?

   (1) Each car sold for $3,400.
   (2) He received a 20 percent commission on each sale.

3. Are A and B on the same committee?

   (1) B is a member of the sales committee.
   (2) A is a member of the planning committee, and members of the sales committee can be on the planning committee.

4. How many gulos are in 8 munos?

   (1) 2 bulos = 8 gulos
   (2) 16 munos = 4 bulos

5. Exactly how many pounds of frankfurters did the boys and girls eat at the party?

   (1) At the party, the boys ate three times as many frankfurters as the girls.
   (2) If the girls ate 6 more frankfurters, then the boys would have eaten only twice as much as the girls.

6.

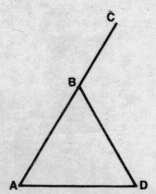

Find the area of the above figure.

   (1) A side of square ABCD = 4
   (2) DEC is an equilateral triangle

7.

In the figure above ABC is a straight line. What is the degree measure of $\angle BDA$?

   (1) $\angle ABD = \angle BAD + \angle BDA$
   (2) $\angle DBC = 90°$

34

8. X and Y are two inscribed polygons whose vertices lie on the same circle. Is the perimeter of X greater than Y?

   (1) The circumference of the circle is 14π
   (2) Polygon X has 3 more sides than polygon Y.

9.

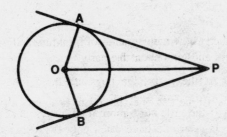

   In the figure above, PA and PB are tangents to circle O at points A and B. What is the length of OP?
   (1) The radius of circle O is 6 in.
   (2) Tangent PA equals 8 in.

10. If A, B, and C are negative integers and t is an integer, is t negative?

    (1) t = A − B
    (2) tC = A

11. What are the values of A and B in the equation $\frac{3A - 2B}{4} = 1$?

    (1) A = 2B
    (2) B = 4

12.

   What is the length of segment BC in the figure above?

   (1) BD = 15
   (2) CD = 10

13.

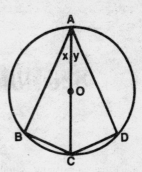

   In the figure above, what is the value of the ratio $\frac{x}{y}$?

   (1) The areas of triangles ABC and ACD are equal.
   (2) Chords BC and CD are equidistant from O, the center of the circle.

14. If A, B, and C are the degree measurements of the three angles of an isosceles triangle, what is the value of B?

    (1) A = 35°
    (2) C = 95°

15. Christine has x + 5 pencils. She distributes equal amounts to her brother and four girl friends and has two pencils left for herself. Exactly how many pencils did she have originally?

    (1) If Christine had only x pencils to give out in the same manner, she would still have two pencils for herself.
    (2) If Christine had eleven less pencils to give out in the same manner she would have none left for herself.

16. In the 5 term series 3, X, Y, M, 12, find the value of M.

    (1) The third term is twice the first term.
    (2) The fourth term is twice the second term.

Stop

END OF SECTION V. IF YOU HAVE ANY TIME LEFT, GO OVER YOUR WORK IN THIS SECTION ONLY. DO NOT WORK IN ANY OTHER SECTION OF THE TEST. WHEN YOUR TIME IS UP, GO ON TO THE NEXT SECTION.

SECTION VI: READING RECALL

30 Minutes

26 Questions

DIRECTIONS: You are allowed 15 minutes to closely read the following passages. Afterwards you will be asked to recall certain ideas and facts about the passages. You are not allowed to refer back to the passages.

Passage 1

That guessing is not always random is scarcely contestable. What is, perhaps, of more interest is the contention that the type of correction for guessing often made in aptitude tests of the multiple-choice variety is inadequate. Evidence has been offered in support of the thesis that guesses have a better than random probability of being right and that therefore "It can pay to guess." The implication seems to be that guessing in this context is a mild form of delinquency and is not sufficiently penalized by applying the usual correction formula. Two points arise and need clarification. The first has to do with item uniqueness, while the second involves more fundamental considerations.

To illustrate the argument, we may use the synonym-type questions of a typical aptitude test. In answering such questions, it can hardly be denied that on balance it pays to guess when in doubt. Two sorts of reasons account for this. First, the subject may have good grounds for rejecting some of the choices, either because he knows their meanings and is sure that they are not synonymous with the word specified, or because they are the wrong part of speech, or for some similar reason. If only one of the distractors is of this form, then a subject's chance of hitting the right answer is not $1/n$ but $1/(n-1)$, and so on. Secondly, as is widely recognized, there is a continuum between ignorance and certainty which may favor guessing in certain circumstances. In vocabulary tests this influence will favor guessing unless the distractors have been specially chosen to mislead the unwary. However, the broad assertion that this influence must favor guessing overlooks the factor of item uniqueness. If we choose items carefully, we can easily demonstrate that guessing raises or lowers scores, or leaves them unaffected.

The following multiple-choice item is a good example:

Condign means the same as
blame, meet, peppery, praiseworthy, slander.

Unless the subject actually knows the right answer he is more likely to choose one of the distractors. The main point of the argument is that it is possible to produce items of this kind and to engineer the distribution of guessing probabilities in any way that takes the fancy. It is a matter of interest to examine why this should be so.

In this particular example we have engineered the situation by:

(A) Using a word that is in any case little known.

(B) Using a target word that has a far more common meaning than the alternative meaning that corresponds to *condign*.

(C) Choosing distractors that are plausible. For example, *condign* has about it a similar ring to *condemn*, and so may easily be thought akin to any word involving value judgments.

(D) Confusing the subject still further by not giving clues as to whether he should be looking for a verb, adjective or noun. Only *peppery* and *praiseworthy* are clearly adjectives; *blame* and *slander* can operate as nouns or verbs; while *meet* in its common form is a verb, although it is as an adjective that it provides a synonym for *condign*.

An experiment was recently carried out in which a vocabulary test was presented to subjects who were also asked to give, with each response, an assessment of their own feelings of confidence or doubt. The subjects—forty in number—were all adults with a good educational background. The *condign* item was added to the end. The null hypothesis was that each word on the *condign* item would be chosen an equal number of times, and that any observed differences would merely be chance variations. The prediction was that those who "guess"—those who express some "doubt" or are "very doubtful"—on this item would tend to choose one of the distractors rather than the target alternative; in other words, less than 20 percent of the subjects would choose *meet*.

All the subjects were doubtful about the *condign* item, and the following results were obtained.

Number of subjects choosing target word—1
Number of subjects choosing distractors—39

Passage 2

The origin of continental nuclei has long been a puzzle. Theories advanced so far have generally failed to explain the first step in continent growth, or have been subject to serious objections. It is the purpose of this article to examine the possible role of the impact of large meteorites or asteroids in the production of continental nuclei.

Unfortunately, the geological evolution of the Earth's surface has had an obliterating effect on the original composition and structure of the continents to such an extent that further terrestrial investigations have small chance of arriving at an unambiguous answer to the question of continental origin. Paradoxically, clues to the origin and early history of the surface features of the Earth may be found on the Moon and planets, rather than on the Earth, because some of these bodies appear to have had a much less active geological history. As a result, relatively primitive surface features are preserved for study and analysis.

In the case of both the Moon and Mars, it is generally concluded from the appearance of their heavily cratered surfaces that they have been subjected to bombardment by large meteoroids during their geological history. Likewise, it would appear a reasonable hypothesis that the Earth has also been subjected to meteoroid bombardment in the past, and that very large bodies struck the Earth early in its geological history.

The largest crater on the Moon listed by Baldwin has a diameter of 285 km. However, if we accept the hypothesis of formation of some of the mare basins by impact, the maximum lunar impact crater diameter is probably as large as 650 km. Based on a lunar analogy, one might expect several impact craters of at least 500 km diameter to have been formed on Earth. By applying Baldwin's equation, the depth of such a crater should be about 20 km. Baldwin admits that his equation gives excessive depths for large craters so that the actual depth should be somewhat smaller. Based on the measured depth of smaller lunar craters, a depth of 10 km is probably a conservative estimate for the depth of a 500 km impact crater. Baldwin's equation gives the depth of the zone of brecciation for such a crater as about 75 km. The plasticity of the Earth's mantle at the depth makes it impossible to speak of "brecciation" in the usual sense. However, local stresses may be temporarily sustained at that depth, as shown by the existence of deep-focus earthquakes. Thus, short-term effects might be expected to a depth of more than 50 km in the mantle.

Even without knowing the precise effects, there is little doubt that the formation of a 500-km crater would be a major geological event. Numerous authors have considered the geological implications of such an event. Donn *et al* have, for example, called on the impact of continent-size bodies of sialic composition to form the original continents. Two major difficulties inherent in this concept are the lack of any known sialic meteorites, and the high probability that the energy of impact would result in a wide dissemination of sialic material, rather than its concentration at the point of impact.

Gilvarry, on the other hand, called on meteoroid impact to explain the production of ocean basins. The major difficulties with this model are that the morphology of most of the ocean basins is not consistent with impact, and that the origin and growth of continents are not adequately explained.

We agree with Donn *et al*. that the impact of large meteorites or asteroids may have caused continent formation, but would rather think in terms of the localized addition of energy to the system, rather than in terms of the addition of actual sialic material.

Passage 3

The communists' preoccupation with economic growth and their whole attitude toward economic progress have been shaped by Marx's theory of long-run development of human society. This theory places economic development at the centre of the entire social philosophy and it is impossible to study the Marxists' political, social and economic views without referring to it. Without the knowledge of this theory it is difficult to understand the communists' dogmatic belief in the superiority of their system, whatever are the observable facts, and their faith in the final victory over capitalism. Economic development has to lead, sooner or later, to socialism and communism and it is necessary to build socialism and, later, communism to make future economic growth possible. This principle is valid for all countries without an exception. They all have to proceed along the same path although they may be placed at different points of it at present. Such is the logic of history.

This theory, which is usually referred to as "historical materialism," "the materialistic conception of history," or "Marx's historical determinism," is believed by the Marxists to be useful not only as the explanation of the past and the present but also as the basis for the prediction of the future course of history. As the final judgment on any prophecy has to be made in the light of the subsequent events, it is interesting to compare the developments since the theory was presented by Marx with the pattern which could have been expected on the basis of Marx's prediction. The purpose of this paper is to outline briefly such a comparison and to discuss the communist explanation of the disparity which has appeared between the actual and the predicted course of events. The paper does not attempt to evaluate the philosophical aspects of theory, its materialism, one-sidedness and methodological oversimplification. Similarly, the value of the theory as a summary of the past historical events preceding the time when it was presented by Marx and its merits and weaknesses as one of numerous "stages of growth" theories are not discussed.

Marx's theory accepts as its basis that man's life is a conscious struggle with the natural environment, the struggle which takes the form of production as "life involves, before everything else, eating and drinking, a habitation, clothing, and many other things." The process of production is the interaction between man and nature and it takes the form of social labour. Man has to improve his instruments of production in order to master the natural environment but "the development of these instruments follows a definite sequence" as "each new improvement and invention can be made only on the basis of those that have preceded it, and must rest upon gradually accumulated production experience, the labour skills and knowledge of the people . . . ." Production is carried on as a social process, because "in the process of producing material wealth, people, whether they like it or not, find themselves in some way linked with one another and the labour of each producer becomes a part of the social labour." These relationships among men are called the "relations of production." They exist independently of human consciousness and this gives them their materialistic character. They are determined by the level of development and the nature of productive forces.

Passage 4

According to Hegel, a conflict between a thesis and its antithesis produces a synthesis which partakes of the natures of both. The general councils of the Church which so far number twenty-one may serve as an illustration of this philosophy. To start from not very far away in the past, the Council of Trent (1545–63) was a reaction to the Lutheran revolt. The first Ecumenical Council of the Vatican (1869–70) was held in the shadow of the French Revolution of 1789, of the revolutions in 1848 and of the rationalist movement. The First Session of the Second Ecumenical Council of the Vatican (1963) was against the atheistic movement, mainly represented by communism, the new scientific irreligious trends and the fact that "The World was too strong for a divided Christianity." The Second Session of this Council, which began on September 29, 1963, and culminated in Pope Paul's visit to the Holy Land in January 1964, is mainly a unitive Council, to try to bring together the various churches in Christendom and to try to have dialogues with other religions for a united stand against disruptive forces in the world. This is the meaning of "ecumenism" in its Christian sense and in its wider and world-wide sense. Islam is only concerned with the latter sense. The thaw which is taking place at the Vatican, a new synthesis, may be regarded as a prelude to a wider thaw with the world religions through continuous dialogue with Islam, Judaism, and other religions.

The dialogue with Islam has a long history. In its beginning, the conflict between Christianity and Islam was violent. One could cite here the Muslim conquests in the seventh and eighth centuries, the Crusades, the Inquisition in Spain, religious persecution and the missionary movements. But throughout this long period there were sometimes peaceful and more rational dialogues and debates. Peter the Venerable in the twelfth century, for instance, wrote in his first book of *Adversus Nefandum Sectum Saracenorum* (Against the Unspeakable Sect of the Saracens) as follows, addressing Muslims: "It appears odd and perhaps is actually so that a man so removed from you by great distance, speaking another language, and having a profession and customs and a manner of life so different from your own, should write from the furthest West to men who live in the countries of the Orient, and should direct his attacks against a people whom he has never seen, and that he assails you not with weapons, as Christians have often done, but by word, not by force but with reasons, not with hate but with love.'' Peter then pleads with the Saracens to enter into discussion. He was indignant that the Latins were living in ignorance of a religion so wide-spread as Islam. A century later, Roger Bacon condemned the method of the crusade and wanted to see the intellectuals taking part in discussions. He gave an illustration from the King of Tartary, who gathered before him people of differing beliefs in order that he might thereby come to a knowledge of the truth. This reminds us of Akbar, the Mughal emperor of India. Raymund Lull appealed in 1312 to Frederick III of Sicily to make representations to the King of Tunis whereby Christians versed in the literature and language of the Arabs might be sent to Tunis, and learned doctors from among the Saracens of Tunis might be invited to Sicily where they could enter into discussion with Christians. He also said, referring to the Crusades, that the Holy Land would never be conquered except by love and prayer. Thomas Aquinas wrote his book *Summa Contra Gentiles* in order to use reason and discussion, especially with Muslims in Spain.

But what has been the attitude of the Muslims to all such approaches? It is one which stems from the Prophet's example given in his dealings with Christians and Jews in Arabia. He used to enjoin his followers not to enter into polemics with their adversaries, but to content themselves with saying to them that they (the Muslims) neither believed nor disbelieved what the others claimed in their Scriptures, but only believed in what was contained in the Quran. A verse in the Quran says: ''Our Lord, we believe in what thou hast revealed and we follow the Apostle.'' Another verse says: ''O followers of the Bible! Come to an equitable proposition between us and you that we shall not serve any but God and that we shall not associate anyone with Him, and that some of us shall not take others for Lords besides God: but if they [the Scriptuaries] turn back, then say: bear witness that we are muslims.'' A third verse says: ''And do not dispute with the people of the Scriptures except by what is best, except those of them who act unjustly, and say: We believe in that which has been revealed to us and revealed to you, and our God and your God is one, and to him do we submit.''

QUESTIONS

DIRECTIONS: You have 15 minutes to answer the following questions based upon the preceding passages. You are not to refer back to the passages.

Passage 1

1. The author of the article believes that

   (A) guessing is always haphazard in nature
   (B) deducting a certain amount of credit for every wrong guess is reasonable and logical
   (C) in a five-choice multiple-choice question, it is safe to assume that if one guesses, one will be correct approximately 20 percent of the time
   (D) there should be more severe penalties for guessing on multiple-choice tests than the penalties usually invoked
   (E) there is a definite correlation between moral delinquency and the tendency to guess on tests

2. The writer is obviously

   (A) opposed to aptitude tests for college entrance but not for graduate school admission
   (B) in disagreement with established practices of penalizing for guessing
   (C) in favor of vocabulary tests to prognosticate success in college
   (D) of the opinion that the essay-type question has greater validity than the multiple-choice question
   (E) interested in developing a test which will tolerate no guessing

3. A multiple-choice vocabulary question

   (A) should never require an opposite meaning as the correct choice
   (B) should have at least one choice which is obviously incorrect
   (C) should, at times, have two correct choices
   (D) should always have a synonym and an antonym among its choices
   (E) should have choices all of which seem possible to many candidates, at first glance

4. The antonym of ''condign'' is

   (A) unconditional
   (B) untidy
   (C) insincere
   (D) undeserved
   (E) interesting

5. Assuming that we wished to add a ''distractor'' sixth-choice for the five-choice ''condign'' question given, we would use

   (A) petite
   (B) indigenous
   (C) destroyed
   (D) blatant
   (E) durable

6. The results of the test in which subjects were asked to give their feelings afterwards, show that the actual percent that chose the correct answer is

   (A) 2.5
   (B) 16.1
   (C) 20
   (D) 39.8
   (E) 78.2

7. If we are dealing with a five-choice multiple-choice question, n in $1/n$ would be

   (A) 1
   (B) 2
   (C) 3
   (D) 4
   (E) 5

Passage 2

8. A mare basin is

   (A) an area where animal life flourished at one time
   (B) a formula for determining the relationship between the depth and width of craters
   (C) a valley that is filled in when a spatial body has impact with the moon or the earth
   (D) a planetoid (small planet) created when a meteorite, upon striking the moon, breaks off a part of the moon
   (E) a dark spot on the moon, once supposed to be a sea, now a plain

9. A lunar crater, at the time it was formed, was approximately

   (A) half as wide as it is today
   (B) twice as wide as it is today
   (C) as wide as it is today
   (D) four times as wide as it is today
   (E) one-fourth as wide as it is today

10. According to the passage, the largest crater that was expected to be found on the moon was about

    (A) 1.6 km across
    (B) 20 km across
    (C) 50 km across
    (D) 500 km across
    (E) 650 km across

11. The writer does *not* believe that

    (A) an asteroid is larger than a meteorite
    (B) material from space, upon hitting the earth, was eventually distributed
    (C) oceans were formerly craters
    (D) the earth, at one time, had craters
    (E) tremendous meteorites, in early times, fell upon our planet

12. The article is primarily concerned with

    (A) the origin of continents
    (B) the craters on the moon
    (C) differences of opinion among authoritative geologists
    (D) the relationship between asteroids and meteorites
    (E) planetary surface features

13. Sialic material refers to

    (A) the broken rock resulting from the impact of a meteorite against the earth
    (B) material that exists on planets other than the earth
    (C) a composite of rocks typical of continental areas of the earth
    (D) the lining of craters
    (E) material that is man-made to simulate materials that existed far back in geological history

14. In order to research how our continents came about, geologists would do well to devote the greater part of their study to

(A) asteroids and meteorites
(B) the earth
(C) the sun
(D) planetoids
(E) other planets and the moon

Passage 3

15. The author indicates that the typical communist

    (A) is more interested in the success of communism than in the welfare of his own family
    (B) no longer adheres to the economic and/or philosophic principles set down by Marx
    (C) has the same fundamental interests as the non-communist
    (D) is afraid to express his true beliefs for fear of punishment
    (E) has an authoritative – if not arrogant – opinion about the advantages of communism over capitalism.

16. A primary feature of Marxism is the stress on

    (A) studying the lessons of history to formulate plans for the eventual victory of communism over capitalism
    (B) the development and management of the material wealth of a government or community
    (C) the need to move ahead with the implementation of the communist philosophy by violent means
    (D) the eventual compromise between communism and the Western world
    (E) the improvement of educational practices and the provision of educational opportunities for all

17. That a state of communism is to be preceded by socialism is

    (A) contrary to Marxist theory
    (B) considered by Marx to be just as feasible as the converse
    (C) a phase of "relations of production"
    (D) the doctrine of historical determinism
    (E) not the concern of advocates of the communist philosophy

18. The writer states or implies that

(A) one cannot accurately appraise a proposed social or political philosophy until the results have been seen
(B) there is essentially no difference in practice between the communistic and the democratic form of government
(C) in the final analysis, man is an animal who cannot be guided by moral considerations
(D) the great majority of individuals are not intelligent enough to govern themselves—a dictator must always be present to make decisions for them
(E) there is no reason to feel that communistic countries and nations with other forms of government cannot exist in peace

19. The writer's attitude toward the Communist Revolution is one of

    (A) righteous indignation
    (B) unnecessary oversimplification
    (C) hardheaded materialism
    (D) studied indifference
    (E) scholarly objectivity

20. The selection does *not*

    (A) refer to the importance of wealth in communistic philosophy
    (B) explain what the productive process involves
    (C) appraise the materialist conception of history
    (D) deal with nations other than those which are now communistic
    (E) quote Marx directly

Passage 4

21. The "rationalist movement" refers to

    (A) the procedure of fixing allowances of food and other goods in time of scarcity
    (B) the reorganization of religion in accordance with up-to-date methods and practices
    (C) the removal of radicals not only in scientific procedures but also in society as well
    (D) the explanation of behavior on grounds ostensibly rational but not in accord with the actual motives
    (E) the reliance upon reason alone, independently of authority or of revelation

22. The leaders of Islam

    (A) have traditionally been averse to religious discussions with the Catholics
    (B) are agreeable to combining their religion with that of the Christians, since there are many features in common, provided certain specified beliefs can be retained by each religion
    (C) are planning ecumenical councils of their own
    (D) have had a continuously friendly relationship with the Christians
    (E) were responsible for conducting the Spanish Inquisition

23. The work, *Adversus Nefandum Sectum Saracenorum*,

    (A) urged a final victory, bloody if necessary, over the followers of Islam
    (B) favored talks with the Saracens in order to arrive at a peaceful settlement of their differences
    (C) presented ideas that could be employed in the conversion of the Muslims
    (D) commended the religious beliefs of the Islamites
    (E) suggested a cultural and professional interchange between the Christians and the Muslims

24. Synonyms for *Muslim* and *Quran* are

    (A) Mussel and Querin
    (B) Muslin and Quorum
    (C) Islam and Queries
    (D) Mohammedan and Koran
    (E) Clay and Cura

25. A major function of the ecumenical councils has been

    (A) to discuss religious persecution and missionary movements
    (B) to determine how to rid the world of evils such as poverty, disease, and war
    (C) to find common ground with the churches other than the Catholic Church
    (D) to arrive at the most efficient means of eliminating atheism
    (E) to plan procedures for converting the rest of the world to Catholicism

26. That the learned men of both Christianity and Islam should meet to iron out their differences was a proposal of a(n)

    (A) apostle
    (B) monk
    (C) general
    (D) pope
    (E) scientist

Stop

END OF SECTION VI. IF YOU HAVE ANY TIME LEFT, GO OVER YOUR WORK IN THIS SECTION ONLY. DO NOT WORK IN ANY OTHER SECTION OF THE TEST. WHEN YOUR TIME IS UP, GO ON TO THE NEXT SECTION.

SECTION VII: ENGLISH USAGE

15 Minutes
25 Questions

DIRECTIONS: In each of the sentences below, four words or phrases have been underlined. Select the underlined part which contains an error in usage, grammar, or punctuation. If there is no error, mark answer space E.

1. When she <u>graduates college</u> she <u>will have</u> to de-
           A   B
cide <u>whether to continue</u> her studies or <u>seek em-</u>
         C   D
<u>ployment</u>. No error.
      E

2. Judging from the <u>beauty</u> of the night, <u>I believe</u>
               A   B
<u>that</u> we are <u>liable</u> to have <u>good</u> weather tomor-
  C   C   D
row. No error.
     E

3. I hope <u>to be able</u> to <u>retaliate</u> <u>for</u> the assistance
         A   B   C
<u>you have given</u> me. <u>No error.</u>
     D   E

4. He fidgeted, <u>like</u> most children <u>do</u>, while the
            A   B
<u>grown-ups</u> <u>were discussing</u> the problem. <u>No er-</u>
  C   D   E
ror.
 E

5. <u>Certainly</u> there <u>can be no objection</u> to the <u>boys'</u>
   A   B   C
<u>working</u> on a <u>volunteer basis</u>. <u>No error.</u>
  C   D   E

6. In his effort <u>to reach</u> a wise decision about these
          A
<u>truants</u>, the attendance officer <u>conferred</u> many
   B   C

times with the dean and <u>I.</u> <u>No error.</u>
               D   E

7. <u>Fortunately for us</u>, at the time of the accident he
      A
<u>was driving</u> someone <u>else's</u> car, <u>not our's.</u> <u>No</u>
   B   C   D   E
error.
 E

8. We were only halfway through the discussion

when <u>somebody</u> voiced <u>their</u> opinion that <u>long</u>
     A   B   C
and dignified masculine tradition <u>demanded con-</u>
           C   D
<u>cealing</u> all sentiments. <u>No error.</u>
  D   E

9. As I <u>said</u>, <u>I have driven</u> thousands of miles in
    A   B
New England and <u>have found</u> many places where
                C
<u>I should be happy</u> to live. <u>No error.</u>
   D   E

10. The <u>underdogs</u> <u>rallied</u> bravely after <u>their burly</u>
     A   B   C
<u>opponents</u> <u>scored</u> three touchdowns. <u>No error.</u>
  C   D   E

11. He <u>could</u> easily <u>have won</u> a scholarship if he
    A   B
<u>would have devoted</u> more time to <u>his school</u>
     C   D
<u>work</u>. <u>No error.</u>
  D   E

12. Reading, <u>writing</u> and revising <u>seem</u> to be the
        A   B

principal activities of the graduate student. No
   C   D   E
error.
  E

13. The clerk who had fainted told me that he felt
                  A

    alright, so I did not make out an accident report.
      B   C   D
    No error.
      E

14. The secretary prepared a notice that was put
            A   B

    into the mailboxes of all employees, including
    B   C

    yourself. No error.
      D   E

15. If any person wants more information on this
      A   B

    topic, they should write to the company. No er-
       C   D   E
    ror.
    E

16. The emigration of large numbers of persons each
       A   B

    year were gradually reducing the excess popula-
            C   D
    tion. No error.
    D   E

17. Although I have attended college until recently,
          A   B
    I left without getting my degree. No error.
    C   D   E

18. Everybody, bustling about, laughing, and even
      A   B
    shrieking, gave himself up to unmitigated joy.
    C   D
    No error.
      E

19. He replied, when she asked him about the proj-
    A   B
    ect, that he hoped to have finished it soon. No
            C   D   E
    error.
    E

20. Not only did he fail to profit from his stock trans-
          A   B
    actions, but he lost all that he had invested. No
        C   D   E
    error.
    E

21. If you ever visit Paris, you would sense for your-
        A   B   C
    self the grace and charm of an old-world city that
    C   D
    is forever new. No error.
          E

22. I think we should treat them with a mixture of

    respect and irreverence; respect for their learning
          A   B
    and experience, irreverence for any alleged infal-
       C   D
    libility. No error.
        E

23. I was appreciative of all his efforts, especially of
     A   B
    him doing that one job for me. No error.
    C   D   E

24. There were among the spectators at least one who
      A   B
    was unaware of the undercurrent of feeling. No
    C   D   E
    error.
    E

25. Can I go to the football game on Saturday if all
    A   B
    my homework is done? No error.
      C   D   E

Stop

END OF SECTION VII. IF YOU HAVE ANY TIME LEFT, GO OVER YOUR WORK IN THIS SECTION ONLY. DO NOT WORK IN ANY OTHER SECTION OF THE TEST. WHEN YOUR TIME IS UP, GO ON TO THE NEXT SECTION.

SECTION VIII: VERBAL ABILITIES

15 Minutes
25 Questions

ANALOGIES

DIRECTIONS: The following questions consist of a related pair of words or phrases, and five lettered pairs of words or phrases. Choose the lettered pair that best expresses a relationship similar to that expressed in the original pair.

1. INTIMIDATE : FEAR ::

   (A) maintain : satisfaction
   (B) astonish : wonder
   (C) sooth : concern
   (D) feed : hunger
   (E) awaken : tiredness

2. STOVE : KITCHEN ::

   (A) window : bedroom
   (B) sink : bathroom
   (C) television : living room
   (D) trunk : attic
   (E) pot : pan

3. CELEBRATE : MARRIAGE ::

   (A) announce : birthday
   (B) report : injury
   (C) lament : bereavement
   (D) face : penalty
   (E) kiss : groom

4. MARGARINE : BUTTER ::

   (A) cream : milk
   (B) lace : cotton
   (C) nylon : silk
   (D) egg : chicken
   (E) oak : acorn

5. NEGLIGENT : REQUIREMENT ::

   (A) careful : position
   (B) remiss : duty
   (C) cautious : injury
   (D) cogent : task
   (E) easy : hard

6. GAZELLE : SWIFT ::

   (A) horse : slow
   (B) wolf : sly
   (C) swan : graceful
   (D) elephant : gray
   (E) lion : tame

7. IGNOMINY : DISLOYALTY ::

   (A) fame : heroism
   (B) castigation : praise
   (C) death : victory
   (D) approbation : consecration
   (E) derelict : martyr

8. SATURNINE : MERCURIAL ::

   (A) Saturn : Venus
   (B) Appenines : Alps
   (C) redundant : wordy
   (D) allegro : adagio
   (E) heavenly : starry

9. ORANGE : MARMALADE ::

   (A) potato : vegetable
   (B) jelly : jam
   (C) tomato : ketchup
   (D) cake : picnic
   (E) sandwich : ham

45

ANTONYMS

DIRECTIONS: The questions in this section consist of one word followed by five lettered words or phrases. Choose the lettered word or phrase that is most nearly opposite in meaning to the numbered word.

10. CONSENSUS

    (A) poll
    (B) disharmony
    (C) conference
    (D) attitude
    (E) agreement

11. INDIGENOUS

    (A) elevating
    (B) destitute
    (C) insulting
    (D) livid
    (E) foreign

12. DESUETUDE

    (A) spasmodic action
    (B) languor induced by hot weather
    (C) state of use
    (D) harmlessness
    (E) platitude

13. MATUTINAL

    (A) growing and developing steadily
    (B) pertaining to the evening
    (C) patriarchal
    (D) regularly established as an annual event
    (E) offering a reward

14. ABSOLVE

    (A) bless
    (B) blame
    (C) melt
    (D) repent
    (E) recount

15. SACROSANCT

    (A) sacerdotal
    (B) sanctimonious
    (C) sacramental
    (D) surreptitious
    (E) unholy

16. POLEMIC

    (A) arctic
    (B) electro-chemical
    (C) agreement
    (D) statistical
    (E) refundable

17. INTRANSIGENT

    (A) impassable
    (B) reconcilable
    (C) harsh
    (D) fly-by-night
    (E) corroborative

SENTENCE COMPLETIONS

DIRECTIONS: For each of the questions below, choose the lettered word or set of words which best fits the meaning of the sentence.

18. Publication of the article was timed to _____ with the professor's fiftieth birthday.

    (A) coincide
    (B) harmonize
    (C) amalgamate
    (D) terminate
    (E) elucidate

19. Few institutions are more_____than France's provincial museums, but lately an effort has been made to rouse them from their lethargy.

    (A) resistant
    (B) conformist
    (C) conservative
    (D) mellifluous
    (E) somnolent

20. The early part of the performance may prove to be only the lively_____to a more sumptuous drama.

    (A) fissure
    (B) consummation
    (C) prelude
    (D) diversion
    (E) incarceration

21. He owes most of his success to his calm, measured, analytical attack on the problems of advertising, making order out of_____.

    (A) procedure
    (B) chaos
    (C) inquiry
    (D) letter
    (E) miscellany

22. Genius, according to Schopenhauer, is_____to the opinions of others—notably of authorities.

    (A) response
    (B) condolence
    (C) pertinence
    (D) malice
    (E) imperviousness

23. His productions are not _____. The ideas usually are slow in building up.

    (A) comprehensible
    (B) conducive
    (C) matriarchal
    (D) spontaneous
    (E) mortified

24. The concept is so_____that no one has succeeded even in defining it.

    (A) fragmentary
    (B) morbid
    (C) elusive
    (D) slanderous
    (E) mastoidal

25. One of the few hard and fast "musts" around here is _____, which Webster defines as the ability to live, grow, and develop.

    (A) malleability
    (B) viability
    (C) flexibility
    (D) mortification
    (E) livid

Stop

END OF SECTION VIII. IF YOU HAVE ANY TIME LEFT, GO OVER YOUR WORK IN THIS SECTION ONLY. DO NOT WORK IN ANY OTHER SECTION OF THE TEST. WHEN YOUR TIME IS UP, GO ON TO THE NEXT SECTION.

SECTION IX: VALIDITY OF CONCLUSION

30 Minutes
39 Questions

DIRECTIONS: Each of the following four sets consists of a reading passage followed by a conclusion drawn from the passage. Each conclusion is followed by statements that have a possible bearing on the conclusion. For each statement, you are to choose from the following the option that best expresses the relationship between the statement and the conclusion:

(A) The statement proves the conclusion.
(B) The statement supports the conclusion but does not prove it.
(C) The statement disproves the conclusion.
(D) The statement weakens the conclusion.
(E) The statement is irrelevant to the conclusion.

SET 1

Early in the afternoon Mrs. Martin noticed two men carrying gasoline cans to the rear of the Boylston Nursing Home next door. Their actions seemed suspicious but she noticed that one of the men was Ned Boylston, the owner of the nursing home. Her suspicions allayed she forgot the matter and went about her business. Two hours later the fire department arrived to find the nursing home ablaze and full of smoke. Though there were no serious injuries the home was completely destroyed. Lt. Macy of the arson squad discovered a half-consumed sweater in the storeroom at the rear of the home where the fire had apparently started. This raised his suspicions that someone had started the fire and he sent the sweater to the arson lab confident that an analysis would reveal that the sweater had been soaked in gasoline. Mrs. Martin told Lt. Macy about seeing Boylston and his companion with gas cans.

CONCLUSION: Lt. Macy concluded that Boylston was in part responsible for deliberately setting the fire.

1. Boylston's companion was Rick Stricker who had three previous convictions for arson.

2. Fred Duffer, a resident of the nursing home and the one who first discovered the blaze, testified that he was the owner of the suspicious sweater which he had used in an attempt to smother the flames.

3. The nursing home, which for the last few years had been a financial disaster for Boylston, had been heavily insured by Boylston.

4. Boylston and his brother-in-law had just returned from a three-week boating trip and had been noticed by Mrs. Martin as they were unloading gas cans and other boating supplies.

5. Boylston had planned a day-long picnic for the residents of the nursing home on the day of the fire. He had been adamant about everyone leaving the home to attend the picnic.

6. The lab analysis revealed that the sweater had not been soaked in gasoline.

7. The sweater was identified as Boylston's boating sweater and the lab analysis revealed that it had been soaked in gasoline.

8. The Boylston antique furniture collection, which was worth a small fortune and had been destroyed in the fire, was uninsured.

9. Boylston was well liked by the nursing home residents as he was always eager to comply with their needs.

10. Four years earlier another Boylston nursing home had been destroyed by fire.

48

SET 2

Field Ballet Company, based in New York City, has in a short time become one of the leading performing dance groups in the country. This ascendancy is due primarily to their having signed a number of leading European dance stars whom American audiences were eager to see. Nonetheless, maintaining a number of European dance stars has been expensive and the company must now raise a substantial sum of cash. Fred Field, the director of the company, sees two alternatives open to him, either of which would solve his problem. One alternative is not to renew the contracts of Rudolf Zahn and his wife Nina, two of the European dancers who joined the company upon receiving lucrative contracts. Though their release would make a substantial amount of money available, the Zahns have become very popular and along with the other European stars have played a role in attracting audiences. The other alternative is to completely reorganize the company's school, at which the dancers train and rehearse, in order to open up large classes to the general public. If such classes become popular, they can provide a substantial income. However, such expansion would involve a risk, since it is always possible that the classes might not become popular. Also, public classes would to some extent disrupt the company's class and rehearsal schedule.

CONCLUSION: After carefully considering both alternatives open to him, Field concludes that it is in the best interest of the company not to renew the contract of the Zahns rather than open its school to the public.

11. Field learns that a substantial number of dancers in the company have come to resent the Zahns' popularity and plan some sort of disruption if the Zahns are once again offered a lucrative contract.

12. Four other major dance companies in New York have realized significant financial success by opening their classes to the general public.

13. Tom and Kristin Baker, who understudy the Zahns and receive a third of their salary, have received critical acclaim and are thought by the company ballet teachers to have even greater talent than the Zahns.

14. It is discovered that Rudolf Zahn is an alcoholic and has been unable to control his drinking as he and his wife become more and more homesick.

15. The Zahns have become popular national figures and a television network plans to make Field an attractive offer to gain the right to televise Zahn performances.

16. It is learned that Zahn has contracted a serious knee injury and is certain to be out for at least six months. Nina will not appear in any role unless her husband is in the male lead.

17. Several European newspapers have criticized European dance stars for leaving their European companies in order to make more money in America.

18. Nancy Kellman, a strong supporter of the company, learns of Field's plans and offers to donate the sum of the Zahns' salary if Field opens his school to the public.

19. It is learned that all of the European dancers, including the Zahns, have strong objections to opening classes to the general public and threaten to leave the company if such a policy is adopted.

20. It seems that, if the Zahns' contract is not renewed, the rest of the European dancers will also leave the company in protest.

SET 3

The accountant for the Longshore Marina in New Orleans, Louisiana, informed Mr. Peers, the president, that the marina's profits had fallen precipitously over the last five years. Mr. Peers called a meeting of the marina members to inform them of the unsound financial situation and to get suggestions for increasing revenues. By the end of the meeting the members had decided upon three courses of action. First, they decided to raise the dues 15 percent. Second, it was decided that if they could obtain a liquor license they would enlarge the yacht club and keep it open during the evening. The third decision was to have a membership drive and to charge an initial $230 for all new families.

CONCLUSION: Profits increased for the first time in

five years when the marina put their new plans into action.

21. The marina could not obtain a liquor license.

22. Membership increased 20 percent after the membership drive.

23. When the increase in dues was announced many members cancelled their membership.

24. With the profits the marina purchased the adjoining boat yard.

25. The accountant announced that profits fell again during the sixth year.

26. The IRS audited the marina's books during the fifth year.

27. During the sixth year the marina built a new, heated swimming pool.

28. The marina had to close during the sixth year because they did not have enough funds to operate.

29. The accountant was found guilty of embezzling marina funds.

SET 4

Tom Webster, returning home from a business trip to Los Angeles at midnight Sunday evening, was shot in the head and killed. Webster's wife, rock singer Linda Harmony, and one of her frequent nightclub escorts, Nolan Sperry, were both in the house when Webster was shot. They both testified that Linda did not expect her husband to be returning that night, mistook him for a prowler and shot him.

CONCLUSION: Lt. Dannon of the Police Department concluded that Linda Harmony had not conspired to murder her husband.

30. According to airline records Webster had never cancelled his reservation to return the Tuesday following his death.

31. On Sunday one of Sperry's friends had overheard Sperry making plans to see Linda that night after learning from Linda that her husband planned to return on Tuesday.

32. Earlier in the evening Linda had reported receiving two threatening phone calls from a stranger.

33. Webster had left a note for a business contact indicating that he would not be able to meet him since his wife, apprehensive about being alone, had requested that he return Sunday evening.

34. According to neighbors there was sufficient lighting for them to recognize Webster when he returned at midnight.

35. Webster, who had suspicions about his wife's friendship with Sperry, told his secretary that he planned to return early in hopes of surprising them.

36. At the time of questioning Linda seemed to be greatly concerned about her husband's death.

37. Linda's fingerprints were found on the gun that was used to shoot Webster.

38. Sperry and Webster had met several times before.

39. According to neighbors it was at least an hour after Webster returned home before they heard a shot.

Stop

END OF EXAMINATION

END OF SECTION IX. IF YOU HAVE ANY TIME LEFT, GO OVER YOUR WORK IN THIS SECTION ONLY. DO NOT WORK IN ANY OTHER SECTION OF THE TEST. WHEN YOUR TIME IS UP, CHECK YOUR ANSWERS WITH THE ANSWER KEY AND EXPLANATORY ANSWERS PROVIDED ON THE FOLLOWING PAGES.

ANSWER KEY

DIRECTIONS: Compare your answers with the correct answers provided below. Add the total number of your correct answers, counting each as one point. Once you have determined your score, refer to the two tables which follow the Explanatory Answers in order to evaluate your performance on the Diagnostic Examination.

SECTION I

1. C	7. B	13. C
2. B	8. C	14. C
3. A	9. B	15. B
4. E	10. D	16. A
5. C	11. A	17. C
6. D	12. C	18. D

SECTION II

1. E	10. C	19. A
2. C	11. B	20. B
3. B	12. C	21. D
4. B	13. E	22. A
5. A	14. D	23. B
6. C	15. B	24. B
7. A	16. A	25. C
8. C	17. C	
9. A	18. B	

SECTION III

1. A	8. B	15. A
2. D	9. A	16. C
3. E	10. C	17. E
4. B	11. B	18. D
5. C	12. C	19. A
6. C	13. E	20. A
7. C	14. B	

SECTION IV

1. E	6. D	11. E
2. D	7. A	12. B
3. A	8. E	13. C
4. C	9. C	14. A
5. B	10. D	15. C

SECTION V

1. D	7. E	12. C
2. C	8. E	13. B
3. E	9. C	14. B
4. C	10. B	15. E
5. E	11. D	16. E
6. C		

SECTION VI

1. D	10. E	19. E
2. B	11. C	20. C
3. E	12. A	21. E
4. D	13. C	22. A
5. B	14. E	23. B
6. A	15. E	24. D
7. E	16. B	25. C
8. E	17. D	26. E
9. B	18. A	

SECTION VII

1. A	10. D	19. D
2. C	11. C	20. C
3. B	12. E	21. B
4. A	13. B	22. E
5. E	14. E	23. C
6. D	15. C	24. A
7. D	16. C	25. A
8. B	17. A	
9. E	18. E	

SECTION VIII

1. B
2. B
3. C
4. C
5. B
6. C
7. A
8. D
9. C

10. B
11. E
12. C
13. B
14. B
15. E
16. C
17. B
18. A

19. E
20. C
21. B
22. E
23. D
24. C
25. B

SECTION IX

1. B
2. D
3. B
4. D
5. B
6. D
7. A
8. D
9. E
10. E
11. B
12. D
13. B

14. B
15. C
16. A
17. E
18. C
19. A
20. C
21. D
22. B
23. D
24. A
25. C
26. E

27. B
28. C
29. B
30. B
31. B
32. B
33. D
34. D
35. B
36. E
37. E
38. E
39. D

EXPLANATORY ANSWERS

SECTION I

1. **(C)** The writer regards the creation of art as part of that process of "conceiving the universe" in which he enjoins the reader to participate. Earlier in the passage, he states that "music and poetry would resound along the streets," as a result of people learning to delight in the realities of the here and now.

2. **(B)** The writer states that children, "who play life, discern its true law and relations more clearly than men, who fail to live it worthily."

3. **(A)** This thought is expressed throughout the passage. It is, in fact, the writer's opening statement.

4. **(E)** The passage states: "Shams and delusions are esteemed for soundest truths, while reality is fabulous," which can be paraphrased as follows: Nonexistent things are taken for realities, while realities are taken to be nonexistent.

5. **(C)** Once again, this is an idea which permeates the passage. It is summed up toward the end of the passage, where the writer states: "And we are enabled to apprehend at all what is sublime and noble by the perpetual instilling and drenching of the reality that surrounds us."

6. **(D)** The passage deals with the nature of reality, our perception of it, and the role of God in the universe—issues which clearly fall into the domain of philosophy and theology.

7. **(B)** The strongest evidence in support of this answer is the author's mention of Somersetshire and Devonshire. These are the names of specific places in England and can be identified as such on the basis of their sound even if the reader is not familiar with them. The author's mention of places outside of England (Normandy and North America) are less specific geographic designations.

8. **(C)** The argument is identical in form to the argument about apples presented in the passage. The author tells us that this "train of reasoning is what logicians call a syllogism."

9. **(B)** This is clearly the best choice. The author uses apples to demonstrate the form of syllogistic reasoning.

10. **(D)** From the context in which the word is used, it is evident that this is a less familiar form of the word premise—an element in the process of syllogistic reasoning.

11. **(A)** The author is concerned with the procedure by which we acquire knowledge about our environment. Of the choices given, a scientist would be the person most concerned with procedural methods of this nature.

12. **(C)** The natural law mentioned is that all hard, green apples are sour. This law is the result of an induction, or generalization, based on several experiences of finding hard, green apples to be sour.

13. **(C)** This is forthrightly stated as follows: "Anyone may mouth out a passage with a theatrical cadence, or get upon stilts to tell his thoughts; but to write or speak with propriety and simplicity is a more difficult task."

14. **(C)** This would be a good place to start a new paragraph because the tone and emphasis of the passage changes at this point. The relationship between writing and speaking had only been generally discussed. Here we begin to go into this subject in more detail.

15. **(B)** The sentence preceding that quoted in the question outlines the extremes of speaking styles and warns against their use. This supports choice (B).

16. **(A)** By definition, cant means the special language of a particular group of people.

17. **(C)** The author has stressed simplicity throughout the passage. He rejects "slipshod allusions."

18. **(D)** Throughout the passage, the author has been criticizing pretentiousness and pomposity. Choice (D) is the only one that is relevant.

SECTION II

1. **(E)** Every hour, the minute hand of a clock goes around once, or 360°. In two hours, it rotates 720°.

2. **(C)** $^{15}/_{45}$ would be ⅓. With a larger denominator, the fraction $^{15}/_{46}$ is less than ⅓.

3. **(B)** Since the perimeter of a square is four times the length of a side, it is

$$4\left(\frac{2x}{3} + 1\right), \text{ or } \frac{8x + 12}{3}$$

4. **(B)** IQ is 100 times this result: the mental age of a person divided by his chronological age. This is $100 \times 160 \div 128$, which equals 125.

5. **(A)** Time does not vary with latitude (distance from the equator), but only with longitude (distance from the prime meridian).

6. **(C)** ABD forms a right triangle with both legs equal to 1 inch. By the Pythagorean Theorem, AD = $\sqrt{2}$.

7. **(A)** Imagine the triangle ACH rotated 180° about AH. C will be lower than the present position of the ABEF plane.

8. **(C)** AX must be shorter than AH, which is $\sqrt{3}$, and longer than AB, which is 1.

9. **(A)** The first rotation puts X where ACGE was. The second leaves X in the same plane. The third rotation returns X to its original position.

10. **(C)** The carpenter needs a total of 33 inches for each board. The total length is 132 inches, or 11 feet.

11. **(B)** CM equals 1000 − 100, or 900.
XL equals 50 − 10, or 40.
IX equals 10 − 1, or 9.
Their sum is 949.

The answers to 12–16 can be readily seen from the diagram below.

12. **(C)**

13. **(E)**

14. **(D)**

15. **(B)**

16. **(A)**

17. **(C)** In the first trip, the motorist travels 120 miles at 60 m.p.h., which takes 2 hours. On the way back, he travels the same distance at 40 m.p.h., which takes 3 hours. His average rate is the total distance (240 miles) divided by the total time (5 hours), which yields 48 m.p.h.

18. **(B)** The proportion to be solved is 2½:4 = 1⅞:x, where x is the length of the shorter dimension of the enlargement. Solving, x=3.

19. **(A)** The area of the circle is π times the square of the radius, or 9π. The area of the square is 36. Thus, the ratio is $\frac{9\pi}{36}$, or $\frac{\pi}{4}$. Approximating π as 3.14, we divide and obtain .785, which is closest to $^4/_5$.

20. **(B)** By simple substitutions, s= 16×8×8, or 1024.

21. **(D)** If angles BAD and BCD are right angles, they are equal. Angle BAC equals angle BCA, since they are base angles of an isosceles triangle. Subtracting equals from equals, angle DAC

equals angle DCA. Therefore, ACD is an isosceles triangle, and AD=CD.

22. **(A)** $10^2 = 100$, or $\wedge\square\square$

23. **(B)** $\triangleright + \exists + \lessgtr = 4+6+3 = 13 = \wedge\lessgtr$

24. **(B)** $\dfrac{\exists}{\times} = \dfrac{6}{8} = \dfrac{3}{4}$

25. **(C)** $\wedge Z \exists - \triangleright\curlyvee + \dfrac{\wedge\square}{Z} = 126 - 47 + \dfrac{10}{2} = 84 = \times\triangleright$

SECTION III

1. **(A)** It is stated that Wingfleet wishes to enter the commercial aircraft field, which is a major reason to try to secure the 2L-1000 contract.

2. **(D)** It is not absolutely certain that the 2L-1000 will not be produced at the bid price, although John Franco is dubious that it can.

3. **(E)** The length of time it will take to produce the 2L-1000 does not seem to concern anyone.

4. **(B)** The possibility that the 2L-1000 can be converted to a commercial plane is a major factor contributing to a major objective of Wingfleet to enter the commercial market.

5. **(C)** The possible liquidation of Ponzol by a foreign government is a factor relating to the exclusive contract held by Wingfleet.

6. **(C)** Since 90 percent of Wingfleet's business is with the government, government reductions in military spending is a major reason why Wingfleet wishes to enter the commercial field.

7. **(C)** The willingness by airlines to make substantial down payments is a minor factor leading to the major factor of a purchase order of 201 passenger planes, which, in turn, influences the major objective of Wingfleet's entrance into the commercial aircraft field.

8. **(B)** The order for 201 passenger planes is a major factor influencing the major objective of Wingfleet's entrance into the commercial aircraft field.

9. **(A)** Diversification is a major objective since Wingfleet has had to depend on the single market of government contracts.

10. **(C)** This is a concern in the event that the project's cost exceeds Wingfleet's bid.

11. **(B)** It is stated that nearly 90 percent of Wingfleet's business is done with the U.S. government.

12. **(C)** It is emphasized that Wingfleet has had to depend on defense contracts which can greatly fluctuate from year to year.

13. **(E)** By being able to modify 2L-1000, the company can enter the commercial aircraft field, which is seen as an advantage.

14. **(B)** Commercial airlines are said to be ready to purchase 201 passenger planes and are willing to make immediate down payments if Wingfleet gets the 2L-1000 contract.

15. **(A)** It is stated that the executive committee suggests making a bid for the 2L-1000 contract, a recommendation which Franco decides to carry to the Board of Directors.

16. **(C)** It is stated that Congress is in an anti-military mood and might frown on paying cost overruns. (A) is incorrect because Congress has been generous with cost overruns before. In (B) the important word is "would," to indicate that Wingfleet would have to pay for the cost overruns. (E) might be true but is not so stated. (D) is obviously untrue.

17. **(E)** The fact that Ponzol engines would be used in the 2L-1000 is assumed to carry great weight with the Pentagon. (A) is wrong; Wingfleet's reputation has not been made in the commercial aircraft field. (B) is exaggerated; many people might be thrown out of work, but failure to get the contract would not throw the huge U.S. economy into a state of chaos. As far as (C) is concerned, many banks would back Wingfleet should

it receive the contract, but it is not stated that this fact would influence the Pentagon's decision. (D) is obviously incorrect.

18. **(D)** John Franco is worried about Ponzol because it is a nationalized company whose foreign government might liquidate it at any time. (B), (C), and (A) are obviously wrong. (E) is incorrect because it is stated that Wingfleet has received orders for 201 aircraft from airlines willing to use the planes commercially.

19. **(A)** It is true that 25 banks would have to lend half a billion dollars for Wingfleet to produce the 2L-1000. (B) is wrong; recently Wingfleet has experienced a deficit. By referring to the tenth paragraph, you can see that (C), (D), and (E) are incorrect.

20. **(A)** It is stated that Wingfleet tried to enter the commercial aircraft field three times without success. Therefore (B) and (E) are incorrect. (C) is wrong; 90 percent of the company's business has been in the military plane field. (D) must be wrong since Wingfleet would not have been able to remain in business had it shown consistent losses on government contracts.

SECTION IV

1. **(E)** The increase from 1900 to 1960 is approximately 100 million.

   $100/75 = 4/3 = 1\frac{1}{3} = 133\frac{1}{3}\% = 135\%$

2. **(D)** In 1900 the population is about 75 million. In 1950 the population is about 150 million. Hence, it doubles in 50 years.

3. **(A)** The greatest increase in population appears to have been from 1950 to 1960 (almost 30 million). Hence, the decade ending 1960 is the correct answer.

4. **(C)** The smallest increase appears to be from 1930 to 1940 (about 5 million). Hence, the decade ending 1940 is the correct answer.

5. **(B)** The ratio of populations is approximately $180/150 = 18/15 = 6:5$.

6. **(D)** 1950: 15% of 11.8 billion = 1,770,000,000. 1965: 25% of 49.2 billion = 12,300,000,000.

   $$\frac{12.3 - 1.77}{1.77} = 5.949 = 595\% \text{ (approx.)}$$

7. **(A)** 25% of 11.8 billion is approximately one-fifth as much as 30% of 49.2 billion.

8. **(E)** The graph gives no breakdown of Canada's manufacturing industry in 1965.

9. **(C)** 1950: 40% of 11.8 billion is less than 20% of 49.2 billion.

10. **(D)** 1.6 billion + 1.4 billion = 3 billion. 3 billion is about 70% of 4.3 billion.

11. **(E)** 25% of 1.8 billion + 45% of 1 billion = 900 million.

12. **(B)** 2.6 billion minus 1.4 billion = 1.2 billion.

    $$\frac{1.2}{1.4} = .857 = 86\% \text{ (approx.)}$$

13. **(C)** 1957: 35% of 3.9 billion = 1 billion, 365 million. 1961: 30% of 4.3 billion = 1 billion, 290 million.

14. **(A)** 35% of 3.9 billion = 1 billion, 365 million. This exceeds the amount of each of the other choices.

15. **(C)** $\frac{1.4}{4.3}$ times 360 degrees is approximately 117 degrees.

SECTION V

1. **(D)** By statement (1) if the rectangle were 6 inches longer, it would be exactly 3 feet, implies it must now be 2½ feet. By statement (2) if the rectangle were 6 inches less it would be exactly 2 feet, implies also it must now be 2½ feet.

2. **(C)** Using the introduction and statement (1) we learn the 3 cars sold for $10,200. Adding statement (2) and taking 20% of the total selling

price, we find the salesman earned $2,040.

3. **(E)** Neither statement (1) nor (2) indicate that A and B are definitely on the same committee.

4. **(C)** By statement (1) if 2 bulos = 8 gulos, 4 bulos = 16 gulos.
By statement (2) if 16 munos = 4 bulos, then using (1) and (2) 4 bulos = 16 gulos = 16 munos.
∴ 16 gulos = 16 munos
and 8 gulos = 8 munos.

5. **(E)** Neither by statement (1) nor (2) can it be determined how many pounds of frankfurters were consumed by the boys and girls.

6. **(C)** To find the area of the entire figure, you must find the area of both geometric figures shown. By statement (1) the area of the square can be found using the formula $A = S^2$. Therefore, $A = 4^2$, $A = 16$. By statement (2) the area of the equilateral triangle can be found by using the formula,
$$A = \frac{S^2}{4}\sqrt{3}.$$
$$A = \frac{4^2}{4}\sqrt{3}, \quad A = 4\sqrt{3}.$$
Combining both statements, the area of the entire figure is $16 + 4\sqrt{3}$.

7. **(E)** Both statements do not provide enough information to find the angle BDA.

8. **(E)** Since the lengths of the sides of both polygons cannot be determined, it is impossible to determine if the perimeter of X is greater than the perimeter of Y.

9. **(C)** The radius drawn to a tangent is perpendicular to the tangent at the point of contact, therefore △ PAO is a rt. triangle. By statement (1) OA = 6 and by statement (2) PA = 8. Hence, using the Pythagorean theorem $(OP)^2 = 8^2 + 6^2$, $(OP)^2 = 64 + 36$; $(OP)^2 = 100$; $OP = 10$.

10. **(B)** By statement (2) tC = A, A is negative. To get a negative answer in multiplication, you must multiply unlike signs; C is negative, therefore t is not negative.

11. **(D)** $\dfrac{3A - 2B}{4} = 1$
$3A - 2B = 4$

By statement (1), A = 2B substituting

$3A - 2B = 4$	$3A - 2B = 4$
$3(2B) - 2B = 4$	$3A - 2(1) = 4$
$6B - 2B = 4$	$3A - 2 = 4$
$4B = 4$	$3A = 6$
$B = 1$	$A = 2$

Knowing A and B, the problem can now be determined.
By statement (2), B = 4 substituting

$$3A - 2B = 4$$
$$3A - 2(4) = 4$$
$$3A - 8 = 4$$
$$3A = 12$$
$$A = 4$$

Knowing A and B, again the problem can be answered.

12. **(C)** By statement (1) BD = 15; by statement (2) CD = 10. Subtracting BD − CD, 15 − 10 = 5, BC = 5.

13. **(B)** By statement (2) chords equidistant from the center of a circle are equal; equal chords have equal arcs ($\overset{\frown}{BC} = \overset{\frown}{CD}$). Angles x and y intercept equal arcs, therefore, x = y. Thus the ratio is 1:1.

14. **(B)** By statement (2) if angle C = 95°, then angles A and B are the equal angles and each are 42½°.

15. **(E)** Neither statement supplies enough information to solve the problem.

16. **(E)** Since the series is not defined, neither statement helps in solving the problem.

SECTION VI

1. **(D)** The author states that, for most questions, the test-taker can narrow his possible choices by

eliminating those choices which he knows to be wrong, thereby improving his chances of guessing the right answer.

2. **(B)** According to the passage, the established procedure for penalizing guessing assumes that all guessed answers are made at random, while in reality guesses are made on the basis of conditioning factors, and that these factors may be controlled to mislead the test-taker who guesses.

3. **(E)** Choice (E) is a logical conclusion to draw from the passage, as this is the method recommended by the author to avoid giving away answers by guess-work.

4. **(D)** Condign means deserved, appropriate.

5. **(B)** Indigenous would be the best distractor to add from the list of possible words, as it is both an adjective and has a sound similar to condign.

6. **(A)** Only one person in forty chose the correct answer to the question, or 2.5%.

7. **(E)** In a five-part question, 1/n represents one part of the five parts making up the whole, or $^1/_5$.

8. **(E)** Though it is not defined in the passage, we may conclude by the context in which it is introduced that a mare basin is a lunar geological feature. This eliminates all possible answers except (E).

9. **(B)** This is determined from the fourth paragraph.

10. **(E)** This is also mentioned in the fourth paragraph.

11. **(C)** Nowhere is this listed as a possibility in the passage although the formation of ocean basins is discussed.

12. **(A)** Although most of the passage seemingly discusses craters, the first paragraph presents the topic as the examination of one of the theories of continent formation. The last paragraph supports this.

13. **(C)** This is deducible from the sixth paragraph which discusses this term in relation to continent formation.

14. **(E)** The author states this quite explicitly in the third paragraph.

15. **(E)** This is made explicit in the first paragraph as the author explains the communists' dogmatic beliefs and the attitudes they hold regarding the superiority of their system.

16. **(B)** As stated in the first paragraph, economic development is at the core of the whole Marxist philosophy. None of the other choices deal with this.

17. **(D)** This is defined in the first and second paragraphs.

18. **(A)** The passage states that "the final judgment on any prophecy has to be made in the light of subsequent events."

19. **(E)** The writer clearly states that he is not going to evaluate Marxism but only outline and discuss certain matters. His observations are based on facts which would lead to choice (E). He is clearly not indifferent (D) since his personal feelings are expressed throughout the passage.

20. **(C)** Capitalism is not discussed in the passage.

21. **(E)** The first paragraph implies that one of the main reasons for the First Ecumenical Council was the rationalist movement. Ecumenism is a bringing together. Choice (E) states that the rationalist movement is a reliance on reason alone, not on revelation or authority—in other words, a turning away from the Catholic Church. This is by far the best choice.

22. **(A)** This is clearly the only possible choice as is made firmly evident in the final paragraph.

23. **(B)** Paragraph two makes this clear.

24. **(D)** This is a matter of common knowledge.

25. **(C)** As quoted in the first paragraph in discussing the meaning of ecumenism, the Council is "to try to bring together the various churches in Christendom."

26. **(E)** Roger Bacon is regarded as one of the first "scientists." He was also one of the leading scholars of his time.

SECTION VII

1. **(A)** When she *graduates from college* she will have to decide whether to continue her studies or seek employment. The correct expression for completing the schoolwork is to *graduate from*. This is more effective than the passive form, *to be graduated from*, although both usages are correct.

2. **(C)** Judging from the beauty of the night, I believe that we are *likely* to have good weather tomorrow. *Liable* is used for undesirable happenings.

3. **(B)** I hope to be able to *reciprocate* for the assistance you have given me. *Retaliate* means to strike back for some injury; *reciprocate* means to pay back for a kindness.

4. **(A)** He fidgeted, *as* most children do, while the grown-ups were discussing the problem. *Like* is a preposition and cannot act as a subordinate conjunction to introduce a clause. *As* does that job.

5. **(E)** There are no errors in this sentence.

6. **(D)** In his effort to reach a wise decision about these truants, the attendance officer conferred many times with the dean and *me*. The objects of the preposition *with* are *dean* and *me*.

7. **(D)** Fortunately for us, at the time of the accident he was driving someone else's car, not *ours*. The possessive pronoun *ours* has no apostrophe.

8. **(B)** We were only halfway through the discussion when somebody voiced *his* opinion that long and dignified masculine tradition demanded concealing all sentiments. *Somebody*, being a singular antecedent, requires a singular possessive pronoun *his*.

9. **(E)** There are no errors in this sentence.

10. **(D)** The underdogs rallied bravely after their burly opponents *had scored* three touchdowns. The past perfect (*had scored*) is required to express the earlier of two past actions.

11. **(C)** He could easily have won a scholarship if he *had devoted* more time to his school work. The contrary-to-fact past condition requires the past perfect subjunctive form (*had devoted*) in the "if" clause.

12. **(E)** There are no errors in this sentence.

13. **(B)** The clerk who had fainted told me that he felt *all right*, so I did not make out an accident report. *Alright* is never correct.

14. **(E)** This sentence is correct.

15. **(C)** If any person wants more information on this topic, *he* should write to the company. A pronoun must agree with its antecedent in number, person and gender. Since the antecedent is singular (*any person*), the pronoun called for is *he*.

16. **(C)** The emigration of large numbers of persons each year *was* gradually reducing the excess population. Since the subject (*emigration*) is singular, the verb must be singular (*was reducing*).

17. **(A)** Although I *attended* college until recently, I left without getting my degree. The past tense (*attended*) is correct here to express a completed action in the past.

18. **(E)** There are no errors in this sentence.

19. **(D)** He replied, when she asked him about the project, that he hoped *to finish* it soon. The present infinitive is required for tense sequence after *hoped*. The present tense of an infinitive is used to indicate that the infinitive has the same time or a future time with relation to the time of the main verb.

20. **(C)** Not only did he fail to profit from his stock transactions, but *he also lost* all that he had invested. The *not only* clause requires a *but also* clause to complete the comparison.

21. **(B)** If you ever visit Paris, you *will sense* for yourself the grace and charm of an old-world city that is forever new. In a future condition which is capable of fulfillment, the principal clause has a verb which is future indicative (*will sense*).

22. **(E)** There are no errors in this sentence.

23. **(C)** I was appreciative of all his efforts, especially of *his* doing that one job for me. The modifier of the gerund *doing* must be an adjective (*his*).

24. **(A)** There *was* among the spectators at least one who was unaware of the undercurrent of feeling. The subject of the verb *was* is *one*.

25. **(A)** *May* I go to the football game on Saturday if all my homework is done? *May* is used for permission. *Can* is used for a physical possibility.

SECTION VIII

1. **(B)** To intimidate is to inspire fear; to astonish is to inspire wonder.

2. **(B)** A stove is an essential part of a kitchen; a sink is an essential part of a bathroom.

3. **(C)** You happily celebrate a marriage; you sorrowfully lament a bereavement.

4. **(C)** Margarine is a manufactured substitute for butter; nylon is a manufactured substitute for silk.

5. **(B)** A person may be negligent in meeting a requirement; he may similarly be remiss in performing his duty.

6. **(C)** A gazelle is known to be swift; a swan is known to be graceful.

7. **(A)** One falls into ignominy if he shows disloyalty; one gains fame if he shows heroism.

8. **(D)** Saturnine and mercurial are antonyms; so are allegro and adagio.

9. **(C)** Marmalade is made from oranges; ketchup is made from tomatoes.

10. **(B)** Consensus means agreement; disharmony is disagreement.

11. **(E)** Indigenous means native; foreign means alien or strange.

12. **(C)** Desuetude means disuse; state of use is the state of being used.

13. **(B)** Matutinal means morning; pertaining to evening is its opposite.

14. **(B)** Absolve means free from blame; blame is to accuse.

15. **(E)** Sacrosanct means sacred; unholy is not sacred.

16. **(C)** Polemic is disputation; agreement is acquiescence.

17. **(B)** Intransigent is unmoving, obstinate; reconcilable is able to make amends.

18. **(A)** Coincide means occur simultaneously.

19. **(E)** Somnolent means sleepy.

20. **(C)** A prelude is an introduction.

21. **(B)** Chaos is disorder.

22. **(E)** Imperviousness is insensitivity.

23. **(D)** Spontaneous means impromptu or off-the-cuff.

24. **(C)** Elusive means evasive, slippery.

25. **(B)** Viability is workability or the capability to live.

SECTION IX

1. **(B)** Combined with the other facts, this would be a strong reason for accepting Macy's conclusion.

A final conclusion awaits the lab analysis of the sweater.

2. **(D)** The suspicion of arson was based primarily on the found sweater, and now that the sweater is accounted for, Macy's conclusion is greatly weakened.

3. **(B)** This gives Boylston a strong motive for starting the fire. His presence with the gas cans is some indication, though not a decisive one, that he acted with this motive.

4. **(D)** This explains Boylston's presence with the gas cans and thus weakens the conclusion that he was there with the gas cans with the intention of starting a fire.

5. **(B)** Such a stress on evacuation could have been due to an intention to set the fire but without an intention to harm anyone.

6. **(D)** The suspicion of arson was based primarily on the found sweater, and thus Macy's conclusion is weakened.

7. **(A)** Boylston's presence with the gas cans and this new information, which indicates gasoline was deliberately used to start the fire, decisively implicates Boylston.

8. **(D)** Such a loss would make Boylston's deliberate involvement in setting the fire extremely unlikely. Still, if the lab analysis indicates the sweater was soaked in gas, then Boylston's presence with the gas cans would continue to make him a prime suspect.

9. **(E)** This tells us nothing about Boylston's possible involvement in setting the fire.

10. **(E)** One previous fire would not in itself raise suspicions about Boylston. The information would become relevant if arson had been established in the previous fire.

11. **(B)** This statement supports the conclusion. Dissent among company members would affect the performance of the company and could even endanger its future. Still, it is possible that the company could survive a period of dissent and enjoy the benefits of keeping the Zahns.

12. **(D)** This statement weakens the conclusion. It provides some reason for thinking that the Field Company could solve its financial problems in a manner similar to that of the other companies mentioned. It does not constitute a disproof, however, since there may be features about the Field Company and its situation which are unique.

13. **(B)** This statement supports the conclusion by opening up the possibility that the Zahns' departure would not really hurt the company since the Zahns could be replaced by the popular and promising Bakers. There can be no guarantee, however, that the Zahns' departure would not hurt the company.

14. **(B)** This statement supports the conclusion. The Zahns' personal problems could make them a liability rather than an asset in the future. There is no certainty, however, that these problems are irremediable.

15. **(C)** This statement disproves the conclusion. With this new and unexpected source of income, there is no longer any reason to take either of the undesirable options.

16. **(A)** This statement proves the conclusion. If Zahn will be unable to dance, and his wife will not dance, there would be no advantage to renewing their contract. Not renewing their contract will solve the problem of funds.

17. **(E)** The attitudes expressed in the European papers have no relevance to Field's decision regarding the Zahns.

18. **(C)** This statement disproves the conclusion. Since the cash problem is solved by this new condition, there is no longer any reason to give up the Zahns.

19. **(A)** This statement proves the conclusion. Since the Zahns' attitude about open classes makes it impossible for Field to keep them and also open up classes, Field has no choice but to not renew their contract.

20. **(C)** This statement disproves the conclusion. Choosing to not renew the Zahns' contract would seem to be disastrous for the company since its success seems dependent upon the European dan-

cers. The option of not renewing the Zahns' contract, therefore, is not in the best interest of the company.

21. **(D)** This statement tends to disprove the result. The way the marina members wanted to increase profits was by enlarging the club and serving liquor. If they couldn't obtain a liquor license they couldn't follow this course of action. But they also had two other ways in mind of increasing profits so the result is not disproved.

22. **(B)** An increased membership means increased profits. This tends to prove the result. But other factors may have decreased the profits; for example, if old members cancelled their memberships because of the increased dues. This statement does not prove the result.

23. **(D)** This statement is really the opposite of question 22. Although profits would decrease with cancelled memberships this does not disprove the result because the marina could have obtained many new members.

24. **(A)** This statement tells us that the marina made a profit, proving the result.

25. **(C)** This statement contradicts the result.

26. **(E)** An audit of the books is irrelevant to whether or not the marina made profits as it is standard practice for the IRS to audit a company's books at random. Also, the audit is during the fifth year and profits are announced for the sixth year.

27. **(B)** This statement tends to affirm the result that the marina increased profits because one would think that the profits were used for the pool. But, the marina could have taken out a loan to build the pool in the hopes of attracting new members. So, this statement does not prove the result.

28. **(C)** This statement disproves the result. If the marina had to close because they didn't have enough funds to operate, we can assume profits did not increase.

29. **(B)** This statement tends to prove the result. It would seem unlikely that the accountant would embezzle the marina's funds unless there was enough money to make it worth his while. But,

we don't know how much money was available, or what year the accountant embezzled. He could have taken the money and then announced that profits were decreasing. This statement does not prove the result.

30. **(B)** Since Webster did not notify the airlines about his change of plans there is some reason to believe that the return was also unexpected by his wife.

31. **(B)** This is a strong but not conclusive reason for believing that Linda did not expect the return of her husband and thus did not plan to murder him on his return.

32. **(B)** If the reports were made in earnest then Linda's shooting of her husband might have been prompted by a fear of intrusion. There is the possibility that they were not made in earnest.

33. **(D)** This indicates that his wife did expect him home and makes it unlikely that she mistook him for a prowler. Still, if she had indeed been extremely agitated over the possibility of an intruder, this could have led to a loss of good judgment.

34. **(D)** If the lighting was sufficient for the neighbors to recognize Webster it seems unlikely, though still possible, that his wife would mistake him for a prowler.

35. **(B)** This establishes that Webster intended to return home unexpectedly, but does not prove that Linda did not intend to murder her husband.

36. **(E)** Her emotional state at the time of questioning is no indication of guilt or innocence.

37. **(E)** This would only establish that Linda fired the gun, a fact she has not denied. The fingerprints would neither support nor weaken Dannon's conclusion.

38. **(E)** Their past meetings have no relevance to Linda's possible guilt.

39. **(D)** The timing of the shot makes it less likely that Webster was mistaken for an intruder. Still it is possible that Webster came in unnoticed and was only later mistaken for an intruder.

EVALUATING YOUR
SCORE ON THE
DIAGNOSTIC EXAMINATION

STEP ONE—Compare your total score with the Unofficial Percentile Ranking Table below. This Table will give you a reasonably good idea of how you stand with others taking the Exam. For example, if your percentile ranking is 61, according to your score, you are superior to 65% and inferior to 39% of those who have taken the Exam. Your percentile ranking on the Examination is a major factor in determining your eligibility.

PERCENTILE RANKING TABLE
(unofficial)

Approximate Percentile Ranking	Score on Test
90–99	148–170
80–89	127–147
70–79	106–126
60–69	85–105
50–59	64–84
40–49	43–63
30–39	22–42
1–29	0–21

STEP TWO—Use the results of the Examination you have just taken to diagnose yourself. Pinpoint the areas in which you show the greatest weakness. Fill in the Diagnostic Table to spotlight the subjects in which you need the most practice.

DIAGNOSTIC TABLE

SUBJECT TESTED	QUESTIONS ANSWERED CORRECTLY ON EXAM		
	Strong	Average	Weak
READING COMPREHENSION	13–18	7–12	0–6
PROBLEM SOLVING	19–25	10–18	0–9
PRACTICAL BUSINESS JUDGMENT	15–20	8–14	0–7
DATA INTERPRETATION	11–15	6–10	0–5
DATA SUFFICIENCY	13–16	7–12	0–6
READING RECALL	19–26	10–18	0–9
ENGLISH USAGE	19–25	10–18	0–9
VERBAL ABILITIES	19–25	10–18	0–9
VALIDITY OF CONCLUSION	29–39	18–28	0–17

Part Three

Three Practice Examinations

PRACTICE EXAMINATION 1

This ARCO Practice Examination is similar to the Graduate Management Admission Test you are going to take in structure, length, and level of difficulty. The examination sections and question-types approximate those of the actual examination.

Take this examination as if you were taking the real test. Follow all instructions and observe the time limits indicated. Remember to mark all your answers on the Answer Sheet provided, which is similar to the one you will find on the actual examination.

An Answer Key and Explanatory Answers for every question in this Practice Examination are provided at the end of the exam. Check your answers to find out your areas of weakness and then concentrate your studies where they are most needed.

The total time allowed for this test is 3 hours.

ANALYSIS AND TIMETABLE: PRACTICE EXAMINATION 1

Subject Tested	Time Allowed
READING COMPREHENSION	30 minutes
PROBLEM SOLVING	35 minutes
PRACTICAL BUSINESS JUDGMENT	20 minutes
DATA SUFFICIENCY	30 minutes
PRACTICAL BUSINESS JUDGMENT	20 minutes
VERBAL ABILITIES	15 minutes
READING RECALL	30 minutes

ANSWER SHEET
PRACTICE EXAMINATION 1
SECTION I: READING COMPREHENSION

1 Ⓐ Ⓑ © Ⓓ Ⓔ	6 Ⓐ Ⓑ © Ⓓ Ⓔ	11 Ⓐ Ⓑ © Ⓓ Ⓔ	16 Ⓐ Ⓑ © Ⓓ Ⓔ	21 Ⓐ Ⓑ © Ⓓ Ⓔ
2 Ⓐ Ⓑ © Ⓓ Ⓔ	7 Ⓐ Ⓑ © Ⓓ Ⓔ	12 Ⓐ Ⓑ © Ⓓ Ⓔ	17 Ⓐ Ⓑ © Ⓓ Ⓔ	22 Ⓐ Ⓑ © Ⓓ Ⓔ
3 Ⓐ Ⓑ © Ⓓ Ⓔ	8 Ⓐ Ⓑ © Ⓓ Ⓔ	13 Ⓐ Ⓑ © Ⓓ Ⓔ	18 Ⓐ Ⓑ © Ⓓ Ⓔ	23 Ⓐ Ⓑ © Ⓓ Ⓔ
4 Ⓐ Ⓑ © Ⓓ Ⓔ	9 Ⓐ Ⓑ © Ⓓ Ⓔ	14 Ⓐ Ⓑ © Ⓓ Ⓔ	19 Ⓐ Ⓑ © Ⓓ Ⓔ	24 Ⓐ Ⓑ © Ⓓ Ⓔ
5 Ⓐ Ⓑ © Ⓓ Ⓔ	10 Ⓐ Ⓑ © Ⓓ Ⓔ	15 Ⓐ Ⓑ © Ⓓ Ⓔ	20 Ⓐ Ⓑ © Ⓓ Ⓔ	25 Ⓐ Ⓑ © Ⓓ Ⓔ

SECTION II: PROBLEM SOLVING

1 Ⓐ Ⓑ © Ⓓ Ⓔ	7 Ⓐ Ⓑ © Ⓓ Ⓔ	13 Ⓐ Ⓑ © Ⓓ Ⓔ	19 Ⓐ Ⓑ © Ⓓ Ⓔ	25 Ⓐ Ⓑ © Ⓓ Ⓔ
2 Ⓐ Ⓑ © Ⓓ Ⓔ	8 Ⓐ Ⓑ © Ⓓ Ⓔ	14 Ⓐ Ⓑ © Ⓓ Ⓔ	20 Ⓐ Ⓑ © Ⓓ Ⓔ	26 Ⓐ Ⓑ © Ⓓ Ⓔ
3 Ⓐ Ⓑ © Ⓓ Ⓔ	9 Ⓐ Ⓑ © Ⓓ Ⓔ	15 Ⓐ Ⓑ © Ⓓ Ⓔ	21 Ⓐ Ⓑ © Ⓓ Ⓔ	27 Ⓐ Ⓑ © Ⓓ Ⓔ
4 Ⓐ Ⓑ © Ⓓ Ⓔ	10 Ⓐ Ⓑ © Ⓓ Ⓔ	16 Ⓐ Ⓑ © Ⓓ Ⓔ	22 Ⓐ Ⓑ © Ⓓ Ⓔ	28 Ⓐ Ⓑ © Ⓓ Ⓔ
5 Ⓐ Ⓑ © Ⓓ Ⓔ	11 Ⓐ Ⓑ © Ⓓ Ⓔ	17 Ⓐ Ⓑ © Ⓓ Ⓔ	23 Ⓐ Ⓑ © Ⓓ Ⓔ	29 Ⓐ Ⓑ © Ⓓ Ⓔ
6 Ⓐ Ⓑ © Ⓓ Ⓔ	12 Ⓐ Ⓑ © Ⓓ Ⓔ	18 Ⓐ Ⓑ © Ⓓ Ⓔ	24 Ⓐ Ⓑ © Ⓓ Ⓔ	30 Ⓐ Ⓑ © Ⓓ Ⓔ

SECTION III: PRACTICAL BUSINESS JUDGMENT

1 Ⓐ Ⓑ © Ⓓ Ⓔ	5 Ⓐ Ⓑ © Ⓓ Ⓔ	9 Ⓐ Ⓑ © Ⓓ Ⓔ	13 Ⓐ Ⓑ © Ⓓ Ⓔ	17 Ⓐ Ⓑ © Ⓓ Ⓔ
2 Ⓐ Ⓑ © Ⓓ Ⓔ	6 Ⓐ Ⓑ © Ⓓ Ⓔ	10 Ⓐ Ⓑ © Ⓓ Ⓔ	14 Ⓐ Ⓑ © Ⓓ Ⓔ	18 Ⓐ Ⓑ © Ⓓ Ⓔ
3 Ⓐ Ⓑ © Ⓓ Ⓔ	7 Ⓐ Ⓑ © Ⓓ Ⓔ	11 Ⓐ Ⓑ © Ⓓ Ⓔ	15 Ⓐ Ⓑ © Ⓓ Ⓔ	19 Ⓐ Ⓑ © Ⓓ Ⓔ
4 Ⓐ Ⓑ © Ⓓ Ⓔ	8 Ⓐ Ⓑ © Ⓓ Ⓔ	12 Ⓐ Ⓑ © Ⓓ Ⓔ	16 Ⓐ Ⓑ © Ⓓ Ⓔ	20 Ⓐ Ⓑ © Ⓓ Ⓔ

SECTION IV: DATA SUFFICIENCY

1 Ⓐ Ⓑ Ⓒ Ⓓ Ⓔ	7 Ⓐ Ⓑ Ⓒ Ⓓ Ⓔ	13 Ⓐ Ⓑ Ⓒ Ⓓ Ⓔ	19 Ⓐ Ⓑ Ⓒ Ⓓ Ⓔ	25 Ⓐ Ⓑ Ⓒ Ⓓ Ⓔ
2 Ⓐ Ⓑ Ⓒ Ⓓ Ⓔ	8 Ⓐ Ⓑ Ⓒ Ⓓ Ⓔ	14 Ⓐ Ⓑ Ⓒ Ⓓ Ⓔ	20 Ⓐ Ⓑ Ⓒ Ⓓ Ⓔ	26 Ⓐ Ⓑ Ⓒ Ⓓ Ⓔ
3 Ⓐ Ⓑ Ⓒ Ⓓ Ⓔ	9 Ⓐ Ⓑ Ⓒ Ⓓ Ⓔ	15 Ⓐ Ⓑ Ⓒ Ⓓ Ⓔ	21 Ⓐ Ⓑ Ⓒ Ⓓ Ⓔ	27 Ⓐ Ⓑ Ⓒ Ⓓ Ⓔ
4 Ⓐ Ⓑ Ⓒ Ⓓ Ⓔ	10 Ⓐ Ⓑ Ⓒ Ⓓ Ⓔ	16 Ⓐ Ⓑ Ⓒ Ⓓ Ⓔ	22 Ⓐ Ⓑ Ⓒ Ⓓ Ⓔ	28 Ⓐ Ⓑ Ⓒ Ⓓ Ⓔ
5 Ⓐ Ⓑ Ⓒ Ⓓ Ⓔ	11 Ⓐ Ⓑ Ⓒ Ⓓ Ⓔ	17 Ⓐ Ⓑ Ⓒ Ⓓ Ⓔ	23 Ⓐ Ⓑ Ⓒ Ⓓ Ⓔ	29 Ⓐ Ⓑ Ⓒ Ⓓ Ⓔ
6 Ⓐ Ⓑ Ⓒ Ⓓ Ⓔ	12 Ⓐ Ⓑ Ⓒ Ⓓ Ⓔ	18 Ⓐ Ⓑ Ⓒ Ⓓ Ⓔ	24 Ⓐ Ⓑ Ⓒ Ⓓ Ⓔ	30 Ⓐ Ⓑ Ⓒ Ⓓ Ⓔ

SECTION V: PRACTICAL BUSINESS JUDGMENT

1 Ⓐ Ⓑ Ⓒ Ⓓ Ⓔ	5 Ⓐ Ⓑ Ⓒ Ⓓ Ⓔ	9 Ⓐ Ⓑ Ⓒ Ⓓ Ⓔ	13 Ⓐ Ⓑ Ⓒ Ⓓ Ⓔ	17 Ⓐ Ⓑ Ⓒ Ⓓ Ⓔ
2 Ⓐ Ⓑ Ⓒ Ⓓ Ⓔ	6 Ⓐ Ⓑ Ⓒ Ⓓ Ⓔ	10 Ⓐ Ⓑ Ⓒ Ⓓ Ⓔ	14 Ⓐ Ⓑ Ⓒ Ⓓ Ⓔ	18 Ⓐ Ⓑ Ⓒ Ⓓ Ⓔ
3 Ⓐ Ⓑ Ⓒ Ⓓ Ⓔ	7 Ⓐ Ⓑ Ⓒ Ⓓ Ⓔ	11 Ⓐ Ⓑ Ⓒ Ⓓ Ⓔ	15 Ⓐ Ⓑ Ⓒ Ⓓ Ⓔ	19 Ⓐ Ⓑ Ⓒ Ⓓ Ⓔ
4 Ⓐ Ⓑ Ⓒ Ⓓ Ⓔ	8 Ⓐ Ⓑ Ⓒ Ⓓ Ⓔ	12 Ⓐ Ⓑ Ⓒ Ⓓ Ⓔ	16 Ⓐ Ⓑ Ⓒ Ⓓ Ⓔ	20 Ⓐ Ⓑ Ⓒ Ⓓ Ⓔ

SECTION VI: VERBAL ABILITIES

1 Ⓐ Ⓑ Ⓒ Ⓓ Ⓔ	6 Ⓐ Ⓑ Ⓒ Ⓓ Ⓔ	11 Ⓐ Ⓑ Ⓒ Ⓓ Ⓔ	16 Ⓐ Ⓑ Ⓒ Ⓓ Ⓔ	21 Ⓐ Ⓑ Ⓒ Ⓓ Ⓔ
2 Ⓐ Ⓑ Ⓒ Ⓓ Ⓔ	7 Ⓐ Ⓑ Ⓒ Ⓓ Ⓔ	12 Ⓐ Ⓑ Ⓒ Ⓓ Ⓔ	17 Ⓐ Ⓑ Ⓒ Ⓓ Ⓔ	22 Ⓐ Ⓑ Ⓒ Ⓓ Ⓔ
3 Ⓐ Ⓑ Ⓒ Ⓓ Ⓔ	8 Ⓐ Ⓑ Ⓒ Ⓓ Ⓔ	13 Ⓐ Ⓑ Ⓒ Ⓓ Ⓔ	18 Ⓐ Ⓑ Ⓒ Ⓓ Ⓔ	23 Ⓐ Ⓑ Ⓒ Ⓓ Ⓔ
4 Ⓐ Ⓑ Ⓒ Ⓓ Ⓔ	9 Ⓐ Ⓑ Ⓒ Ⓓ Ⓔ	14 Ⓐ Ⓑ Ⓒ Ⓓ Ⓔ	19 Ⓐ Ⓑ Ⓒ Ⓓ Ⓔ	24 Ⓐ Ⓑ Ⓒ Ⓓ Ⓔ
5 Ⓐ Ⓑ Ⓒ Ⓓ Ⓔ	10 Ⓐ Ⓑ Ⓒ Ⓓ Ⓔ	15 Ⓐ Ⓑ Ⓒ Ⓓ Ⓔ	20 Ⓐ Ⓑ Ⓒ Ⓓ Ⓔ	25 Ⓐ Ⓑ Ⓒ Ⓓ Ⓔ

SECTION VII: READING RECALL

1 Ⓐ Ⓑ Ⓒ Ⓓ Ⓔ	6 Ⓐ Ⓑ Ⓒ Ⓓ Ⓔ	11 Ⓐ Ⓑ Ⓒ Ⓓ Ⓔ	16 Ⓐ Ⓑ Ⓒ Ⓓ Ⓔ	21 Ⓐ Ⓑ Ⓒ Ⓓ Ⓔ
2 Ⓐ Ⓑ Ⓒ Ⓓ Ⓔ	7 Ⓐ Ⓑ Ⓒ Ⓓ Ⓔ	12 Ⓐ Ⓑ Ⓒ Ⓓ Ⓔ	17 Ⓐ Ⓑ Ⓒ Ⓓ Ⓔ	22 Ⓐ Ⓑ Ⓒ Ⓓ Ⓔ
3 Ⓐ Ⓑ Ⓒ Ⓓ Ⓔ	8 Ⓐ Ⓑ Ⓒ Ⓓ Ⓔ	13 Ⓐ Ⓑ Ⓒ Ⓓ Ⓔ	18 Ⓐ Ⓑ Ⓒ Ⓓ Ⓔ	23 Ⓐ Ⓑ Ⓒ Ⓓ Ⓔ
4 Ⓐ Ⓑ Ⓒ Ⓓ Ⓔ	9 Ⓐ Ⓑ Ⓒ Ⓓ Ⓔ	14 Ⓐ Ⓑ Ⓒ Ⓓ Ⓔ	19 Ⓐ Ⓑ Ⓒ Ⓓ Ⓔ	24 Ⓐ Ⓑ Ⓒ Ⓓ Ⓔ
5 Ⓐ Ⓑ Ⓒ Ⓓ Ⓔ	10 Ⓐ Ⓑ Ⓒ Ⓓ Ⓔ	15 Ⓐ Ⓑ Ⓒ Ⓓ Ⓔ	20 Ⓐ Ⓑ Ⓒ Ⓓ Ⓔ	25 Ⓐ Ⓑ Ⓒ Ⓓ Ⓔ

SECTION I: READING COMPREHENSION

30 Minutes
25 Questions

DIRECTIONS: Below each of the following passages, you will find questions or incomplete statements about the passage. Each statement or question is followed by lettered words or expressions. Select the word or expression that most satisfactorily completes each statement or answers each question in accordance with the meaning of the passage.

As the world's population grows, the part played by man in influencing plant life becomes more and more important. In old and densely populated countries, as in central Europe, man determines almost wholly what shall grow and what shall not grow. In such regions, the influence of man on plant life is in large measure a beneficial one. Laws, often centuries old, protect plants of economic value and preserve soil fertility. In newly settled countries the situation is unfortunately quite the reverse. The pioneer's life is too strenuous a one for him to think of posterity.

Some years ago Mt. Mitchell, the highest summit east of the Mississippi, was covered with a magnificent forest. A lumber company was given full rights to fell the trees. Those not cut down were crushed. The mountain was left a wasted area where fire would rage and erosion would complete the destruction. There was no stopping the devastating foresting of the company, for the contract had been given. Under a more enlightened civilization this could not have happened. The denuding of Mt. Mitchell is a minor chapter in the destruction of lands in the United States; and this country is by no means the only or chief sufferer. China, India, Egypt, and East Africa all have their thousands of square miles of waste land, the result of man's indifference to the future.

Deforestation, grazing, and poor farming are the chief causes of the destruction of land fertility. Wasteful cutting of timber is the first step. Grazing then follows lumbering in bringing about ruin. The Caribbean slopes of northern Venezuela are barren wastes owing first to ruthless cutting of forests and then to destructive grazing. Hordes of goats have roamed these slopes until only a few thorny acacias and cacti remain. Erosion completed the devastation. What is there illustrated on a small scale is the story of vast areas in China and India, countries where famines are of regular occurrence.

Man is not wholly to blame, for Nature is often merciless. In parts of India and China, plant life, when left undisturbed by man, cannot cope with either the disastrous floods of wet seasons or the destructive winds of the dry season. Man has learned much; prudent land management has been the policy of the Chinese people since 2700 B.C., but even they have not learned enough.

When the American forestry service was in its infancy, it met with much opposition from legislators who loudly claimed that the protected land would in one season yield a crop of cabbages of more value than all the timber on it. Herein lay the fallacy, that one season's crop is all that need be thought of. Nature, through the years, adjusts crops to the soil and to the climate. Forests usually occur where precipitation exceeds evaporation. If the reverse is true, grasslands are found; and where evaporation is still greater, desert or scrub vegetation alone survives. The phytogeographic map of a country is very similar to the climatic map based on rainfall, evaporation, and temperature. Man ignores this natural adjustment of crops and strives for one "bumper" crop in a single season; he may produce it, but "year in and year out the yield of the grassland is certain, that of the planted fields, never."

Man is learning; he sprays his trees with insecticides and fungicides; he imports ladybugs to destroy aphids; he irrigates, fertilizes, and rotates his crops; but he is still indifferent to many of the consequences of his short-sighted policies. The great dust storms of the western United States are proof of this indifference.

In spite of the evidence to be had from this country, the people of other countries, still in the pioneer

73

stage, farm as wastefully as did our own pioneers. In the interiors of Central and South American Republics, natives fell superb forest trees and leave them to rot in order to obtain virgin soil for cultivation. Where the land is hillside, it readily washes and after one or two seasons is unfit for crops. So the frontier farmer pushes back into the primeval forest, moving his hut as he goes, and fells more monarchs to lay bare another patch of ground for his plantings to support his family. Valuable timber which will require a century to replace is destroyed and the land laid waste to produce what could be supplied for a pittance.

How badly man can err in his handling of land is shown by the draining of extensive swamp areas, which to the uninformed would seem to be a very good thing to do. One of the first effects of the drainage is the lowering of the water-table, which may bring about the death of the dominant species and leave to another species the possession of the soil, even when the difference in water level is little more than an inch. Frequently, bog country will yield marketable crops of cranberries and blueberries but, if drained, neither these nor any other economic plant will grow on the fallow soil. Swamps and marshes have their drawbacks but also their virtues. When drained they may leave waste land, the surface of which rapidly erodes to be then blown away in dust blizzards disastrous to both man and wild beasts.

1. The best title for this passage is

   (A) How to Increase Soil Productivity
   (B) Conservation of Natural Resources
   (C) Man's Effect on Soil
   (D) Soil Conditions and Plant Growth
   (E) Mountain Vegetation

2. A policy of good management is sometimes upset by

   (A) the indifference of man
   (B) centuries-old laws
   (C) insecticides
   (D) grazing animals
   (E) floods and winds

3. Areas in which the total amounts of rain and snow falling on the ground are greater than that which is evaporated will support

   (A) forests
   (B) grasslands
   (C) scrub vegetation

   (D) cranberries and blueberries
   (E) no plants

4. Pioneers do not have a long range view on soil problems since they

   (A) are not protected by laws
   (B) live under adverse conditions
   (C) use poor methods of farming
   (D) must protect themselves from famine
   (E) have no access to information on soil

5. Phytogeographic maps are those that show

   (A) areas of grassland
   (B) areas of bumper crops
   (C) areas of similar climate
   (D) areas of similar plants
   (E) forest areas

6. The basic cause of frequent famines in China and India is probably due to

   (A) allowing animals to roam wild
   (B) drainage of swamps
   (C) over-grazing of the land
   (D) destruction of forests
   (E) lack of any system of crop rotation

7. One way to help prevent soil erosion is by

   (A) draining unproductive swamp areas
   (B) legislating against excess lumbering
   (C) trying to raise bumper crops each year
   (D) irrigating desert areas
   (E) lowering the water table

8. What is meant by "the yield of the grassland is certain; that of the planted field, never" is that

   (A) it is impossible to get more than one bumper crop from any one cultivated area
   (B) crops, planted in former grassland, will not give good yields
   (C) through the indifference of man, dust blizzards have occurred in former grasslands
   (D) if man does not interfere, plants will grow in the most suitable environment
   (E) grass is the most abundant form of vegetation

9. The first act of prudent land management might be to

(A) prohibit drainage of swamps

(B) use irrigation and crop rotation in planted areas

(C) increase use of fertilizers

(D) institute land-reclamation programs

(E) prohibit excessive forest lumbering

10. The results of good land management may usually be found in

(A) heavily populated areas

(B) areas not given over to grazing

(C) underdeveloped areas

(D) ancient civilizations

(E) temperate climates

Regarding physical changes that have been and are now taking place on the surface of the earth, the sea and its shores have been the scene of the greatest stability. The dry land has seen the rise, the decline, and even the disappearance, of vast hordes of various types and forms within times comparatively recent, geologically speaking; but life in the sea is today virtually what it was when many of the forms now extinct on land had not yet been evolved. Also, it may be parenthetically stated here, the marine habitat has been biologically the most important in the evolution and development of life on this planet. Its rhythmic influence can still be traced in those animals whose ancestors have long since left that realm to abide far from their primary haunts. For it is now generally held as an accepted fact that the shore area of an ancient sea was the birthplace of life.

Still, despite the primitive conditions still maintained in the sea, its shore inhabitants show an amazing diversity, while their adaptive characters are perhaps not exceeded in refinement by those that distinguish the dwellers of dry land. Why is this diversity manifest? We must look for an answer into the physical factors obtained in that extremely slender zone surrounding the continents, marked by the rise and fall of the tides.

It will be noticed by the most casual observer that on any given seashore the area exposed between the tide marks may be roughly divided into a number of levels each characterized by a certain assemblage of animals. Thus in proceeding from high- to low-water mark, new forms constantly become predominant while other forms gradually drop out. Now, provided that the character of the substratum does not change, these differences in the types of animals are determined almost exclusively by the duration of time that the individual forms may remain exposed to the air without harm. Indeed, so regularly does the tidal rhythm act on certain animals (the barnacles, for instance), that certain species have come to require a definite period of exposure in order to maintain themselves, and will die out if kept continuously submerged. Although there are some forms that actually require periodic exposure, the number of species inhabiting the shore that are able to endure exposure every twelve hours, when the tide falls, is comparatively few.

With the alternate rise and fall of the tides, the successive areas of the tidal zone are subjected to force of wave-impact. In certain regions the waves often break with considerable force. Consequently, wave-shock has had a profound influence on the structure and habits of shore animals. It is characteristic of most shore animals that they shun definitely exposed places, and seek shelter in nooks and crannies and such refuges as are offered under stones and seaweed; particularly is this true of those forms living on rock and other firm foundations. Many of these have a marked capacity to cling closely to the substratum; some, such as anemones and certain snails, although without the grasping organs of higher animals, have special powers of adhesion; others, such as sponges and sea squirts, remain permanently fixed, and if torn loose from their base are incapable of forming a new attachment. But perhaps the most significant method of solving the problem presented by the surf has been in the adaptation of body-form to minimize friction. This is strikingly displayed in the fact that seashore animals are essentially flattened forms. Thus, in the typically shore forms the sponges are of the encrusting type, the non-burrowing worms are leaflike, the snails and other mollusks are squat forms and are without the spines and other ornate extensions such as are often produced on the shells of many mollusks in deeper and quieter waters. The same influence is no less marked in the case of the crustaceans; the flattening is either lateral, as in the amphipods, or dorso-ventral, as in the isopods and crabs.

In sandy regions, because of the unstable nature of substratum, no such means of attachment as indicated in the foregoing paragraph will suffice to maintain the animals in their almost ceaseless battle with the billows. Most of them must perforce depend on their ability quickly to penetrate into the sand for safety. Some forms endowed with less celerity, such as the sand dollars, are so constructed that their bodies offer no more resistance to wave impact than does a flat pebble.

Temperature, also, is a not inconsiderable factor among those physical forces constantly operating to produce a diversity of forms among seashore animals. At a comparatively shallow depth in the sea, there is small fluctuation of temperatures; and life there exists in surroundings of serene stability; but as the shore is approached, the influence of the sun becomes more and more manifest and the variation is greater. This variation becomes greatest between the tide marks where, because of the very shallow depths and the fresh water from the land, this area is subjected to wide changes in both temperature and salinity.

Nor is a highly competitive mode of life without its bearing on structure as well as habits. In this phase of their struggle for existence, the animals of both the sea and the shore have become possessed of weapons for offense and defense that are correspondingly varied.

Although the life in the sea has been generally considered and treated as separate and distinct from the more familiar life on land, that supposition has no real basis in fact. Life on this planet is one vast unit, depending for its existence chiefly on the same sources of supply. That portion of animal life living in the sea, notwithstanding its strangeness and unfamiliarity, may be considered as but the aquatic fringe of the life on land. It is supported largely by materials washed into the sea, which are no longer available for the support of land animals. Perhaps we have been misled in these considerations of sea life because of the fact that approximately three times as many major *types* of animals inhabit salt water as live on the land; of the major types of animals no fewer than ten are exclusively marine, that is to say, nearly half again as many as land-dwelling types together. A further interesting fact is that despite the greater variety in the form and structure of sea animals about three-fourths of all known *kinds* of animals live on the land, while only one-fourth live in the sea. In this connection it is noteworthy that sea life becomes scarcer with increasing distance from land; toward the middle of the oceans it disappears almost completely. For example, the central south Pacific is a region more barren than is any desert area on land. Indeed, no life of any kind has been found in the surface water, and there seems to be none on the bottom.

Sea animals are largest and most abundant on those shores receiving the most copious rainfall. Particularly is this true on the most rugged and colder coasts where it may be assumed that the material from the land finds its way to the sea unaltered and in greater quantities.

11. The best title for this passage is

    (A) Between the Tides
    (B) Seashore Life
    (C) The Tides
    (D) The Seashore
    (E) Primitive Life Forms

12. Of the following adaptations, the one that would enable an organism to live on a sandy beach is

    (A) the ability to move rapidly
    (B) the ability to burrow deeply
    (C) a flattened shape
    (D) spiny extensions of the shell
    (E) the ability to adhere to hard surfaces

13. The absence of living things in mid-ocean might be due to

    (A) lack of rainfall in mid-ocean
    (B) the distance from material washed into the sea
    (C) larger animals feeding on smaller ones which must live near the land
    (D) insufficient dissolved oxygen
    (E) the high salt content of mid-ocean water

14. A greater variety of living things exist on a rocky shore than on a sandy beach because

    (A) rocks offer a better foothold than sand
    (B) foodstuffs are trapped in rocky areas
    (C) temperature changes are less drastic in rocky areas
    (D) the water in rock pools is less salty
    (E) sandy areas are continually being washed by the surf

15. Organisms found living at the high-tide mark are adapted to

    (A) maintain themselves in the air for a long time
    (B) offer no resistance to wave impact
    (C) remain permanently fixed to the substratum
    (D) burrow in the ground
    (E) withstand the sun's rays

16. The author holds that living things in the sea represent the aquatic fringe of life on land. This is so because

    (A) there are relatively fewer marine forms of animals than there are land-living forms

(B) there is greater variety among land-living forms

(C) marine animals ultimately depend upon material from the land

(D) there are three times as many kinds of animals on land than there are in the sea

(E) life began in the sea

17. A biologist walking along the shore at the low tide line would not easily find many live animals since

(A) their flattened shapes make them indistinguishable

(B) they are washed back and forth by the waves

(C) they burrow deeply

(D) they move rapidly

(E) most die of exposure to the open air

18. The intent of the author in the next to the last paragraph is to show that

(A) the temperature and salinity of the sea determine the variety among shore animals

(B) marine animals are vastly different from terrestrial organisms

(C) colder areas can support more living things than warm areas

(D) marine forms have the same problems as terrestrial animals

(E) sea life occurs in great variety

19. A scientist wishing to study a great variety of living things would do well to hunt for them

(A) in shallow waters

(B) on a rocky seashore

(C) on a sandy seashore

(D) on any shore between the tide lines

(E) in deep waters

20. The most primitive forms of living things in the evolutionary scale are to be found in the sea because

(A) the influence of the sea is found in land animals

(B) the sea is relatively stable

(C) many forms have become extinct on land

(D) land animals are supposed to have evolved from sea organisms

(E) the sea environment retards evolutionary development

Those early principles discovered in 1775 are the same as those upon which blueprinting is based today. Light, be it sun or electric, has a decided effect on a chemical compound known as ferro-prussiate; it turns the color from a pale green to a deep blue. Thus, if a sheet of white paper is coated with a solution of ferro-prussiate and is so covered that only a portion of it is exposed to light, that exposed part will turn blue while the unexposed section remains its original color. Then, if the paper is washed in water which both removes the unexposed coating, revealing the white paper, and fixes (makes permanent) the exposed blue coating, a print is obtained in blue and white. This, then, is a blueprint.

The principles of all copying processes which depend on sensitized paper to obtain a print are similar. In photography, photostating, blueprinting, and so on, light, to make a print, must reach and react upon a chemically sensitized surface only in the places permitted by an original copy.

There are several of these processes divided into two general groups: (1) direct, and (2) indirect. Of these two, direct copying is the more widely used because it is less expensive and requires less equipment.

Blueprinting, probably the best known and most widely used direct copying method, prints from a tracing of the original or from the original itself, according to the process involved. Because of possible shrinkage or stretch of the tracings as well as inaccuracies accrued in the tracing process, the direct copying method does not ordinarily produce copies as true as those obtained by the indirect.

Chief process of the indirect method is photostating. Known as "Indirect" because it takes the print through a lens, it can always work from the original without a tracing and can enlarge or reduce the copy as desired. This flexibility and photographic accuracy have made indirect copying popular.

21. According to the paragraph, the most accurate statement is that

(A) blueprinting was discovered in 1775

(B) the principles behind blueprinting were discovered in 1775

(C) since 1775, no new information has been discovered regarding blueprinting

(D) the effect of electricity on a chemical compound was discovered in 1775

(E) blueprinting was discovered because of the start of the American Revolution

22. In making a blueprint, a sheet is covered with a chemical compound and light is permitted to fall on those parts which later on are seen as

    (A) white
    (B) black
    (C) pale green
    (D) deep blue
    (E) yellow

23. Photostating, compared with blueprinting,

    (A) is cheaper
    (B) is a more direct method
    (C) requires a tracing
    (D) makes possible enlargement of copy
    (E) is more expensive

24. Where the lowest cost and least equipment is desired, the copying would be done by the

    (A) direct method with a lens
    (B) direct method without a lens
    (C) indirect method with a lens
    (D) indirect method without a lens
    (E) indirect-direct method combination

25. Generally, a more accurate copy of the original can be obtained by the

    (A) direct method without a lens
    (B) indirect method with or without a lens
    (C) indirect method without a lens
    (D) indirect method with a lens
    (E) direct method with a lens

Stop

END OF SECTION I. IF YOU HAVE ANY TIME LEFT, GO OVER YOUR WORK IN THIS SECTION ONLY. DO NOT WORK IN ANY OTHER SECTION OF THE TEST. WHEN YOUR TIME IS UP, GO ON TO THE NEXT SECTION.

SECTION II: PROBLEM SOLVING

35 Minutes
30 Questions

DIRECTIONS: For each of the following questions, select the choice which best answers the question or completes the statement.

1. Which one of these quantities is the smallest?

   (A) $^4/_5$
   (B) $^7/_9$
   (C) .76
   (D) $^5/_7$
   (E) $^9/_{11}$

2. A girl earns twice as much in December as in each of the other months. What part of her entire year's earnings does she earn in December?

   (A) $^2/_{11}$
   (B) $^2/_{13}$
   (C) $^3/_{14}$
   (D) $^1/_6$
   (E) $^1/_7$

3. If $x = -1$, then $3x^3 + 2x^2 + x + 1 =$

   (A) -1
   (B) 1
   (C) -5
   (D) 5
   (E) 2

4. How many twelfths of a pound are equal to $83\frac{1}{3}\%$ of a pound?

   (A) 5
   (B) 10
   (C) 12
   (D) 14
   (E) 16

5. An equilateral triangle 3 inches on a side is cut up into smaller equilateral triangles one inch on a side. What is the greatest number of such tri-

angles that can be formed?

   (A) 3
   (B) 6
   (C) 9
   (D) 12
   (E) 15

6. If $\dfrac{a}{b} = \dfrac{3}{5}$ then $15a =$

   (A) 3b
   (B) 5b
   (C) 6b
   (D) 9b
   (E) 15b

7. A square 5 units on a side has one vertex at the point $(1, 1)$. Which one of the following points *cannot* be diagonally opposite the vertex?

   (A) $(6, 6)$
   (B) $(-4, 6)$
   (C) $(-4, -4)$
   (D) $(6, -4)$
   (E) $(4, -6)$

8. Five equal squares are placed side by side to make a single rectangle whose perimeter is 372 inches. Find the number of square inches in the area of one of these squares.

   (A) 72
   (B) 324
   (C) 900
   (D) 961
   (E) 984

9. Which is the smallest of the following numbers?

   (A) $\sqrt{3}$

79

(B) $\dfrac{1}{\sqrt{3}}$

(C) $\dfrac{\sqrt{3}}{3}$

(D) ⅓

(E) $\dfrac{1}{3\sqrt{3}}$

10. In the figure, what percent of the area of rectangle PQRS is shaded?

    (A) 20
    (B) 25
    (C) 30
    (D) 33⅓
    (E) 40

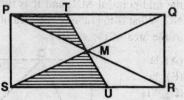

11. ⅙ of an audience consisted of boys and ⅓ of it consisted of girls. What percent of the audience consisted of children?

    (A) 66²/₃
    (B) 50
    (C) 37½
    (D) 40
    (E) 33⅓

12. One wheel has a diameter of 30 inches and a second wheel has a diameter of 20 inches. The first wheel traveled a certain distance in 240 revolutions. In how many revolutions did the second wheel travel the same distance?

    (A) 120
    (B) 160
    (C) 360
    (D) 420
    (E) 480

13. If x and y are two different real numbers and rx = ry, then r =

    (A) 0
    (B) 1
    (C) $\dfrac{x}{y}$
    (D) $\dfrac{y}{x}$
    (E) x − y

14. If $\dfrac{m}{n} = \dfrac{5}{6}$, then what is 3m + 2n?

    (A) 0
    (B) 2
    (C) 7
    (D) 10
    (E) cannot be determined from the information given

15. If x > 1, which of the following increase(s) as x increase(s)?

    I. $x - \dfrac{1}{x}$

    II. $\dfrac{1}{x^2 - x}$

    III. $4x^3 - 2x^2$

    (A) only I
    (B) only II
    (C) only III
    (D) only I and III
    (E) I, II, and III

16. In the figure, PQRS is a parallelogram, and ST = TV = VR. What is the ratio of the area of triangle SPT to the area of the parallelogram?

    (A) ¹/₆
    (B) ¹/₅
    (C) ¹/₃
    (D) ²/₇
    (E) cannot be determined from the information given

17. One angle of a triangle is 82°. The other two angles are in the ratio 2:5. Find the number of degrees in the smallest angle of the triangle.

    (A) 14
    (B) 25
    (C) 28
    (D) 38
    (E) 82

18. If a boy can mow a lawn in t minutes, what part can he do in 15 minutes?

    (A) t − 15
    (B) $\dfrac{t}{15}$
    (C) 15t
    (D) 15 − t
    (E) $\dfrac{15}{t}$

19. A typist uses lengthwise a sheet of paper 9 inches by 12 inches. She leaves a 1-inch margin on each side and a 1½ inch margin on top and bottom. What fractional part of the page is used for typing?

    (A) $^{21}/_{22}$
    (B) $^{7}/_{12}$
    (C) $^{5}/_{9}$
    (D) $^{3}/_{4}$
    (E) $^{5}/_{12}$

20. It takes a boy 9 seconds to run a distance of 132 feet. What is his speed in miles per hour?

    (A) 8
    (B) 9
    (C) 10
    (D) 11
    (E) 12

21. A rectangular sign is cut down by 10% of its height and 30% of its width. What percent of the original area remains?

    (A) 30
    (B) 37
    (C) 57
    (D) 70
    (E) 63

22. How many of the numbers between 100 and 300 begin or end with 2?

    (A) 20
    (B) 40
    (C) 180
    (D) 100
    (E) 110

23. If Mary knows that y is an integer greater than 2 and less than 7 and John knows that y is an integer greater than 5 and less than 10, then Mary and John may correctly conclude that

    (A) y can be exactly determined
    (B) y may be either of 2 values
    (C) y may be any of 3 values
    (D) y may be any of 4 values
    (E) there is no value of y satisfying these conditions

24. The area of a square is $49x^2$. What is the length of a diagonal of the square?

    (A) 7x
    (B) $7x \sqrt{2}$
    (C) 14x
    (D) $7x^2$
    (E) $\dfrac{7x}{\sqrt{2}}$

25. In the figure, MNOP is a square of area 1, Q is the mid-point of MN, and R is the mid-point of NO. What is the ratio of the area of triangle PQR to the area of the square?

    (A) ¼
    (B) ⅓
    (C) $^{1}/_{16}$
    (D) ⅜
    (E) ½

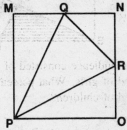

26. If a rectangle is 4 feet by 12 feet, how many two-inch tiles would have to be put around the outside edge to completely frame the rectangle?

    (A) 32
    (B) 36
    (C) 192
    (D) 196
    (E) 200

27. One-tenth is what part of three-fourths?

    (A) $^{40}/_{3}$
    (B) $^{3}/_{40}$
    (C) $^{15}/_{2}$
    (D) ⅛
    (E) $^{2}/_{15}$

28. The area of square PQRS is 49. What are the coordinates of Q?

    (A) $\left(\dfrac{7}{2} \sqrt{2}, 0 \right)$

    (B) $\left(0, \dfrac{7}{2} \sqrt{2} \right)$
    (C) (0, 7)
    (D) (7, 0)
    (E) $(0, 7\sqrt{2})$

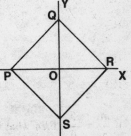

29. Village A has a population of 6800, which is decreasing at a rate of 120 per year. Village B has a population of 4200, which is increasing at a rate of 80 per year. In how many years will the population of the two villages be equal?

    (A) 9
    (B) 11
    (C) 13
    (D) 14
    (E) 16

30. The average of 8 numbers is 6; the average of 6 other numbers is 8. What is the average of all 14 numbers?

    (A) 6
    (B) $6^6/_7$
    (C) 7
    (D) $7^2/_7$
    (E) $8^1/_7$

Stop

END OF SECTION II. IF YOU HAVE ANY TIME LEFT, GO OVER YOUR WORK IN THIS SECTION ONLY. DO NOT WORK IN ANY OTHER SECTION OF THE TEST. WHEN YOUR TIME IS UP, GO ON TO THE NEXT SECTION.

SECTION III: PRACTICAL BUSINESS JUDGMENT

20 Minutes
20 Questions

DIRECTIONS: This section consists of a reading selection which details a business situation followed by two sets of questions, data evaluation and data application. In the first set, data evaluation, you will be asked to classify certain of the facts presented in the passage on the basis of their importance. The second set, data application, will test your grasp of specific details of the situation.

Mary and Robert Johnson run a flower-and-vegetable seed business, which Robert inherited from his father who started it in 1926. Although confined to the state of Colorado, the business has made over $200,000 in sales revenue during each of the past three years. The Johnsons have netted a profit of about $30,000 per annum after corporate taxes have been paid.

Only 25% of the volume comes from retail stores. The remainder is the result of direct-mail campaigns. The company's "special customer" list, comprised of people who have ordered one or more times, produces most of the direct-mail revenue. The average order is $15.20, and the average customer purchases seeds for five years. This high company loyalty speaks well for the Johnsons and the quality of their products.

Robert Johnson has always been fascinated by printing presses. Indeed, the most interesting part of the business to him is the creation of the catalog. Not only does he write it, he also designs it and works closely with the printer in producing it.

Now he has an opportunity to buy a press of his own. He reasons that now production would be in his absolute control. Four years ago, his printer was hit with a strike while producing the Johnson catalog. The spring issue went out two weeks late—a disaster in a business in which timing is so important. Sales volume dropped $39,000 that year. Johnson believes that ownership of a press would prevent this from happening again.

There would be a saving in money as well, even though he would have to pay in the neighborhood of

$4,000 a year for a part-time pressman. Printing costs at present run $40,000 a year. After carefully investigating prices of paper and inks, Johnson figures that his printing costs would drop to $16,000, excluding the compensation for his moonlighting pressman. The offset press costs $18,000. He reasons that he will make up the price of the machine in one year.

Mary opposes the purchase. First of all, she believes that owning a press is impractical. She points out that Robert hasn't figured into his calculations how much more time he would have to devote to printing. Even with the part-time pressman, Robert would still have to be highly involved in the printing process, much more than he is now. She is sure that this activity would take him away from the more important duties of overseeing the selection of seeds, managing the cash flow, and making sure that orders get out quickly and accurately.

Furthermore, she says, mechanical breakdowns are inevitable. Even though home printing is Robert's hobby, there is a big difference between running a small hand-cranked press and the maintenance of a commercial high-speed press. Robert is a good amateur but not a professional printer. She also doubts that the quality of the catalog will be as good as it has been in the past.

Robert considers Mary's objections carefully and decides to postpone making a decision for six months.

DATA EVALUATION

DIRECTIONS: Based on your analysis of the business situation, classify each of the following elements in one of five categories. Mark:

(A) if the element is a MAJOR OBJECTIVE in making the decision; that is, the outcome or result sought by the decision maker.

(B) if the element is a MAJOR FACTOR in arriving at the decision; that is, a consideration explicitly mentioned in the passage that is basic in determining the decision.

(C) if the element is a MINOR FACTOR in making the decision; that is, a secondary consideration in determining the decision.

(D) if the element is a MAJOR ASSUMPTION made in deliberating; that is, a supposition or projection made by the decision maker before weighing the variables.

(E) if the element is an UNIMPORTANT ISSUE in getting to the point; that is, a factor that is insignificant or not immediately relevant to the situation.

1. Possible drop in quality of catalog.

2. Absolute control of production.

3. Expansion of sales revenue.

4. Mailing catalog on most advantageous date.

5. Printing cost reduction.

6. Making up cost of purchase of printing press within one year.

7. Increase profit.

8. Strike at outside printer's plant.

9. Failure to estimate cost of increased time Robert would have to spend on printing press.

10. Robert's fascination with printing.

DATA APPLICATION

DIRECTIONS: Based on your understanding of the business situation, answer the following questions testing your comprehension of the information supplied in the passage. For each question, select the choice which best answers the question or completes the statement.

11. In the past three years, the Johnson Seed Company has produced an average profit when compared with sales revenue of about

    (A) 5%
    (B) 10%
    (C) 15%
    (D) 30%
    (E) 50%

12. The volume of sales revenue resulting from direct mail has for the past three years averaged about

    (A) $30,000
    (B) $40,000
    (C) $150,000
    (D) $200,000
    (E) $230,000

13. One reason Robert Johnson wishes to buy a press is that

    (A) his printer has gone out of business
    (B) his spring catalogs have often gone out late
    (C) he could have another business on the side
    (D) he would avoid delays caused by strikes of printing plants
    (E) he believes it will increase sales volume

14. Even though a part-time printer would have to be paid, Robert estimates he could reduce his yearly printing costs by

    (A) $16,000
    (B) $20,000
    (C) $22,000
    (D) $36,000
    (E) $40,000

15. The business of the Johnsons is

    (A) seasonal
    (B) spread throughout the year
    (C) varied throughout the year as far as sales are concerned
    (D) dropping off
    (E) countrywide

16. According to Mary, Robert's calculations have not included the

    (A) costs of paper
    (B) compensation for the part-time pressman
    (C) cost of the printing press
    (D) price of ink
    (E) cost of his own time

7. According to Mary, an important function performed by Robert is

    (A) the supervision of a part-time pressman
    (B) order processing
    (C) reducing the number of names on the expen-

sive ''special customer'' list
(D) working closely with an outside printer
(E) settling strikes of outside suppliers

18. One of Mary's objections to purchasing a printing press is that she believes

    (A) Robert does not have personal contact with customers
    (B) the sales volume has been on a plateau for three years
    (C) Robert spends too much time now working on the catalog
    (D) Robert has had too little experience in direct mail
    (E) Robert is not competent in running a high-speed press

19. Mary implies that the possible purchase of a press is

    (A) a practical and reasonable idea
    (B) due to the fact that Robert is bored with the seed business
    (C) due to sentiment on Robert's part
    (D) foolish because the company cannot afford the purchase price
    (E) the result of panic due to a drop in sales

20. Mary seems to believe that the quality of the catalog

    (A) will drop if the press is purchased
    (B) is of less importance than prompt delivery
    (C) will be better when Robert controls the printing
    (D) will remain the same if they buy the press
    (E) has never been of a high standard

Stop

END OF SECTION III. IF YOU HAVE ANY TIME LEFT, GO OVER YOUR WORK IN THIS SECTION ONLY. DO NOT WORK IN ANY OTHER SECTION OF THE TEST. WHEN YOUR TIME IS UP, GO ON TO THE NEXT SECTION.

SECTION IV: DATA SUFFICIENCY

30 Minutes
30 Questions

DIRECTIONS: Each question below is followed by two numbered facts. You are to determine whether the data given in the statements is sufficient for answering the question. Use the data given, plus your knowledge of math and everyday facts, to choose between the five possible answers. Mark

(A) if statement 1 alone is sufficient to answer the question, but statement 2 alone is not sufficient.
(B) if statement 2 alone is sufficient to answer the question, but statement 1 alone is not sufficient.
(C) if both statements together are needed to answer the question, but neither statement alone is sufficient.
(D) if either statement by itself is sufficient to answer the question asked.
(E) if not enough facts are given to answer the question.

1. How much did a man earn in 1962?

   (1) He earned $6500 in 1963 which is 12½% more than he earned in 1962.
   (2) His wife (who earned half the amount he earned) and he earned $8666.62 together in 1962.

2. A merchant has gone bankrupt. How much will his creditors receive?

   (1) With debts of $43,250, he will pay off 15 cents on the dollar.
   (2) His total loss is $125,000.

3. What is a student's over-all average?

   (1) He receives 90 in English, 84 in Algebra, 75 in French, and 76 in Music.
   (2) The subjects have the following weights: English 4, Algebra 3, French 3, and Music 1.

4. How long will it take two pipes to empty a tank that is ¾ full?

   (1) Pipe A can fill the tank in 12 minutes.
   (2) Pipe B can empty it in 8 minutes.

5. What is the average of the walking speeds of two men?

   (1) One man travels at four miles an hour.
   (2) The other man completes 60 miles.

6. A desk has a marked price of $100. Discounts of first 20% and then 25% are made. What did the dealer pay for the desk?

   (1) The dealer's profit is 30% of the selling price.
   (2) The dealer's cost of doing business is 10% of the selling price.

7. How many letters can two typists complete in one day?

   (1) A working day consists of six hours and thirty minutes,
   (2) Four typists can type 600 letters in three days.

8. What time is it on a certain watch?

   (1) The minute hand is at 6.
   (2) The hour hand is halfway between 9 and 10.

9. How much pie did the fourth man eat?

   (1) The first three men ate $^1/_4$, $^2/_7$, and $^3/_{11}$ of the pie respectively.
   (2) Together the four men ate the whole pie.

10. How long is a bridge that crosses a river which is 760 feet wide?

    (1) One bank of the river holds $^1/_5$ of the bridge.
    (2) The other bank holds $^1/_6$ of the bridge.

11. What is the non-voting population of a certain European country?

(1) Only males over 20 years of age are permitted to vote.
(2) The country has a total population of 5,362,486.

12. Was Pericles a famous historian of ancient Greece?

   (1) Pericles is the greatest Greek historian.
   (2) Pericles lived in Greece (490–429 B.C.).

13. What tax is to be paid on $60,000 worth of land?

   (1) The tax rate is $2.56 per $1000.
   (2) The land is assessed at 20% of its value.

14. What is the annual interest which a bank will pay on a principal of $10,000?

   (1) The interest is paid every six months.
   (2) The interest rate is 4%.

15. A wine merchant wishes to reduce the price of his wine on hand by adding water. How many gallons of water must he add to reduce the price from $1.50 a gallon to $1.20 a gallon?

   (1) He has 32 gallons of wine on hand.
   (2) The wine originally contained 14% alcohol.

16. How many full jars will be needed to fill a bowl of punch with a capacity of 5 gallons?

   (1) The punch bowl is hemispherical.
   (2) Each jar holds one quart.

17. How long did Gottfried Wilhelm von Leibnitz live?

   (1) He was born in 1646.
   (2) He died in the year MDCCXVI.

18. Is a bullfrog an amphibian?

   (1) The bullfrog belongs to the genus Rana.
   (2) The genus Rana is part of the amphibian group.

19. How many degrees are there in the smaller acute angle of a right triangle?

   (1) The hypotenuse is twice the length of the shorter arm.
   (2) The larger acute angle is 60°.

20. How many times more calories are there in a hamburger than in an apple?

   (1) A banana has twice the calories that an apple has.
   (2) A hamburger has 1½ times as many calories as a banana.

21. What is the third term in a series of numbers?

   (1) The first number in the series is 3.
   (2) The second number in the series is 9.

22. What is the amount of a deposit in the 16th week of a regular series of deposits?

   (1) A depositor starts off a bank account with $5; the next week he deposits $7.
   (2) The deposits form an arithmetic progression.

23. How much does a certain length of ribbon cost?

   (1) The length is 63 inches.
   (2) A yard and a half remains on the bolt after the ribbon is cut.

24. What is the second angle (in degrees) of a triangle?

   (1) The first angle is three times the second angle.
   (2) The third angle is 20 degrees more than the second angle.

25. How many gallons are needed to raise the water level of a rectangular swimming pool 4 inches?

   (1) The pool is 75 feet long by 42 feet wide by 12 feet deep.
   (2) The present water level is 7 feet.

26. Is Socrates mortal?

   (1) All men are mortal.
   (2) Socrates is a man.

27. What is the meaning of the adjective *monanthous*?

   (1) *Mon* means single (Greek).
   (2) *Anthous* means flower (Greek).

28. What is the number of cubic feet of soil required to fill a flower box?

(1) The box is 8 inches wide.
(2) The box is 3 feet long.

29. What is the part of speech of *skates*?
    (1) It cannot be modified by an adjective.
    (2) It is modified by *quickly*.

30. What is the difference between *testimony* and *evidence*.
    (1) Both are legal terms.
    (2) Testimony means information given orally only.

Stop

END OF SECTION IV. IF YOU HAVE ANY TIME LEFT, GO OVER YOUR WORK IN THIS SECTION ONLY. DO NOT WORK IN ANY OTHER SECTION OF THE TEST. WHEN YOUR TIME IS UP, GO ON TO THE NEXT SECTION.

SECTION V: PRACTICAL BUSINESS JUDGMENT

20 Minutes
20 Questions

DIRECTIONS: This section consists of a reading selection which details a business situation followed by two sets of questions, data evaluation and data application. In the first set, data evaluation, you will be asked to classify certain of the facts presented in the passage on the basis of their importance. The second set, data application, will test your grasp of specific details of the situation.

Ogden Sporting Shoe Company has been in business for over fifty years. It is a family-run company that manufactures a small but very high quality line of sporting shoes. It has always had a very good relationship with its employees, most of whom have been working for the Ogden family for over twenty years. The Ogdens have taken special pride in their development of a high-quality all-leather running shoe, which they consider to be unique to the industry. Several national athletic shoe manufacturers have attempted to buy out the family-owned business, but the Ogdens, content with their modest profits, have always resisted these attractive offers. In the past two years, however, the company has operated at a deficit. The sharp decline in profits has been due, on the one hand, to a sharp rise in competition as a number of new shoe manufacturers have attempted to involve themselves in the vast new market for running shoes. A second factor has been the significant rise in the cost of quality raw materials, which the Ogdens exclusively use. The Ogdens cannot continue to operate their business at a deficit. Selling the business would be an easy solution but an unattractive one, since the Ogdens gain a great satisfaction in providing their superior products for discriminating customers.

The company has considered two alternatives as a compromise solution to their problem. The first alternative would be to produce a moderately priced running shoe, the expected quality of which could bring the company out of deficit. A proposed part of this plan would be an endorsement from the winner of the Boston Marathon. The production of this moderately priced shoe would involve some sacrificing of their standards, but the popularity of the shoe would hopefully enable them to continue manufacturing their usual line. The second alternative would be to merge with the Brill Shoe Company, another small family-owned company in the region that insists on a high quality product. The merger would permit the Ogdens to keep all of their employees and to offer the same high quality line that they have produced in the past. The continued production of this line, however, would be subject to review by the board of directors of the proposed company. Thus the Ogdens would no longer have complete autonomy over the line of products they have carefully developed over the years.

DATA EVALUATION

DIRECTIONS: Based on your analysis of the business situation, classify each of the following elements in one of five categories. Mark:

(A) if the element is a MAJOR OBJECTIVE in making the decision; that is, the outcome or result sought by the decision maker.

(B) if the element is a MAJOR FACTOR in arriving at the decision; that is, a consideration explicitly mentioned in the passage that is basic in determining the decision.

(C) if the element is a MINOR FACTOR in making the decision; that is, a secondary consideration in determining the decision.

(D) if the element is a MAJOR ASSUMPTION made in deliberating; that is, a supposition or projection made by the decision maker before weighing the variables.

(E) if the element is an UNIMPORTANT ISSUE in getting to the point; that is, a factor that is insignificant or not immediately relevant to the situation.

1. Maintaining their production of their high quality products.

2. Not wanting to operate the business on a deficit.

3. Autonomy over their products.

4. An endorsement from the Boston Marathon winner.

5. The experience of the Brill Company in manufacturing running shoes.

6. Keeping the workers at Ogden employed.

7. A continuing consumer interest in quality sporting shoes.

8. Willingness to sacrifice standards.

9. Offsetting the high costs of raw materials.

10. The effectiveness of product endorsements by well-known personalities on consumers.

11. A decision by Brill to move outside the region.

12. A decision by Brill to sell out to a large national firm.

13. The winning of the Boston Marathon by a woman.

14. Refusal to consider offers by a national shoe manufacturer to buy out the business.

15. How well the Brill and Ogden executives work together.

DATA APPLICATION

DIRECTIONS: Based on your understanding of the business situation, answer the following questions testing your comprehension of the information supplied in the passage. For each question, select the choice which best answers the question or completes the statement.

16. Which of the following are factors in the Ogdens' decision to make a change in their business?

    I. their business operating at a deficit
    II. a sharp rise in competition
    III. the desire to make a moderately priced running shoe

(A) I only
(B) II only
(C) I and II only
(D) III only
(E) I, II, and III

17. What are the reasons given for the recent decline in profits?

    I. the size of the company
    II. rise in competition
    III. increase costs of raw materials

(A) I only
(B) II only
(C) II and III only
(D) I, II, and III
(E) I, and II

18. The reason that the Ogdens have declined to sell their business to a national shoe company is

    I. They had no interest in operating at a profit.
    II. They wanted to provide the discriminating customer with a high quality product.
    III. They found none of the offers attractive.

(A) I only
(B) II only
(C) III only
(D) I and II only
(E) II and III only

19. Merging with the Brill Company is attractive because

    I. Brill also makes an all-leather running shoe.
    II. They would not lose any of their present employees.
    III. It would allow them to keep their autonomy.

(A) I only
(B) II only
(C) III only
(D) II and III only
(E) I and III only

20. An expected advantage of producing a moderately priced running shoe is that

I. The sales could bring the company out of its deficit.
II. The production would enable them to merge with Brill.
III. There would be very little competition in this area.

(A) I only
(B) II only
(C) III only
(D) I and III only
(E) I, II, and III

Stop

END OF SECTION V. IF YOU HAVE ANY TIME LEFT, GO OVER YOUR WORK IN THIS SECTION ONLY. DO NOT WORK IN ANY OTHER SECTION OF THE TEST. WHEN YOUR TIME IS UP, GO ON TO THE NEXT SECTION.

SECTION VI: VERBAL ABILITIES

15 Minutes
25 Questions

ANTONYMS

DIRECTIONS: The questions in this section consist of one word followed by five lettered words or phrases. Choose the lettered word or phrase that is most nearly opposite in meaning to the numbered word.

1. FETID

   (A) in an embryonic state
   (B) easily enraged
   (C) acclaimed by peers
   (D) reduced to skin and bones
   (E) having a pleasant odor

2. CHIMERICAL

   (A) nimble
   (B) realistic
   (C) powerful
   (D) underrated
   (E) remarkable

3. APOCALYPTIC

   (A) concealed
   (B) pure
   (C) steep
   (D) paralyzed
   (E) authentic

4. ABERRANCE

   (A) refusal
   (B) criticism
   (C) adherence
   (D) exhuming
   (E) easing

5. DISCRETE

   (A) orderly
   (B) antisocial
   (C) crude
   (D) joking
   (E) grouped

6. CONTUMACIOUS

   (A) swollen
   (B) scandalous
   (C) sanguine
   (D) concise
   (E) obedient

7. CAMARADERIE

   (A) deviation
   (B) comrades
   (C) aristocracy
   (D) ill will
   (E) plunder

ANALOGIES

DIRECTIONS: The following questions consist of a related pair of words or phrases and five lettered pairs of words or phrases. Choose the lettered pair that best expresses a relationship similar to that expressed in the original pair.

8. DIETING : OVERWEIGHT : :

   (A) overeating : gluttony
   (B) gourmet : underweight
   (C) poverty : sickness
   (D) doctor : arthritis
   (E) resting : fatigue

92

9. HOUSE : MORTGAGE : :

   (A) car : lien
   (B) inventory : merchandise
   (C) word : promise
   (D) security : price
   (E) equity : interest

10. MONEY : EMBEZZLEMENT : :

   (A) bank : cashier
   (B) writing : plagiarism
   (C) remarks : insult
   (D) radiation : bomb
   (E) success : deference

11. FOIL : FENCE : :

   (A) pencil : mark
   (B) road : run
   (C) gloves : box
   (D) train : travel
   (E) bow : bend

12. CLIMB : TREE : :

   (A) row : canoe
   (B) ascend : cliff
   (C) throw : balloon
   (D) file : finger
   (E) rise : top

13. LION : CUB : :

   (A) duck : drake
   (B) rooster : chicken
   (C) human : child
   (D) mother : daughter
   (E) fox : vixen

14. DIET : WEIGHT : :

   (A) food : fat
   (B) dinner : supper
   (C) bread : starchy
   (D) drug : pain
   (E) reduce : increase

15. HYGROMETER : BAROMETER : :

   (A) water : mercury
   (B) snow : rain
   (C) humidity : pressure
   (D) temperature : weather
   (E) forecast : rain

16. CORRESPONDENCE : CLERK : :

   (A) office : manager
   (B) secretary : stenographer
   (C) orders : accountant
   (D) records : archivist
   (E) paper : author

SENTENCE COMPLETIONS

DIRECTIONS: For each of the sentences below, choose the lettered word or set of words which best fit the meaning of the sentence.

17. An _____ study should reveal the influence of environment on man.

   (A) ecumenical
   (B) endemic
   (C) ecological
   (D) epigraphic
   (E) incidental

18. The researcher in the field of _____ was interested in race improvement.

   (A) euthenics
   (B) euthanasia
   (C) euphuism
   (D) euphonics
   (E) philology

19. Through a _____ circumstance, we unexpectedly found ourselves on the same steamer with Uncle Harry.

   (A) fortuitous
   (B) fetid
   (C) friable
   (D) lambent
   (E) habitual

20. I had a terrible night caused by an _____ during my sleep.

   (A) epilogue
   (B) insipidity
   (C) insouciance
   (D) optimum
   (E) incubus

21. The Romans depended on the _____ for the _____ of their homes.

(A) lares . . . protection
(B) caries . . . painting
(C) aborigines . . . blessing
(D) mores . . . erection
(E) resilience . . . insolvency

22. In the study of grammatical forms, the _____ is very helpful.

    (A) syllogism
    (B) mattock
    (C) paradigm
    (D) pimpernel
    (E) palladium

23. The _____ method is used to _____ admission.

    (A) plutonic . . . offer
    (B) Socratic . . . elicit
    (C) sardonic . . . bar

(D) Hippocratic . . . prepare
(E) refrigerant . . . desist

24. They had a wonderful view of the bay through the _____ .

    (A) nadir
    (B) behemoth
    (C) oriel
    (D) fiat
    (E) pastorate

25. There is no reason to insult and _____ the man simply because you do not agree with him.

    (A) depict
    (B) enervate
    (C) defame
    (D) distort
    (E) enhance

Stop

END OF SECTION VI. IF YOU HAVE ANY TIME LEFT, GO OVER YOUR WORK IN THIS SECTION ONLY. DO NOT WORK IN ANY OTHER SECTION OF THE TEST. WHEN YOUR TIME IS UP, GO ON TO THE NEXT SECTION.

SECTION VII: READING RECALL

30 Minutes
25 Questions

DIRECTIONS: You are allowed 15 minutes to closely read the following passages. Afterwards you will be asked to recall certain ideas and facts about the passages. You are not allowed to refer back to the passages.

Passage 1

What is to happen about transport? Evidently there are huge and important changes in prospect. A decade or so from now, there will have been yet another transformation in the way in which people and their goods are moved from place to place. Old techniques are being faced with attenuation or even extinction, sometimes because better methods of travelling have come along but sometimes simply because the old methods have become intolerable.

The development of recent decades most obviously likely to be continued is the tendency for alternative methods of travel to co-exist, and so to offer potential travellers a choice. Within large cities, underground transport is usually an alternative to several ways of travelling on the surface. Roads, railways and airlines are in competition, and there are still people who cross the North Atlantic by sea. (Most freight goes that way, of course.) Choices between co-existing alternatives are usually made on rational grounds, although this does not imply that cheapness is all that matters.

In circumstances like these, even minor technical developments can trigger off marked changes in the pattern of transport. In Britain, electric traction promises to increase the distance over which railways can win passengers from airlines. Quite modest improvements of public transport in cities could do much to diminish congestion from motor cars. Oil tankers displacing 300,000 tons like that ordered from a Japanese yard by Gulf Oil could decisively affect the pattern of petroleum distribution from the major oilfields and—at the same time—encourage the pipeline oper-

ators, who offer the simplest and often the cheapest means of bulk transport. Then, there is the Boeing 747 aircraft, which is likely to do for people what the huge tankers will do for petroleum—trunk route transport will flourish, but getting off the beaten track will be increasingly troublesome. All these changes, promised or merely possible in the pattern of transport, have in common what is, in the broadest sense, an economic stimulus.

From this point of view, the benefits of new technical developments may be different from what their supporters intend. Thus, ironically, it could be that the first—and perhaps even the only—beneficial consequence of the Anglo-French project to build the *Concorde* supersonic airliner will be to ensure that the operating costs of slower aircraft are steadily reduced. More soberly, there could well be a time, in the early '70s, when huge subsonic aircraft ply across the North Atlantic and similar routes, and smaller and faster aircraft travel less busy but longer routes. (It does not, of course, follow that the British and French Governments will recover their expenditure on the *Concorde*.) Yet again, diversity seems to promise that the pattern of transport will be helped to find its most economic form. But what kind of diversity would be best?

Fast transport between cities separated by a few hundred miles is becoming urgently necessary in densely populated areas, particularly in Europe, North America and Japan. The United States Government is financing a number of exploratory investigations bearing on specific problems such as linking the major cities on the Atlantic seaboard. However, it remains to be seen whether the result will really reach beyond schemes for patching up the existing railway network to some of the more ambitious schemes which are sometimes heard of—monorails, pneumatic tubes with trains inside, and deep-bored tunnels intended to enable trains to oscillate from one city to another with no expenditure of energy except for overcoming friction and air resistance. One difficulty is that these transport studies, although well supported, are not being given the kind of attention lavished, for example, on getting to the Moon. In Britain, the somewhat comparable development of hovercraft, also likely to be important over distances of a few hundred miles (by sea or dry land), is not moving forward as vigorously as it might because of a tendency to expect that this device should show a profit from the beginning. Then intra-city transport systems of radically new design are being explored chiefly on the backs of envelopes.

There may eventually be even greater benefits to be won by planning cities, and indeed whole countries, in such a way that the advantages of novel kinds of transport networks can be exploited to the full. Within existing cities, for example, populations tend to be uniformly distributed on the ground, although with a density decreasing outwards from some central zone. The interactions between the distribution of population and an existing transport network tend to be limited to the proclivity for population to distribute itself, over the course of time, in such a way that all transport links are equally congested. It is, however, entirely conceivable that some quite different pattern of population would lend itself more easily to the use of fast transport links. If, within cities, populations were to be gathered into a number of more or less separate concentrations, it might be possible to win great advantages from potentially fast means of travel—monorails for example—which are not likely to be economic as simple replacements for existing underground railways. In other words, there is a strong case for asking that the fabric of a city and the means of transport used within it be designed as a delicately integrated whole. Similarly, cities should be designed or encouraged to develop in such a way as to cater more efficiently for the need to move people and goods easily from one to the next. This, after all, is how the great oil companies organize their affairs (although even they find it difficult to regulate the disposition of the eventual users of petroleum products).

Passage 2

Chemical engineering was not originally science-based in the same sense as electrical engineering. Although the chemical industry was firmly based on the science of chemistry, the role of the chemical engineer was originally merely to provide vessels, pipes, pumps and so on to enable a reaction to be carried out under the conditions specified by the chemist. It is true that there are early examples in which the engineering interacted with and influenced the process—for example, the lead-chamber sulphuric acid process, the Solvay ammonia-soda process and the Haber-Bosch ammonia synthesis. In general, however, the chemical engineer had little influence on the process, and there was very little science involved in chemical engineering. The most difficult part of the job was the choice of the right materials of construction—but until quite recently science has been of little help in this respect.

The type of chemical engineer I have just described—typical, perhaps, of the year 1900—has given way to someone who occupies a very different position. The scientific and unspecialized nature of the training of the chemical engineer fits him for employment in many industries apart from the chemical industry—for example, combustion engineering, food processing and extraction metallurgy. The proportion of chemical engineers employed in non-chemical industries in our country has risen steadily in the past decade, and now amounts to about 25 percent. This wider dissemination of the philosophy of chemical engineering is an important feature of the development of the profession, and is likely to be of great benefit to certain industries which have been somewhat isolated from the mainstream of technological development.

I shall use the phrase "chemical engineering science" to mean the science employed by chemical engineers in their various activities. It is clear that the chemical engineer does not himself always have to develop scientific methods for solving the problems which he encounters. For example, although he is professionally very deeply concerned with the properties of materials, he is not usually thought to be responsible for developing the science and technology of materials—metallurgy, corrosion, refractories, and so on. Other technologists have assumed this responsibility, which on the whole requires a different scientific background from that of the chemical engineer. Chemical engineering science is, therefore, the body of applied science developed by chemical engineers for their own purposes, in fields not covered by other branches of technology. It would be a great mistake to think of the content of chemical engineering science as permanently fixed. It is likely to alter greatly over the years in response to the changing requirements of industry and to the occasional technological breakthrough.

The functions of chemical engineering science are mainly economic. One is the development of quantitative design procedures, so that full-scale plants can be designed by calculation, if necessary with the help of laboratory-scale experiments, but if possible without the need for expensive and time-consuming pilot-scale experiments. The more precise the design procedures which can be developed, the more precisely is it possible to optimize the design of the plant, and the narrower becomes the wasteful margin of safety imposed by ignorance. There is also the need to improve the efficiency of processes and of the plant in which they are carried out—for example, to obtain a higher yield in a chemical reaction, a higher plate-efficiency in a distillation column, or a machine which will produce granular material of a more nearly uniform size. There is also the matter of true invention, leading to quite new processes and devices. Although science may not always provide the inspiration for inventions, it must usually be called in to develop them properly. Finally, there is the need to develop not only automatic but also self-optimizing processes and plants; in the chemical factory of the near future we shall have replaced not only the workman but the management by instruments.

Passage 3

Educators are seriously concerned about the high rate of dropouts among the doctor of philosophy candidates and the consequent loss of talent to a nation in need of Ph.D.'s. Some have placed the dropout loss as high as 50 percent. The extent of the loss was, however, largely a matter of expert guessing.

Last week a well-rounded study was published. It was based on 22,000 questionnaires sent to former graduate students who were enrolled in 24 universities between 1950 and 1954 and seemed to show many past fears to be groundless.

The dropout rate was found to be 31 percent and in most cases the dropouts, while not completing the Ph.D. requirements, went on to productive work.

They are not only doing well financially, but, according to the report, are not far below the income levels of those who went on to complete their doctorates.

The study, called "Attrition of Graduate Students at the Ph.D. Level in the Traditional Arts and Sciences," was made at Michigan State University under a $60,000 grant from the United States Office of Education. It was conducted by Dr. Allan Tucker, former assistant dean of the university and now chief academic officer of the Board of Regents of the State University System of Florida.

Discussing the study last week, Dr. Tucker said the project was initiated "because of the concerns frequently expressed by graduate faculties and administrators that some of the individuals who dropped out of Ph.D. programs were capable of completing the requirements for the degree.

"Attrition at the Ph.D. level is also thought to be a waste of precious faculty time and a drain on university resources already being used to capacity. Some people expressed the opinion that the shortage of highly trained specialists and college teachers could be reduced by persuading the dropouts to return to graduate school to complete the Ph.D. program."

"The results of our research," Dr. Tucker concluded, "did not support these opinions."

The study found that:

(1) Lack of motivation was the principal reason for dropping out.

(2) Most dropouts went as far in their doctoral programs as was consistent with their levels of ability or their specialties.

(3) Most dropouts are now engaged in work consistent with their education and motivation.

(4) The dropout rate was highest in the humanities (50 percent) and lowest in the natural sciences (29 percent)—and is higher in lower-quality graduate schools.

Nearly 75 percent of the dropouts said there was no academic reason for their decision, but those who mentioned academic reasons cited failure to pass qualifying examinations, uncompleted research and failure to pass language exams.

"Among the single most important personal reasons identified by dropouts for noncompletion of their Ph.D. program," the study found "lack of finances was marked by 19 percent."

As an indication of how well the dropouts were doing, a chart showed that 2 percent whose studies were in the humanities were receiving $20,000 and more annually while none of the Ph.D.'s with that background reached this figure. The Ph.D.'s shone in the $7,500 to $15,000 bracket with 78 percent at that level against 50 percent for the dropouts. This may also be an indication of the fact that top salaries in the academic fields, where Ph.D.'s tend to rise to the highest salaries, are still lagging behind other fields.

In the social sciences 5 percent of the Ph.D.'s reached the $20,000 plus figure as against 3 percent of the dropouts but in the physical sciences they were neck-and-neck with 5 percent each.

Academic institutions employed 90 percent of the humanities Ph.D.'s as against 57 percent of the humanities dropouts. Business and industry employed 47 percent of the physical science Ph.D.'s and 38 percent of the physical science dropouts. Government agencies took 16 percent of the social science Ph.D.'s and 32 percent of the social science dropouts.

As to the possibility of getting dropouts back on campus, the outlook was glum.

"The main conditions which would have to prevail for at least 25 percent of the dropouts who might consider returning to graduate school would be to guarantee that they would retain their present level of income and in some cases their present job."

Passage 4

It is a part of the charm of little Tahiti, or Otaheite, whose double island is not more than a hundred miles about, that it has been the type of the oceanic island in story.

With its discovery begins the interest that awoke Europe by the apparent realization of man in his earliest life—a life that recalled the silver if not the golden age. Here men and women made a beautiful race, living free from the oppression of nature, and at first sight also free from the cruel and terrible superstitions of many savage tribes. I have known people who could recall the joyous impression made upon them by these stories of new paradises, only just opened; and both Wallis's and Bougainville's short and official reports are bathed in a feeling of admiration, that takes no definite form, but refers both to the people and the place and the gentleness of the welcome.

The state of nature had just then been the staple reference in the polemic literature of the latter part of the eighteenth century. The refined and dry civilization of the few was troubled by the confused sentiments, the dreams, and the obscure desires of the ignorant and suffering many. Their inarticulate voice was suddenly phrased by Rousseau. With that cry came the literary belief in the natural man, in the possibility of analyzing the foundations of government and civilization, in the perfectibility of the human race and its persistent goodness when freed from the weight of society's blunders and oppressions.

Later, Byron:—

"—the happy shores without a law,
Where all partake the earth without dispute,
And bread itself is gathered as a fruit;
Where none contest the fields, the woods, the streams:
The goldless age, where gold disturbs no dreams."

There is no doubt that at the moment of the discovery our islanders had reached the full extent of their civilization; that, numerous, splendid, and untainted in their physical development, they seemed to live in a facility of existence, in an absence of anxiety emphasized by their love of pleasure and fondness for society—by a simplicity of conscience which found no fault in what we reprobate—in a happiness which is not and could not be our own. The "pursuit of happiness" in which these islanders were engaged, and in which they seemed successful, is the catchword of the eighteenth century.

People were far then from the cruel ideas of Hobbes; and the more amiable views of the nature of man, and of his rights, echo in the sentimentality of the eighteenth century like the sound of the island surf about Tahiti.

The name recalls so many associations of ideas, so much romance of reading, so much of the history of thought, that I find it difficult to disentangle the varying strands of the threads. There are many boyish recollections behind the charm of Melville's *Omoo* and Stoddard's *Idylls*, or even the mixed pleasure of Loti's *Marriage*.

I believe too that my feelings are intensified because they are directed towards an island, a word, a thing of all time marked by man as something wherein to place the ideal, the supernatural, the home of the blest, the abode of the dead, the fountain of eternal youth, as in Heine's song about the island of Bimini:

"Little birdling Colibri,
    Lead us thou to *Tahiti*!"

QUESTIONS

DIRECTIONS: You have 15 minutes to answer the following questions based upon the preceding passages. You are not to refer back to the passages.

Passage 1

1. Basically, transportation plans for the future are made in the light of

    (A) economic considerations
    (B) government regulations
    (C) moral and ethical standards
    (D) political interrelations
    (E) anticipated growth of cities

2. The article brings out that

    (A) there is much less intra-city transport congestion in the small cities than in the large cities
    (B) population increases as one leaves the center of an average-sized city
    (C) the next ten years should, if we are to judge by what has happened in the last decade, bring few changes in the means of transportation
    (D) eventually there will be, for reasons of efficiency, only one mode of transportation
    (E) transportation of commercial goods from Boston and New York to London and Paris is, for the most part, by boat

3. The selection makes it clear that our government is spending money so that it will be easier in the future to transport goods and passengers between New York,

    (A) Los Angeles, and San Francisco
    (B) Minneapolis, and Omaha
    (C) Chicago, and Kansas City
    (D) Savannah, and Jacksonville
    (E) Denver, and Tulsa

4. The least expensive way to ship oil is most often by

    (A) freighter
    (B) plane
    (C) railroad
    (D) truck
    (E) none of the above

5. The author states that old means of travel are becoming extinct largely because

    (A) transport studies are being heavily financed
    (B) the means of transportation have become centrally controlled
    (C) the old means of travel have become intolerable
    (D) radically new forms of travel have become popular
    (E) massive planning efforts have recently been successful

6. The author states or implies that

    (A) an innovator of a transportation technique may find such a technique advantageous, but not in the way originally anticipated
    (B) the giant French jet planes are now actively transporting oil but ships are still being used by Britain for oil transportation
    (C) Japanese oil tankers are, at the present time, being rapidly replaced by pipelines for the transportation of oil
    (D) supersonic planes will, before long, carry freight rather than passengers
    (E) railroads are doomed as more efficient means of transportation are developed

7. The writer would *not* agree that

    (A) future communities should be planned with transportation efficiency as a major consideration
    (B) the replacement of current railways by monorails would save money in a short period of time
    (C) an oil company would do well to use more than one type of transportation for its product
    (D) we should divert some of the money being used for putting a man on the moon to the improvement of transportation in our own country
    (E) electric locomotives have helped to make railroad transportation more ''palatable'' to the passenger

Passage 2

8. The general tenor of the article is that

(A) the chemical engineer does not have the prestige of the other engineers

(B) great strides have been made—and will continue to be made—in the chemical engineering profession

(C) engineering, in general, is a profession which does not receive adequate recognition financially as well as socially

(D) there is much difference of opinion among scientists in regard to whether chemical engineering is a true science

(E) the most trying field of all engineering is chemical engineering

9. The word "refractories" in the third paragraph means materials which

(A) rust readily

(B) do not behave as expected

(C) crack easily

(D) are highly resistant to intense heat

(E) are made in a chemical factory

10. "The functions of chemical engineering science are mainly economic." This statement implies that

(A) chemicals are more costly today than ever before

(B) other engineering sciences are relatively uninterested in the profit motive

(C) the chemical engineer is not concerned with moral issues

(D) chemical engineering is the most lucrative of all engineering professions

(E) chemical engineering, by securing maximum efficiency, will save money

11. The author implies that

(A) faith plays as important a part as science in chemical engineering

(B) the chemical engineer should not be concerned with working with metals

(C) the science of chemical engineering is far from set in regard to its function

(D) the chemical engineer ought not to employ a scientific method

(E) more often than not, the chemical engineer has the same content background as the electrical engineer

12. At the beginning of the twentieth century, the chemical engineer

(A) knew little about science

(B) did not put his scientific background to much use

(C) was not capable of selecting appropriate materials to do the job required

(D) frequently did the work of the electrical engineer

(E) was not required to have a degree

13. The selection indicates that

(A) chemical engineering is an art rather than a science

(B) about one-fourth of the nation's engineers are chemical engineers

(C) the prototype of all engineers was the chemical engineer

(D) the chemical engineer no longer concerns himself with pumps and pipes

(E) the development of certain processes required a scientific approach on the part of the chemical engineer

14. After reading this article, one would think that the writer

(A) is opposed to labor unions

(B) believes that creativity is to be discouraged among engineers

(C) feels that the majority of chemical engineers have selfish interests

(D) stresses the need for a technological revolution

(E) urges chemical engineers to develop their own procedures to solve problems—not to depend on other technologists

Passage 3

15. Dr. Tucker's report showed that

(A) the rate of attrition is highest in lower-quality graduate schools

(B) since the dropout does just about as well financially as the Ph.D. degree-getter, there is no justifiable reason for the former to return to his studies

(C) the high dropout rate is largely attributable to the lack of stimulation on the part of faculty members

(D) the dropout should return to a lower quality

school to continue his studies

(E) the Ph.D. holder is generally a better adjusted person than the dropout

16. The article states that

(A) not having sufficient funds to continue accounts for more Ph.D. dropouts than all the other reasons combined

(B) in fields such as English, philosophy, and the arts, the dropouts are doing better in the higher salary brackets than the Ph.D.'s

(C) at the $10,000 earning level, there is a higher percentage of dropouts than the percentage of Ph.D.'s

(D) in physics, geology, and chemistry, the Ph.D.'s are twice as numerous in the higher salary brackets than the dropouts

(E) the government agencies employ twice as many dropouts as they do Ph.D.'s

17. Research has shown that

(A) dropouts are substantially below Ph.D.'s in financial attainment

(B) the incentive factor is a minor one in regard to pursuing Ph.D. studies

(C) the Ph.D. candidate is likely to change his field of specialization if he drops out

(D) about one-third of those who start Ph.D. work do not complete the work to earn the degree

(E) there are comparatively few dropouts in the Ph.D. humanities disciplines

18. Meeting foreign language requirements for the Ph.D.

(A) is the most frequent reason for dropping out

(B) is more difficult for the science candidate than for the humanities candidate

(C) is considered part of the so-called "qualification" examination

(D) is an essential for acquiring a Ph.D. degree

(E) does not vary in difficulty among universities

19. Dr. Tucker felt that

(A) a primary purpose of his research project was to arrive at a more efficient method for dropping incapable Ph.D. applicants

(B) a serious aspect of the dropout situation was

the deplorable waste of productive talent

(C) one happy feature about the dropout situation was that the dropouts went into college teaching rather than into research

(D) his project should be free of outside interference and so he rejected outside financial assistance for the project

(E) Ph.D. dropouts were responsible for considerable loss of time and money on the part of the university

20. After reading the article, one would refrain from concluding that

(A) colleges and universities employ a substantial number of Ph.D. dropouts

(B) Ph.D.'s are not earning what they deserve in nonacademic positions

(C) the study, *Attrition of Graduate Students at the Ph.D. Level in the Traditional Arts and Sciences,* was conducted with efficiency and validity

(D) a Ph.D. dropout, by and large, does not have what it takes to earn the degree

(E) optimism reigns in regard to getting Ph.D. dropouts to return to their pursuit of the degree

Passage 4

21. Tahiti

(A) adjoins the island of Otaheite

(B) is more or less circular with a diameter of approximately 100 miles

(C) was visited by Rousseau

(D) was known for the beauty of its inhabitants

(E) had among its natives many well-educated persons

22. Byron looks upon Tahiti as a land where

(A) individuals are loath to complete their tasks

(B) money is of relatively little importance

(C) lawlessness prevails

(D) inhabitants substitute fruit for bread

(E) the people live in dire poverty

23. Wallis and Bougainville were primarily

(A) scientists

(B) historians

(C) navigators

(D) philosophers

(E) cannot be determined

24. Literature in the latter part of the eighteenth century was characterized by

(A) stress on the importance of the individual

(B) a reversion to classical patterns by imitating the Latin and Greek poets

(C) religious views comparable to those of the early theologians

(D) bold references to the vices of mankind

(E) a divorcement from the realities of life

25. The author considers the Tahitians

(A) superstitious and savage until visitors to their island showed them a better way of life

(B) a backward race who were happy in their stupidity

(C) a troubled people suffering from lack of adequate diet and deprived of the comforts of civilization

(D) a well-adjusted folk who did not especially benefit from the influence of the visiting white men

(E) a refined community, highly civilized, quite unlike the natives of other Pacific islands

Stop

END OF EXAMINATION

END OF SECTION VII. IF YOU HAVE ANY TIME LEFT, GO OVER YOUR WORK IN THIS SECTION ONLY. DO NOT WORK IN ANY OTHER SECTION OF THE TEST. WHEN YOUR TIME IS UP, CHECK YOUR ANSWERS WITH THE ANSWER KEY AND EXPLANATORY ANSWERS PROVIDED ON THE FOLLOWING PAGES.

ANSWER KEY

SECTION I

1. C	6. D	11. B	16. C	21. B
2. E	7. B	12. A	17. D	22. D
3. A	8. D	13. B	18. D	23. D
4. B	9. E	14. E	19. D	24. B
5. D	10. A	15. A	20. B	25. D

SECTION II

1. D	7. E	13. A	19. B	25. D
2. B	8. D	14. E	20. C	26. D
3. A	9. E	15. D	21. E	27. E
4. B	10. B	16. A	22. E	28. B
5. C	11. B	17. C	23. A	29. C
6. D	12. C	18. E	24. B	30. B

SECTION III

1. C	5. B	9. C	13. D	17. B
2. A	6. D	10. B	14. B	18. E
3. E	7. A	11. C	15. A	19. C
4. A	8. C	12. C	16. E	20. A

SECTION IV

1. D	7. B	13. C	19. D	25. A
2. A	8. B	14. E	20. C	26. C
3. C	9. C	15. A	21. E	27. C
4. C	10. C	16. B	22. C	28. E
5. E	11. E	17. C	23. E	29. D
6. C	12. C	18. C	24. C	30. E

SECTION V

1. A	5. E	9. A	13. E	17. C
2. D	6. A	10. C	14. D	18. B
3. B	7. D	11. B	15. B	19. B
4. C	8. B	12. B	16. C	20. A

SECTION VI

1. E	6. E	11. C	16. D	21. A
2. B	7. D	12. B	17. C	22. C
3. A	8. E	13. C	18. A	23. B
4. C	9. A	14. D	19. A	24. C
5. E	10. B	15. C	20. E	25. C

SECTION VII

1. A	6. A	11. C	16. B	21. D
2. E	7. B	12. B	17. D	22. B
3. D	8. B	13. E	18. D	23. E
4. E	9. D	14. E	19. E	24. A
5. C	10. E	15. A	20. E	25. D

EXPLANATORY ANSWERS

SECTION I

1. **(C)** The passage is concerned specifically with the effects of man's activity on the environment.

2. **(E)** This is stated in the passage; even the best efforts of man are sometimes thwarted by nature.

3. **(A)** This is also stated in the passage.

4. **(B)** As the passage states, "the pioneer's life is too strenuous a one for him to think of posterity."

5. **(D)** Phytogeographic maps are "very similar to the climatic map based on rainfall, evaporation, and temperature," which the passage states are the essential elements in determining an area's vegetation.

6. **(D)** The destruction of forests is the only cause listed which is mentioned in the passage as a cause of land destruction in China and India.

7. **(B)** This is the only solution to preventing soil erosion mentioned in the passage.

8. **(D)** While grasslands may be converted to agricultural uses, their yield is uncertain owing to climatic conditions. The only plants certain to grow in grasslands are grasses.

9. **(E)** Excessive clearing of forests is the abuse with most long-term effects, as it may take a century or more for a forest to grow back, and as such should be given priority in a program of good land management.

10. **(A)** The passage tells us that in heavily populated areas, elaborate laws have been evolved, of necessity, to "protect plants of economic value and preserve soil fertility."

11. **(B)** "Seashore Life" is the most specific expression of the passage's subject.

12. **(A)** To live on a sandy beach, an animal must be able to move quickly and burrow into the sand; the passage says nothing about their ability to burrow deeply.

13. **(B)** The passage states that life in the sea is "supported largely by materials washed into the sea."

14. **(E)** Because of the violence of breaking waves, shore animals prefer living among the rocks than on a sandy beach.

15. **(A)** The passage tells us that certain organisms living at the high-tide mark actually require exposure to the open air, as well as occasional immersion.

16. **(C)** That marine animals depend in large part upon material washed into the sea for their subsistence is a more important factor in the author's conclusion than the relative number or variety of land and sea animals.

17. **(D)** The ability of shore animals to move quickly was established in question twelve.

18. **(D)** The next to last paragraph in the passage is concerned with establishing the essential similarity between land- and sea-dwellers, despite their apparent differences.

19. **(D)** Although there may be more life in shallow waters, the greatest variety of life is found between the high- and low-tide lines.

20. **(B)** The first paragraph tells us that "the sea and its shores have been the scene of the greatest stability."

21. **(B)** This is directly stated in the first sentence of the passage.

22. **(D)** This process is explained in the first paragraph.

23. **(D)** Because it captures the image through a lens, photostating makes it possible to enlarge or reduce the copy.

24. **(B)** Direct copying is called direct because it doesn't use a lens. The passage tells us that this is the least expensive method, and that it uses the least equipment.

25. **(D)** The direct method of copying with a lens is most accurate, as it will not cause shrinkage or stretching of the original.

SECTION II

1. **(D)** $\frac{4}{5} = .8$

$$\frac{7}{9} = 9\overline{)7.00} \quad .78$$

$$\frac{5}{7} = 7\overline{)5.00} \quad .71$$

$$\frac{9}{11} = 11\overline{)9.00} \quad .82$$

Thus $\frac{5}{7}$ is the smallest quantity.

2. **(B)** Let x = amount earned each month
$2x$ = amount earned in December
Then $11x + 2x = 13x$ (entire earnings)
$$\frac{2x}{13x} = \frac{2}{13}$$

3. **(A)** $3x^3 + 2x^2 + x + 1$
$= 3(-1)^3 + 2(-1)^2 + (-1) + 1$
$= 3(-1) + 2(1) - 1 + 1$
$= -3 + 2 + 0$
$= -1$

4. **(B)** $\dfrac{x}{12} = \dfrac{83\frac{1}{3}}{100} = \dfrac{250}{300}$

or $\dfrac{x}{12} = \dfrac{25}{30} = \dfrac{5}{6}$

$6x = 60$
$x = 10$

5. **(C)** Since the ratio of the sides is $3:1$, the ratio of the areas is $9:1$.

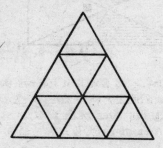

The subdivision into 9 △ is shown

6. **(D)** $\dfrac{a}{b} = \dfrac{3}{5}$

$5a = 3b$

Multiply both sides by 3.

$15a = 9b$

7. **(E)** The opposite vertices may be any of the number pairs $(1 \pm 5,\ 1 \pm 5)$ or $(6,6)$, $(-4,\ -4)$, $(-4,6)$, $(6,-4)$

Thus $(4,\ -6)$ is not possible.

8. **(D)**

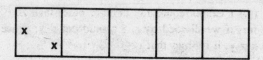

Perimeter of rectangle $= x + 5x + x + 5x$

Thus $12x = 372$

$x = 31$

Area of square $= 31^2 = 961$

9. **(E)** $\sqrt{3} = 1.73$ (approx.)

$$\frac{1}{\sqrt{3}} = \frac{\sqrt{3}}{3} = \frac{1.73}{3} = .57$$

$$\frac{\sqrt{3}}{3} = \frac{1.73}{3} = .57$$

$$\frac{1}{3} = .3333\ldots\ldots$$

$$\frac{1}{3\sqrt{3}} = \frac{\sqrt{3}}{3.3} = \frac{\sqrt{3}}{9} = \frac{1.73}{9} = .19$$

Thus the smallest is $\dfrac{1}{3\sqrt{3}}$

10. **(B)**

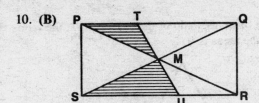

Since $\triangle$ TQM $\cong$ $\triangle$ SMU, it follows that the shaded area = Area of $\triangle$ PTM + Area of $\triangle$ TQM = Area of $\triangle$ PMQ. But Area of $\triangle$ PMQ = ½ Area of $\triangle$ PQS = ¼ Area of $\square$ PQRS; ¼ = 25%

11. **(B)** Let x = number of people in audience
then $\frac{1}{6}$ x = no. of boys
$\frac{1}{3}$ x = no. of girls
$\frac{1}{6}x + \frac{1}{3}x = \frac{1}{6}x + \frac{2}{6}x = \frac{3}{6}x = \frac{1}{2}x$ =
no. of children
½ = 50%

12. **(C)** The number of revolutions is inversely proportional to size of wheel.
Thus $\frac{30}{20} = \frac{n}{240}$
Where n = no. of revolutions for 2nd wheel.
2n = 720
n = 360

13. **(A)** r cannot equal any number other than zero, for, if we divided by r, x would equal y. Since x $\neq$ y, it follows that r = 0.

14. **(E)** $\frac{m}{n} = \frac{5}{6}$
6m = 5n
6m − 5n = 0
However, it is not possible to determine from this the value of 3m + 2n.

15. **(D)** I. As x increases, $\frac{1}{x}$ decreases and
$x - \frac{1}{x}$ increases.

II. $\frac{1}{x^2 - x} = \frac{1}{x(x-1)}$ As x increases, both
x and (x − 1) increase, and $\frac{1}{x(x-1)}$ decreases.

III. $4x^3 - 2x^2 = 2x^2(2x - 1)$. As x increases, both $2x^2$ and $(2x - 1)$ increase and their product increases. Therefore, I and III increase.

16. **(A)** Area of $\triangle$ SPT = 1/3 Area of $\triangle$ PSR since they have common altitude and the base ST = 1/3 SR. But Area of $\triangle$ PSR = ½ Area of $\square$ PQRS. Hence, Area of $\triangle$ SPT = 1/3 × 1/2 Area of $\square$ PQRS = 1/6 $\square$ PQRS.

17. **(C)** Let the other two angles be 2x and 5x. Thus,
2x + 5x + 82 = 180
7x = 98
x = 14
2x = 28
5x = 70
Smallest angle = 28°

18. **(E)** His rate is $\frac{1}{t}$ of the lawn per minute.
Hence, in 15 minutes, he will do
$15 \cdot \frac{1}{t} = \frac{15}{t}$ of the lawn

19. **(B)** Typing space is 12 − 3 = 9 inches long and 9 − 2 = 7 inches wide. Part used =
$\frac{9 \times 7}{9 \times 12} = \frac{7}{12}$

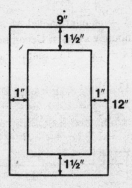

20. **(C)** Since there are 5,280 ft. in a mile, the boy runs 1/40 mile (132/5,280) in 9 seconds. At this speed, he will run 1 mile in 6 minutes (9 × 40 = 360 seconds or 6 minutes), or 10 miles in 60 minutes (1 hr.).

21. **(E)** Let the original sign be 10 by 10.

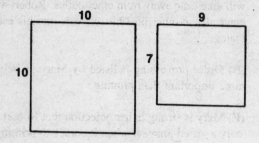

Then the new sign is 9 by 7

$$\frac{63}{100} = 63\%$$

22. **(E)** All the numbers from 200 to 299 begin with 2. There are 100 of these. Then all numbers like 102, 112, _____, 192 end with 2. There are ten of these.
Hence, there are 110 such numbers.

23. **(A)** If $2 < y < 7$ and $5 < y < 10$, then $5 < y < 7$ (intersection of 2 sets). Since y is an integer, it must be 6.

24. **(B)** If the area is $49x^2$, the side of the square is 7x. Therefore, the diagonal of the square must be the hypotenuse of a right isosceles triangle of leg 7x.
Hence diagonal $= 7x \sqrt{2}$

25. **(D)** Since MP = 1 and MQ = ½, the area of △ PMQ = area of △ POR = ½ · 1 · ½ = ¼
The area of △ QNR = ½ · ½ · ½ = ⅛
Area of △ PQR = 1 − 2(¼) − ⅛ = 1 − ⅝ = ⅜

26. **(D)** 72 tiles along each length. 24 tiles along each width. 2 × 96 = 192 tiles along perimeter. But 4 more are needed for the corners of the frame.

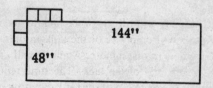

Hence, 196 tiles are needed.

27. **(E)** $\dfrac{1}{10} = \dfrac{3x}{4}$

Cross-multiplying, we obtain
$$30x = 4$$
$$x = {}^2/_{15}$$

28. **(B)** Since QR = 7, and QOR is a right, isosceles triangle, $OQ = \dfrac{7}{\sqrt{2}} = \dfrac{7\sqrt{2}}{2}$
Hence, coordinates of Q are $(0, {}^7/_2\sqrt{2})$

29. **(C)** Let x = no. of years for 2 populations to be equal.
Then $6800 - 120x = 4200 + 80x$
$$2600 = 200x$$
$$x = 13$$

30. **(B)** 8 × 6 = 48 (sum of first eight numbers)
6 × 8 = 48 (sum of last six numbers)
96 = sum of all 14 numbers
Average = 96/14 = 6 6/7

SECTION III

1. **(C)** That there may be a possible drop in the quality of the catalog is a minor factor.

2. **(A)** It is Robert's aim to be able to control production so that he can avoid outside delays.

3. **(E)** Increased sales revenue resulting from his ownership of a printing press does not seem to enter into Robert's calculations.

4. **(A)** The date on which the catalog is mailed is of critical importance; having this date assured is a major objective.

5. **(B)** Reduction of printing costs is a major factor since it directly influences the major objective of increasing profit.

6. **(D)** Making up the price of the printing press within one year is an assumption on Robert's part, which can only be proved if he actually buys the press and tries it for a year.

7. **(A)** Robert wishes to increase profits by lowering printing costs.

8. **(C)** The strike at the printing plant is a minor factor that led to a major factor of delaying the catalog mailing.

9. **(C)** Failure to correctly estimate costs of his time devoted to printing should a press be purchased is a minor factor that obviously leads him to postpone making a decision. It bears directly on the major factor to reduce printing costs, which in turn leads to the major objective of increasing profits.

10. **(B)** Robert's fascination with printing seems to be a major factor in his desire to own a press.

11. **(C)** It is stated that the Johnsons make $30,000 on an average annual sales revenue of $200,000.

12. **(C)** It is stated that 25% of the $200,000 sales revenue comes from retail outlets, and the rest (75%) from direct mail.

13. **(D)** It is stated that Robert wishes to own his own press so he can avoid the sharp drop in sales that resulted from a late mailing of his catalog, caused by a strike at his printer. (B) is wrong; we have only been told about one late mailing. (C) is wrong; Robert apparently has no desire to have an additional business. It is never mentioned that acquisition of a press will help increase sales volume, so (E) is wrong. We are not told that his printer is out of business; thus (A) is incorrect.

14. **(B)** His present printing cost is $40,000. If he owned his own press, he would have to pay $16,000 for paper and ink and $4,000 for a part-time pressman, making a total of $20,000, or a reduction of $20,000.

15. **(A)** It is a seasonal business, of course, dealing in seeds which must be planted at a certain time. That is the reason why sales volume dropped sharply when the Johnson catalog was mailed only two weeks late. (D) is incorrect; we are told that the company made over $200,000 in sales revenue during each of the past three years. (E) is wrong; the business is confined to the state of Colorado.

16. **(E)** Mary points out that Robert has not figured into his calculations how much more time he will now have to spend in the printing process, which will take time away from other duties. Robert did enter all the other possible answers into his estimates.

17. **(B)** Order processing is listed by Mary as being more important than printing.

18. **(E)** Mary is strong in her objection that Robert is only a gifted amateur when it comes to printing, not a professional pressman.

19. **(C)** She calls it his hobby. (B) is wrong; we are not told that Robert is bored with the business. (A) is also incorrect; she does not think that buying the press is practical. (D) is wrong because the purchase price of the press does not seem to be a concern. Sales have been about $200,000 for each of the past three years; therefore (E) is wrong.

20. **(A)** So stated. That does not mean she believes the catalog is of no importance, (B), or that it has never been of a high standard, (E); we are not told her opinions on these.

SECTION IV

1. **(D)** According to Statement 1, he earned 87½% of $6500 in 1962 = $5777.77. According to Statement 2, he earned ⅔ of $8666.67 in 1962 = $5777.77.

2. **(A)** $43,250 × .15 will be the sum that creditors will receive.

3. **(C)** (90 × 4 + 84 × 3 + 75 × 3 + 76 × 1) ÷ 11 will give the student's over-all average.

4. **(C)** Pipe A will fill ¹/₁₂ of the tank in one minute. Pipe B will empty ⅛ of the tank in one minute. Together, in one minute, A and B will empty ⅛ − ¹/₁₂ = ¹/₂₄ of the tank. The time required to empty 3/4 or 18/24 of the tank can now be determined (18 minutes).

5. **(E)** To arrive at the average rate, it would be necessary to know how many miles per hour *each* man walked.

6. **(C)** The double discount will bring the selling price down to $60. Since the dealer's profit is 30% of this (from Statement 1), he has bought the desk for $60 × .7 = $42. His cost of doing business is $60 × 10% = $6 (from Statement 2). The cost of the desk to him is $42 minus $6 = $36.

7. **(B)** The length of the working day is irrelevant in this solution. From Statement 2 we can determine that the two typists can type 300 letters in three days—therefore, 100 letters in one day.

8. **(B)** If the hour hand is exactly half-way between 9 and 10, the minute hand must be on the 6—it's 9:30.

9. **(C)** From Statement 1 we know that the first three men ate $^{249}/_{308}$ of the pie. From Statement 2 we learn that the fourth man ate the rest of the pie = $^{59}/_{308}$.

10. **(C)** Let x = the length of the bridge. Then, $^1/_5$ x + $^1/_6$ x + 760 feet = x.

11. **(E)** To solve, it is necessary to know the number of males over 20.

12. **(C)** Statement 1 tells us that Pericles was a historian. Statement 2 tells us that he lived in ancient times.

13. **(C)** The tax to be paid is arrived at as follows: $2.56 × 60 × .20

14. **(E)** The bank's compounding practice is required for solution.

15. **(A)** The wine will lose 30¢ worth of quality per gallon—that is, $^1/_5$ of the original quality. In other words, $^1/_5$ of each gallon of wine will be replaced by 1/3 gallon of water. Therefore, 8 will be the total number of gallons of water to be added.

16. **(B)** Statement 1, in no way, contributes to the solution of the problem. Statement 2 tells us that each jar holds one quart = ¼ gallon. 20 × ¼ gallon = 5 gallons.

17. **(C)** MDCCXVI = 1716. 1716 − 1646 = 70 years.

18. **(C)** The amphibian group includes Rana (Statement 2). Rana includes the bullfrog (Statement 1). Therefore, the amphibian group must include the bullfrog.

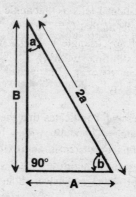

19. **(D)**
From Statement 1, we learn that side A, as shown in the diagram, is ½ side 2a.
$$\text{Sin A} = \frac{\text{length of leg opposite angle a}}{\text{length of hypotenuse}} = ½$$
The table of sine ratios which mathematicians have constructed for all acute angles between 0° and 90° should tell us that if sin A = .5, then angle a = 30°. Statement 2 tells us that angle b = 60°. The three angles of any triangle add up to 180°. Therefore, angle a = 30°.

20. **(C)** Statement 1 tells us that the calories of 2 apples = the calories of a banana. Therefore, 2A = 1B. Statement 2 tells us that the calories in 1 hamburger = the calories in $^3/_2$ bananas. Therefore, 1H = $^3/_2$B. So 2H = 3B. Since 1B = 2A, let us substitute in the relationship of 2H = 3B.
2H = 3B = 3 × 2A = 6A
$$H = \frac{6A}{2} \text{ and } H = 3A$$

Therefore, 1 hamburger has 3 times as many calories as 1 apple.

21. **(E)** The series pattern is not brought out by the first and second numbers of the series.

22. **(C)** Statements 1 and 2 indicate that the first three deposits are in the sequence of 5,7,9. We can, therefore, establish that we have here an arithmetic series which progresses by 2's.

23. **(E)** Statement 1 indicates the length of the ribbon. What we need to know in order to solve the problem is the cost per unit of that particular ribbon. The latter information is not provided.

24. **(C)** Statement 1 tells us that angle A = 3B. Statement 2 tells us that C = 20 + B. Since the three angles of any triangle = 180°, A + B + C = 180. Substituting, we have
3B + B + 20 + B = 180
5B = 160; B = 32°.

25. **(A)** Statement 1 indicates that the volume of the added water = $75 \times 42 \times \frac{1}{3}$ = 1050 cubic feet. 7.5 gallons of water is approximately 1 cubic foot of water. Therefore, 1050×7.5 = 7,875 gallons of water = Answer. Statement 2 is irrelevant.

26. **(C)** In this syllogism, Statement 1 is the major premise, Statement 2 is the minor premise, and the conclusion, by deductive reasoning, is that Socrates is mortal.

27. **(C)** By putting together the information of the two statements, we may conclude that monanthous means having but one flower.

28. **(E)** The third dimension of the box is lacking. Without this third dimension, we cannot solve the problem.

29. **(D)** *Skates* can be a noun or a verb. Statement 1 shows that *skates* is not a noun (nouns can be modified by adjectives). Statement 2 shows that *skates* is a verb (adverbs modify verbs, but not nouns).

30. **(E)** The information in Statement 1 is of too general a nature to be of any help. Statement 2 tells us what *testimony* means but tells us nothing about what *evidence* means.

SECTION V

1. **(A)** Major Objective. It is clear from the passage that the production of their quality products is even more important to the Ogdens than realizing a large profit, which they could easily have achieved by selling out to one of the national shoe companies.

2. **(D)** Major Assumption. It is this given assumption that leads the Ogdens to consider their various alternatives. The various alternatives open to them are on the supposition that they do not want to operate on a deficit.

3. **(B)** Major Factor. This is a major factor in making their decision since if the Ogdens are unwilling to give up autonomy over their products they would have to choose the first alternative and exclude the merger alternative.

4. **(C)** Minor Factor. This is a minor factor since such an endorsement would contribute to the desirability of the first option. It is not a major factor since the lack of such an endorsement could be overcome by other endorsements or an alternative promotional plan that was successful.

5. **(E)** Unimportant Issue. Brill's experience in the area of running shoes is unimportant to the merger since Ogden will be bringing that experience to the merger.

6. **(A)** Major Objective. Though this is not the foremost objective in making the decision, it is one of the desirable outcomes sought by the decision maker. It was stated that the Ogdens were on close terms with their employees and that even if they were to merge with Brill, they would be allowed to keep all their employees, an obvious desirable outcome.

7. **(D)** Major Assumption. Ogden's search for alternatives to maintain the production of their high quality products is based on the assumption that there will continue to be a market for these products.

8. **(B)** Major Factor. This is a major factor in their decision since the sacrifice of standards is a necessary component of the first alternative. An unwillingness to do so would eliminate the first alternative.

9. **(A)** Major Objective. This is one of the desirable outcomes sought by the decision maker that comes out of their major objective of maintaining the production of their quality products. The success of either alternative would offset the costs of the raw materials.

10. **(C)** Minor Factor. This is a factor since the success of the first alternative would be enhanced by such effectiveness. It is not a major factor since the success of the first alternative would not necessarily depend upon the impact of an endorsement.

11. **(B)** Major Factor. The second alternative requires that Brill be in the same region as Ogden. Brill's move outside of the area would virtually eliminate the second alternative.

12. **(B)** Major Factor. This would seem to completely rule out the merger option which was founded on the rationale of two very similar companies sharing a demand for high quality products.

13. **(E)** Unimportant Issue. Such an outcome would have no predictable effect on the option involving an endorsement from the marathon winner.

14. **(D)** Major Assumption. The two alternatives that Ogden considers are based on the assumption that the option to sell out to a national shoe manufacturer is ruled out.

15. **(B)** Major Factor. How well the two companies can work together will be a major factor in considering the possibility of a merger.

16. **(C)** Ogden is led to make a change because they cannot continue to operate at a deficit, and one of the causes of their operating at a deficit is the sharp rise in competition. Alternative III is not a factor in the decision but one of the compromises that could be forced upon them.

17. **(C)** Alternatives II and III are explicitly given as reasons for decline in profits. The passage gives no indication that the size of the company has anything to do with a decline in profits.

18. **(B)** Only alternative II is a reason. The passage states that they did receive attractive offers and that they would not consider operating at a loss. Their overriding concern was obviously their desire to market a high quality product.

19. **(B)** Alternative II is stated as one of the attractions. Alternative I is eliminated since there is

nothing in the passage to indicate that Brill does not make such a shoe. Alternative III is explicitly denied in the passage.

20. **(A)** The passage indicates that an expected advantage of producing the moderately priced shoe is that it will be a means of bringing the company out of its deficit. The production plan is completely independent of the plan to merge with Brill and the passage makes it clear that there will be a great deal of competition in the sale of such a shoe.

SECTION VI

1. **(E)** Fetid means having an offensive smell; thus, (E) is clearly opposite.

2. **(B)** Chimerical means fantastic or improbable. Something realistic would be its opposite.

3. **(A)** Apocalyptic can mean prophetic. This then would be something that is revealed and not hidden or concealed.

4. **(C)** An aberrance would be a turning away from, not an adherence to.

5. **(E)** Discrete would be unconnected, not grouped.

6. **(E)** Contumacious means disobedient; thus, (E) is clearly opposite in meaning.

7. **(D)** The opposite of camaraderie or good fellowship would be ill will.

8. **(E)** Dieting cures overweight; resting cures fatigue.

9. **(A)** A mortgage is taken out on a house; a lien may be taken out against a car.

10. **(B)** Embezzlement is the theft of another's money; plagiarism is the appropriation of another person's written work without his permission.

11. **(C)** You fence with a foil; you box with gloves.

12. **(B)** You climb up a tree and ascend a cliff.

13. **(C)** A young lion is a cub; a young person is a child.

14. **(D)** Diet reduces weight; drug reduces pain.

15. **(C)** A hygrometer measures humidity while a barometer measures atmospheric pressure.

16. **(D)** A clerk looks after correspondence while an archivist looks after records.

17. **(C)** Ecological studies are those which deal with the interrelationships of organisms and their environments.

18. **(A)** Euthenics deals with the improvement of the human condition.

19. **(A)** The context of the sentence suggests that the meeting was a lucky or fortuitous event.

20. **(E)** A nightmare or incubus would cause a bad night.

21. **(A)** The household gods or lares looked after the well-being of each Roman household.

22. **(C)** A paradigm would be an example of a grammatical form.

23. **(B)** The use of the Socratic method helps to find out the truth or the reality of a situation.

24. **(C)** One can see a view through an oriel or window.

25. **(C)** One should not insult and defame or slander a person because he does not agree with him.

SECTION VII

1. **(A)** The passage states: "All these changes, promised or merely possible in the pattern of transport, have in common what is, in the broadest sense, an economic stimulus."

2. **(E)** The passage states that most freight goes by sea.

3. **(D)** The passage states: "The United States Government is financing a number of exploratory investigations bearing on specific problems such as linking the major cities on the Atlantic seaboard." Option (D) is the only one in which both cities mentioned are on the Atlantic seaboard.

4. **(E)** The answer would be by pipeline which is not offered as a choice.

5. **(C)** The passage states: "Old techniques are being faced with attenuation or even extinction, sometimes because better methods of traveling have come along but sometimes simply because the old methods have become intolerable."

6. **(A)** The author states: "In circumstances like these, even minor technical developments can trigger off marked changes in the patterns of transport."

7. **(B)** The author feels that new innovations, such as the British hovercraft, often are not developed as rapidly as possible because there is no guarantee that they would yield a profit immediately. The author speaks of monorails as one of these new innovations.

8. **(B)** All of the other options involve a defensive or polemical attitude. This is clearly not the tenor of the passage. The author discusses the development of the profession since the turn of the century and makes specific mention of a number of developments in the field.

9. **(D)** As a common adjective, the word refractory denotes something which is immune or stubborn. From this knowledge we can isolate (D) as the correct answer.

10. **(E)** The fourth paragraph details several of the ways that the work of the chemical engineer can save money in an industrial context.

11. **(C)** The passage states: "It would be a great mistake to think of the content of chemical engineering as being permanently fixed."

12. **(B)** Of chemical engineering in the past, the author says: "there was very little science involved in chemical engineering."

13. **(E)** The passage states: "There is also the matter of true invention, leading to quite new processes

and devices. Although science may not always provide the inspiration for inventions, it must usually be called in to develop them properly."

14. **(E)** The author is throughout the passage stressing the need for invention on the chemical engineer's part.

15. **(A)** This is one of the findings listed as a factor in many students' decisions to drop out. (B) and (D) are incorrect because the report gives no advice to dropouts for their future plans. (C) and (E) are not mentioned in the passage.

16. **(B)** The passage states: "As an indication of how well the dropouts were doing, a chart showed that 2 percent whose studies were in the humanities were receiving $20,000 and more annually while none of the Ph.D.s with that background reached this figure."

17. **(D)** According to the research study cited in the passage, "the dropout rate was found to be 31 percent."

18. **(D)** This is more or less an item of common knowledge. This option is supported by the fact that failure to pass language exams is, according to the passage, one of the reasons commonly cited for dropping out of Ph.D. programs.

19. **(E)** None of the opinions mentioned in the other options can be attributed explicitly or implicitly to Dr. Tucker.

20. **(E)** The passage states: "As to the possibility of getting dropouts back on campus, the outlook was glum." The passage goes on to give the economic reason for this glum outlook.

21. **(D)** The physical beauty of the race inhabiting the island is stressed in the passage.

22. **(B)** The Byron passage cited speaks of a "goldless age, where gold disturbs no dreams."

23. **(E)** This cannot be definitely determined from the passage.

24. **(A)** This is articulated in the third paragraph with the mention of Rousseau and his belief in the natural man.

25. **(D)** This view is brought forth by the author who states that "at the moment of the discovery our islanders had reached the full extent of their civilization; that, numerous, splendid, and untainted in their physical development, they seemed to live in a facility of existence . . . in a happiness which is not and could not be our own."

PRACTICE EXAMINATION 2

This ARCO Practice Examination is similar to the Graduate Management Admission Test you are going to take in structure, length, and level of difficulty. The examination sections and question-types have been changed from those in previous Practice Examinations, but have been kept approximate to those found in the actual GMAT.

Take this examination as if you were taking the real test. Follow all instructions and observe the time limits indicated. Remember to mark all your answers on the Answer Sheet provided, which is similar to the one you will find on the actual examination.

An Answer Key and Explanatory Answers for every question in this Practice Examination are provided at the end of the exam. Check your answers to find out your areas of weakness and then concentrate your studies where they are most needed.

The total time allowed for this test is 3 hours.

ANALYSIS AND TIMETABLE: PRACTICE EXAMINATION 2

Subject Tested	Time Allowed
READING COMPREHENSION	30 minutes
DATA INTERPRETATION	35 minutes
PRACTICAL BUSINESS JUDGMENT	20 minutes
DATA SUFFICIENCY	30 minutes
ENGLISH USAGE	15 minutes
PRACTICAL BUSINESS JUDGMENT	20 minutes
VALIDITY OF CONCLUSION	30 minutes

ANSWER SHEET
PRACTICE EXAMINATION 2
SECTION I: READING COMPREHENSION

1 (A)(B)(C)(D)(E)	6 (A)(B)(C)(D)(E)	11 (A)(B)(C)(D)(E)	16 (A)(B)(C)(D)(E)	21 (A)(B)(C)(D)(E)
2 (A)(B)(C)(D)(E)	7 (A)(B)(C)(D)(E)	12 (A)(B)(C)(D)(E)	17 (A)(B)(C)(D)(E)	22 (A)(B)(C)(D)(E)
3 (A)(B)(C)(D)(E)	8 (A)(B)(C)(D)(E)	13 (A)(B)(C)(D)(E)	18 (A)(B)(C)(D)(E)	23 (A)(B)(C)(D)(E)
4 (A)(B)(C)(D)(E)	9 (A)(B)(C)(D)(E)	14 (A)(B)(C)(D)(E)	19 (A)(B)(C)(D)(E)	24 (A)(B)(C)(D)(E)
5 (A)(B)(C)(D)(E)	10 (A)(B)(C)(D)(E)	15 (A)(B)(C)(D)(E)	20 (A)(B)(C)(D)(E)	25 (A)(B)(C)(D)(E)

SECTION II: DATA INTERPRETATION

1 (A)(B)(C)(D)(E)	7 (A)(B)(C)(D)(E)	13 (A)(B)(C)(D)(E)	19 (A)(B)(C)(D)(E)	25 (A)(B)(C)(D)(E)
2 (A)(B)(C)(D)(E)	8 (A)(B)(C)(D)(E)	14 (A)(B)(C)(D)(E)	20 (A)(B)(C)(D)(E)	26 (A)(B)(C)(D)(E)
3 (A)(B)(C)(D)(E)	9 (A)(B)(C)(D)(E)	15 (A)(B)(C)(D)(E)	21 (A)(B)(C)(D)(E)	27 (A)(B)(C)(D)(E)
4 (A)(B)(C)(D)(E)	10 (A)(B)(C)(D)(E)	16 (A)(B)(C)(D)(E)	22 (A)(B)(C)(D)(E)	28 (A)(B)(C)(D)(E)
5 (A)(B)(C)(D)(E)	11 (A)(B)(C)(D)(E)	17 (A)(B)(C)(D)(E)	23 (A)(B)(C)(D)(E)	29 (A)(B)(C)(D)(E)
6 (A)(B)(C)(D)(E)	12 (A)(B)(C)(D)(E)	18 (A)(B)(C)(D)(E)	24 (A)(B)(C)(D)(E)	30 (A)(B)(C)(D)(E)

SECTION III: PRACTICAL BUSINESS JUDGMENT

1 (A)(B)(C)(D)(E)	5 (A)(B)(C)(D)(E)	9 (A)(B)(C)(D)(E)	13 (A)(B)(C)(D)(E)	17 (A)(B)(C)(D)(E)
2 (A)(B)(C)(D)(E)	6 (A)(B)(C)(D)(E)	10 (A)(B)(C)(D)(E)	14 (A)(B)(C)(D)(E)	18 (A)(B)(C)(D)(E)
3 (A)(B)(C)(D)(E)	7 (A)(B)(C)(D)(E)	11 (A)(B)(C)(D)(E)	15 (A)(B)(C)(D)(E)	19 (A)(B)(C)(D)(E)
4 (A)(B)(C)(D)(E)	8 (A)(B)(C)(D)(E)	12 (A)(B)(C)(D)(E)	16 (A)(B)(C)(D)(E)	20 (A)(B)(C)(D)(E)

SECTION IV: DATA SUFFICIENCY

1 Ⓐ Ⓑ Ⓒ Ⓓ Ⓔ	7 Ⓐ Ⓑ Ⓒ Ⓓ Ⓔ	13 Ⓐ Ⓑ Ⓒ Ⓓ Ⓔ	19 Ⓐ Ⓑ Ⓒ Ⓓ Ⓔ	25 Ⓐ Ⓑ Ⓒ Ⓓ Ⓔ
2 Ⓐ Ⓑ Ⓒ Ⓓ Ⓔ	8 Ⓐ Ⓑ Ⓒ Ⓓ Ⓔ	14 Ⓐ Ⓑ Ⓒ Ⓓ Ⓔ	20 Ⓐ Ⓑ Ⓒ Ⓓ Ⓔ	26 Ⓐ Ⓑ Ⓒ Ⓓ Ⓔ
3 Ⓐ Ⓑ Ⓒ Ⓓ Ⓔ	9 Ⓐ Ⓑ Ⓒ Ⓓ Ⓔ	15 Ⓐ Ⓑ Ⓒ Ⓓ Ⓔ	21 Ⓐ Ⓑ Ⓒ Ⓓ Ⓔ	27 Ⓐ Ⓑ Ⓒ Ⓓ Ⓔ
4 Ⓐ Ⓑ Ⓒ Ⓓ Ⓔ	10 Ⓐ Ⓑ Ⓒ Ⓓ Ⓔ	16 Ⓐ Ⓑ Ⓒ Ⓓ Ⓔ	22 Ⓐ Ⓑ Ⓒ Ⓓ Ⓔ	28 Ⓐ Ⓑ Ⓒ Ⓓ Ⓔ
5 Ⓐ Ⓑ Ⓒ Ⓓ Ⓔ	11 Ⓐ Ⓑ Ⓒ Ⓓ Ⓔ	17 Ⓐ Ⓑ Ⓒ Ⓓ Ⓔ	23 Ⓐ Ⓑ Ⓒ Ⓓ Ⓔ	29 Ⓐ Ⓑ Ⓒ Ⓓ Ⓔ
6 Ⓐ Ⓑ Ⓒ Ⓓ Ⓔ	12 Ⓐ Ⓑ Ⓒ Ⓓ Ⓔ	18 Ⓐ Ⓑ Ⓒ Ⓓ Ⓔ	24 Ⓐ Ⓑ Ⓒ Ⓓ Ⓔ	30 Ⓐ Ⓑ Ⓒ Ⓓ Ⓔ

SECTION V: ENGLISH USAGE

1 Ⓐ Ⓑ Ⓒ Ⓓ Ⓔ	6 Ⓐ Ⓑ Ⓒ Ⓓ Ⓔ	11 Ⓐ Ⓑ Ⓒ Ⓓ Ⓔ	16 Ⓐ Ⓑ Ⓒ Ⓓ Ⓔ	21 Ⓐ Ⓑ Ⓒ Ⓓ Ⓔ
2 Ⓐ Ⓑ Ⓒ Ⓓ Ⓔ	7 Ⓐ Ⓑ Ⓒ Ⓓ Ⓔ	12 Ⓐ Ⓑ Ⓒ Ⓓ Ⓔ	17 Ⓐ Ⓑ Ⓒ Ⓓ Ⓔ	22 Ⓐ Ⓑ Ⓒ Ⓓ Ⓔ
3 Ⓐ Ⓑ Ⓒ Ⓓ Ⓔ	8 Ⓐ Ⓑ Ⓒ Ⓓ Ⓔ	13 Ⓐ Ⓑ Ⓒ Ⓓ Ⓔ	18 Ⓐ Ⓑ Ⓒ Ⓓ Ⓔ	23 Ⓐ Ⓑ Ⓒ Ⓓ Ⓔ
4 Ⓐ Ⓑ Ⓒ Ⓓ Ⓔ	9 Ⓐ Ⓑ Ⓒ Ⓓ Ⓔ	14 Ⓐ Ⓑ Ⓒ Ⓓ Ⓔ	19 Ⓐ Ⓑ Ⓒ Ⓓ Ⓔ	24 Ⓐ Ⓑ Ⓒ Ⓓ Ⓔ
5 Ⓐ Ⓑ Ⓒ Ⓓ Ⓔ	10 Ⓐ Ⓑ Ⓒ Ⓓ Ⓔ	15 Ⓐ Ⓑ Ⓒ Ⓓ Ⓔ	20 Ⓐ Ⓑ Ⓒ Ⓓ Ⓔ	25 Ⓐ Ⓑ Ⓒ Ⓓ Ⓔ

SECTION VI: PRACTICAL BUSINESS JUDGMENT

1 Ⓐ Ⓑ Ⓒ Ⓓ Ⓔ	5 Ⓐ Ⓑ Ⓒ Ⓓ Ⓔ	9 Ⓐ Ⓑ Ⓒ Ⓓ Ⓔ	13 Ⓐ Ⓑ Ⓒ Ⓓ Ⓔ	17 Ⓐ Ⓑ Ⓒ Ⓓ Ⓔ
2 Ⓐ Ⓑ Ⓒ Ⓓ Ⓔ	6 Ⓐ Ⓑ Ⓒ Ⓓ Ⓔ	10 Ⓐ Ⓑ Ⓒ Ⓓ Ⓔ	14 Ⓐ Ⓑ Ⓒ Ⓓ Ⓔ	18 Ⓐ Ⓑ Ⓒ Ⓓ Ⓔ
3 Ⓐ Ⓑ Ⓒ Ⓓ Ⓔ	7 Ⓐ Ⓑ Ⓒ Ⓓ Ⓔ	11 Ⓐ Ⓑ Ⓒ Ⓓ Ⓔ	15 Ⓐ Ⓑ Ⓒ Ⓓ Ⓔ	19 Ⓐ Ⓑ Ⓒ Ⓓ Ⓔ
4 Ⓐ Ⓑ Ⓒ Ⓓ Ⓔ	8 Ⓐ Ⓑ Ⓒ Ⓓ Ⓔ	12 Ⓐ Ⓑ Ⓒ Ⓓ Ⓔ	16 Ⓐ Ⓑ Ⓒ Ⓓ Ⓔ	20 Ⓐ Ⓑ Ⓒ Ⓓ Ⓔ

SECTION VII: VALIDITY OF CONCLUSION

1 Ⓐ Ⓑ Ⓒ Ⓓ Ⓔ	8 Ⓐ Ⓑ Ⓒ Ⓓ Ⓔ	15 Ⓐ Ⓑ Ⓒ Ⓓ Ⓔ	22 Ⓐ Ⓑ Ⓒ Ⓓ Ⓔ	29 Ⓐ Ⓑ Ⓒ Ⓓ Ⓔ	36 Ⓐ Ⓑ Ⓒ Ⓓ Ⓔ
2 Ⓐ Ⓑ Ⓒ Ⓓ Ⓔ	9 Ⓐ Ⓑ Ⓒ Ⓓ Ⓔ	16 Ⓐ Ⓑ Ⓒ Ⓓ Ⓔ	23 Ⓐ Ⓑ Ⓒ Ⓓ Ⓔ	30 Ⓐ Ⓑ Ⓒ Ⓓ Ⓔ	37 Ⓐ Ⓑ Ⓒ Ⓓ Ⓔ
3 Ⓐ Ⓑ Ⓒ Ⓓ Ⓔ	10 Ⓐ Ⓑ Ⓒ Ⓓ Ⓔ	17 Ⓐ Ⓑ Ⓒ Ⓓ Ⓔ	24 Ⓐ Ⓑ Ⓒ Ⓓ Ⓔ	31 Ⓐ Ⓑ Ⓒ Ⓓ Ⓔ	38 Ⓐ Ⓑ Ⓒ Ⓓ Ⓔ
4 Ⓐ Ⓑ Ⓒ Ⓓ Ⓔ	11 Ⓐ Ⓑ Ⓒ Ⓓ Ⓔ	18 Ⓐ Ⓑ Ⓒ Ⓓ Ⓔ	25 Ⓐ Ⓑ Ⓒ Ⓓ Ⓔ	32 Ⓐ Ⓑ Ⓒ Ⓓ Ⓔ	39 Ⓐ Ⓑ Ⓒ Ⓓ Ⓔ
5 Ⓐ Ⓑ Ⓒ Ⓓ Ⓔ	12 Ⓐ Ⓑ Ⓒ Ⓓ Ⓔ	19 Ⓐ Ⓑ Ⓒ Ⓓ Ⓔ	26 Ⓐ Ⓑ Ⓒ Ⓓ Ⓔ	33 Ⓐ Ⓑ Ⓒ Ⓓ Ⓔ	40 Ⓐ Ⓑ Ⓒ Ⓓ Ⓔ
6 Ⓐ Ⓑ Ⓒ Ⓓ Ⓔ	13 Ⓐ Ⓑ Ⓒ Ⓓ Ⓔ	20 Ⓐ Ⓑ Ⓒ Ⓓ Ⓔ	27 Ⓐ Ⓑ Ⓒ Ⓓ Ⓔ	34 Ⓐ Ⓑ Ⓒ Ⓓ Ⓔ	
7 Ⓐ Ⓑ Ⓒ Ⓓ Ⓔ	14 Ⓐ Ⓑ Ⓒ Ⓓ Ⓔ	21 Ⓐ Ⓑ Ⓒ Ⓓ Ⓔ	28 Ⓐ Ⓑ Ⓒ Ⓓ Ⓔ	35 Ⓐ Ⓑ Ⓒ Ⓓ Ⓔ	

SECTION I: READING COMPREHENSION

30 Minutes
25 Questions

DIRECTIONS: Below each of the following passages, you will find questions or incomplete statements about the passage. Each statement or question is followed by five lettered words or expressions. Select the word or expression that most satisfactorily completes each statement or answers each question in accordance with the meaning of the passage.

As befits a nation made up of immigrants from all over the Christian world, Americans have no distinctive Christmas symbols; but we have taken the symbols of all the nations and made them our own. The Christmas tree, the holly and the ivy, the mistletoe, the exchange of gifts, the myth of Santa Claus, the carols of all nations, the plum pudding and the wassail bowl are all elements in the American Christmas of the mid-twentieth century. Though we have no Christmas symbols of our own, the American Christmas still has a distinctive aura by virtue of two characteristic elements.

The first of these is that, as might be expected in a nation as dedicated to the carrying on of business as the American nation, the dominant role of the Christmas festivities has become to serve as a stimulus to retail business. The themes of Christmas advertising begin to appear as early as September, and the open season on Christmas shopping begins in November. Fifty years ago, Thanksgiving Day was regarded as the opening day of the season for Christmas shopping; today, the season opens immediately after Halloween. Thus virtually a whole month has been added to the Christmas season—for shopping purposes.

Second, the Christmas season of festivities has insensibly combined with the New Year's celebration into one lengthened period of Saturnalia. This starts with the "office parties" a few days before Christmas, continues on Christmas Eve, now the occasion in America of one of two large-scale revels that mark the season—save that the Christmas Eve revels are often punctuated by a visit to one of the larger churches for midnight Mass, which has increasingly tended to become blended into a part of the entertainment aspect of the season—and continues in spirited euphoria until New Year's Eve, the second of the large-scale revels. New Year's Day is spent resting, possibly regretting one's excesses, watching a football "bowl" game, and indulging in the lenitive of one's choice. January 2 marks, for most, the return to temperance and decorum and business as usual.

1. The author's attitude toward the manner in which Christmas is celebrated in the United States is one of

    (A) great disapproval
    (B) humorous confusion
    (C) laudatory acclaim
    (D) objective appraisal
    (E) great optimism

2. A statement which is most closely associated with the main idea of this passage is the following:

    (A) In Puritan Massachusetts Bay Colony, it was a crime, punishable by the stocks, to observe Christmas.
    (B) Christmas customs in Europe and America that are associated with the Feast of the Nativity were not originally Christian.
    (C) Rudolph the Red Nosed Reindeer has become a traditional aspect of Christmas, yet was created only a few years ago by commercial interests.
    (D) The custom of wassailing continued well into the nineteenth century.
    (E) In widely separated areas of the world, religious observances tend to cluster around striking natural phenomena.

3. According to the passage, Americans in regard to the Christmas season have

119

(A) demonstrated great originality
(B) little justification for merrymaking
(C) departed completely from the example of early settlers
(D) made little attempt to promote a variety of entertainment
(E) borrowed extensively from the traditions of other countries

4. Which of the following does the author point out as being distinctively American?

(A) the selling of Christmas items as part of the season's activities
(B) the extension of Christmas festivities from Thanksgiving to New Year's Eve
(C) the extensive use of the Santa Claus myth
(D) the attending of sports activities on New Year's Day
(E) the spirited euphoria on New Year's Eve

The operation of the gelatin process is undoubtedly the simplest of all modern duplicating methods. In order to reproduce copies of typewritten matter, for example, the copy is typed on an ordinary sheet of paper by any typist in the customary way. The only difference between this first operation and regular everyday typing is that a special typewriter ribbon impregnated with hectograph ink is necessary. The typed copy is then transferred to the gelatin by pressing the typed matter tightly against the gelatin surface, leaving it for a few minutes, and then removing the paper that bore the original copy. The gelatin is simply a spongy, jelly-like material in sheet form that absorbs and holds in reverse any copy done in hectograph ink. Thus, when blank impression paper is pressed against the inked portion of the gelatin it picks up a print of the image. This can be repeated as many as 100 times, with the gelatin releasing just a little of the ink each time. This factor of single inking is the reason for the gradual lightening of copies on a run of more than fifty copies.

After the desired copies have been made the gelatin may be used again, but not at a future time or for different copy without additional preparation. Aniline inks sink gradually down into the gelatin; after an hour of either use or non-use, they no longer reproduce satisfactory copies. The gelatin's preparation for further use consists simply of allowing it to remain untouched for about eight hours. At the end of this time the ink will have sunk far enough below the gelatin surface so that it will no longer print. New copy can then be transferred from a new master to the newly cleared surface. This gelatin sheet may thus be used over and over again for a considerable length of time. It is time and exposure to natural elements rather than usage that determine the life of this gelatin duplicating medium.

5. When preparing typed material for transfer to the gelatin, the typing is done

(A) with a regular typewriter ribbon
(B) with a special typewriter ribbon impregnated with hectograph ink
(C) with a special carbon paper ribbon
(D) without any ribbon so that the type can cut into the gelatin
(E) with gelatin ribbon

6. When preparing typed material for transfer to the gelatin, the material should first be typed on

(A) regular paper
(B) carbon paper
(C) gelatin paper
(D) waxed paper
(E) tissue paper

7. The typed material is transferred to the gelatin by pressing the typed side of the paper against the

(A) gelatin surface
(B) reverse of the gelatin surface
(C) blank impression paper
(D) reverse of the blank impression paper
(E) typewriter carriage

8. Copy done in hectograph ink is absorbed and held by the gelatin

(A) from the blank impression paper
(B) from the carbon copy
(C) upside down
(D) in reverse
(E) by osmosis

9. Blank impression paper picks up its material directly from

(A) the uninked portion of the gelatin
(B) the uninked portion of the original copy
(C) the inked portion of the gelatin
(D) the inked portion of the original copy
(E) the inked portion of the carbon copy

A vast health checkup is now being conducted in the western Swedish province of Varmland with the use of an automated apparatus for high-speed multiple-blood analyses. Developed by two brothers, the apparatus can process more than 4,000 blood samples a day, subjecting each to 10 or more tests. Automation has cut the cost of the analyses by about 90 percent.

The results so far have been astonishing, for hundreds of Swedes have learned that they have silent symptoms of disorders that neither they nor their physicians were aware of. Among them were iron-deficiency anemia, hypercholesterolemia, hypertension and even diabetes.

The automated blood analysis apparatus was developed by Dr. Gunnar Jungner, 49-year-old associate professor of clinical chemistry at Goteborg University, and his brother, Ingmar, 39, the physician in charge of the chemical central laboratory of Stockholm's Hospital for Infectious Diseases.

The idea was conceived 15 years ago when Dr. Gunnar Jungner was working as clinical chemist in Western Sweden and was asked by local physicians to devise a way of performing multiple analyses on a single blood sample. The design was ready in 1961.

Consisting of calorimeters, pumps and other components, many of them American-made, the Jungner apparatus was set up here in Stockholm. Samples from Varmland Province are drawn into the automated system at 90-second intervals.

The findings clatter forth in the form of numbers printed by an automatic typewriter.

The Jungners predict that advance knowledge about a person's potential ailments made possible by the chemical screening process will result in considerable savings in hospital and other medical costs. Thus, they point out, the blood analyses will actually turn out to cost nothing.

In the beginning, the automated blood analyses ran into considerable opposition from some physicians who had no faith in machines and saw no need for so many tests. Some laboratory technicians who saw their jobs threatened also protested. But the opposition is said to be waning.

10. Automation is viewed by the writer with

(A) animosity
(B) indecision
(C) remorse
(D) indifference
(E) favor

11. The results of the use of the Jungner apparatus indicate that

(A) persons may become aware of an ailment not previously detected
(B) blood diseases can be cured very easily
(C) diabetes does not respond to the apparatus
(D) practically all Swedish physicians have welcomed the invention
(E) only one analysis may be made at a time

12. All of the following statements about automated blood analysis are true EXCEPT:

(A) the analysis is recorded in a permanent form
(B) the idea for the apparatus involved an international effort
(C) the system has met opposition from physicians and technicians
(D) the machine is more efficient than other types of analysis
(E) the process is a means to save on hospital costs

13. The main purpose of the passage is to

(A) predict the future of medical care
(B) describe a health check-up system
(C) show how Sweden has superior health care
(D) warn about the dangers of undetected disease
(E) describe in detail the workings of a new machine

14. The prediction process that the Jungners use is essentially

(A) biological
(B) physiological
(C) chemical
(D) anatomical
(E) biophysical

In discussing human competence in a world of change, I want to make it crystal-clear that I am not ready to accept all the changes that are being pressed on us. I am not at all prepared to suggest that we must blindly find new competences in order to adjust to all the changes or in order to make ourselves inconspicuous in the modern habitat. Let me be specific. I see no reason in the world why modern man should develop any competence whatsoever to pay high rents in order to be permitted to live in buildings with walls that act as soundtracks rather than sound-absorbers. Nor do I believe that this problem can or should be overcome by developing such novel engineering competences as "acoustical perfume"—artificial noise to drown out next-door noises. When I don't wish to be a silent partner to the bedroom conversation of the neighbors, I am not at all satisfied by having the sound effects of a waterfall, the chirping of crickets, or incidental music superimposed on the disturbance, just to cover up the incompetence or greed of modern builders.

The other day I found myself wandering through the desolate destruction of Pennsylvania Station in New York, thoroughly incompetent in my efforts to find a ticket office. Instead I found a large poster which said that "your new station" was being built and that this was the reason for my temporary inconvenience. Nonsense! my station was not being built at all. My station is being destroyed, and I do not need the new competence of an advertising copy writer or a public relations consultant to obscure the facts. The competence that was needed—and which I and great numbers of like-minded contemporaries lacked—was the competence to prevent an undesirable change. In plain language—the competence to stop the organized vandalism which, in the name of progress and change, is tearing down good buildings to put up flimsy ones; is dynamiting fine landmarks to replace them with structures that can be ripped down again twenty years later without a tear.

When the packaging industry finds it increasingly easy to design containers that make reduced contents appear to be an enlarged value at a steeper price, the change does not call for the competence of a consumer psychologist to make the defrauded customer feel happy. The change calls simply for a tough public prosecutor.

Lest I be mistaken for a political or even a sentimental reactionary who wants to halt progress and change, let me add another example of modern life the improvement of which may call for radical public action rather than for any new competence. Commuter rail transportation has fallen into decline in many parts of the country. Persons dependent on it find themselves frustrated and inconvenienced. In reply to their plight, they are given explanations such as the economic difficulties facing the railroad. Explanations, however, are no substitute for remedies. The competence required here is not technological or mechanical. After all, it would be difficult to persuade any sane citizen that a technology able to dis-

patch men into space and return them on schedule is mechanically incapable of transporting commuters from the suburbs to the cities in comfort, in safety, and on time.

The competence lacking here is one of general intelligence of the kind that is willing to shed doctrinaire myths when they stand in the way of the facts of modern life. To make millions of commuters suffer (and I use this example only because it is readily familiar, not because it is unique today) merely because the doctrine of free, competitive enterprise must be upheld, even after competition has disappeared as a vital ingredient, is an example of ludicrous mental incompetence. So is the tendency to worry whether a public takeover of a public necessity that is no longer being adequately maintained by private enterprise constitutes socialism or merely the protection of citizens' interests.

We ought to place the stress of competence in such a fashion that we can use it to mold, control, and—in extreme instances—even to block change rather than merely to adjust or submit to it.

—by Fred M. Hechinger (reprinted with permission)

15. The attitude of the writer is one of

(A) conciliation
(B) indignation
(C) amiability
(D) self-pity
(E) optimism

16. As used in the passage, the term "doctrinaire myth" (next to last paragraph) may be defined as a belief based on premises that are

(A) universally accepted
(B) politically motivated
(C) based on self-interest
(D) logical
(E) obsolete

17. The author's main purpose in the passage is to

(A) develop an ideology
(B) argue against a belief
(C) describe a problem and urge action
(D) deride modern life
(E) show the ironies of commuter travel

18. An appropriate title for the passage would be

    (A) Antidotes for Incompetence
    (B) The Suffering Commuter
    (C) Technological Methods
    (D) Consumer Satisfaction
    (E) Advertising Notes

19. The passage, in no way, states or implies that

    (A) much construction today is inferior to what it was in other years
    (B) the razing of Pennsylvania Station was justifiable
    (C) consumers are often deceived
    (D) some engineering devices are not worth the trouble spent in contriving them
    (E) space scientists have made great progress

Every profession or trade, every art, and every science has its technical vocabulary, the function of which is partly to designate things or processes which have no names in ordinary English, and partly to secure greater exactness in nomenclature. Such special dialects, or jargons, are necessary in technical discussion of any kind. Being universally understood by the devotees of the particular science or art, they have the precision of a mathematical formula. Besides, they save time, for it is much more economical to name a process than to describe it. Thousands of these technical terms are very properly included in every large dictionary, yet, as a whole, they are rather on the outskirts of the English language than actually within its borders.

Different occupations, however, differ widely in the character of their special vocabularies. In trades and handicrafts and other vocations, like farming and fishing, that have occupied great numbers of men from remote times, the technical vocabulary is very old. It consists largely of native words, or of borrowed words that have worked themselves into the very fibre of our language. Hence, though highly technical in many particulars, these vocabularies are more familiar in sound, and more generally understood, than most other technicalities. The special dialects of law, medicine, divinity, and philosophy have also, in their older strata, become pretty familiar to cultivated persons, and have contributed much to the popular vocabulary. Yet every vocation still possesses a large body of technical terms that remain essentially foreign, even to educated speech. And the proportion has been much increased in the last fifty years, particularly in the various departments of natural and political science and in the mechanic arts. Here new terms are coined with the greatest freedom, and abandoned with indifference when they have served their turn. Most of the new coinages are confined to special discussions, and seldom get into general literature or conversation. Yet no profession is nowadays, as all professions once were, a closed guild. The lawyer, the physician, the man of science, the cleric, associates freely with his fellow-creatures, and does not meet them in a merely professional way. Furthermore, what is called "popular science" makes everybody acquainted with modern views and recent discoveries. Any important experiment, though made in a remote or provincial laboratory, is at once reported in the newspapers, and everybody is soon talking about it—as in the case of the Roentgen rays and wireless telegraphy. Thus our common speech is always taking up new technical terms and making them commonplace.

20. This passage is primarily concerned with

    (A) a new language
    (B) technical terminology
    (C) various occupations and professions
    (D) scientific undertakings
    (E) popular science

21. Special words used in technical discussion

    (A) never last long
    (B) should be confined to scientific fields
    (C) should resemble mathematical formulae
    (D) are considered artificial speech
    (E) may become part of common speech

22. It is true that

    (A) the average man often uses in his own vocabulary what was once technical language not meant for him
    (B) various professions and occupations often interchange their dialects and jargons
    (C) there is always a clearcut non-technical word that may be substituted for the technical word
    (D) an educated person would be expected to know most technical terms
    (E) everyone is interested in scientific findings

23. In recent years, there has been a marked increase in the number of technical terms in the nomenclature of

    (A) farming
    (B) government
    (C) handicrafts
    (D) fishing
    (E) sports

24. The writer of this article was, no doubt,

    (A) a linguist
    (B) an attorney
    (C) a scientist
    (D) a politician
    (E) a physician

25. The author's main purpose in the passage is to

    (A) describe a phenomenon
    (B) argue a belief
    (C) propose a solution
    (D) stimulate action
    (E) be entertaining

Stop

END OF SECTION I. IF YOU HAVE ANY TIME LEFT, GO OVER YOUR WORK IN THIS SECTION ONLY. DO NOT WORK IN ANY OTHER SECTION OF THE TEST. WHEN YOUR TIME IS UP, GO ON TO THE NEXT SECTION.

SECTION II: DATA INTERPRETATION

35 Minutes
30 Questions

DIRECTIONS: The following questions are to test your ability to read and interpret graphs and tables. Answer each question based on your reading of the graphs or tables provided.

Questions 1–7

The chart below shows the annual average number of administrative actions completed for the four divisions of a bureau. Assume that the figures remain stable from year to year.

Administrative Actions	DIVISIONS				
	W	X	Y	Z	Totals
Telephone Inquiries Answered	8,000	6,800	7,500	4,800	27,100
Interviews Conducted	[I]	630	550	500	2,180
Applications Processed	15,000	18,000	14,500	9,500	57,000
Letters Typed	2,500	[II]	4,350	3,250	14,500
Reports Completed	200	250	100	50	600
Totals	26,200	30,080	27,000	18,100	[III]

1. What is the value of I?

   (A) 480
   (B) 500
   (C) 530
   (D) 620
   (E) None of these or cannot be calculated from data provided.

2. What is the value of II?

   (A) 4,400
   (B) 4,080
   (C) 3,400
   (D) 3,050
   (E) None of these or cannot be calculated from data provided.

3. What is the value of III?

   (A) 100,350
   (B) 100,380
   (C) 101,350
   (D) 101,380
   (E) None of these or cannot be calculated from data provided.

4. In which division is the number of Applications Processed the greatest percentage of the total Administrative Actions for that division?

   (A) W
   (B) X
   (C) Y
   (D) Z
   (E) Cannot be calculated from data provided.

5. The bureau chief is considering a plan that would consolidate the typing of letters in a separate unit. This unit would be responsible for the typing of letters for all divisions in which the number of letters typed exceeds 15 percent of the total number of administrative actions. Under this plan which of the following divisions would *continue* to type its own letters?

   (A) W and X
   (B) W and X and Y
   (C) X and Y
   (D) X and Z
   (E) Y and Z

6. The setting up of a central information service that would be capable of answering 25 percent of the whole bureau's telephone inquiries is under consideration. Under such a plan, the divisions would gain for other activities that time previously spent on telephone inquiries. Approximately how much total time would such a service gain for all four divisions if it requires 5 minutes to answer the average telephone inquiry?

125

(A) 500 hours
(B) 515 hours
(C) 565 hours
(D) 581 hours
(E) 585 hours

7. Assume that the rate of production shown in the table can be projected as accurate for the coming year and that monthly output is constant for each type of administrative action within a division. Division Y is scheduled to work exclusively on a 4-month long special project during that year. During the period of the project, Division Y's regular workload will be divided evenly among the remaining divisions. Using the figures in the table, what would be, most nearly, the percentage increase in the total Administrative Actions completed by Division Z for the year?

(A) 8%
(B) 16%
(C) 25%
(D) 50%
(E) 86%

Questions 8–11

The graph below indicates at 5 year intervals the number of citations issued for various offenses from the year 1950 to the year 1970.

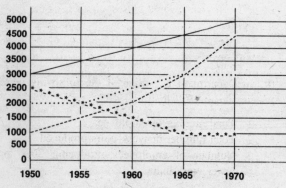

1950   1955   1960   1965   1970

LEGEND:

_____ **PARKING VIOLATIONS**

- - - - - **DRUG USE**

.... **DANGEROUS WEAPONS**

*_*_*_* **IMPROPER DRESS**

8. Over the 20-year period, which offense shows an average rate of increase of more than 150 citations per year?

(A) parking violations
(B) dangerous weapons
(C) drug use
(D) none of the above
(E) all of the above

9. Over the 20-year period, which offense shows a constant rate of increase or decrease?

(A) parking violations
(B) drug use
(C) dangerous weapons
(D) improper dress
(E) none of the above

10. Which offense shows a total increase or decrease of 50% for the full 20-year period?

(A) parking violations
(B) drug use
(C) dangerous weapons
(D) improper dress
(E) none of the above

11. The percentage increase in total citations issued from 1955 to 1960 is most nearly

(A) 7%
(B) 11%
(C) 21%
(D) 41%
(E) 56%

Questions 12–16

The Payroll Summary below represents payroll for a monthly period for a particular agency.

		DEDUCTIONS				
PAYROLL SUMMARY						
Employee	Total Earnings	FICA	Withhold. Tax	State Tax	Other	Net Pay
W	450.00	27.00	67.00	18.00	6.00	332.00
X	235.00	14.10	33.00	8.00	2.00	177.90
Y	341.00	20.46	52.00	14.00	5.00	249.54
Z	275.00	I	30.00	6.00	2.40	220.10
Totals	1301.00	II	182.00	46.00	15.40	III

12. What is the Value of I?

    (A) $16.00
    (B) $16.50
    (C) $17.50
    (D) $18.00
    (E) $18.50

13. What is the Value of II?

    (A) $78.06
    (B) $78.56
    (C) $78.60
    (D) $79.56
    (E) Cannot be calculated from data given.

14. Based on the data given above, the amount of' cash that would have to be available to pay the employees on payday is

    (A) $1301.00
    (B) $979.54
    (C) $905.60
    (D) $1057.60
    (E) Cannot be calculated from data given.

5. Based on the data given above, the amount required to be deposited with a governmental depository is

    (A) $243.40
    (B) $182.00
    (C) $306.06
    (D) $321.46
    (E) Cannot be determined from data given.

16. Based on the data given above, what would be the amount of cash deducted for FICA from the salary of an employee who earns $300 per month?

    (A) $16.50
    (B) $17.00
    (C) $18.00
    (D) $24.00
    (E) Cannot be calculated from data given.

Questions 17–19

The following chart shows the differences between the rates of production of employees in Department D in 1961 and 1971. Answer questions 17 to 19 solely on the basis of the information given in the chart.

NUMBER OF EMPLOYEES PRODUCING WORK-UNITS WITHIN RANGE IN 1961	NUMBER OF WORK-UNITS PRODUCED	NUMBER OF EMPLOYEES PRODUCING WORK-UNITS WITHIN RANGE IN 1971
7	500 – 1000	4
14	1001 – 1500	11
26	1501 – 2000	28
22	2001 – 2500	36
17	2501 – 3000	39
10	3001 – 3500	23
4	3501 – 4000	9

17. Assuming that within each range of work-units produced, the average production was at the midpoint of that range (e.g., category 500–1000 = 750), then the average number of work-units produced per employee in 1961 fell into the range

    (A) 1001–1500
    (B) 1501–2000
    (C) 2001–2500
    (D) 2501–3000
    (E) Cannot be calculated from data given.

18. The ratio of the number of employees producing more than 2000 work-units in 1961 to the number of employees producing more than 2000 work-units in 1971 is most nearly

    (A) 1:2
    (B) 2:3
    (C) 3:4
    (D) 4:5
    (E) 5:6

19. In Department D, which of the following were greater in 1971 than in 1961?

    1. Total number of employees
    2. Total number of work-units produced
    3. Number of employees producing 2000 or fewer work-units

    (A) 1, 2 and 3
    (B) 1 and 2, but not 3
    (C) 1 and 3, but not 2
    (D) 2 and 3, but not 1
    (E) 2 only

Questions 20–30

In the table that follows, lettered entries have been substituted for some of the numbers. In answering the questions about the lettered entries, you are to compute the number that should be in the space where the lettered entry appears. In those questions which concern tokens, consider the worth of a token as 35 cents.

				DAILY FARE REPORT		
Date: 3/12/76						**Booth No. S-50**
Name: John Brown Time: From 7 A.M. to 3 P.M.				Name: Mary Smith Time: From 3 P.M. to 11 P.M.		
			TURNSTILES			
TURN-STILE	OPENING READING	CLOSING READING	DIFFER-ENCE	OPENING READING	CLOSING READING	DIFFER-ENCE
1	5123	5410	287	5410	6019	609
2	3442	Entry F	839	4281	4683	402
3	8951	9404	453	Entry G	9757	353
4	7663	8265	602	8265	8588	Entry H
Totals:	Entry I	27360	2181	27360	Entry J	1687
Total Fares			2181	Total Fares		1687
Deduct: Slugs, Foreign Coins			12	Deduct: Slugs, Foreign Coins		Entry K
Deduct: Test Rings-Turnstile #			0	Deduct: Test Rings-Turnstile #3		3
Net Fares			2169	Net Fares		1680
(a) Net Fares at Token Value			Entry L	(a) Net Fares at Token Value		$588.00
Token Reserve at Start			4200	Token Reserve at Start		5000
Add: Tokens Received			2200	Add: Tokens Received		Entry M
Deduct: Tokens Transferred Out			1400	Deduct: Tokens Transferred Out		0
Total Token Reserve			Entry N	Total Token Reserve		6450
Deduct: Total Reserve at End			4330	Deduct: Total Reserve at End		5674
No. of Reserve Tokens Sold			670	No. of Reserve Tokens Sold		Entry O
(b) Value of Reserve Tokens Sold			Entry P	(b) Value of Reserve Tokens Sold		$271.60
Net Amount Due: (a) + (b)			$993.65	Net Amount Due: (a) + (b)		Entry Q

20. Entry F for Brown's tour of duty should be a closing reading of

(A) 2603
(B) 3873
(C) 4281
(D) 4571
(E) 5123

21. Entry G for Smith's tour of duty should be an opening reading of

(A) 8642
(B) 3932
(C) 9404
(D) 9857
(E) 8964

22. Entry H for Smith's tour of duty should be a difference of

(A) 303
(B) 323
(C) 344
(D) 402
(E) 502

23. Entry I for Brown's tour of duty should be a total of

(A) 24299
(B) 25179
(C) 26288

(D) 27168
(E) 29541

24. Entry J for Smith's tour of duty should be a total of

(A) 28036
(B) 29047
(C) 29556
(D) 30437
(E) 25673

25. Entry K for Smith's tour of duty should indicate that the number of slugs and foreign coins is

(A) 0
(B) 2
(C) 4
(D) 7
(E) 9

26. Entry L for Brown's tour of duty should indicate that the net fares at token value amount to

(A) $493.80
(B) $542.25
(C) $650.70
(D) $759.15
(E) $763.35

27. Entry M for Smith's tour of duty should indicate that the tokens received number

(A) 674
(B) 1000
(C) 1200
(D) 1450
(E) 2200

28. Entry N for Brown's tour of duty should indicate a total token reserve of

(A) 670
(B) 5000
(C) 6400
(D) 7800
(E) 600

29. Entry O for Smith's tour of duty should indicate that the number of reserve tokens sold was

(A) 776
(B) 1450
(C) 3250
(D) 12124
(E) 674

30. Entry P for Brown's tour of duty should indicate that the value of reserve tokens sold should be

    (A) $210.00
    (B) $234.50
    (C) $490.00
    (D) $523.35
    (E) $770.00

Stop

END OF SECTION II. IF YOU HAVE ANY TIME LEFT, GO OVER YOUR WORK IN THIS SECTION ONLY. DO NOT WORK IN ANY OTHER SECTION OF THE TEST. WHEN YOUR TIME IS UP, GO ON TO THE NEXT SECTION.

SECTION III: PRACTICAL BUSINESS JUDGMENT

20 Minutes
20 Questions

DIRECTIONS: This section consists of a reading selection which details a business situation followed by two sets of questions, data evaluation and data application. In the first set, data evaluation, you will be asked to classify certain of the facts presented in the passage on the basis of their importance. The second set, data application, will test your grasp of specific details of the situation.

Hans Muller's Restaurant has been a landmark on Route 77 for 59 years. The present owner is the third Hans Muller to run the establishment. It is profitable and busy all year around.

Muller is approached by Afsky Limited, a large conglomerate that owns a number of widely diversified businesses. Recently, Afsky has bought a chain of motels and wishes to combine them with excellent restaurants. They have discovered that Muller owns a large lot next to his restaurant, which they see as a spot on a major highway upon which to build a motel. They offer to buy Muller out with an offer of $250,000 in cash for the restaurant and $50,000 for the lot.

The offer is intriguing at first to Muller. He is a widower and his children are now adults, married, and living far away. None of them are interested in carrying on the restaurant business. He himself has always dreamed of retiring to Florida.

However, the restauranteur thinks over the offer carefully. He is 55 years old, too young to become inactive. On the other hand, he feels too old to enter a new line of work or even to start a new restaurant in Florida. He has not tired of running his establishment and he enjoys the company of those steady customers he has known personally for years.

Also, a cash payment is not in his best interests. Taxes would eat up most of the money.

Muller makes a counteroffer to Afsky. He wishes $50,000 in cash and $400,000 of Afsky stock.

He also wishes to remain as manager of the restaurant. He would like a ten-year employment contract at an annual salary of $25,000 plus three percent of the total revenue. Furthermore, at the end of five years, he would like to be able to sell his Afsky stock for not more than $50,000 a year. Afsky can receive full title to his lot.

He points out to the conglomerate executives that they are newcomers to the restaurant business and liable to make mistakes that could result in heavy financial losses. By remaining as manager, he could save them from such a disaster. Furthermore, he adds, he has built personal good will and a friendly local clientele throughout the years. Afsky, by bringing in outsiders to run the place, would run the danger of losing the regular customers.

DATA EVALUATION

DIRECTIONS: Based on your analysis of the business situation, classify each of the following elements in one of five categories. Mark:

(A) if the element is a MAJOR OBJECTIVE in making the decision; that is, the outcome or result sought by the decision maker.

(B) if the element is a MAJOR FACTOR in arriving at the decision; that is, a consideration explicitly mentioned in the passage that is basic in determining the decision.

(C) if the element is a MINOR FACTOR in making the decision; that is, a secondary consideration in determining the decision.

(D) if the element is a MAJOR ASSUMPTION made in deliberating; that is, a supposition or projection made by the decision maker before weighing the variables.

(E) if the element is an UNIMPORTANT ISSUE in getting to the point; that is, a factor that is insignificant or not immediately relevant to the situation.

1. Making a deal for the restaurant and the lot.

2. Afsky's possible loss of regular restaurant customers.

3. Hans Muller's desire to remain in the restaurant business.

130

4. Afsky's ability to pay for the restaurant and lot.

5. Restaurant's 59-year existence.

6. Advantage of having motel on busy highway.

7. Hans Muller's enjoyment in running his restaurant.

8. Muller's disinclination to start a Florida restaurant.

9. Afsky shares as a good form of payment.

10. Afsky's desire to build a motel.

DATA APPLICATION

DIRECTIONS: Based on your understanding of the business situation, answer the following questions testing your comprehension of the information supplied in the passage. For each question, select the choice which best answers the question or completes the statement.

11. Hans Muller's Restaurant can be described as

   (A) a seasonal business, making most money during the winter when skiers visit the area
   (B) an old restaurant that is nearly bankrupt because of poor management
   (C) off the beaten path and does a marginal business
   (D) profitable
   (E) managed by the founder

12. Which of the following best describes Afsky, Ltd.?

   (A) It consists entirely of a motel chain.
   (B) It has been in the restaurant field for 59 years.
   (C) It is a widely diversified conglomerate.
   (D) It is a small local real-estate firm.
   (E) It wishes to avoid entering the restaurant business.

13. Which of the following does Afsky, Ltd. wish to buy?

   I. Muller's Restaurant
   II. A lot next to Muller's Restaurant
   III. A motel near Muller's Restaurant

   (A) I only
   (B) II only
   (C) I and II only
   (D) I and III only
   (E) I, II and III

14. Afsky, Ltd. believes that Muller's lot is desirable because

   (A) it is inexpensive
   (B) Muller wishes to go to Florida
   (C) it is on a busy highway
   (D) Muller's present customers will use the motel
   (E) there is not another motel for miles

15. Which of the following is included in Afsky's offer to Hans Muller?

   I. $250,000 in cash for the restaurant
   II. $25,000 annual salary for ten years
   III. $50,000 in cash for the lot

   (A) I only
   (B) II only
   (C) I and II only
   (D) I and III only
   (E) I, II and III

16. One reason Muller turns down Afsky's offer is that he

   (A) doesn't think he will be getting enough money
   (B) wants his sons to carry on the restaurant
   (C) would like to build the motel himself
   (D) doesn't want to retire
   (E) is opposed to letting Afsky, Ltd, start operations in this area

17. Which of the following is included in Muller's counteroffer?

   I. 3% of the restaurant's revenue
   II. $50,000 in cash
   III. 10-year employment contract

   (A) I only
   (B) II only
   (C) I and II only
   (D) I and III only
   (E) I, II and III

18. The reason Muller desires a great deal of stock and a relatively small amount in cash is that he

    (A) could live in comfort on the stock dividends
    (B) would have to pay a heavy tax if the settlement was in cash only
    (C) believes Afsky stock will greatly increase in value
    (D) could sell all the stock within five years
    (E) could put the stock in trust for his children

19. Which of the following are factors Muller thinks might affect Afsky adversely in running the restaurant?

    I.   lack of restaurant management experience
    II. local resentment against a motel
    III. loss of present clientele

    (A) I only
    (B) II only
    (C) I and II only
    (D) I and III only
    (E) I, II and III

20. As part of his counteroffer, Hans Muller

    (A) wants a 5-year employment contract
    (B) wishes to continue managing the restaurant
    (C) proposes that he manage the motel
    (D) asks for a million dollars
    (E) would keep title to the lot

Stop

END OF SECTION III. IF YOU HAVE ANY TIME LEFT, GO OVER YOUR WORK IN THIS SECTION ONLY. DO NOT WORK IN ANY OTHER SECTION OF THE TEST. WHEN YOUR TIME IS UP, GO ON TO THE NEXT SECTION.

SECTION IV: DATA SUFFICIENCY

30 Minutes
30 Questions

DIRECTIONS: Each question below is followed by two numbered facts. You are to determine whether the data given in the statements is sufficient for answering the question. Use the data given, plus your knowledge of math and everyday facts, to choose between the five possible answers. Mark

(A) if statement 1 alone is sufficient to answer the question, but statement 2 alone is not sufficient.
(B) if statement 2 alone is sufficient to answer the question, but statement 1 alone is not sufficient.
(C) if both statements together are needed to answer the question, but neither statement alone is sufficient.
(D) if either statement by itself is sufficient to answer the question asked.
(E) if not enough facts are given to answer the question.

1. What is the value of f?

   (1) $2f+g=9$
   (2) $18-3g=4f-g$

2. Is ABC an isosceles triangle?

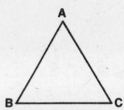

   (1) Angle B + angle C = angle A
   (2) A lies on the perpendicular bisector of BC.

3. If Tim is the fourth smallest boy in the class, how many boys are there in the class?

   (1) Half the boys are taller than Tim.
   (2) No boy is exactly Tim's height.

4. If c is a positive whole number, what is the value of c?

   (1) $c^2+2c+1=4c+4$
   (2) $c^2+1=16-2c$

5. Is X greater than zero?

   (1) $X^2=(4+X)^2$
   (2) $X-4=2X+6$

6. Is it raining today?

   (1) I watch television only on rainy days.
   (2) I will not watch television today.

7. How fast does steamboat S travel in still water?

   (1) When steamboat S left port, it was 3:00 P.M.
   (2) After traveling ten miles up a river (with a certain current) and ten miles back, it arrived at 7:00 P.M.

8. How many brothers does Marty have?

   (1) Marty's two sisters are twins.
   (2) Marty's uncle has only one nephew.

9. If Bill owns two pets, is one of them a snake?

   (1) Everyone on Bill's block who owns a snake also keeps a hamster.
   (2) Bill has a rabbit for a pet.

10. Is m evenly divisible by n?

   (1) $m+n=m^2$
   (2) $mn=m+n$

11. What is the area of $\triangle$ ABC if AB is parallel to CD?

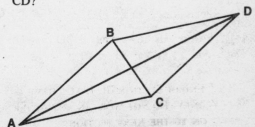

133

(1) The area of $\triangle$BCD = 10 square inches.
(2) The area of $\triangle$ABD = 12 square inches.

12. What day of the week is today?

(1) I went to the movies nine days ago.
(2) I go to the movies only on Thursdays.

13. Is it possible to place a wooden block with a square base in a circular hole?

(1) A side of the square is longer than the radius of the circle.
(2) The square has half the area of the circle.

14. If each man weighs 170 lbs. and each boy weighs 100 lbs., how many men are there on a barge which weighs two tons when empty?

(1) The barge weighs 4950 lbs. when full.
(2) There are five times as many men as there are boys on the barge.

15. How many days are there in a certain month?

(1) There is no "r" in its name.
(2) There are four letters in its name.

16. Find the number of degrees in angle BDC, assuming that AD=DC.

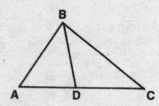

(1) AB=BC
(2) BD=BC

17. How much does Joe earn each week?

(1) Joe works six hours a day at $1.75 an hour.
(2) If Joe worked at $3.50 an hour, he would make $63 a week.

18. Is A less than B?

(1) AB=9
(2) A+B=10

19. Is ABCD a parallelogram?

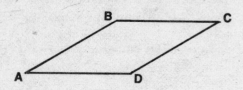

(1) Angle B = angle D and BC = AD
(2) AB=CD and AD=BC

20. Jim, a carpenter, lives with his brother Joe, a policeman. What street does Jim live on?

(1) All policemen live on Byron Avenue.
(2) Anyone who lives on Simpson Street is a carpenter.

21. Is A evenly divisible by B?

(1) A $=x^5+1$
(2) B$=x^4-x^3+x^2-x+1$

22. Does Jimmy play the piano?

(1) Jimmy is an accomplished violinist.
(2) All accomplished violinists must play the piano.

23. What is the score of the baseball game between the Smashers and the Thunderbolts?

(1) The Thunderbolts are winning by four runs.
(2) Last inning, when the Smashers scored two runs, they doubled their score, and haven't scored since.

24. Is ABC a right triangle?

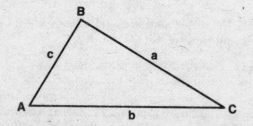

(1) a+b is greater than c

(2) The area of ABC is ½ac

25. What is the value of r, given that r is a real number?

    (1) $r=4-r$

    (2) $(r-2)(r^2+1)=0$

26. Find the number of degrees in angle A.

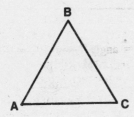

    (1) ABC is an isosceles triangle.

    (2) $B=75°$

27. Is G less than x^2+4?

    (1) $G=4x-1$

    (2) x is a whole number greater than -2

28. A man has eleven coins totalling $.35. How many nickels does he have?

    (1) He has no dimes

    (2) He has exactly five pennies

29. Is x an even number?

    (1) (x^2+x) is even

    (2) (x^2+2x) is odd

30. Is S evenly divisible by T? (S and T are both positive whole numbers.)

    (1) $S=T+4$

    (2) $2S=T+11$

Stop

END OF SECTION IV. IF YOU HAVE ANY TIME LEFT, GO OVER YOUR WORK IN THIS SECTION ONLY. DO NOT WORK IN ANY OTHER SECTION OF THE TEST. WHEN YOUR TIME IS UP, GO ON TO THE NEXT SECTION.

SECTION V: ENGLISH USAGE

15 Minutes
25 Questions

DIRECTIONS: In each of the sentences below, four words or phrases have been underlined. Select the underlined part which contains an error in usage, grammar, or punctuation. If there is no error, mark answer space E.

1. She <u>gathered up</u> all the apples and, <u>putting</u> them
         A   B
   in a basket, <u>carries</u> them <u>into the house.</u> <u>No error.</u>
             C   D   E

2. There was a time when <u>the Arctic</u> was unknown
                   A
   territory; now scientists <u>manning</u> research sta-
                   B
   tions there and the mysteries <u>of this frozen con-</u>
                         C
   tinent are <u>being</u> revealed. <u>No error.</u>
           D   E

3. Mary was so <u>disinterested</u> in the <u>baseball</u> game
                A   B
   <u>that</u> she <u>yawned</u> unashamedly. <u>No error.</u>
    C   D   E

4. Nigeria, a <u>former</u> British colony and <u>protecto-</u>
             A   B
   <u>rate,</u> <u>it is</u> now a member <u>of</u> the British Common-
    B   C   D
   wealth of Nations. <u>No error.</u>
                 E

5. John Kennedy <u>effected</u> many <u>executive</u> reforms
               A   B
   during the <u>tragically</u> numbered years he served as
             C
   <u>President</u> of the United States. <u>No error.</u>
      D   E

6. <u>Tuck a dish towel over the potatoes to keep them</u>
    A   B
   warm and to absorb steam <u>so they</u> will not be-
                     C
   come <u>soggily.</u> <u>No error.</u>
        D   E

7. The symbolic <u>interpretation</u> of <u>visions</u> <u>renders</u>
               A   B   C
   the interpreter <u>a prophet.</u> <u>No error.</u>
             D   E

8. I loved the <u>morning and should go down</u> the dirt
             A   B
   road with my tin <u>pail toward</u> the stream where
                 C
   there were <u>gooseberries.</u> <u>No error.</u>
           D   E

9. <u>Their</u> are <u>still</u> people who say that <u>it has</u> never
    A   B   C
   been <u>proved</u> that our earth is round. <u>No error.</u>
       D   E

10. Until <u>nearly</u> the end of the century, the <u>workshop</u>
         A   B
    was the <u>quite most</u> popular supplier of madonnas
           C
    for the <u>public patrons</u> of Florence. <u>No error.</u>
          D   E

11. <u>Harvard's</u> football <u>captain</u> could <u>tackle,</u> block
       A   B   C
    and pass better than <u>any</u> on the team. <u>No error.</u>
                D   E

12. A <u>round and white</u> sun <u>emblazoned</u> at the <u>summit</u>
          A   B   C
    <u>of the sky.</u> <u>No error.</u>
      D   E

13. When the <u>members</u> of the committee are <u>at odds</u>
           A   B
    and they are in the process of offering <u>their</u> res-
                            C
    ignations, problems become <u>insoluble.</u> <u>No error.</u>
                     D   E

14. One of the requirements <u>was</u> a course in <u>sixteenth</u>
       A   B   C
    <u>centuries</u> literature. <u>No error.</u>
       D   E

15. Further acquaintance with the memoir's of Eliz-
    A   B

    abeth Barrett Browning and Robert Browning en-
                                         C

    ables us to appreciate the depth of influence that
    C   D

    two people of talent can have on each other. No
                                       E

    error.
    E

16. When my commanding officer first looked up
              A   B

    from his desk, he took Lieutenant Baxter to be I.
    B   C   D

    No error.
    E

17. Though he had awakened before the birds began
              A

    to twitter, he laid in bed until long after the sun
       B   C

    had arisen. No error.
    D   E

18. As she dived off the springboard, she was horri-
          A   B

    fied to see that the water was drained from the
    B   C

    pool the night before. No error.
            D   E

19. When the reviews appeared in the morning pa-
                                A

    pers, we saw that everybody but Carolyn and him
    A   B   C

    had received averse notices. No error.
          D   E

20. The ceremonies were opened by a drum and bu-
             A

    gle corps of Chinese school children parading up
       B   C   D

    the street in colorful uniforms. No error.
                            E

21. Irregardless of what other members of the board
        A   B

    say, I must repeat, as chairman, that these are the
                     C

    facts concerning the requirements for the posi-
         D

    tion. No error.
        E

22. There would have been no objections to him join-
            A   B

    ing the party if he had been amenable to the plans
                  C   D

    of the group. No error.
             E

23. I was not at all surprised to hear that Wallace
        A   B

    Dolan, one of the most promising young men in
                   C

    the community won the poetry contest. No error.
       D   E

24. Little Mary, in her naiveté, explained her ab-
                 A

    sence from school with an incredulous tale in
                        B   C

    which she played the role of the daring heroine.
    C   D

    No error.
    E

25. The mourners past solemnly through the great
              A   B

    doors of the cathedral in keeping with the low
                       C

    tones of the organ. No error.
    D   E

Stop

END OF SECTION V. IF YOU HAVE ANY TIME LEFT, GO OVER YOUR WORK IN THIS SECTION
ONLY. DO NOT WORK IN ANY OTHER SECTION OF THE TEST. WHEN YOUR TIME IS UP, GO
ON TO THE NEXT SECTION.

SECTION VI: PRACTICAL BUSINESS JUDGMENT

20 Minutes
20 Questions

DIRECTIONS: This section consists of a reading section which details a business situation followed by two sets of questions, data evaluation and data application. In the first set, data evaluation, you will be asked to classify certain of the facts presented in the passage on the basis of their importance. The second set, data application, will test your grasp of specific details of the situation.

Six years ago Peter Williams formed an unusual enterprise. His company creates unique electronic toys, but does not sell them through retail outlets. Instead, Peter Williams creates a prototype toy and then takes it to toy companies. A firm which sees market potential for the idea contracts with Williams for its full development. Williams then receives a substantial fee, which is in actuality an advance against royalty.

Early in the history of Williams' business, he found that he needed investment money for personnel expansion and expensive electronic equipment. He contacted a group of five men who had banded together to search for venture capital projects. They bought one-third of the company stock for $100,000.

At first, everyone was pleased. Business went up from $151,000 in the second year of existence to $896,000 in the fourth year. The only problem was that the company never seemed to make any money. The costs of contracts usually were greater than contract fees. When the investors became concerned, Williams admitted that he perhaps had underestimated costs, but that anticipated royalties would make up the deficit and produce a substantial profit.

Williams sought no further investment, but kept the company solvent by bank loans and what he called "bouncing," that is, by paying the costs of one contract with the fees of the next. This did not make outside suppliers too happy, as some of them had to wait up to six months to get paid. Nonetheless, the company staggered on, and Williams was even able to add to his staff until there were 22 employees.

However, in the fifth year, business fell off sharply

to $304,000. The sixth year was even worse; Williams only got one contract for $136,000.

The investors' grumbles, meanwhile, have increased to a roar. They point out that the overall debt of the company, including their outlay, is close to a quarter of a million dollars. Royalties, which they expected to produce a flood of cash by this time, are hardly a trickle. They are suspicious that Peter Williams' creativity has run dry.

They suggest two alternatives. The first is that the company discontinue business after completion of the one remaining contract in the house. In this way, debts will eventually be paid. After that, all shareholders, including Williams, will possibly receive very substantial dividends from future royalty revenue.

The second alternative is that Peter Williams assign to them the royalties from the ten most potential contracts. For these considerations, they will surrender their shares. The advantages to Williams, they claim, are many. He would be rid of disgruntled shareholders who are looking for any legal excuse to force him out. He would then own all the shares and would be free to dictate policy unopposed. Very possibly he might be able to make more royalty money from the five contracts remaining to him than by sharing in the total fifteen contracts.

Peter Williams thinks over the alternatives for one month. Then he turns both down.

It is true, he admits, that relations between him and the investors have become very acrimonious. Board meetings are far from pleasant and usually end in shouting matches.

However, he does not feel that he has run out of creative ideas. To the contrary, he points out that he has been making prototypes right along, and he is sure that they will eventually result in contracts.

He attributes the business slowdown to a general decline in the toy industry. This, in turn, is due to an acute recession throughout the nation. But national

138

business indicators seem to predict a sharp upturn in the economy in the very near future.

He has initiated many economies. He has reduced the staff to only five people, including himself. He has cut his own salary in half. He has sublet two of the three floors of his rented premises.

He feels that the royalties will soon produce considerable funds. He regrets having the investors unhappy, but he reminds them that he is the majority shareholder; as such, he can dictate policy as long as he stays within the law and makes full and frequent disclosure of the company's financial position to them.

DATA EVALUATION

DIRECTIONS: Based on your analysis of the business situation, classify each of the following elements in one of five categories. Mark:

(A) if the element is a MAJOR OBJECTIVE in making the decision; that is, the outcome or result sought by the decision maker.

(B) if the element is a MAJOR FACTOR in arriving at the decision; that is, a consideration explicitly mentioned in the passage that is basic in determining the decision.

(C) if the element is a MINOR FACTOR in making the decision; that is, a secondary consideration in determining the decision.

(D) if the element is a MAJOR ASSUMPTION made in deliberating; that is, a supposition or projection made by the decision maker before weighing the variables.

(E) if the element is an UNIMPORTANT ISSUE in getting to the point; that is, a factor that is insignificant or not immediately relevant to the situation.

1. Coming to terms with stockholders' dissatisfaction.

2. Recent reduction of staff.

3. Williams' desire to remain in business.

4. Unpleasant board meetings.

5. Lack of substantial royalties so far.

6. Williams is a majority stockholder.

7. Purchase of expensive electronic equipment.

8. Assuring stockholders that business will grow

9. Propositions made by stockholders.

10. The company has been kept solvent by bank loans and "bouncing."

DATA APPLICATION

DIRECTIONS: Based on your understanding of the business situation, answer the following questions testing your comprehension of the information supplied in the passage. For each question, select the choice which best answers the question or completes the statement.

11. Peter Williams' company is basically a

(A) retail business
(B) wholesaler
(C) service firm
(D) manufacturer
(E) middleman operation

12. When the venture capital group invested, the company's worth was estimated at

(A) $100,000
(B) $300,000
(C) $33,000
(D) $151,000
(E) $896,000

13. Peter Williams hopes to make up losses by

(A) securing further investment
(B) income from future royalties
(C) bank loans
(D) "bouncing"
(E) reducing his salary

14. The company's deficits seem to be the result of

(A) incorrect estimation of contract costs
(B) Williams' high salary
(C) overstaffing
(D) a lack of business
(E) a national recession

15. "Bouncing" is a system by which Peter Williams

(A) overdraws the company's bank account
(B) contracts with two companies to make the same toy
(C) makes bank loans by using future royalties as collateral
(D) sublets part of the business premises
(E) pays the costs of one contract with the fees of a subsequent one

16. Williams attributes the sharp decline in business to the

    (A) lack of interest in the kinds of toys he makes
    (B) desire of toy companies to develop their own products
    (C) lack of toy company funds to develop new toys
    (D) company's lack of electronic equipment
    (E) national recession

17. Excluding the shareholders' investment, the company's deficit is more nearly

    (A) $96,000
    (B) $150,000
    (C) $236,000
    (D) $280,000
    (E) $500,000

18. One of the investors' suggestions is that the company

    (A) discontinue business
    (B) declare bankruptcy

(C) seek further investment
(D) assign them royalties from all completed projects
(E) let Williams buy back their shares

19. One of the things the investors would like is

    (A) Williams' resignation
    (B) a further cut in staff
    (C) Williams to sublet all of the business premises
    (D) future royalties from certain projects
    (E) Williams to stop making prototypes

20. The reason that Peter Williams is able to turn down the two alternatives offered by the investors is that

    (A) he has initiated internal economies
    (B) he can prove he is still creative
    (C) the company is not technically bankrupt
    (D) he is the majority shareholder
    (E) there will be an upturn in the national economy

Stop

END OF SECTION VI. IF YOU HAVE ANY TIME LEFT, GO OVER YOUR WORK IN THIS SECTION ONLY. DO NOT WORK IN ANY OTHER SECTION OF THE TEST. WHEN YOUR TIME IS UP, GO ON TO THE NEXT SECTION.

SECTION VII: VALIDITY OF CONCLUSION

30 Minutes
40 Questions

DIRECTIONS: Each of the following 4 sets consists of a reading passage followed by a conclusion drawn from the passage. Each conclusion is followed by statements which have a possible bearing on the conclusion. For each statement, you are to choose from the following the option which best expresses the relationship between the statement and the conclusion:

(A) The statement proves the conclusion.
(B) The statement supports the conclusion but does not prove it.
(C) The statement disproves the conclusion.
(D) The statement weakens the conclusion.
(E) The statement is irrelevant to the conclusion.

SET 1

The Rare Foods Eating Club met weekly for a luncheon of unusual foods. As it was one of the hottest days of the summer, only ten guests arrived for the luncheon. The first course was a choice between shark or porcupine soup. For the main course the guests were given a choice between yak meat and a rare mushroom dish. The meal was somewhat hurried since the air conditioning unit was malfunctioning. Two hours after the meal the four Jones brothers, who had been placed next to the air conditioner, began to vomit and run high temperatures. Holmes, who knew of the difficulties in distinguishing some varieties of poisonous mushrooms from non-poisonous ones, was quite certain that poisonous mushrooms had brought on their sickness.

CONCLUSION: The local doctor concluded that the mushroom dish did not cause the Jones brothers' sickness.

1. The Jones brothers were the only guests that had sampled the mushroom dish.

2. The mushroom dish had been ordered by everyone but Holmes.

3. The cook had forgotten to refrigerate the yak meat the night before.

4. The Jones brothers were all sensitive to high temperatures.

5. At a past luncheon when the air conditioner malfunctioned two guests who had been near the unit began to vomit and run high temperatures.

6. Though the edible varieties were in season, none of the poisonous varieties of mushrooms were in season.

7. Only the poisonous varieties of mushrooms were in season.

8. The Jones brothers had just come from a drinking party.

9. The symptoms associated with mushroom poisoning are known to appear between 12 and 15 hours after the mushrooms are eaten.

10. Holmes, an international expert on the varieties of mushrooms, had been responsible for the gathering and preparation of the mushrooms.

SET 2

The Bay City Kickers have, in a brief time, become one of the leading teams in their soccer league. This ascendancy has been due primarily to the signing of the Kellman brothers, famous European stars whom American audiences were eager to see and who have since become popular with local fans. Nevertheless, the acquisition of the Kellman brothers was costly and the team must now raise a substantial sum of cash. Tom Marks, the general manager of the team, sees

141

that there are two possibilities open to him that would solve his cash problem. One possibility would be not to renew the lucrative contracts of the Kellman brothers. Though their release would make a substantial amount of money available, their loss would almost certainly affect attendance figures and hence potential income. The other possibility is to run weekend soccer clinics, which if popular would provide substantial income. Such clinics, however, would substantially interfere with the team's practice sessions and would certainly affect their play in competition.

CONCLUSION: It is in the best interest of the team to release the Kellman brothers rather than open weekend clinics.

11. Many of the team players have come to resent the Kellman brothers and plan some sort of disruption if they are once again offered lucrative contracts.

12. Several other soccer teams in the league have achieved significant financial success by running weekend clinics.

13. Two new rookies from South America, who will receive less than a third of the Kellmans' salary, are thought by the coaches to be even better than the Kellman brothers.

14. It is discovered that the Kellmans have become more and more homesick and are considering returning to Europe.

15. Since the Kellmans have become popular national figures, a major television network plans to make Marks an attractive offer to gain the rights to televise the Bay City games.

16. It is learned that both Kellmans have serious knee problems and may have to be out of action for a year or more.

17. Several European newspapers have criticized European soccer stars for leaving European teams in order to make more money in America.

18. A local foundation has planned to donate a substantial sum of money to the team if the team goes ahead with the plan to open a weekend clinic.

19. All of the players, including the Kellmans, have strong objections to weekend clinics and threaten to leave the team if such a plan is adopted.

20. The Kellmans have become very popular with their teammates and if their contract is not renewed the other members of the team have threatened to quit.

SET 3

The Haleys and the MacVeys, two mountaineer families, had been feuding with one another for years. The Haleys were hunters and expert riflemen. The MacVeys, who refused to use guns, were expert animal trappers and skinners. One day Zeb Haley returned to his cabin surprised to find a large keg of whiskey to which a note had been attached. It was signed "Sam MacVey," the head of the MacVey clan. The keg was apparently a peace offering and the note indicated that Sam thought it was time the two families resolved their disputes. The note included an invitation to a venison dinner at Sam MacVey's cabin. Zeb, who was touched by this, set out for his meeting with Sam. Zeb was later found on the Arrow Creek Trail on MacVey property. He had been crushed to death by a grizzly bear trap.

CONCLUSION: Sam MacVey was guilty of murdering Zeb Haley.

21. In his note to Zeb, Sam had advised him not to take the Arrow Creek Trail.

22. Grizzly bears had not been in the area for over 10 years and grizzly bear traps were no longer being used.

23. Sam had been furious a week earlier when his highly prized, but no longer used, grizzly bear trap was found to be missing.

24. MacVey strongly urged Zeb to take the Arrow Creek Trail, advising him that the other trails had a number of coyote traps.

25. Sam was considered to be the best trapper in the whole North woods.

26. Near the trap there was a warning sign clearly indicating the location of the trap.

27. A week earlier two different neighbors had reported to Sam that they had seen a grizzly bear on the Arrow Creek Trail and requested that he set a trap.

28. MacVey, who was unable to write even his name, said he knew nothing of a note or a keg of whiskey.

29. Investigation revealed that Zeb had dragged himself and the trap onto the trail from a thick underbrush off the trailway.

30. Sam had been seen leaving the vicinity of the trap just as Zeb was seen coming down the trail.

SET 4

Mr. Green had sent Wilma, his secretary, to pick up his station wagon from Acme Auto Repair. Mr. Green had instructed Acme to repair the brakes that had been failing. While returning with Mr. Green's car from Acme, Wilma, driving on Main Street, entered the intersection at Elm after the light changed from green to red. She sounded her horn but nevertheless collided with the car of Mr. Jenkins who had entered the intersection from Elm Street after the light had turned green.

CONCLUSION: The damages to Mr. Jenkins' car are due to Wilma's poor driving.

31. Jenkins could easily have avoided Wilma but, in his anger at her running a red light, he increased his speed in order to hit her.

32. There are a high number of accidents at the intersection of Main and Elm.

33. Wilma, driving without a license, had failed her driving test due to color blindness.

34. Wilma, who was in a hurry, did not heed the garage's warning that the station wagon had not yet been serviced.

35. Due to a mix-up the mechanic had inspected the brakes of another station wagon, and Mr. Green's station wagon had received only an engine tune-up.

36. The collision would not have occurred had Jenkins, who was intoxicated, not been making an illegal U-turn at the intersection.

37. Wilma had been seen coming out of a bar shortly before she picked up the station wagon.

38. Since Acme Service Department was several hours behind schedule, a salesman, instead of a mechanic, was asked to inspect Mr. Green's station wagon.

39. Wilma, who was in the way of a high-speeding fire truck, had been waved on through the intersection by the fire truck.

40. Wilma, who was already an hour late, had accelerated when she saw the light about to change to red.

Stop

END OF EXAMINATION

END OF SECTION VII. IF YOU HAVE ANY TIME LEFT, GO OVER YOUR WORK IN THIS SECTION ONLY. DO NOT WORK IN ANY OTHER SECTION OF THE TEST. WHEN YOUR TIME IS UP, CHECK YOUR ANSWERS WITH THE ANSWER KEY AND EXPLANATORY ANSWERS PROVIDED ON THE FOLLOWING PAGES.

ANSWER KEY

SECTION I

1. D	6. A	11. A	16. E	21. E
2. C	7. A	12. B	17. C	22. A
3. E	8. D	13. B	18. A	23. B
4. A	9. C	14. C	19. B	24. A
5. B	10. E	15. B	20. B	25. A

SECTION II

1. B	7. B	13. A	19. B	25. C
2. A	8. C	14. B	20. C	26. D
3. D	9. A	15. C	21. C	27. D
4. B	10. C	16. C	22. B	28. B
5. A	11. B	17. C	23. B	29. A
6. C	12. B	18. A	24. B	30. B

SECTION III

1. A	8. C	15. D
2. C	9. B	16. D
3. B	10. B	17. E
4. D	11. D	18. B
5. E	12. C	19. D
6. B	13. C	20. B
7. B	14. C	

SECTION IV

1. E	7. E	13. A	19. D	25. D
2. B	8. B	14. A	20. A	26. E
3. C	9. C	15. E	21. C	27. A
4. D	10. E	16. A	22. C	28. B
5. D	11. B	17. C	23. C	29. B
6. E	12. C	18. E	24. B	30. C

SECTION V

1. C	6. D	11. D	16. D	21. A
2. B	7. E	12. B	17. C	22. B
3. A	8. B	13. E	18. C	23. D
4. C	9. A	14. D	19. D	24. B
5. E	10. C	15. B	20. E	25. A

SECTION VI

1. A	6. D	11. C	16. E
2. C	7. E	12. B	17. B
3. B	8. A	13. B	18. A
4. C	9. B	14. A	19. D
5. C	10. C	15. E	20. D

SECTION VII

1. D	9. A	17. E	25. E	33. B
2. A	10. C	18. D	26. C	34. A
3. B	11. B	19. A	27. C	35. D
4. B	12. D	20. C	28. D	36. D
5. A	13. B	21. D	29. D	37. E
6. B	14. B	22. B	30. B	38. D
7. C	15. C	23. C	31. D	39. C
8. B	16. A	24. B	32. E	40. A

EXPLANATORY ANSWERS

SECTION I

1. **(D)** The author presents a clear exposition of circumstances as they exist. His passage expresses neither strong condemnation nor approval of the facts at hand. He appears to have a good grasp of his subject and does not express any confusion.

2. **(C)** The main purpose of the passage is to discuss the two characteristics unique to American Christmas celebrations: the role of commercial interests, and the combination of Christmas and New Year's holidays to create one continuous period of "Saturnalia." Statement (C) is clearly pertinent to the first of these concerns.

3. **(E)** The passage states that Americans have "taken the [Christmas] symbols of all the nations and made them [their] own."

4. **(A)** According to the passage, one of the characteristics of Christmas in America is the fact that ". . . the dominant role of the Christmas festivities has become to serve as a stimulus to retail business."

5. **(B)** The passage states: ". . . the copy typed is on an ordinary sheet of paper by any typist in the customary way. The only difference . . . is that a special typewriter ribbon impregnated with hectograph ink is necessary."

6. **(A)** As is mentioned above, the material should first be typed on regular paper.

7. **(A)** The passage states: "The typed copy is then transferred to the gelatin by pressing the typed matter tightly against the gelatin surface."

8. **(D)** The passage states that the gelatin "holds in reverse any copy done in hectograph ink."

9. **(C)** According to the passage "when blank impression paper is pressed against the inked portion of the gelatin it picks up a print of the image."

10. **(E)** The author deals at some length with the advantages of automation. He devotes only his final paragraph to opposition to automation. His treatment of the opposition is very brief and indicates no support.

11. **(A)** The passage states: "hundreds of Swedes have learned that they have silent symptoms of disorders that neither they nor their physicians were aware of."

12. **(B)** We are told that the idea was conceived by Dr. Gunnar Jungner alone.

13. **(B)** As is announced in the first sentence, the passage deals with the health check-up system being implemented in Sweden. The passage deals with the results and advantages of the system and the leading figures involved.

14. **(C)** The passage explicitly states that a "chemical screening process" is used by the Jungners to predict potential ailments.

15. **(B)** The author is discussing inconveniences and affronts of contemporary life which, in many cases, affect him personally, and which he is not willing to passively accept.

16. **(E)** According to the passage, a doctrinaire myth is a belief based on circumstances which no longer exist. The writer cites the example of the commuter railroads which justify poor service on the principle of competitive free enterprise when all competition has ceased to exist.

17. **(C)** The author's purpose is to describe the problem of technological changes which hinder or inconvenience, rather than help, the average citizen. The author urges that people carefully examine the dubious principles used to justify such innovations and to refuse to accept changes which do not serve the common good.

18. **(A)** A recurring idea in the passage is that of "competence," which the writer frequently uses ironically to denote the willingness or ability of the consumer to passively accept incompetence on the part of those who provide his goods and services.

19. **(B)** The writer nowhere states or implies that the razing of Pennsylvania Station was justifiable. He feels that the remodeling of the station was useless and undesired.

20. **(B)** The passage concerns itself with technical terminology solely. The first paragraph talks about it in general terms; the second goes into the relationship between occupations and special terminology in detail.

21. **(E)** The last three lines of the passage emphasize this point which is referred to in the second paragraph.

22. **(A)** This clearly follows from the second paragraph. The other choices cannot be determined from the passage.

23. **(B)** This can be determined from the middle of the second paragraph.

24. **(A)** A linguist is a language specialist; the passage is concerned with highly specialized language.

25. **(A)** The tone of the passage is descriptive; the other choices would not be suitable.

SECTION II

1. **(B)** To find the value of I using the lowest possible figures, add the number of *Interviews Conducted* by divisions X, Y, and Z. Then subtract this figure from the *Total Interviews* conducted.

Thus: $630 + 550 + 500 = 1680$
$2180 - 1680 = 500$

2. **(A)** To find the value of II using the lowest figures (which allow for the fewest mistakes), add the number of letters typed by Divisions W, Y, and Z. Then subtract from the *Total Letters Typed*.

Thus: $2500 + 4350 + 3250 = 10100$
$14500 - 10100 = 4400$

3. **(D)** To find the value of III, add all the totals of all *Administrative Actions*.

$27100 + 2180 + 57000 + 14500 + 600 = 101380$

4. **(B)** There are three steps necessary to the solution of this problem: Establish a ratio of *Applications Processed: Total Administrative Actions* for each division.

Div. W	15000 : 26200
Div. X	18000 : 30080
Div. Y	14500 : 27000
Div. Z	9500 : 18100

Simplify each ratio by dividing the first term by the second term and convert this figure to a percentage by multiplying by 100.

Div. W	$15000 \div 26200 = .572 \times 100 = 57.2\%$
Div. X	$18000 \div 30080 = .598 \times 100 = 59.8\%$
Div. Y	$14500 \div 27000 = .537 \times 100 = 53.7\%$
Div. Z	$9500 \div 18100 = .525 \times 100 = 52.5\%$

The division in which the number of applications processed is the greatest percentage of total *Administrative Actions* is Division X.

5. **(A)** The easiest way to solve this type of problem is to take 15 percent of the total *Administrative Actions* for each Division and then determine by inspecting the chart whether or not the number of letters typed exceeds this figure.

Div. W $26200 \times .15 = 3930$ which is greater than 2500 (number of letters typed)

Div. X $30080 \times .15 = 4512$ which is greater than 4400 (number of letters typed)

Div. Y $27000 \times .15 = 4050$ which is less than

4350 (number of letters typed)

Div. Z $18100 \times .15 = 2715$ which is less than 3250 (number of letters typed)

Therefore under the new plan only Division W and X would continue to do their own typing since the number of letters typed in these two divisions does not exceed 15 percent of the total *Administrative Actions* of each division.

6. **(C)** 27100 Total Telephone Inquiries Answered by all Divisions

$\times .25$ Calls that could be answered by a Central Information Service

6775 Number of Telephone Inquiries that could be answered by a Central Information Service

At 5 minutes per call that means 6775×5 or 33875 minutes could be saved by having a Central Information Service.

Since there are 60 minutes in an hour, $33,875 \div 60 = 564.5$ hours could be gained by all four divisions if such a service were instituted.

7. **(B)** Division Y is responsible for 27,000 *Administrative Actions* annually. Therefore in 4 months, which is $^4/_{12}$ or $^1/_3$ year, Division Y would be responsible for $27000 \times ^1/_3$ or 9,000 *Administrative Actions*.

Nine thousand *Administrative Actions* divided evenly among Divisions W, X and Z = $9000 \div 3$ or 3000 *Administrative Actions* to be added to each division's work load for the coming year. An increase of 3000 *Actions* over the 18100 actions completed by Division Z for the current year is equal to $3000 \div 18100 = .16$ or 16% (approx.).

8. **(C)** An average rate of increase of 150 citations per year over a 20 year period = 150×20 or an increase of 3000 citations in 20 years. Reading from the graph one can see that *parking violations* increased from 3000 in 1950 to 5000 in 1970. This is an increase of 2000 citations in 20 years. Also, *drug use* increased from 1000 in 1950 to 4500 in 1970. This is an increase of 3500 in 20 years. *Dangerous weapons* increased from 2000 in 1950 to 3000 in 1970. This is an increase

of 1000 in 20 years. *Improper dress* obviously *decreased* over the 20-year period shown and so is not to be considered in this question. The only offense which shows an increase of 3000 (or more) over the 20-year period is *drug use*.

9. **(A)** A constant rate of increase or decrease is indicated on a graph by a straight line. Inspection of this graph shows that only citations for *Parking Violations* progress in a straight line from 1950 to 1970, increasing by 500 citations for each five-year period.

10. **(C)** Over the full 20-year period citations for *Parking Violations* increased from 3000 to 5000.

% of Increase $= \dfrac{\text{Amount of Increase}}{\text{Original Amount}} \times 100$

% of Increase (Parking Violations) $= \dfrac{2000}{3000} \times 100$
$= .66 \times 100 = 66\%$

% of Increase (Drug Use) $= \dfrac{3500}{1000} \times 100$
$= 3.5 \times 100 = 350\%$

% of Increase (Dangerous Weapons) $= \dfrac{1000}{2000} \times 100$
$= .5 \times 100 = 50\%$

% of Decrease (Improper Dress) $= \dfrac{1500}{2500} \times 100$
$= .6 \times 100 = 60\%$

The only offense which shows a total increase or decrease of 50% is *Dangerous Weapons*.

11. **(B)** To find the percentage increase in total citations issued from 1955 to 1960, you must first find the number of citations issued in 1955 and 1960.

Citations issued
in 1955 = 3500 (Parking Violations)
2000 (Improper Dress)
2000 (Dangerous Weapons)
1500 (Drug Use)
9000 Total Citations Issued

Citations issued
in 1960 =   4000 (Parking Violations)
            2500 (Dangerous Weapons)
            2000 (Drug Use)
            <u>1500</u> (Improper Dress)
          10000 Total Citations Issued

$10000 - 9000 = 1000$ Increase

% Increase $= \dfrac{1000}{9000} \times 100 = .11 \times 100 = 11\%$ (approx.)

12. **(B)** "I" is FICA or one of the Deductions made from the Total Earnings of Employee Z. To find the value of "I," first find the Total Deductions for Employee Z:

Total Deductions = Total Earnings − Net Pay
$$= 275.00 - 220.10$$
$$= \$54.90.$$

Next, find the total known deductions for Employee Z: $30.00 + 6.00 + 2.40 = 38.40$

FICA ("I") = Total Deductions − Known Deductions
$$= 54.90 - 38.40 = 16.50$$

13. **(A)** Using the information you have just gained from the previous question, substitute $16.50 for "I" in the table and then add all the figures in the FICA column to arrive at the Total.

$$\$27.00 + 14.10 + 20.46 + 16.50 = \$78.06$$

14. **(B)** The amount of cash necessary to pay the employees is the total of Net Pay. This figure is represented on the chart as "III." However, its value can be calculated by adding all the figures in the Net Pay column.

$$\$332.00 + 177.90 + 249.54 + 220.10 = \$979.54$$

Alternative (A) is incorrect because it represents Total Earnings which includes taxes and other deductions which are not paid to the employees.

15. **(C)** The amount which must be deposited with a governmental depository is the total of FICA + Withholding Tax + State Tax or

$$\$78.06 + 182.00 + 46.00 = \$306.06$$

The $15.40 (Total of the "Other" column) covers such employee benefits as health and life insurance and does not have to be paid to a governmental depository.

16. **(C)** To answer this question, it is necessary to determine the percentage of each employee's Total Earnings which his FICA deduction represents.

Employee W: $\dfrac{27.00}{450.00} = .06$ or 6%

Employee X: $\dfrac{14.10}{235.00} = .06$ or 6%

Employee Y: $\dfrac{20.46}{341.00} = .06$ or 6%

Employee Z: $\dfrac{16.50}{275.00} = .06$ or 6%

Since FICA represents 6% of the Total Earnings of each employee appearing on the Payroll Summary, it will also represent 6% of the Total Earnings of any other employee. Thus, $300 × .06 = $18.00 (FICA deduction for an employee earning $300 per month).

17. **(C)** First find the number of employees in 1961:

$7 + 14 + 26 + 22 + 17 + 10 + 4 = 100$ employees

Then find total number of work-units produced using midpoint of each range:

```
 7 ×  750 =  5250
14 × 1250 = 17500
26 × 1750 = 45500
22 × 2250 = 49500
17 × 2750 = 46750
10 × 3250 = 32500
 4 × 3750 = 15000
212000 Total Work-Units
            Produced
```

Divide number of work-units produced by number of workers to get average number of work-units per employee:

$212,000 \div 100 = 2120$ Work-Units per Employee

This falls in the range of 2001–2500.

18. **(A)** Number of employees producing more than 2000 work-units in 1961 $= 22 + 17 + 10 + 4 = 53$

Number of employees producing more than 2000 work-units in 1971 $= 36 + 39 + 23 + 9 = 107$

Ratio of employees producing more than 2000 work-units in 1961 to those producing more than

2000 work-units in 1971 = 53:107 which is most nearly 1:2.

19. **(B)**

1. Number of employees in 1961 = 100 (See question 17)
   Number of employees in 1971 = 150
   (4 + 11 + 28 + 36 + 39 + 23 + 9 = 150)

2. Work-units produced in 1961 = 212000 (See question 17)
   Work-units produced in 1971 = 362500

   $$
   \begin{aligned}
   4 \times 750 &= 3000 \\
   11 \times 1250 &= 13750 \\
   28 \times 1750 &= 49000 \\
   36 \times 2250 &= 81000 \\
   39 \times 2750 &= 107250 \\
   23 \times 3250 &= 74750 \\
   9 \times 3750 &= \underline{33750} \\
   &\ 362500
   \end{aligned}
   $$
   362500 Total Work-Units produced in 1971

3. Employees producing 2000 or fewer work-units in 1961= 7 + 14 + 26 = 47
   Employees producing 2000 or fewer work-units in 1971 = 4 + 11 + 28 = 43

Therefore, 1 (Total number of employees) and 2 (Total number of work-units produced) were greater in 1971 than in 1961.

20. **(C)** It is possible to answer this question by careful reading of the two reports shown, without any computation at all. John Brown's report covers Turnstiles 1, 2, 3, and 4 from 7 AM to 3 PM, and Mary Smith's report covers the same Turnstiles from 3 PM to 11 PM. Therefore, the Closing Reading for Turnstile 2 on John Brown's report (Entry F) will be the same figure as the Opening Reading for Turnstile 2 on Mary Smith's report.

To compute the Closing Reading, simply add the Difference shown for Turnstile 2 to the Opening Reading given:
$$3442 + 839 = 4281$$

21. **(C)** This figure can be supplied by simply reading the report. The Opening Reading for Turnstile 3 (Entry G) on Mary Smith's report will be the same as the Closing Reading for Turnstile 3 on John Brown's report.

To compute the Opening Reading, subtract the Difference (or number of turns made) from the Closing Reading given:
$$9759 - 353 = 9404$$

22. **(B)**
      8588 Closing Reading
     −8265 Opening Reading
       323 Difference or Entry H

23. **(B)** Entry I is the sum of all Opening Readings
     5123
     3442
     8951
     <u>7663</u>
   25179

24. **(B)** Entry J is the sum of all Closing Readings
     6019
     4683
     9757
     <u>8588</u>
   29047

25. **(C)** The difference between Total Fares and Net Fares = 1687 − 1680 = 7. Since Test Rings = 3, the remainder of the difference must be made up of Slugs and Foreign Coins.

     7 Difference between Total Fares and Net Fares
   −3 Test Rings
     4 Slugs and Foreign Coins

26. **(D)**
       2169 Net Fares
    ×   .35 Token Value
   $759.15 Net Fares at Token Value or Entry L

27. **(D)** Since no tokens were transferred out, Mary Smith's Total Token Reserve = Tokens at Start + Tokens Received.

     6450 Total Token Reserve
   −5000 Token Reserve at Start
     1450 Tokens Received or Entry M

28. **(B)**
     4200 Token Reserve at Start
   +2200 Tokens Received
     6400
   −1400 Tokens Transferred Out
     5000 Total Token Reserve or Entry N

29. **(A)**   6450 Total Token Reserve
     −5674 Total Reserve at End
       776 No. of Reserve Tokens Sold or
            Entry O

30. **(B)**   670 No. of Reserve Tokens Sold
      × .35 Value of Each Token
    $234.50 Value of Reserve Tokens Sold
            or Entry P

SECTION III

1. **(A)** Making a deal is the main objective for both parties.

2. **(C)** Afsky's possible loss of regular customers is a minor factor.

3. **(B)** Muller's desire to remain in the restaurant business is a major factor in coming to an agreeable deal for the restaurant and lot.

4. **(D)** Afsky's financial stability is a major assumption.

5. **(E)** The age of the restaurant is unimportant.

6. **(B)** The advantage of having a motel on Route 77 is a major factor in Afsky's desire to purchase.

7. **(B)** Muller's enjoyment in running his restaurant must be a major factor, as it influences his counteroffer and his major objective of a satisfactory deal.

8. **(C)** Muller's disinclination to start all over again in Florida leads him to think about the major factors that influence his decision to stay.

9. **(B)** Shares of stock rather than a great deal of cash are part of Muller's considerations in forming his counteroffer.

10. **(B)** Building a motel is a major factor influencing Afsky's desire to make a deal for the restaurant and the adjoining lot.

11. **(D)** It is stated that the restaurant is profitable. It is not seasonal, as (A) states, but busy all year round. It is certainly not near bankruptcy, as it says in (B). (C) is wrong because it is stated that the restaurant is on a major highway, which is one of the reasons Afsky wants to build a motel next to the restaurant. (E) is also incorrect. Hans Muller is not the founder, but the "third Hans Muller to run the establishment."

12. **(C)** It is stated that Afsky, Ltd, is widely diversified. Thus, (A) and (D) are incorrect. (B) is wrong; Afsky is new to the restaurant business and wishes to build up its holdings in this field.

13. **(C)** Afsky wants to buy the restaurant and adjoining lot. It cannot buy a motel since there is none there, but it wishes to build one.

14. **(C)** Afsky believes that a motel on Route 77 would be desirable. (A) is wrong since we are not told whether or not $50,000 is a high price for the lot. Hans Muller does not wish to go to Florida yet, so (B) is incorrect. It is not stated if Muller's present customers would use the motel, but as they are local people, they probably would not. We are not told whether there is another motel in the area.

15. **(D)** Afsky offered $250,000 cash for the restaurant, and $50,000 cash for the lot. The annual salary was part of Muller's counteroffer.

16. **(D)** After thinking it over, Muller decides against retiring. His sons do not wish to carry on the restaurant. He is not necessarily against the price offered. He does not indicate any desire to build the motel himself, and he does not have any bias against Afsky coming into the area.

17. **(E)** Muller wants 3% of the restaurant's revenue, $50,000 in cash, and a 10-year employment contract.

18. **(B)** Taxes comprise the only reason Muller turns the cash offer down.

19. **(D)** Muller tells the Afsky people that they run a strong possibility of financial loss because they are inexperienced in restaurant management. Furthermore, he has a strong personal relationship with his customers which Afsky might lose. There seems to be no local resentment against a motel on the site.

20. **(B)** Muller definitely wishes to continue managing the restaurant. (A) is wrong since he wants a 10-year contract. (C) is wrong; he displays no interest in running the motel. (D) and (E) are wrong; he wants a total of $400,000, mostly in stock, and he is willing to give up title to the lot.

SECTION IV

1. **(E)** If we manipulate equation (1) a little, it becomes $4f + 2g = 18$, which has the same infinite number of solutions as equation (2).

2. **(B)** If A is on the perpendicular bisector of BC, then AB must equal AC. (Check this with the Pythagorean Theorem.)

3. **(C)** If Tim is the fourth smallest boy in the class, there are three shorter than he. Since half the boys are taller than Tim, the whole class must consist of the taller half, plus the shorter half, which includes Tim and the three other short boys. Thus, there are eight boys altogether.

4. **(D)** Since c must be a positive number, either equation taken alone yields c=3 as a solution.

5. **(D)** In equation (1), X must equal $(-4-X)$, and therefore, $X+2=0$, $X=-2$. In equation (2), $X+10=0$, $X=-10$. Both times, X is less than zero.

6. **(E)** The fact that I watch television *only* on rainy days does not imply that I watch it on *every* rainy day. Therefore, I may refrain from watching television on any day, regardless of the weather.

7. **(E)** While the algebra involved is not difficult, it is unnecessary here, as long as you remember that the answer will always be affected by the rate of the current, which was not given.

8. **(B)** If Marty had a brother, the brother would also be the nephew of Marty's uncle. However, Marty is the only nephew. Therefore, Marty has no brothers.

9. **(C)** If Bill owned a snake, he would have to own a hamster also. Since Bill has a rabbit, and he has only two pets, he cannot, therefore, own a snake.

10. **(E)** If m and n are both 2, then in cases (1) and (2), both conditions are satisfied. However, m and n may also both be zero, and no number can be divided by zero.

11. **(B)** Since CD is parallel to AB, any point on CD will have the same distance from AB. Therefore, all triangles formed by AB and a point on CD have the same area, and therefore, the area of $\triangle$ ABC = 12 square inches.

12. **(C)** If I went to the movies nine days ago, it must have been on a Thursday. Therefore, it was also Thursday two days ago, and today is Saturday.

13. **(A)** By equation (1), the diagonal of the square must be larger than the circle's diameter, and the block will *not* fit. Using Statement (2) alone, we cannot deduce anything about the relative sizes of the block and hole.

14. **(A)** The total of the men and boys must be 950 lbs. Thus, the total weight of the men must end in 50. The only possibility is 5 men, weighing 850 lbs., and one boy, weighing 100 lbs.

15. **(E)** The month may be either June or July.

16. **(A)** If AB=BC, then BD is part of the perpendicular bisector of AC, and therefore, angle BDC equals 90°.

17. **(C)** Since Joe earns exactly half of what is assumed in (2), he makes exactly half of $63, or $31.50.

18. **(E)** Since A and B may be interchanged, either one may equal 1, the other one being 9. Therefore, we cannot tell which is greater.

19. **(D)** Either of these conditions is sufficient to prove that ABCD is a parallelogram. (To prove it for (1), draw AC and flip triangle ADC over so that AD and BC form an isosceles triangle.)

20. **(A)** Since Joe is a policeman, he and Jim must both live on Byron Avenue. B is insufficient because a carpenter does not necessarily live on Simpson Street.

21. **(C)** Yes. $x^5+1=(x+1)(x^4-x^3+x^2-x+1)$

22. **(C)** Yes. If he is an accomplished violinist he must play the piano, because of (2). Because of (1), he is accomplished.

23. **(C)** The Smashers must now have 4 runs, because of (2). Therefore the Thunderbolts have 8.

24. **(B)** If the area is ½ac, then a must be the base, and c the altitude of the triangle (or vice versa). This can be proven by use of the formula: area = ½ (side 1) (side 2) sin (angle between).

25. **(D)** Both yield r=2 as solutions. In (2), r^2+1 cannot equal zero, since r^2 can never equal -1.

26. **(E)** The angles may be either $75°-75°-30°$, or $75°-52½°-52½°$.

27. **(A)** $(x-2)^2$ is greater than -1. $x^2-4x+4>-1$, so that $x^2+4>4x-1$.

28. **(B)** He has six coins to total 30¢, none of which are pennies. Therefore, all six are nickels.

29. **(B)** In (1), the statement is always true (take 1 and 2 for examples). In (2), $(x^2+2x)=(x+1)^2-1$. Therefore, if (2) is true, then $(x+1)$ must be even, so x must be odd.

30. **(C)** No. S=7 and T=3.

SECTION V

1. **(C)** Parallel sentence structure (parts of a sentence that are parallel in meaning should be parallel in structure) dictates that the verb be in the past tense; *carried*, not *carries*.

2. **(B)** *Manning* is a gerund. It should be *man*, the present tense of the verb *to man*.

3. **(A)** *Disinterested*, which is an adjective meaning unbiased, should be *uninterested*, which means having no interest in.

4. **(C)** The pronoun *it* is superfluous in this sentence. Only the verb *is* is required.

5. **(E)** There are no errors in this sentence.

6. **(D)** *Soggily* is an adverb. It should be *soggy*, an adjective which modifies potatoes.

7. **(E)** There are no errors in this sentence.

8. **(B)** *Should go down* is an incorrect verb form. It should be *would go down*.

9. **(A)** *Their* should be the adverb *there* in an impersonal construction where the real subject follows the verb.

10. **(C)** *Quite most* is redundant. It should be *quite* or *most*.

11. **(D)** *Any* is the incorrect pronoun. It should be *anyone*.

12. **(B)** *Emblazoned* is the incorrect verb choice. It should be *blazed*.

13. **(E)** There are no errors in this sentence.

14. **(D)** *Centuries* is the plural. It should be the singular *century*.

15. **(B)** *Memoir's* is possessive. It should be the non-possessive plural *memoirs*. "Of" denotes possession, making the apostrophe redundant.

16. **(D)** *I* is the object of the infinitive to be and should be *me*.

17. **(C)** *Laid*, the past tense of lay when it connotes to set or put, should be *lay*, which connotes recline.

18. **(C)** *Was drained*, simple past, is the incorrect verb tense. It should be *had been drained*, past perfect.

19. **(D)** *Averse*, which means unwilling, should be *adverse*, which means unfavorable.

20. **(E)** There are no errors in this sentence.

21. **(A)** *Irregardless* is a nonstandard word form. It should be *regardless*.

22. **(B)** *Him*, an objective pronoun, should be *his*, a possessive pronoun modifying the gerund joining. (Gerunds take the possessive, participles the objective case.)

23. **(D)** *Community won* should be *community, won*. The comma is necessary to set off the dependent clause that modifies Wallace Dolan.

24. **(B)** The adjective *incredulous* more appropriately modifies a person and should be *incredible*.

25. **(A)** *Past,* which is an adjective or adverb, should be *passed,* the past tense of the verb to pass.

SECTION VI

1. **(A)** The decision maker in this passage is Williams. The decision he must make is to accept or reject the shareholders' demands. The objective is to come to terms with stockholder dissatisfaction.

2. **(C)** The recent reduction of staff is a minor factor that relates to the major factor of the financial position of Williams' company.

3. **(B)** Williams' desire to remain in business is a major factor in his decision.

4. **(C)** Unpleasant board meetings are a minor factor that resulted in the major factor of propositions being made by the stockholders.

5. **(C)** Lack of substantial royalties is a minor factor that relates to the major factor of shareholder dissatisfaction and to the financial position of the company.

6. **(D)** It is assumed that Williams is a majority stockholder.

7. **(E)** The purchase of expensive electronic equipment is not related to the present decision.

8. **(A)** Assuring stockholders that business will grow is a major objective.

9. **(B)** The propositions made by the shareholders are a major factor in necessitating the decision made by Williams.

10. **(C)** The way the company has been kept solvent relates to the general financial position of Williams' company.

11. **(C)** Basically, Peter Williams' company is a service firm, its service being the creation of new products for toy companies.

12. **(B)** Since the investors bought one-third of the company's stock for $100,000, the total value must be $300,000.

13. **(B)** Williams states that the royalties will soon produce considerable funds. It is true that he has reduced his own salary, but this is a stopgap method of reducing present operating costs and would not make up a quarter-million dollar deficit. He did not mention getting bank loans or seeking more investment money. "Bouncing" cannot reduce losses.

14. **(A)** Contract-cost overruns have certainly been the major factor in creating the large deficit. We do not know what Williams' salary is, but the investors did not object to it so we can assume it is not too high. Williams has pared down his staff, but they too did not seem to bother the investors. The recession and the resulting lack of business are unfortunate for the company, but the deficit existed prior to the decline; it merely grew during the bad times.

15. **(E)** "Bouncing" is defined in the story.

16. **(E)** So stated.

17. **(B)** We are told that the company's deficit, which includes the investors' money, is nearly a quarter of a million dollars. The investors put in $100,000. Therefore, when we subtract that figure, the result is under $150,000.

18. **(A)** So stated. The investors do not go so far as to suggest bankruptcy proceedings, nor do they recommend more investment or that Williams buy back their shares. They want royalties only from some of the completed projects, not all.

19. **(D)** The investors want the royalties from ten of the fifteen completed projects.

20. **(D)** Williams tells the investors bluntly that policy is in his hands because he is the majority shareholder.

SECTION VII

1. **(D)** This fact may indicate that the mushroom dish is the cause of the sickness. It remains to be established that the mushrooms are of the poisonous variety. Also, other possible causes remain, such as the brothers' placement next to the air conditioner.

2. **(A)** Since only four of the nine ordering the mushroom dish were taken ill, this establishes that the mushroom dish was not the agent.

3. **(B)** Improper refrigeration and the extreme heat may have caused the meat to spoil and thus provide an alternative explanation of the sickness.

4. **(B)** This fact in conjunction with the malfunctioning air conditioner could provide an alternative explanation of the sickness.

5. **(A)** This seems to establish that it is the air conditioner that is the source of the problem.

6. **(B)** This establishes that the mushrooms were not poisonous. Still it is remotely possible that the mushrooms are in some way the agent of the sickness.

7. **(C)** This establishes that the mushrooms are poisonous and thus certain to have some effect on the guests.

8. **(B)** It is possible that the alcohol in conjunction with the extreme heat and a hurried meal of exotic foods jointly contributed to the brothers' sickness.

9. **(A)** The two-hour time lapse rules out the mushrooms as the agent.

10. **(C)** Holmes' expertise and his responsibility for the dish makes it extremely unlikely that he was in the wrong about the poisoning which he obviously conspired to bring about.

11. **(B)** This statement supports the conclusion. This sort of dissent definitely seems against the best interests of the team. Still it is possible that the team could survive a period of dissent and still enjoy the benefits of keeping the Kellmans.

12. **(D)** This statement weakens the conclusion. This condition provides a reason for thinking that Bay City clinics could be a financial success and could thus eliminate the necessity of releasing the Kellmans.

13. **(B)** This statement supports the conclusion. The two rookies, who are much less costly than the Kellmans, might make up for any loss that resulted from a departure of the Kellmans. There can be no guarantee, however, that in the end a Kellman departure would not hurt the team.

14. **(B)** This statement supports the conclusion. These personal problems could make the Kellmans a liability rather than an asset. There is no certainty, however, that these problems cannot be overcome.

15. **(C)** This statement disproves the conclusion. With the new source of income, there is no longer any reason to take either of the undesirable options.

16. **(A)** This statement proves the conclusion. Such serious problems make it unlikely that the Kellmans will be available to play and hence provide conclusive reasons for releasing them in order to solve the problem of funds.

17. **(E)** The attitudes expressed in the European newspapers have no bearing on what is in the best interest of the team.

18. **(D)** This statement weakens the conclusion. This new development makes the clinic option an even more likely option of solving the problem of funds. Still it is true that the clinics interfere with practice sessions, and that in the long run might hurt the team.

19. **(A)** This statement proves the conclusion. Since the team as a whole has ruled out the clinic option, this leaves the team no choice but to release the Kellmans.

20. **(C)** This statement disproves the conclusion. Releasing the Kellmans would seem to result in disaster and so this option is ruled out.

21. **(D)** This statement weakens the conclusion. If Sam was hoping that Zeb would follow his advice, then Sam was not intending to trap Zeb on the Arrow Creek Trail. There is still the possibility that the advice was part of a scheme to get Zeb to take the trail.

22. **(B)** This statement supports the conclusion. Since the traps were no longer in use, the presence of the trap on the trail requires an explanation. That the trap was intended for Zeb would provide an explanation of its presence.

23. **(C)** This statement disproves the conclusion. Sam obviously could not be responsible for what was done with the stolen bear trap.

24. **(B)** This statement supports the conclusion. If one assumes that Zeb was ignorant of the bear trap while knowledgeable of the coyote traps, then Sam's directions seem to involve malicious intent. Still there is the possibility that Sam was ignorant of the bear trap's presence.

25. **(E)** This condition does not contribute any information relevant to Sam's guilt or innocence.

26. **(C)** This statement disproves the conclusion. The warning rules out the intentional killing of Zeb.

27. **(C)** This statement disproves the conclusion. The condition establishes a legitimate reason for placing the trap on the trail and that it was not placed there to harm Zeb.

28. **(D)** This statement weakens the conclusion. Sam's inability to write rules him out as the one who wrote the note. Still it is possible that Sam was in some way behind a plot to murder Zeb.

29. **(D)** This statement weakens the conclusion. Since the trap was in thick underbrush off the trailway, it seems unlikely that it was intended for Zeb or anyone walking along the trailway.

30. **(B)** This statement supports the conclusion. This condition strongly indicates that Sam set the trap for Zeb. There are still the possibilities, though somewhat remote, that Sam did not set the trap and that no harm was intended for Zeb.

31. **(D)** This statement weakens the conclusion. Since

Jenkins himself could have avoided the damages to his car, the damages are not entirely due to Wilma's negligence. Wilma is not absolved of all responsibility since her car was in the intersection when it should not have been.

32. **(E)** The condition tells us nothing about the extent to which Wilma is responsible for the accident.

33. **(B)** This statement supports the conclusion. This condition gives us a reason to believe that her running the red light was due to a failure on her part. Still it is possible that in this instance the brakes were at fault and not Wilma.

34. **(A)** This statement proves the conclusion. Since Wilma knew that the brakes had not been repaired, she must take complete responsibility for the station wagon's performance at the intersection.

35. **(D)** This statement weakens the conclusion. The condition indicates that Wilma's entry into the intersection may have been due to faulty brakes and not to her poor driving.

36. **(D)** This statement weakens the conclusion. The condition makes it clear that Jenkins must share responsibility for what went wrong at the intersection. But Wilma is not absolved of all responsibility since her car was in the intersection when it should not have been.

37. **(E)** This statement is irrelevant. The condition alone gives us no reason to believe that Wilma's driving ability was impaired.

38. **(D)** This statement weakens the conclusion. Wilma's entry into the intersection may have been due to faulty brakes and not her poor driving.

39. **(C)** This statement disproves the conclusion. It is clear that Wilma's entry into the intersection was due to an emergency situation, one to which Jenkins himself should have responded.

40. **(A)** This statement proves the conclusion. The condition makes it clear that Wilma herself, and not faulty brakes, is completely responsible for her entry into the intersection.

PRACTICE EXAMINATION 3

This ARCO Practice Examination is similar to the Graduate Management Admission Test you are going to take in structure, length, and level of difficulty. The examination sections and question-types have been changed from those in previous Practice Examinations, but have been kept approximate to those found in the actual GMAT.

Take this examination as if you were taking the real test. Follow all instructions and observe the time limits indicated. Remember to mark all your answers on the Answer Sheet provided, which is similar to the one you will find on the actual examination.

An Answer Key and Explanatory Answers for every question in this Practice Examination are provided at the end of the exam. Check your answers to find out your areas of weakness and then concentrate your studies where they are most needed.

The total time allowed for this test is 3 hours.

ANALYSIS AND TIMETABLE: PRACTICE EXAMINATION 3

Subject Tested	Time Allowed
READING RECALL	35 minutes
PROBLEM SOLVING	40 minutes
PRACTICAL BUSINESS JUDGMENT	20 minutes
DATA SUFFICIENCY	25 minutes
VERBAL ABILITIES	15 minutes
PRACTICAL BUSINESS JUDGMENT	20 minutes
READING COMPREHENSION	25 minutes

ANSWER SHEET
PRACTICE EXAMINATION 3
SECTION I: READING RECALL

1 Ⓐ Ⓑ Ⓒ Ⓓ Ⓔ   7 Ⓐ Ⓑ Ⓒ Ⓓ Ⓔ   13 Ⓐ Ⓑ Ⓒ Ⓓ Ⓔ   19 Ⓐ Ⓑ Ⓒ Ⓓ Ⓔ   25 Ⓐ Ⓑ Ⓒ Ⓓ Ⓔ

2 Ⓐ Ⓑ Ⓒ Ⓓ Ⓔ   8 Ⓐ Ⓑ Ⓒ Ⓓ Ⓔ   14 Ⓐ Ⓑ Ⓒ Ⓓ Ⓔ   20 Ⓐ Ⓑ Ⓒ Ⓓ Ⓔ   26 Ⓐ Ⓑ Ⓒ Ⓓ Ⓔ

3 Ⓐ Ⓑ Ⓒ Ⓓ Ⓔ   9 Ⓐ Ⓑ Ⓒ Ⓓ Ⓔ   15 Ⓐ Ⓑ Ⓒ Ⓓ Ⓔ   21 Ⓐ Ⓑ Ⓒ Ⓓ Ⓔ   27 Ⓐ Ⓑ Ⓒ Ⓓ Ⓔ

4 Ⓐ Ⓑ Ⓒ Ⓓ Ⓔ   10 Ⓐ Ⓑ Ⓒ Ⓓ Ⓔ   16 Ⓐ Ⓑ Ⓒ Ⓓ Ⓔ   22 Ⓐ Ⓑ Ⓒ Ⓓ Ⓔ   28 Ⓐ Ⓑ Ⓒ Ⓓ Ⓔ

5 Ⓐ Ⓑ Ⓒ Ⓓ Ⓔ   11 Ⓐ Ⓑ Ⓒ Ⓓ Ⓔ   17 Ⓐ Ⓑ Ⓒ Ⓓ Ⓔ   23 Ⓐ Ⓑ Ⓒ Ⓓ Ⓔ   29 Ⓐ Ⓑ Ⓒ Ⓓ Ⓔ

6 Ⓐ Ⓑ Ⓒ Ⓓ Ⓔ   12 Ⓐ Ⓑ Ⓒ Ⓓ Ⓔ   18 Ⓐ Ⓑ Ⓒ Ⓓ Ⓔ   24 Ⓐ Ⓑ Ⓒ Ⓓ Ⓔ   30 Ⓐ Ⓑ Ⓒ Ⓓ Ⓔ

SECTION II: PROBLEM SOLVING

1 Ⓐ Ⓑ Ⓒ Ⓓ Ⓔ   7 Ⓐ Ⓑ Ⓒ Ⓓ Ⓔ   13 Ⓐ Ⓑ Ⓒ Ⓓ Ⓔ   19 Ⓐ Ⓑ Ⓒ Ⓓ Ⓔ   25 Ⓐ Ⓑ Ⓒ Ⓓ Ⓔ

2 Ⓐ Ⓑ Ⓒ Ⓓ Ⓔ   8 Ⓐ Ⓑ Ⓒ Ⓓ Ⓔ   14 Ⓐ Ⓑ Ⓒ Ⓓ Ⓔ   20 Ⓐ Ⓑ Ⓒ Ⓓ Ⓔ   26 Ⓐ Ⓑ Ⓒ Ⓓ Ⓔ

3 Ⓐ Ⓑ Ⓒ Ⓓ Ⓔ   9 Ⓐ Ⓑ Ⓒ Ⓓ Ⓔ   15 Ⓐ Ⓑ Ⓒ Ⓓ Ⓔ   21 Ⓐ Ⓑ Ⓒ Ⓓ Ⓔ   27 Ⓐ Ⓑ Ⓒ Ⓓ Ⓔ

4 Ⓐ Ⓑ Ⓒ Ⓓ Ⓔ   10 Ⓐ Ⓑ Ⓒ Ⓓ Ⓔ   16 Ⓐ Ⓑ Ⓒ Ⓓ Ⓔ   22 Ⓐ Ⓑ Ⓒ Ⓓ Ⓔ   28 Ⓐ Ⓑ Ⓒ Ⓓ Ⓔ

5 Ⓐ Ⓑ Ⓒ Ⓓ Ⓔ   11 Ⓐ Ⓑ Ⓒ Ⓓ Ⓔ   17 Ⓐ Ⓑ Ⓒ Ⓓ Ⓔ   23 Ⓐ Ⓑ Ⓒ Ⓓ Ⓔ   29 Ⓐ Ⓑ Ⓒ Ⓓ Ⓔ

6 Ⓐ Ⓑ Ⓒ Ⓓ Ⓔ   12 Ⓐ Ⓑ Ⓒ Ⓓ Ⓔ   18 Ⓐ Ⓑ Ⓒ Ⓓ Ⓔ   24 Ⓐ Ⓑ Ⓒ Ⓓ Ⓔ   30 Ⓐ Ⓑ Ⓒ Ⓓ Ⓔ

SECTION III: PRACTICAL BUSINESS JUDGMENT

1 Ⓐ Ⓑ Ⓒ Ⓓ Ⓔ   5 Ⓐ Ⓑ Ⓒ Ⓓ Ⓔ   9 Ⓐ Ⓑ Ⓒ Ⓓ Ⓔ   13 Ⓐ Ⓑ Ⓒ Ⓓ Ⓔ   17 Ⓐ Ⓑ Ⓒ Ⓓ Ⓔ

2 Ⓐ Ⓑ Ⓒ Ⓓ Ⓔ   6 Ⓐ Ⓑ Ⓒ Ⓓ Ⓔ   10 Ⓐ Ⓑ Ⓒ Ⓓ Ⓔ   14 Ⓐ Ⓑ Ⓒ Ⓓ Ⓔ   18 Ⓐ Ⓑ Ⓒ Ⓓ Ⓔ

3 Ⓐ Ⓑ Ⓒ Ⓓ Ⓔ   7 Ⓐ Ⓑ Ⓒ Ⓓ Ⓔ   11 Ⓐ Ⓑ Ⓒ Ⓓ Ⓔ   15 Ⓐ Ⓑ Ⓒ Ⓓ Ⓔ   19 Ⓐ Ⓑ Ⓒ Ⓓ Ⓔ

4 Ⓐ Ⓑ Ⓒ Ⓓ Ⓔ   8 Ⓐ Ⓑ Ⓒ Ⓓ Ⓔ   12 Ⓐ Ⓑ Ⓒ Ⓓ Ⓔ   16 Ⓐ Ⓑ Ⓒ Ⓓ Ⓔ   20 Ⓐ Ⓑ Ⓒ Ⓓ Ⓔ

SECTION IV: DATA SUFFICIENCY

1 Ⓐ Ⓑ Ⓒ Ⓓ Ⓔ   6 Ⓐ Ⓑ Ⓒ Ⓓ Ⓔ   11 Ⓐ Ⓑ Ⓒ Ⓓ Ⓔ   16 Ⓐ Ⓑ Ⓒ Ⓓ Ⓔ   21 Ⓐ Ⓑ Ⓒ Ⓓ Ⓔ

2 Ⓐ Ⓑ Ⓒ Ⓓ Ⓔ   7 Ⓐ Ⓑ Ⓒ Ⓓ Ⓔ   12 Ⓐ Ⓑ Ⓒ Ⓓ Ⓔ   17 Ⓐ Ⓑ Ⓒ Ⓓ Ⓔ   22 Ⓐ Ⓑ Ⓒ Ⓓ Ⓔ

3 Ⓐ Ⓑ Ⓒ Ⓓ Ⓔ   8 Ⓐ Ⓑ Ⓒ Ⓓ Ⓔ   13 Ⓐ Ⓑ Ⓒ Ⓓ Ⓔ   18 Ⓐ Ⓑ Ⓒ Ⓓ Ⓔ   23 Ⓐ Ⓑ Ⓒ Ⓓ Ⓔ

4 Ⓐ Ⓑ Ⓒ Ⓓ Ⓔ   9 Ⓐ Ⓑ Ⓒ Ⓓ Ⓔ   14 Ⓐ Ⓑ Ⓒ Ⓓ Ⓔ   19 Ⓐ Ⓑ Ⓒ Ⓓ Ⓔ   24 Ⓐ Ⓑ Ⓒ Ⓓ Ⓔ

5 Ⓐ Ⓑ Ⓒ Ⓓ Ⓔ   10 Ⓐ Ⓑ Ⓒ Ⓓ Ⓔ   15 Ⓐ Ⓑ Ⓒ Ⓓ Ⓔ   20 Ⓐ Ⓑ Ⓒ Ⓓ Ⓔ   25 Ⓐ Ⓑ Ⓒ Ⓓ Ⓔ

SECTION V: VERBAL ABILITIES

1 Ⓐ Ⓑ Ⓒ Ⓓ Ⓔ   6 Ⓐ Ⓑ Ⓒ Ⓓ Ⓔ   11 Ⓐ Ⓑ Ⓒ Ⓓ Ⓔ   16 Ⓐ Ⓑ Ⓒ Ⓓ Ⓔ   21 Ⓐ Ⓑ Ⓒ Ⓓ Ⓔ

2 Ⓐ Ⓑ Ⓒ Ⓓ Ⓔ   7 Ⓐ Ⓑ Ⓒ Ⓓ Ⓔ   12 Ⓐ Ⓑ Ⓒ Ⓓ Ⓔ   17 Ⓐ Ⓑ Ⓒ Ⓓ Ⓔ   22 Ⓐ Ⓑ Ⓒ Ⓓ Ⓔ

3 Ⓐ Ⓑ Ⓒ Ⓓ Ⓔ   8 Ⓐ Ⓑ Ⓒ Ⓓ Ⓔ   13 Ⓐ Ⓑ Ⓒ Ⓓ Ⓔ   18 Ⓐ Ⓑ Ⓒ Ⓓ Ⓔ   23 Ⓐ Ⓑ Ⓒ Ⓓ Ⓔ

4 Ⓐ Ⓑ Ⓒ Ⓓ Ⓔ   9 Ⓐ Ⓑ Ⓒ Ⓓ Ⓔ   14 Ⓐ Ⓑ Ⓒ Ⓓ Ⓔ   19 Ⓐ Ⓑ Ⓒ Ⓓ Ⓔ   24 Ⓐ Ⓑ Ⓒ Ⓓ Ⓔ

5 Ⓐ Ⓑ Ⓒ Ⓓ Ⓔ   10 Ⓐ Ⓑ Ⓒ Ⓓ Ⓔ   15 Ⓐ Ⓑ Ⓒ Ⓓ Ⓔ   20 Ⓐ Ⓑ Ⓒ Ⓓ Ⓔ   25 Ⓐ Ⓑ Ⓒ Ⓓ Ⓔ

SECTION VI: PRACTICAL BUSINESS JUDGMENT

1 Ⓐ Ⓑ Ⓒ Ⓓ Ⓔ   5 Ⓐ Ⓑ Ⓒ Ⓓ Ⓔ   9 Ⓐ Ⓑ Ⓒ Ⓓ Ⓔ   13 Ⓐ Ⓑ Ⓒ Ⓓ Ⓔ   17 Ⓐ Ⓑ Ⓒ Ⓓ Ⓔ

2 Ⓐ Ⓑ Ⓒ Ⓓ Ⓔ   6 Ⓐ Ⓑ Ⓒ Ⓓ Ⓔ   10 Ⓐ Ⓑ Ⓒ Ⓓ Ⓔ   14 Ⓐ Ⓑ Ⓒ Ⓓ Ⓔ   18 Ⓐ Ⓑ Ⓒ Ⓓ Ⓔ

3 Ⓐ Ⓑ Ⓒ Ⓓ Ⓔ   7 Ⓐ Ⓑ Ⓒ Ⓓ Ⓔ   11 Ⓐ Ⓑ Ⓒ Ⓓ Ⓔ   15 Ⓐ Ⓑ Ⓒ Ⓓ Ⓔ   19 Ⓐ Ⓑ Ⓒ Ⓓ Ⓔ

4 Ⓐ Ⓑ Ⓒ Ⓓ Ⓔ   8 Ⓐ Ⓑ Ⓒ Ⓓ Ⓔ   12 Ⓐ Ⓑ Ⓒ Ⓓ Ⓔ   16 Ⓐ Ⓑ Ⓒ Ⓓ Ⓔ   20 Ⓐ Ⓑ Ⓒ Ⓓ Ⓔ

SECTION VII: READING COMPREHENSION

1 Ⓐ Ⓑ Ⓒ Ⓓ Ⓔ   5 Ⓐ Ⓑ Ⓒ Ⓓ Ⓔ   9 Ⓐ Ⓑ Ⓒ Ⓓ Ⓔ   13 Ⓐ Ⓑ Ⓒ Ⓓ Ⓔ   17 Ⓐ Ⓑ Ⓒ Ⓓ Ⓔ

2 Ⓐ Ⓑ Ⓒ Ⓓ Ⓔ   6 Ⓐ Ⓑ Ⓒ Ⓓ Ⓔ   10 Ⓐ Ⓑ Ⓒ Ⓓ Ⓔ   14 Ⓐ Ⓑ Ⓒ Ⓓ Ⓔ   18 Ⓐ Ⓑ Ⓒ Ⓓ Ⓔ

3 Ⓐ Ⓑ Ⓒ Ⓓ Ⓔ   7 Ⓐ Ⓑ Ⓒ Ⓓ Ⓔ   11 Ⓐ Ⓑ Ⓒ Ⓓ Ⓔ   15 Ⓐ Ⓑ Ⓒ Ⓓ Ⓔ   19 Ⓐ Ⓑ Ⓒ Ⓓ Ⓔ

4 Ⓐ Ⓑ Ⓒ Ⓓ Ⓔ   8 Ⓐ Ⓑ Ⓒ Ⓓ Ⓔ   12 Ⓐ Ⓑ Ⓒ Ⓓ Ⓔ   16 Ⓐ Ⓑ Ⓒ Ⓓ Ⓔ   20 Ⓐ Ⓑ Ⓒ Ⓓ Ⓔ

SECTION I: READING RECALL

35 Minutes
30 Questions

DIRECTIONS: You are allowed 15 minutes to closely read the following passages. Afterwards you will be asked to recall certain ideas and facts about the passages. You are not allowed to refer back to the passages.

Passage 1

The job of attracting the right young people into business will be facilitated if businessmen and the world at large understand the real benefits of an education designed to prepare young people for business and the fact that such an education does breed the broad-gauge man who can stand with feet planted in both Column A and Column B. The continued success of our business democracy requires no less.

Education for business must avoid the purely intellectual for something with a more pragmatic focus. And what is wrong with an education that has a pragmatic focus? Plato—in his *Republic*—was far more pragmatic than we ever think of being.

But even if education for business should be unashamedly pragmatic, it cannot be an end in itself. Any young person entering management, from school, regardless of what degree he has earned, is going to have to continue his education throughout his life. Things are happening too fast today for anyone to feel fully educated after four years, or six years, or ten years! What he will have to do is to be retrained or retooled as the years go by. The kind of education needed is that which opens the young person's eyes to the need for a lifetime of study and gives him the foundations on which his continued study can be based.

Rather than being narrowly vocational, modern business education in many ways leads in the liberality of its approach. Beginning with courses in human relations, and ending up permeating all its activities, is the concept of participative management. Why? Because as business becomes more scientific, more intellectual, more complex, no one man can have the total knowledge required to make sound decisions arbitrarily. When things become so highly complex, group management is the logical answer.

It is in modern business education that this type of leadership is taught and researched. This is of crucial importance to the well-being of our nation, because if the leaders of our business democracy cannot meet the challenge of the collective economy which boasts it will bury us, we may indeed be buried—and not just economically. Modern business education teaches how to lead without a sacrifice of freedom; how to exercise control and direction, while at the same time respecting opinions of others more qualified in highly specialized areas, as well as respecting their essential dignity as humans; and how to learn to lead by freeing the latent potentialities of gifted advisers—not by stifling them.

Perhaps it will be the business schools of this nation which will remind American education not only that democracy and strong leadership are *not* contradictory terms, but that leadership can and *must* be taught. No other part of our university system seemingly is paying much, if any, attention to *doing* something about, rather than talking about, education for democratic leadership. To some faculties, leadership itself is a jingoistic word harking back echoes of Teddy Roosevelt. Not so to the faculties of our modern business schools—and not so to the masses of American students who are revolting against the lofty disengagement of many academics from the complex—and often unclean—realities of our world.

Thus business will be serving the nation's interest as well as its own—*if* it recognizes that the *right* kind of young people it needs for tomorrow's managers are the brighter students who are not purely intellectual, or purely pragmatic; *if* it offers them a career that will satisfy their values; and *if* it does what it can to encourage their development.

Passage 2

While the Soviet regime has accepted monetary incentives and self-interest as key motivating forces for both managers and workers for decades, the Chinese regime takes a less sanguine·view toward such rewards. During the 1952–1957 period, great stress was placed on monetary incentives for spurring productivity. Many workers were put on piece-rate schemes, and enterprise managers as well as party officials were paid bonuses primarily in relation to gross output results. This led to some complaints in the press and journals about undesirable managerial practices similar to those found in Russia.

During the Great Leap Forward of 1958–1961, the regime tried to wipe out self-interest—and hence monetary incentives—as a key motivating force. With the Reds in charge, it was felt that they could organize and motivate the work force to respond to nonmaterial stimuli. When the experts once again gained favor in 1961, worker as well as managerial incentives were also revived. However, profit rather than gross output became the key success indicator. Profit could be a reasonably meaningful measure of efficiency, it was felt, since enterprise managers were given greater independence over product decisions, marketing, and procurement, and more say in the pricing of their products. By 1964 some articles had begun to appear about the ideological conflict involved in stressing profit as the key success indicator and in emphasizing monetary incentives and personal gain. That was at a time when economic conditions were once again favorable and when China and Russia were engaged in an open, heated feud about proper ideology and revisionism.

I found during my visits to 38 Chinese factories that piece-rate incentives for workers had been completely abolished. However, at about 80 percent of the factories, workers could still earn monthly or quarterly bonuses. And, interestingly enough, such bonuses were not based solely upon productivity; politics and helping co-workers were also key criteria.

Passage 3

Middle level managers, such as department heads and workshop directors, can still earn bonuses at about 80 percent of the factories surveyed. It is the middle managers who are usually the experts because of their formal education and training. (By contrast, the director of a factory is likely to be more Red than expert, and the vice directors are typically a mixture of Reds and experts.) For middle managers to earn bonuses, the fulfillment of certain enterprise targets is a required condition at only about 20 percent of the factories; they are more commonly evaluated for their "contributions" rather than on the basis of overall enterprise performance. Where enterprise targets have to be fulfilled for bonuses to be paid, in most cases profit is not the only success indicator. Quantity and value of production, sales, production costs, labor productivity, and/or quality are other key success indicators at various enterprises.

During the past few years, directors, vice directors, and party secretaries have not been eligible to receive bonuses at any enterprises. Can top-level enterprise managers (or middle managers, too, for that matter) be adequately motivated over time to perform efficiently without bonuses? I doubt it. At present there seems to be considerable dedication, zeal, patriotism, and other nonmaterial stimuli motivating many of them to do the best job they can. But these stimuli cannot do the job alone for long. Compounding the difficulty is the fact that salaries, powers, and living conditions of top managers are relatively low in relation to those of their subordinates.

Just as the nonmanager is dependent on his boss for motivational opportunities, so is the manager dependent on his boss for conditions of motivation which have meaning at his level. Since the motivation of an employee at any level is strongly related to the supervisory style of his immediate boss, sound motivation patterns must begin at the top. Being closer to the policy-making level, the manager has more opportunity to understand and relate his work to company goals. However, high position alone does not guarantee motivation or self-actualization.

Motivation for the manager, as well as the nonmanager, is usually both a consequence and a symptom of effective job performance. Job success is dependent on cyclical conditions created by interpersonal competence, meaningful goals, and helpful systems. After sustained conditioning in the developmental cycle, an individual has amazing capacity and incentive to remain in it. Moreover, if forced into the reductive cycle, unless he has pathological needs to remain there, organizational conditions must be remarkably and consistently bad to suppress his return to the developmental cycle.

Sustained confinement of a large percentage of the work force in the reductive cycle is symptomatic of organizational illness. It is usually a culmination of a chain of events beginning with top management, and is reversible only by changes at the top. Consequences of reductive conditions such as militant unionism and other forms of reactive behavior usually provoke management into defensive and manipulative behavior which only reinforces the reductive cycle. The vicarious pleasure sought by the rank and file through seeing the management giant felled by their union is a poor substitute for the self-actualization of being a whole person doing a meaningful job, but, in the absence of motivational opportunities, it is an understandable compromise.

The seeds of concerted reactive behavior are often brought to the job from broadly shared frustrations arising from social injustice, economic deprivation, and moral decadence either to sprout in a reductive climate or become infertile in a developmental climate. Hence, the unionization of a work group is usually precipitated by management failure to provide opportunities for employees to achieve personal goals through the achievement of organization goals. Organizations survive these failures only because most other companies are equally handicapped by the same failures.

Management failures in supervision do not, of course, stem from intentional malice. They may result, in part, from a lingering tradition of "scientific management" which fractionated tasks and "protected" employees from the need to think, and perpetrated management systems based on automaton conformity. But more often such failures stem from the manager's insensitivity to the needs and perceptions of others, particularly from his inability to see himself as others see him.

Insensitivity or the inability to empathize is manifested not only as interpersonal incompetence, but also as the failure to provide meaningful goals, the misuse of management systems, or a combination of both. Style of supervision, then, is largely an expression of the personality characteristics and mental health of the manager, and his potential for inducing developmental or reductive cyclical reactions.

QUESTIONS

DIRECTIONS: You have 20 minutes to answer the following questions based upon the preceding passages. You are not to refer back to the passages.

Passage 1

1. According to the author, the business community can be best served by the student who is

   (A) practical
   (B) intellectual
   (C) a Liberal Arts major

(D) practical as well as intellectual
(E) jingoistic

2. The passage implies that

   (A) a business education is more easily obtained than a Liberal Arts education
   (B) business schools are in the forefront in the matter of liberalizing curricula
   (C) a Liberal Arts education is superior to a Technical education
   (D) education is of little importance to success in the business world
   (E) business is not challenging to most students

3. According to the passage, the economic health of our country depends mainly on

   (A) businessmen
   (B) business school faculties
   (C) government supervision
   (D) the general public
   (E) group management

4. According to the author

   (A) business is an end in itself
   (B) the college-trained business leader should continue his education throughout life
   (C) the role of the businessman in business education has not been clearly defined
   (D) Plato disengaged himself from the realities of life
   (E) business education is essential to success in the business world

5. Which of the following describes business education today?

   I. Interest in human relations
   II. Realization of individual limitations
   III. Concept of participative management

   (A) I only
   (B) II only
   (C) II and III only
   (D) I and III only
   (E) I, II, and III

6. It is obvious that

(A) our business leaders are incapable of competing with the collective economy system
(B) things are going along at an unwholesome rate of speed
(C) business is growing less complex
(D) Teddy Roosevelt is favorably regarded by the author
(E) students prefer that their professors take an active role in solving world problems

7. The author views the business schools of this country as a prod to education to see to it that

(A) the ability to lead must be part of the curriculum
(B) business education is just as important as any other type of education
(C) professors get off their "high horses" and teach realistically
(D) a new emphasis is to be placed upon innovation
(E) businessmen must not be disregarded in what they have to offer educators

8. The author indicates that

(A) business methods have drastically changed in the last decade
(B) there has been too much government interference in business
(C) the larger universities are far too impersonal in their dealings with students
(D) the importance of vocational education is much over-rated
(E) business success, in the final analysis, spells success for the entire nation

9. Businessmen, according to the passage, must recognize that

(A) they must set an example for young people
(B) greater financial support of business schools is necessary
(C) business schools must be autonomous to function properly
(D) a primary result of a business education should be the development of individuals with a wide range
(E) government intervention in business schools is inevitable

10. The most appropriate title for this passage is

(A) Businessmen and Business Schools
(B) Youth and Business
(C) Business Schools
(D) Bright Students and Business
(E) The Relationship between Business Education and Business

Passage 2

11. The "Great Leap Forward" period was characterized by

(A) the emergence of intellectual leadership
(B) the attempt to eliminate the stimulus of money as a spur to production
(C) a series of one-year plans
(D) the acceptance of some capitalistic innovations
(E) a wave of corruption among the managers

12. During the period 1958–1961, who was in charge of China's production facilities?

(A) the workers
(B) Soviet engineers
(C) Chinese experts
(D) the proletariat
(E) the Communist Party

13. The feud between China and Russia, which came out into the open in 1964, concerned itself with

(A) monetary vs. non-material incentives
(B) trading with the West
(C) ideology
(D) military matters
(E) border disputes

14. In the period 1952–1957 in China, which of the following were incentives for encouraging greater production?

I. Piece-rate schemes
II. Bonuses to managers in relation to gross output
III. Bonuses to managers in relation to profits

(A) I only
(B) II only
(C) III only
(D) I and II only
(E) II and III only

15. The author's attitude toward production techniques now used by the Chinese is

    (A) sanguine
    (B) gloomy
    (C) indifferent
    (D) sarcastic
    (E) biased

16. When the writer visited the factories in China, he found that

    (A) the factories were badly in need of repair
    (B) most workers were still offered monetary incentives
    (C) the level of intelligence among the workers was high
    (D) politics played no part in the granting of bonuses
    (E) most workers were discontented

17. In 1961, the major change from previous incentive plans was the emphasis on

    (A) profits
    (B) output
    (C) better living conditions
    (D) working comforts
    (E) social opportunities

18. Who is usually the factory expert in China's economic system?

    (A) the director
    (B) the middle manager
    (C) the party secretary
    (D) the vice director
    (E) whoever proves that he has the greatest ability

19. Who cannot receive a bonus in any enterprise?

    I. the director
    II. the worker
    III. the middle manager

    (A) I only
    (B) II only
    (C) III only
    (D) I and III only
    (E) I, II, and III

Passage 3

20. According to the passage, where enterprise targets have to be fulfilled for bonuses to be paid to middle management, which of the following are success indicators?

    I. Profits
    II. Sales
    III. Production costs

    (A) I only
    (B) II only
    (C) III only
    (D) I and II only
    (E) I, II, and III

21. Managers and other employees are most often dependent upon whom for their motivation?

    (A) wives
    (B) owner of the firm
    (C) their union
    (D) their fellow-workers
    (E) themselves

22. The writer is especially critical of

    (A) automation
    (B) unions
    (C) employees
    (D) personnel
    (E) management

23. A reductive cycle is one in which

    (A) an employer attempts to reduce costs
    (B) the work-force is gradually reduced in number
    (C) costs decrease as a firm gains experience
    (D) a union, step-by-step, takes over control of a business
    (E) there is less productive effort on the part of employees

24. The passage brings out that job success is contingent upon cyclical conditions created by which of the following?

    I. interpersonal competence
    II. meaningful goals
    III. monetary rewards

(A) I only
(B) II only
(C) I and II only
(D) I and III only
(E) I, II, and III

25. If a substantial number of the employees remain in the reductive cycle, one may assume that

(A) the organization is enjoying increased business
(B) the personnel department has been functioning effectively
(C) the boss is not giving sufficient attention to the business
(D) there is an unwholesome behavior pattern among the employees
(E) they belong to unions

26. Which of the following is likely to result initially from reductive conditions in an organization?

   I. militant unionism
  II. pension plans
 III. higher wages

(A) I only
(B) II only
(C) I and II only
(D) I and III only
(E) I, II, and III

27. The passage indicates that the unionization of a work group is most commonly brought about by management's failure to provide

(A) opportunities for the workers to realize individual objectives by way of group objectives
(B) opportunities for the workers to achieve a feeling of self-identification
(C) more pleasant working surroundings including modern conveniences available both at

their work and during rest-periods and lunch-periods
(D) greater fringe benefits including more holidays and health insurance
(E) opportunities for socialization during working hours as well as after work

28. According to the author, management failures in supervision are mainly attributable to

(A) currying favor with the boss
(B) a soft-hearted attitude
(C) ignorance
(D) lack of consideration
(E) inability to gain respect

29. The style of supervision is

   I. an expression of the manager's personality
  II. an expression of the manager's mental health
 III. an expression of the manager's own job skills

(A) I only
(B) II only
(C) III only
(D) I and II only
(E) II and III only

30. Employees will get together to seek an improvement of conditions because of dissatisfactions stemming from

   I. social injustice
  II. economic deprivation
 III. moral decadence

(A) I only
(B) II only
(C) I and II only
(D) I and III only
(E) I, II, and III

Stop

END OF SECTION I. IF YOU HAVE ANY TIME LEFT, GO OVER YOUR WORK IN THIS SECTION ONLY. DO NOT WORK IN ANY OTHER SECTION OF THE TEST. WHEN YOUR TIME IS UP, GO ON TO THE NEXT SECTION.

SECTION II: PROBLEM SOLVING

40 Minutes
30 Questions

DIRECTIONS: For each of the following questions, select the choice which best answers the question or completes the statement.

1. Of the following, the one that is *not* a meaning of ⅔ is

   (A) 1 of the 3 equal parts of 2
   (B) 2 of the 3 equal parts of 1
   (C) 2 divided by 3
   (D) a ratio of 2 to 3
   (E) 4 of the 6 equal parts of 2

2. If the average weight of boys of John's age and height is 105 lbs. and if John weighs 110% of average, then John weighs

   (A) 110 lbs.
   (B) 110.5 lbs.
   (C) 106.05 lbs.
   (D) 126 lbs.
   (E) 115½ lbs.

3. On a house plan on which 2 inches represents 5 feet, the length of a room measures 7½ inches. The actual length of the room is

   (A) 12½ feet
   (B) 15¾ feet
   (C) 17½ feet
   (D) 18¾ feet
   (E) 13¾ feet

Questions 4–7 are to be answered with reference to the following diagram.

The figure shown in the diagram is made of pieces of plastic, each piece half a centimeter thick and one centimeter wide.

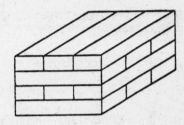

4. What is the volume of the figure?

   (A) 12 cu cm
   (B) 18 cu cm
   (C) 27 cu cm
   (D) 36 cu cm
   (E) cannot be determined from the given information

5. How many pieces are touched by at least 8 other pieces?

   (A) 1
   (B) 2
   (C) 3
   (D) 4
   (E) 5

6. If all the pieces had been cut from one strip of plastic, how long a piece of ½ cm × 1 cm material would have been required?

   (A) 15 cm
   (B) 18 cm
   (C) 27 cm
   (D) 12 cm
   (E) 36 cm

7. What is the total surface in square centimeters of all the pieces?

(A) 10
(B) 18
(C) 72
(D) 120
(E) 42

8. ABCD is a parallelogram, and DE = EC

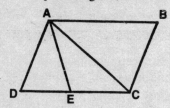

What is the ratio of triangle ADE to the area of the parallelogram?

(A) 1:2
(B) 1:3
(C) 2:5
(D) 1:4
(E) cannot be determined from the given information

9. If pencils are bought at 35 cents per dozen and sold at 3 for 10 cents, the total profit on 5½ dozen is

(A) 25 cents
(B) 27½ cents
(C) 28½ cents
(D) 31½ cents
(E) 35 cents

10. Of the following, the one which may be used correctly to compute 26 × 3½ is

(A) (26 × 30) + (26 × ½)
(B) (20 × 3) + (6 × 3½)
(C) (20 × 3½) + (6 × 3)
(D) (20 × 3) + (26 × ½) + (6 × 3½)
(E) (26 × ½) + (20 × 3) + (6 × 3)

11. It costs 31 cents a square foot to lay linoleum. To lay 20 square yards of linoleum it will cost

(A) $16.20
(B) $18.60
(C) $62.80
(D) $62.00
(E) $55.80

12. A piece of wood 35 feet, 6 inches long was used

to make 4 shelves of equal length. The length of each shelf was

(A) 9 feet, 1½ inches
(B) 8 feet, 10½ inches
(C) 7 feet, 10½ inches
(D) 7 feet, 1½ inches
(E) 6 feet, 8½ inches

13. A class punch ball team won 2 games and lost 10. The fraction of its games won is correctly expressed as

(A) ¹/₆
(B) ¹/₅
(C) ⁴/₅
(D) ⁵/₆
(E) ¹/₁₀

14. 10 to the fifth power may correctly be expressed as

(A) 10 × 5
(B) 5^{10}
(C) 5√10
(D) 10 × 10 × 10 × 10 × 10
(E) $10^{10} \div 10^2$

15. The total cost of 3½ pounds of meat at $1.10 a pound and 20 oranges at $.60 a dozen will be

(A) $4.65
(B) $4.85
(C) $5.05
(D) $4.45
(E) none of these

Questions 16–18 are to be answered with reference to the following number system:

The following symbols are used in the same fashion as Roman numerals are used.

I   = |
V   =   ∩
X   =   ?
L   =   ⌠
C   =   ₢
D   =   ⊝
M   =   ⅄

For example, ?|∩ = 14.

Thousands are indicated by drawing a line over the symbol. For example, $\overline{\text{ʼ}}$ = 5000.

16. $\overline{\text{ʔ}}$ 0 ʃ equals?

(A) 1915
(B) 10,315
(C) 10,915
(D) 10,150
(E) 11,050

17. $4(10^4) + 5(10^3) + 4(100)$ is represented by

(A) ʒ ₵₵₵₵ ∩
(B) $\overline{\text{????}}$ ₵∩
(C) ∩ʃ ₵₵₵₵
(D) ??? 0 ʃ
(E) ʔʃ ₵ ∩∩

18. Select the correct expression for $\overline{\text{ʒ ᑫ ||||}}$

(A) $1,000,000 + 100 + 2,000 + 100,000 + 2$
(B) $2(10^6) + 2(10^4) + 10 + 1,000 + 2$
(C) $2(100) + 2(10^3) + 5(10) + 10(1,000,000) + 2$
(D) $10^6 + 50(10,000) + 2,000 + 2$
(E) $100 \times 10^5 + 5 \times 10^5 + 20 \times 10^2 + 2 \times 10^1$

19. The total number of eighths in two wholes and three fourths is

(A) 11
(B) 14
(C) 19
(D) 22
(E) 24

20. The difference between one hundred five thousand eighty-four and ninety-three thousand seven hundred nine is

(A) 37,215
(B) 12,131
(C) 56,294
(D) 56,375
(E) 11,375

21. A recipe for a cake calls for 2½ cups of milk and 3 cups of flour. With this recipe, a cake was baked using 14 cups of flour. How many cups of milk were required?

(A) 10 ¹/₃
(B) 10 ³/₄
(C) 11
(D) 11 ³/₅
(E) 11 ²/₃

Questions 22–24 are to be answered with reference to the following explanation and diagram.

A cube may be rotated about any one of its three axes, a, b, or c. The rotation of the cube 90° about "a" in the direction of the arrow may be denoted by a; the rotation of the cube 90° about "b" in the direction of the arrow by b; and rotation of the cube 90° about "c" in the direction of the arrow by c.

If operation a is performed twice, the whole operation may be indicated as a^2; if three times, as a^3; etc. Similarly, the same holds for b and c. If operation b is performed, and then c, the result is bc.

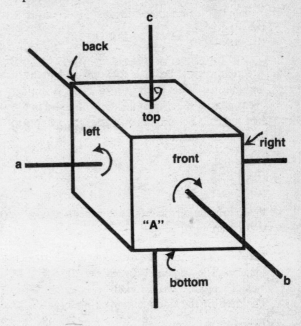

22. After the operation a^3b, where is face "A"?

(A) back
(B) bottom
(C) left
(D) top
(E) right

23. Where was the face which is on the bottom after the operation bc before the operation?

(A) back
(B) left
(C) right
(D) top
(E) bottom

24. Which operation leaves the cube in the same position as it is after $a^2b^2c^2$?

(A) $(bc)^2$
(B) b^3c^3
(C) c^4
(D) c^3ba^3
(E) $(ab)^3$

25. What would be the marked price of an article if the cost was $12.60 and the gain was 10% of the selling price?

(A) $13.66
(B) $13.86
(C) $11.34
(D) $12.48
(E) $14.00

26. A certain type of board is sold only in lengths of multiples of 2 feet from 6 ft. to 24 ft. A builder needs a large quantity of this type of board in 5½ foot lengths. For minimum waste, the lengths to be ordered should be

(A) 6 ft.
(B) 12 ft.
(C) 24 ft.
(D) 22 ft.
(E) 18 ft.

27. The tiles in the floor of a bathroom are 15/16 inch squares. The cement between the tiles is 1/16 inch. There are 3240 individual tiles in this floor. The area of the floor is approximately

(A) 225 sq. yds.
(B) 2.5 sq. yds.
(C) 250 sq. ft.
(D) 22.5 sq. yds.
(E) 225 sq. ft.

28. A group of 15 children received the following scores in a reading test: 36 36 30 30 30 29 27 27 27 26 26 26 26 18 13. What was the median score?

(A) 25.4
(B) 26
(C) 27
(D) 30
(E) 24.5

Questions 29–30 are to be answered with reference to the following diagram and explanation.

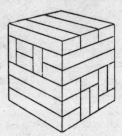

The 6-inch cube shown in the diagram is made up of pieces each 1 inch thick, 2 inches wide, and 6 inches long. Each block is painted in three colors, red, blue, and yellow according to its position as shown in the diagram. The top side of each block is red. The bottom side of each piece is blue, and the vertical sides are yellow.

29. How many $1 \times 2 \times 6$ blocks are there in the 6-inch cube?

(A) 15
(B) 18
(C) 27
(D) 36
(E) 24

30. How many square inches of block are painted blue?

(A) 150
(B) 316
(C) 210
(D) 256
(E) 180

Stop

END OF SECTION II. IF YOU HAVE ANY TIME LEFT, GO OVER YOUR WORK IN THIS SECTION ONLY. DO NOT WORK IN ANY OTHER SECTION OF THE TEST. WHEN YOUR TIME IS UP, GO ON TO THE NEXT SECTION.

SECTION III: PRACTICAL BUSINESS JUDGMENT

20 Minutes
20 Questions

DIRECTIONS: This section consists of a reading selection which details a business situation followed by two sets of questions, data evaluation and data application. In the first set, data evaluation, you will be asked to classify certain of the facts presented in the passage on the basis of their importance. The second set, data application, will test your grasp of specific details of the situation.

Handborn, Inc., a major publisher, is offered the autobiography of a fabulous and mysterious business tycoon. However, there is a question as to whether or not the offer is genuine, and whether this is the kind of book Handborn should publish. If the autobiography is truly the billionaire's life story, a great deal of money can be made. The logical step would be to approach the billionaire directly to ascertain if he did indeed write the book, but the go-between warns that if this is done, Handborn will be turned down. Should the publisher make a contract with the go-between?

Handborn, Inc., is one of the world's largest publishers. A great part of its sales revenue is derived from scientific textbooks and magazines. Its trade book division, which publishes novels and general non-fiction, is a recently organized branch of the eighty-year-old company. This division has been unprofitable through most of its existence, although high hopes are held for it.

Peter Handborn, who has been president for two years, listens carefully to a proposal made by John Robinson, head of the trade book division, at an executive editorial meeting where major projects are approved or turned down. Robinson states that William Milton, a Handborn author of four novels and three non-fiction books, has established contact with Lawrence Magnerson, a brilliant business tycoon. The eccentric Magnerson has tentatively agreed to allow Handborn to publish his autobiography, provided that Milton does the actual writing based on taped interviews between the author and the business executive. Magnerson has shunned interviews and any public contact for almost two decades. He has become a

"man of mystery," although his fabulous business deals have been national news.

Milton is to receive $100,000 as an advance against royalties. Magnerson is to receive $250,000 as an advance against royalties. The royalty will be 15 percent of the price of the book. Handborn also must share on a fifty-fifty basis all subsidiary revenue, such as would result from the publication of excerpts in magazines, etc., with Milton and Magnerson. According to Milton, the billionaire will only deal with him and no one else.

Robinson asserts that such a book would be a coup for Handborn. Robinson has had informal contacts with *National,* a news magazine with a very large circulation; Twinights, a major book club; and Vale, a very large paperback publisher. Representatives of these firms have expressed strong interest in the Magnerson autobiography. Payments to Handborn from these companies would be substantial and would probably pay for the printing of the book. Robinson predicts that 100,000 copies of the Handborn edition would be sold, adding that this figure is probably low. An excellent profit could be realized.

Robinson is questioned on the authenticity of Milton's tale in light of Magnerson's obvious distaste for the public spotlight. Robinson says he considers Milton to be completely honest, an opinion he has formed over years of acquaintance with the writer. But why, Robinson is asked, cannot Handborn deal with Magnerson directly? He replies that Magnerson apparently wishes to keep his contacts with the outside world to a bare minimum. According to Milton, the billionaire would scuttle the deal if Handborn attempted to meet with him.

Robinson produces a handwritten agreement, signed "Lawrence Magnerson," which authorizes Milton as his sole agent. The note has been checked by a leading handwriting expert who, after checking samples of Magnerson's writing of 20 years ago, has declared it to be authentic.

Peter Handborn considers the matter carefully. On the negative side, there is some doubt as to whether the manuscript is indeed Magnerson's. Moreover, this is not the type of book that Handborn would ordinarily publish. It smacks a little of sensationalism which might reflect upon the conservative, solid image of Handborn, Inc.

On the other hand, as Robinson said, publication certainly would be a coup. Profits are almost guaranteed. Robinson seems to have taken adequate precautions concerning the validity of Milton's story.

Peter Handborn thinks about contacting Magnerson directly or through the tycoon's executives or friends. This he rejects because Magnerson might call off the deal and go to another publisher. He defers the decision until further proof of authenticity is forthcoming. Too much delay might result in the book going to another publisher.

He finally decides to publish without reaching Magnerson directly, persuaded by the available documents and the confidence inspired by Mr. Milton. Despite misgivings and the problems involved, Peter Handborn approves the project.

DATA EVALUATION

DIRECTIONS: Based on your analysis of the business situation, classify each of the following elements in one of five categories. Mark:

(A) if the element is a MAJOR OBJECTIVE in making the decision; that is, the outcome or result sought by the decision maker.

(B) if the element is a MAJOR FACTOR in arriving at the decision; that is, a consideration explicitly mentioned in the passage that is basic in determining the decision.

(C) if the element is a MINOR FACTOR in making the decision; that is, a secondary consideration in determining the decision.

(D) if the element is a MAJOR ASSUMPTION made in deliberating; that is, a supposition or projection made by the decision maker before weighing the variables.

(E) if the element is an UNIMPORTANT ISSUE in getting to the point; that is, a factor that is insignificant or not immediately relevant to the situation.

1. The trade division will realize a profit from the Magnerson book.

2. The company can pay the advance.

3. The subsidiary rights would bring in substantial revenue.

4. Milton might not be telling the truth.

5. Handborn would sell at least 100,000 copies.

6. The public is interested in Magnerson.

7. Magnerson's handwriting on the agreement seems to be authentic.

8. The trade division has been unprofitable.

9. If Handborn circumvents Milton and contacts Magnerson directly, the deal might be called off.

10. Delay might mean that Magnerson's autobiography might be published by another company.

DATA APPLICATION

DIRECTIONS: Based on your understanding of the business situation, answer the following questions testing your comprehension of the information supplied in the passage. For each question, select the choice which best answers the question or completes the statement.

11. Which of the following would be the strongest factor in persuading Peter Handborn to publish Magnerson's autobiography?

(A) He desires to make the book division profitable

(B) He would like to enhance Handborn's public image

(C) He would like to develop a new line of books

(D) He desires the opportunity to develop good subsidiary relationships with other companies

(E) He desires to solidify his position as president

12. Robinson's belief in Milton's integrity is based on

(A) Milton's record as an author of several books for Handborn

(B) Robinson's opinion after working with Milton for several years

(C) Milton's producing an agreement between himself and Magnerson

(D) Milton's receipt of a minor part of the total royalty advance

(E) Milton coming to Handborn rather than to another publisher with a stronger trade book division

13. It was decided that Magnerson could not be approached directly by Handborn because

    (A) Milton wouldn't allow it
    (B) Robinson strongly opposed it
    (C) Magnerson might feel that Handborn doubted the authenticity of the manuscript
    (D) it would be difficult to establish contact with the recluse
    (E) Magnerson might then refuse to allow the book to be published by Handborn

14. What are the terms of the subsidiary rights of the proposal being considered by Handborn, Inc.?

    (A) Fifty percent of revenue from this market must be given to Milton and Magnerson.
    (B) The author and the tycoon would receive all the money.
    (C) The total revenue from this source would be in excess of a million dollars.
    (D) More than half would be given directly to Magnerson.
    (E) The revenue given to Magnerson and Milton would be counted as part of the advance against royalties

15. Concern over the possibility that Magnerson's autobiography is not authentic arises because

    (A) the only proof is the agreement between Milton and Magnerson
    (B) the figure that Magnerson asks as an advance is surprisingly low
    (C) the tone of the autobiography does not sound authentic
    (D) Handborn has never dealt with an intermediary before
    (E) Magnerson has long avoided publicity concerning himself

16. Robinson believes that subsidiary rights contracts would

    (A) be the main source of revenue
    (B) be difficult to negotiate
    (C) probably cover the printing costs of the book
    (D) be dangerous to accept because of the possibility that the manuscript might not be authentic

    (E) not be desirable since they might hurt the sales of the Handborn edition

17. The agreement between Magnerson and Milton states that

    (A) only Handborn should be the publisher
    (B) the manuscript will be edited from taped interviews
    (C) Milton is Magnerson's sole agent
    (D) the terms of the agreement will be kept secret
    (E) Milton is to receive an advance of $100,000

18. Robinson believes that the sales of the Handborn edition of the book

    (A) would be less than 50,000 copies
    (B) would be more than a million copies
    (C) should not be a factor in deciding whether to publish the book or not
    (D) would be about 100,000 copies at a conservative estimate
    (E) cannot be estimated

19. One reason Handborn, Inc. might consider publishing Magnerson's autobiography is that

    (A) Magnerson's life is the kind of subject that falls within the general Handborn publishing program
    (B) Magnerson is an enigma whose mystery is fascinating to the public
    (C) Magnerson will contribute a substantial amount toward publication costs
    (D) Magnerson has been the subject of several successful books
    (E) Magnerson owns the companies that would pay for the subsidiary rights

20. Handborn derives most of its income from

    (A) specialized magazines
    (B) novels and general non-fiction
    (C) elementary school textbooks
    (D) scientific and technical textbooks and magazines
    (E) subsidiary rights

Stop

END OF SECTION III. IF YOU HAVE ANY TIME LEFT, GO OVER YOUR WORK IN THIS SECTION ONLY. DO NOT WORK IN ANY OTHER SECTION OF THE TEST. WHEN YOUR TIME IS UP, GO ON TO THE NEXT SECTION.

SECTION IV: DATA SUFFICIENCY

25 Minutes
25 Questions

DIRECTIONS: Each question below is followed by two numbered facts. You are to determine whether the data given in the statements is sufficient for answering the question. Use the data given, plus your knowledge of math and everyday facts, to choose between the five possible answers. Mark

(A) if statement 1 alone is sufficient to answer the question, but statement 2 alone is not sufficient.
(B) if statement 2 alone is sufficient to answer the question, but statement 1 alone is not sufficient.
(C) if both statements together are needed to answer the question, but neither statement alone is sufficient.
(D) if either statement by itself is sufficient to answer the question asked.
(E) if not enough facts are given to answer the question.

1. Is Denise older than Andrea?

   (1) Denise's father and Andrea's father were born the same year.
   (2) Andrea's grandfather is 5 years older than Denise's grandfather.

2. Is A less than B?

   (1) $A^2 = 25$
   (2) $B = 6$

3. How much did Edna spend for dress material?

   (1) The material cost 25 cents per square yard.
   (2) If she bought three times as much material, she could have made four more dresses.

4. Does Devin weigh more than 180 lbs?

   (1) If Devin loses 10 lbs., he will be less than 180 lbs.
   (2) If Devin loses 10 lbs., he will weigh less than 180 lbs. but more than 170 lbs.

5. What is the value of x?

   (1) $3x - y = 24$
   (2) $x + y = 10$

6. How many days will it take 12 men to paint 12 rooms?

   (1) Any group of 4 men can paint 3 rooms per day.
   (2) Each man can paint three-fourths of a room per day.

7. Find the value of a + b + c.

   (1) $abc = 0$
   (2) $a + b = 4$

8. If ⊙ is one of the operations addition or multiplication, which is it?

   (1) $0 \odot 0 = 0$
   (2) $0 \odot 1 = 1$

9. In the figure below, are lines A and B parallel?

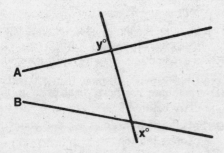

   (1) $x = y$
   (2) $x + y = 180°$

10. There are four plateaus on a mountain labeled A, B, C, and D.

    A is 2,200 feet above the ground.
    B is 600 feet higher than A.
    D is 1,000 feet higher than C.
    Is B higher than C?

174

(1) D is 2,600 feet above the ground.

(2) D is 400 feet higher than A.

11. If triangle ABC lies wholly within square DEFG, what is the area of the region of DEFG not overlapped by △ABC?

(1) No point on △ABC touches any point on sq. DEFG.

(2) The area of △ABC is 20 and the area of sq. DEFG is 50.

12. What is the distance from city A to city C?

(1) City A is 60 miles from city B.

(2) City B is 40 miles from city C.

13. ABCD is a square. Find the perimeter of QRST.

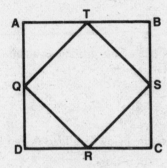

(1) The area of ABCD is 16.

(2) Q, R, S, and T are the mid-points of the four sides of ABCD.

14. If A is positive, is B more than 100 percent of A?

(1) B = ⅔A

(2) B = A − 4

15. If Y is a member of the set of numbers {8,12,15,16,20} what number is Y?

(1) Y is a multiple of 4.

(2) Y is a multiple of 5.

16. Is A ÷ 5 even?

(1) A ÷ 15 is an integer

(2) A ÷ 10 is not odd

17. What is the value of $\dfrac{x - y}{y}$?

(1) $\dfrac{x}{y} = 2$

(2) $y = 4$

18. In the two triangles below, what is the value of p + q + r + s?

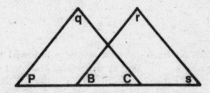

(1) p + q = r + s

(2) B + C = 90°

19. In a class of 28 students, how many boys scored over 90% on the last geometry test?

(1) Exactly 5 girls in the class scored over 90% on the geometry test.

(2) One-fourth of the class scored over 90% on the geometry test.

20. What is the average of w, x, y, and z?

(1) w + x + y − 20 = z + 4

(2) 3(w + x + y) = 63 and z = 3

21. How many members belong to club A?

(1) All the members of club A also belong to club B.

(2) There are exactly 40 members of club B.

22. What is the value of $a^2 - b^2$?

(1) a − b = 4

(2) a + b = 6

23. Find the length of XY.

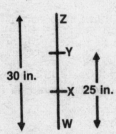

(1) XZ = 18 in.

(2) XW = 12 in.

24. In △PQR, is the measure of ∠ Q greater than 90°?

   (1) The measure of ∠ R is 100°
   (2) The measure of ∠ P is 30°

25. In the figure below, K ∥ L. Is <x ≅ <y?

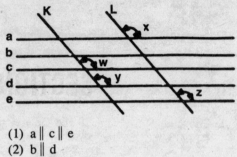

   (1) a ∥ c ∥ e
   (2) b ∥ d

Stop

END OF SECTION IV. IF YOU HAVE ANY TIME LEFT, GO OVER YOUR WORK IN THIS SECTION ONLY. DO NOT WORK IN ANY OTHER SECTION OF THE TEST. WHEN YOUR TIME IS UP, GO ON TO THE NEXT SECTION.

SECTION V: VERBAL ABILITIES

15 Minutes
25 Questions

ANALOGIES

DIRECTIONS: The following questions consist of a related pair of words or phrases, and five lettered pairs of words or phrases. Choose the lettered pair that best expresses a relationship similar to that expressed in the original pair.

1. ADVERSITY : HAPPINESS ::

   (A) fear : misfortune
   (B) solace : adversity
   (C) vehemence : serenity
   (D) troublesome : petulance
   (E) graduation : felicitation

2. MARACAS : RHYTHM ::

   (A) flute : base
   (B) xylophone : percussion
   (C) drum : harmony
   (D) violin : concert
   (E) piano : octave

3. FEATHERS : PLUCK ::

   (A) goose : duck
   (B) garment : weave
   (C) car : drive
   (D) wool : shear
   (E) duck : down

4. MODESTY : ARROGANCE ::

   (A) debility : strength
   (B) cause : purpose
   (C) passion : emotion
   (D) finance : Wall Street
   (E) practice : perfection

5. BLOW : HORN ::

   (A) switch : tracks
   (B) turn on : lights
   (C) go over : map
   (D) accelerate : engine
   (E) tune : radio

6. BAY : SEA ::

   (A) mountain : valley
   (B) plain : forest
   (C) peninsula : land
   (D) cape : reef
   (E) island : sound

7. DECEMBER : WINTER ::

   (A) April : showers
   (B) September : summer
   (C) June : fall
   (D) March : spring
   (E) February : autumn

8. NECKLACE : ADORNMENT ::

   (A) medal : decoration
   (B) bronze : medal
   (C) scarf : dress
   (D) window : house
   (E) pearl : diamond

9. LIQUOR : ALCOHOLISM ::

   (A) pill : dope
   (B) tranquilizer : emotions
   (C) perfume : smell
   (D) candy : overweight
   (E) atomizer : sinusitis

177

ANTONYMS

DIRECTIONS: The questions in this section consist of one word followed by five lettered words or phrases. Choose the lettered word or phrase that is most nearly opposite in meaning to the numbered word.

10. IMMUTABLE

    (A) erudite
    (B) abject
    (C) changeable
    (D) fantastic
    (E) aura

11. DUCTILE

    (A) feted
    (B) alluvial
    (C) stubborn
    (D) abnormal
    (E) belabor

12. FASTIDIOUS

    (A) factitious
    (B) absurd
    (C) indifferent
    (D) sloppy
    (E) chary

13. TEMERITY

    (A) affinity
    (B) cherubim
    (C) humility
    (D) degenerate
    (E) celerity

14. ITINERANT

    (A) animosity
    (B) metaphor
    (C) perpetrator
    (D) resident
    (E) cerebrum

15. TACITURN

    (A) malevolent
    (B) loquacious
    (C) paltry
    (D) opaque
    (E) morbid

16. NEFARIOUS

    (A) grotesque
    (B) virtuous
    (C) jovial
    (D) pious
    (E) cerement

17. OBSEQUIOUS

    (A) harbinger
    (B) bold
    (C) heredity
    (D) quaff
    (E) falchion

SENTENCE COMPLETIONS

DIRECTIONS: For each of the sentences below, choose the lettered word or set of words which best fit the meaning of the sentence.

18. The admiration the Senator earns is _____ by his _____ instinct for getting onto the front pages.

    (A) concocted . . . proverbial
    (B) evolved . . . haughty
    (C) belied . . . aggressive
    (D) engendered . . . unerring
    (E) transcended . . . dogged

19. The accelerated growth of public employment _____ the dramatic expansion of budgets and programs.

    (A) parallels
    (B) contains
    (C) revolves
    (D) escapes
    (E) populates

20. So great is the intensity of Shakespeare's dramatic language that the audience becomes _____ and sees messages and equivocations everywhere, until the play becomes an apocalypse of _____ and fall.

    (A) stunned . . . rise
    (B) hallucinated . . . temptation
    (C) aroused . . . doubt
    (D) dulled . . . zeal
    (E) weary . . . disgust

21. Not every _____ mansion, church, battle site, theater, or other public hall can be preserved.

    (A) novel
    (B) structured
    (C) comparative
    (D) unknown
    (E) venerable

22. Man is still a _____ in the labor market.

    (A) glut
    (B) possibility
    (C) commodity
    (D) resumption
    (E) provision

23. As we moved on to Melford shortly after noon on Saturday, the clear air and the rolling _____ made one wonder whether this festival would lead all others, at least in altitude.

    (A) stones
    (B) hovels
    (C) skyline
    (D) oaks
    (E) terrain

24. Witness the long waiting list for the overworked psychiatrists and psychologists and the twentieth-century _____ for lying on the couch talking about oneself and the neuroses that have resulted from a too intense _____ with oneself.

    (A) wish . . . inspection
    (B) process . . . tirade
    (C) plan . . . understanding
    (D) fad . . . preoccupation
    (E) garb . . . implication

25. The book will be _____ by every Western student of the USSR, and it will be a thrilling adventure for any reader.

    (A) skimmed
    (B) perused
    (C) rejected
    (D) blasphemed
    (E) borrowed

Stop

END OF SECTION V. IF YOU HAVE ANY TIME LEFT, GO OVER YOUR WORK IN THIS SECTION ONLY. DO NOT WORK IN ANY OTHER SECTION OF THE TEST. WHEN YOUR TIME IS UP, GO ON TO THE NEXT SECTION.

SECTION VI: PRACTICAL BUSINESS JUDGMENT

20 Minutes
20 Questions

DIRECTIONS: This section consists of a reading selection which details a business situation followed by two sets of questions, data evaluation and data application. In the first set, data evaluation, you will be asked to classify certain of the facts presented in the passage on the basis of their importance. The second set, data application, will test your grasp of specific details of the situation.

A billionaire's autobiography turns out to be a fake. It can't be published, since the putative writer and subject states that he doesn't know a thing about it and never heard of William Milton to whom the book was allegedly dictated. Naturally, he threatens suit if the book is published. Having paid large sums of money, expending a great deal of time in preparing the project, and incurring a bad name for gullibility, what can Handborn now do to recoup its losses?

After Peter Handborn approves the project, John Robinson sends Milton two contracts, one for him and one for Magnerson. The contracts are returned promptly, duly signed. Then two checks are sent to Milton. The first, for $50,000, is made out to Milton and represents half of the royalty advance he is to receive. He will get the balance upon acceptance of the manuscript by Handborn. A $250,000 check made out to Magnerson is also sent, covering his entire advance against royalties.

Four months later, Milton delivers a portion of the manuscript. He also states that Magnerson has changed his mind about the advance. Now the eccentric tycoon demands a total advance of one million dollars!

This is a blow indeed. But it is softened somewhat by the knowledge that Handborn has signed substantial subsidiary rights contracts with National magazine, Twinights Book Club, and Vale Paperback Company. After long consultation with John Robinson, Peter Handborn gives permission to increase the advance, but he limits this to a total of $650,000 or $400,000 additional.

Two weeks later, Milton informs Handborn that he has spoken to Magnerson and persuaded the billionaire to accept the new terms. A revised contract is sent to Milton and returned with Magnerson's signature. A check for $400,000 is sent to Milton.

Handborn's comptroller is dubious. Why, he asks, would a man of Magnerson's enormous wealth, in the highest tax bracket, bargain for new terms? Other Handborn executives agree that it is strange, but then Magnerson certainly is not the usual author.

A month later, the Handborn comptroller reveals that the Magnerson checks have been deposited in a foreign bank by a woman. The checks are endorsed "Hannah Magnerson." Milton is asked about this. He states that Magnerson, like God, moves in mysterious ways, and therefore there's no need for alarm.

Subsequently, Milton turns in the rest of the manuscript. He also delivers tapes on which he has recorded the conversations between himself and Magnerson.

Robinson and his editors are elated after reading the manuscript. They are sure they have an excellent book. It is pithy, humorous in parts, and reveals much about leading public figures. The manuscript is accepted, and Milton is given his final advance payment of $50,000.

As soon as Handborn publicly announces the forthcoming publication, a letter is received from Magnerson's lawyer, stating that the book must be a complete fabrication since Magnerson has never met Milton, nor has he had any communication with him. Legal action is threatened.

The letter does not cause consternation at Handborn. They reason that Magnerson might be getting cold feet because of his revelations concerning public figures. Then again, there has been some conflict among executives in the Magnerson industrial empire. This letter could be a result of that struggle. Also, there is the verification of Magnerson's signature by the handwriting expert. Lastly, Robinson asks three people who know Magnerson personally to listen to the tapes. All three agree it is the voice of the billionaire.

Confidence in the project starts to fade, though, when the comptroller informs Peter Handborn that the Magnerson money has been withdrawn from the foreign bank by the mysterious "Hannah Magnerson." The government of the country in which the bank is located is most concerned since it suspects that fraud is involved. No one knows where "Hannah" took the money. Furthermore, a description of the woman sounds very much like Milton's wife.

Peter Handborn and John Robinson have a conference with William Milton. The writer insists that the manuscript is 100% authentic and that he met with Magnerson on several occasions. He does admit, however, that "Hannah" is indeed his wife, but that Magnerson asked him to handle the money in this manner. He claims Magnerson ordered him to remove the cash from the foreign bank without divulging its present location.

Later investigation turns up several people who are willing to swear that they were with Milton on the dates he said he met with Magnerson . . . and none of these people remember meeting the billionaire.

It is obvious to Mr. Handborn that publication must be aborted. The advances against subsidiary rights must be returned at once.

But what can be done about recouping the money that Handborn, Inc., has invested in this project? William Milton can be prosecuted, of course, resulting in bad publicity for Handborn, Inc. But that does not mean that the advances will be returned. In fact, Peter Handborn doubts that the advance money will ever find its way back into the company's coffers. Yet the picture here is not entirely bleak since Handborn, Inc., is insured against fraud. They can recover $500,000.

That would leave a loss of $250,000 from the advances. Other costs (overhead, editorial charges, prepublication advertising, etc.) would increase this amount to a total of around $400,000.

John Robinson has an idea. Why not write an insider's story of the whole affair? This would be of great interest and might sell better than the ill-starred autobiography.

Peter Handborn considers the possibilities. The danger of publishing such a book is that it might expose the gullibility of the Handborn executives, including himself, and thus might harm the company's public image. How would this affect the company's relationships with the banks on which it, like any other major publisher, depends?

Peter Handborn approves Robinson's project. He reasons thus: Handborn, Inc., will receive some adverse publicity, despite any attempt it might make to keep the matter quiet. Why not make an asset out of a liability? Admit that the company executives, although cautious men, were completely fooled. Probably a great deal of sympathy might be engendered, for who has not been taken in by a con artist at some time? And quite possibly Handborn might recoup most or all of its losses.

DATA EVALUATION

DIRECTIONS: Based on your analysis of the business situation, classify each of the following elements in one of five categories. Mark:

(A) if the element is a MAJOR OBJECTIVE in making the decision; that is, the outcome or result sought by the decision maker.

(B) if the element is a MAJOR FACTOR in arriving at the decision; that is, a consideration explicitly mentioned in the passage that is basic in determining the decision.

(C) if the element is a MINOR FACTOR in making the decision; that is, a secondary consideration in determining the decision.

(D) if the element is a MAJOR ASSUMPTION made in deliberating; that is, a supposition or projection made by the decision maker before weighing the variables.

(E) if the element is an UNIMPORTANT ISSUE in getting to the point; that is, a factor that is insignificant or not immediately relevant to the situation.

1. Handborn, Inc., has invested a great deal of money in the project.

2. Handborn, Inc., must extricate itself from the "fraud" situation as quickly as possible.

3. Either Milton or Magnerson renegotiated the contract.

4. The advance money given to Milton may not be recovered.

5. Substantial subsidiary rights contracts have been signed.

6. There is an executive struggle going on within the Magnerson organization.

7. The manuscript is a fake.

8. Handborn hopes to recoup some or all of its losses.

9. Handborn, Inc., is insured against fraud.

10. If a book about the hoax is published, it is almost certain to be a best-seller.

DATA APPLICATION

DIRECTIONS: Based on your understanding of the business situation, answer the following questions testing your comprehension of the information supplied in the passage. For each question, select the choice which best answers the question or completes the statement.

11. Partway through the project, before the entire manuscript was delivered,

   (A) Magnerson threatened to sue
   (B) Milton demanded more money for himself
   (C) the contract had to be renegotiated
   (D) the Magnerson money was withdrawn from the foreign bank
   (E) the Magnerson advance was increased to a million dollars

12. The main reason Handborn decided to increase the advance was that

   (A) prepublication orders for the book were enormous
   (B) Magnerson refused to finish the manuscript
   (C) the publishing company didn't think Milton was receiving enough for his work
   (D) substantial subsidiary rights contracts had been signed
   (E) the treasurer insisted on it

13. How was the advance to Magnerson handled by the Handborn Company?

   (A) Upon signing the contract, the company deposited a check for the full amount in a foreign bank.
   (B) Upon signing the contract, the company sent a check to Milton for one half the advance to Magnerson.
   (C) Upon signing the contract, the company held a check in escrow for the full advance to Magnerson.
   (D) Upon signing the contract, the company sent a check to Milton for the full advance to Magnerson.
   (E) Upon signing the contract, the company paid an advance to Magnerson which they limited to $650,000.

14. The woman who deposited the Magnerson checks was finally identified as

   (A) Milton's wife
   (B) Magnerson's wife
   (C) a Magnerson aide
   (D) Milton in disguise
   (E) a Handborn employee

15. The person who first voiced suspicion was

   (A) Peter Handborn
   (B) John Robinson
   (C) Magnerson's lawyer
   (D) a friend of Magnerson who listened to the tape recording
   (E) the Handborn comptroller

16. All of the following are reasons why the letter from Magnerson's lawyer did not raise much concern at Handborn except

   (A) Magnerson had possibly revealed too much about his relationships with certain public figures.
   (B) The handwriting expert had examined Magnerson's signatures carefully.
   (C) Qualified people had listened to the tapes of the interviews.
   (D) The letter could be the result of an executive conflict within the Magnerson industrial complex.
   (E) Milton had notified the company that Magnerson had asked him to conceal the whereabouts of the advance paid to the billionaire.

17. When John Robinson and his editors examined the complete manuscript, they came to the conclusion that it was

   (A) poor but would sell well
   (B) concise and entertaining
   (C) an obvious and crude fake
   (D) in need of extensive revision
   (E) technically well written but dull

18. After it was learned that the advance money had been withdrawn from a foreign bank, Peter Handborn met with William Milton. At this meeting, Milton

   (A) admitted the book was a fraud
   (B) denied that "Hannah" was his wife
   (C) stuck to his story that the manuscript was genuine

(D) offered to return his advance

(E) threatened a lawsuit for libel

19. One reason Handborn might NOT initiate legal proceedings against Milton is that

    (A) unfavorable publicity might result for Handborn, Inc.

    (B) the manuscript might be authentic after all

    (C) Magnerson would dislike the publicity

    (D) there is no ample proof of fraud

    (E) the money received from subsidiary rights would have to be returned

20. One consequence considered by Handborn should they publish a book revealing details of the fraud is that

    (A) readers would sympathize with the company

    (B) the company would lose even more money

    (C) the relationships with the banks might be improved

    (D) Magnerson might then publish his autobiography with Handborn, Inc.

    (E) the insurance company might refuse to pay money to cover damages

Stop

END OF SECTION VI. IF YOU HAVE ANY TIME LEFT, GO OVER YOUR WORK IN THIS SECTION ONLY. DO NOT WORK IN ANY OTHER SECTION OF THE TEST. WHEN YOUR TIME IS UP, GO ON TO THE NEXT SECTION.

SECTION VII: READING COMPREHENSION

25 Minutes
20 Questions

Recent scientific discoveries are throwing new light on the basic nature of viruses and on the possible nature of cancer, genes and even life itself. These discoveries are providing evidence for relationships among these four subjects which indicate that one may be dependent upon another to an extent not fully appreciated heretofore. Too often one works and thinks within too narrow a range and hence fails to recognize the significance of certain facts for other areas. Sometimes the important new ideas and subsequent fundamental discoveries come from the borderline areas between two well-established fields of investigation. This will result in the synthesis of new ideas regarding viruses, cancer, genes and life. These ideas in turn will result in the doing of new experiments which may provide the basis for fundamental discoveries in these fields.

There is no doubt that of the four topics, life is the one most people would consider to be of the greatest importance. However, life means different things to different people and it is in reality difficult to define just what we mean by life. There is no difficulty in recognizing an agent as living so long as we contemplate structures like a man, a dog or even a bacterium, and at the other extreme a piece of iron or glass or an atom of hydrogen or a molecule of water. The ability to grow or reproduce and to change or mutate has long been regarded as a special property characteristic of living agents along with the ability to respond to external stimuli. These are properties not shared by bits of iron or glass or even by a molecule of hemoglobin. Now if viruses had not been discovered, all would have been well. The organisms of the biologist would have ranged from the largest of animals all the way down to the smallest of the bacteria which are about 200 millimicra. There would have been a definite break with respect to size; the largest molecules known to the chemist were less than 20 millimicra in size. Thus life and living agents would have been represented by those structures which possessed the ability to reproduce themselves and to mutate and were about ten times larger than the largest known molecule. This would have provided a comfortable area of separation between living and non-living things.

Then came the discovery of the viruses. These infectious, disease-producing agents are characterized by their small size, by their ability to grow or reproduce within specific living cells, and by their ability to change or mutate during reproduction. This was enough to convince most people that viruses were merely still smaller living organisms. When the sizes of different viruses were determined, it was found that some were actually smaller than certain protein molecules. When the first virus was isolated in the form of a crystallizable material it was found to be a nucleoprotein. It was found to possess all the usual properties associated with protein molecules yet was larger than any molecule previously described. Here was a molecule that possessed the ability to reproduce itself and to mutate. The distinction between living and nonliving things seemed to be tottering. The gap in size between 20 and 200 millimicra has been filled in completely by the viruses, with some actual overlapping at both ends. Some large viruses are larger than some living organisms, and some small viruses are actually smaller than certain protein molecules.

Let us consider the relationship between genes and viruses since both are related to life. Both genes and viruses seem to be nucleoproteins and both reproduce only within specific living cells. Both possess the ability to mutate. Although viruses generally reproduce many times within a given cell, some situations are known in which they appear to reproduce only once with each cell division. Genes usually reproduce once with each cell division, but here also the rate can be changed. Actually the similarities between genes and viruses are so remarkable that viruses were referred to as ''naked genes'' or ''genes on the loose.''

Despite the fact that today viruses are known to cause cancer in animals and in certain plants, there exists a great reluctance to accept viruses as being of importance in human cancer. Basic biological phenomena generally do not differ strikingly as one goes from one species to another. It should be recognized that cancer is a biological problem and not a problem that is unique for man. Cancer originates when a normal cell suddenly becomes a cancer cell which multiplies widely and without apparent restraint. Cancer may originate in many different kinds of cells, but the cancer cell usually continues to carry certain traits of the cell of origin. The transformation of a normal cell into a cancer cell may have more than one kind of cause, but there is good reason to consider the relationships that exist between viruses and cancer.

Since there is no evidence that human cancer, as generally experienced, is infectious, many persons believe that because viruses are infectious agents they cannot possibly be of importance in human cancer. However, viruses can mutate and examples are known in which a virus that never kills its host can mutate to form a new strain of virus that always kills its host. It does not seem unreasonable to assume that an innocuous latent virus might mutate to form a strain that causes cancer. Certainly the experimental evidence now available is consistent with the idea that viruses as we know them today could be the causative agents of most, if not all cancer, including cancer in man.

1. People were convinced that viruses were small living organisms, because viruses

   (A) are disease-producing
   (B) reproduce within living cells
   (C) could be grown on artificial media
   (D) consist of nucleoproteins
   (E) resemble bacteria

2. Scientists very often do not apply the facts learned in one subject area to a related field of investigation because

   (A) the borderline areas are too close to both to give separate facts
   (B) scientists work in a very narrow range of experimentation
   (C) new ideas are synthesized only as a result of new experimentation
   (D) fundamental discoveries are based upon

finding close relationships in related sciences

   (E) experimental evidence is subject to error

3. Before the discovery of viruses, it might have been possible to distinguish living things from non-living things by the fact that

   (A) animate objects can mutate
   (B) non-living substances cannot reproduce themselves
   (C) responses to external stimuli are characteristic of living things
   (D) living things were greater than 20 millimicra in size
   (E) all of the above

4. The size of viruses is presently known to be

   (A) between 20 and 200 millimicra
   (B) smaller than any bacterium
   (C) larger than any protein molecule
   (D) larger than most nucleoproteins
   (E) the same size as cancer cells

5. That genes and viruses seem to be related might be shown by the fact that

   (A) both are ultra-microscopic
   (B) each can mutate but once in a cell
   (C) each reproduces but once in a cell
   (D) both appear to have the same chemical structure
   (E) they possess the same dimensions

6. Viruses were called ''genes on the loose'' because they

   (A) are able to reproduce very freely
   (B) like genes, seem to be able to mutate
   (C) seemed to be genes without cells
   (D) can loosen genes from cells
   (E) travel through the bloodstream

7. Cancer should be considered to be a biological problem rather than a medical one because

   (A) viruses are known to cause cancers in animals
   (B) at present, human cancer is not believed to be contagious
   (C) there are many known causes for the transformation of a normal cell to a cancer cell
   (D) results of experiments on plants and animals

do not vary greatly from species to species

(E) biologists are better scientists than doctors

8. The possibility that a virus causes human cancer is indicated by

   (A) the fact that viruses have been known to mutate
   (B) the fact that a cancer-immune individual may lose his immunity
   (C) the fact that reproduction of human cancer cells might be due to a genetic factor
   (D) the fact that man is host to many viruses
   (E) concrete experimental evidence

9. The best title for this passage is

   (A) New Light on the Cause of Cancer
   (B) The Newest Theory on the Nature of Viruses
   (C) Viruses, Genes, Cancer and Life
   (D) On the Nature of Life
   (E) Viruses and Disease

10. According to the passage, cancer cells are

    (A) similar to the cell of origin
    (B) mutations of viruses
    (C) unable to reproduce
    (D) among the smallest cells known
    (E) present in small amounts in all individuals

An action of apparent social significance among animals is that of migration. But several different factors are at work causing such migrations. These may be concerned with food-getting, with temperature, salinity, pressure and light changes; with the action of sex hormones and probably other combinations of these factors.

The great aggregations of small crustaceans, such as copepods found at the surface of the ocean, swarms of insects about a light, or the masses of unicellular organisms making up a part of the plankton in the lakes and oceans, are all examples of nonsocial aggregations of organisms brought together because of the presence or absence of certain factors in their environment, such as air currents, water currents, food or the lack of it, oxygen or carbon dioxide, or some other contributing causes.

Insects make long migrations, most of which seem due to the urge for food. The migrations of the locust, both in this country and elsewhere, are well known. While fish, such as salmon, return to the same stream where they grew up, such return migrations are rare

in insects, the only known instance being in the monarch butterfly. This is apparently due to the fact that it is long-lived and has the power of strong flight. The mass migrations of the Rocky Mountain and the African species of locust seem attributable to the need for food. Locusts live, eat, sun themselves and migrate in groups. It has been suggested that their social life is in response to the two fundamental instincts, aggregation and imitation.

Migrations of fish have been studied carefully by many investigators. Typically the migrations are from deep to shallow waters, as in the herring, mackerel and many other marine fish. Fresh-water fish in general exhibit this type of migration in the spawning season. Spawning habits of many fish show a change in habitat from salt to fresh water. Among these are the shad, salmon, alewife and others. In the North American and European eels, long migrations take place at the breeding season. All these migrations are obviously not brought about by a quest for food, for the salmon and many other fish feed only sparingly during the spawning season, but are undoubtedly brought about by metabolic changes in the animal initiated by the interaction of sex hormones. If this thesis holds, then here is the beginning of social life.

Bird migrations have long been a matter of study. The reasons for the migration of the golden plover from the Arctic regions to the tip of South America and back in a single year are not fully explainable. Several theories have been advanced, although none have been fully proved. The reproductive "instinct," food scarcity, temperature and light changes, the metabolic changes brought about by the activity of the sex hormones and the length of the day, all have been suggested, and ultimately several may prove to be factors. Aside from other findings, it is interesting to note that bird migrations take place year after year on about the same dates. Recent studies in the biochemistry of metabolism, showing that there is a seasonal cycle in the blood sugar that has a definite relation to activity and food, seem to be among the most promising leads.

In mammals the seasonal migrations that take place, such as those of the deer, which travel from the high mountains in summer to the valleys in winter, or the migration of the caribou in the northern areas of Canada, are based on the factor of temperature which regulates the food supply. Another mystery is the migration of the lemming, a small ratlike animal found in Scandinavia and Canada. The lemming population varies greatly from year to year, and, at times when it greatly increases, a migration occurs in which hordes of lemmings march across the country, swimming rivers and even plunging into the ocean if it bars their way. This again cannot be purely social association of animals. The horde is usually made up entirely of males, as the females seldom migrate.

11. The migration of the lemmings cannot be considered one of social association since

    (A) only males migrate
    (B) migrations occur only with population increases
    (C) it is probably due to the absence of some factor in the environment
    (D) the migrants do not return
    (E) migrations occur when there is a food scarcity

12. Animals which apparently migrate in quest of food are the

    (A) fish
    (B) birds
    (C) amphibians
    (D) insects
    (E) crustaceans

13. A characteristic of migration is the return of the migrants to their former home areas. This is, however, not true of the

    (A) birds
    (B) insects
    (C) mammals
    (D) fish
    (E) lemmings

14. The reproductive instinct is probably not a factor in the actual migration of

    (A) shad
    (B) lemming
    (C) golden plover
    (D) monarch butterfly
    (E) deer

15. In paragraph 1, several probable factors causing migrations are given. None of these seem to explain the migrations of

    (A) lemming
    (B) caribou
    (C) salmon

    (D) locusts
    (E) rats

16. The reasons for the migrations of birds may ultimately be determined by scientists working in the field of

    (A) population studies
    (B) ecology
    (C) metabolism chemistry
    (D) reproduction
    (E) genetics

17. According to the passage, the reproductive process seems to be a known factor in the migration of many

    (A) fish
    (B) insects
    (C) mammals
    (D) birds
    (E) carnivores

18. Animals which migrate back and forth between the same general areas are

    (A) locusts and salmon
    (B) salmon and golden plover
    (C) golden plover and lemming
    (D) monarch butterfly and caribou
    (E) monarch butterfly and locusts

19. The shortest distance covered by any migrating group is taken by

    (A) insects
    (B) fish
    (C) birds
    (D) mammals
    (E) both A and B

20. The main purpose of the passage is to

    (A) show how a natural event effects change in different species
    (B) present a new theory in regard to biological evolution
    (C) teach the reader how to evaluate a natural phenomenon
    (D) describe a phenomenon that has not yet been satisfactorily explained
    (E) show how species behave similarly under the same conditions

Stop

END OF EXAMINATION

END OF SECTION VII. IF YOU HAVE ANY TIME LEFT, GO OVER YOUR WORK IN THIS SECTION ONLY. DO NOT WORK IN ANY OTHER SECTION OF THE TEST. WHEN YOUR TIME IS UP, CHECK YOUR ANSWERS WITH THE ANSWER KEY AND EXPLANATORY ANSWERS PROVIDED ON THE FOLLOWING PAGES.

ANSWER KEY

SECTION I

1. D	7. A	13. C	19. A	25. D
2. B	8. E	14. D	20. E	26. A
3. E	9. D	15. B	21. B	27. A
4. B	10. E	16. B	22. E	28. D
5. E	11. B	17. A	23. E	29. D
6. E	12. E	18. B	24. C	30. E

SECTION II

1. E	7. D	13. A	19. D	25. E
2. E	8. D	14. D	20. E	26. D
3. D	9. B	15. B	21. E	27. B
4. B	10. E	16. D	22. C	28. C
5. B	11. E	17. C	23. C	29. B
6. E	12. B	18. D	24. C	30. E

SECTION III

1. A	6. D	11. A	16. C
2. D	7. B	12. B	17. C
3. B	8. C	13. E	18. D
4. B	9. B	14. A	19. B
5. B	10. D	15. E	20. D

SECTION IV

1. E	6. D	11. B	16. B	21. E
2. C	7. E	12. E	17. A	22. C
3. E	8. B	13. C	18. B	23. D
4. B	9. A	14. D	19. C	24. A
5. C	10. D	15. C	20. B	25. E

SECTION V

1. C	6. C	11. C	16. B	21. E
2. B	7. D	12. D	17. B	22. C
3. D	8. A	13. C	18. D	23. E
4. A	9. D	14. D	19. A	24. D
5. B	10. C	15. B	20. B	25. B

SECTION VI

1. B	6. C	11. C	16. E
2. A	7. D	12. D	17. B
3. E	8. A	13. D	18. C
4. D	9. D	14. A	19. A
5. E	10. B	15. E	20. A

SECTION VII

1. B	6. B	11. A	16. C
2. B	7. D	12. D	17. A
3. D	8. A	13. B	18. B
4. A	9. C	14. B	19. D
5. D	10. A	15. A	20. A

EXPLANATORY ANSWERS

SECTION I

1. **(D)** The passage stresses throughout that the best students should be practical as well as intellectual; they should be "not purely intellectual, or purely pragmatic" but a mixture of both.

2. **(B)** This is stated explicitly in the opening of the fourth paragraph.

3. **(E)** As is stated in the passage about the complexity of modern business: "When things become so highly complex, group management is the logical answer."

4. **(B)** This is stated early in the reading. The college-trained business leader needs the kind of education which opens his eyes to "the need for a lifetime of study and gives him the foundations on which his continued study can be based."

5. **(E)** All of these concepts are espoused in the passage.

6. **(E)** The passage stresses the idea that leadership must be taught and that the universities must not be removed from the world but take an active role in it.

7. **(A)** At the opening of paragraph six, the author states: "Perhaps it will be the business schools of this nation which will remind American education not only that democracy and strong leadership are *not* contradictory terms, but that leadership can and *must* be taught."

8. **(E)** The implication is quite clear since the author states that "business will be serving the nation's interests as well as its own."

9. **(D)** This is implied throughout the passage with its stressing the liberality of the business education, and, as is stated in the opening paragraph, businessmen should recognize that a business education does breed "the broad-gauge man who can stand with feet planted in both Column A and Column B."

10. **(E)** Although choice (A) would also seem to have some bearing, the thrust of the passage is on how a modern business education has responded to modern business needs.

11. **(B)** The passage states that during this period "the regime tried to wipe out self-interest—and hence monetary incentives—as a key motivating force."

12. **(E)** Members of the Communist Party were in charge.

13. **(C)** The passage explicitly states that China and Russia "were engaged in an open, heated feud about proper ideology and revisionism."

14. **(D)** The passage does not mention profits in connection with bonuses for the 1952–57 period.

15. **(B)** The author favors monetary incentives as a motivating force. He seems pessimistic about current trends.

16. **(B)** The author gives a figure of 80 percent of factory workers earning monthly or quarterly bonuses.

17. **(A)** The passage states: "However, profit rather than gross output became the key success indicator."

18. **(B)** The decision-making role of the managers is stressed in the second paragraph.

19. **(A)** The director's benefits are not mentioned.

20. **(E)** This is stated at the end of the first paragraph.

21. **(B)** As the passage states: "sound motivation patterns must begin at the top."

22. **(E)** The implication of the passage is that all the ills are a "culmination of a chain of events beginning with top management."

23. **(E)** The reductive cycle is related to poor motivation and thus would lead to less productive effort.

24. **(C)** The passage states: "Job success is dependent upon cyclical conditions created by inter-personal competence, meaningful goals, and helpful systems."

25. **(D)** It is pointed out that being in the developmental cycle is better for the worker while being in the reductive cycle has unhealthy connotations. "Sustained confinement of a large percentage of the work force in the reductive cycle is symptomatic of organizational illness."

26. **(A)** Militant unionism is expressly stated to be a consequence of reductive conditions. The other two options are not mentioned.

27. **(A)** The passage states that "the unionization of a work group is usually precipitated by management failure to provide opportunities for employees to achieve personal goals through the achievement of organization goals.

28. **(D)** This is stated in the next to the last paragraph.

29. **(D)** This is defined in the last paragraph.

30. **(E)** This is stated in the sixth paragraph.

SECTION II

1. **(E)** 4 of the 6 equal parts of 2 means

$$\frac{4}{6} \times 2, \text{ or } \frac{4}{3}$$

2. **(E)** 110% of 105 is 1.1×105, or 115.5

3. **(D)** This is a proportion: 2 inches: 7½ inches = 5 feet: x, so x = 18¾ feet.

4. **(B)** The horizontal edges are each 3 cm. long, and the vertical edges are 2 cm. long. Therefore, the volume is $3 \times 3 \times 2$, or 18 cc.

5. **(B)** The only pieces that touch eight other pieces are the shaded ones in this diagram:

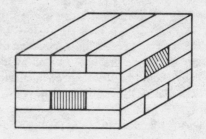

6. **(E)** In order to have a volume of 18 cc., the piece of material must be ½ cm. $\times$ 1 cm. $\times$ 36 cm.

7. **(D)** Each piece has two faces which are 1 cm. $\times$ ½ cm., or ½ sq. cm., two faces which are 1 cm. $\times$ 3 cm., or 3 sq. cm., and two faces which are ½ cm. $\times$ 3 cm., or 1½ sq. cm. The surface area of each piece is therefore 10 sq. cm. Since there are 12 such pieces, the total area is 120 sq. cm.

8. **(D)** The area of triangle ADE equals the area of triangle AEC, since they have the same base and altitude. The area of triangle ABC equals that of triangle ADC, since the diagonal of a parallelogram divides it equally.

9. **(B)** At 3 for 10¢, one dozen pencils cost 40¢, so the profit on each dozen is 5¢. With 5½ dozen, the profit is 27½¢.

10. **(E)** $26 \times 3½ = (26 \times 3) + (26 \times ½)$ by the distributive law. $26 \times 3 = (20 \times 3) + (6 \times 3)$ by the distributive law. Therefore, $26 \times 3½ = (26 \times ½) + (20 \times 3) + (6 \times 3)$.

11. **(E)** 20 square yards equals 180 square feet. At 31¢ per square foot, it will cost $55.80.

12. **(B)** 35 feet, 6 inches equals 426 inches. One-fourth of this is 106½ inches, or 8 feet, 10½ inches.

13. **(A)** Out of 12 total games, two were won. Thus, the fraction is $^2/_{12}$ or $^1/_6$.

14. **(D)** 10^5 is defined as $10 \times 10 \times 10 \times 10 \times 10$, or 100,000. $10 \times 5 = 50$; $5^{10} = 25^5$, $\sqrt[5]{10}$ is between 1 and 2; and $10^{10} \div 10^2 = 10^8$.

15. **(B)** $3\frac{1}{2} \times \$1.10 = \$3.85$. At 60¢ a dozen, one orange costs 5¢, and 20 cost \$1.00. The total is \$4.85.

16. **(D)** $\overline{\text{XCL}}$ = 10,150.

17. **(C)** $4(10^4) + 5(10^3) + 4(100) = 45,400 =$

18. **(D)** = 1,502,002 = 10^6 + 50(10,000) + 2,000 + 2.

19. **(D)** $2\frac{3}{4} \div \frac{1}{8} = \frac{11}{4} \div \frac{1}{8} = \frac{11}{4} \times 8 = 22$

20. **(E)** $105,084 - 93,709 = 11,375$.

21. **(E)** This is a proportion → $2\frac{1}{2} : 3 = x : 14$; x = $^{35}/_3$, or $11\frac{2}{3}$.

22. **(C)** After a^3, "A" is on the bottom. After this, then b; "A" moves to the left.

23. **(C)** Starting on the right, b brings the face in question to the bottom, and c then leaves it in the same position.

24. **(C)** $a^2b^2c^2$ returns the cube to its original position, and so does c^4.

25. **(E)** If the gain was 10% of the selling price, then \$12.60 was 90% so 100% was equal to \$14.00.

26. **(D)** There will be no waste if the lengths are multiples of 5½ feet. This occurs between 6 and 24 only for 22 feet.

27. **(B)** Each tile, including half of the cement around it, has an area of 1 square inch. 3240 square inches equals 22.5 square feet, or 2.5 square yards.

28. **(C)** A median score is the middle score when all scores are arranged in ascending or descending order. This is 27 here.

29. **(B)** The volume of the large cube is 6^3, or 216 cubic inches. Each $1'' \times 2'' \times 6''$ block has a volume of 12 cubic inches. Dividing, there are 18 cubes.

30. **(E)** 12 blocks have their $2'' \times 6''$ faces painted blue. 6 more have their $1'' \times 6''$ faces painted blue. The total area of blue is 180 sq. in.

SECTION III

1. **(A)** To make a profit is a major objective.

2. **(D)** It is assumed the company has the resources to pay the advance.

3. **(B)** Certainly the subsidiary revenues play a large part in getting an affirmative decision.

4. **(B)** The possibility that Milton might not be telling the truth is a major consideration.

5. **(B)** The potential sales of the book is a major factor.

6. **(D)** An assumption certainly, since no one at Handborn has conducted a survey to find out if the public is interested in Magnerson.

7. **(B)** Magnerson's signature seems to establish the credibility of Milton's story.

8. **(C)** A minor factor. The trade division's unprofitability is mentioned at the very beginning, but not after that. Peter Handborn doesn't seem to think about it.

9. **(B)** A strong factor. No one seems to want to do anything that might ruin the deal.

10. **(D)** It's highly possible that another company would publish the Magnerson autobiography, but this is still an assumption.

11. **(A)** The trade book division has been unprofitable. Magnerson's story might very well put it

into the black. None of the other answers are given.

12. **(B)** Robinson specifically states that his belief in Milton's honesty has been developed over years of working with him.

13. **(E)** Robinson states that Magnerson might very well call the whole thing off if Handborn approached him directly. (B) is nearly right, but it cannot be said that Robinson "strongly" opposed this possible move.

14. **(A)** The agreement states that Magnerson and Milton get half of the subsidiary revenues. What the figure will be is unknown. Magnerson's share is also unknown. The subsidiary revenue has nothing to do with the advance against royalties.

15. **(E)** Magnerson has been avoiding the public spotlight for years. To suddenly allow his autobiography to be published seems out of character.

16. **(C)** Robinson has stated that he is sure the subsidiary rights income would be very substantial and probably would cover printing costs.

17. **(C)** The agreement is between Milton and Magnerson only and does not involve Handborn. The agreement was signed and is judged to be genuine by the handwriting expert.

18. **(D)** Robinson states that at least 100,000 copies would be sold. This is a conservative guess, but he does not commit himself to any other figure.

19. **(B)** The mystery of Magnerson fascinates the general public.

20. **(D)** So stated in the first paragraph.

SECTION IV

1. **(E)** Statements (1) and (2) mention only the fathers and grandfathers; no information is given about the ages of Andrea and Denise.

2. **(C)** From statement (1) A = ±5 and statement

(2) B = 6, hence B > A.

3. **(E)** In order to do the problem, you must know how much material is required for one dress, and neither statement supplies the information.

4. **(B)** By statement (2) if Devin loses 10 lbs., he still weighs more than 170 lbs. He must weigh more than 180 lbs. to begin with.

5. **(C)** Add statements (1) and (2) together to get 4x = 34, then x = 8½.

6. **(D)** By statement (1), 4 men paint 3 rooms in 1 day; 1 man paints ¾ room in 1 day (divide by 4); 1 man paints 12 rooms in 16 days (divide by ¾); 12 men paint 12 rooms in 1½ days (multiply and divide by 10). By statement (2) same as above.

7. **(E)** For three unknowns, you need three equations, and only two are given.

8. **(B)** By statement (1) the operation could be either addition or multiplication. By statement (2) it could only be addition.

9. **(A)** By statement (1) if x and y are equal, their vertical angles are also equal. Their vertical angles are alternate interior angles, thus the lines are parallel.

10. **(D)** By statement (1)
A = 2,200
B = 2,800
D = 2,600
C = 1,600
 B > C
By statement (2)
A = 2,200
D = 2,600
B = 2,800
C = 1,600
 B > C

11. **(B)** Using statement (2), the area of square DEFG minus the area of triangle ABC equals 30, the region not overlapped by triangle ABC.

12. **(E)** This is a question on the locus of points from a fixed point. City A is within a 60 mile radius of City B and City B is within a 40 mile radius of City C. Not knowing the exact location of either

city it is impossible to determine the number of miles from City A to City C.

13. **(C)** By statement (1) if the area of the square is 16, then each side is 4. By statement (2) since Q, R, S, and T are the midpoints of the four sides, it is now possible to find the 4 sides of Q, R, S, T. Using the theorem

$$(QT)^2 = 2^2 + 2^2$$
$$(QT)^2 = 4 + 4$$
$$(QT)^2 = 8$$
$$QT = 2\sqrt{2}$$

Hence, the perimeter of QRST equals $8\sqrt{2}$.

14. **(D)** By statement (1) if B = ⅔A, then A > B and by statement (2) if B = A − 4, then A is also greater than B.

15. **(C)** By statements (1) and (2), 20 is the only possible answer.

16. **(B)** By statement (2) if A ÷ 10 is not odd, it must be even. Hence A ÷ 5 must also be even because 10 is an even multiple of 5.

17. **(A)** $\dfrac{x - y}{y} = \dfrac{x}{y} - \dfrac{y}{y} = \dfrac{x}{y} - 1$;

therefore, to solve the problem the value of x/y must be known. Statement (1) x/y = 2.

18. **(B)** The number of degrees in a △ = 180; there are two triangles, hence angles p, q, r, s, B, and C must equal 360°. By statement (2) if angles B and C equal 90°, then angles p + q + r + s must equal 360° − 90° or 270°.

19. **(C)** By statement (2) ¼ of 28 = 7. It is now known that 7 in the class scored over 90%. Using statement (1) if 5 out of the 7 are girls, then 2 boys scored over 90%.

20. **(B)** To find the average of four terms you must find their total. This can be accomplished in statement (2).

3(w + x + y) = 63 and z = 3
w + x + y = 21 and z = 3
w + x + y + z = 24

Therefore, their average is 6.

21. **(E)** Impossible to determine from information given.

22. **(C)** The question contains two unknowns and requires 2 equations to solve. Statement (1) is an equation and statement (2) is an equation.

23. **(D)** By statement (1) add XZ and WY and subtract WZ from their total. In statement (2) subtract XW from WY.

24. **(A)** By statement (1) if one angle of a triangle is 100°, then the sum of the other two angles equals 80°. Hence ∠Q could not be greater than 90°.

25. **(E)** If a, b, c, d, and e were parallel to each other, it could be determined that x = y. But there is no indication that these lines are all parallel to each other.

SECTION V

1. **(C)** Adversity (a condition of suffering) will disrupt happiness; vehemence (passion and intensity) will disrupt serenity (peacefulness, calm).

2. **(B)** Maracas are rhythm instruments; the xylophone is a percussion instrument.

3. **(D)** To remove feathers, one has to pluck them; to remove wool, one has to shear it.

4. **(A)** Modesty is the opposite of arrogance; debility is the opposite of strength.

5. **(B)** To blow a horn makes it work; to turn on lights makes them work.

6. **(C)** A bay is a prominence of sea water into land; a peninsula is a prominence of land into the sea.

7. **(D)** December is a month in winter; March is a month in spring.

8. **(A)** Necklace is a kind of adornment; medal is a kind of decoration.

9. **(D)** Too much liquor can bring on alcoholism; too much candy can make someone overweight.

10. **(C)** Immutable means unchangeable; changeable

is its opposite.

11. **(C)** Ductile means supple, capable of being molded; stubborn is rigid.

12. **(D)** Fastidious is extreme attention to detail; sloppy is careless, messy.

13. **(C)** Temerity is brashness; humility is submission.

14. **(D)** An itinerant is someone who moves from place to place; a resident remains in one location.

15. **(B)** Taciturn is terse, quiet; loquacious is talkative.

16. **(B)** Nefarious is evil; virtuous is good.

17. **(B)** Obsequious is toadying; bold is independent.

18. **(D)** Engendered means originated; unerring means never false.

19. **(A)** Parallels means happening at the same time and in the same way.

20. **(B)** Hallucinated means to have become filled with delusion; temptation is enticement (apocalypse means prophetic revelation).

21. **(E)** Venerable means deserving of respect because of old age.

22. **(C)** A commodity is something to be bought and sold.

23. **(E)** Terrain is landscape.

24. **(D)** A fad is a craze or fashion; a preoccupation is complete absorption.

25. **(B)** Perused means studied with care.

SECTION VI

1. **(B)** The money is paramount in Peter Handborn's mind.

2. **(A)** That is why Peter Handborn wishes to cancel

publication immediately and return the subsidiary rights money.

3. **(E)** The renegotiated contract is of little interest. The company's more immediate need is to get out of the spiderweb.

4. **(D)** An assumption certainly. Peter Handborn presumably believes that Milton will risk going to prison because he will be a rich man when he gets out and collects his loot.

5. **(E)** The return of subsidiary rights money is hardly important in this dilemma.

6. **(C)** The struggle within the Magnerson organization has been mentioned as a fact, but this is of little interest to Peter Handborn as he considers what his company should do.

7. **(D)** By the time Peter Handborn thinks about what he must do, he is sure that the company has been the victim of a fraud.

8. **(A)** This is the main reason for adopting Robinson's idea to publish a book on the affair.

9. **(D)** A major assumption is the ability to collect some money from the insurance company.

10. **(B)** A major factor is the decision to publish an exposé.

11. **(C)** is the only correct statement. (A), (B), and (E) are false. (D) is true, but happened after the entire manuscript was delivered.

12. **(D)** The subsidiary rights revenues were substantial, so there seemed to be no financial danger in agreeing to an increase in the royalty advance to Magnerson. (B) is nearly right, but not quite because Magnerson made no threat to withdraw publication, although the implication was there.

13. **(D)** This is the only correct statement of the five possible answers.

14. **(A)** Milton admitted his wife had deposited the Magnerson advance money.

15. **(E)** The Handborn comptroller wondered why a

billionaire would feel he had to get more advance money. This happened long before the letter from Magnerson's lawyer.

16. **(E)** All the possible answers were true, but it was after the letter from the Magnerson lawyer that Milton asserted the billionaire had told him to hide his advance money.

17. **(B)** is the only correct statement.

18. **(C)** is the only correct statement.

19. **(A)** Peter Handborn is concerned about bad publicity for his company.

20. **(A)** (B) is possible, but not probable. (C) is wrong since Peter Handborn thinks that publication might prejudice his company's relationships with banks. (D) and (E) are not considered at all by Peter Handborn.

SECTION VII

1. **(B)** This is stated in the beginning of the third paragraph.

2. **(B)** The opening paragraph clearly states that often "one works and thinks within too narrow a range and hence fails to recognize the significance of certain facts for other areas."

3. **(D)** Size, as discussed in paragraphs two and three, would be the determinant.

4. **(A)** This is explicitly stated in the third paragraph: "The gap in the size between 20 and 200 millimicra has been filled in completely by the viruses, with some actual overlapping at both ends."

5. **(D)** Paragraph four states that they both appear to be nucleoproteins. Thus, they would both have a similar chemical structure.

6. **(B)** The choice would be the one which refers to a shared characteristic between the two. This would be (B).

7. **(D)** This is quite unequivocally stated: "Basic biological phenomena generally do not differ strikingly as one goes from one species to the other. It should be recognized that cancer is a biological problem and not a problem that is unique to man."

8. **(A)** This is the whole point of the discussion in the final paragraph.

9. **(C)** The passage examines the relationship and new ideas regarding these four things. The other choices stress one to the exclusion of the others.

10. **(A)** This is so stated: "Cancer may originate in different kinds of cells, but the cancer cell usually continues to carry certain traits of the cell of origin." Choice (B) is presented in the passage as a theory, not as a proven fact.

11. **(A)** As is stated: "This again cannot be purely social association of animals. The horde is usually made up entirely of males, as the females seldom migrate."

12. **(D)** This is quite clearly stated in the opening sentence of the second paragraph.

13. **(B)** The second paragraph states that this trait is rare in insects except for the migration of the monarch butterfly.

14. **(B)** The lemming migration is considered a mystery and the final paragraph discounts the reproductive instinct.

15. **(A)** Once again, the final paragraph must be referred to.

16. **(C)** Paragraph five discusses that several theories have been advanced which have not been fully proved. But of late there have been "studies in the biochemistry of metabolism, showing that there is a seasonal cycle in the blood sugar that has a definite relation to activity and food."

17. **(A)** This is quite obvious for the passage goes into detail about the spawning habits of fish.

18. **(B)** The passage states that "salmon return to the same stream where they grew up." And as for the golden plover, the passage states that it migrates from the Arctic regions to the tip of South

America and returns in a single year.

19. **(D)** The implication is that mammalian migrations are not as spectacular in degree. From the examples given in the passage, they travel to nearby areas in search of food.

20. **(A)** Each paragraph discusses a different species in regard to migration.

Part Four

Review of GMAT Subject Areas and Question-Types

VOCABULARY PROFICIENCY

Etymology is the science of the formation of words, and this somewhat frightening-sounding science can be of great help to you in learning new words and identifying words which may be unfamiliar to you. You will also find that the progress you make in studying the following pages will help to improve your spelling.

A great many of the words which we use every day have come into our language from the Latin and Greek. In the process of being absorbed into English, they appear as parts of words, many of which are related in meaning to each other.

For your convenience, this material is presented in easy-to-study form. Latin and Greek syllables and letter-combinations have been categorized into three groups:

1. *Prefixes:* letter combinations which appear at the beginning of a word.
2. *Suffixes:* letter combinations which appear at the end of a word.
3. *Roots or stems:* which carry the basic meaning and are combined with each other and with prefixes and suffixes to create other words with related meanings.

With the prefixes and suffixes, which you should study first, we have given examples of word formation with meanings, and additional examples. If you find any unfamiliar words among the samples, consult your dictionary to look up their meanings.

The list of roots or stems is accompanied by words in which the letter combinations appear. Here again, use the dictionary to look up any words which are not clear in your mind.

After you have done your preliminary work and have gotten a better idea of how words are formed in English, schedule the various vocabulary tests and quizzes we have provided in this chapter. They cover a wide variety of the vocabulary questions commonly encountered on examinations. They are short quizzes, not meant to be taken all at one time. Space them out. Adhere closely to the directions which differ for the different test types. Keep an honest record of your scores. Study your mistakes. Look them up in your dictionary. Concentrate closely on each quiz . . . and watch your scores improve.

ETYMOLOGY –
A KEY TO WORD RECOGNITION
Prefixes

PREFIX	MEANING	EXAMPLE	PREFIX	MEANING	EXAMPLE
ab, a	away from	absent, amoral	mal	bad	malcontent
ad, ac, ag, at	to	advent, accrue, aggressive, attract	mis	wrong	misnomer
an	without	anarchy	non	not	nonentity
ante	before	antedate	ob	against	obstacle
anti	against	antipathy	per	through	permeate
bene	well	beneficent	peri	around	periscope
bi	two	bicameral	poly	many	polytheism
circum	around	circumspect	post	after	post-mortem
com, con, col	together	commit confound, collate	pre	before	premonition
contra	against	contraband	pro	forward	propose
de	from, down	descend	re	again	review
dis, di	apart	distract, divert	se	apart	seduce
ex, e	out	exit, emit	semi	half	semicircle
extra	beyond	extracurricular	sub	under	subvert
in, im, il, ir, un	not	inept, impossible, illicit	super	above	superimpose
inter	between	interpose	sui	self	suicide
intra, intro, in	within	intramural, introspective	trans	across	transpose
			vice	instead of	vice-president

Suffixes

SUFFIX	MEANING	EXAMPLE
able, ible	capable of being	capable, reversible
age	state of	storage
ance	relating to	reliance
ary	relating to	dictionary
ate	act	confiscate
ation	action	radiation
cy	quality	democracy

SUFFIX	MEANING	EXAMPLE
ence	relating to	confidence
er	one who	adviser
ic	pertaining to	democratic
ious	full of	rebellious
ize	to make like	harmonize
ment	result	filament
ty	condition	sanity

Roots

STEM	MEANING	EXAMPLE
ag, ac	do	agenda, action
agr	farm	agriculture
aqua	water	aqueous
cad, cas	fall	cadence, casual
cant	sing	chant
cap, cep	take	captive, accept
capit	head	capital
cede	go	precede
celer	speed	celerity
cide, cis	kill, cut	suicide, incision
clud, clus	close	include, inclusion
cur, curs	run	incur, incursion
dict	say	diction
duct	lead	induce
fact, fect	make	factory, perfect
fer, lat	carry	refer, dilate
fring, fract	break	infringe, fracture
frater	brother	fraternal
fund, fus	pour	refund, confuse
greg	group	gregarious
gress, grad	move forward	progress, degrade
homo	man	homicide
ject	throw	reject
jud	right	judicial
junct	join	conjunction
lect, leg	read, choose	collect, legend
loq, loc	speak	loquacious, interlocutory
manu	hand	manuscript
mand	order	remand
mar	sea	maritime
mater	mother	maternal
med	middle	intermediary
min	lessen	diminution
mis, mit	send	remit, dismiss
mort	death	mortician
mote, mov	move	remote, remove
naut	sailor	astronaut
nom	name	nomenclature
pater	father	paternity
ped, pod	foot	pedal, podiatrist
pend	hang	depend
plic	fold	implicate
port	carry	portable
pos, pon	put	depose, component
reg, rect	rule	regicide, direct
rupt	break	eruption
scrib, scrip	write	inscribe, conscription
anthrop	man	anthropology

STEM	MEANING	EXAMPLE
arch	chief, rule	archbishop
astron	star	astronomy
auto	self	automatic
biblio	book	bibliophile
bio	life	biology
chrome	color	chromosome
chron	time	chronology
cosmo	world	cosmic
crat	rule	autocrat
dent, dont	tooth	dental, indent
eu	well, happy	eugenics
gamos	marriage	monogamous
ge	earth	geology
gen	origin, people	progenitor
graph	write	graphic
gyn	women	gynecologist
homo	same	homogeneous
hydr	water	dehydrate
logy	study of	psychology
meter	measure	thermometer
micro	small	microscope
mono	one	monotony
onomy	science	astronomy
onym	name	synonym
pathos	feeling	pathology
philo	love	philosophy
phobia	fear	hydrophobia
phone	sound	telephone
pseudo	false	pseudonym
psych	mind	psychic
scope	see	telescope
soph	wisdom	sophomore
tele	far off	telepathic
theo	god	theology
thermo	heat	thermostat
sec	cut	dissect
sed	remain	sedentary
sequ	follow	sequential
spect	look	inspect
spir	breathe	conspire
stat	stand	status
tact, tang	touch	tactile, tangible
ten	hold	retentive
term	end	terminal
vent	come	prevent
vict	conquer	evict
vid, vis	see	video, revise
voc	call	convocation
volv	roll	devolve

WORD LIST

The words that appear in the Verbal Abilities questions of the GMAT are ones that are frequently encountered in textbooks, "intellectual" nonfiction, and reputable fiction. Such are the words that make up the following GMAT Word List. It is important that you study this list. A great many of these words have appeared time and again on previous GMAT tests—and may well appear on the test that you take.

The definitions given here are deliberately brief. This should help you master the word meanings more quickly. For many of the words in this list, there are other meanings besides the common definition given here. The linguistic scholar, Senator S. I. Hayakawa,

has said in this connection, "It is surprising that with so many meanings to the words, people don't misunderstand one another oftener than they do." Use your dictionary frequently—learn the other meanings as well if you have the time.

Since the GMAT has antonyms (opposites) rather than synonyms, you are advised to try to give the opposite meanings for those words on this list that do have an antonym.

Learn 20 words each day and in less than three months you will have mastered the entire list. It should make a marked difference in your score.

A

abase —to degrade
abash —to embarrass
abate —to decrease
aberration —variation
abeyance —temporary suspension
abject —miserable
abjure —to renounce
ablution —cleansing
abnegate —to reject
abominate —to abhor
aborigine —original inhabitant
abortive —futile
abrade —to rub off
abrogate —to abolish
absolve —to acquit
absolution —forgiveness
abstemious —sparing in diet
abstruse —difficult to understand
abut —adjoin
accolade —praise
accoutre —to equip
acerbity —bitterness
acolyte —assistant
acrimony —bitterness
actuary —insurance computer
actuate —to incite
acumen —sharpness of mind
adage —proverb
adamant —inflexible

adduce —to bring forth proof
adipose —fatty
adjunct —attachment
adjure —to demand, request
admonish —to warn
adroit —skillful
adulation —praise
adumbration —omen, warning
advent —coming
adventitious —accidental
adversity —misfortune
affable —friendly
affected —assumed artificially
affidavit —sworn statement in writing
affinity —relationship
affirmation —positive statement
affluent —plentiful
agenda —things to be done
agglomerate —to gather into one mass
aggrandize —to increase
aggregate —total
agnostic —doubter
agrarian —rural
akimbo —with hands on hips
alacrity —speed
albino —white
alchemy —medieval

chemistry
alienist —psychiatrist
alimentary —pert. to food
allay —to calm
allocate —to apportion
allude —to refer
alluvial —left by departing water
altercate —to quarrel
altruism —unselfishness
amatory —loving
ambidextrous —versatile, skillful
ambrosia —food for ancient gods
ambulant —able to walk
ameliorate —to improve
amenable —submissive
amenity —pleasing manner
amnesty —pardon
amulet —charm
anachronism —something out of time
analgesic —pain-reliever
analogous—corresponding (to)
anathema —curse
anchorite —hermit
aneroid —using no fluid
aneurism —swelling of artery
animadversion —criticism
animalcule —microscopic animal

annals —records by the year
anneal —to toughen
anomaly —irregularity
antediluvian —old
anterior —front; earlier
anthropoid —resembling man
anthropology —the science of man
antithesis —direct opposite
antipathy —dislike
apartheid—South African racial segregation
apathetic —indifferent
aperture —opening
apex —peak
aphorism —proverb
apiary —place where bees are kept
aplomb —poise
apocalypse —revelation
apocryphal —of doubtful authority
apogee —highest point
apostasy —forsaking one's religion
apothegm —aphorism
apotheosis —deification
appall —to horrify
appellation —name; title
append —to attach
apposite —appropriate
apprise —to give notice

aquiline —hooked
arabesque —ornament; ballet position
arable —plowable
arbiter —judge
arboreal —living among trees
archetype —example
archipelago —group of islands
archive —record
arduous —laborious
argot —slang
armada —fleet of armed ships
arraign —to bring before a court
arrogate —to claim without right
arroyo —dry river bed
artifacts —products of primitive art
artifice —deception
ascetic —practicing self-denial
aseptic —free from bacteria
asperity —harshness
aspersion —slanderous remark
assay —to evaluate
asseverate —to assert
assiduous —constant; devoted
assimilate —to absorb
assuage —to ease
astral —relating to stars
astute —shrewd
athwart —in opposition to
atoll —a ring-shaped island
atrophy —wasting away
attenuate —to make slender
attest —to bear witness to
attrition —rubbing against
atypical —not normal
augur —to foretell
aural —pert. to hearing
aureate —gilded
auspices —protection
auspicious —indicating success
austerity —severity
austral —southern
autocrat —absolute monarch
autonomy —self-government
autopsy —inspection of corpse

avarice —greed
averse —reluctant
avocation —hobby
avoirdupois —system of weights
avuncular —like an uncle
awry —in the wrong direction

B

badger —to tease or annoy
badinage —playful teasing
baleful —destructive
banal —commonplace
bandy —to give and take
baneful —evil
banter —good-natured ridicule
baroque —highly ornate
barrister —counselor-at-law
bastion —fortification
bauble —trinket
beatify —to make happy
bedizen —to adorn gaudily
beguile —to cheat
belabor —to beat soundly
belles-lettres —literature
bellicose —warlike
benediction —blessing
beneficence —charity
benign —kindly
berate —to scold vehemently
besom —a broom
bestride —to straddle
bicameral —consisting of two branches
biennial —every two years
biped —two-footed animal
blanch —to bleach
blasphemy —contempt for God
blatant —noisy
blithe —joyous
bluster —to be noisy
bombastic —pompous
bourgeois —pert. to the middle class
bourne —boundary
bourse —a foreign exchange
bovine —cowlike
brigand —bandit
broach —introduce
bromidic —tiresome; dull
bruit —to rumor

brusque —blunt in manner
bucolic —rustic
buffoon —a clown
bull —a papal letter
bullion —gold or silver in bars
burgeon —to sprout
burnish —to polish by rubbing

C

cabal —conspiracy
cabala —any occult science
cache —hiding place
cacophony —discord
cadaver —dead body
cadence —rhythm
cadre —framework
caduceus —symbol of the medical profession
cairn —heap of stones used as a tombstone
caitiff —scoundrel
cajole —coax
caliph —Moslem head
calk, caulk —to fill a seam
calligraphy —penmanship
callow —immature; innocent
calumniate —to slander
camaraderie —fellowship
canaille —rabble; mob
cant —slang; pretense
canter —easy gallop
cantilever —type of bridge
canvass —to solicit (note spelling)
capacious —spacious
capitulate —to surrender
capricious —whimsical; fickle
captious —faultfinding
carafe —bottle
carcinoma —cancer
careen —to tip to one side
carnal —of the body
carnivorous —flesh-eating
carrion —decaying flesh
carte blanche —unrestricted authority
cassock —long church garment
castigate —to criticize; punish
casuistry —false reasoning
cataclysm —sudden, violent change

catalyst —substance causing change
catastrophe —calamity
catechism —elementary religious book
categorical —certain
cathartic —cleansing
catholic —universal
caudal —near the tail
causerie —a chat
cauterize —to cut with a hot iron
caveat —warning
cavil —to find fault
celerity —swiftness
celibacy —unmarried state
cenotaph —monument for the dead
cephalic —pert. to the head
cerebral —pert. to the brain
cerebration —process of thought
cervical —pert. to the neck
chaff —rubbish; to tease
chagrin —disappointment, vexation
challis —soft cotton fabric
chamberlain —official
chameleon —lizard
champ —to bite
chandler —dealer in candles
charlatan —impostor
charnel —burial place
chary —careful, stingy
chaste —pure
chastisement —punishment
chattel —property
chauvinism —zealous patriotism
chicanery —fraud
chide —to rebuke
chimerical —imaginary
chiropractic —healing by manipulating
chivalrous —gallant
chrysalis —the pre-butterfly stage
churlish —rude
chutney —seasoning
cicada —locust
circuitous —roundabout
circumlocution —talking around a subject
circumspect —watchful
circumvent —to go around

cirrus —thin, fleecy cloud
citadel —fortress
cite —to quote
clack —to chatter
clairvoyant —foretelling the future
clandestine —secret
claque —hired applauders
claustrophobia —fear of enclosed places
clavicle —collarbone
clavier —musical keyboard
cleave —to adhere; to split
cliché —overworked expression
climacteric —critical
coadjutor —helper
coalesce —to grow together
coddle —to boil gently
codicil —addition
coerce —to compel
coffer —box
cogent —convincing
cogitate —to think
cognate —related
cohesion —sticking together
cohort —a company or band
colander —strainer
collateral —accompanying
collate —to collect in order
collation —a light meal
colligate —arrange in order
collocation —arrangement
colloquialism —informal conversation
colloquy —conference
collusion —secret agreement
colophon —inscription in a book
comatose —lethargic
comity —friendly feeling
commensurate —equal; corresponding
comminuted —reduced to fine particles
commiseration —sympathy
commodious —roomy
commutation —substitution
compact —agreement
complacence —calm
complacent —self-satis-

fied
complement —full quantity
component —ingredient
compunction —remorse
concatenate —to connect
concentric —with the same center
conclave —a private meeting
concomitant —accompanying
concordat —covenant
concupiscent —lustful
concurrent —running together
condign —well-deserved
condiment —spice
condole —to express sympathy
condone —to pardon
conduce —to lead to
conduit —pipe
confidant —one confided in
configuration —form resulting from arrangement of parts
conflagration —large fire
confute —to overwhelm by argument
congeal —to change from a fluid to a solid
congenital —dating from birth
conglomerate —mixture
congruent —in agreement
congruous —becoming
conic —cone-shaped
conifer —cone-bearing tree
conjecture —guess
conjoin —to unite
conjugal —pert. to marriage
conjure —to produce by magic
connive —to assist in wrong-doing
connubial —pert. to marriage
consanguinity —blood relationship
consecrate —to dedicate
consign —to transfer merchandise
consonance —agreement
consort —wife or husband
constituency —body of voters
constrain —to compel

consummate —to complete
contemn —to despise
contentious —quarrelsome
contiguous —next to
contingent —conditional
contravene —to oppose
contrition —repentance
controvert —to dispute
contumacious —stubbornly disobedient
contumely —contempt
contusion —bruise
conundrum —puzzle
conversant —having knowledge of
convivial —gay
convoke —to call together
copious —plentiful
cordillera —chain of mountains
cordovan —type of leather
cornucopia —horn of plenty
coronary —pert. to the arteries
corporeal —bodily
corpulent —very fat
correlate —to have a relationship
corroborate —to confirm
corollary —something that follows; result
corona —crown
cortege —procession
cosmopolitan —belonging to the world
coterie —small informal group
cotillion —a social dance
cotter —pin
couchant —lying down
coulee —gulch
countermand —to revoke an order
coup d'état —overthrow of government
couplet —two lines that rhyme
couturier —dressmaker
cozen —to cheat
covenant —agreement
covert —hidden
covetous —envious
cower —to shrink from fear
crag —rock
crass —stupid
craven —cowardly
credence —belief
credulous —inclined to

believe
cremate —to burn a dead body
cretinism —dwarfism
crimp —to make wavy
criterion —standard of judging
crouton —piece of toasted bread
cruciate —cross-shaped
crux —vital point
cryptic —mysterious
cudgel —thick stick
culinary —relating to the kitchen
culmination —acme
culpable —guilty
cuneate —wedge-shaped
cumulus —rounded cloud
cupidity —greed
curmudgeon —churlish person
cursory —superficial
cygnet —young swan

D

dactyl —a metrical foot
daguerreotype —type of early photograph
dale —valley
dalliance —dawdling
damask —a figured fabric
dank —damp
dappled —marked with small spots
dastard —coward
davit —crane for hoisting boats
dawdle —to waste time
dearth —scarcity
debase —to reduce in dignity
debauch —to corrupt
debilitate —to weaken
debonair —courteous
decadence —deterioration
decamp —to depart; flee
decant —to pour off gently
decanter —ornamental wine bottle
deciduous —leaf-shedding
declivity —downward slope
décolleté —low-necked
decorous —proper
decrepit —old
decry —to clamor against
deduce —to derive by reasoning
de facto —actual

defalcation—embezzlement
defamation—slander
defection—desertion
deference—act of respect
definitive—final
defunct—dead
deify—to make as a god
deign—to condescend
de jure—according to law
delectable—delightful
delete—to erase; remove
deleterious—harmful
delineate—to mark off
delta—flat plain at river mouth
demagogue—leader who incites
demean—to debase
demesne—possession of land
demur—to hesitate
demure—serious
denizen—inhabitant
dénouement—solution
deposition—testimony outside court
deprecate—to belittle
depreciate—decrease in value
depredation—plundering
derelict—something abandoned
derogatory—disparaging
descant—to talk or write lengthily
descry—to spy
desecrate—to profane
despicable—contemptible
despoil—to plunder
desultory—aimless
deterrent—thing which discourages
detonate—to explode
deviate—to stray
devolve—to hand down
dexterity—skill
diabolic—devilish
diadem—a crown
diapason—full range of notes
diaphanous—translucent; filmy
dichotomy—division
dictum—authoritative statement
didactic—instructive
diffidence—timidity
diffuse—to spread out
digress—to wander
dilate—to expand

dilatory—dawdling
dilettante—a dabbler
diluvial—pert. to the flood
diminution—reduction in size
diocese—district of bishop
dipsomaniac—an alcoholic (persón)
dirk—a kind of dagger
discernible—identifiable
disciple—student
disclaim—to renounce
discomfit—to defeat
disconcert—to throw into confusion
disconsolate—hopeless
discordant—not harmonious
discountenance—to disapprove
discursive—rambling
disdain—to reject
disingenuous—not innocent
disinterested—unprejudiced
disjoin—to separate
disparage—to belittle
disparity—inequality
disputation—controversy
disquisition—discussion of a subject
dissemble—to disguise
disseminate—to spread
dissertation—formal essay
dissimulation—disguise
dissipate—to squander
dissolute—immoral
dissonant—inharmonious
dissuade—to advise against
distend—to stretch
distortion—twisting out of shape
distraught—bewildered
dithyramb—choral song
diurnal—daily
diva—prima donna
diverge—to extend in different directions
diversity—variety
divest—to deprive
divination—foreseeing the future
divot—turf cut out by a stroke
docile—easily led
doggerel—poorly written poetry

dogma—system of beliefs
dogmatic—arbitrary
doldrums—boredom
dole—free food or money
doleful—sorrowful
dolorous—grievous
dolphin—porpoise
dolt—blockhead
doomsday—day of judgment
dormant—sleeping
dorsal—referring to the back
dossier—file on a person
dotage—senility
dotard—senile person
doublet—man's coat
doughty—valiant
dour—sullen
dowry—money given at time of marriage
doxology—hymn praising God
dray—open cart
drivel—foolish talk
droll—amusing
dross—waste matter
dryad—wood nymph
dubious—doubtful
ductile—able to be molded
dudgeon—resentment
duenna—Spanish chaperone
dupe—to deceive
duplicity—hypocrisy
durance—imprisonment

E

ebullience—boiling up
ecclesiastical—pert. to the church
eclat—brilliancy of achievement
ecology—science of environment
eclogue—pastoral poem
eclectic—selective
ecstasy—extreme happiness
ecumenical—general
edict—public notice
edifice—a building (especially large)
edify—to instruct
educe—to bring out
efface—to wipe out
effete—worn-out
effigy—image
effluence—a flowing out
effrontery—boldness
effulgent—illuminated
effusive—gushing

egocentric—self-centered
egotism—conceit
egress—exit
elated—elevated in spirt
electorate—voting body
eleemosynary—devoted to charity
elegy—mournful poem
elicit—to draw out
elucidate—to make clear
emanate—to issue forth
embellish—to adorn
embody—to render concrete
embolism—blood clot
embrocate—to rub with a lotion
emendation—a correction
emetic—inducing vomiting
emissary—messenger
emollient—soothing
empirical—pert. to experience
emporium—trade center
empyreal—celestial
empyrean—heavenly
emulate—to try to equal
enclave—area within foreign territory
encomium—praise
encroach—to infringe
encyclopedic—covering a wide range
endemic—peculiar to an area
endive—lettuce-like plant
endogenous—originating from within
enervate—to weaken
enfranchise—to give the right to vote; set free
engender—to produce
engrossed—fully absorbed
engulf—to swallow up
enhance—to improve; add to
ennui—weariness
enormity—outrageous offense
ensnare—to trap
enteric—intestinal
enthrall—to charm; subjugate
entrepreneur—employer
enunciate—to pronounce clearly
envenom—to embitter
eolithic—stone age
epic—long poem of grandeur

epicure —lover of good food

epigram —witty thought

epilogue —concluding literary portion

epistle —a letter

epithet —descriptive adjective

epitome —condensation

equanimity —calm temper

equestrian —pert. to horses

equinox —equal day and night

equipoise —equilibrium

equivocate —to deceive

ergo —therefore

erode —to wear away

erotic —amatory

eruct —to belch

erudite —scholarly

escadrille —airplane squadron

escarpment —a steep slope

eschew —to avoid

escritoire —writing desk

esculent —edible

escutcheon —shield

esoteric —secret

esthetic —beautiful; artistic

estuary —river mouth

ethereal —spirit-like

ethnic —referring to a race

ethnology —study of origin of races

etiolate —to whiten

etiology —study of causes of disease

etude —musical composition

etymology —derivation of words

eugenics —improvement in offspring

eulogy —praise

euphemism —mild expression

euphonious —pleasant-sounding

euphoria —sense of well-being

euphuism —affected way of writing

euthanasia —painless death

evacuate —to empty

evanescent —transitory

evasion —to subterfuge

evince —to make evident

eviscerate —to disembowel

evoke —to call forth

evolve —to develop gradually

exacting —severe

exchequer —treasury

excise —indirect tax

excoriate —to skin; denounce

execrable —extremely bad

execrate —to abhor

exemplary —deserving imitation

exhort —to incite

exhortation —recommendation

exhume —to dig out

exigency —necessity

existentialism —philosophy of a purposeless world

exodus —a going forth

exogenous —derived externally

exonerate —to free from guilt

exorbitant —unreasonable

exorcise —to expel evil spirits

exordium —beginning part of an oration

expatiate —to elaborate (especially in speech)

expedient —advantageous

expedite —to speed up

expiate —to atone

expeditious —prompt

explicate —to explain

expostulate —to protest

expound —to state in detail

expulsion —driving out

expunge —to erase or delete

expurgate —to remove objectionable matter

exquisite —carefully selected

extant —still existing

extemporaneously —on the spur of the moment

extirpate —to destroy entirely

extol —to praise

extort —to obtain by threat of violence

extradite —to transfer a prisoner

extricate —to free

extrinsic —foreign; external

extrude —to expel

F

fabricate —to build

facade —front of a building

facetious —humorous

facilitate —to make easy

facile —expert

factious —contrary; petulant

factotum —employee with many duties

faculty —a natural or acquired ability

fallible —capable of erring

fallow —lying idle

falter —to hesitate

farraginous —mixed; jumbled

farrier —blacksmith

fasces —emblem of power

fastidious —very critical

fathom —six feet

fatuous —foolish

feasible —suitable

feckless —ineffective

feculent —foul; impure

fecund —fertile

felicity —happiness

ferret —to search

ferrous —containing iron

fetid —stinking

fetish —superstition

fettle —state of fitness

fetus —unborn babe

fiasco —ridiculous failure

fief —estate under feudal control

finesse —subtlety; craftiness

fiord —sea inlet

firth —narrow inlet

fissure —crack

flaccid —not firm

flagitious —wicked

flagrant —openly disgraceful

flail —to beat

flatulent —causing gas

flaunt —to show off

fledge —to furnish with feathers

flex —to bend

florescence —flowering

florid —flowery; having a ruddy color

flotsam —ship wreckage

flout —to scoff at; mock or jeer

fluctuate —to rise and fall

flume —valley

foible —weakness

foliaceous —leaflike

font —religious receptacle; type assortment

foray —plundering raid

forensic —pert. to debate

formidable —frightening; impressive

fortuitous —accidental

fractious —unruly

fray —fight

frenetic —frantic

frivolous —not serious

frizzle —to make crisp or curly

frond —divided leaf

frugal —thrifty

fugue —musical composition

fulminate —to denounce loudly

fulsome —objectionably excessive

furbelow —trimming

fustian —worthless

G

gabble —to talk without meaning

galaxy —large system of stars

gall —to wear away

gallinaceous —pert. to fowl

gainsay —to deny

gambol —to frolic

gamut —the complete range

garble —to confuse such as facts

garish —flashy; showy

garrulous —talkative

gauntlet —type of glove

gelid —icy

generic —pert. to a race

genus —a kind or class

geriatrics —care for the aged

germane —pertinent

gerund —a verbal noun

gestation —pregnancy

ghoul —grave-robber

gibber —to talk foolishly

gird —to encircle

gist (jist) —essence

glaucous —sea-green

glib —speaking fluently without sincerity

glucose —sugar

gluttonous—greedy for food
gnostic—wise
goad—to urge on
golgotha—a place of sacrifice; cemetery
gonad—sex gland
gossamer—sheer
gourmet—a judge of food
gradient—degree of rising or falling
grail—a shallow vessel
grandee—person of high rank
grandeur—splendor
granular—grain-like
graphology—study of handwriting
gratuitous—free
gratuity—tip
gregarious—sociable
grimace—to distort the features
grimalkin—old cat
grimly—fiercely
grist—a thing used to one's advantage
grommet—a metal ring
grouse—to complain
grub—to toil unceasingly
gudgeon—simpleton
guile—deceit
gull—to swindle
gut—to destroy
guzzle—to drink much
gynecology—science of women's diseases
gyrate—to spin
gyroscope—rotating wheel
gyve—shackle

H

habiliment—clothes
habitable—livable
haft—handle
haggard—gaunt; careworn
halberd—axlike weapon
halcyon—peaceful
hale—to compel to go
hallow—to make holy
hallucination—delusion
harass—to annoy
harbinger—forecast
harridan—vicious old woman
hassock—cushion used as stool
hauteur—pride
hawser—a large rope
hearth—floor of fireplace
hedonist—lover of

pleasure
hegemony—leadership
heinous—hateful; atrocious
helix—coil of wire
heptagon—seven-sided polygon
herbivorous—feeding on herbs
heretical—not agreeing
hermitage—monastery
heterodox—having unorthodox opinions
heterogeneous—different
hexapod—having six feet
heyday—period of great vigor
hidalgo—Spanish nobleman
hieratic—priestly
hinder—to retard
hirsute—hairy
histology—science of organic tissue
histrionic—theatrical
hoary—white with age
hoi polloi—masses
holocaust—great destruction
holograph—personally written document
homage—respect
homeopathy—method of treating disease
homiletics—art of preaching
homily—sermon
homogeneous—essentially alike
homogenous—derived from the same source
homologous—similar
homunculus—dwarf
hone—to sharpen
hormone—internal secretion
hortatory—encouraging
horticulture—the science of gardening
hoyden—tomboy
humanist—classical scholar
humerus—arm bone
hummock—small hill
humus—fertilizer
hurtle—to clash; rush headlong
husbandry—occupation of farming
hustings—electioneering platform
hydrophobia—rabies; fear of water

hydrous—containing water
hygroscope—instrument indicating humidity
hymeneal—pert. to marriage
hyperbole—exaggeration
hypertension—high blood pressure
hypochondria—fancies of bad health
hypothesis—assumption

I

ichthyology—science of fish
iconoclast—image breaker
ideology—body of ideas
idiosyncrasy—peculiar tendency
idyllic—simple or poetic
igneous—of volcanic origin
ignoble—base, unworthy
ignominious—contemptible
illusory—unreal
imbibe—to drink in
imbrue—to stain or drench
imbue—to saturate
impale—to fix on a point
impalpable—not evident
impassioned—animated; excited
impeach—to accuse (not to find guilty)
impeccable—faultless
impecunious—poor
impede—to hinder
imperceptible—not easily seen
imperishable—indestructible
imperturbable—tranquil
impervious—not to be penetrated
impetuous—impulsive
implicit—absolute; implied
importune—to beg
impotent—incapable
imprecation—curse
impresario—manager
imprimatur—license to publish
impudence—shamelessness
impugn—to question
impunity—exemption from punishment
impute—to blame

inadvertence—carelessness
inalienable—not transferable
inarticulate—not distinct
incarcerate—to imprison
incarnadine—flesh-colored
incendiary—inflammatory
incognito—with identity concealed
incommensurate—not adequate
incongruous—not suitable
inconsiderable—trivial
incorrigible—beyond reform
incubus—burden
inculpate—to blame
indenture—contract
indigenous—native
indigent—poor
indiscriminate—not selective
indite—to write
indolent—lazy
indubitable—undeniably true
indurate—hardened
inebriated—drunk
ineffable—indescribable
inert—sluggish
inexorable—unyielding
inference—conclusion
inflammable—burnable
ingenuous—innocent
ingratiate—to establish in favor
iniquitous—sinful
innocuous—harmless
innuendo—insinuation
inscrutable—unfathomable
insensate—without sensation
insidious—treacherous
insinuate—to suggest subtly
insolvent—bankrupt
insouciant—carefree
insular—pert. to an island
intangible—not touchable
interdict—official order
interpolate—to insert new material
interregnum—interval between reigns
intractable—stubborn
intransigent—uncom-

promising
intravenous—through a vein
intrepid—brave
intrinsic—essential
introvert—to turn inward
inveigh—to attack
investiture—act of giving an office or right to
inveterate—firmly established
invidious—odious
invocation—calling on God
ionosphere—outer layers
isobar—weather map line
isotope—chemical element
isthmus—narrow land strip
iterate—to repeat
itinerant—traveling on a circuit

J
jaded—worn out
jargon—confused talk
jaundiced—envious
jeremiad—lamentation
jettison—to cast overboard
jocose—humorous
jodhpurs—riding pants
juridical—legal
juxtaposed—close together

K
kaleidoscope—optical instrument
karat—1/24 part gold
kinetics—science of pure motion
kiosk—stand which is open on one side
kith—friends

L
lacerate—to tear
laconic—brief
lachrymose—tearful
laity—the people collectively as distinguished from clergymen
lampoon—satire or ridicule
landed—having an estate in land
languish—to become weak
lascivious—lewd
lassitude—weariness

latent—concealed
latex—milky fluid
latitude—allowance
legerdemain—trickery
lethargic—drowsy
lexicon—dictionary
libel—defamation
libretto—verbal text of an opera
licentiate—one who has a license
liege—feudal lord
limn—to portray
litany—prayer
lithe—supple
litigation—legal action
liturgy—religious ritual
livid—black and blue
loquacious—talkative
lucid—clear
lucre—money or riches
ludicrous—ridiculous
lugubrious—sad
lymph—transparent body fluid

M
macabre—gruesome
macadamize—to cover with broken stones
macerate—to soften by dipping
madrigal—short musical poem
maelstrom—whirlpool
magisterial—authoritative
magnanimous—generous
mahatma—extraordinary person
mahout—elephant driver
maladroit—clumsy
malaise—discomfort
malapropism—word misused ridiculously
malfeasance—wrongful act
mandate—a specific order
mange—skin disease
mantilla—head scarf
marline—a nautical cord
marquee—canopy
marsupial—pert. to animals such as kangaroos
martinet—disciplinarian
matrix—a mold
masticate—to chew
maw—mouth of a voracious animal
mawkish—nauseating
maxim—proverb

medley—mixture
mega—million
megrim—low spirits
melange—mixture
mellifluent—sweetly flowing
menage—household
mendacious—lying
mendicant—beggar
meniscus—crescent-shaped
mercurial—lively
meretricious—showily attractive
mesa—high, wide tableland with rocky slopes
metamorphose—to transform
metaphor—a comparison
mete—to distribute
mettle—courage
microcosm—a little world
mien—manner or bearing
militate—to operate against
misanthropy—dislike mankind
miscegenation—interbreeding of races
misconstruction—wrong interpretation
miscreant—villain
missal—prayer book
mistral—cold dry northerly wind
mitigate—to lessen
mnemonics—memory device
modicum—small quantity
modulate—to soften
monolith—large piece of stone
montage—blending of pictures
mordant—biting; sarcastic
moribund—dying
mortar—container for crushing
mosque—Moslem temple
motley—miscellaneous
mufti—civilian dress
mulct—to defraud
mummery—pretentious ritual
murrain (mur-rin)—cattle disease
muzhik—Russian peasant
myopia—nearsightedness

myriad—a great many

N
nacre—mother-of-pearl
nadir—lowest point
naiad—mythical water nymph
nape—back of neck
narcissism—love of oneself
natatorial—pert. to swimming
nebulous—hazy
nefarious—wicked
neophyte—new convert
neolithic—pert. to later Stone Age
neurasthenia—nervous exhaustion
niggardly—stingy
nihilism—disbelief in religion
nimbus—halo
nirvana—freedom from pain
noctambulist—sleepwalker
nocturne—a piece of dreamy music
node—knob
noisome—offensive
nomenclature—names of things
nonagenarian—person in his 90's
nonpareil—without equal
nonplus—to perplex
non sequitur—illogical argument
nosegay—bouquet
noxious—harmful
nuncio—representative of Pope
nurture—to provide food

O
obdurate—callous; hardened
obeisance—bowing
obelisk—four-sided pillar
obesity—excessive fatness
obfuscate—to confuse
oblation—solemn offering
obloquy—disgrace
obsequious—servile
obsolescent—becoming out-of-date
obstreperous—noisy
obtrude—to thrust forth**

obturate —to stop or close
obtuse —dull
obviate —to prevent
occidental —Western
occipital —pert. to back of head
occlude —to close
ocellated —having eye-like spots
octamerous —having eight parts
odoriferous —fragrant
officious —meddling
oleaginous —oily
olfactory —pert. to sense of smell
oligarchy —rule by a few
omega —last letter
ominous —threatening
omnipotent —all-powerful
omnivorous —eating everything
onerous —difficult
opprobrious —shameful
optimum —the best
opulence —riches
oracular —prophetic
orbicular —circular
ordnance —military weapons
ordinance —law
ordure —filth
oriel —bay window
orifice —opening
orthography —science of spelling
oscillate —to vibrate
ossify —to become rigid or bonelike
ostensible —apparent
ostentatious —pretentious
overt —open to view

P

pachyderm —elephant
pacific —calm
paisley —colorful fabric
paean —song of praise
palanquin —bed carried on poles
palatable —tasty
palaver (puh-lav-ur) — smooth or empty talk
pall —to become dull
palliate —to mitigate
palpable —evident
panacea —remedy for all ills
panegyric —eulogy
panoply —set of armor

pantheism —belief of God-nature unity
paradigm —model
paradox —contradiction
parapet —barricade
paregoric —pain-reliever
pariah —outcast
parietal —pert. to side of skull
parity —equality
parochial —provincial
paroxysm —a fit
parsimonious —stingy
pastoral —pert. to rural life
patriarch —leader of a tribe
patrimony —an inheritance
pavilion —a large tent
peccadillo —a small fault
pectoral —pert. to chest
peculate —to embezzle
pecuniary —financial
pedantic —bookish
pediculous —infested with lice
peduncle —flower stalk
peignoir —dressing gown
pejorative —disparaging
pelagic —pert. to ocean
pelf —stolen property
penchant —strong inclination
pendant —anything hanging from something
pensile —hanging
pennate —winged
penurious —stingy
perambulate —to walk about
perception —awareness
percussion —impact
peregrination —traveling
peremptory —positive
perigee —point nearest earth
periphery —external surface
peristaltic —pert. to alternate waves
permeable —penetrable
permutation —changing
perquisite —incidental compensation
peroration —last part of a speech
perspective —the effect of distance
perspicuity —clearness of style or expression
pert —saucy
peruse —to read carefully

pervade —to spread to every part
perverse —contrary
pestle —that which pounds
petulance —peevishness
phalanx —any massed body
philistine —narrow-minded person
philology —study of words or literature
phylum —grouping in biology
picaresque —pert. to rogues
pilaster —part of a column
pileous —pert. to hair
pillory —structure for exposing to scorn
piquant —pungent
pique —to wound
piscatorial —pert. to fishing
pixilated —amusingly eccentric
plagiarism —stealing ideas from someone else
plait —to braid or pleat
platitude —trite remark
plectrum —small piece used to pluck
plenipotentiary —possessing full power
plethora —oversupply
plinth —lower part of column
plumb —to test the depth of
plutocracy —rule by the rich
poach —to trespass
pogrom —organized massacre
poignant —keenly affecting
polemics —art of disputing
polity —method of government
polonaise —slow Polish dance
polymer —chemical compound
pontificate —to speak pompously
porringer —soup plate
posterity —succeeding generations
portend —to warn
pottage —a stew

poultice —a soft moist mass
pragmatic —practical
prate —chatter
precarious —uncertain
precipitous —steep
preclude —to prevent
precursor —predecessor
predatory —plundering
predilection —preference
preeminent —superior
premeditation —forethought
preposterous —very absurd
prerogative —privilege
presbyter —ordained clergyman
prescience —foresight
presentiment —foreboding
presentment —report made by a grand jury
preternatural —supernatural
prevaricate —to lie
primogeniture —state of being first-born
primordial —first in order
pristine —primitive; unspoiled
probity —integrity
proclivity —tendency
procrastinate —to put off
prodigious —large
proffer —to offer
profligate —utterly immoral
progeny —offspring
proletarian —pert. to workers
prolix —long-winded
promontory —a high point of land
propinquity —nearness
propitious —favorable
proscenium —front stage
proselyte —a convert
prosody —science of verse forms
protagonist —leading character
prototype —example
protuberance —projection
provender —food for animals
providential —fortunate
psychoneurosis —emotional disorder
puissant —powerful
punctilious —exact
purloin —to embezzle

purulent —discharging pus
pusillanimous —afraid
putative —supposed
putrefy —to decay
Pyrrhic victory —victory at great cost
pythonic —prophetic

Q

quadrennial —comprising four years
qualm —feeling of fear
quandary —doubt
quasi —resembling but not genuine
query —question
quidnunc —curious person
quiescent —inactive
quietus —a silencing
quintessence —concentrated essence
quirk —a turn
quixotic —visionary
quotidian —daily

R

rabbet —groove
rabble —vulgar, noisy people
rabid —furious
raillery —banter
raiment —clothing
ramification —a division
rampant —springing; climbing
ramshackle —out of repair
rancor —anger
rankle —to irritate
rapacity —greediness
ratiocination —reasoning
recalcitrant —stubborn
recapitulate —to summarize
reciprocal —in return
recitative —ordinary speech set to music
recrimination —countercharge
rectitude —uprightness
refractory —obstinate
regale —to entertain
regicide —killing of a king
regimen —manner of living
relegate —to assign
reliquary —receptacle
remission —pardon
remonstrate —to protest
renascent —being reborn

renegade —deserter
repine —to complain
replete —full
reprehension —rebuke
reprisal —injury in return
reproof —a scolding
respite —pause or rest
repudiate —to refuse
requital —repayment
resilient —rebounding
resplendent —shining
restitution —compensation
résumé —summary
resurgent —rising again
resuscitate —to revive
reticulate —net-like
retroactive —applying to the past
retrogression —going back
retroussé —turned up
revile —to scold
rhesus —type of monkey
rhinitis —inflammation of nose
risibility —disposition to laughter
rote —mechanical routine
rubicund —red
rudiment —first stage; non-functioning organ

S

sable —black
sabot —wooden shoe
saccharine --pert. to sugar
sagacious —wise
salacious —obscene
salient —prominent
saline —salty
salubrious —healthful
salutary —wholesome
salutatory —pert. to a greeting
sanctimonious —affectedly holy
sanctity —holiness
sanguine —confident
saponify —to make fat into soap
sardonic —ironical
satiate —to supply to excess
satrap —governor of province
saturate —to fill
saturnine —gloomy
scapular —pert. to shoulder
scarab —ornament

scarify —to make scratches
schism —division
schist —a type of rock
sciatic —pert. to the hip
scintilla —bit
scintillation —a sparkling
scrip —paper money less than a dollar
scruple —reluctance
scurrilous —insulting
secular —not religious
sedentary —sluggish
sedulous —painstaking
seismic —caused by an earthquake
semantic —pert. to meaning
senescent —growing old
sententious —magisterial
sentient —feeling
sequester —to seclude
seraglio —harem
serrated —sawtoothed
shamble —something destroyed or in disorder
shibboleth —a pet phrase
shunt —to turn aside
sidereal —pert. to stars
silicosis —lung disease
simian —pert. to a monkey
simile —comparison using as or like
simony —profit from sacred things
simper —self-conscious smile
sinecure —job requiring little work
sinuous —with many curves
slake —to lessen
slatternly —sloppy
slothful —lazy
slough —soft, muddy ground
sluice —a water channel
sojourn —temporary residence
solicitude —concern
soliloquy —monologue
somatic —bodily
sonorous —resonant
sophism —fallacy
spatula —flat, broad instrument
specious —deceptive
spectre —ghost
speculum —mirror
splenetic —peevish
spontaneous —uncon-

strained
sporadic —occasional
spume —foam
stalactite —hanging calcium deposit
stalagmite —calcium deposit on cave floor
steppe —vast treeless plain
sternum —the breastbone
stigma —blemish
stilted —elevated
stint —to be frugal
stoical —impassive
stratagem —scheme
stricture —severe criticism
strident —grating
suave —smoothly polite
subcutaneous —beneath the skin
subjoin —to add
sublimate —to purify or refine
subpoena —summons for witness
subsidy —financial aid
subterfuge —a false excuse
succinct —brief
succor —comfort; aid
succulence —juiciness
suffuse —to overspread
sully —to soil
supercilious —proud and haughty
supernal —heavenly
supersede —to take the place of
supervene —to interrupt
supplicate —to beg
surfeit —excess
surreptitious —secret
surrogate —deputy
surveillance —watching
swathe —to bind or wrap
sybarite —person devoted to luxury
sycophant —flatterer
syllogism —deductive reasoning
sylvan —pert. to woods
symposium —meeting for discussion
syncope —contraction of a word
synonymy —the quality of being the same
synthesis —combination

T

tableau —a striking scene
taboret —small stool

tachometer —instrument for measuring speed
taciturn —silent
talus —slope
tankard —large drinking vessel
tantamount —equal to
tautology —needless repetition
temerity —rashness
terminus —limit
thesaurus —treasury
thoracic —between neck and abdomen
thrall —slave
threnody —song of lamentation
thrombosis —blood clot
tiara —headdress
tirade —vehement speech
tithe —tax of one-tenth
tocsin —bell
tome —volume
toque —hat without a brim
torpor —dullness
tortilla —large round thin cake
trachea —windpipe
tractable —easily led
traduce —to slander
tranquillity —calmness
transcendent —surpassing others
transfuse —to pour from one to another
transmute —to change
transpire —to become known

transubstantiation —to change to another substance
transverse —lying across
trauma —wound
travail —labor
treacle —molasses
treble —triple
tremulous —shaking
trenchant —sharp
trepidation —trembling from fear
tribulation —trouble
truncheon —club
trundle —small wheel
tumbrel —farmer's cart
tumid —swollen
turbulent —violent
turgid —swollen
turpitude —shameful depravity
tutelage —instruction
twit —to tease
tyke —mischievous child
tyro —novice

U

ubiquity —omnipresence
ukase —Russian government order
ululation —a wailing
umbilicus —navel
umbrage —offense
unctuous —oily or smooth
undulating —waving
ungainly —clumsy
upbraid —to reproach
uproarious —noisy

urbane —refined
ursine —pert. to bears
usurpation —wrongful seizure
uxorious —fond of a wife

V

vacuous —empty
vapid —dull
varicosity —swollen veins
vacillation —unsteadiness
vacuity —stupidity
vagary —whim
vanguard —leaders
vaquero —cowboy
variegate —to diversify
vaunt —to boast
vendetta —feud
venerate —to revere
venous —pert. to veins
ventricle —cavity
verdant —green; fresh
verisimilitude —appearance of truth
verity —honesty
vernacular —native language
vernal —pert. to spring
vertex —top
vertigo —dizziness
vestige —trace
viable —capable of living
vicissitude —change
vilify —to defame
vindicate —to uphold
viridity —greenness
vituperate —to defame
vociferate —to shout
volatility —frivolity

volition —will
voracious —ravenous
votary —devoted person

W

waft —current of wind
waggery —mischievous merriment
wainscot —wood paneling
wassail —a toast
wastrel —spendthrift
wean —to detach
welter —to roll about
wheedle —to coax
whimsical —fantastic; quaint
whey —milk water
wizened —withered
wont —custom
woof —fabric
wraith —ghost

X

xylem —woody tissue of plants

Y

yak —species of ox
yen —monetary unit of Japan
yogi —an ascetic

Z

zany —clown
zeal —enthusiasm
zenith —highest point

ANTONYMS

SUGGESTIONS FOR ANSWERING ANTONYM TESTS

1. Read all of the directions carefully so that you are sure you know what you are being asked to do. This applies to all tests. The time spent in reading the directions is NOT wasted.
2. In answering antonym questions be careful that you do not trick yourself. The choices may include a synonym for the word as well as an antonym.

Procedure

3. If you know the meaning of the word, think of an antonym before you look for an answer because this will help prevent you from picking a synonym.
4. Choose the answer which is most nearly correct from among the answer choices you are given. Sometimes the choices that are given may not be the same word you would use as an antonym. If you find a word that seems to be the best of the possible choices, there is a good chance that you have the correct answer.
   Example:

   SADNESS
   (A) interest
   (B) happiness
   (C) elation
   (D) sorrow
   (E) freedom

   Although all of the words except sorrow have some element that shows the lack of sadness, the word "elation" is the furthest from "sadness" and is the BEST answer.
5. If you are not sure of the meaning of the word, you may still be able to make an intelligent guess.
   A. See if you can get a feeling for the connotation of the word.
   Example:

PUSILLANIMOUS
(A) dishonest
(B) evil
(C) lost
(D) brave
(E) unneeded

Although you may not know the meaning of the word, you may well get a negative feeling about the word. It is probably not something you would like to be called. Therefore, pick a word with a positive connotation; in this case (D) for your answer.

B. Look at the prefixes, suffixes, and root words because these can often tell you enough about a word to help you make an intelligent choice.
Example:

OMNISCIENT
(A) swift
(B) stupid
(C) willing
(D) kind
(E) upset

If you can recognize that the root of the word is the same as the word science, you will know that the word has something to do with knowledge, and answer (B) becomes a logical choice.

C. If you have no knowledge of the word at all, you can sometimes make a more or less intelligent guess by looking at the answer choices and trying to find information from them.
Example:

ANTEDILUVIAN
(A) modern
(B) abundant
(C) ancient
(D) interested
(E) slow

Notice that "modern" and "ancient" are antonyms. Since testmakers often place a synonym and an antonym among the possible answers, there is a better than

213

"haphazard" chance that one of these is the correct answer, and it is to your advantage to pick one of them. In this case the prefix "ante" meaning *before* should have led you to pick a meaning leaning to "after" or "modern."

ANTONYMS: TEST 1

Directions: Each of the following questions consists of a word printed in capital letters followed by five (5) lettered words or phrases. Select the word or phrase which is most nearly opposite to the capitalized word in meaning. Circle the letter preceding your answer.

1. PIQUANT
   (A) factitious
   (B) vain
   (C) insipid
   (D) vulture
   (E) chromatic

2. OPPORTUNE
   (A) dialectical
   (B) mutable
   (C) unplanned
   (D) weird
   (E) ill-timed

3. PETULANT
   (A) irascible
   (B) cheerful
   (C) uncouth
   (D) abnormal
   (E) ambulant

4. SAVORY
   (A) apathetic
   (B) clandestine
   (C) pliant
   (D) unpalatable
   (E) capillary

5. SATIATED
   (A) satirical
   (B) centaur
   (C) gorgeous
   (D) delectable
   (E) hungry

6. RECLUSIVE
   (A) empyreal
   (B) obscure
   (C) gregarious
   (D) rustic
   (E) chilblain

7. COURTEOUS
   (A) flaccid
   (B) emolient
   (C) insolent
   (D) scrupulous
   (E) flinching

8. USURP
   (A) repair
   (B) reduce
   (C) produce quickly
   (D) hold carefully
   (E) own rightfully

9. ACRIMONIOUS
   (A) alluvial
   (B) apocalyptic
   (C) cursive
   (D) harmonious
   (E) flippant

10. SKEPTICAL
    (A) cryptic
    (B) credulous
    (C) discursive
    (D) eminent
    (E) caricatured

11. RECONDITE
    (A) miniature
    (B) ceramic
    (C) arable
    (D) caraway
    (E) obvious

12. REDUNDANT
    (A) dilatory
    (B) apocryphal
    (C) astute
    (D) insufficient
    (E) calumnious

13. **INDUBITABLE**
    (A) fetid
    (B) aesthetic
    (C) unmitigated
    (D) questionable
    (E) belabored

14. **RESTITUTION**
    (A) inflation
    (B) cataclysm
    (C) deprivation
    (D) misogyny
    (E) changeling

15. **ROTUNDITY**
    (A) clemency
    (B) ebullience
    (C) angularity
    (D) contumely
    (E) chicory

16. **SAGACIOUS**
    (A) derelict
    (B) hazardous
    (C) articulate
    (D) verbose
    (E) ignorant

17. **SANGUINARY**
    (A) kind
    (B) sanctified
    (C) gastronomical
    (D) turgid
    (E) embittered

18. **PARSIMONY**
    (A) miasma
    (B) antimony
    (C) clinch
    (D) fustian
    (E) prodigality

19. **PERSPICUITY**
    (A) cupidity
    (B) salubriousness
    (C) ambiguity
    (D) discrimination
    (E) chrysolite

20. **PREPOSTEROUS**
    (A) complaisant
    (B) conceited
    (C) apologetic
    (D) rational
    (E) castellated

ANSWER KEY

1.	C	11.	E
2.	E	12.	D
3.	B	13.	D
4.	D	14.	C
5.	E	15.	C
6.	C	16.	E
7.	C	17.	A
8.	E	18.	E
9.	D	19.	C
10.	B	20.	D

EXPLANATORY ANSWERS

1. **(C)** Piquant means lively or interesting; the opposite would be insipid.

2. **(E)** Something opportune would be at the right time; therefore, ill-timed would be the correct choice.

3. **(B)** Petulant means irritable; the opposite would be cheerful.

4. **(D)** Savory means pleasant; the antonym would be unpalatable.

5. **(E)** Satiated means satisfied to the full; the opposite would be hungry.

6. **(C)** To be reclusive means to be withdrawn from others; the opposite is gregarious.

7. **(C)** When you are courteous, you are polite; the opposite would be insolent.

8. **(E)** To usurp means to seize without legal right; the antonym is to own rightfully.

9. **(D)** Something acrimonious is characterized by harshness; the best answer here would be harmonious.

10. **(B)** When you are skeptical, you are doubtful; the opposite would be credulous.

11. **(E)** Something recondite is obscure; the opposite would be obvious.

12. **(D)** Redundant can mean being in excess; its opposite meaning would therefore be insufficient.

13. **(D)** Something indubitable is unquestionable or that which cannot be doubted; the opposite is questionable.

14. **(C)** Restitution means the restoration of something; the best answer here would be deprivation.

15. **(C)** Rotundity is characterized by roundness; its opposite would be angularity.

16. **(E)** A sagacious person is wise or intelligent; the opposite would be ignorant.

17. **(A)** Sanguinary means cruel; its opposite would be kind.

18. **(E)** Parsimony is extreme frugality, in other words, stinginess; its antonym would be prodigality.

19. **(C)** Perspicuity indicates clarity and clearness; its antonym would be ambiguity.

20. **(D)** When something is preposterous, it is absurd, completely contrary to reason; the opposite is rational.

ANTONYMS: TEST 2

Directions: Each of the following questions consists of a word printed in capital letters followed by five (5) lettered words or phrases. Select the word or phrase which is most nearly opposite to the capitalized word in meaning. Circle the letter preceding your answer.

1. PROFUSION
   (A) travesty
   (B) validity
   (C) scarcity
   (D) ordinance
   (E) laudanum

2. AGNOSTIC
   (A) aged
   (B) fanatic
   (C) truncated
   (D) productive
   (E) inebriate

3. MITIGATION
   (A) aggravation
   (B) verdancy
   (C) obscenity
   (D) restriction
   (E) interregnum

4. MISANTHROPIC
   (A) angelic
   (B) cauterized
   (C) supercilious
   (D) biologic
   (E) humanitarian

5. INIQUITY
   (A) equity
   (B) rectitude
   (C) peace
   (D) apostasy
   (E) calmness

6. PROTUBERANCE
   (A) cadence
   (B) habitation
   (C) indentation
   (D) appendage
   (E) timbrel

7. INGENUOUS
   (A) genuflecting
   (B) hypothetical
   (C) spasmodic
   (D) genuine
   (E) hypocritical

8. SANCTIMONIOUS
   (A) proud
   (B) stubborn
   (C) wealthy
   (D) ingenuous
   (E) impervious

9. EXTIRPATE
   (A) propagate
   (B) inseminate
   (C) ingratiate
   (D) emasculate
   (E) daub

10. CAPRICIOUS
    (A) redoubtable
    (B) constant
    (C) bellicose
    (D) cretaceous
    (E) ignominious

11. CASUISTRY
    (A) wright
    (B) trilogy
    (C) sediment
    (D) verity
    (E) beauty

12. CONTUMELY
    (A) willingness
    (B) imminence
    (C) praise
    (D) augmentation
    (E) tractability

13. CREDULITY
    (A) litany
    (B) drollery
    (C) ablution
    (D) badinage
    (E) cynicism

14. PREDILECTION
    (A) sobriety
    (B) hostility
    (C) euphony

(D) emollient
(E) contention

15. EFFULGENT
    (A) murky
    (B) petulant
    (C) mercenary
    (D) ludicrous
    (E) mundane

16. SEDULOUS
    (A) vociferous
    (B) indolent
    (C) concomitant
    (D) itinerant
    (E) onerous

17. IMPERTURBABLE
    (A) militant
    (B) cynical
    (C) conical
    (D) agitated
    (E) Martian

18. CAPTIOUS
    (A) eulogistic
    (B) whimsical
    (C) jocose
    (D) lethargic
    (E) empyreal

19. DENOUEMENT
    (A) fusillade
    (B) redundance
    (C) modicum
    (D) limpet
    (E) introduction

20. TAUTOLOGY
    (A) oscillation
    (B) succinctness
    (C) investiture
    (D) urbanity
    (E) curvature

ANSWER KEY

1.	C	11.	D
2.	B	12.	C
3.	A	13.	E
4.	E	14.	B
5.	A	15.	A
6.	C	16.	B
7.	E	17.	D
8.	D	18.	A
9.	A	19.	E
10.	B	20.	B

EXPLANATORY ANSWERS

1. **(C)** A profusion is an abundance; its opposite would be scarcity.

2. **(B)** An agnostic admits to uncertainty regarding absolutes; a fanatic will take an uncritically extreme position.

3. **(A)** Mitigation refers to a lessening of intensity; its opposite would be aggravation.

4. **(E)** Misanthropic means mankind-hating; its opposite would be humanitarian.

5. **(A)** Iniquity is injustice; its opposite would be fairness or equity.

6. **(C)** A protuberance is a projection or bulge; its opposite would be an indentation.

7. **(E)** Ingenuous means sincere and frank; therefore, the opposite of hypocritical.

8. **(D)** Sanctimonious means hypocritical behavior in certain matters; its opposite is ingenuous.

9. **(A)** To extirpate is to destroy totally; the opposite would be to increase in number or to propagate.

10. **(B)** Capricious means inconstant; the opposite is constant.

11. **(D)** Casuistry may refer to intellectual dishonesty; verity or truth is opposite in meaning.

12. **(C)** Contumely is an insult; its opposite is praise.

13. **(E)** Credulity is a state of trusting too easily; the opposite is cynicism.

14. **(B)** A predilection is a preference for; its antonym would be hostility.

15. **(A)** Effulgent means to shine forth brightly; its opposite would be murky.

16. **(B)** Sedulous means diligent and persevering; therefore, not lazy or indolent.

17. **(D)** Imperturbable means calm; therefore, agitated is its opposite.

18. **(A)** When you are captious, you fault-find; when you are eulogistic, you praise.

19. **(E)** The denouement refers to the final outcome or the resolution of a plot and thus the opposite of the introduction.

20. **(B)** Tautology refers to needless repetition and verbosity; the opposite is succinctness.

ANTONYMS: TEST 3

Directions: Each of the following questions consists of a word printed in capital letters followed by five (5) lettered words or phrases. Select the word or phrase which is most nearly opposite to the capitalized word in meaning. Circle the letter preceding your answer.

1. CATEGORICAL
   (A) cancelled
   (B) doglike
   (C) ambiguous
   (D) unregenerate
   (E) voluptuous

2. PREMEDITATED
   (A) superannuated
   (B) tractable
   (C) syncopated
   (D) impromptu
   (E) sebaceous

3. PROPINQUITY
   (A) remoteness
   (B) succulence
   (C) antiquity
   (D) tedium
   (E) glebe

4. SANGUINE
   (A) real
   (B) alive
   (C) moving
   (D) skillful
   (E) morose

5. ALTERCATION
   (A) adversity
   (B) consonance
   (C) provender
   (D) encomium
   (E) contrition

6. COLLIGATION
   (A) juxtaposition
   (B) coxswain
   (C) emendation
   (D) derangement
   (E) integration

7. ADJURE
   (A) assist
   (B) retain

(C) ask facetiously
(D) jump quickly
(E) remove instantly

8. POSTULATE
   (A) undulate
   (B) prove
   (C) peculate
   (D) palpitate
   (E) disenchant

9. ARROGATE
   (A) earn
   (B) confabulate
   (C) imprecate
   (D) interpose
   (E) litigate

10. ALIENATE
    (A) protract
    (B) profligate
    (C) conjoin
    (D) liberate
    (E) desiccate

11. APOCRYPHAL
    (A) authentic
    (B) winsome
    (C) zealous
    (D) nefarious
    (E) crooked

12. IMPETUOUS
    (A) migratory
    (B) hypothetical
    (C) incidental
    (D) obstreperous
    (E) controlled

13. AMELIORATE
    (A) emulsify
    (B) vitiate
    (C) clasp
    (D) dissemble
    (E) curl

14. BENIGN
    (A) dulcet
    (B) dogmatic
    (C) dolorous

(D) malignant
(E) morose

15. ABRIDGE
    (A) epitomize
    (B) encourage
    (C) augment
    (D) cloy
    (E) subdue

16. AVERSION
    (A) amnesty
    (B) augury
    (C) affinity
    (D) wassail
    (E) valance

17. SOLICITUDE
    (A) nonchalance
    (B) truncheon
    (C) ebullition
    (D) dereliction
    (E) diffidence

18. STOICISM
    (A) anemia
    (B) sensitivity
    (C) detritus
    (D) escutcheon
    (E) gossamer

19. EXCULPATION
    (A) hyperbole
    (B) anticipation
    (C) condemnation
    (D) implication
    (E) cessation

20. SUBJOIN
    (A) delete
    (B) regress
    (C) infer
    (D) interpolate
    (E) upgrade

ANSWER KEY

1.	C	11.	A
2.	D	12.	E
3.	A	13.	B
4.	E	14.	D
5.	B	15.	C
6.	D	16.	C
7.	C	17.	A
8.	B	18.	B
9.	A	19.	C
10.	C	20.	A

EXPLANATORY ANSWERS

1. **(C)** Categorical means absolute or unqualified; opposite in meaning would be ambiguous or uncertain.

2. **(D)** Premeditated means thought out beforehand; impromptu means done on the spur of the moment.

3. **(A)** Propinquity means nearness; remoteness would therefore be opposite in meaning.

4. **(E)** Sanguine means cheerfulness; moroseness, or gloominess, would be opposite in meaning.

5. **(B)** An altercation is a dispute or noisy controversy; consonance, in this instance meaning harmony or agreement, is the correct antonym.

6. **(D)** Colligation means a coming together; derangement would be a disarrangement or falling apart.

7. **(C)** Adjure is to request earnestly; its opposite would be to ask lightly or facetiously.

8. **(B)** To postulate is to assume without proof; to prove would therefore be its antonym.

9. **(A)** To arrogate is to take without right; to earn is to merit something by working for it.

10. **(C)** To alienate is to estrange; to conjoin is to bring together.

11. **(A)** Apocryphal means of doubtful authenticity; authentic would be its true opposite.

12. **(E)** Impetuous means impulsive or rash; controlled, meaning restrained, would be the correct antonym.

13. **(B)** Ameliorate means to improve; vitiate means to make faulty.

14. **(D)** Benign means benevolent; malignant means malevolent.

15. **(C)** To abridge means to shorten; to augment means to add.

16. **(C)** An aversion is a strong feeling of dislike; an affinity is a natural liking.

17. **(A)** When you show solicitude you show concern for; nonchalance is a lack of concern.

18. **(B)** Stoicism is a philosophy extolling the repression of emotions; sensitivity, or emotional feeling, would be opposite in meaning.

19. **(C)** Exculpation means to free from blame; condemnation would be the act of blaming.

20. **(A)** Subjoin means to add on; to delete means to cut out.

ANTONYMS: TEST 4

Directions: Each of the following questions consists of a word printed in capital letters followed by five (5) lettered words or phrases. Select the word or phrase which is most nearly opposite to the capitalized word in meaning. Circle the letter preceding your answer.

1. CONCOMITANT
   (A) hymeneal
   (B) synthetic
   (C) pellucid
   (D) lineal
   (E) discrete

2. PROCLIVITY
   (A) insipidity
   (B) repugnance
   (C) effrontery
   (D) doxology
   (E) contingency

3. ETHEREAL
   (A) synchronous
   (B) advantageous
   (C) ponderous
   (D) contagious
   (E) egregious

4. EXTRANEOUS
   (A) doubled
   (B) facetious
   (C) germane
   (D) toxic
   (E) sequential

5. ANALOGOUS
   (A) expletive
   (B) septic
   (C) virulent
   (D) heterogeneous
   (E) defunct

6. ASSUAGE
   (A) corrugate
   (B) detest
   (C) provoke
   (D) traduce
   (E) reverberate

7. ASSEVERATE
   (A) striate
   (B) deny

(C) wrap
(D) mislead
(E) integrate

8. TEMPORAL
   (A) firm
   (B) permanent
   (C) kaleidoscopic
   (D) placid
   (E) lucid

9. FUSION
   (A) schism
   (B) paradox
   (C) lenity
   (D) analogy
   (E) monasticism

10. CAJOLE
    (A) inveigle
    (B) proselytize
    (C) antagonize
    (D) synthesize
    (E) dissimulate

11. DILETTANTE
    (A) titmouse
    (B) pilaster
    (C) strophe
    (D) professional
    (E) seraglio

12. INCREMENT
    (A) injunction
    (B) argot
    (C) conjunction
    (D) badinage
    (E) reduction

13. AVERSE
    (A) reasonable
    (B) agreeable
    (C) coincidental
    (D) palatable
    (E) porous

14. COMMENSURATE
    (A) inadequate
    (B) incompetent
    (C) sedimentary

(D) amalgamated
(E) propitious

15. DISCIPLE
    (A) artisan
    (B) craven
    (C) renegade
    (D) wench
    (E) dastard

16. TERMINUS
    (A) sarcophagus
    (B) marina
    (C) spontaneity
    (D) commencement
    (E) replica

17. MUCILAGINOUS
    (A) portable
    (B) sanctimonious
    (C) rotund
    (D) separable
    (E) prolix

18. PROCRASTINATE
    (A) eulogize
    (B) invest
    (C) expedite
    (D) insinuate
    (E) mediate

19. VENERATE
    (A) abominate
    (B) involve
    (C) adapt
    (D) instigate
    (E) correlate

20. EMBELLISH
    (A) suffice
    (B) disfigure
    (C) forfeit
    (D) demolish
    (E) derogate

ANSWER KEY

1.	E	11.	D
2.	B	12.	E
3.	C	13.	B
4.	C	14.	A
5.	D	15.	C
6.	C	16.	D
7.	B	17.	D
8.	B	18.	C
9.	A	19.	A
10.	C	20.	B

EXPLANATORY ANSWERS

1. **(E)** Concomitant means accompanying; discrete, meaning separate, would be opposite in meaning.

2. **(B)** Proclivity would be a leaning toward; repugnance, meaning aversion, is its antonym.

3. **(C)** Ethereal means light; ponderous means heavy.

4. **(C)** When something is extraneous, it is not pertinent; something germane is relevant or pertinent.

5. **(D)** Analogous means alike; heterogeneous means unlike or dissimilar.

6. **(C)** To assuage is to pacify; to provoke is to incite.

7. **(B)** Asseverate means to affirm positively; to deny would be its opposite.

8. **(B)** Temporal means temporary; permanent, or everlasting, would be opposite in meaning.

9. **(A)** A fusion is a coming together; a schism means a disunion.

10. **(C)** To cajole means to persuade by flattery; to antagonize means to make hostile.

11. **(D)** A dilettante is an amateur, a dabbler; a professional is the correct antonym.

12. **(E)** Increment means a measured increase while reduction indicates a decrease.

13. **(B)** Averse means opposed or not agreeable; the opposite would naturally be agreeable.

14. **(A)** Commensurate means having the same measure; inadequate, meaning insufficient and incommensurate, is its antonym.

15. **(C)** A disciple is a follower, an adherent to the doctrine of another; a renegade is a deserter from a party or cause.

16. **(D)** The terminus is the end of something; a commencement is a beginning.

17. **(D)** Mucilaginous, meaning of the nature of mucilage or glue, connotes a sticking together or adhesion; opposite in meaning would be separable.

18. **(C)** To procrastinate means to delay; to expedite means to speed up the progress of something.

19. **(A)** To venerate means to revere; to abominate means to loathe.

20. **(B)** To embellish means to beautify, to adorn; to disfigure, or to mar the beauty of, is opposite in meaning.

ANTONYMS: TEST 5

Directions: Each of the following questions consists of a word printed in capital letters followed by five (5) lettered words or phrases. Select the word or phrase which is most nearly opposite to the capitalized word in meaning. Circle the letter preceding your answer.

1. DELETERIOUS
   (A) fractious
   (B) salubrious
   (C) pathetic
   (D) eulogistic
   (E) antipathetic

2. PUISSANCE
   (A) bicuspid
   (B) approbation
   (C) impotence
   (D) repudiation
   (E) erudition

3. SYCOPHANCY
   (A) colloquialism
   (B) innuendo
   (C) nihilism
   (D) frankness
   (E) apotheosis

4. ABERRATION
   (A) correctness
   (B) empathy
   (C) attenuation
   (D) consanguinity
   (E) reticence

5. ANOMALOUS
   (A) capacious
   (B) vicious
   (C) explicated
   (D) covetous
   (E) explainable

6. COGNIZANCE
   (A) idiom
   (B) ignorance
   (C) abeyance
   (D) anecdote
   (E) fetish

7. QUIESCENT
   (A) restless
   (B) exempt

   (C) malignant
   (D) mendicant
   (E) farcical

8. ESCHEW
   (A) traduce
   (B) escheat
   (C) greet
   (D) emanate
   (E) subvene

9. TACITURN
   (A) dubious
   (B) garrulous
   (C) eucharistic
   (D) iniquitous
   (E) gullible

10. SENTENTIOUS
    (A) stalled
    (B) laconic
    (C) frustrated
    (D) prolix
    (E) sadistic

11. INAUGURATE
    (A) facilitate
    (B) ameliorate
    (C) inculcate
    (D) gesticulate
    (E) terminate

12. DUBIOUS
    (A) concomitant
    (B) cadaverous
    (C) immutable
    (D) hypochondriac
    (E) iconoclastic

13. CASTIGATION
    (A) cliché
    (B) panegyric
    (C) esthete
    (D) euphemism
    (E) gourmet

14. FORTUITY
    (A) transient
    (B) extenuation
    (C) corpuscle

(D) foreordination
(E) opportunity

15. **PLEONASM**
  (A) succinctness
  (B) ambiversion
  (C) braggadocio
  (D) connoisseur
  (E) demagogue

16. **EMANCIPATION**
  (A) scintillation
  (B) imprisonment
  (C) misadventure
  (D) pertinacity
  (E) segregation

17. **INVIDIOUS**
  (A) contingent
  (B) promiscuous
  (C) benignant
  (D) inadvertent
  (E) envious

18. **BUCOLIC**
  (A) circumspect
  (B) urbane
  (C) abortive
  (D) laconic
  (E) punctilious

19. **LUGUBRIOUS**
  (A) cheerful
  (B) hungry
  (C) skillful
  (D) jealous
  (E) wise

20. **INEXORABLE**
  (A) erudite
  (B) impregnable
  (C) indulgent
  (D) perspicacious
  (E) quixotic

ANSWER KEY

1.	B	11.	E
2.	C	12.	C
3.	D	13.	B
4.	A	14.	D
5.	E	15.	A
6.	B	16.	B
7.	A	17.	C
8.	C	18.	B
9.	B	19.	A
10.	D	20.	C

EXPLANATORY ANSWERS

1. **(B)** Deleterious means injurious to health; salubrious means promoting health.

2. **(C)** Puissance means power; impotence means weakness.

3. **(D)** Sycophancy means self-seeking flattery, saying yes for advancement; frankness, meaning honesty of opinion, is clearly opposite in meaning.

4. **(A)** Aberration is a deviation from what is correct; correctness is the antonym.

5. **(E)** Something anomalous is strange or contradictory; something explainable would therefore be its antonym.

6. **(B)** Cognizance means knowledge; the opposite would be ignorance or lack of knowledge.

7. **(A)** Quiescent means being at rest, quiet; restless, its antonym, means characterized by an inability to remain at rest.

8. **(C)** To eschew means to avoid; most opposite in meaning would be to greet.

9. **(B)** Taciturn means silent; garrulous means talkative.

10. **(D)** Sententious means pithy or succinct; therefore, prolix which means unnecessarily long is its opposite.

11. **(E)** To inaugurate is to begin; to terminate is to end.

12. **(C)** Dubious can mean fluctuating; immutable, meaning changeless, is its opposite.

13. **(B)** Castigation means a reproof; its opposite would be panegyric, a commendation.

14. **(D)** A fortuity is an accidental occurrence, happening by chance; a foreordination is something that has been ordained beforehand.

15. **(A)** Pleonasm is redundancy, the use of more words than is necessary; succinctness, meaning expressed in few words, is its antonym.

16. **(B)** Emancipation means freedom; its opposite is imprisonment.

17. **(C)** Invidious means harmful; benignant means beneficial.

18. **(B)** Bucolic means rustic and unsophisticated; its antonym is urbane which means having the polish characteristic of sophisticated city life.

19. **(A)** Lugubrious means gloomy; its opposite is cheerful.

20. **(C)** Inexorable means unyielding; indulgent, meaning giving in to another, is its opposite.

SENTENCE COMPLETIONS

This question-type requires that you complete a sentence in which one or two words are represented by blank spaces. Here you must look for the underlying meaning of a sentence. You must then be able to discriminate between the choices given. Usually this understanding does not require a special background, but it does require the possession of a solid vocabulary plus sufficient reasoning ability.

SUCCESS IN SENTENCE COMPLETIONS

We suggest the following steps for success in sentence completion questions:

1. Fit each choice into the blank(s) provided.
2. Determine which choice completes the sentence so that the sentence makes good sense.

Let us illustrate with this question:

The Citizens Budget Commission criticized the proposed legislation as _____ and wasteful.
- (A) helpful
- (B) possible
- (C) completed
- (D) praiseworthy
- (E) illogical

After fitting each choice into the blank, you will, as a result of clear thinking, arrive at the conclusion that (E) *illogical* is the only reasonable choice.

SENTENCE COMPLETIONS: TEST 1

Directions: Each of the questions below contains one or more blank spaces, each blank indicating an omitted word. Each sentence is followed by five (5) lettered words or sets of words. Read and determine the general sense of each sentence. Then choose the word or set of words which, when inserted in the sentence, best fits the meaning of the sentence. Circle the letter preceding your answer.

1. He believed that poverty was ineradicable and that no social legislation could be more than _____.
   - (A) interpretive
   - (B) palliative
   - (C) ambivalent
   - (D) desultory
   - (E) excruciating

2. Even while he was openly accusing his partners of dishonesty, he was making _____ arrangements to flee the country.
   - (A) covert
   - (B) quiescent
   - (C) subcutaneous
   - (D) egregious
   - (E) ephemeral

3. Although he spoke well, his writing was _____ under the circumstances.
   - (A) maladroit
   - (B) imperturbable
   - (C) malignant
   - (D) relevant
   - (E) indigenous

229

4. The hot, humid day made me feel completely
   _____; I sank back weakly into the
   hammock.
   (A) sedulous
   (B) sapient
   (C) enervated
   (D) energetic
   (E) protracted

5. The painter demurred and procrastinated so
   much that it was clear he would take on the
   job with great _____.
   (A) furor
   (B) fervency
   (C) redolence
   (D) reluctance
   (E) proclivity

6. Rich people usually feel revulsion mingled
   with pity at the sight of the _____ of
   slum areas.
   (A) temerity
   (B) squalor
   (C) serendipity
   (D) pallor
   (E) candor

7. After seven hours of listening to his
   interminable story-telling, we finally escaped
   from the _____ old man.
   (A) evasive

(B) surreptitious
(C) garrulous
(D) dogmatic
(E) replenished

8. In its search for means of inducing sleep in
   the grievously sick, modern researchers have
   analyzed many of the _____
   compounds that primitive peoples have
   discovered.
   (A) bubonic
   (B) soporific
   (C) biographic
   (D) crepuscular
   (E) inferential

9. John wanted nothing more than to
   _____ the pain.
   (A) alleviate
   (B) allegate
   (C) subordinate
   (D) alliterate
   (E) castigate

10. Her status in the hat shop was that of a mere
    _____.
    (A) millenary
    (B) minim
    (C) millinery
    (D) menial
    (E) militant

ANSWER KEY

1.	B		6.	B
2.	A		7.	C
3.	A		8.	B
4.	C		9.	A
5.	D		10.	D

EXPLANATORY ANSWERS

1. **(B)** The meaning of the sentence is that the man feels that poverty is a "necessary evil." It will always be with us and social measures provide only a relief, not a cure. In other words, legislation is only palliative.

2. **(A)** The sentence indicates that the man was outwardly doing one thing while secretly doing another. He was thus making covert, or secret, plans to leave the country.

3. **(A)** The sentence expresses a seemingly contradictory fact that although he spoke well, he wrote badly. Maladroit would be the correct word expressing his writing ability.

4. **(C)** The weather is described as causing the speaker to become tired—it depleted him of energy. In other words, it enervated him.

5. **(D)** The painter's unwillingness to do the job shows that he would only take it on with great reluctance.

6. **(B)** The feelings of the rich indicate their reaction to the misery of the slums. The squalor elicits their revulsion and pity.

7. **(C)** If someone has been talking without stopping for seven hours, we could easily describe him as garrulous.

8. **(B)** Soporific means causing sleep. This is the only choice which fits into the sentence.

9. **(A)** One usually wants to relieve or alleviate pain.

10. **(D)** The sentence suggests she had only a subordinate position; in other words, she had a menial job.

SENTENCE COMPLETIONS: TEST 2

Directions: Each of the questions below contains one or more blank spaces, each blank indicating an omitted word. Each sentence is followed by five (5) lettered words or sets of words. Read and determine the general sense of each sentence. Then choose the word or set of words that, when inserted in the sentence, best fits the meaning of the sentence. Circle the letter preceding your answer.

1. Through his _____, he deceived us all.
   (A) wit
   (B) selvage
   (C) canard
   (D) petard
   (E) telescope

2. The lover of democracy has an _____ toward totalitarianism.
   (A) antipathy
   (B) empathy
   (C) antipode
   (D) idiopathy
   (E) predilection

3. An _____ may connect the names of members of a partnership.
   (A) addendum
   (B) idiograph
   (C) epigram
   (D) encomium
   (E) ampersand

4. A _____ person cannot be expected to resist _____.
   (A) profligate —money
   (B) raucous —temptation
   (C) recreant —aggression
   (D) squalid —quarreling
   (E) strong —vice

5. He hated his father so intensely that he committed _____.
   (A) parricide
   (B) fratricide
   (C) genocide
   (D) matricide
   (E) suicide

6. Because he was _____, people often confided in him.
   (A) circumlocutory
   (B) choleric
   (C) caustic
   (D) circumspect
   (E) circuitous

7. The convicted man resorted to _____ in attacking his accusers.
   (A) nepotism
   (B) anathema
   (C) panoply
   (D) bravura
   (E) entropy

8. The _____ woman was the _____ of all eyes.
   (A) titled —cupola
   (B) lonely —sinecure
   (C) ugly —doggerel
   (D) attractive —cynosure
   (E) fat —vacuum

9. A _____ is likely to give you the wrong advice.
   (A) nuance
   (B) panacea
   (C) charlatan
   (D) virago
   (E) halberd

10. The _____ professor put his wife out and went to sleep with the cat.
   (A) diurnal
   (B) distrait
   (C) dubious
   (D) dilatory
   (E) distinguished

ANSWER KEY

1.	C	6.	D
2.	A	7.	B
3.	E	8.	D
4.	C	9.	C
5.	A	10.	B

EXPLANATORY ANSWERS

1. **(C)** The sentence implies that he used some means of deception. A canard is a lie and would thus be the means of deceit.

2. **(A)** Democracy and totalitarianism are opposite and incompatible forms of government. A lover of democracy would be antagonistic toward totalitarianism. Antipathy best expresses this relationship.

3. **(E)** By definition, an ampersand is a character meaning "and." It would thus be the connecting word between the names of a business partnership.

4. **(C)** By determining the meaning of the different sets, the best choice is clearly (C). A coward or recreant would not be expected to fight or resist aggressive behavior.

5. **(A)** Parricide is the crime of killing one's father and would thus be the correct choice.

6. **(D)** People would trust a prudent or circumspect person. They would therefore be likely to tell such a person confidential matters.

7. **(B)** An anathema can mean a threat or curse (without the religious connotations usually attached to the word). Thus a convicted man would want to get back at his accusers in this fashion.

8. **(D)** The sentence implies that someone was the focus of all the eyes. Thus an attractive woman could very well be the center of attention—the cynosure of all eyes.

9. **(C)** By definition a charlatan is a fraud and would be quite likely to impart false information.

10. **(B)** The sentence clearly indicates that the professor was absentminded and distracted. He was thus distrait.

SENTENCE COMPLETIONS: TEST 3

Directions: Each of the questions below contains one or more blank spaces, each blank indicating an omitted word. Each sentence is followed by five (5) lettered words or sets of words. Read and determine the general sense of each sentence. Then choose the word or set of words that, when inserted in the sentence, best fits the meaning of the sentence. Circle the letter preceding your answer.

1. Art is long and time is _____.
   - (A) fervid
   - (B) fallow
   - (C) nebulous
   - (D) evanescent
   - (E) flaccid

2. The _____ flower was also _____.
   - (A) pretty —redolent
   - (B) drooping —potable
   - (C) pale —opulent
   - (D) blooming —amendable
   - (E) thorny—resurgent

3. The _____ effects of the drug made her very weary.
   - (A) succinct
   - (B) spurious
   - (C) soporific
   - (D) supine
   - (E) suggestive

4. Being _____, the child was not permitted to have his supper.
   - (A) refractory
   - (B) reticent
   - (C) vernal
   - (D) unctuous
   - (E) nubile

5. The chairman's _____ speech swayed the audience to favor his proposal.
   - (A) cursory
   - (B) blatant
   - (C) ancillary
   - (D) cogent
   - (E) irregular

6. He is quite _____ and, therefore, easily _____.
   - (A) callow —deceived
   - (B) lethal —perceived
   - (C) fetal —conceived
   - (D) limpid —received
   - (E) intransigent —sieved

7. That _____ seems so out of place with those lovely little girls.
   - (A) shard
   - (B) hoyden
   - (C) tyro
   - (D) vanguard
   - (E) sylph

8. The sculptor will convert this _____ piece of clay into a beautiful bust.
   - (A) virulent
   - (B) morose
   - (C) taciturn
   - (D) salient
   - (E) amorphous

9. His _____ had no place in our serious conversation.
   - (A) badinage
   - (B) viscosity
   - (C) concatenation
   - (D) valence
   - (E) sibling

10. Her _____ manner embarrassed the others at the party.
   - (A) affable
   - (B) tractable
   - (C) sapid
   - (D) gauche
   - (E) astute

ANSWER KEY

1.	D	6.	A
2.	A	7.	B
3.	C	8.	E
4.	A	9.	A
5.	D	10.	D

EXPLANATORY ANSWERS

1. **(D)** This sentence implies the age-old theme of art is long and life is short. Evanescent best expresses this condition.

2. **(A)** You must find two words that express complementary qualities appropriate to a flower. Redolent, meaning fragrant, would suit pretty.

3. **(C)** A soporific drug would be one inducing sleep and drowsiness. It would cause a person to be weary.

4. **(A)** The sentence suggests that the child was not permitted to have supper as a punishment. Refractory, meaning stubborn or uncontrollable, would best fit the sense of the sentence.

5. **(D)** A speech which could sway people would be compelling and one which also appealed to reason. Thus, the speech was cogent.

6. **(A)** Someone callow is unsophisticated and therefore able to be fooled or deceived.

7. **(B)** A hoyden is an ill-bred or boisterous girl. She would therefore be out of place with the others as described in the sentence.

8. **(E)** A sculptor forms something out of shapeless clay. Amorphous means without definite form and thus is the correct fill-in.

9. **(A)** Badinage means silly repartee or banter. It would be out of place to use it in a serious discussion.

10. **(D)** When someone lacks social grace, he or she is usually awkward with others, and this could be embarrassing at a party. Gauche means lacking in social refinement.

SENTENCE COMPLETIONS: TEST 4

Directions: Each of the questions below contains one or more blank spaces, each blank indicating an omitted word. Each sentence is followed by five (5) lettered words or sets of words. Read and determine the general sense of each sentence. Then choose the word or set of words that, when inserted in the sentence, best fits the meaning of the sentence. Circle the letter preceding your answer.

1. In a state of _____, we are likely to have _____.
   - (A) ochlocracy—havoc
   - (B) bureaucracy—respect
   - (C) theocracy—sin
   - (D) desuetude—activity
   - (E) anarchy—order

2. Knowledge cannot thrive where there is _____.
   - (A) parturition
   - (B) nescience
   - (C) protocol
   - (D) neoclassicism
   - (E) solipsism

3. _____ is a phase of the study of penology.
   - (A) Recidivism
   - (B) Eclecticism
   - (C) Hematosis
   - (D) Hydrometry
   - (E) Parturition

4. The _____ of war is death and cruelty.
   - (A) sirocco
   - (B) rutabaga
   - (C) beldam
   - (D) quiddity
   - (E) oriel

5. The conceited soldier was forward and _____ in his attitude.
   - (A) mundane
   - (B) thrasonical

   - (C) gratuitous
   - (D) laconic
   - (E) narcose

6. Being a man of maxims, he was _____ in what he said.
   - (A) bawdy
   - (B) transmogrified
   - (C) sebaceous
   - (D) sentient
   - (E) sententious

7. His _____ remarks are too stupid to be taken _____.
   - (A) empyreal—lightly
   - (B) puerperal—slowly
   - (C) lacunal—violently
   - (D) vapid—seriously
   - (E) spurious—nonchalantly

8. The _____ was very informative during the trip.
   - (A) censer
   - (B) centaur
   - (C) cicerone
   - (D) burgeon
   - (E) hellion

9. A _____ and the principle of monogamy are poles apart.
   - (A) seraglio
   - (B) purlieu
   - (C) shallop
   - (D) benison
   - (E) cathode

10. The mourning throng was preparing for a _____.
   - (A) wimple
   - (B) cirque
   - (C) riposte
   - (D) monody
   - (E) tricot

ANSWER KEY

1.	A	6.	E
2.	B	7.	D
3.	A	8.	C
4.	D	9.	A
5.	B	10.	D

EXPLANATORY ANSWERS

1. **(A)** Ochlocracy means mob rule. In such a state there would be havoc. These two choices are therefore best suited.

2. **(B)** Knowledge cannot thrive in a state of nescience or ignorance.

3. **(A)** Recidivism means a relapse into criminal behavior and would thus be the correct choice.

4. **(D)** War is made up of death and cruelty. Quiddity means essence and this would fit the meaning of the sentence.

5. **(B)** One needs an adjective describing the forward, conceited soldier. Thrasonical means boastful or braggart and would thus be an appropriate choice.

6. **(E)** In order to fill in the blank space, you must know what maxims are. They can loosely be defined as proverbs or rules of conduct. If the man spoke in a sententious manner, he would be moralistic in expression. He could very well then be a man of maxims.

7. **(D)** The general meaning behind the sentence is that the remarks are so stupid that they can't be important; in other words, they can't be taken seriously. Vapid, meaning insipid or uninteresting, makes sense in this context.

8. **(C)** A cicerone is a guide and would be informative during a trip. It is the only choice which makes any sense.

9. **(A)** A seraglio is another name for a harem, the place where the wives and concubines in a Muslim household are housed. This set up would be far from the principle of monogamy wherein only one mate is taken at a time.

10. **(D)** A monody is a dirge and thus likely to be heard by a funeral party.

SENTENCE COMPLETIONS: TEST 5

Directions: Each of the questions below contains one or more blank spaces, each blank indicating an omitted word. Each sentence is followed by five (5) lettered words or sets of words. Read and determine the general sense of each sentence. Then choose the word or set of words which, when inserted in the sentence, best fits the meaning of the sentence. Circle the letter preceding your answer.

1. The will did not require _____ of witnesses since it was _____.
   (A) subordination—genocidic
   (B) bribery—histrionic
   (C) attestation—holographic
   (D) consternation—ballistic
   (E) approval—heraldic

2. Man's fate is _____.
   (A) ineluctable
   (B) cerulean
   (C) estivated
   (D) spatulated
   (E) antipodean

3. How can you depend upon a person who is so _____?
   (A) protean
   (B) somatic
   (C) pensile
   (D) empirical
   (E) sedentary

4. A _____ would be interested in a _____ of that type.
   (A) botanist—hibiscus
   (B) soldier—maverick
   (C) musician—caterwaul
   (D) butcher—brioche
   (E) dancer—canton

5. In India, a wealthy person may travel in a _____ borne by means of poles resting on men's shoulders.
   (A) carapace
   (B) bibelot
   (C) gambrel
   (D) lampoon
   (E) palanquin

6. Suffering from _____, he decided to stay indoors.
   (A) claustrophobia
   (B) agoraphobia
   (C) chicanery
   (D) patois
   (E) hydrophobia

7. _____ that my uncle is, he can do just about everything.
   (A) Dipsomaniac
   (B) Factotum
   (C) Numismatist
   (D) Pachyderm
   (E) Pragmatist

8. His _____ features reminded me of the missing link.
   (A) simian
   (B) euphemistic
   (C) vicarious
   (D) vertiginous
   (E) serpentine

9. For insisting on "It is I" instead of "It is me," he was charged with _____.
   (A) caligraphy
   (B) anomaly
   (C) bellicosity
   (D) preciosity
   (E) blasphemy

10. In certain tropical areas, malaria is an _____ disease.
    (A) endocrine
    (B) introversive
    (C) endemic
    (D) interstitial
    (E) incumbent

ANSWER KEY

1.	C		6.	B
2.	A		7.	B
3.	A		8.	A
4.	A		9.	D
5.	E		10.	C

EXPLANATORY ANSWERS

1. **(C)** The will did not have to be authenticated by witnesses since it was written in the party's own handwriting. By substituting synonyms for the choices, choice (C) proves the only logical answer.

2. **(A)** Fate is something which is inevitable or ineluctable.

3. **(A)** One can depend upon a person who is steady and always the same. However, a person who is changeable or protean cannot be relied upon.

4. **(A)** A botanist is a specialist in plants; a hibiscus is in the plant family. None of the other choices are suitable.

5. **(E)** By definition, a palanquin is an Asian vehicle—a litter borne on the shoulders of men by means of poles.

6. **(B)** Agoraphobia is the fear of open spaces and would thus be the best of the possible choices.

7. **(B)** The sentence suggests that the uncle is a jack-of-all-trades or a man of many parts. By definition, a factotum is a person able to do many different kinds of jobs.

8. **(A)** The missing link is the hypothetical link between man and his apelike progenitors. Simian means apelike and is thus the correct choice.

9. **(D)** The sentence implies that he was being too insistent on a small point. He could be accused of preciosity or being overly refined.

10. **(C)** Endemic means particular to a region. Within the context of the sentence, this is the only possible choice.

ANALOGIES

SUGGESTIONS FOR
ANSWERING
ANALOGY QUESTIONS

1. An analogy question tests your ability to reason. Usually, the vocabulary on this test is not as difficult as the vocabulary on the antonym tests or the sentence completion tests. An analogy expresses a similarity between the relationships of things to one another. On the GMAT this relationship is between the meanings and/or the usages of English words and is usually offered as a sentence written in an abbreviated form.

Example:

MARE : COLT : : COW : CALF

As a sentence this reads: A mare is related to a colt in the same way as a cow is related to a calf.

2. An analogy question tests your ability to discover the relationships between the first pair of words (the question pair) and then to find the second pair of words (the answer pair) that is MOST similar in their relationship. Remember to look for the BEST answer, not just a good answer.

Procedure

3. The KEY to answering analogy questions is analyzing the relationship between the question pair of words. If you do a good job working out this relationship, the answer often becomes obvious. Remember, there is most often more than one relationship between two words.

(a) Analyze the relationships between the question pair.

(b) Look for the pair of words with a similar relationship.

(c) If more than one pair of words fit, return to the question pair.

(d) Refine and expand the relationships in the question pair.

(e) Eliminate answers that do not appear to be the *best* answer.

(f) Always return to the question pair for more clarification if you have trouble selecting the best answer. *The key is always in the question pair.*

Example:
SLAVERY : FREEDOM : :
(A) disease : health
(B) work : play
(C) in : out
(D) war : peace
(E) enemy : friend

Analysis	*Answer*
Opposite	→ All are opposites (return to the question pair).
Negative — positive.	→ Eliminate (B) and (C) since they may be either negative or positive depending on the situation (return to the question pair).
Involve people.	→ Eliminate (A) since it involves all living things and not just people (return to question pair).
A state or condition in which people find themselves.	→ Eliminate (E) since these are people themselves and not just conditions or states of being

The best answer must be (D).

Note: Thoroughly analyze the relationships between the question pair *before* you attempt to find the *best* answer. In the above problem if your original analysis had been: A negative condition in which people find themselves: A positive condition in which people find themselves, the answer would then have been obvious.

4. In an analogy the same sequence of ideas must be found in both pairs of words.

Example:
AUTHOR : NOVEL : :
  (A) bust : sculptor
  (B) drama : playwright
  (C) composer : song
  (D) poem : poet
  (E) sermon : preacher

Analysis	*Answer*
A person and the thing he creates.	All of the answers include a person and the thing he creates. In the question pair the person comes first, and for the answer to be correct the person must be in the same position. This eliminates all answers but (C).

5. In an analogy the parts of speech must keep the same relationship.

Example:
ENEMY : BAD : :
  (A) ally : strong
  (B) dictatorship : evil
  (C) foe : dangerously
  (D) Satan : sin
  (E) friend : good

Analysis	*Answer*
Noun and describing adjective.	Eliminate (C) (dangerously —adverb) and (D) (sin —noun or verb) (return to the question pair).
Noun and adjective that describe relationship to you.	Eliminate (A) (may just as easily be weak) (return to question pair).
An enemy is a person, with bad being adjective describing your relationship to this person.	Eliminate (B) since dictatorship is not a person (dictator is the person).

Answer must be (E).

Note: If the words in the question pair are the same part of speech, the answer pair must also be the same part of speech, but not necessarily the same part of speech as the question pair.

Example:
NOUN : NOUN : : ? : ? (Your answer may be noun : noun; verb : verb; adjective: adjective; etc. It cannot be noun : adjective; verb : adverb; etc.)

If the words in the question pair are different parts of speech, the answer pair must be the same parts of speech as the question pair and in the same order as in the question pair.

Example:
NOUN : ADJECTIVE : : ? : ? (Your answer must be noun : adjective; it cannot be adjective : noun; verb : adverb; etc.)

6. In an analogy you are concerned with the relationship between pairs of words and not with the individual meanings of words. Do not compare the individual meanings of words in the question pair with individual words in possible answer pairs. In the analogy A : B : : C : D,

you are concerned with the relationship of A : B as a unit and the relationship of C : D as another unit. Do not concern yourself about the meaning of word A as it relates to word C or D.

Example:

CAGE : PARROT : :
(A) soar : eagle
(B) bowl : goldfish
(C) nest : sparrow
(D) corral : livestock
(E) imprisoned : lion

Analysis	*Answer*
A home and the animal staying there.	Eliminate (A) and (E) as they are not homes. Also, cage is a noun, soar a verb, and imprisoned an adjective.
A man-made object and the animal kept there.	Eliminate (C); a nest is not man-made.
A man-made object and the specific animal kept there.	Eliminate (D) because livestock is a general term including horses, cattle, etc.

The answer is (B) even though a bowl and a cage or a parrot and a goldfish have very little in common. It is the relationship between the question pair of words that is important. That relationship is most similar in answer pair (B).

7. Work as rapidly as you can without becoming careless. If you do not know the meanings of the words in the question pair, it may be best to skip that question. If you are able to eliminate any of the answers but cannot find one answer that is best, guess at the answer and mark the question as one to return to if you have time. Do not spend a lot of time on one or two difficult questions just to find you cannot finish the test. You may miss out on doing some easier questions.

ANALOGIES: TEST 1

Directions: In each of the following questions, you are given a related pair of words or phrases in capital letters. Each capitalized pair is followed by five (5) lettered pairs of words or phrases. Choose the pair that best expresses a relationship similar to that expressed by the original pair. Circle the letter preceding your answer.

1. CONDONE : OFFENSE ::
   (A) punish : criminal
   (B) mitigate : penitence
   (C) overlook : aberration
   (D) mistake : judgment
   (E) ignore : loyalty

2. SPASM : PAIN ::
   (A) flash : light

(B) respite : thought
(C) tender : touch
(D) pinch : taste
(E) sound : noise

3. CORRUGATED : STRIPED ::
   (A) box : zebra
   (B) paint : crayon
   (C) roughness : smoothness
   (D) pit : dot
   (E) wall : board

4. BRASS : COPPER ::
   (A) zinc : iron
   (B) pewter : tin

(C) lead : gold
(D) mercury : antimony
(E) silicon : carbon

5. OXYGEN : GASEOUS ::
(A) feather : light
(B) mercury : fluid
(C) iron : heavy
(D) sand : grainy
(E) mountain : high

6. AGILE : ACROBAT ::
(A) grease : mechanic
(B) peanuts : vendor
(C) plant : fruit
(D) eloquent : orator
(E) fast : car

7. CAT : MOUSE ::
(A) bird : worm
(B) dog : tail
(C) trap : cheese
(D) hide : seek
(E) lion : snake

8. POWER : BATTERY ::
(A) vitamins : metabolism
(B) recuperation : convalescence
(C) exercise : strength
(D) automobile : engine
(E) light : kerosene

9. VANILLA : BEAN ::
(A) tabasco : stem
(B) chili : flower
(C) mint : fruit
(D) ginger : root
(E) sage : berry

10. ENERGY : DISSIPATE ::
(A) battery : recharge
(B) atom : split
(C) food : heat
(D) money : squander
(E) gas : generate

11. NOSE : FACE ::
(A) ring : finger
(B) stem : root
(C) knob : door
(D) shoe : foot
(E) leaf : vine

12. PECK : BUSHEL ::
(A) pound : ounce
(B) quart : gallon
(C) pint : cup
(D) minute : second
(E) rod : yard

13. RIFLE : SOLDIER ::
(A) bow : arrow
(B) sword : knight
(C) horse : cowboy
(D) canteen : marine
(E) lock : robber

14. DEER : VENISON ::
(A) pig : hog
(B) sheep : mutton
(C) lamb : veal
(D) duck : roast
(E) beef : stew

15. DEPRESSION : UNEMPLOYMENT ::
(A) legislation : lobbying
(B) emaciation : debilitation
(C) capital : interest
(D) deterioration : rust
(E) recession : inefficiency

16. INTEGER : DECIMAL ::
(A) 100 : 10
(B) 1 : 0
(C) decimal : fraction
(D) whole number : fraction
(E) 100 : percent

17. ICING : CAKE ::
(A) veneer : table
(B) frost : lake
(C) pastry : bakery
(D) slicing : rake
(E) paper : page

18. CHALK : BLACKBOARD ::
(A) door : handle
(B) table : chair
(C) ink : paper
(D) dog : tail
(E) type : paint

19. THROW : BALL ::
    (A) shoot : trigger
    (B) pat : dog
    (C) mew : cat
    (D) boil : shell
    (E) finish : furniture

20. YELL : UTTER ::
    (A) scream : deafen
    (B) shout : call
    (C) child : infant
    (D) bend : break
    (E) speak : sing

ANSWER KEY

1.	C	6.	D	11.	C	16.	D
2.	A	7.	A	12.	B	17.	A
3.	D	8.	E	13.	B	18.	C
4.	B	9.	D	14.	B	19.	B
5.	B	10.	D	15.	D	20.	B

EXPLANATORY ANSWERS

1. **(C)** One pardons or overlooks an offense; one can also overlook a wrong or an aberration.

2. **(A)** A painful spasm is a sudden onset of pain; a flash is a brief glimpse of light. Both are sudden, unexpected sensory impressions.

3. **(D)** Something striped may be corrugated just as a dot may be pitted.

4. **(B)** Brass is an alloy made from copper; pewter is an alloy made from tin.

5. **(B)** Oxygen in its natural state is gaseous; mercury in its natural state is a liquid.

6. **(D)** An acrobat must be agile; an orator eloquent.

7. **(A)** A cat is the natural predator of a mouse; a bird is the natural predator of a worm.

8. **(E)** A battery may be a source of power; kerosene can be the source of light.

9. **(D)** Vanilla comes from a bean, ginger from a root.

10. **(D)** Energy can be wasted or dissipated just as money can be wasted or squandered.

11. **(C)** A nose must be on a face; a knob must be on a door.

12. **(B)** Bushels are made up of pecks; gallons are made up of quarts.

13. **(B)** A rifle is the weapon of a soldier, a sword the weapon of a knight.

14. **(B)** Venison is deer meat; mutton is sheep meat.

15. **(D)** Unemployment can be caused by a depression; rust can be caused by a deterioration.

16. **(D)** An integer can be expressed by decimals just as a whole number can be expressed by fractions.

17. **(A)** The icing is the outer coating of a cake; the veneer is the outer coating of a table.

18. **(C)** You use chalk to write on a blackboard; you use ink to write on paper.

19. **(B)** You can throw a ball; you can pat a dog.

20. **(B)** Yell is the extreme of utter; shout is the extreme of call.

ANALOGIES: TEST 2

Directions: In each of the following questions, you are given a related pair of words or phrases in capital letters. Each capitalized pair is followed by five (5) lettered pairs of words or phrases. Choose the pair that best expresses a relationship similar to that expressed by the original pair. Circle the letter preceding your answer.

1. ARCHAEOLOGIST : ANTIQUITY ::
   (A) flower : horticulture
   (B) ichthyologist : marine life
   (C) theology : minister
   (D) Bible : psalms
   (E) gold : silver

2. COURT : JUSTICE ::
   (A) doctor : sickness
   (B) chief : boss
   (C) machinist : product
   (D) policeman : government
   (E) auditor : accuracy

3. SCHOOL : DISCIPLINE ::
   (A) pupil : dean
   (B) report card : marks
   (C) society : conformity
   (D) underworld : gangster
   (E) writing : pencil

4. INSULT : INVULNERABLE ::
   (A) success : capable
   (B) poverty : miserable
   (C) purchase : refundable
   (D) assault : impregnable
   (E) research : difficult

5. FINGER : HAND ::
   (A) leg : toe
   (B) dictionary : word
   (C) toe : foot
   (D) medicine : doctor
   (E) wound : injure

6. COOLNESS : NIGHT ::
   (A) black : yellow
   (B) humidity : sunshine
   (C) warmth : day
   (D) fear : fright
   (E) evening : dusk

7. GIRL : WOMAN ::
   (A) student : teacher
   (B) adult : child
   (C) black : white
   (D) infant : child
   (E) nephew : niece

8. SHOE : LEATHER ::
   (A) passage : ship
   (B) trail : wagon
   (C) journey : boat
   (D) highway : asphalt
   (E) car : engine

9. PEDAGOGUE : LEARNING ::
   (A) teaching : books
   (B) professor : erudition
   (C) Plato : pedant
   (D) schoolmaster : ABC's
   (E) books : knowledge

10. THIRST : PARCHED ::
    (A) fever : flushed
    (B) water : sink
    (C) hunger : strangled
    (D) laughter : appeased
    (E) promise : honored

11. FRAME : PICTURE ::
    (A) cup : saucer
    (B) table : floor
    (C) radio : sound
    (D) cover : book
    (E) base : lamp

12. ROOM : HOUSE :: ‾
    (A) refrigerator : kitchen
    (B) chair : room
    (C) cabin : ship
    (D) wheel : chair
    (E) cockpit : plane

13. BACTERIA : ILLNESS ::
    (A) medicine : germs
    (B) calcium : bone
    (C) knife : laceration
    (D) fire : explosion
    (E) flood : dam

14. PLASTER : MORTAR BOARD ::
    (A) brush : paint
    (B) drink : soda
    (C) paint : palette
    (D) blow : bubble
    (E) mail : hammer

15. NAIVE : CHEAT ::
    (A) sensible : succeed
    (B) contentious : scorn
    (C) gullible : convince
    (D) hurt : retaliate
    (E) simple : win

16. NEGOTIABLE : CHECK ::
    (A) frozen : asset
    (B) inventory : merchandise
    (C) bank : money
    (D) trade : tariff
    (E) flowing : river

17. PROJECTILE : TRAJECTORY ::
    (A) satellite : orbit
    (B) bullet : weapon
    (C) project : tragedy

    (D) rejection : renunciation
    (E) bullet : target

18. ERASER : CHALK ::
    (A) sponge : water
    (B) cloth : air
    (C) shovel : dirt
    (D) filter : air
    (E) separator : cream

19. BLISTER : SKIN ::
    (A) sore : toe
    (B) ball : pitcher
    (C) sty : eye
    (D) store : street
    (E) cut : finger

20. 20 : 21 ::
    (A) 5 : 10
    (B) A : B
    (C) 10 : 9
    (D) S : V
    (E) 3 : 17

ANSWER KEY

1.	B	6.	C	11.	D	16.	E
2.	E	7.	D	12.	C	17.	A
3.	C	8.	D	13.	C	18.	A
4.	D	9.	B	14.	C	19.	C
5.	C	10.	A	15.	C	20.	B

EXPLANATORY ANSWERS

1. **(B)** An archaeologist is a specialist in the study of antiquity; an ichthyologist is a specialist in the study of marine life.

2. **(E)** A court's duty is to provide justice; an auditor's duty is to provide accuracy in financial matters.

3. **(C)** A school demands discipline of its students; a society demands conformity of its members.

4. **(D)** An insult cannot hurt one who is invulnerable; an assault cannot hurt a city which is impregnable.

5. **(C)** A finger is an appendage of a hand; a toe is an appendage of a foot.

6. **(C)** Coolness is usually a quality of the night; warmth is usually a quality of the day.

7. **(D)** A girl becomes a woman; an infant becomes a child.

8. **(D)** A shoe can be made of leather; a highway can be made of asphalt.

9. **(B)** A pedagogue encourages learning; a professor encourages erudition.

10. **(A)** Thirst is evidenced by a parched throat; fever is evidenced by a flushed face.

11. **(D)** A frame is put on a picture; a cover is put on a book.

12. **(C)** The living quarters of houses are rooms; the living quarters of ships are cabins.

13. **(C)** Bacteria can lead to illness; a knife can cause a laceration.

14. **(C)** You can mix plaster on a mortar board; you can mix paint on a palette.

15. **(C)** A naive person can be easily cheated; a gullible person is easily convinced.

16. **(E)** A check is a negotiable asset; a river is a flowing body of water.

17. **(A)** A trajectory is the path of a projectile; an orbit is the path of a satellite.

18. **(A)** An eraser removes chalk; a sponge picks up and absorbs water.

19. **(C)** A blister forms on the skin; a sty forms on the eye.

20. **(B)** 21 immediately follows 20; B immediately follows A.

ANALOGIES: TEST 3

Directions: In each of the following questions, you are given a related pair of words or phrases in capital letters. Each capitalized pair is followed by five (5) lettered pairs of words or phrases. Choose the pair that best expresses a relationship similar to that expressed by the original pair. Circle the letter preceding your answer.

1. ERRORS : INEXPERIENCE ::
   - (A) skill : mistakes
   - (B) training : economy
   - (C) success : victory
   - (D) news : publication
   - (E) losses : carelessness

2. CAUCASIAN : SAXON ::
   - (A) lamp : stove
   - (B) hammer : nail
   - (C) furniture : chair
   - (D) carriage : horse
   - (E) city : house

3. CLOTH : TEXTURE ::
   - (A) wool : silk
   - (B) book : text
   - (C) wood : grain
   - (D) linen : flax
   - (E) paper : weight

4. CHILD : FAMILY ::
   - (A) flower : bunch
   - (B) bird : set
   - (C) calf : herd
   - (D) fish : brace
   - (E) deer : gang

5. ACORN : OAK ::
   - (A) fig : bush
   - (B) flower : stalk
   - (C) seed : nut
   - (D) bulb : tulip
   - (E) leaf : limb

6. SORROW : DEATH ::
   - (A) laugh : cry
   - (B) plum : peach
   - (C) happiness : birth
   - (D) fear : hate
   - (E) confusion : anger

7. TEPID : HOT ::
   - (A) pat : slap
   - (B) winter : summer
   - (C) topple : tumble
   - (D) bing : bang
   - (E) storm : rain

8. HYPOTHESIS : PROBLEM ::
   - (A) forecast : warning
   - (B) prognosis : condition
   - (C) cause : worry
   - (D) effect : solution
   - (E) preparation : conclusion

9. OCTAVO : BINDING ::
   - (A) pica : printing
   - (B) music : octave
   - (C) day : week
   - (D) pamphlet : book
   - (E) ruler : artist

10. GOVERNMENT : EXILE ::
    - (A) police : arrest
    - (B) judge : convict
    - (C) constitution : amendment
    - (D) church : excommunicate
    - (E) society : reform

11. RIBS : UMBRELLA ::
    - (A) rafter : roof
    - (B) hub : wheel
    - (C) crank : engine
    - (D) trunk : tree
    - (E) wall : fence

12. PEDAL : BICYCLE ::
    - (A) run : race
    - (B) climb : hill
    - (C) wind : clock
    - (D) switch : motor
    - (E) twist : cork

13. EXPLOSION : DEBRIS ::
    (A) fire : ashes
    (B) flood : water
    (C) famine : war
    (D) disease : germ
    (E) heat : injury

14. WOOL : SHEEP ::
    (A) quill : porcupine
    (B) mohair : goat
    (C) scale : fish
    (D) shell : lobster
    (E) feather : bird

15. CAT : FELINE ::
    (A) horse : equine
    (B) tiger : carnivorous
    (C) bird : vulpine
    (D) chair : furniture
    (E) sit : recline

16. CLASSIC : GREECE ::
    (A) Empire : France
    (B) Edwardian : Rome
    (C) Victorian : Germany
    (D) Modern : Russia
    (E) Peasant : Arabia

17. ORGANISM : STIMULUS ::
    (A) horse : spur
    (B) bacteria : microscope
    (C) organ : dissection
    (D) owl : observe
    (E) tree : remove

18. RUSTICITY : URBANITY ::
    (A) silk : wool
    (B) rust : steel
    (C) caution : daring
    (D) publicity : television
    (E) verbose : windy

19. CLOTHES : CLOSET ::
    (A) feet : rug
    (B) actor : script
    (C) ink : pen
    (D) beetle : insect
    (E) book : literature

20. TADPOLE : FROG ::
    (A) gander : goose
    (B) caterpillar : butterfly
    (C) husband : wife
    (D) frog : fish
    (E) daisy : rose

ANSWER KEY

1.	E	6.	C	11.	A	16.	A
2.	C	7.	A	12.	C	17.	A
3.	C	8.	B	13.	A	18.	C
4.	C	9.	A	14.	B	19.	C
5.	D	10.	D	15.	A	20.	B

EXPLANATORY ANSWERS

1. **(E)** Inexperience may cause errors; carelessness can cause losses.

2. **(C)** A chair is a piece of furniture; a Saxon is a member of the Caucasian race.

3. **(C)** A quality of cloth is its texture; a quality of wood is its grain.

4. **(C)** A child is the young member of a human family; a calf a young member of a herd of animals.

5. **(D)** Oaks grow from acorns; tulips from bulbs.

6. **(C)** You express sorrow when someone dies; happiness is expressed at a baby's birth.

7. **(A)** Something tepid is mildly hot; a pat is a mild slap.

8. **(B)** You present a hypothesis to a problem; you make a prognosis to a condition.

9. **(A)** An octavo is a measurement unit in book binding; a pica is a unit of measurement used in printing.

10. **(D)** A government can punish a person by exile; a church can punish by excommunication. Both forms of punishment cast the individual out of the original organization.

11. **(A)** Ribs support an umbrella covering; rafters support a roof.

12. **(C)** You pedal a bicycle to get it to move; you wind a clock to get it to run.

13. **(A)** Debris are the remains after an explosion; ashes are the remains after a fire.

14. **(B)** Wool is a fiber from sheep; mohair is a fiber from goats.

15. **(A)** Feline means relating to cats; equine means relating to horses.

16. **(A)** Greece had its Classic Age; France had its Empire.

17. **(A)** A spur is used to urge on a horse; a stimulus is used to arouse an organism.

18. **(C)** Rusticity is the opposite of urbanity; caution is the opposite of daring.

19. **(C)** Clothes are put in a closet; ink is put in a pen.

20. **(B)** A tadpole is a young frog; a caterpillar a young butterfly.

ANALOGIES: TEST 4

Directions: In each of the following questions, you are given a related pair of words or phrases in capital letters. Each capitalized pair is followed by five (5) lettered pairs of words or phrases. Choose the pair that best expresses a relationship similar to that expressed by the original pair. Circle the letter preceding your answer.

1. CONTROL : ORDER ::
   (A) joke : clown
   (B) teacher : pupil
   (C) disorder : climax
   (D) anarchy : chaos
   (E) government : legislator

2. WOOD : CARVE ::
   (A) trees : sway
   (B) paper : burn
   (C) clay : mold
   (D) pipe : blow
   (E) statue : model

3. STATE : BORDER ::
   (A) nation : state
   (B) flag : loyalty
   (C) Idaho : Montana
   (D) planet : satellite
   (E) property : fence

4. SOLDIER : REGIMENT ::
   (A) navy : army
   (B) lake : river
   (C) star : constellation
   (D) amphibian : frog
   (E) flock : geese

5. APOGEE : PERIGEE ::
   (A) dog : pedigree
   (B) opposite : composite
   (C) paradoxical : incredible
   (D) effigy : statue
   (E) inappropriate : apposite

6. ASYLUM : REFUGEE ::
   (A) flight : escape
   (B) peace : war
   (C) lunatic : insanity
   (D) accident : injury
   (E) destination : traveler

7. WORRIED : HYSTERICAL ::
   (A) hot : cold
   (B) happy : ecstatic
   (C) lonely : crowded
   (D) happy : serious
   (E) skilled : careful

8. WORD : CHARADE ::
   (A) phrase : act
   (B) idea : philosophy
   (C) fun : party
   (D) message : code
   (E) graph : chart

9. PLAYER : TEAM ::
   (A) fawn : doe
   (B) book : story
   (C) ball : bat
   (D) fish : school
   (E) tennis : racket

10. INTERRUPT : SPEAK ::
    (A) shout : yell
    (B) intrude : enter
    (C) interfere : assist
    (D) telephone : telegraph
    (E) concede : defend

11. ENCOURAGE : RESTRICT ::
    (A) gain : succeed
    (B) deprive : supply
    (C) see : believe
    (D) detain : deny
    (E) finish : complete

12. SETTING : STONE ::
    (A) pen : paper
    (B) glass : window
    (C) socket : bulb
    (D) ring : finger
    (E) locket : chain

13. ITALY : MILAN ::
    (A) Paris : Moscow
    (B) Moscow : Russia
    (C) Spain : Madrid
    (D) Manhattan : New York
    (E) Norway : Sweden

14. MIST : RAIN
    (A) wind : hurricane
    (B) hail : thunder
    (C) snow : freeze
    (D) clouds : sky
    (E) sun : warm

15. GUN : HOLSTER ::
    (A) shoe : soldier
    (B) sword : warrior
    (C) ink : pen
    (D) books : school bag
    (E) cannon : plunder

16. MACE : MAJESTY ::
    (A) king : crown
    (B) sword : soldier
    (C) diploma : knowledge
    (D) book : knowledge
    (E) house : security

17. VIXEN : SCOLD ::
    (A) wound : scar
    (B) hero : win
    (C) bee : sting
    (D) pimple : irritate
    (E) duck : walk

18. DEBATE : SOLILOQUY ::
    (A) crowd : mob
    (B) Hamlet : Macbeth
    (C) Lincoln : Douglas
    (D) group : hermit
    (E) fight : defend

19. THREAT : INSECURITY ::
    (A) challenge : fight
    (B) reason : anger
    (C) thunder : lightning
    (D) speed : acceleration
    (E) discipline : learning

20. LARGE : ENORMOUS ::
    (A) cat : tiger
    (B) warmth : frost
    (C) plump : fat
    (D) royal : regal
    (E) happy : solemn

ANSWER KEY

1.	D	6.	E	11.	B	16.	C
2.	C	7.	B	12.	C	17.	C
3.	E	8.	D	13.	C	18.	D
4.	C	9.	D	14.	A	19.	A
5.	E	10.	B	15.	D	20.	C

EXPLANATORY ANSWERS

1. **(D)** Control results in order; anarchy results in chaos.

2. **(C)** One creates something by carving wood; one creates something by molding clay.

3. **(E)** A border separates one state from another; a fence separates one property from another.

4. **(C)** A soldier is part of a regiment; a star is part of a constellation.

5. **(E)** Apogee and perigee are opposites; so are inappropriate and apposite.

6. **(E)** A refugee seeks asylum; a traveler seeks a destination.

7. **(B)** One who is greatly worried may become hysterical; one who is very happy may well be ecstatic.

8. **(D)** A word may be disguised by a charade; a message may be disguised by a code.

9. **(D)** A player is part of a team; a fish is part of a school.

10. **(B)** You interrupt another's conversation, when you speak; you intrude upon someone else, when you enter the place where he is. In other words, the second action is causing a disruption of some kind.

11. **(B)** When you encourage, you help and give—you do not restrict; when you deprive, you take away—you do not supply.

12. **(C)** A stone is fitted into a setting; a bulb is screwed into a socket.

13. **(C)** Italy is a country; Milan is one of its cities. Spain likewise is a country in which the city of Madrid is located.

14. **(A)** Mist can be considered as incipient rain; wind is a fraction of the force of a hurricane. The relationship is one of degree.

15. **(D)** A gun is placed in a holster in order to be carried; books are placed in a school bag in order to be carried.

16. **(C)** A mace is a symbol of majesty; it signifies authority. A diploma also signifies that a person has graduated from a place of learning. It therefore can signify that someone possesses knowledge.

17. **(C)** A vixen attacks by scolding; a bee by stinging.

18. **(D)** A debate is a formal argument involving more than one person; a soliloquy is a dramatic speech given by an individual expressing his interior state. A group is a social unit composed of more than one person. A hermit is an anti-social individual.

19. **(A)** A threat may cause insecurity; a challenge may cause a fight.

20. **(C)** To be enormous is to be very large; to be fat is to be very plump.

ENGLISH USAGE: TEST 1

DIRECTIONS: In each of the sentences below, four words or phrases have been underlined. Select the underlined part which contains an error in usage, grammar, or punctuation. If there is no error, select choice E. Write in your answer next to the question number.

1. The Peace Corps, <u>instituted</u> <u>by</u> President Ken-
                A   B
   nedy, <u>appealed</u> to the generosity, idealism, and
          C
   <u>to their</u> sense of adventure of the American peo-
     D
   ple. <u>No error.</u>
        E

2. <u>Regardless</u> of the <u>amount</u> of obstacles to be <u>over-</u>
     A   B   C
   come, the program will be <u>a success.</u> <u>No error.</u>
                      D   E

3. The <u>repeated</u> occurrence of accidents of <u>this sort</u>
        A   B
   <u>call</u> into question the safety of the <u>machine's</u> de-
   C   D
   sign. <u>No error.</u>
         E

4. An inexperienced liar, Mary explained her absence from school with an <u>incredulous</u> tale of
                          A
   <u>daring</u> in which she played the <u>role</u> of the <u>hero-</u>
   B   C   D
   ine. <u>No error.</u>
        E

5. <u>Irregardless</u> of <u>what</u> people say, I must repeat
     A   B
   that these are the facts <u>concerning</u> the <u>require-</u>
                    C   D
   ments for the position. <u>No error.</u>
                  E

6. There <u>is</u> no objection to <u>him</u> joining the <u>party</u> if
        A   B   C
   he is willing to fit <u>in</u> with the plans of the group.
                  D

<u>No error.</u>
 E

7. If you <u>saw</u> the <u>number</u> of pancakes he <u>consumed</u>
         A   B   C
   at breakfast this morning, you <u>would have under-</u>
                             D
   stood why he is so overweight. <u>No error.</u>
                        E

8. The <u>test results</u> <u>ought</u> to be <u>available</u> <u>inside of</u>
        A   B   C   D
   three days. <u>No error.</u>
           E

9. <u>Neither</u> Charlotte Brontë <u>nor</u> her brother
     A   B
   Branwell <u>are</u> remembered as <u>healthy</u> or happy.
            C   D
   <u>No error.</u>
    E

10. The children stared, silent and <u>intently</u>, <u>as</u> the
                          A   B
    spectacle of the ice palace <u>unfolded</u> <u>before</u> their
                          C   D
    eyes. <u>No error.</u>
          E

11. Such a habit is not <u>only</u> dangerous to the <u>individ-</u>
                   A   B
    ual's health, but a man will find <u>it</u> a serious <u>drain</u>
                          C   D
    on his finances. <u>No error.</u>
               E

12. She saw that there was nothing <u>else</u> she could <u>do</u>;
                          A   B
    the room was clean <u>like</u> it had <u>never been</u> before.
                C   D
    <u>No error.</u>
     E

13. The teacher was <u>justly</u> annoyed by <u>him</u> walking
                 A   B
    in <u>late</u> and <u>disturbing</u> the class. <u>No error.</u>
       C   D   E

14. Each of the nurses were scrupulously careful
                        ‾‾‾‾   ‾‾‾‾‾‾‾‾‾‾‾
                          A   B
    about personal cleanliness. No error.
    ‾‾‾‾‾   ‾‾‾‾‾‾‾‾‾‾ ‾‾‾‾‾‾‾‾
     C   D   E

15. I enjoy eating in good restaurants and to go to the
      ‾‾‾‾‾   ‾‾‾‾   ‾‾‾‾‾
       A   B   C
    theater afterwards. No error.
            ‾‾‾‾‾‾‾‾‾‾ ‾‾‾‾‾‾‾‾
                D   E

ANSWER KEY

1. D	6. B	11. C
2. B	7. A	12. C
3. C	8. D	13. B
4. A	9. C	14. A
5. A	10. A	15. C

EXPLANATORY ANSWERS

1. **(D)** The phrase *to their* is unnecessary and violates the parallel structure of nouns in a series. Omit it.

2. **(B)** Use *number* for a quantity thought of as a collection of individual things *(obstacles)*.

3. **(C)** The verb should be *calls* to agree with the singular subject *occurrence*.

4. **(A)** *Incredible,* not incredulous. The latter means disbelieving.

5. **(A)** *Regardless.* There is no such word as irregardless.

6. **(B)** . . . to *his* joining the party. . . Joining is a gerund, or verbal noun, so the possessive "his" precedes it.

7. **(A)** If you *had seen.* This is a conditional sentence.

8. **(D)** In formal English, *inside of* cannot refer to time. Use *within*.

9. **(C)** *Is.* The verb must agree in number with the part of the sentence's subject that is closer to the verb, in this case, Branwell.

10. **(A)** The adjective form *(intent)* is required.

11. **(C)** The habit, not it. "It" can refer to habit or health and is therefore ambiguous.

12. **(C)** . . . *as it* had never been. . . . "Like" applies to nouns and pronouns; "as" goes before phrases and clauses.

13. **(B)** . . . by *his* walking. "Walking" is a gerund, or verbal noun, so the possessive pronoun "his" precedes it.

14. **(A)** Each. . . *was.* . . .

15. **(C)** . . . and *going.* . . . "Going" relates to "eating"; there should be parallel construction.

ENGLISH USAGE: TEST 2

DIRECTIONS: In each of the sentences below, four words or phrases have been underlined. Select the underlined part which contains an error in usage, grammar, or punctuation. If there is no error, select choice E. Write in your answer next to the question number.

1. He had a chance to invest <u>wisely</u>, establish <u>his</u>
A   B
position, and <u>displaying</u> his ability <u>as</u> an execu-
C   D
tive. <u>No error.</u>
E

2. <u>Inspecting</u> <u>Robert's</u> report card, his mother noted
A   B
that he <u>had received</u> high ratings in Latin and
C
<u>History.</u> <u>No error.</u>
D   E

3. When one buys tickets in <u>advance</u>, there is no
A
sure guarantee that <u>you</u> will be free <u>to attend</u> the
B   C
play on the night of the <u>performance.</u> <u>No error.</u>
D   E

4. <u>His</u> brother, the <u>captain of the squad</u> <u>scored</u> <u>many</u>
A   B   C   D
points. <u>No error.</u>
E

5. People who are <u>too</u> <u>credulous</u> are <u>likely</u> <u>to be de-</u>
A   B   C   D
<u>ceived</u> by unscrupulous individuals. <u>No error.</u>
E

6. <u>Due</u> to <u>his being hospitalized</u>, the <u>star</u> halfback
A   B   C

<u>was unable to play</u> in the championship game.
D
<u>No error.</u>
E

7. Lifeguards <u>have been known</u> to <u>effect</u> rescues
A   B
even <u>during</u> <u>tumultuous</u> storms. <u>No error.</u>
C   D   E

8. The <u>mayor</u> <u>expressed</u> concern about the large
A   B
<u>amount</u> of people injured at street <u>crossings.</u> <u>No</u>
C   D   E
<u>error.</u>

9. "Leave us <u>face</u> the fact that <u>we're</u> in <u>trouble!</u>"
A   B   C   D
he shouted. <u>No error.</u>
E

10. Jones seems <u>slow</u> on the track, but you will find
A
few boys <u>quicker</u> <u>than</u> <u>him</u> on the basketball
B   C   D
court. <u>No error.</u>
E

11. We had <u>swam</u> <u>across</u> the lake <u>before</u> the sun <u>rose.</u>
A   B   C   D
<u>No error.</u>
E

12. The <u>loud noise</u> of the cars and trucks <u>annoys</u>
A   B
<u>those</u> who live <u>near</u> the road. <u>No error.</u>
C   D   E

13. I know that you <u>will enjoy</u> <u>receiving</u> flowers that
A   B

258

smell so sweetly. No error.
<u>C</u>   <u>D</u>   <u>E</u>

14. He is at least ten years older then she is. No er-
<u>ror.</u>   <u>A</u>   <u>B</u> <u>C</u> <u>D</u>   <u>E</u>

15. I found one of them books that tell you how to
   <u>A</u>   <u>B</u>   <u>C</u>
build a model airplane. No error.
<u>D</u>   <u>E</u>

ANSWER KEY

1. C	6. A	11. A
2. D	7. E	12. E
3. B	8. C	13. D
4. C	9. A	14. C
5. E	10. D	15. B

EXPLANATORY ANSWERS

1. **(C)** *Display.* "Display" must agree with "invest" and "establish" for parallel construction.

2. **(D)** *history,* not History.

3. **(B)** . . . that *one* will be free. . . . "One" must agree with "one buys" of the introductory clause.

4. **(C)** . . . , the captain of the *squad,* . . . . This is an appositional phrase.

5. **(E)** There are no errors in this sentence.

6. **(A)** *Because of,* not due to.

7. **(E)** There are no errors in this sentence. (*To effect* is correct; in this case it means to complete. To affect means to pretend.)

8. **(C)** . . . large *number* of people. . . .

9. **(A)** *Let* us. . . .

10. **(D)** . . . quicker than *he.* . . .

11. **(A)** *Swum,* not swam.

12. **(E)** There are no errors in this sentence.

13. **(D)** *Sweet,* not sweetly. The latter is an adverb and would imply the flowers do the smelling.

14. **(C)** . . . *than* she is.

15. **(B)** . . . one of *those.* . . .

ENGLISH USAGE: TEST 3

DIRECTIONS: In each of the sentences below, four words or phrases have been underlined. Select the underlined part which contains an error in usage, grammar, or punctuation. If there is no error, select choice E. Write in your answer next to the question number.

1. Why <u>should we give</u> him our <u>books</u>, when he had
          A   B
   <u>extras</u> why did he <u>refuse to share</u> them with us?
    C   D
   <u>No error.</u>
     E

2. Jack <u>likes</u> all <u>sports</u>: tennis, basketball, <u>football,</u>
         A   B   C
   <u>and etc.</u> <u>No error.</u>
     D   E

3. <u>That</u> <u>Bill's</u> reasoning was <u>fallacious</u> was soon
     A   B   C
   <u>apparent to all.</u> <u>No error.</u>
       D   E

4. Neither John <u>nor</u> his <u>children</u> <u>is</u> likely to attend
      A   B   C
   the <u>ceremonies.</u> <u>No error.</u>
       D   E

5. He <u>will give</u> the <u>message</u> to <u>whoever</u> <u>opens</u> the
       A   B   C   D
   door. <u>No error.</u>
       E

6. The <u>boy</u>, <u>as well as</u> his mother, <u>desperately</u> <u>need</u>
      A   B   C   D
   help. <u>No error.</u>
       E

7. Because he <u>has always been</u> popular and <u>with</u>
             A   B
   <u>abundant</u> wealth, he <u>thoroughly</u> enjoyed his col-
                             C

lege years. <u>No error.</u>
            E

8. <u>Having studied your report carefully,</u> <u>I am con-</u>
             A   B
   vinced that <u>neither</u> of your <u>solutions are</u> correct.
             C   D
   <u>No error.</u>
     E

9. If he is successful in his attempt <u>to cross</u> the lake,
                               A
   he <u>will have swum</u> a <u>distance</u> of <u>twelve miles.</u>
           B   C   D
   <u>No error.</u>
     E

10. In spite of his youth, <u>no</u> faster <u>runner</u> than <u>him</u>
                       A   B   C
    <u>will be found</u> in our school. <u>No error.</u>
        D   E

11. <u>Because of the poor lighting,</u> they <u>mistakenly</u>
          A   B
    supposed the <u>intruder</u> to be <u>I.</u> <u>No error.</u>
             C   D   E

12. <u>None</u> of the <u>diplomats</u> at the conference was able
      A   B
    either <u>to comprehend</u> or <u>solve</u> the problem. <u>No</u>
              C   D   E
    error.

13. It was <u>agreed</u> by a majority of the signers of the
          A
    compact that truth <u>as well as</u> justice <u>was</u> to be
               B   C
    <u>there</u> rule of life. <u>No error.</u>
      D   E

14. Everybody was <u>up</u> early on Monday because <u>our</u>
              A   B
    local <u>store</u> was having <u>it's</u> annual sale. <u>No error.</u>
      C   D   E

15. A careful driver <u>watches</u> the road and goes <u>slowly</u>
                  A   B

   or quickly <u>depending upon</u> the condition of the
                        C

   road, the <u>visibility</u>, and the traffic. <u>No error.</u>
              D   E

ANSWER KEY

1. B	6. D	11. D
2. D	7. B	12. E
3. E	8. D	13. D
4. C	9. E	14. D
5. E	10. C	15. E

EXPLANATORY ANSWERS

1. **(B)** Why should we give him our *books? When* he had extras why did he refuse to share them with us? These are two complete questions, not one.

2. **(D)** Jack likes all sports: tennis, basketball, football, *etc. Etc.* means *and so forth*. Do not use *and* with *etc.*

3. **(E)** This sentence is correct.

4. **(C)** Neither John nor his children *are* likely to attend the ceremonies. When one singular subject and one plural subject are joined by *or* or *nor,* the subject closer to the verb (in this case *children*) determines the number of the verb.

5. **(E)** This sentence is correct.

6. **(D)** The boy, as well as his mother, desperately *needs* help. The singular verb *needs* is necessary to agree with the singular subject *boy.*

7. **(B)** Because he has always been popular and *abundantly wealthy,* he thoroughly enjoyed his college years. The predicate adjective *wealthy* is needed for parallelism with *popular.*

8. **(D)** Having studied your report carefully, I am convinced that neither of your solutions *is* correct. The verb must be singular to agree with the singular subject *neither.*

9. **(E)** This sentence is correct.

10. **(C)** In spite of his youth, no faster runner than *he* will be found in our school. The meaning is: no faster runner than *he is.* Therefore, the nominative *he* is needed.

11. **(D)** Because of the poor lighting, they mistakenly supposed the intruder to be *me.* The verb *to be* takes the same case after it as before it. Since the subject of an infinitive is in the objective case, the word following it must also be in the objective case.

12. **(E)** This sentence is correct.

13. **(D)** It was agreed by a majority of the signers of the compact that truth as well as justice was to be *their* rule of life. *There* means in that place; *their* means belonging to them.

14. **(D)** Everybody was up early on Monday because our local store was having *its* annual sale. *It's* means *it is; its* means belonging to it.

15. **(E)** This sentence is correct.

READING COMPREHENSION

The standardized educational or psychological tests that are widely used to aid in selecting, classifying, assigning, or promoting students, employees, and military personnel have been the target of recent attacks in books, magazines, the daily press, and even in Congress. The target is wrong, for in attacking the tests, critics divert attention from the fault that lies with ill-informed or incompetent users. The tests themselves are merely tools, with characteristics that can be measured with reasonable precision under specified conditions. Whether the results will be valuable, meaningless, or even misleading depends partly upon the tool itself but largely upon the user.

All informed predictions of future performance are based upon some knowledge of relevant past performance: school grades, research productivity, sales records, batting averages, or whatever is appropriate. How well the predictions will be validated by later performance depends upon the amount, reliability, and appropriateness of the information used and on the skill and wisdom with which it is interpreted. Anyone who keeps careful score knows that the information available is always incomplete and that the predictions are always subject to error.

Standardized tests should be considered in this context. They provide a quick, objective method of getting some kinds of information about what a person has learned, the skills he has developed, or the kind of person he is. The information so obtained has, qualitatively, the same advantages and shortcomings as other kinds of information. Whether to use tests, other kinds of information, or both in a particular situation depends, therefore, upon the empirical evidence concerning comparative validity, and upon such factors as cost and availability.

In general, the tests work most effectively when the traits or qualities to be measured can be most precisely defined (for example, ability to do well in a particular course or training program) and least effectively when what is to be measured or predicted cannot be well defined (for example, personality or creativity). Properly used, they provide a rapid means of getting comparable information about many people. Sometimes they identify students whose high potential has not been previously recognized. But there are many things they do not do. For example, they do not compensate for gross social inequality, and thus do not tell how able an underprivileged youngster might have been had he grown up under more favorable circumstances.

Professionals in the business and the conscientious publishers know the limitations as well as the values. They write these things into test manuals and in critiques of available tests. But they have no jurisdiction over users; an educational test can be administered by almost anyone, whether he knows how to interpret it or not. Nor can the difficulty be controlled by limiting sales to qualified users; some attempts to do so have been countered by restraint-of-trade suits.

In the long run it may be possible to establish better controls or to require higher qualifications. But in the meantime, unhappily, the demonstrated value of these tests under many circumstances has given them a popularity that has led to considerable misuse. Also unhappily, justifiable criticism of the misuse now threatens to hamper proper use. Business and government can probably look after themselves. But school guidance and selection programs are being attacked for using a valuable tool, because some of the users are unskilled.

> —by Watson Davis, Sc.D., Director of Science
> Service (reprinted with permission)

1. The essence of this article on educational tests is:

 (A) These tests do not test adequately what they set out to test.
 (B) Don't blame the test—blame the user.
 (C) When a student is nervous or ill, the test results are inaccurate.

(D) Publishers of tests are without conscience.

(E) Educators are gradually losing confidence in the value of the tests.

2. Tests like the College Entrance Scholastic Aptitude Test are, it would seem to the author,

(A) generally unreliable
(B) generally reliable
(C) meaningless
(D) misleading
(E) neither good nor bad

3. The selection implies that, more often, the value of an educational test rests with

(A) the interpretation of results
(B) the test itself
(C) the testee
(D) emotional considerations
(E) the directions

4. Which statement is not true, according to the passage, about educational tests?

(A) Some students "shine" unexpectedly.
(B) Predictions do not always hold true.
(C) Personality tests often fail to measure the true personality.
(D) The supervisor of the test must be very well trained.
(E) Publishers cannot confine sales to highly skilled administrators.

5. According to the passage, the validity of a test requires most of all

(A) cooperation on the part of the person tested
(B) sufficient preparation on the part of the applicant
(C) clearcut directions
(D) one answer—and only one—for each question
(E) specificity regarding what is to be tested

When the television is good, nothing—not the theatre, not the magazines, or newspapers—nothing is better. But when television is bad, nothing is worse. I invite you to sit down in front of your television set when your station goes on the air and stay there without a book, magazine, newspaper, or anything else to distract you and keep your eyes glued to that set until the station signs off. I can assure you that you will observe a vast wasteland. You will see a procession of game shows, violence, audience participation shows, formula comedies about totally unbelievable families, blood and thunder, mayhem, more violence, sadism, murder, Western badmen, Western goodmen, private eyes, gangsters, still more violence, and cartoons. And, endlessly, commercials that scream and cajole and offend. And most of all, boredom. True, you will see a few things you will enjoy. But they will be very, very few. And if you think I exaggerate, try it.

Is there no room on television to teach, to inform, to uplift, to stretch, to enlarge the capacities of our children? Is there no room for programs to deepen the children's understanding of children in other lands? Is there no room for a children's news show explaining something about the world for them at their level of understanding? Is there no room for reading the great literature of the past, teaching them the great traditions of freedom? There are some fine children's shows, but they are drowned out in the massive doses of cartoons, violence, and more violence. Must these be your trademarks? Search your conscience and see whether you cannot offer more to your young beneficiaries whose future you guard so many hours each and every day.

There are many people in this great country, and you must serve all of us. You will get no argument from me if you say that, given a choice between a Western and a symphony, more people will watch the Western. I like Westerns and private eyes, too—but a steady diet for the whole country is obviously not in the public interest. We all know that people would more often prefer to be entertained than stimulated or informed. But your obligations are not satisfied if you look only to popularity as a test of what to broadcast. You are not only in show business; you are free to communicate ideas as well as to give relaxation. You must provide a wider range of choices, more diversity, more alternatives. It is not enough to cater to the nation's whims—you must also serve the nation's needs. The people own the air. They own it as much in prime evening time as they do at 6 o'clock in the morning. For every hour that the people give you—you owe them something. I intend to see that your debt is paid with service.

—excerpt from speech by Newton H. Minow, chairman of the Federal Communications Commission, before the National Association of Broadcasters.

6. The wasteland referred to describes

(A) Western badmen and Western goodmen

(B) average television programs

(C) the morning shows

(D) television shows with desert locales

(E) children's programs

7. The author's attitude toward television is one of

(A) sullenness

(B) reconciliation

(C) determination

(D) rage

(E) hopelessness

8. The National Association of Broadcasters probably accepted Minow's remarks with

(A) considerable enthusiasm

(B) shocked wonderment

(C) complete agreement

(D) some disagreement

(E) absolute rejection

9. The Federal Communications Commission chairman is, in effect, telling the broadcasters that

(A) the listener, not the broadcaster, should make decisions about programs

(B) children's shows are worthless

(C) mystery programs should be banned

(D) television instruction should be a substitute for classroom lessons

(E) they had better mend their ways

10. Concerning programs for children, Minow believes that programs should

(A) eliminate cartoons

(B) provide culture

(C) be presented at certain periods during the day

(D) eliminate commercials

(E) not deal with the West

11. The statement that ''the people own the air'' implies that

(A) citizens have the right to insist on worthwhile television programs

(B) television should be socialized

(C) the government may build above present structures

(D) since air is worthless, the people own nothing

(E) the broadcasters have no right to commer-

cialize on television

12. It can be inferred from the passage in regard to television programming that the author believes

(A) the broadcasters are trying to do the right thing but are failing

(B) foreign countries are going to pattern their programs after ours

(C) there is a great deal that is worthwhile in present programs

(D) the listeners do not necessarily know what is good for them

(E) 6 A.M. is too early for a television show

If Johnny can't write, one of the reasons may be a conditioning based on speed rather than respect for the creative process. Speed is neither a valid test of nor a proper preparation for competence in writing. It makes for murkiness, glibness, disorganization. It takes the beauty out of the language. It rules out respect for the reflective thought that should precede expression. It runs counter to the word-by-word and line-by-line reworking that enables a piece to be finely knit.

This is not to minimize the value of genuine facility. With years of practice, a man may be able to put down words swiftly and expertly. But it is the same kind of swiftness that enables a cellist, after having invested years of efforts, to negotiate an intricate passage from Haydn. Speed writing is for stenographers and court reporters, not for anyone who wants to use language with precision and distinction.

Thomas Mann was not ashamed to admit that he would often take a full day to write 500 words, and another day to edit them, out of respect for the most difficult art in the world. Flaubert would ponder a paragraph for hours. Did it say what he wanted it to say—not approximately but exactly? Did the words turn into one another with proper rhythm and grace? Were they artistically and securely fitted together? Were they briskly alive, or were they full of fuzz and ragged edges? Were they likely to make things happen inside the mind of the reader, igniting the imagination and touching off all sorts of new anticipations? These questions are relevant not only for the established novelist but for anyone who attaches value to words as a medium of expression and communication.

E. B. White, whose respect for the environment of good writing is exceeded by no word-artist of our time, would rather have his fingers cut off than to be guilty of handling words lightly. No sculptor chipping away at a granite block in order to produce a delicate curve or feature has labored more painstakingly than White in fashioning a short paragraph. Obviously, we can't expect our schools to make every Johnny into a White or a Flaubert or a Mann, but it is not unreasonable to expect more of them to provide the conditions that promote clear, careful, competent expression. Certainly the cumulative effort of the school experience should not have to be undone in later years.

—by Norman Cousins, Editor of *Saturday Review* (reprinted with permission)

13. According to the passage, competence in writing is

(A) an art that takes practice
(B) a skill that requires dexterity
(C) a technique that is easy to learn
(D) a result of the spontaneous flow of words
(E) an inate ability that few people have

14. The main purpose of the passage is to

(A) present an original idea
(B) describe a new process
(C) argue against an established practice
(D) comment on a skill and its techniques
(E) urge the reader to action

15. Our schools, according to the passage,

(A) are providing proper conditions for good writing
(B) should not stress writing speed on a test
(C) should give essay tests rather than multiple-choice tests
(D) teach good writing primarily through reading
(E) correlate art and music with writing instruction

16. In describing White as a "word-artist," the author means that White

(A) was also a cartoonist
(B) illustrated his stories
(C) was colorful in his descriptions
(D) had artistic background
(E) was a great writer

17. It can be inferred from the passage that the author values good literature primarily for its ability to

(A) relieve the boredom of everyday life
(B) accurately describe events as they occur
(C) prevent disorder in society
(D) communicate ideas and experience
(E) provide individuals with skills for success

ANSWER KEY

1. B	7. C	13. A
2. B	8. D	14. D
3. A	9. E	15. B
4. D	10. B	16. E
5. E	11. A	17. D
6. B	12. D	

EXPLANATORY ANSWERS

1. **(B)** This is explicitly stated in the first paragraph where the author lays the blame on the test user rather than on the test.

2. **(B)** The author stresses the general reliability of the tests throughout the passage.

3. **(A)** Since the passage directly criticizes the test users and administrators, the people who interpret the results, the implication is that some measure of the test's validity depends on the interpretation of results.

4. **(D)** This is clearly stated in the fifth paragraph: "an educational test can be administered by almost anyone, whether he knows how to interpret it or not."

5. **(E)** This is also stated quite clearly in the opening of the fourth paragraph.

6. **(B)** The first paragraph portrays the whole gamut of television programs as a "vast wasteland."

7. **(C)** The speaker's attitude is one of a determined reformer. He understands the great potential of the medium and knows that television is capable of providing fine viewing (see the opening sentence). Therefore, he is determined to raise the level of television programs.

8. **(D)** Since he is criticizing them, (A) and (B) are automatically ruled out. Since the passage implies that television does offer a wider variety of programming on occasion, the group would know the value of the average show. Both (C) and (E) would suggest they were totally in the dark about the quality of television programming.

9. **(E)** This is clearly implied in the final paragraph where the speaker is telling his audience that he intends to see that the quality of television programming is upgraded.

10. **(B)** This is explicitly stated in the second paragraph. Nowhere does the passage state the need to eliminate commercial television or do away with purely entertaining shows. But the speaker wants more shows that "enlarge the capacities of our children."

11. **(A)** This statement, coming near the end of the final paragraph, is fairly straightforward in meaning. The speaker states that television owes something to the viewing public which they, the public, have the right to demand.

12. **(D)** This is clearly implied in the third paragraph when the speaker states that "people would more often prefer to be entertained than stimulated or informed."

13. **(A)** The passage specifically describes writing as the most difficult art in the world. And as is clearly implied in the opening paragraph, competence is the result of craft, not of speed.

14. **(D)** The writer is describing how the skill of good writing is attained. He elaborates on this theme by describing the techniques of famous writers.

15. **(B)** The passage stresses the idea that one of the reasons our schools are turning out poor writers is that they are stressing writing speed rather than craft.

16. **(E)** The author uses White as a model of the writer-artist. He would be the great writer, the model one should try to imitate to attain competence.

17. **(D)** The author stresses the value of words as a medium of expression and communication. Words should express what the writer wants to say.

READING RECALL

DIRECTIONS: You are to closely read the following passages. Afterwards you will be asked to recall certain facts and ideas about the passages. You are not allowed to refer back to the passages.

Passage 1

It is almost a definition of a gentleman to say he is one who never inflicts pain. This description is both refined and, as far as it goes, accurate. He is mainly occupied in merely removing the obstacles which hinder the free and unembarrassed action of those about him; and he concurs with their movements rather than takes the initiative himself. His benefits may be considered as parallel to what are called comforts or conveniences in arrangements of a personal nature: like an easy chair or a good fire, which do their part in dispelling cold and fatigue, though nature provides both means of rest and animal heat without them. The true gentleman, in like manner, carefully avoids whatever may cause a jar or a jolt in the minds of those with whom he is cast;—all clashing of opinion, or collision of feeling, all restraint, or suspicion, or gloom, or resentment; his great concern being to make everyone at their ease and at home. He has his eyes on all his company; he is tender towards the bashful, gentle towards the distant, and merciful towards the absurd; he can recollect to whom he is speaking; he guards against unseasonable allusions, or topics which may irritate; he is seldom prominent in conversation, and never wearisome. He makes light of favors while he does them, and seems to be receiving when he is conferring. He never speaks of himself except when compelled, never defends himself by a mere retort, he has no ears for slander or gossip, is scrupulous in imputing motives to those who interfere with him, and interprets everything for the best. He is never mean or little in his disputes, never takes unfair advantage, never mistakes personalities or sharp sayings for arguments, or insinuates evil which he dare not say out. From a longsighted prudence, he observes the maxim of the ancient sage, that we should ever conduct ourselves towards our enemy as if he were one day to be our friend. He has too much good sense to be affronted at insults, he is too well employed to remember injuries, and too indolent to bear malice. He is patient, forbearing, and resigned, on philosophical principles; he submits to pain, because it is inevitable, to bereavement, because it is irreparable, and to death, because it is his destiny. If he engages in controversy of any kind, his disciplined intellect preserves him from the blundering discourtesy of better, perhaps, but less educated minds, who, like blunt weapons, tear and hack instead of cutting clean; who mistake the point in argument, waste their strength on trifles, misconceive their adversary, to leave the question more involved than they find it. He may be right or wrong in his opinion, but he is too clear-headed to be unjust; he is as simple as he is forcible, and as brief as he is decisive. Nowhere shall we find greater candor, consideration, indulgence: he throws himself into the minds of his opponents, he accounts for their mistakes. He knows the weakness of human reason as well as its strength, its province, and its limits. If he be an unbeliever, he will be too profound and large-minded to ridicule religion or to act against it; he is too wise to be a dogmatist or fanatic in his infidelity. He respects piety and devotion; he even supports institutions as venerable, beautiful, or useful, to which he does not assent; he honors the ministers of religion, and it contents him to decline its mysteries without assailing or denouncing them. He is a friend of religious toleration, and that, not only because his philosophy has taught him to look on all forms of faith with an impartial eye, but also from the gentleness and effeminacy of feeling, which is the attendant on civilization.

Not that he may not hold a religion too, even when he belongs to no formal congregation. In that case his religion is one of imagination and sentiment; it is the embodiment of those ideas of the sublime, majestic, and beautiful, without which there can be no large philosophy. Sometimes he acknowledges the being of God, sometimes he invests an unknown principle or quality with the attributes of perfection. And this deduction of his reason, or creation of his fancy, he makes the occasion of such excellent thoughts, and the starting-point of so varied and systematic a teaching, that he even seems like a disciple of Christianity itself. From the very accuracy and steadiness of his logical powers, he is able to see what sentiments are consistent in those who hold any religious doctrine at all, and he appears to others to feel and to hold a whole circle of theological truths, which exist in his mind not otherwise than as a number of deductions.

Passage 2

Monseigneur, one of the great lords in power at the Court, held his fortnightly reception in his grand hotel in Paris. Monseigneur was in his inner room, his sanctuary of sanctuaries, the Holiest of Holiests to the crowd of worshippers in the suite of rooms without. Monseigneur was about to take his chocolate. Monseigneur could swallow a great many things with ease, and was by some few sullen minds supposed to be rather rapidly swallowing France; but, his morning's chocolate could not so much as get into the throat of Monseigneur, without the aid of four strong men besides the Cook.

Yes. It took four men, all four a-blaze with gorgeous decoration, and the Chief of them unable to exist with fewer than two gold watches in his pocket, emulative of the noble and chaste fashion set by Monseigneur, to conduct the happy chocolate to Monseigneur's lips. One lacquey carried the chocolate-pot into the sacred presence; a second milled and frothed the chocolate with the little instrument he bore for that function; a third presented the favoured napkin; a fourth (he of the two gold watches) poured the chocolate out. It was impossible for Monseigneur to dispense with one of these attendants on the chocolate and hold his high place under the admiring Heavens. Deep would have been the blot upon his escutcheon if his chocolate had been ignobly waited on by only three men; he must have died of two.

Monseigneur had been out at a little supper last night, where the Comedy and the Grand Opera were charmingly represented. Monseigneur was out at a little supper most nights, with fascinating company. So polite and so impressible was Monseigneur, that the Comedy and the Grand Opera had far more influence with him in the tiresome articles of state affairs and state secrets, than the needs of all France. A happy circumstance for France, as the like always is for all countries similarly favoured!—always was for England (by way of example), in the regretted days of the merry Stuart who sold it.

Monseigneur had one truly noble idea of general public business, which was, to let everything go on in its own way; of particular public business, Monseigneur had the other truly noble idea that it must all go his way—tend to his own power and pocket. Of his pleasures, general and particular, Monseigneur had the other truly noble idea, that the world was made for them. The text of his order (altered from the original by only a pronoun, which is not much) ran: "The earth and the fulness thereof are mine, saith Monseigneur."

Passage 3

If a man were called to fix the period in the history of the world, during which the condition of the human race was most happy and prosperous, he would, without hesitation, name that which elapsed from the death of Domitian to the accession of Commodus [96–180 A.D.]. The vast extent of the Roman empire was governed by absolute power, under the guidance of virtue and wisdom. The armies were restrained by the firm but gentle hand of four successive emperors, whose characters and authority commanded involuntary respect. The forms of the civil administration were carefully preserved by Nerva, Trajan, Hadrian, and the Antonines, who delighted in the image of liberty, and were pleased with considering themselves as the accountable ministers of the laws. Such princes deserved the honour of restoring the republic, had the Romans of their days been capable of enjoying a rational freedom.

The labours of these monarchs were overpaid by the immense reward that inseparably waited on their success; by the honest pride of virtue, and by the exquisite delight of beholding the general happiness of which they were the authors. A just, but melancholy reflection embittered, however, the noblest of human enjoyments. They must often have recollected the instability of a happiness which depended on the character of a single man. The fatal moment was perhaps approaching, when some licentious youth, or some jealous tyrant, would abuse, to the destruction, that absolute power, which they had exerted for the benefit of their people. The ideal restraints of the senate and the laws might serve to display the virtues, but could never correct the vices, of the emperor. The military force was a blind and irresistible instrument of oppression; and the corruption of Roman manners would always supply flatterers eager to applaud, and ministers prepared to serve, the fear or the avarice, the lust or the cruelty, of their masters.

These gloomy apprehensions had been already justified by the experience of the Romans. The annals of the emperors exhibit a strong and various picture of human nature, which we should vainly seek among the mixed and doubtful characters of modern history. In the conduct of those monarchs we may trace the utmost lines of vice and virtue; the most exalted perfection, and the meanest degeneracy of our own species. The golden age of Trajan and the Antonines had been preceded by an age of iron. It is almost superfluous to enumerate the unworthy successors of Augustus. Their unparalleled vices, and the splendid theater on which they were acted, have saved them from oblivion. The dark unrelenting Tiberius, the furious Caligula, the feeble Claudius, the profligate and cruel Nero, the beastly Vitellius, and the timid inhuman Domitian, are condemned to everlasting infamy. During fourscore years (excepting only the short and doubtful respite of Vespasian's reign) Rome groaned beneath an unremitting tyranny, which exterminated the ancient families of the republic, and was fatal to almost every virtue and every talent that arose in that unhappy period.

QUESTIONS

DIRECTIONS: You are to answer the following questions based upon the preceding passages. You are not to refer back to the passages. Circle the letter preceding your answer.

Passage 1

1. According to the passage, the gentleman when engaged in debate is

    (A) soothing and conciliatory
    (B) brilliant and insightful
    (C) opinionated and clever
    (D) concise and forceful
    (E) quiet and charming

2. A gentleman, here, is equated with

    (A) a jar or jolt
    (B) an easy chair or a good fire
    (C) a blunt weapon
    (D) a sharp saying
    (E) collisions and restraints

3. A person who is "scrupulous in imputing motives" is

    (A) careful about accusing others
    (B) eager to prove another guilty
    (C) willing to falsify
    (D) unable to make decisions
    (E) suspicious concerning the actions of others

4. This passage does not take into account a commonly held concept of a gentleman—namely,

    (A) consideration for others
    (B) refusal to slander
    (C) leniency toward the stupid
    (D) neatness in attire
    (E) willingness to forgive

5. The most appropriate title for this passage would be

    (A) A Gentleman Now and Before
    (B) Definition of a Gentleman
    (C) Intellectualism and the Gentleman
    (D) Can a Gentleman Be Religious?

    (E) Gentlemen Prefer Easy Chairs

6. The word "effeminacy" as used in this selection really means

    (A) femininity
    (B) childishness
    (C) cowardice
    (D) indecision
    (E) delicacy

Passage 2

7. The locale of this passage is

    (A) the opera
    (B) a sweet shop
    (C) the field of battle
    (D) an apartment
    (E) a church

8. The tone of the selection is

    (A) serious
    (B) sarcastic
    (C) inquiring
    (D) objective
    (E) informative

9. The chronological placement is the

    (A) twentieth century
    (B) eighteenth century
    (C) sixteenth century
    (D) fourteenth century
    (E) indefinite past or future

10. Monseigneur represents

    (A) a person who elicits sympathy
    (B) a simpleton who cannot provide for himself
    (C) a profligate who cares little about others
    (D) an intellectual who dabbles in business matters
    (E) a miser who has moments of extravagance

11. The style of the passage suggests that it is part of

    (A) an historical document
    (B) a textbook on sociology

(C) an essay against political favoritism

(D) a magazine article on good etiquette

(E) a story about abuse of power

12. The author is, with his reference to Monseigneur, using a literary device called

(A) onomatopoeia

(B) denouement

(C) symbolism

(D) psychogenesis

(E) euphemism

Passage 3

13. The emperor group which is spoken of favorably consists of

(A) Trajan, Caligula, Hadrian

(B) the Antonines, Vespasian, Domitian

(C) Nerva, Claudius, Vitellius

(D) Claudius, Caligula, the Antonines

(E) Nerva, Trajan, Hadrian

14. The period during which the Roman Empire showed greatest stability was the

(A) second century B.C.

(B) first century B.C.

(C) second century A.D.

(D) first century A.D.

(E) none of the above

15. Which of the following can be inferred about the Roman emperors?

(A) They all had trouble controlling the military

(B) Some had doubts about the virtue of one-man rule

(C) Most of them were superior to leaders in other countries

(D) The later Roman emperors built upon the success of earlier ones

(E) They each in their own way worked for the happiness of all citizens

16. According to the author, Roman emperors are unique in that

(A) they represent greater variety of moral conduct than any other group of leaders

(B) they are unmatched for their cruelty

(C) their life spans were shorter than those of any other group of rulers

(D) they were the most capable leaders in all history

(E) they encouraged the building of roads and temples

17. According to the passage, Vespasian's reign can best be characterized as

(A) violent

(B) prosperous

(C) victorious

(D) democratic

(E) short

ANSWER KEY

1. D	7. D	13. E
2. B	8. B	14. C
3. A	9. B	15. B
4. D	10. C	16. A
5. B	11. E	17. E
6. E	12. C	

EXPLANATORY ANSWERS

Passage 1

1. **(D)** This is clearly expressed in the middle of the passage.

2. **(B)** This is explicitly stated in the opening.

3. **(A)** This is a matter of definition.

4. **(D)** This is not mentioned in the passage.

5. **(B)** Since the passage is primarily concerned with enumerating the attributes of a gentleman, the best choice would be (B).

6. **(E)** In the context in which it is used, effeminacy refers to sensitivity or delicacy.

Passage 2

7. **(D)** The opening says that Monseigneur is at home, in rooms in his large house. A suite of rooms can be termed an apartment.

8. **(B)** The ironic and taunting attitude displayed toward Monseigneur throughout can be truly termed sarcastic.

9. **(B)** Mention of the English Stuarts places the passage as referring to post-17th-century events. More importantly, from the tone of the author concerning the aristocracy and the writing style itself, the obvious placement is 18th century.

10. **(C)** Monseigneur is said to care only about one person—himself.

11. **(E)** The passage is critical of Monseigneur and the decadent ruling class he represents; however, it is written in a fictionalized mode. The only appropriate choice is (E).

12. **(C)** Monseigneur stands for something else—the French upper class. The literary device of having one thing represent something else is termed symbolism.

Passage 3

13. **(E)** The passage states: "The forms of civil administration were carefully preserved by Nerva, Trajan, Hadrian, and the Antonines, who delighted in the image of liberty etc." Also Caligula, Claudius, and Domitian, whose names appear in all the other options, are all spoken of unfavorably.

14. **(C)** The period which the passage praises for its stability, and which constitutes the prime subject of the passage, is the period between 96 and 180 A.D., which is mainly the second century A.D.

15. **(B)** The passage states: "They [the emperors] must often have recollected the instability of a happiness which depended on the character of a single man."

16. **(A)** The passage states: "The annals of the emperors exhibit a strong and various picture of human nature, which we should vainly seek among the mixed and doubtful characters of modern history. In the conduct of these monarchs we may trace the utmost lines of vice and virtue. . . ."

17. **(E)** The passage refers to the "short and doubtful respite of Vespasian's reign."

GLOSSARY OF BUSINESS TERMS

ABATEMENT. A deduction or allowance, as, a discount given for prompt payment.

ACCOUNT. A detailed statement of items affecting property or claims, listed respectively as Debits or Credits, and showing excess of Debits or Credits in form of a balance. Sufficient explanatory matter should be given to set forth the complete history of the account. There need not be both Debits and Credits, nor more than one of either of these. If Debits and Credits, or both are made frequently, the account is active. Items held in suspense awaiting future classification or allocation may be charged or credited to an adjustment account. When desirable to keep a separate accounting for specific shipments of goods, it is known as an Adventure Account. If more than one party is interested in such shipment, it is a joint venture account.

Asset Accounts record value owned.

Book Accounts are kept in books, and show in formal manner the details regarding transactions between parties. To be of legal effect the entries must be original, not transferred or posted.

Capital Accounts show the amounts invested in an enterprise either net, as in case of the Capital Accounts of proprietors, partners, and stockholders shown on the liability side of Balance Sheets; or gross, as in case of the Asset Accounts which show both owned and borrowed Capital invested.

Cash Accounts set forth receipts and disbursements of cash as well as balance on hand at beginning and end of period.

Clearing Accounts are employed to collect items preliminary to their allocation to a more detailed classification of the accounts, or preliminary to the determination of the accounts to which such items properly belong.

Contingent Accounts are those which list liabilities or assets dependent for their validity upon some event which may or may not occur.

Contra Accounts are those which offset each other.

Controlling Accounts are those which summarize and afford an independent check upon detailed accounts of a given class which are usually kept in a subordinate ledger. The controlling accounts are kept in the General Ledger. The balance of the controlling account equals the aggregate of the balances of the detailed accounts when all postings affecting these accounts are completed.

Current Accounts are open or running accounts not balanced or stated.

Deficiency Accounts supplement statements of affairs of an insolvent enterprise, showing what items comprise the deficiency of assets subject to lien for payment of unsecured creditors.

Depreciation Accounts are expense accounts which are charged periodically with the amounts credited to the respective Depreciation Reserve Accounts.

Depreciation Reserve Accounts are credited periodically with the amounts charged to contra depreciation expense accounts. Depreciation Reserve Accounts are valuation accounts because they supplement or evaluate the asset accounts for the ultimate replacement of which they are intended.

Discount Accounts are accounts which are either charged with discounts allowed to customers or credited with discounts secured from creditors; or accounts which are charged with amounts paid to have Notes Discounted; or accounts which are carried unamortized differences between par of Bonds sold and the amounts realized at time of sale, such amounts realized being less than the par of the Bonds.

Dividend Accounts are credited with amounts declared payable as dividends by boards of directors. These accounts are charged for amounts disbursed in payment, the charge being made either at time checks are sent out and for full amount of dividend, or for the amounts of the individual checks as they are returned for payment.

Impersonal Accounts record expenses and revenues, assets and liabilities, but do not make reference to persons in their titles.

Income Accounts show sources and amounts of operating revenues, expenses incurred for operations, sources and amounts of nonoperating revenues, fixed charges, net income and disposition thereof.

Investment Accounts record property owned but not used for operating purposes.

Liability Accounts record value owed.

Merchandise Accounts are charged with cost of buying goods and crediting with sales, thus exhibiting Gross Profit when opening and closing inventories are taken into consideration.

Nominal Accounts are those which, during the accounting period, record changes which affect proprietorship favorably or unfavorably.

Open Accounts are those not balanced or closed.

Personal Accounts are those with individuals, usually customers and creditors.

Profit and Loss Account is an account into which all earnings and expenses are closed.

Real Accounts record Assets and Liabilities.

Revenue Accounts are equivalent to nominal accounts, showing income and expense.

Sales Accounts are rendered by agents to principals in explanation of consigned goods sold.

Sinking Fund Accounts record periodic installments paid into sinking funds and interest accretions added thereto.

Surplus Accounts record accretions to capital from profits.

ACCOUNTING. The science of accounts, their construction, classification and interpretation.

ACCRUE. Accumulation of wealth or liabilities based on passage of time.

ACCRUED EXPENSE. A liability representing expense that has accrued but is not yet due and payable. It is in reality postpaid expense, and therefore the opposite of prepaid expense, which is an asset.

ACCRUED INCOME. Income that has accrued but is not yet due. It is in reality postpaid income, and therefore the opposite of prepaid income, which is a liability.

AGENT. One possessing authority to act for another to a more or less limited extent.

ALLOCATION. Determination of the proper distribution of a given sum among a series of accounts.

AMORTIZATION. Extinction of a debt by systematic application of installments to a sinking fund, or reduction of premiums or discount incurred on sale or purchase of bonds by application of the effective interest rate.

ANNUITY. A sum of money payable periodically in installments.

APPRECIATION. Increase in value of assets.

ASSET. Wealth owned. Assets may be classified in various ways. From the point of view of ease of liquidation they are Quick or Fixed in varying degrees.

AUDIT. Verification of the accuracy of account books by examination of supporting vouchers, making tests of postings and computations and determining whether all entries are made according to correct accounting principles, and making sure that there are no omissions.

BALANCE. The excess of the sum of the items on one side of an account over the sum of the items on the other side.

BALANCE SHEET. A schedule of Assets and Liabilities so classified and arranged as to enable an intelligent study to be made of the important financial ratios existing between different classes of assets, between different classes of liabilities and between assets and liabilities; also to enable one to observe the origin of the equity existing in the assets and to determine to whom it belongs.

BOND. A bond is a written promise under seal to pay a certain sum of money at a specified time. Bonds bear interest at a fixed rate, usually payable semiannually. Bonds may be sold either above or below par, in which case the coupon rate of interest differs from the effective rate when the bonds are sold below par and higher when bonds are sold above par.

BURDEN. Elements of production cost which, not being directly allocable to output, must be distributed on a more or less arbitrary basis.

CAPITAL. In accounting, capital is excess of assets over liabilities of a given enterprise.

Fixed Capital consists of wealth in form of land, buildings, machinery, furniture and fixtures, etc.

Floating Capital is capital which can be readily converted into cash.

Nominal Capital is the authorized capital stock of a corporation.

Paid-Up Capital is the amount of capital stock issued and fully paid.

Working Capital is the excess of current assets over current liabilities.

CASH. All forms of exchange media which by custom are received in settlement of debts.

CHARGES. Items debited in accounts.

CHECK OR CHEQUE. See Draft.

COLLATERAL SECURITY. Personal property transferred by the owner to another to secure the carrying out of an obligation.

CONSIGNEE. An agent who receives shipments of goods from his principal to be sold on commission basis, title to goods remaining in the principal or consignor.

CONSIGNMENT. A shipment of goods to another and held by him for account of the principal or consignor.

CONSIGNOR. One who ships goods to an agent or factor who holds them for account of the principal or consignor.

CONSOLIDATION. Unification or affiliation of enterprises engaged in competitive or supplementary undertakings.

CONTINGENT. That which depends upon some happening or occurrence; doubtful, conditional.

CORPORATION. An artificial person created by law to carry out a certain purpose or purposes.

COST. Cost is the outlay, usually measured in terms of money, necessary to buy or to produce a commodity. The two elements of Cost are Prime Cost and Overhead or Burden. Prime Cost is the outlay on direct labor and raw materials necessary to produce a commodity. Burden includes all elements of Cost other than direct labor and raw materials.

COST ACCOUNTING. Determination, by means of applying accounting principles, of the elements of Cost entering into the production of a commodity or service.

CREDITOR. One who gives credit in business matters; one to whom money is due.

DEBT. An obligation to pay money or that which one owes to another.

DEBTOR. One who owes money.

DEFERRED ASSET OR CHARGE. See Prepaid Expense.

DEFERRED CREDIT & INCOME OR LIABILITY. See Prepaid Income.

DEFICIENCY. Insufficiency of assets to discharge debts or other obligations.

DEPRECIATION. Decline in value of assets resulting from one or more of the following:

1. Wear and tear
2. Tenure of holding
3. Permanency or steadiness of industry
4. Exhaustion of raw materials
5. Obsolescence
6. Accidents
7. Fluctuations in trade
8. Inadequacy

DISBURSEMENTS. Cash payments.

DISCOUNT. Deduction from a listed or named figure, usually computed on a percentage basis.

DIVIDEND. Division of profits among stockholders on a pro rata basis.

DRAFT. A draft or bill of exchange is defined by Uniform Negotiable Instrument Law as, "an unconditional order in writing addressed by one person to another, signed by the person giving it, requiring the person to whom it is addressed to pay on demand or at a fixed or determinable future time a certain sum in money to order or to bearer."

DRAWEE. The person against whom a draft is drawn and who becomes primarily liable upon acceptance.

DRAWER. The maker of a draft or bill of exchange.

ENTRY. Written description of a business transaction or adjustment made in books of accounts.

ESTATE. A right of ownership in property.

FIXED ASSETS. Those assets which are not readily convertible into cash and in the usual routine of business are not so converted.

FRANCHISE. A privilege or liberty given by the Government to certain individuals.

GOOD WILL. Present right to receive expected future superprofits, superprofits being the amount by which future profits are expected to exceed all economic expenditure incident to its production.

IMPREST SYSTEM. Plan used to account for petty cash disbursements whereby the cashier is at intervals reimbursed for the amount disbursed by him through a check drawn to Cash and charged to the accounts against which such disbursements were made.

INCOME. A flow of benefits from wealth over a period of time.

INTEREST. Expense or income resulting from use of wealth over a period of time.

INVENTORY. An itemized list of goods giving amounts and prices.

INVOICE. A statement issued by a seller of goods to the purchaser giving details regarding quantities, prices and terms of payment.

JOURNAL. The book of original entry in double entry bookkeeping.

Cash Journal is a combination cash book and journal, containing columns for both cash and non-cash transactions.

Purchases Journal records purchases made and the names of persons credited therefor.

Sales Journal records sales and the names of persons charged therefor.

LEDGER. A ledger is the book in which transactions are classified according to function. When subordinate ledgers are used, the General Ledger becomes a digest of details kept in subordinate ledgers, as well as the record of all usual ledger accounts.

Accounts Receivable Ledger contains a record of all transactions affecting trade debtors.

Accounts Payable Ledger contains a record of all transactions affecting trade creditors.

LIABILITY. A debt.

Capital Liabilities are those which are incurred in the acquisition of permanent assets, and which are usually in form of bonded indebtedness having a maturity date removed more than a year.

Contingent Liabilities are those which may or may not become definite obligations, depending upon some event.

Current Liabilities are those which will fall due within a period of a year.

Deferred Liabilities are income received but not yet due; see Prepaid Income.

Fixed Liabilities are those in form of bonds or long term notes.

NOTES PAYABLE. The sum of all notes and acceptances upon which a concern is primarily liable as maker, endorser or acceptor.

NOTES RECEIVABLE. The sum of all notes and acceptances upon which others are liable to the holding concern.

NOTES RECEIVABLE DISCOUNTED. Contingent Liability for all notes receivable discounted at bank but not yet liquidated by the makers.

OVERDRAFT. A debit balance in a deposit account which should normally have a credit balance.

POSTING. Transferring items from journals to ledgers, and making the necessary cross-references in folio columns.

PREMIUM ON BONDS. Amount above par at which bonds are bought or sold.

PREPAID EXPENSE. An asset representing expenditures for services not yet rendered. Also known as Deferred Charge or Deferred Asset.

PREPAID INCOME. Income received for services not yet rendered. It is therefore a liability. Also known as Deferred Credit or Deferred Liability.

PROFIT. Increase in net worth resulting from business operations.

PROPRIETORSHIP. Equity in assets over and above liability.

QUICK ASSETS. Assets that can ordinarily be readily converted into cash without involving heavy loss.

RESERVE. A segregation of surplus, or a retention of revenues equivalent to losses in asset values. In the former case it is a reserve of surplus, in the latter case, a valuation reserve.

RESERVE FUND. An amount set aside in form of cash or investments for general or special purposes.

REVENUE. Income from all sources.

SINKING FUND. An amount set aside in form of cash or investments for the purpose of liquidating some liability.

STATEMENT. To set forth in systematic form all data with reference to some phase of a business undertaking. To present essential details, subordinate schedules are frequently appended. A statement of Assets and Liabilities.

Balance Sheets set forth the status of a business as of a given date.

Consolidated Balance Sheets set forth the status of affiliated businesses as of a given time.

Consolidated Income Statements set forth the results of operations of affiliated enterprises over a period.

Income Statements set forth the result of operations over a period.

Statements of Affairs set forth the status of an insolvent business as of a given time, the arrangement being such as to show both book value of assets, what they are expected to realize, and gross liabilities, and how they are expected to rank.

STOCK. Share issued by a corporation, evidenced by formal certificates representing ownership therein. The total amount of such shares is known as the Capital Stock of the corporation.

Common Stock is that upon which dividends are paid only after dividend requirements on preferred stock and interest requirements on bonds are met.

Donated Stock is stock of a corporation which has been given back to be sold at a discount, usually to afford working capital in cases where the stock was originally issued in payment for fixed assets.

Guaranteed Stock is that which is guaranteed as to principal or interest or both by some other corporation or corporations.

Inactive Stock is that which is seldom traded on the exchange.

Preferred Stock is that which has prior rights over common stock either as to dividends or assets or both. Various provisions are found relative to the voting power, as for example, the preferred stock may be given control of the corporation if dividends thereon remain unpaid for two consecutive years. In case of cumulative preferred stock, unpaid dividends become a lien upon profits of following years.

Treasury Stock is that which has been returned to the treasury of the issuing corporation.

Unissued Stock is the excess of Authorized over Issued Stock.

STOCK BONUSES. Gifts of stock offered to furnish incentive to investors to buy some other security of the issuing company.

STOCK RIGHTS. Privileges extended to stockholders to subscribe to new stock at a price below the market value of outstanding stock.

STOCK SUBSCRIPTIONS. Agreements to purchase the stock of a corporation. They become effective only when ratified by the corporation, unless accepted by a trustee in behalf of the corporation.

SURPLUS. In case of corporations having only par value stock, surplus ordinarily measures excess of net worth or proprietorship over par value of stock outstanding.

Capital Surplus is that derived from extraordinary sources, as sale of stock at premium or sale of fixed assets at a profit.

Surplus from Operations is that derived from undertakings from the carrying out of which the business was established.

TRIAL BALANCE. A list of balances of all General Ledger accounts made to determine the correctness of postings from books of original entry as well as the correctness of the work of determining these balances.

TURNOVER. Rapidity of replacement of capital invested in inventories, accounts receivable, etc.

VOUCHER. Any document which serves as proof of a transaction.

VOUCHER SYSTEM. A scheme of accounting under which distribution of all expenditures is made on vouchers preliminary to their entry in the voucher register.

WORK IN PROCESS. Materials in process of manufacture, partly finished goods including all material, labor and overhead costs incurred on those goods up to the time of taking inventory.

PRACTICAL BUSINESS JUDGMENT

TEST 1

DIRECTIONS: This section consists of a reading selection which details a business situation followed by two sets of questions, data evaluation and data application. In the first set, data evaluation, you will be asked to classify certain of the facts presented in the passage on the basis of their importance. The second set, data application, will test your grasp of specific details of the situation.

The Bowton Company's supermarkets are situated in Illinois, Wisconsin, and Indiana. The company is dynamic and aggressive, having grown from eight stores ten years ago to 26 today.

Fords Lake is a town 40 miles from the Chicago Loop. It has not shown the spectacular growth of other suburbs, but its population has increased from 16,000 to over 30,000 in the past decade. With no other Bowton supermarket within 20 miles of the area, the Bowton Company is considering opening a store in Fords Lake.

Some Bowton executives oppose the project as a poor risk. They point to the proposed site, which is in a shopping center three miles from the Fords Lake business district. Two other food chains have failed on this site because, they claim, most new residences are on the other side of the community.

Moreover, the shopping-center owners demand a five-year lease. Bowton would have to try to find another business to take over the lease should its own store fail before the end of that time.

If a Bowton market must be opened in Fords Lake, it would be far better, these executives argue, to build it in the heart of the community. But, they point out, another supermarket is already there.

The majority of the executives maintain that the site has great potential. A new east-west highway is being built which will pass Fords Lake to the north and force the car-commuters to Chicago to pass by the shopping center. A housing project of 3,000 units is going to be constructed nearby. This project will have three- and four-bedroom homes. The average household is expected to consist of five people with over $35,000 of income to dispose of annually.

They also argue that the center of Fords Lake is now congested with traffic and has extremely poor parking facilities, while there is excellent parking in the shopping center. Investment in a new building in Fords Lake proper would thus be a bad risk and would prove far more costly than a five-year lease should the store fail.

They are not too concerned about the other supermarket in Fords Lake. There is enough business for both. Besides, the competitor's prices are higher than Bowton's.

They also discount past supermarket failures in the shopping center. They claim these were caused more by poor management than by the shopping center's being slightly off the beaten path.

The board of directors listens to both sides and then votes to open a Bowton store at the Fords Lake shopping center.

DATA EVALUATION

DIRECTIONS: Based on your analysis of the business situation, classify each of the following elements in one of five categories. Mark:

(A) if the element is a MAJOR OBJECTIVE in making the decision; that is, the outcome or result sought by the decision maker.

(B) if the element is a MAJOR FACTOR in arriving at the decision; that is, a consideration explicitly mentioned in the passage that is basic in determining the decision.

(C) if the element is a MINOR FACTOR in making the decision; that is, a secondary consideration in determining the decision.

(D) if the element is a MAJOR ASSUMPTION made in deliberating; that is, a supposition or projection made by the decision maker before weighing the variables.

(E) if the element is an UNIMPORTANT ISSUE in getting to the point; that is, a factor that is insignificant or not immediately relevant to the situation.

1. The residents at the projected residential development will shop in the Bowton store

2. No Bowton store within 20 miles

3. New east-west highway

4. Competition from another store

5. The expansion of the Bowton Company to a new location

6. An increase of the population flow through the shopping center site

7. Failure of two supermarkets at the Fords Lake shopping center

8. Bowton activities confined to three states

9. Establishing a new store

10. New housing development

DATA APPLICATION

DIRECTIONS: Based on your understanding of the business situation, answer the following questions testing your comprehension of the information supplied in the passage. For each question, select the choice which best answers the question or completes the statement. Circle the letter preceding your answer.

11. In the last ten years, the Bowton Company has increased its number of supermarkets by

    (A) 18%
    (B) 26%
    (C) 200%
    (D) 325%
    (E) 480%

12. In the last decade the population of Fords Lake has increased about

    (A) 50%
    (B) 100%
    (C) 150%
    (D) 200%
    (E) 250%

13. Which of the following arguments are used by some Bowton executives to oppose a Bowton store in the shopping center?

    I. The center is far from the new residences.

II. Another Bowton store is five miles away.
III. The owners demand a five-year lease.

(A) I only
(B) II only
(C) I and II only
(D) I and III only
(E) I, II and III

14. Which of the following are arguments used to oppose Bowton's opening a store in the heart of the Fords Lake business district?

    I. A rival store is already there.
    II. Two supermarkets already failed in that area.
    III. Parking facilities are poor.

(A) I only
(B) III only
(C) I and III only
(D) II and III only
(E) I, II and III

15. The shopping-center site is favored by

    (A) only a minority of Bowton executives
    (B) the residents of Fords Lake
    (C) the majority of Bowton executives
    (D) less than half of the Bowton board of directors
    (E) the stockholders of the Bowton Company

16. One argument presented in favor of the shopping-center site is that

    (A) it is at present close to a dense residential area
    (B) the shopping-center owners would waive rent for two years
    (C) no supermarket has ever been in this area of the community
    (D) a new highway will pass nearby
    (E) Bowton has been very successful in shopping-center locations

17. The average family that will occupy the housing project soon to be constructed will

    (A) be considered as a typical lower-middle-income family
    (B) probably go into the Fords Lake business district to shop
    (C) consist of three people
    (D) be able to spend $35,000 a year after taxes

(E) probably have little economic effect on the shopping center

18. The population increase in the Fords Lake community expected to result from the new housing project is

(A) 3,000
(B) 10,000
(C) 15,000
(D) 30,000
(E) 46,000

19. Which of the following arguments are used to ease the fear of those who worry about competition from a rival Fords Lake supermarket?

I. There is enough business for both stores.
II. The other store is badly managed.
III. Bowton's prices are lower.

(A) I only
(B) II only
(C) I and II only
(D) I and III only
(E) I, II and III

20. Which of the following reason(s) given explain the failure of two supermarkets in the shopping center?

I. Poor parking facilities
II. Off the beaten path
III. Poor management

(A) I only
(B) II only
(C) III only
(D) II and III only
(E) I, II and III

ANSWER KEY

1. D	8. E	15. C
2. C	9. A	16. D
3. C	10. C	17. D
4. E	11. D	18. C
5. A	12. B	19. D
6. B	13. D	20. D
7. C	14. C	

EXPLANATORY ANSWERS

1. (D) is correct. It is assumed that the future development residents will go to the shopping center rather than all the way to the Fords Lake business district.

2. (C) The fact that no other Bowton store is within 20 miles is a minor factor in seeking a site in Fords Lake.

3. (C) The new east-west highway is a minor factor influencing the major factor that more people will now pass the shopping center, which, in turn, influences the decision to open a store in the shopping center.

4. (E) Competition from the other supermarket in the area does not influence the decision to open a Bowton store.

5. (A) The Bowton Company has shown rapid growth.

6. (B) Increase of population through the shopping center is the major factor.

7. (C) The board of directors feels that Bowton can overcome whatever difficulties caused these failures.

8. (E) The geographic area of Bowton's activities has no bearing on the decision.

9. (A) The establishment of a new store is a major objective.

10. (C) The future residential development certainly influences the decision to open a new store nearby.

11. (D) The stores increased from 8 to 26.

12. (B) The population increased from 16,000 to slightly over 30,000.

13. (D) It is stated that no other Bowton supermarket is within 20 miles of Fords Lake. The opposing executives refer only to the new residences already occupied, not to the projected housing development near the shopping center.

14. (C) It is stated there is a rival store in the heart of Fords Lake and that parking facilities are poor. The two supermarkets that failed were in the shopping center, not in the business district.

15. (C) So stated in the story.

16. (D) So stated in the story. (A) is wrong since the shopping center is not as yet close to a residential area of any size. (C) is incorrect; we are told that two supermarkets failed in the shopping center. (E) is wrong; we are not told what success Bowton has had in other shopping centers.

17. (D) Disposable income is what is left after taxes, social security, and so forth, are taken out of a salary check; in short, it is take-home pay. (A) is wrong; $35,000 disposable income is far higher than lower-middle income. (C) is wrong; we are told the average family will consist of five people. (B) and (E) are assumptions that are not stated in the story.

18. **(C)** is correct. There will be 3,000 new housing units with an average of five people in each, or a total of 15,000.

19. **(D)** represents the correct statements; **(E)** is wrong; we don't know if the rival store is badly managed.

20. **(D)** We are told that the shopping center is off the beaten path at the moment. We are also told that poor management was the reason given by a majority of Bowton executives for failure of the two previous supermarket ventures.

TEST 2

DIRECTIONS: This section consists of a reading selection which details a business situation followed by two sets of questions, data evaluation and data application. In the first set, data evaluation, you will be asked to classify certain of the facts presented in the passage on the basis of their importance. The second set, data application, will test your grasp of specific details of the situation.

Bob Bensen is a California entrepreneur. He has owned twelve businesses and is 42 years old. His present firm, Bensen Bamboo Company, purchases mock-bamboo siding from Japan and resells it to contractors building fast-food restaurants in the northeastern United States—most notably in Boston. He has run the medium-sized firm for three years and has seen its liquid assets increase from $4 million to $10 million in that time. He has had several opportunities to sell the company and has one standing offer from a former business partner who said he will purchase it at any time for $15 million. Because Bensen is determined to run a business that will give him a solid future, he has held on to the Bamboo Company on the strength of its past performance; he feels it will continue to do well. His wife and his doctor have encouraged him to "slow down," and he is not eager to go through the headaches involved in selling another business. He is hoping the company will be a solid one for the next twenty years or so.

Recently, however, he was approached by someone offering to trade companies. He met with a young man named Wilson who said he had been involved in purchasing bricks from Thailand and distributing them to major builders and contractors throughout the South and Southwest. He managed to convince Bensen

there is a more secure future in the brick business than there is in the mock-bamboo trade and that because he was interested in quick money, he wanted to exchange operations with Bensen. He said his company, Thailand Bricks, Inc., would (after some initial investments) continue to grow moderately but steadily for many years, and that he was sure Bensen Bamboo would do extremely well for two or three more years and then lose its market. Each company had the same net worth and liquid assets of $10 million. There would be no difficulty making transfers of ownership. Bensen was interested. He called a meeting.

At the meeting, Bensen outlined what Wilson had told him. He explained that after three months, their assets would be down $5 million, then after three more months, up to $12 million . . . . "leaving us a nice $2 million profit and a solid future," he said confidently. "I've been thinking, all this talk about the Sunbelt makes sense to me. The future's there. I'm ready to try one more company by trading. Let's get out of Boston."

Bensen's chief sales advisor looked confused. "The Company has been doing so well, I don't see why you want to switch. My research tells me we stand to have a $14 million liquidity at the end of the next six months, and, with a similar $5 million expenditure, we'll be way ahead on profits. Besides, we know the Boston market is strong this year. Even though we expect transportation problems and there is the possibility of some labor difficulties in Japan, we'll be in better shape after six months than if we trade with Wilson."

The financial advisor said the trade was an attractive venture, but explained: "If we wait six months, we'll have more money, and we can shop around. We'll look better in the market; we can even find a better trade."

Bensen said he liked the looks of this trade and that he did not want to shop around in six months. But he agreed to think it over on the "profits" issue.

DATA EVALUATION

DIRECTIONS: Based on your analysis of the business situation, classify each of the following elements in one of five categories. Mark:

(A) if the element is a MAJOR OBJECTIVE in making the decision; that is, the outcome or result sought by the decision maker.

(B) if the element is a MAJOR FACTOR in arriving at the decision; that is, a consideration explicitly mentioned in the passage that is basic in determining the decision.

(C) if the element is a MINOR FACTOR in making the decision; that is, a secondary consideration in determining the decision.

(D) if the element is a MAJOR ASSUMPTION made in deliberating; that is, a supposition or projection made by the decision maker before weighing the variables.

(E) if the element is an UNIMPORTANT ISSUE in getting to the point; that is, a factor that is insignificant or not immediately relevant to the situation.

1. Wife and doctor's advice that Bensen "slow down."

2. Solid future for Bensen's business ventures.

3. Fifteen million dollar offer to purchase Bensen Bamboo Company.

4. The future is in the Sunbelt.

5. Transportation problems.

6. Bensen wants to trade and not buy.

7. Boston market is strong this year.

8. Labor difficulties in Japan.

9. To be ahead in profits.

10. To be able to shop around for a better deal in six months.

DATA APPLICATION

DIRECTIONS: Based on your understanding of the business situation, answer the following questions testing your comprehension of the information supplied in the passage. For each question, select the choice which best answers the question or completes the statement. Circle the letter preceding your answer.

11. Bensen assumed control of the Bamboo Company when he was

    (A) 39
    (B) 38
    (C) 24
    (D) 40
    (E) cannot be determined

12. Since Bensen took over, the Bamboo Company has increased its liquid assets by

    (A) 80%
    (B) 15%
    (C) 120%
    (D) 150%.
    (E) cannot be determined

13. **A major reason for Bensen's not selling Bensen Bamboo is**

    (A) he could not find a buyer
    (B) despite plenty of buyers, no one offered enough money
    (C) he had owned twelve companies, and, being superstitious, preferred not to own a thirteenth
    (D) he thought the company had a solid future
    (E) none of the above

14. Wilson's reason for wanting to trade was

    (A) he was tired of his business and wanted a change
    (B) he saw the opportunity to build his own personal, building-material empire
    (C) he wanted to make quick money
    (D) he liked Bensen; he knew he was a good businessman and wanted to go into partnership
    (E) he preferred the Boston market to the South and the Southwest

15. If, according to Wilson, after six months the brick venture would have decreased the company's liquid assets by $5 million, then they would have increased by what percent after another three months?

    (A) 120%
    (B) 140%
    (C) 80%
    (D) 240%
    (E) cannot be determined

16. Bensen's chief sales advisor

    I. expected Bensen's interest in trading
    II. agreed the market was better in the South and the Southwest
    III. wanted to be ahead on profits
    IV. said the Boston market shows a strong future in the long run

(A) I
(B) II
(C) III
(D) I and III
(E) I, II, III, and IV

17. Liquid assets after six months in the mock-bamboo venture will be

   (A) $3 million
   (B) $6 million
   (C) no profits after six months
   (D) $4 million
   (E) $14 million

18. The sales manager expects

   (A) transportation and currency devaluation problems
   (B) labor difficulties in California
   (C) labor difficulties in Boston
   (D) loss of Southwest market
   (E) none of the above

19. The financial advisor said

   I. The trade looked "attractive."
   II. "If we wait six months, we'll be ruined."
   III. "If we wait six months, we'll be way ahead on profits."
   IV. "We should look for better deals next year."

   (A) I only
   (B) I and II
   (C) III
   (D) III and IV
   (E) IV only

20. Bensen said

   (A) he liked the looks of Bensen Bamboo Company this year
   (B) he wants to retire for the next twenty years
   (C) he didn't want to shop around in six months
   (D) "Profits are my only concern."
   (E) none of the above

ANSWER KEY

1. C	8. C	15. B
2. A	9. A	16. C
3. E	10. E	17. E
4. D	11. A	18. E
5. C	12. D	19. A
6. B	13. D	20. C
7. D	14. C	

EXPLANATORY ANSWERS

1. **(C)** Minor Factor. The trade with Wilson would be an extra strain on Bensen, but not a deciding factor in his acceptance or rejection of the trade.

2. **(A)** The passage tells us Bensen is hoping the Bamboo Company "will be a solid one for the next twenty years," but is considering the trade because "there is a more secure future in the brick business." A solid future is obviously a major objective of Bensen's.

3. **(E)** The fifteen million dollar offer was made by by a former partner of Bensen's, and while it still stands, it is not under consideration and is therefore irrelevant.

4. **(D)** Major Assumption. Bensen wants a solid future for his business ventures, and feels a move to the Sunbelt would be to his advantage, despite a lack of hard statistics.

5. **(C)** Minor Factor. Problems of transportation exist with Bensen's current business, but according to the sales advisor, they will not affect the Bamboo Company's profits significantly.

6. **(B)** Trading is obviously a major factor in Bensen's decision, as he could have sold out of the Bamboo Company for fifteen million dollars to a former partner long ago, if he had wanted to sell.

7. **(D)** The strength of the Boston market is a major assumption made by the chief sales advisor in arguing against the trade with Wilson. The assumption may have a strong base in statistical data, but it is still a projection for the future.

8. **(C)** Labor difficulties in Japan are a potential source of trouble to the Bamboo Company, but according to the chief sales advisor, this is only a minor factor in deciding about the trade.

9. **(A)** Maximizing his profit figures is obviously a major objective of Bensen's, as it is upon this consideration that he will decide whether or not to make the trade.

10. **(E)** Irrelevant. Bensen states that he has no interest in shopping around in six months' time.

11. **(A)** The passage states that Bensen has run the company for three years and that he is forty-two years old.

12. **(D)** The passage states that liquid assets went from $4 million to $10 million under Bensen; this means a 150% increase.

13. **(D)** The passage states Bensen has held on to the Bamboo Company because he wants a business with a solid future, and he thinks his company will be solid for "the next twenty years or so."

14. **(C)** The passage states that Wilson was "interested in quick money" and that he wanted to exchange companies because he felt Bensen Bamboo would do well for two or three more years, then lose its market.

15. **(B)** The passage states the brick venture would up the liquid assets $7 million to yield a final liquid asset figure of $12 million. Seven million is 140% of $5 million.

16. **(C)** The sales advisor said, in comparing the two companies, "we'll be way ahead on profits after six months." (Number IV seems a plausible choice, but the advisor said the Boston market would be strong for the next *year* only.)

17. **(E)** The passage states that after six months, the Bamboo Company will have "a $14 million liquidity."

18. **(E)** There is no mention of currency values (A); labor difficulties are expected in Japan, not California (B) or Boston (C); no one speaks of losing a Southwest market (E).

19. **(A)** The financial advisor said "the trade was attractive." (Though IV seems a plausible selection, the advisor was optimistic about a better trade in six months only.)

20. **(C)** In the last paragraph, Bensen says "he does not want to shop around in six months."

TEST 3

DIRECTIONS: This section consists of a reading selection which details a business situation followed by two sets of questions, data evaluation and data application. In the first set, data evaluation, you will be asked to classify certain of the facts presented in the passage on the basis of their importance. The second set, data application, will test your grasp of specific details of the situation.

Laker Health Spa, only two years in business and completing an extremely successful year, has capital to invest in the expansion of its facilities. The club management is particularly interested in exploring alternative exercise programs to those currently in use. One possible direction of expansion is to introduce a system of exercise machines into the club. Several of the leading health clubs in the city already have in use such systems in order to provide a basic exercise program for their members. Those who favor such systems claim that it makes all other exercise methods obsolete. The machines allow only for a very precise movement and they are constructed so that one can progressively increase the difficulty of the movements. Maxon, a leading manufacturer of such a system, says that they are prepared to make Laker an unusually attractive offer. Critics of such systems say that those who use such machines are more prone to

injury while exercising and that the machines do not develop natural body movements of the sort one finds in yoga exercises.

A very different alternative for Laker would be to create a spacious exercise area free of any sort of equipment. This would provide a space for large classes using natural exercise methods without machines. Tony Barnes, who has received attention in the media for his revolutionary exercise techniques, has expressed interest in becoming a part of the Laker organization and in organizing equipment-free exercise programs. Barnes would join Laker on the conditions that the option of partial ownership be open to him and that he have complete autonomy over the club's exercise program.

DATA EVALUATION

DIRECTIONS: Based on your analysis of the business situation, classify each of the following elements in one of five categories. Mark:

(A) if the element is a MAJOR OBJECTIVE in making the decision; that is, the outcome or result sought by the decision maker.

(B) if the element is a MAJOR FACTOR in arriving at the decision; that is, a consideration explicitly mentioned in the passage that is basic in determining the decision.

(C) if the element is a MINOR FACTOR in making the decision; that is, a secondary consideration in determining the decision.

(D) if the element is a MAJOR ASSUMPTION made in deliberating; that is, a supposition or projection made by the decision maker before weighing the variables.

(E) if the element is an UNIMPORTANT ISSUE in getting to the point; that is, a factor that is insignificant or not immediately relevant to the situation.

1. The institution of new exercise programs.

2. A continuing public interest in physical fitness and exercise.

3. Comparative cost of creating a large exercise area and introducing a system of exercise machines.

4. The attractiveness of Maxon's offer.

5. Barnes' experience in working with exercise machines.

6. The number of people who don't join exercise clubs because of confined and crowded exercise areas.

7. The number of years that Laker has been in business.

8. Safety record of exercise machines.

9. Club members' demand that the current exercise programs not be changed.

10. Expansion of facilities.

11. There is some merit to natural non-machine techniques.

12. Desirability of the exercise program being controlled by one individual.

13. Maintenance and service of exercise machines.

14. Barnes' ability to work with subordinates.

15. Growing use of natural techniques by Olympic trainers.

DATA APPLICATION

DIRECTIONS: Based on your understanding of the business situation, answer the following questions testing your comprehension of the information supplied in the passage. For each question, select the choice which best answers the question or completes the statement. Circle the letter preceding your answer.

16. According to the passage a system of exercise machines

   I. would be less costly than other exercise programs
   II. would be safer than other exercise programs
   III. are thought by some to be the superior method of exercise

   (A) I only
   (B) I and II only
   (C) III only
   (D) I and III only
   (E) I, II, and III

17. Barnes could be an asset to the Laker Spa because of

I. his knowledge of natural exercise methods
II. his recent coverage in the media
III. his demand for autonomy over the exercise program

   (A) I only
   (B) II only
   (C) III only
   (D) I and III only
   (E) I and II only

18. Barnes would only be hired if

   I. Laker decides against a system of exercise machines.
   II. Laker is willing to offer an option of partial ownership to him.
   III. He comes into the club with complete autonomy over the exercise program.

   (A) I only
   (B) II only
   (C) III only
   (D) II and III only
   (E) I, II, and III

19. Which of the following conditions would have to be met if Laker were to bring in a system of exercise machines?

   I. an attractive offer from Maxon
   II. someone other than Barnes were in charge of the exercise program
   III. a greater demand for yoga classes

   (A) I only
   (B) II only
   (C) I and II
   (D) II and III
   (E) I, II, and III

20. Which of the following is not an objective of the Laker Health Spa?

   I. to institute the most economic plan available
   II. to expand its facilities
   III. to bring about new exercise programs

   (A) I only
   (B) II only
   (C) III only
   (D) II and III only
   (E) I, II, and III

ANSWER KEY

1. A	8. B	15. E
2. D	9. B	16. C
3. B	10. A	17. E
4. B	11. D	18. E
5. E	12. B	19. B
6. C	13. C	20. A
7. E	14. B	

EXPLANATORY ANSWERS

1. **(A)** Major Objective. It is this objective that is behind Laker's exploration of the two alternative exercise programs.

2. **(D)** Major Assumption. It is only on this assumption that it would make sense to consider the expansion of exercise facilities.

3. **(B)** Major Factor. This would be a major factor in determining which of the two alternative directions they wanted to take. If it turns out that only one of the alternative programs is within range of what they are prepared to spend, then the more feasible program would be the obvious choice.

4. **(B)** Major Factor. This is a major factor in making the choice since an unusually attractive offer from Maxon could give the first alternative a clear edge. There appear to be no special bargains tied up with the second alternative and it could be costly if, for example, they were to meet all of Barnes' demands.

5. **(E)** Unimportant Issue. This is an unimportant factor since Barnes would only be brought in if Laker decided to initiate a non-machine program.

6. **(C)** Minor Factor. This could be a factor in the decision since if a number of people stay away from health clubs because of the confined exercise area, then the second alternative would meet a need in health club exercise programs that the first alternative would not meet. This is not a major factor since the primary objective is not to bring people into health clubs who would not ordinarily come into health clubs.

7. **(E)** Unimportant Issue. This factor would have no bearing on Laker's present decision to expand its facilities.

8. **(B)** Major Factor. This is a major factor since a poor safety record would virtually eliminate the first of the two alternatives.

9. **(B)** Major Factor. If this demand were serious enough and Laker felt the need to respond to the demands of its club members, then this factor could bring about a major revision of their expansion plans.

10. **(A)** Major Objective. This factor correctly describes the general objective of the club, which has a particular interest in expanding exercise facilities.

11. **(D)** Major Assumption. It is only on this assumption that the club is prepared to consider the second alternative as a possibility.

12. **(B)** Major Factor. This is a major factor since if it is undesirable that one individual have control of the exercise program, then the desirability of the second alternative is greatly weakened. Barnes will only come to Laker if he can have complete control over the exercise programs.

13. **(C)** Minor Factor. The care and upkeep of the machines would certainly be relevant to the option of adopting a machine system. But it is a consideration that could easily be overridden by other factors, such as an attractive offer from Maxon.

14. **(B)** Major Factor. This is a major factor since if Barnes lacked this ability the alternative involving his control of the exercise program would seem to be unworkable.

15. **(E)** Unimportant Issue. This factor has no bearing on which of the alternatives under consideration is the more attractive one.

16. **(C)** It is clearly stated that those who favor the machine system think that such systems make other methods obsolete. There is nothing in the passage about the comparative cost of exercise programs and it is stated that the safety of the machine system has been one of the issues raised by the critics of the machine system.

17. **(E)** Barnes could be of value to Laker because of his special knowledge of natural exercise techniques. His being well covered in the media could contribute to the promotion and success of the new program. His autonomy is not an asset but one of the things he expects in return for the assets he has to offer.

18. **(E)** Alternatives II and III must be included since it is only on those conditions that Barnes will take the job. Alternative I must be included since Barnes would not be hired if Laker adopted a system of exercise machines.

19. **(B)** Only the second alternative would have to be met. The hiring of Barnes, who uses only natural methods and demands autonomy over the program, would be incompatible with adopting a system of machines. Laker could adopt a machine system without using Maxon's and a demand for yoga classes is in no way essential to adopting a machine system.

20. **(A)** Alternatives I and II are clearly stated as objectives, but there is nothing in the passage to indicate that economy would be the deciding factor in making their decision.

VALIDITY OF CONCLUSION

DIRECTIONS: Each of the following four sets consists of a reading passage followed by a conclusion drawn from the passage. Each conclusion is followed by statements which have a possible bearing on the conclusion. For each statement, you are to choose from the following the option which best expresses the relationship between the statement and the conclusion:

(A) The statement proves the conclusion.
(B) The statement supports the conclusion but does not prove it.
(C) The statement disproves the conclusion.
(D) The statement weakens the conclusion.
(E) The statement is irrelevant to the conclusion.

Write in the correct letter next to each question number.

SET 1

D. Rivers, the president of WAS Airlines, sent a memorandum to all WAS stockholders on January 13 describing three alternative plans for continued profits on their roundtrip, New York to London flight. The price of WAS's London flight had for some time been $400, but a rival firm, Camel Airlines, had recently introduced a 279-dollar bargain flight from New York to London. Plan 1 called for the investment of one million dollars in new luxury items for WAS planes. Rivers felt that many people would rather pay more money for a flight to Europe if they would be provided with wider seats, free champagne, and flight attendants dressed in designer uniforms. Plan 2 suggested lowering the price of the flight to $325. Rivers felt that, although this price was higher than Camel's, he would be able to sell more flights than Camel on the basis of WAS's reputation as the safest and most reliable airline in the business. Plan 3 was to lower the fare to $278, while increasing the number of seats on the planes by 15%.

CONCLUSION: Plan 3 was put into effect on February 15, 1977.

1. Sixty percent of the stockholders preferred Plan 2.

2. On January 17, the Civil Aeronautics Board prohibited airline fares below $325.

3. On March 2, 1977, Jenny Malone paid her travel agent $278 for her roundtrip, New York-London ticket on WAS airlines.

4. The public relations department at WAS began receiving complaints on February 25 about cramped conditions on their New York to London flight.

5. Molly Parks, a stewardess on WAS airlines, loved her designer uniform so much that she wore it to a party after working hours.

6. In 1978, WAS merged with Balia Airlines.

7. Joe Buck celebrated his anniversary and WAS's new low fares by taking his wife to London.

8. WAS announced increased profits in 1978, despite the competition from Camel Airlines.

9. While drinking free champagne and watching the flight attendants in their designer uniforms, Todd Craig fell asleep in his extra wide seat on WAS Airlines' Flight #345 to London, feeling that WAS Airlines was certainly justified in charging $400 for so much service.

10. On January 25, 1977, Camel Airlines raised the price of their New York to London charter flight to $300.

SET 2

Ted Johnson owns a small grocery business that has been on the decline for over a year since the advent of a large supermarket in a nearby town. He is seriously considering accepting an offer made by the owner of the adjoining store, Frank North. North, a prospering hardware dealer and an avid fishing and boating enthusiast, wants more space to accommodate a line of fishing tackle and boating accessories. North has told Johnson that he has received a substantial demand for boating and fishing equipment which he has been unable to meet and he wants to expand his business to cater to this market. North offers to buy Johnson's property and take him in as a partner in the new boating and fishing business. Johnson, who wants an active and prosperous business and who is strongly against retirement, sees two alternatives open to him: either maintaining his present business or accepting North's offer.

CONCLUSION: Of the visible alternatives open to him, Johnson concludes that it is in his best interest to reject North's offer and maintain his present business.

11. The Conservation Department is about to release a report that recommends the banning of all water sports in the area for at least the next five years. There is every indication that this recommendation will be acted upon.

12. A recreational development is being planned for the area and a number of people from nearby cities have decided to purchase tracts of land in the area to take advantage of the new boating and fishing opportunities.

13. Kramer, another hardware dealer in the area, tells Johnson that he never receives calls for fishing or boating equipment.

14. Johnson learns that North, before he was successful in the hardware business, had gone bankrupt in the sporting goods business.

15. It is learned that another supermarket is about to open nearby.

16. The chain that owns the large supermarket has been unhappy with the store's business and will sell the store to a large sporting goods chain who will stock the store in boating and fishing equipment.

17. Johnson learns that North's wife has strong moral objections against fishing and hunting activities.

18. Johnson learns that North is expected to live only a year, and North's wife, who will be taking

over his business interests, has moral objections against hunting and fishing activities.

19. A number of fishermen tell Johnson that North, who claims to be a very successful fisherman, cannot be expected to tell the truth about the size and number of his catch.

20. The Be Kind to All Animals Society has recently become active in the area and intends to disrupt those businesses that are involved with game sports.

SET 3

When the Secretary of Commerce of the United States received a report stating that the country's stockpiles of copper had increased from a quarter of a million tons in 1988 to 1.5 million tons in 1993, he became alarmed. World stockpiles of copper, and copper prices, had remained stable during the past years. Because of the higher quality of American copper, it had always been 3 cents per pound more expensive than the rest of the world's copper, the price of which was determined by the London Metal Exchange. The secretary had three ideas to choose among in order to remedy the situation. He considered lowering the price of American copper by 1.5 cents per pound. He felt that, because of the higher quality of American copper, the copper-buying corporations of the world would start to purchase American copper at this reduced price. Next, he considered mixing the copper with a cheaper metal so that he could drop prices to below the world standard. His third idea was to request that the United States Treasury Department issue copper quarters rather than silver ones. This course of action would have the beneficial effect of reducing American stockpiles of copper, and would thus keep the price of copper at its current level. At the same time, it would help to build up silver stockpiles which had recently fallen to a critically low level.

CONCLUSION: Now that the price of American copper has been reduced by 1.5 cents per pound, stockpiles have started to decrease.

21. A scientific investigation committee could discover no metal which could successfully be mixed

with copper.

22. The secretary received a pledge from 89% of the world's copper-buying corporations that they would start and continue to buy American copper if the price were lowered to 1.5 cents per pound.

23. The president of the London Metal Exchange informed the secretary that, in his opinion, the world's supply of copper was sufficient to meet any need.

24. The president of Boeing Airlines informed the secretary that he could substitute copper for steel in his planes, but that he would only purchase American copper if the price were dropped.

25. At the end of the fiscal year, the secretary received a report that silver stockpiles in the United States had started to increase for the first time in four years.

26. Liechtenstein, a small country in Europe, announced that it would continue to buy its copper from the London Metal Exchange.

27. The new copper quarter was issued in 1994. It had a picture of the Secretary of Commerce on one side.

28. Carl Saunders, a scientist in Pascal, North Dakota, discovered that he could mix iron, a cheap metal, with copper, and the resulting compound would have all the properties of copper.

29. The President of the United States refused to allow the quality of American copper to be reduced. He also vetoed the proposal to issue copper quarters.

30. The London Metal Exchange kept the price of copper constant in 1994 and 1995.

SET 4

In 1975, Walter Hinckle, the sole owner of the Handy-Dandy Dry Cleaning Company, located out-side Keene, New Hampshire, began investigating various options which would allow him to expand his business and increase his profits. A vacant lot adjacent to the left side of his building was for sale. If he expanded his business into this lot, he would be able to stay in the same location while having enough space for a much needed parking lot. However, a friend in the real estate business told Hinckle about a piece of land available closer to the university in town which would be suitable for a dry cleaning business. Also, because many of his relatives and friends had moved to Florida, Hinckle considered the option of moving his business to Fort Lauderdale.

CONCLUSION: In 1976, construction of a new addition to the Handy-Dandy Dry Cleaning Company was completed on the vacant lot adjacent to the former establishment.

31. Silas Silverman built a fast food store on the lot adjacent to the left side of the Handy-Dandy Dry Cleaning building.

32. Pride Cleaner Company opened a store in 1974 across the street from Handy-Dandy.

33. The interest rate on municipal bonds rose 7% between 1974 and 1976.

34. The dry cleaning business relies heavily on customer loyalty.

35. Census reports showed a reflux of population into the University district of Keene, New Hampshire.

36. Hinckle hired the Wellington Construction Company to erect the addition and new parking lot on the vacant lot adjacent to his building.

37. Figures published by the U.S. Department of Commerce showed that the rate of failure of small businesses is higher in the Northeast than in the Southeast.

38. Land values in the University district were rising during this period.

39. The new Democratic mayor of Keene promised strong affirmative action programs.

ANSWER KEY

1. D	11. A	21. B	31. C
2. C	12. D	22. A	32. D
3. A	13. B	23. E	33. E
4. B	14. B	24. B	34. B
5. D	15. D	25. D	35. D
6. E	16. A	26. E	36. A
7. B	17. E	27. C	37. D
8. E	18. B	28. D	38. B
9. C	19. E	29. A	39. E
10. D	20. B	30. E	

EXPLANATORY ANSWERS

1. **(D)** Because 60% constitutes a majority, one might be inclined to think that the statement disproves the conclusion. However, this is not necessarily the case. For example, there is a chance that the decision would be made by those stockholders holding majority shares of WAS stock. These stockholders could have preferred Plan 3.

2. **(C)** If fares below $325 were prohibited, Plan 3, which called for a fare of $278, could not be put into effect.

3. **(A)** The amount paid to the travel agent is exactly the airfare called for by Plan 3.

4. **(B)** Plan 3 called for increased seating on the New York to London flights and this could engender complaints. This statement, however, does not absolutely prove the conclusion. For example, WAS could have decided to add more seats with Plan 2. The passage does not preclude this possibility.

5. **(D)** Plan 1 is the plan which called for designer uniforms. However, as was the case in question 4, there is a possibility that WAS decided to include the new uniforms as part of Plan 3. While it is unlikely that a budget plan such as Plan 3 would include designer uniforms, this unlikeliness does not constitute a disproof.

6. **(E)** A merger with Balia is irrelevant to the conclusion.

7. **(B)** Plan 2, as well as Plan 3, called for lowered fares.

8. **(E)** All three plans were intended to increase profits. This statement offers no specific information regarding Plan 3.

9. **(C)** This statement disproves the conclusion. It mentions all of the options which were a part of Plan 1.

10. **(D)** The prime reason for the proposals to lower WAS's fare was the competition from Camel. If Camel raised their price to $300, it is not likely that WAS would find it necessary to lower their rates to $278. They might, however, have wanted to do so anyway.

11. **(A)** This statement proves the conclusion. A ban on all water sports would completely rule out the option of going into the boating and fishing supplies business.

12. **(D)** This statement weakens the conclusion. New recreational opportunities in the area would provide a good reason for Johnson to accept North's offer. But, of course, such a new development should contribute to other sorts of business as well, including the grocery business.

13. **(B)** This statement supports the conclusion. The information provided by Kramer calls into question North's contention that there will be a large

demand for boating and fishing equipment. We do not know, however, if Kramer's statement is accurate or if Kramer's experience is applicable to Johnson's situation.

14. **(B)** This statement supports the conclusion. It can be taken as an indication that North does not have a good business judgment in the area of sporting goods. However, it is possible that the bankruptcy did not have anything to do with the type of business and may have been due to conditions which are no longer present.

15. **(D)** This statement weakens the conclusion. The added competition would make Johnson's business an even greater risk and hence provide some reason for accepting North's offer.

16. **(A)** This statement proves the conclusion. It removes the initial condition which made Johnson consider leaving the grocery business and, at the same time, makes North's proposal more of a risk.

17. **(E)** Irrelevant. It is North's attitude, not his wife's, which is relevant to the success of the proposed business.

18. **(B)** This statement supports the conclusion. It would seem undesirable for Johnson to be involved, as he inevitably would be, in a business venture with someone who has moral qualms about such a venture.

19. **(E)** North's fish stories would have no relevance to his reliability as a businessman.

20. **(B)** This statement supports the conclusion. Such disruptions would no doubt have some negative effect on the proposed business and hence provide some reason for rejecting North's offer.

21. **(B)** This statement supports the conclusion. If no metal could be found that would mix successfully with copper, the secretary's second option would be eliminated. This leaves the option of reducing the price by 1.5 cents per pound, and that of issuing copper quarters. As the statement makes no mention of copper quarters one way or the other, this possibility cannot be excluded, and the conclusion, therefore, is not absolutely proven.

22. **(A)** This statement proves the conclusion. The main objective set up in the passage is to find a way to sell more copper. A pledge on the part of 89% of the world's copper-buying nations to buy American copper if the price were lowered gives the secretary ample reason to adopt the course of action mentioned by the conclusion.

23. **(E)** This statement is irrelevant. It has been stated in the passage that there is a surplus of copper in stockpiles throughout the world. The problem that the Secretary of Commerce must solve is how to sell American copper. The fact that the world-wide copper supply is adequate has no bearing on the secretary's decision to lower the price of American copper.

24. **(B)** This statement supports the conclusion. The secretary might have decided to drop the price to accommodate Boeing. He could have assumed that if Boeing were willing to buy the copper at the reduced price, others would as well. He also could have decided, however, that Boeing was not a large enough company to warrant this decision, and could therefore have opted for one of the other alternatives.

25. **(D)** This statement weakens the conclusion. If silver stockpiles increased, as the statement asserts, it could have been due to a decision to mint copper quarters (and, implicitly, a decision not to reduce copper prices). The increased silver stockpiles, however, could have been the result of any number of other causes.

26. **(E)** The statement asserts that Liechtenstein is a small country. The announcement that it would continue to buy copper from the Metal Exchange would therefore have little effect on the secretary's decision, and is, consequently, irrelevant to the conclusion.

27. **(C)** This statement disproves the conclusion. The passage tells us that the secretary had to choose among three options. If copper quarters were issued, we can deduce that the price of copper was not changed.

28. **(D)** This statement weakens the conclusion. If a cheaper alloy having all the properties of copper

could be made, the secretary might have decided to use this alloy in the future, lower prices below world levels, and thereby reduce stockpiles. There is no conclusive proof, however, that this was his course of action.

29. **(A)** This statement proves the conclusion by eliminating all courses of action other than the one mentioned in the conclusion.

30. **(E)** This statement is irrelevant to the conclusion. There is no indication in the passage that the secretary's decision was in any way contingent upon the future activities of the London Metal Exchange.

31. **(C)** This statement disproves the conclusion. If Silverman had bought the lot adjacent to the Handy-Dandy Dry Cleaning Company, then it would be impossible for Hinckle to buy it and expand his building.

32. **(D)** This statement weakens the conclusion. If the Pride Cleaner Company were competing for the business in Hinckle's location, it is not likely that he would want to remain there.

33. **(E)** Irrelevant. There is no relationship between municipal bonds and the dry cleaning business.

34. **(B)** This statement supports the conclusion. It offers a reason why Hinckle would want to stay where he was and keep the clientele he already had.

35. **(D)** This statement weakens the conclusion. If the population of the University district of Keene was growing, then it would be a good idea for Hinckle to take the option of relocating closer to the city.

36. **(A)** The hiring of a construction company to build the addition proves the conclusion.

37. **(D)** This statement weakens the conclusion. It offers a reason why Hinckle would want to move his business to Fort Lauderdale.

38. **(B)** This statement supports the conclusion. The price of relocating the Handy-Dandy Dry Cleaning Company in the University district where land values had increased might have proved too expensive.

39. **(E)** Irrelevant. The new mayor's promise of strong affirmative action programs has nothing to do with the dry cleaning business.

MATH REFRESHER

The accompanying illustrative problems and solutions are followed in the Problem Solving Section by practice problems in general mathematics, algebra and geometry. These are the only areas of mathematics usually encountered on the quantitative ability sections of the GMAT.

ILLUSTRATIVE PROBLEMS AND SOLUTIONS

I. Formulas

1. In the formula, $F = 9/5C + 32$, find C when $F = 68$.

   Solution:
   Substituting in the formula

   $68 = 9/5C + 32$

   Subtracting 32 from both sides

   $36 = 9/5C$

   Multiply both sides by 5 to get $180 = 9C$

   $C = 20$ *Answer*.

2. Solve the formula $s = \dfrac{at}{a + t}$ for t.

   Solution:
   Multiply both sides by $a + t$.

   $s(a + t) = at$

   $as + st = at$

   Subtract st from both sides: $as = at - st$

   Factor the right side, getting $as = (a - s)t$

   $t = \dfrac{as}{a - s}$ *Answer*.

3. In the formula $V = \pi r^2 h$, if r is doubled, what must be done to h to keep V constant?

   Solution:
   If r is doubled, the effect is to quadruple V since

the r is squared in the formula. Hence, h must be divided by 4 to keep V the same in value. *Answer*.

4. A package weighing 15 lb. is to be sent by parcel post. It costs x cents for the first 10 lb. and y cents for each additional lb. Express the cost, C, in terms of x and y.

   Solution:
   The first 10 lb. cost x cents; the remaining 5 lb. cost $5y$ cents. Hence, the total cost C is given by the formula

   $C = x + 5y$ *Answer*.

II. Fractions

1. Reduce to lowest terms: $\dfrac{y(y - 5)}{y^2 - 4y - 5}$

   Solution:
   Factor numerator and denominator

   $\dfrac{y(y - 5)}{(y + 1)(y - 5)}$

   Divide numerator and denominator by $(y - 5)$ giving

   $\dfrac{y}{y + 1}$ *Answer*.

2. Multiply $\dfrac{x^2}{xy - y^2} \cdot \dfrac{x^2 - y^2}{x^2 + xy}$

Solution:
Factor numerators and denominators

$$\frac{x^2}{y(x-y)} \cdot \frac{(x+y)(x-y)}{x(x+y)}$$

Divide numerators and denominators by common factors x, $(x-y)$, $(x+y)$

$$\frac{x \cdot x}{y(x-y)} \cdot \frac{(x+y)(x-y)}{x(x+y)} = \frac{x}{y} \ Answer.$$

3. Divide: $\dfrac{b+5}{b} \div \dfrac{b^2-25}{b^2}$

Solution:
Invert second fraction and multiply

$$\frac{b+5}{b} \cdot \frac{b^2}{b^2-25} = \frac{b+5}{b} \cdot \frac{b \cdot b}{(b+5)(b-5)}$$

$$= \frac{b}{(b-5)} Answer.$$

4. If a man buys several articles for n cents per dozen and sells them for $n/9$ cents per article, what is his profit, in cents, on each article?

Solution:
Profit = S.P. − Cost

$$= \frac{n}{9} - \frac{n}{12}$$

Common denominator is 36.

Profit $\dfrac{4n}{36} - \dfrac{3n}{36}$

$$= \frac{n}{36} Answer.$$

5. Simplify: $\left(\dfrac{1}{a} - \dfrac{1}{b} \right) \div \left(1 - \dfrac{a}{b} \right)$

Solution:
Convert each expression in parentheses to a single fraction

$$\frac{b-a}{ab} \div \frac{b-a}{b} = \frac{b-a}{ab} \cdot \frac{b}{b-a}$$

$$= 1/a \ Answer.$$

6. Simplify: $\dfrac{3 + 1/x}{9 - 1/x^2}$

Solution:
Multiply numerator and denominator by x^2

$$\frac{3x^2 + x}{9x^2 - 1} = \frac{x(3x+1)}{(3x-1)(3x+1)}$$

$$= \frac{x}{3x-1} Answer.$$

7. Simplify: $\dfrac{\sin^4 A - \cos^4 A}{\sin^2 A - \cos^2 A}$

Solution:
Factor the numerator, giving

$$\frac{(\sin^2 A + \cos^2 A)(\sin^2 A - \cos^2 A)}{(\sin^2 A - \cos^2 A)}$$

but $\sin^2 A + \cos^2 A = 1$ *Answer.*

8. If $y = 1 - 1/x$, $x > 0$, what effect does an increase in x have on y?

Solution:
As x increases, $1/x$ decreases. Therefore, we are subtracting a smaller quantity from 1 and, consequently, y increases. *Answer.*

III. Sets

1. How many elements in the set $\{x|3 < x < 9,\}$ where x is an integer?

   Solution:
   The indicated set contains only the elements 4, 5, 6, 7, and 8. Hence, there are **5** elements. *Answer.*

2. If A is the set of all prime numbers and B is the set of all even integers, then what set is represented by $A \cap B$?

   Solution:
   The only even, prime integer is 2. Hence

   $$A \cap B = \{2\} \ Answer.$$

3. Find the solution set of the equation $x^2 = 3x$, if x is the set of real numbers.

   Solution:

   $$x^2 - 3x = 0$$
   $$x(x-3) = 0$$
   $$x = 0 \text{ or } x - 3 = 0$$
   $$x = 3$$

   Hence, the solution set is

   $$\{0,3\} \ Answer.$$

4. Find the solution set of $3x - 4 > x + 2$, where x is the set of the real numbers.

Solution:

$$3x - 4 > x + 2$$
$$3x - x > 4 + 2$$
$$2x > 6$$
$$x > 3 \; Answer.$$

5. Find the solution set of the system:

$A = \{(x,y)/x^2 + y^2 = 25\}$ and
$B = \{(x,y)/y = x + 1\}.$

Solution:
Substituting $y = x + 1$ into the first equation, we obtain

$$x^2 + (x + 1)^2 = 25$$
$$x^2 + x^2 + 2x + 1 = 25$$
$$2x^2 + 2x - 24 = 0$$
$$x^2 + x - 12 = 0$$
$$(x + 4)(x - 3) = 0$$

Thus $x + 4 = 0$ or $x - 3 = 0$
so that $x = -4$ or $x = 3$
When $x = -4$, $y = -3$ and
when $x = 3$, $y = 4$
Thus $A \cap B$ has only two elements:

$$(3,4) \text{ and } (-4,-3) \; Answer.$$

IV. Functions

1. If $f(x) = x^2 + 2x - 5$, find the value of $f(2)$.

Solution:
Substitute $x = 2$ in the polynomial, giving

$$2^2 + 2(2) - 5$$
$$f(2) = 4 + 4 - 5 = 3 \; Answer.$$

2. If $f(y) = \tan y + \cot y$, find the value of $f\left(\dfrac{\pi}{4}\right)$

Solution:

$$f\left(\frac{\pi}{4}\right) = \tan \frac{\pi}{4} + \cot \frac{\pi}{4}$$
$$= 1 + 1$$
$$f\left(\frac{\pi}{4}\right) = 2 \; Answer.$$

3. If $f(t) = t^2 + 1$, find $f(a - 1)$

Solution:
Substitute $t = a - 1$, giving

$$f(a - 1) = (a - 1)^2 + 1$$
$$= (a^2 - 2a + 1) + 1$$
$$f(a - 1) = a^2 - 2a + 2 \; Answer.$$

4. If $f(x) = 2x + 3$ and $g(x) = x - 3$, find $f[g(x)]$.

Solution:
In $f(x)$, substitute $g(x)$ for x.

$$f[g(x)] = 2[g(x)] + 3$$
$$= 2(x - 3) + 3$$
$$= 2x - 6 + 3$$
$$f[g(x)] = 2x - 3 \; Answer.$$

5. What are the *domain* and *range* of the function $y = |x|$?

Solution:
The function is defined for all real values of x. Hence, the *domain* is $\{x| -\infty < x < +\infty, x$ is a real number$\}$ *Answer*.
Since $y = |x|$ can only be a positive number or zero, the *range* of the function is given by the set $\{y| 0 \leq y < +\infty, y$ a real number$\}$ *Answer*.

6. If $f(t) = \dfrac{1 + t}{t}$ then $f(t) =$

(A) $+f(-t)$

(B) $f\left(\dfrac{1}{t}\right)$

(C) $f\left(-\dfrac{1}{t}\right)$

(D) $\dfrac{1}{t} f\left(\dfrac{1}{t}\right)$

(E) none of these

Solution:

(A) $f(-t) = \dfrac{1 - t}{-t} = \dfrac{t - 1}{t} \neq f(t)$

(B) $f\left(\dfrac{1}{t}\right) = \dfrac{1 + \dfrac{1}{t}}{1 \; \dfrac{1}{t} - \dfrac{1}{t}} = t + 1 \neq f(t)$

(C) $f\left(-\dfrac{1}{t}\right) = \dfrac{1\dfrac{1}{t} - \dfrac{1}{t}}{-\dfrac{1}{t}} = \dfrac{-t+1}{1} \neq f(t)$

(D) $\dfrac{1}{t}f\left(\dfrac{1}{t}\right) = (t+1) \cdot \dfrac{1}{t}$ from (B)

$\dfrac{1}{t}f\left(\dfrac{1}{t}\right) = \dfrac{t+1}{t} = f(t)$ *Answer.*

V. Exponents

1. Find the value of $2x^0 + x^{2/3} + x^{-2/3}$ when $x = 27$.

   Solution:
   Substitute $x = 27$ in given expression

   $2(27)^0 + (27)^{2/3} + 27^{-2/3}$

   $= 2 \cdot 1 + (\sqrt[3]{27})^2 + \dfrac{1}{27^{2/3}}$

   $= 2 + 9 + 1/9 = 11\ 1/9$ *Answer.*

2. If $y = 3^x$, then $3^{x+2} =$

   (A) y^2
   (B) $2y$
   (C) $y + 3$
   (D) $9y$
   (E) $y + 9$

   Solution:

   $$3^{x+2} = 3^x \cdot 3^2$$
   $$= y \cdot 9 = 9y\ Answer.$$

3. If 0.00000784 is written in the form 7.84×10^n, what does n equal?

   Solution:
   Writing the given number in scientific notation, we get $0.00000784 = 7.84 \times 10^{-6}$

   Hence, $n = -6$ *Answer.*

4. The length of an electromagnetic wave is given by the formula $L = \dfrac{C}{F}$ where C is the velocity of light $(3 \times 10^{10}$ cm. per sec.$)$ and F is the frequency. What is the value of L when $F = 3000$ megacycles per second?

   Solution:
   $F = 3000 \times 10^6 = 3 \times 10^9$
   Substitute in formula

   $$L = \dfrac{3 \times 10^{10}}{3 \times 10^9} = 1 \times 10^1$$
   $$= 10\ cm.\ Answer.$$

5. Solve the exponential equation $3^{2x-1} = 81$

   Solution:

   $3^{2x-1} = 3^4$
   Equating exponents, since the bases are equal, we get

   $$2x - 1 = 4$$
   $$2x = 5$$
   $$x = 2\tfrac{1}{2}\ Answer.$$

6. If $4^y = 125$, between what two consecutive integers does y lie?

   Solution:

   $$4^3 = 64$$
   $$4^4 = 256$$

   Since 125 is between 64 and 256 and 4^y is a steadily increasing function, it follows that y is between 3 and 4. *Answer.*

7. Solve the equation: $9^{x+3} = \dfrac{1}{27}$

   Solution:
   $(3^2)^{x+3} = \dfrac{1}{3^3} = 3^{-3}$ or $3^{2x+6} = 3^{-3}$

   Since the bases are equal, the exponents may be set equal.

   $$2x + 6 = -3$$
   $$2x = -9$$
   $$x = -4\tfrac{1}{2}\ Answer.$$

VI. Logarithms

1. Find the value of $\log_4 64$

   Solution:
   Let $x = \log_4 64$

Then, in exponential notation,

$$4^x = 64$$

$$x = 3 \; Answer.$$

2. If log 63.8 = 1.8048, what is log 6.38?

Solution:

$$\log 6.38 = \log \frac{63.8}{10}$$

$$= \log 63.8 - \log 10$$

$$= 1.8048 - 1$$

$$= 0.8048 \;\; Answer.$$

3. If log 2 = a and log 3 = b, express log 12 in terms of a and b.

Solution:

$$\log 12 = \log (4 \cdot 3)$$

$$= \log 4 + \log 3$$

$$= \log 2^2 + \log 3$$

$$= 2 \log 2 + \log 3$$

$$= 2a + b \;\; Answer.$$

4. In the formula $A = P (1 + r)^n$, express n in terms of A, P and r.

Solution:

$$\frac{A}{P} = (1 + r)^n$$

$$\log \frac{A}{P} = \log (1 + r)^n = n \log (1 + r)$$

$$\log A - \log P = n \log (1 + r)$$

$$n = \frac{\log A - \log P}{\log (1 + r)} \;\; Answer.$$

5. If log t^2 = 0.8762, then log 100t = ?

Solution:

$$2 \log t = 0.8762$$

$$\log t = 0.4381$$

$$\log 100t = \log 100 + \log t$$

$$= 2 + 0.4381$$

$$= 2.4381 \;\; Answer.$$

6. If log tan x = 0, find the smallest positive value of x.

Solution:
If log tan x = 0, then tan x = 1. Therefore x = $\frac{\pi}{4}$ *Answer.*

VII. Equations

1. Find the roots of the equation $x^2 - 5x + 6 = 0$.

Solution: Factor the left member

$$(x - 3)(x - 2) = 0$$

Either $x - 3 = 0$ or $x - 2 = 0$, yielding $x = 3$ and $x = 2$ *Answer.*

2. Solve the following system of equations:

$$x^2 - 3y^2 = 13$$

$$x = 1 - 3y$$

Solution:
Substitute the value of x from the second equation into the first

$$(1 - 3y)^2 - 3y^2 = 13$$

$$1 - 6y + 9y^2 - 3y^2 = 13$$

$$6y^2 - 6y - 12 = 0$$

$$y^2 - y - 2 = 0$$

$$(y - 2)(y + 1) = 0$$

$$y = 2$$

$$x = 1 - 3y$$

$$x = 1 - 3(2)$$

$$x = -5$$

$$y = -1$$

$$x = 1 - 3y$$

$$x = 1 - 3(-1)$$

$$x = 4$$

Group the roots	x	-5	4
	y	2	-1 *Answer.*

3. Find the nature of the roots of the equation:

$$2x^2 - 4x - 3 = 0$$

Solution:

discriminant $(D) = b^2 - 4ac$

$$D = (-4)^2 - 4(2)(-3)$$

$$D = 16 + 24 = 40$$

Since D is positive but not a perfect square, the roots are real, unequal, and irrational *Answer*.

4. Solve the equation: $\sqrt{y - 2} = 14 - y$

Solution:
Square both sides

$$y - 2 = (14 - y)^2$$

$$y - 2 = 196 - 28y + y^2$$

$$y^2 - 29y + 198 = 0$$

$$(y - 11)(y - 18) = 0$$

$$y = 11 \text{ and } y = 18$$

It is essential that these roots now be checked in the original equation.
Substitute $y = $ in the equation, giving $\sqrt{11 - 2} = 14 - 11$ or $\sqrt{9} = 3$, which checks.
Now substitute $y = 18$, giving $\sqrt{18 - 2} = 14 - 18$ or $\sqrt{16} = -4$. This value does not check and $y = 11$ is the only root. *Answer*.

5. For what value of a in the equation $ax^2 - 6x + 9 = 0$ will the roots of the equation be equal?

Solution:
Set the discriminant equal to zero

$$(-6)^2 - 4 \cdot 9 \cdot a = 0$$

$$36 = 36a$$

$$a = 1 \text{ *Answer*}.$$

6. If 2 is one root of the equation

$$x^3 - 4x^2 + 14x - 20 = 0,$$

find the other two roots.
Solution: Use synthetic division

1	−4	14	−20	$\lfloor 2$
	2	−4	20	
1	−2	10	$\lfloor 0$	

Thus the resulting equation is

$$x^2 - 2x + 10 = 0$$

Solve by the quadratic formula

$$x = \frac{2 \pm \sqrt{4 - 40}}{2} = \frac{2 \pm 6i}{2}$$

$$x = 1 \pm 3i \text{ *Answer*}.$$

7. Find K so that 5 is a root of the equation

$$y^4 - 4y^3 + Ky - 10 = 0.$$

Solution:
Substitute $y = 5$ into the equation.

$$625 - 4(125) + 5K - 10 = 0$$

$$625 - 500 + 5K - 10 = 0$$

$$5K = -115$$

$$K = -23 \text{ *Answer*}.$$

8. Find all positive values of t less than $180°$ that satisfy the equation

$$2\sin^2 t - \cos t - 2 = 0.$$

Solution:
Substitute $1 - \cos^2 t$ for $\sin^2 t$.

$$2(1 - \cos^2 t) - \cos t - 2 = 0$$

$$2 - 2\cos^2 t - \cos t - 2 = 0$$

$$2\cos^2 t + \cos t = 0$$

$$\cos t(2\cos t + 1) = 0$$

$$\cos t = 0$$

$$\text{or } 2\cos t + 1 = 0$$

$$t = 90° \qquad \cos t = -1/2$$

$$t = 120°$$

$90°, 120°$ *Answer*.

VIII. Inequalities

1. What is the solution set of the inequality

$$8y - 5 > 4y + 3$$

Solution:
Subtract $4y$ from both sides and add 5.

$$8y - 4y > 5 + 3$$

$$4y > 8$$

$$y > 2 \text{ } Answer.$$

2. Find the solution set of the inequality

$$|x + 3| < 5$$

Solution:
When $x + 3 \geq 0$, then $|x + 3| = x + 3$
Thus $x \geq -3$ and $x + 3 < 5$ or $x < 2$

When $x + 3 < 0$, then $|x + 3| = -(x + 3)$
thus $x < -3$ and $-(x + 3) < 5$

$$\text{or } x + 3 > -5$$

$$x > -8$$

Thus the solution set is the interval:

$$-8 < x < -3 \text{ } Answer.$$

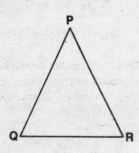

3. In $\triangle PQR$, $PQ = PR = 5$ and $60° < P < 90°$. What is the possible range of values of QR?

Solution:
When $\angle P = 60°$, $\triangle PQR$ is equilateral and $QR = 5$. When $\angle P = 90°$, $\triangle PQR$ is right, isosceles and $QR = 5\sqrt{2}$
Therefore, $5 < QR < 5\sqrt{2}$ *Answer.*

4. For what values of x between 0 and 360° is $\sin x > \cos x$?

Solution:
Graph the two functions on the same set of axes.

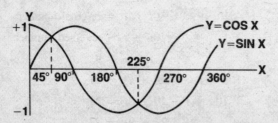

From the graph it is apparent that $\sin x > \cos x$ in the interval

$$45° < x < 225° \text{ } Answer.$$

5. A triangle has sides of 5 and 7. What is the possible range of values for the third side?

Solution:
Since the sum of two sides must be greater than the third side, the third side must be less than 12.
Call the third side x. Then, by the same principle, $5 + x > 7$ or $x > 2$

Hence, $2 < x < 12$ *Answer.*

6. In $\triangle KLM$, $\angle K = 60°$ and $\angle M = 50°$. Which side of the triangle is the longest?

Solution:
The longest side lies opposite the largest angle. Since the sum of two angles is 110°, the third angle, L, must be 70°. Hence the longest side must lie opposite $\angle L$ and is, therefore, KM. *Answer.*

IX. Verbal Problems

1. The area of a rectangular plot is 204 square feet and its perimeter is 58 feet. Find its dimensions.

Solution:
Let

$$x = \text{length}$$
$$y = \text{width}$$
$$xy = 204$$
$$2x + 2y = 58$$
$$x + y = 29$$
$$y = 29 - x$$

Substitute this value in the area equation

$$x(29 - x) = 204$$
$$29x - x^2 = 204$$
$$x^2 - 29x + 204 = 0$$
$$(x - 12)(x - 17) = 0$$

$x - 12 = 0$	$x - 17 = 0$
$x = 12$	$x = 17$
$y = 17$	$y = 12$

The length is 17 and the width is 12 *Answer*.

2. Ten pounds of a salt water solution is 20% salt. How much water must be evaporated to strengthen it to a 25% solution?

   Solution:

   ORIGINAL SOLUTION   NEW SOLUTION

   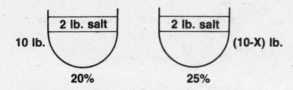

   Let x = lb. of water evaporated

   $$2 = .25(10 - x) = \frac{1}{4}(10 - x)$$

   $$8 = 10 - x$$

   $$x = 10 - 8 = 2 \text{ lb. } Answer.$$

3. A man walked out into the country at the rate of 3 miles an hour and hurried back over the same road at 4 miles an hour. The round trip took 5¼ hours. How far out into the country did he walk?

   Solution:

   $$\frac{d}{3} + \frac{d}{4} = 5\frac{1}{4} = \frac{21}{4}$$

   Multiply both sides by 12:

   $$4d + 3d = 63$$

   $$7d = 63$$

   $$d = 9 \, Answer.$$

4. If the price of eggs drops 10 cents per dozen, it becomes possible to buy 2 dozen more eggs for $6.00 than was possible at the higher price. Find the original, higher price.

   Solution:

   Let

   p = original price in cents per dozen

   n = original number of $6.00 dozens

$$pn = 600$$

$$(p - 10)(n + 2) = 600$$

$$pn - 10n + 2p - 20 = 600$$

Substitute $pn = 600$ and $n = \dfrac{600}{p}$ in second equation.

$$600 - \frac{6000}{p} + 2p - 20 = 600$$

Multiply through by p.

$$2p^2 - 20p - 6000 = 0$$

$$p^2 - 10p - 3000 = 0$$

$$(p - 60)(p + 50) = 0$$

$$p = 60 \text{ or } p = -50 \text{ (reject)}$$

thus $p = 60$ cents per doz. *Answer*.

5. Two planes start from the same place at the same time. One travels east at r miles per hour and the other north at s miles per hour. How far apart will they be after t hours?

   Solution:

   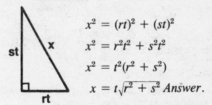

   $$x^2 = (rt)^2 + (st)^2$$

   $$x^2 = r^2t^2 + s^2t^2$$

   $$x^2 = t^2(r^2 + s^2)$$

   $$x = t\sqrt{r^2 + s^2} \; Answer.$$

6. The sum of the digits of a two-digit number is 9. If the digits are reversed, the resulting number exceeds the original number by 27. What is the original number?

   Solution:

   Let t = ten's digit

   and u = unit's digit

   $10t + u$ = original number

   $10u + t$ = reversed number

   $$t + u = 9$$

   $$(10u + t) - (10t + u) = 27$$

   $$10u + t - 10t + u = 27$$

   $$9u - 9t = 27$$

$$u - t = 3$$
$$u + t = 9$$
$$2u = 12$$
$$u = 6$$
$$t = 3$$

Original No. is 36 *Answer*.

X. Geometry

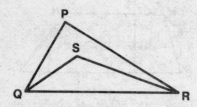

1. In the figure, QS and RS are angle-bisectors. If $\angle P = 80°$, how many degrees in $\angle QSR$?

   Solution:

   $$\angle Q + \angle R = 180° - P = 180 - 80 = 100°$$

   Therefore $\angle SQR + \angle SRQ = \frac{1}{2} \; 100° = 50°$

   Then $\angle QSR = 180° - 50° = 130°$ *Answer*.

2. What is the locus of points equidistant from two intersecting lines and at a given distance d from their point of intersection?

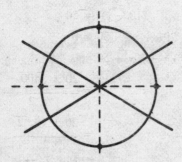

   Solution:
   The locus of points equidistant from two intersecting lines consists of the two angle-bisectors of the angles formed by the lines.

   At the intersection draw a circle of radius d.

   The desired locus is the four points where this

circle intersects the angle-bisectors. *Answer*.

3. Find the ratio of the area of the circle inscribed in the square to the area of the circle circumscribed about the square.

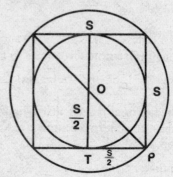

   Solution:
   Let the side of the square be s. Then the radius of the inscribed circle is $s/2$.
   Since $\triangle OTP$ is right isosceles, the radius OP of the circumscribed circle is $\frac{s}{2} \sqrt{2}$

   Area of inner circle $= \pi \left(\frac{s}{2}\right)^2 = \frac{\pi s^2}{4}$

   Area of outer circle $= \pi \left(\frac{s}{2}2\right)^2 =$

   $$= \frac{\pi s^2}{4} \; 2 = \frac{\pi s^2}{2}$$

   Ratio $= \dfrac{\dfrac{\pi s^2}{4}}{\dfrac{\pi s^2}{2}} = \dfrac{\dfrac{1}{4}}{\dfrac{1}{2}} = \dfrac{2}{4} = \dfrac{1}{2}$. *Answer*.

4. A boat travels 40 miles east, 80 miles south, then 20 miles east again. How far is it from the starting point?

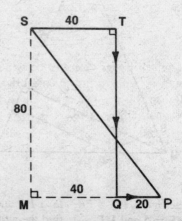

Solution:

In the figure, draw $SM \parallel TQ$. Then

$$SM = TQ = 80$$
$$MQ = ST = 40$$

In the right $\triangle PMS$, $MP = 60$ and $SM = 80$. By the Pythagorean theorem, it follows that

$$SP = 100 \; Answer.$$

5. If the radius of a right circular cylinder is tripled, what must be done to the altitude to keep the volume the same?

Solution:

$V = \pi r^2 h$

Thus, tripling r will have the effect of multiplying V by 9. Hence, to keep the volume constant, h will have to be divided by 9. *Answer.*

6. Two parallel planes are 6 inches apart. Find the locus of points equidistant from the two planes, and 4 inches from a point P in one of them.

Solution:

The locus of points equidistant from the two planes is a parallel plane midway between them (3 inches from each). The locus of points 4 inches from P is a sphere with P as center and radius 4 inches. The intersection of this sphere with the mid-plane is a *circle*, which is the desired locus. *Answer.*

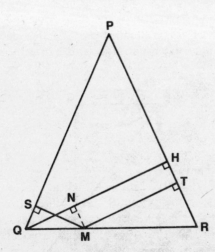

7. In the figure, $PQ = PR$, $MS \perp PQ$ and $MT \perp PR$. If $MS = 5$ and $MT = 7$, find the altitude QH.

Solution:

Draw $MN \perp QH$. Since $MNHT$ is a rectangle, it follows that $NH = MT = 7$. Since $\triangle QMS$ is congruent to $\triangle QMN$, then $QN = MS = 5$.

$$QH = QN + NH = 5 + 7 = 12 \; Answer.$$

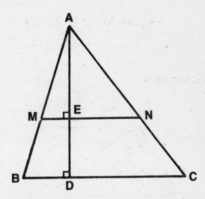

8. In the figure, $MN \parallel BC$ and MN bisects the area of $\triangle ABC$.
If $AD = 10$, find ED.

Solution:

Let $ED = x$

$$AE = 10 - x$$

Since $\triangle AMN \sim \triangle ABC$, it follows that

$$\frac{\text{Area of } \triangle AMN}{\text{Area of } \triangle ABC} = \frac{(10 - x)^2}{10^2} = \frac{1}{2}$$

Cross multiplying,

$$2(10 - x)^2 = 100$$
$$(10 - x)^2 = 50$$
$$100 - 20x + x^2 - 50 = 0$$
$$x^2 - 20x + 50 = 0$$
$$x = \frac{20 \pm \sqrt{400 - 200}}{2}$$
$$= \frac{20 \pm 10\sqrt{2}}{2}$$
$$= 10 \pm 5\sqrt{2}$$

Reject positive value since $x < 10$

$$ED = 10 - 5\sqrt{2} \quad Answer.$$

XI. Trigonometry

1. Express $(1 + \sec y)(1 - \cos y)$ as a product of two

trigonometric functions of y.

Solution:
Multiply the two binomials. $1 + \sec y - \cos y - \sec y \cos y$

Substitute $\dfrac{1}{\cos y}$ for $\sec y$.

$1 + \dfrac{1}{\cos y} - \cos y - \dfrac{1}{\cos y} \cdot \cos y$

$= 1 + \dfrac{1}{\cos y} - \cos y - 1 = \dfrac{1}{\cos y} - \cos y$

$= \dfrac{1 - \cos^2 y}{\cos y} = \dfrac{\sin^2 y}{\cos y} = \dfrac{\sin y}{\cos y} \cdot \sin y$

$= \tan y \cdot \sin y$ *Answer*.

2. If $\log \tan x = K$, express $\log \cot x$ in terms of K.

Solution:

$\log \cot x = \log \dfrac{1}{\tan x}$

$= \log 1 - \log \tan x$

$= 0 - K$

$= -K$ *Answer*.

XII. Graphs and Coordinate Geometry

1. M is the mid-point of line segment PQ. The coordinates of point P are $(5, -3)$ and of point M are $(5, 7)$. Find the coordinates of point Q.

Solution: Let the coordinates of Q be (x, y). Then

$5 = \dfrac{1}{2}(5 + x)$ and $7 = \dfrac{1}{2}(-3 + y)$

$10 = 5 + x$ $\qquad$ $14 = -3 + y$

$x = 5$ $\qquad\qquad$ $17 = y$

Coordinates of Q are $(5, 17)$ *Answer*.

2. A triangle has vertices R $(1, 2)$, S $(7, 10)$ and T $(-1, 6)$. What kind of a triangle is RST?

Solution:

slope of $RS = \dfrac{10 - 2}{7 - 1} = \dfrac{8}{6} = \dfrac{4}{3}$

slope of $RT = \dfrac{6 - 2}{-1 - 1} = \dfrac{4}{-2} = -2$

slope of $ST = \dfrac{10 - 6}{7 - (-1)} = \dfrac{4}{8} = \dfrac{1}{2}$

Since the slope of ST is the negative reciprocal of the slope of RT, then $RT \perp ST$, and the triangle is a right triangle. *Answer*.

3. Find the equation of the straight line through the point $(5, -4)$ and parallel to the line $y = 3x - 2$.

Solution:
The slope of $y = 3x - 2$ is 3. The desired line, therefore, has slope 3. By the point-slope form, the equation is

$$y - (-4) = 3(x - 5)$$

$$y + 4 = 3x - 15$$

$$\text{or } y = 3x - 19 \, Answer.$$

4. If the following equations are graphed on the same set of axes, how many points of intersection are there?

$$x^2 + y^2 = 16$$

$$y = x^2 + 2$$

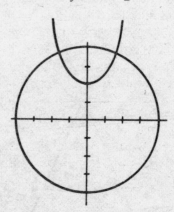

Solution:
Sketch both graphs as indicated. $x^2 + y^2 = 16$ is a circle of radius 4 and center at origin. $y = x^2 + 2$ is a parabola. Some points are $(0,2)$, $(\pm 1, 3)$, $(\pm 2, 6)$. The graphs intersect in two points. *Answer*.

5. Which of the following points lies inside the circle $x^2 + y^2 = 25$?

(A) (3,4)
(B) (−4,3)
(C) (4,2$\sqrt{2}$)
(D) (4,2$\sqrt{3}$)
(E) none of these

Solution:

The given circle has a radius of 5 and center at the origin. Points A and B are at distance 5 from the origin, and lie on the circle. The distance of D from the origin $= \sqrt{4^2 + (2\sqrt{3})^2} = \sqrt{16 + 12} = \sqrt{28} > 5$.

Hence D lies outside the circle. The distance of point C from the origin is $\sqrt{4^2 + (2\sqrt{2})^2} = \sqrt{16 + 8} = \sqrt{24} < 5$.

Hence point C lies inside the circle. *Answer.*

6. For what value of K is the graph of the equation $y = 2x^2 - 3x + K$ tangent to the x-axis?

Solution:

If this parabola is tangent to the x-axis, then the roots of the equation $2x^2 - 3x + K = 0$ are equal, and the discriminant of this equation must be zero.
Hence,

$$(-3)^2 - 4(2)K = 0$$

$$9 = 8K$$

$$K = 9/8 \; Answer.$$

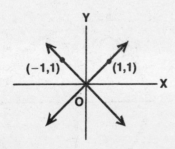

7. What is the equation of the graph in the figure?

Solution:

The graph consists of the two straight lines $y = x$ in the first and third quadrants, and $y = -x$ in the second and fourth. The equation is, therefore, $|y| = |x|$ *Answer.*

8. What is the equation of the locus of points equidistant from the points (3, 0) and (0, 3)?

Solution:

The locus is the perpendicular bisector of the line PQ. This locus is a line bisecting the first quadrant angle. Its equation is $y = x$. *Answer.*

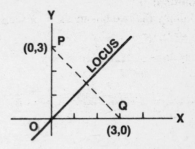

XIII. Number Systems and Concepts

1. Under which arithmetic operations is the set of *even* integers (including zero) closed?

Solution:

Represent two *even* integers by $2x$ and $2y$ where x and y are integers.
Then $2x + 2y = 2(x + y)$. Since $(x + y)$ is an integer, $2(x + y)$ is an even integer. $2x - 2y = 2(x - y)$. Since $(x - y)$ is an integer, $2(x - y)$ is an even integer.
$(2x) \cdot (2y) = 2(2xy)$. Since $2xy$ is an integer, $2(2xy)$ is an even integer.
But $\dfrac{2x}{2y} = \dfrac{x}{y}$, which need not be an integer.
Hence the even integers (including zero) are closed under addition, subtraction, and multiplication. *Answer.*

2. What complex number (in the form $a + bi$) is the multiplicative inverse of $1 + i$?

Solution:

$$(1 + i)x = 1$$

$$x = \frac{1}{1 + i} \cdot \frac{1 - i}{1 - i}$$

$$x = \frac{1 - i}{1 - i^2} = \frac{1 - i}{1 - (-1)} = \frac{1 - i}{2}$$

$$x = \frac{1}{2} - \frac{1}{2}i \; Answer.$$

3. If $\odot$ is an operation on the positive, real numbers, for which of the following definitions of $\odot$ is $r \odot s = s \odot r$? (commutative property)

(A) $r \odot s = r - s$

(B) $r \odot s = \dfrac{r}{s}$

(C) $r \odot s = r^2 s$

(D) $r \odot s = \dfrac{r + s}{rs}$

(E) $r \odot s = r^2 + rs + s^4$

Solution:

(A) is not commutative because $r - s \neq s - r$

(B) is not commutative because $\dfrac{r}{s} \neq \dfrac{s}{r}$

(C) is not commutative because $r^2 s \neq s^2 r$

(E) is not commutative because $r^2 + rs + s^4 \neq$

$s^2 + sr + r^4$

(D) *is* commutative because

$$\frac{r + s}{rs} = \frac{s + r}{sr} \, Answer.$$

4. If $a^2 - 2ab + b^2 = m$, where a is an odd and b is an even integer, then what kind of an integer is m?

Solution:

$(a - b)^2 = m$, so that m is a *perfect square*, since $a - b$ is an integer.

Also, the difference between an odd and an even integer is odd, so that $(a - b)$ is odd and $(a - b)^2$ is odd.

Therefore m is an odd, perfect square. *Answer.*

5. Consider the number 144_b, which is written to the base b, b a positive integer. For what values of b is the number a perfect square?

Solution:

$$144_b = 1 \cdot b^2 + 4b + 4$$
$$= (b + 2)^2$$

So that the number will be a perfect square for any integral value of b. However, since the digits up to 4 are used to write the number, $b > 4$. *Answer.*

6. Which of the following is an irrational number?

(A) 2/3

(B) $^3\sqrt{-8}$

(C) $\sqrt{\dfrac{32}{50}}$

(D) $5/\sqrt{5}$

(E) none of these

Solution:

(A) is apparently rational (a fraction).

(B) $^3\sqrt{-8} = -2$ which is rational $\left(\dfrac{-2}{1}\right)$

(C) $\sqrt{\dfrac{32}{50}} = \sqrt{\dfrac{16}{25}} = \dfrac{4}{5}$ which is rational

(D) $\dfrac{5}{\sqrt{5}} = \dfrac{5\sqrt{5}}{\sqrt{5}\sqrt{5}} = \dfrac{5\sqrt{5}}{5} = \sqrt{5}$

Hence, (D) is irrational. *Answer.*

BUSINESS MATH REVIEW

PERCENTS

1. The percent sign (%) is a symbol used to indicate percentage, but no operations can be performed with the number to which it is attached. For convenience, then, it is sometimes required to attach a percent sign; but to perform operations with the number, it is necessary to remove the percent sign.
   a. In general, to add a % sign, multiply the number by 100.

   Example: 3 = 300%

   b. In general, to remove a % sign, divide the number by 100.

   Example: 200% = 2

   c. A percent may be expressed as a decimal or a fraction by dividing it by 100.

   Example: 57% = .57
   $$9\% = {}^9/_{100}$$

   d. A decimal may be expressed as a percent by multiplying it by 100.

   Example: .67 = 67%

2. To change a fraction or a mixed number to a percent:
   a. Multiply the fraction or mixed number by 100.
   b. Reduce, if possible.
   c. Add a % sign.

   ILLUSTRATION: Change $^1/_7$ to a percent.
   Solution:
   $$^1/_7 \times 100 = {}^{100}/_7$$
   $$= 14^2/_7$$
   $$^1/_7 = 14^2/_7\%$$

   Answer: $14^2/_7\%$

   ILLUSTRATION: Change 4⅔ to a percent.

   Solution:
   $$4^{2}/_3 \times 100 = {}^{14}/_3 \times 100 = {}^{1400}/_3$$

$$= 466^{2}/_3\%$$
Answer: 466⅔%

3. To remove a % sign attached to a decimal and to keep it as a decimal, divide the decimal by 100.

   Example: .5% = .5 ÷ 100 = .005

4. To remove a % sign attached to a decimal and to change the number to a fraction:
   a. Divide the decimal by 100.
   b. Change this result to a fraction.
   c. Reduce, if necessary.

   ILLUSTRATION: Change 15.05% to a fraction.
   Solution:
   $$15.05\% = 15.05 \div 100 = .1505$$
   $$= 1505/10000$$
   $$= 301/2000$$

   Answer: 301/2000

5. To remove a % sign attached to a fraction or mixed number and to keep it as a fraction, divide the fraction or mixed number by 100.

   ILLUSTRATION: Change ¾ % to a fraction.
   Solution:
   $$^3/_4 \% = {}^3/_4 \div 100 = {}^3/_4 \times 1/100$$
   $$= 3/400$$

   Answer: 3/400

6. To remove a % sign attached to a fraction or mixed number and to change the number to a decimal:
   a. Divide the fraction or mixed number by 100.
   b. Change this result to a decimal.

   ILLUSTRATION: Change 3/5% to a decimal.
   Solution:
   $$3/5\% = 3/5 \div 100 = 3/5 \times 1/100$$
   $$= 3/500$$

$$.006$$
$$3/500 = 500\overline{)3.000}$$

Answer: .006

7. To remove a % sign attached to a decimal including a fraction and to keep it as a decimal, divide
the decimal by 100.

   Example: $.5\frac{1}{3}\% = .005\frac{1}{3}$

8. To remove a % sign attached to a decimal including a fraction and to change the number to a fraction:
   a. Divide the decimal by 100.
   b. Change this result to a fraction.
   c. Clear this mixed fraction.
   d. Reduce, if necessary.

   ILLUSTRATION: change $.14\frac{1}{6}\%$ to a fraction.
   Solution: $.14\frac{1}{6}\% = .0014\frac{1}{6}$
   $$= \frac{14\frac{1}{6}}{10000}$$
   $$= 14\frac{1}{6} \div 10000$$
   $$= 85/6 \times 1/10000$$
   $$= 85/60000$$
   $$= 17/12000$$
   Answer: 17/12000

9. In a percentage problem, the whole is 100% (or
1).

   Example: If a problem involves 10% of a quantity,
   the rest of the quantity is 90%.

INTEREST

1. Interest is the price paid for the use of money.
   There are three items considered in interest:
   a. The principal which is the amount of money
      bearing interest.
   b. The interest rate, expressed in percent on an
      annual basis.
   c. The time, during which the principal is used.

2. Since the interest rate is an annual rate, the time
   must be expressed annually, too.
   a. If the time is given in years, or part of a year,
      do not change the figures given.
   b. If the time is given in months it should be
      expressed as a fraction, the numerator of
      which is the number of months given, and the

denominator of which is 12.
   c. If the time is given in days, it should be ex-
      pressed as a fraction, the numerator of which
      is the number of days given, and the denomi-
      nator of which is 360. (Sometimes, it is re-
      quired to find the exact interest, in which case
      365 is the denominator.)
   d. If the time is given in terms of years and
      months, change it all to months and form a
      fraction, the numerator of which is the num-
      ber of months, and the denominator of which
      is 12.
   e. If the time is given in terms of years, months,
      and days, or months and days, or years and
      days, change it all to days and form a frac-
      tion, the numerator of which is the number of
      days, and the denominator of which is 360 (or
      365, if so required.) A month is considered as
      30 days.

3. To find the interest when the three items are
   given:
   a. Change the rate of interest to a fraction.
   b. Express the time as a fractional part of a year.
   c. Multiply all three items.

   ILLUSTRATION: Find the interest on $400 at $2\frac{1}{4}\%$
   for 3 months and 16 days.
   Solution:
   $$2\frac{1}{4}\% = \frac{9}{400}$$
   3 months and 16 days $= \frac{106}{360}$ of a year
   $$\text{(30 days to a month)}$$
   $$400 \times \frac{9}{400} \times \frac{106}{360} = \frac{53}{20}$$
   $$= \$2.65$$

   Answer: Interest $2.65

4. If the interest, interest rate, and time are given,
   to find the principal:
   a. Change the interest rate to a fraction.
   b. Express the time as a fractional part of a year.
   c. Multiply the rate by the time.
   d. Divide the interest by this product.

   ILLUSTRATION: What amount of money invested
   at 6% would receive interest of $18 over $1\frac{1}{2}$
   years?
   Solution:
   $$6\% = \frac{6}{100}$$
   $$1\frac{1}{2} \text{ years} = \frac{3}{2} \text{ years}$$
   $$6/100 \times 3/2 = 9/100$$
   $$\$18 \div 9/100 = 18 \times 100/9$$

Answer: Amount=$200

5. If the principal, time and interest are given, to find the rate:
   a. Change the time to a fractional part of a year.
   b. Multiply the principal by the time.
   c. Divide the interest by this product.
   d. Convert to a percent.

ILLUSTRATION: At what interest rate should $300 be invested for 40 days to accrue $2 in interest?
Solution:

$$40 \text{ days} = {}^{40}/_{360} \text{ of a year}$$
$$300 \times {}^{40}/_{360} = {}^{100}/_{3}$$
$$\$2 \div 100/3 = 2 \times 3/100$$
$$= {}^{3}/_{50}$$
$$ {}^{3}/_{50} = 6\%$$

Answer: Interest rate= 6%

6. If the principal, interest, and interest rate are given, to find the time (in years):
   a. Change the interest rate to a fraction (or decimal).
   b. Multiply the principal by the rate.
   c. Divide the interest by this product.

ILLUSTRATION: Find the length of time for which $240 must be invested at 5% to accrue $16 in interest.
Solution:

$$5\% = .05$$
$$240 \times .05 = 12$$
$$16 \div 12 = 1\frac{1}{3}$$

Answer: Time=1⅓ years

COMPOUND INTEREST

7. Interest may be computed on a compound basis; that is, the interest at the end of a certain period (half year, full year, or whatever time stipulated) is added to the principal for the next period. The interest is then computed on the new increased principal, and for the next period, the interest is again computed on the new increased principal. Since the principal constantly increases, compound interest yields more than simple interest.

COMPOUND INTEREST RATE

8. Since the interest rate is an annual rate, it must be proportionately reduced if the interest is compounded on less than a yearly basis. In general, if the interest is computed for some fractional part of a year, use that same fractional part of the interest rate. Specifically:
   a. If the interest is compounded annually, use the rate given.
   b. If compounded semi-annually, use ½ the rate given.
   c. If compounded quarterly, use ¼ the rate given, etc.

9. To find the compound interest when given the principal, the rate, and time period:
   a. Determine the rate to be used, and change it to a decimal.
   b. Multiply the principal by this rate to ascertain the interest for the first period.
   c. Add the interest to the principal.
   d. Multiply the new principal by the determined rate to find the interest for the second period.
   e. Add this interest to form a new principal.
   f. Continue the same procedure until all periods required have been accounted for.
   g. Subtract the original principal from the final principal to find the compound interest.

ILLUSTRATION: Find the amount that $200 will become if compounded semi-annually at 4% for 1½ years.
Solution:
Since it is to be compounded semi-annually for 1½ years, the interest will have to be computed 3 times, and the rate to be used is 2%=.02

Interest for the first period: $200×.02=$4
First new principal: $200+$4=$204
Interest for the second period: $204×.02=$4.08
Second new principal: $204+$4.08=$208.08
Interest for the third period:
$208.08×.02 = $4.1616
Final principal: $208.08+$4.16=$212.24
Answer: $212.24

BANK DISCOUNTS

10. When a note is cashed by a bank in advance of

its date of maturity, the bank deducts a discount from the principal and pays the rest to the depositor.

11. To find the bank discount:
    a. Find the time between the date the note is deposited and its date of maturity, and express this time as a fractional part of a year.
    b. Change the rate to a fraction.
    c. Multiply the principal by the time and the rate to find the bank discount.
    d. If required, subtract the bank discount from the original principal to find the amount the bank will pay the depositor.

ILLUSTRATION: A $400 note drawn up on August 12, 1962 for 90 days is deposited at the bank on September 17, 1962. The bank charges a 6½% discount on notes. How much will the depositor receive?

Solution:

From August 12, 1962, to September 17, 1962 is 36 days. This means that the note has 54 days to run.

54 days $= {}^{54}/_{360}$ of a year

$6½\% = {}^{13}/_{200}$

$\$400 \times 13/200 \times 54/360 = 39/10 = \$3.90$

$\$400 - \$3.90 = \$396.10$

Answer: The depositor will receive $396.10

PROBLEM SOLVING

TEST 1

DIRECTIONS: For each of the following questions, select the choice which best answers the question or completes the statement. Circle the letter preceding your answer.

1. Which of the following fractions is more than ¾?

   (A) $^{35}/_{71}$
   (B) $^{13}/_{20}$
   (C) $^{71}/_{101}$
   (D) $^{19}/_{24}$
   (E) $^{15}/_{20}$

2. If $820 + R + S - 610 = 342$, and if $R = 2S$, then $S =$

   (A) 44
   (B) 48
   (C) 132
   (D) 184
   (E) 192

3. What is the cost, in dollars, to carpet a room x yards long and y yards wide, if the carpet costs two dollars per square foot?

   (A) xy
   (B) 2xy
   (C) 3xy
   (D) 6xy
   (E) 18xy

4. If $7M = 3M - 20$, then $M + 7 =$

   (A) 0
   (B) 2
   (C) 5
   (D) 12
   (E) 17

5. In circle O below, AB is a diameter, angle BOD contains 15° and angle EOA contains 85°. Find the number of degrees in angle ECA.

   (A) 15

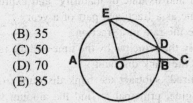

   (B) 35
   (C) 50
   (D) 70
   (E) 85

6. The diagonal of a rectangle is 10. The area of the rectangle

   (A) must be 24
   (B) must be 48
   (C) must be 50
   (D) must be 100
   (E) cannot be determined from the data given

7. In triangle PQR in the figure below, angle P is greater than angle Q and the bisectors of angle P and angle Q meet in S. Then

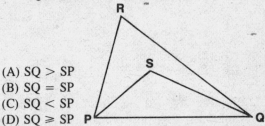

   (A) SQ > SP
   (B) SQ = SP
   (C) SQ < SP
   (D) SQ ≥ SP
   (E) no conclusion concerning the relative lengths of SQ and SP can be drawn from the data given

8. The coordinates of vertices X and Y of an equilateral triangle XYZ are $(-4, 0)$ and $(4, 0)$, respectively. The coordinates of Z may be

   (A) $(0, 2\sqrt{3})$
   (B) $(0, 4\sqrt{3})$
   (C) $(4, 4\sqrt{3})$
   (D) $(0, 4)$
   (E) $(4\sqrt{3}, 0)$

9. Given: All men are mortal. Which statement expresses a conclusion that logically follows from the given statement?

   (A) All mortals are men.
   (B) If X is a mortal, then X is a man.

(C) If X is not a mortal, then X is not a man.

(D) If X is not a man, then X is not a mortal.

(E) Some mortals are not men.

10. In the accompanying figure, ACB is a straight angle and DC is perpendicular to CE. If the number of degrees in angle ACD is represented by x, the number of degrees in angle BCE is represented by

(A) 90 − x

(B) x − 90

(C) 90 + x

(D) 180 − x

(E) 45 + x

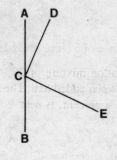

11. What is the smallest positive number which, when it is divided by 3, 4, or 5, will leave a remainder of 2?

(A) 22

(B) 42

(C) 62

(D) 122

(E) 182

12. A taxi charges 20 cents for the first quarter of a mile and 5 cents for each additional quarter of a mile. The charge, in cents, for a trip of d miles is

(A) 20 + 5d

(B) 20 + 5 (4d − 1)

(C) 20 + 20d

(D) 20 + 4 (d − 1)

(E) 20 + 20 (d − 1)

13. In a certain army post, 30% of the men are from New York State, and 10% of these are from New York City. What percent of the men in the post are from New York City?

(A) 3

(B) .3

(C) .03

(D) 13

(E) 20

14. From 9 A.M. to 2 P.M., the temperature rose at a constant rate from −14°F to +36°F. What was the temperature at noon?

(A) −4°

(B) +6°

(C) +16°

(D) +26°

(E) +31°

15. There are just two ways in which 5 may be expressed as the sum of two different positive (non-zero) integers; namely, 5 = 4 + 1 = 3 + 2. In how many ways may 9 be expressed as the sum of two different positive (non-zero) integers?

(A) 3

(B) 4

(C) 5

(D) 6

(E) 7

16. A board 7 feet 9 inches long is divided into three equal parts. What is the length of each part?

(A) 2 ft. 7 in.

(B) 2 ft. 6⅓ in.

(C) 2 ft. 8⅓ in.

(D) 2 ft. 8 in.

(E) 2 ft. 9 in.

17. In the figure below, the largest possible circle is cut out of a square piece of tin. The area of the remaining piece of tin is approximately (in square inches)

(A) .75

(B) 3.14

(C) .14

(D) .86

(E) 1.0

18. Which of the following is equal to 3.14×10^6?

(A) 314

(B) 3,140

(C) 31,400

(D) 314,000

(E) 3,140,000

19. $$\dfrac{36}{29 - \dfrac{4}{0.2}} =$$

(A) ⁴/₃

(B) 2
(C) 4
(D) ¾
(E) 18

20. In terms of the square units in the figure below, what is the area of the semicircle?

(A) 32π
(B) 16π
(C) 8π
(D) 4π
(E) 2π

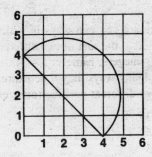

21. The sum of three consecutive odd numbers is always divisible by I. 2, II. 3, III. 5, IV. 6

(A) only I
(B) only II
(C) only I and II
(D) only I and III
(E) only II and IV

22. In the diagram, triangle ABC is inscribed in a circle and CD is tangent to the circle. If angle BCD is 40° how many degrees are there in angle A?

(A) 20
(B) 30
(C) 40
(D) 50
(E) 60

23. If a discount of 20% off the marked price of a suit saves a man $15, how much did he pay for the suit?

(A) $35
(B) $60
(C) $75
(D) $150
(E) $300

24. The ice compartment in a refrigerator is 8 inches deep, 5 inches high, and 4 inches wide. How many ice cubes will it hold, if each cube is 2 inches on a side?

(A) 16
(B) 20
(C) 40
(D) 80
(E) 160

25. Find the last number in the series: 8, 4, 12, 6, 18, 9, ?

(A) 19
(B) 20
(C) 22
(D) 24
(E) 27

26. A 15-gallon mixture of 20% alcohol has 5 gallons of water added to it. The strength of the mixture, as a percent, is near

(A) 15
(B) 13⅓
(C) 16⅔
(D) 12½
(E) 20

27. In the figure below, QXRS is a parallelogram and P is any point on side QS. What is the ratio of the area of triangle PXR to the area of QXRS?

(A) 1:4
(B) 1:3
(C) 2:3
(D) 3:4
(E) 1:2

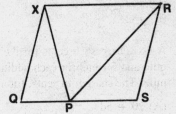

28. If x (p + 1) = M, then p =

(A) M − 1
(B) M
(C) $\dfrac{M - 1}{x}$
(D) M − x − 1
(E) $\dfrac{M}{x} - 1$

29. If T tons of snow fall in 1 second, how many tons fall in M minutes?

(A) 60 MT
(B) MT + 60

(C) MT

(D) $\dfrac{60\,M}{T}$

(E) $\dfrac{MT}{60}$

(A) 14

(B) 13

(C) − 1

(D) 3

(E) cannot be determined from the information given

30. If $\dfrac{P}{Q} = \dfrac{4}{5}$, what is the value of 2 P + Q?

ANSWER KEY·

1. D	7. A	13. A	19. C	25. E
2. A	8. B	14. C	20. D	26. A
3. E	9. C	15. B	21. B	27. E
4. B	10. A	16. A	22. C	28. E
5. B	11. C	17. D	23. B	29. A
6. E	12. B	18. E	24. A	30. E

EXPLANATORY ANSWERS

1. **(D)** ¾ = .75

   $\frac{35}{71}$ is slightly less than $\frac{35}{70}$ = .5

   $\frac{13}{20} = \frac{13 \times 5}{20 \times 5} = \frac{65}{100}$ = .65

   $\frac{71}{101}$ is very close to $\frac{7}{10}$ or .7

   $\frac{15}{20} = \frac{15 \times 5}{20 \times 5} = \frac{75}{100}$ = .75

   which equals ¾

   $\frac{19}{24}$ = $24\overline{)19.00}$ $\frac{.79}{}$ which is more than ¾

   $\frac{168}{220}$
   $\frac{216}{}$

2. **(A)**

   $$820 + R+S - 610 = 342$$
   $$R + S + 210 = 342$$
   $$R + S = 132$$
   If R = 2S, then $2S + S = 132$
   $$3S = 132$$
   $$S = 44$$

3. **(E)**

   Area = xy sq. yd.
   = 9 xy sq. ft.
   9 xy·2 = 18 xy

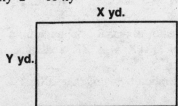

   X yd.

   Y yd.

4. **(B)**

   $$7 M = 3 M - 20$$
   $$4 M = - 20$$
   $$M = - 5$$
   $$M + 7 = - 5 + 7 = 2$$

5. **(B)** Arc EA = 85° and arc BD = 15°, since a central angle is measured by its arc then
   angle ECA = ½ (AE — BD)
   = ½ (85 — 15)
   = ½ · 70
   = 35°

6. **(E)** If we know only the hypotenuse of a right triangle, we cannot determine its legs. Hence, the area of the rectangle cannot be determined from the data given.

7. **(A)** If angle P > angle Q, then ½ angle P > ½ angle Q; then angle SPQ > angle SQP. Since the larger side lies opposite the larger angle, it follows that SQ > SP.

8. **(B)** Since Z is equidistant from X and Y, it must lie on the Y–axis. Then △ OZY is a 30° − 60° − 90° triangle with YZ = 8
   Hence OZ = $^8/_2 \sqrt{3}$ = $4\sqrt{3}$
   Coordinates of Z are
   $(0, 4\sqrt{3})$ (−4,0)   (4,0)

9. **(C)** (A) is a converse and not necessarily true.
   (B) is also based on the truth of the converse.
   (C) is based on the contrapositive, which is logically equivalent to the given statement.
   (D) is based on the converse and not necessarily true.
   (E) does not necessarily follow.
   Hence (C) is the correct answer.

10. **(A)** Since ACB is a straight angle and angle DCE is a right angle, then angle ACD and angle BCE are complementary. Hence BCE = 90 − x.

11. **(C)** The smallest positive number divisible by 3, 4, or 5 is $3 \cdot 4 \cdot 5 = 60$. Hence the desired number is

    60 + 2 = 62

12. **(B)** Since there are 4d quarter miles in d miles, the charge = 20 + 5 (4d − 1)

13. **(A)** Assume that there are 100 men on the post; then 30 are from New York State and $^1/_{10} \times 30$ = 3 are from New York City.
    $^3/_{100} = 3\%$

14. **(C)** Rise in temp. = 36 − (−14) = 36 + 14 = 50°. $^{50}/_5 = 10°$ (hourly rise)
    Hence, at noon, temp. = −14 + 3 (10) = −14 + 30 = + 16°

15. **(B)** 9 = 8 + 1 = 7 + 2 = 6 + 3 = 5 + 4
    Thus, 4 ways.

16. **(A)** $\dfrac{7 \text{ ft. 9 in.}}{3} = \dfrac{6 \text{ ft. 21 in.}}{3}$ = 2 ft. 7 in.

17. **(D)** Area of Square = 2^2 = 4
    Area of Circle = $\pi \cdot 1^2 = \pi$
    Difference = 4 − π = 4 − 3.14 = .86

18. **(E)** $3.14 \times 10^6 = 3.14 \times 1,000,000$
    $\qquad\qquad = 3,140,000$

19. **(C)** $\dfrac{36}{29 - \dfrac{4}{0.2}} = \dfrac{36}{29 - 20} = \dfrac{36}{9} = 4$

20. **(D)** Diameter = $4\sqrt{2}$, since it is the hypotenuse of a right isosceles $\triangle$ of leg 4
    Then the radius = $2\sqrt{2}$
    Area of semicircle = $1 \times \pi(2\sqrt{2})^2$
    $\qquad = 1 \times \pi \cdot 8 = 4\pi$

21. **(B)** Consecutive odd numbers may be represented as 2n + 1
    $\qquad\qquad\qquad\quad$ 2n + 3
    $\qquad\qquad\qquad\quad \underline{2n + 5}$
    Sum = $\qquad$ 6n + 9

Always divisible by 3. Thus, only II.

22. **(C)** Angle BCD is formed by tangent and chord and is equal to one-half arc BC. Angle A is an inscribed angle and also equal to one-half of arc BC.
    Hence angle A = angle BCD = 40°

23. **(B)** Let x = amount of marked price.
    Then $^1/_5$ x = 15
    $\qquad\quad$ x = 75
    75 − 15 = $60

24. **(A)** Since the ice cubes are 2 inches on an edge, there can be only 2 layers of 8 cubes each or a total of 16 cubes.

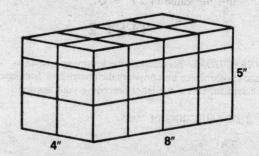

25. **(E)** There is a double recurring pattern here as indicated: Multiply by .5; then multiply by 3. Hence, the last term is 27.

26. **(A)** The new solution is $^3/_{20}$ pure alcohol or 15%.

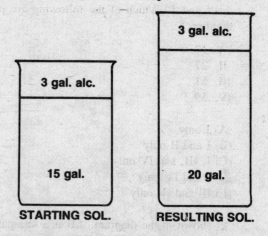

27. **(E)** Area of ▣ = XR × altitude from P to XR.
    Area of $\triangle$XPR = ½ XR × altitude from P to XR.
    Hence, ratio of area of $\triangle$ to ▣ = 1:2

28. **(E)** x(p + 1) = M. Divide both sides by x.

$$p + 1 = \frac{M}{x}$$

$$\text{or } p = \frac{M}{x} - 1$$

29. **(A)** $\frac{T}{1} = \frac{x}{60M}$

$$x = 60MT$$

30. **(E)** If $\frac{P}{Q} = \frac{4}{5}$

Then $5P = 4Q$

However, there is no way of determining from this the value of $2P + Q$.

TEST 2

DIRECTIONS: For each of the following questions, select the choice which best answers the question or completes the statement. Circle the letter preceding your answer.

1. What is 40% of $^{10}/_7$?

    (A) $^2/_7$
    (B) $^4/_7$
    (C) $^{10}/_{28}$
    (D) $^1/_{28}$
    (E) $^{28}/_{10}$

2. A prime number is one which is divisible only by itself and 1. Which of the following are prime numbers?

    I. 17
    II. 27
    III. 51
    IV. 59

    (A) I only
    (B) I and II only
    (C) I, III, and IV only
    (D) I and IV only
    (E) III and IV only

3. As shown in the diagram, AB is a straight line and angle BOC = 20°. If the number of degrees in angle DOC is 6 more than the number of degrees in angle x, find the number of degrees in angle x.

    (A) 77

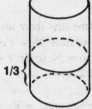

(B) 75
(C) 78
(D) 22
(E) 87

4. As shown in the figure, a cylindrical oil tank is ⅓ full. If 3 more gallons are added, the tank will be half-full. What is the capacity, in gallons, of the tank?

    (A) 15
    (B) 16
    (C) 17
    (D) 18
    (E) 19

5. A boy receives grades of 91, 88, 86, and 78 in four of his major subjects. What must he receive in his fifth major subject in order to average 85?

    (A) 86
    (B) 85
    (C) 84
    (D) 83
    (E) 82

6. If a steel bar is 0.39 feet long, its length in *inches* is

    (A) less than 4
    (B) between 4 and 4½
    (C) between 4½ and 5
    (D) between 5 and 6
    (E) more than 6

7. In the figure, PS is perpendicular to QR. If PQ = PR = 26 and PS = 24, then QR =

    (A) 14
    (B) 16
    (C) 18
    (D) 20
    (E) 22

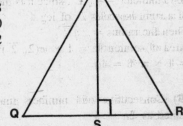

8. If x = 0, for what value of y is the following equation valid?

$5x^3 + 7x^2 - (4y + 13)x - 7y + 15 = 0$

(A) $-2^1/_7$
(B) 0
(C) $+2^1/_7$
(D) $^{15}/_{11}$
(E) $3^1/_7$

9. If a man walks $^2/_5$ mile in 5 minutes, what is his average rate of walking in miles per hour?

(A) 4
(B) 4½
(C) $4^4/_5$
(D) $5^1/_5$
(E) 5¾

10. One end of a dam has the shape of a trapezoid with the dimensions indicated. What is the dam's area in square feet?

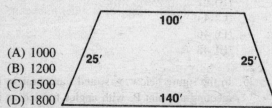

(A) 1000
(B) 1200
(C) 1500
(D) 1800
(E) cannot be determined from the information given

11. If $1 + \dfrac{1}{t} = \dfrac{t + 1}{t}$, what does t equal?

(A) + 2 only
(B) + 2 or − 2 only
(C) + 2 or − 1 only
(D) − 2 or + 1 only
(E) is any number except 0.

12. Point A is 3 inches from line b as shown in the diagram. In the plane that contains point A and line b, what is the total number of points which are 6 inches from A and also 1 inch from b?

(A) 0
(B) 1
(C) 2
(D) 3
(E) 4

13. If R and S are different integers, both divisible by 5, then which of the following is *not necessarily* true?

(A) R − S is divisible by 5
(B) RS is divisible by 25
(C) R + S is divisible by 5
(D) $R^2 + S^2$ is divisible by 5
(E) R + S is divisible by 10

14. If a triangle of base 7 is equal in area to a circle of radius 7, what is the altitude of the triangle?

(A) 8π
(B) 10π
(C) 12π
(D) 14π
(E) cannot be determined from the information given

15. If the following numbers are arranged in order from the smallest to the largest, what will be their correct order?

I. $\dfrac{9}{13}$

II. $\dfrac{13}{9}$

III. 70%

IV. $\dfrac{1}{.70}$

(A) II, I, III, IV
(B) III, II, I, IV
(C) III, IV, I, II
(D) II, IV, III, I
(E) I, III, IV, II

16. The coordinates of the vertices of quadrilateral PQRS are P(0, 0), Q(9, 0), R(10, 3) and S(1, 3) respectively. The area of PQRS is

(A) $9\sqrt{10}$
(B) $^9/_2\sqrt{10}$
(C) $^{27}/_2$
(D) 27
(E) not determinable from the information given

17. In the circle shown, AB is a diameter. If secant AP = 8 and tangent CP = 4, find the number of units in the diameter of the circle.

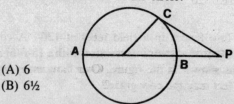

(A) 6
(B) 6½

(C) 8

(D) $3\sqrt{2}$

(E) cannot be determined from the information given

18. A certain type of siding for a house costs $10.50 per square yard. What does it cost for the siding for a wall 4 yards wide and 60 feet long?

(A) $800

(B) $840

(C) $2520

(D) $3240

(E) $5040

19. A circle whose radius is 7 has its center at the origin. Which of the following points are outside the circle?

I. (4, 4)

II. (5, 5)

III. (4, 5)

IV. (4, 6)

(A) I and II only

(B) II and III only

(C) II, III, and IV only

(D) II and IV only

(E) III and IV only

20. A merchant sells a radio for $80, thereby making a profit of 25% of the cost. What is the ratio of cost to selling price?

(A) $^4/_5$

(B) ¾

(C) $^5/_6$

(D) ⅔

(E) $^3/_5$

21. How many degrees between the hands of a clock at 3:40?

(A) 150°

(B) 140°

(C) 130°

(D) 125°

(E) 120°

22. Two fences in a field meet at 120°. A cow is tethered at their intersection with a 15-foot rope, as shown in the figure. Over how many square feet may the cow graze?

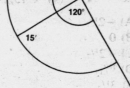

(A) 50π

(B) 75π

(C) 80π

(D) 85π

(E) 90π

23. If $^{17}/_{10}$ y = 0.51, then y =

(A) 3

(B) 1.3

(C) 1.2

(D) .3

(E) .03

24. A junior class of 50 girls and 70 boys sponsored a dance. If 40% of the girls and 50% of the boys attended the dance, approximately what percent attended?

(A) 40

(B) 42

(C) 44

(D) 46

(E) 48

25. In the figure below, r, s, and t are straight lines meeting at point P, with angles formed as indicated; then y =

(A) 30°

(B) 120°

(C) 3x

(D) 180 − x

(E) 180 − 3x

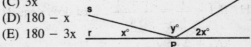

26. $^{18}/_{33} = \dfrac{\sqrt{36}}{\sqrt{?}}$

(A) 11

(B) 121

(C) 66

(D) 144

(E) 1089

27. If we write all the whole numbers from 200 to 400, how many of these contain the digit 7 once and only once?

(A) 32

(B) 34

(C) 35

(D) 36

(E) 38

28. $(r + s)^2 - r^2 - s^2 = (?)$

 (A) 2rs
 (B) rs
 (C) rs^2
 (D) 0
 (E) 2r^2 + 2s^2

29. In the figure, angle S is obtuse, PR = 9, PS = 6 and Q is any point on RS. Which of the following inequalities expresses possible values of the length of PQ?

 (A) 9≥PQ≥6
 (B) 9≥6≥PQ
 (C) 6≥PQ≥9
 (D) PQ≥9≥6
 (E) 9≤PQ≤6

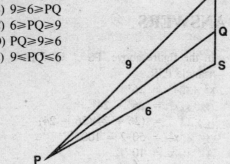

30. If a man buys several articles for K cents per dozen and sells them for $\dfrac{K}{8}$ cents per article, what is his profit, in cents, per article?

 (A) $\dfrac{K}{48}$

 (B) $\dfrac{K}{12}$

 (C) $\dfrac{3K}{4}$

 (D) $\dfrac{K}{18}$

 (E) $\dfrac{K}{24}$

ANSWER KEY

1. B	7. D	13. E	19. D	25. E
2. D	8. C	14. D	20. A	26. B
3. A	9. C	15. E	21. C	27. D
4. D	10. D	16. D	22. B	28. A
5. E	11. E	17. A	23. D	29. A
6. C	12. E	18. B	24. D	30. E

EXPLANATORY ANSWERS

1. **(B)** $40\% = \frac{2}{5}$
$\frac{2}{5} \times \frac{10}{7} = \frac{4}{7}$

2. **(D)** 27 and 51 are each divisible by 3. 17 and 59 are prime numbers.
Hence, I and IV only.

3. **(A)** Angle DOC = $6 + x$
Angle AOC = $(6 + x) + x = 180 - 20$
$6 + 2x = 160$
$2x = 154$
$x = 77$

4. **(D)** Let C = the capacity in gallons.
Then $\frac{1}{3}C + 3 = \frac{1}{2}C$
Multiplying through by 6, we obtain
$2C + 18 = 3C$
or $C = 18$

5. **(E)** $\dfrac{91+88+86+78+x}{5} = 85$
$343 + x = 425$
$x = 82$

6. **(C)** $12 \times .39 = 4.68$ inches; that is, between $4\frac{1}{2}$ and 5.

7. **(D)**

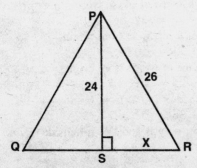

In the figure above, PS ⊥ QR. Then, in right triangle PSR,
$x^2 + 24^2 = 26^2$
$ x^2 = 26^2 - 24^2$
$ = (26 + 24)(26 - 24)$
$ x^2 = 50 \cdot 2 = 100$
$ x = 10$
Thus, QR = 20

8. **(C)** All terms involving x are 0.
Hence, the equation reduces to
$0 - 7y + 15 = 0$
or $7y = 15$
$y = 2\frac{1}{7}$

9. **(C)** $\text{rate} = \dfrac{\text{distance}}{\text{time}} = \dfrac{\frac{2}{5} \text{ mile}}{\frac{5}{60} \text{ hour}} = \dfrac{\frac{2}{5}}{\frac{1}{12}}$
$\text{rate} = \frac{2}{5} \cdot \frac{12}{1} = \frac{24}{5} = 4\frac{4}{5}$ miles per hour

10. **(D)** Draw the altitudes indicated. A rectangle and two right triangles are produced. From the figure, the base of each triangle is 20 feet. By the Pythagorean theorem, the altitude is 15 feet. Hence, the area

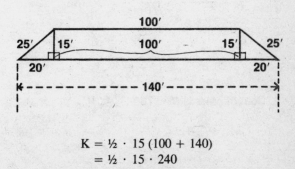

$K = \frac{1}{2} \cdot 15 \,(100 + 140)$
$ = \frac{1}{2} \cdot 15 \cdot 240$

= 15 · 120

= 1800 square feet

11. **(E)** If $1 + \dfrac{1}{t} = \dfrac{t + 1}{1}$, then the right hand fraction can also be reduced to $1 + \dfrac{1}{t}$, and we have an identity, which is true for all values of t except 0.

12. **(E)** All points 6 inches from A are on a circle of radius 6 with center at A. All points 1 inch from b are on 2 straight lines parallel to b and 1 inch from it on each side. These two parallel lines intersect the circle in 4 points.

13. **(E)** Let R = 5P and S = 5Q where P and Q are integers.
Then R − S = 5P − 5Q = 5(P−Q) is divisible by 5.
RS = 5P · 5Q = 25PQ is divisible by 25.
R + S = 5P + 5Q = 5(P + Q) is divisible by 5.
$R^2 + S^2 = 25P^2 + 25Q^2 = 25(P^2 + Q^2)$ is divisible by 5.
R + S = 5P + 5Q = 5(P + Q), which is not necessarily divisible by 10.

14. **(D)** $\frac{1}{2} \cdot 7 \cdot h = \pi \cdot 7^2$
Dividing both sides by 7, we get
$\frac{1}{2}h = 7\pi$
or $h = 14\pi$

15. **(E)**

$$^9/_{13} = \dfrac{.69}{13\overline{)9.00}} \qquad ^{13}/_9 = \dfrac{1.44}{9\overline{)13.00}} \qquad 70\% = .7$$

$$\begin{array}{r} .69 \\ 13\overline{)9.00} \\ 78 \\ \hline 120 \\ 117 \end{array} \qquad \begin{array}{r} 1.44 \\ 9\overline{)13.00} \\ 9 \\ \hline 40 \\ 36 \\ \hline 40 \\ 36 \end{array}$$

$$\dfrac{1}{70} = \dfrac{\frac{1}{7}}{10} = \dfrac{10}{} = \dfrac{1.42}{7\overline{)10.00}}$$

$$\begin{array}{r} 1.42 \\ 7\overline{)10.00} \\ 7 \\ \hline 30 \\ 28 \\ \hline 20 \end{array}$$

Correct order is $^9/_{13}, 70\%, \dfrac{1}{.70}, ^{13}/_9$

or I, III, IV, II

16. **(D)**

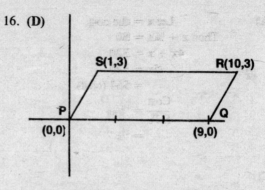

Since PQ and RS are parallel and equal, the figure is a parallelogram of base = 9 and height = 3
Hence, area = 9 · 3 = 27

17. **(A)**

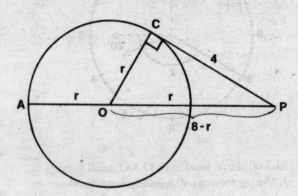

From the figure, in right △ PCO,
$PO^2 = r^2 + 4^2$
$(8 − r)^2 = r^2 + 16$
$64 − 16r + r^2 = r^2 + 16$
$48 = 16r$
r = 3
Diameter = 6

18. **(B)** Area of wall = 4 · $^{60}/_3$ = 4 · 20 = 80 sq. yd.
Cost = 80 × $10.50 = $840.00

19. **(D)** Distance of (4, 4) from origin = $\sqrt{16 + 16} = \sqrt{32} < 7$
Distance of (5, 5) from origin = $\sqrt{25 + 25} = \sqrt{50} > 7$
Distance of (4, 5) from origin = $\sqrt{16 + 25} = \sqrt{41} < 7$
Distance of (4, 6) from origin = $\sqrt{16 + 36} = \sqrt{52} > 7$
Hence, only II and IV are outside circle.

20. (A)

$$\text{Let } x = \text{the cost.}$$
$$\text{Then } x + \tfrac{1}{4}x = 80$$
$$4x + x = 320$$
$$5x = 320$$
$$= \$64 \text{ (cost)}$$
$$\frac{\text{Cost}}{\text{S.P.}} = {}^{64}/_{80}$$
$$= {}^{4}/_{5}$$

21. (C)

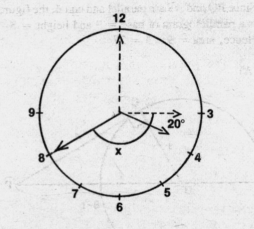

At 3:00, large hand is at 12 and small hand is at 3. During the next 40 minutes, large hand moves to 8 and small hand moves $\dfrac{40}{60} = \dfrac{2}{3}$ of distance

between 3 and 4; $\dfrac{2}{3} \times 30° = 20°$

Since there is 30° between two numbers of clock
$<x = 5 \,(30°) - 20° = 150° - 20° = 130°$

22. (B) Area of sector $= {}^{120}/_{360} \cdot \pi \cdot 15^2$
$$= \tfrac{1}{3} \cdot \pi \cdot 15 \cdot 15$$
$$= 75\pi$$

23. (D) ${}^{17}/_{10}y = 0.51$
Multiplying both sides by 10, we get
$$17\,y = 5.1$$
$$y = .3$$

24. (D) $40\% = {}^{2}/_{5} \times 50 = 20$ girls attended
$50\% = \tfrac{1}{2} \times 70 = 35$ boys attended

$$\frac{55}{50 + 70} = \frac{55}{120} = \frac{11}{24}$$

$$\begin{array}{r} .458 \\ 24\,)\overline{11.000} \\ \underline{96} \\ 140 \\ \underline{120} \\ 200 \\ \underline{192} \end{array} = 45.8\%$$

Approx. 46%

25. (E) Since $x + 2x + y = 180°$, it follows that
$$3x + y = 180$$
$$y = 180 - 3x$$

26. (B) ${}^{18}/_{33} = {}^{6}/_{11}$
$$= \frac{\sqrt{6^2}}{\sqrt{11^2}} = \frac{\sqrt{36}}{\sqrt{121}}$$
Missing denominator is $\sqrt{121}$.

27. (D) There are 20 numbers that contain 7 in the unit's place. There are 20 more that contain 7 in the ten's place. Thus, there are 40 numbers with 7 in either unit's or ten's place. But the numbers 277 and 377 must be rejected, and they have each been counted twice.
Hence, $40 - 4 = 36$

28. (A) $(r + s)^2 - r^2 - s^2 =$
$r^2 + 2rs + s^2 - r^2 - s^2 =$
$\qquad\qquad 2rs$

29. (A) As Q moves from R to S, PQ gets smaller. Its largest possible value would be 9.
Hence, $9 \geqslant PQ \geqslant 6$

30. (E) Selling price per article $= \dfrac{K}{8}$

Cost per article $= \dfrac{K}{12}$

Profit per article $= \dfrac{K}{8} - \dfrac{K}{12} = \dfrac{3K - 2K}{24} = \dfrac{K}{24}$

DATA INTERPRETATION

TEST 1

DIRECTIONS: The following questions are to test your ability to read and interpret graphs and tables. Answer each question based on your reading of the graphs or tables provided. Circle the letter preceding your answer.

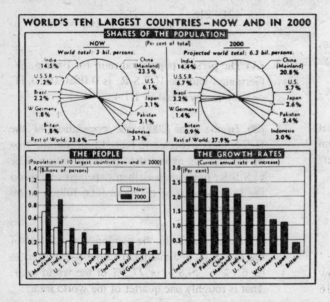

1. The population of Brazil in 2000 is expected to be about:

   (A) 100 million
   (B) 150 million
   (C) 200 million
   (D) 250 million
   (E) 300 million

2. The growth rate of India, Japan, and Britain expressed as a combined average percent of increase is approximately:

   (A) 1%
   (B) 2%
   (C) 3%

   (D) 4%
   (E) 5%

3. The percent change in the population of the U.S.S.R. from now to 2000 is expected to be about:

   (A) 50%
   (B) 60%
   (C) 70%
   (D) 80%
   (E) 90%

4. The present population ratio for Britain, W. Germany, and the U.S.S.R. is:

   (A) 1:1:4
   (B) 1:1:2
   (C) 1:2:3
   (D) 1:3:5
   (E) 1:3:3

5. In 2000 the U.S.S.R. population is expected to exceed that of the United States by about:

   (A) 40 million
   (B) 60 million
   (C) 80 million
   (D) 100 million
   (E) 120 million

6. The combined population of the U.S.S.R. and China (Mainland) is expected to be approximately what part of the world population in 2000?

   (A) one-tenth
   (B) three-quarters
   (C) one-fifth
   (D) one-quarter
   (E) one-half

ANSWER KEY

1. C	4. A
2. A	5. B
3. E	6. D

EXPLANATORY ANSWERS

1. **(C)** From the chart "The People," the population of Brazil in the year 2000 is expected to be slightly over 200 million persons. This is close to 200 million in answer (C).

2. **(A)** The growth rates (in percent) of India, Japan, and Britain are 2.1, 1.1, and 0.4%, respectively. The combined average of these is $(2.1+1.1+0.4)/3 = 3.6/3 = 1.2\%$; or about 1%.

3. **(E)** From the chart "The People," we find that the population of the U.S.S.R. will increase from about 220 million to 420 million—giving a percentage increase of

$$\frac{420-220}{220} \times 100 = \frac{200}{220} \times 100 = 91\%$$

More accurately, we can find from the "Share" charts that the population of the U.S.S.R. is now 7.2% of the world total of 3 billion, or about 216 million persons. In 2000, it will be 6.7% of the world total of 6.3 billion, or about 421 million persons. The percentage increase is then

$$\frac{421-216}{216} \times 100 = \frac{205}{216} \times 100 = 95\%$$

4. **(A)** The present population ratio for Britain, W. Germany, and the U.S.S.R. is 0.05:0.05:0.21, or very nearly equal to 1:1:4.

5. **(B)** In the year 2000, the population of the U.S.S.R. is expected to be 0.42 billion and that of the U.S. is expected to be 0.36 billion. The U.S.S.R. population is then expected to exceed the U.S. population by about 0.06 billion or 60 million people.

6. **(D)** In the year 2000, the combined population of the U.S.S.R. and mainland China is expected to be 6.7% + 20.8%, or 27.5% of the world total. That is roughly one quarter of the world total.

TEST 2

DIRECTIONS: The following questions are to test your ability to read and interpret graphs and tables. Answer each question based on your reading of the graphs or tables provided. Circle the letter preceding your answer.

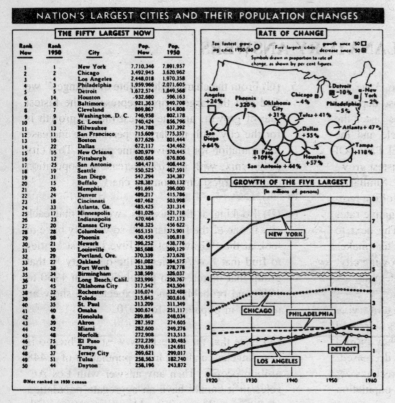

NATION'S LARGEST CITIES AND THEIR POPULATION CHANGES

THE FIFTY LARGEST NOW

Rank Now	Rank 1950	City	Pop. New	Pop. 1950
1	1	New York	7,710,346	7,891,957
2	2	Chicago	3,492,945	3,620,962
3	4	Los Angeles	2,448,018	1,970,358
4	3	Philadelphia	1,959,966	2,071,605
5	5	Detroit	1,612,574	1,849,568
6	14	Houston	932,680	596,163
7	6	Baltimore	921,363	949,708
8	7	Cleveland	869,867	914,808
9	9	Washington, D. C.	746,958	802,178
10	8	St. Louis	740,424	856,796
11	13	Milwaukee	734,788	637,392
12	11	San Francisco	715,609	775,357
13	10	Boston	677,626	801,444
14	22	Dallas	672,117	434,462
15	15	New Orleans	620,979	570,445
16	12	Pittsburgh	600,684	676,806
17	25	San Antonio	584,471	408,442
18	19	Seattle	550,525	467,591
19	31	San Diego	547,294	334,387
20	15	Buffalo	528,387	580,132
21	26	Memphis	491,691	396,000
22	24	Denver	489,217	415,786
23	18	Cincinnati	487,462	503,998
24	33	Atlanta, Ga.	485,425	331,314
25	17	Minneapolis	481,026	521,718
26	23	Indianapolis	470,464	427,173
27	20	Kansas City	458,325	456,622
28	98	Columbus	465,151	375,901
29	98	Phoenix	430,459	106,818
30	21	Newark	396,252	438,776
31	30	Louisville	385,688	369,129
32	29	Portland, Ore.	370,339	373,628
33	27	Oakland	361,082	384,575
34	38	Fort Worth	353,388	278,778
35	34	Birmingham	338,569	326,037
36	41	Long Beach, Calif.	323,996	250,767
37	45	Oklahoma City	317,542	243,504
38	32	Rochester	316,074	332,488
39	36	Toledo	315,643	303,616
40	35	St. Paul	313,209	311,349
41	40	Omaha	300,674	251,117
42		Honolulu	289,864	248,034
43	39	Akron	287,592	274,605
44	42	Miami	282,600	249,276
45	48	Norfolk	272,908	213,513
46	75	El Paso	272,239	130,485
47	84	Tampa	270,610	124,681
48	37	Jersey City	269,621	299,017
49	51	Tulsa	258,563	182,740
50	44	Dayton	258,196	243,872

*Not ranked in 1950 census

RATE OF CHANGE

Ten fastest growing cities 1950-'60 ○   Five largest cities ●   growth since '50 ☐   decrease since '50 ▨

Symbols drawn in proportion to rate of change, as shown by per cent figures.

Los Angeles +24%   Phoenix +320%   Chicago -4%   Detroit -10%   New York -2%   Philadelphia -5%   Oklahoma City +31%   Tulsa +41%   Dallas +55%   Atlanta +47%   San Diego +64%   El Paso +109%   San Antonio +44%   Houston +57%   Tampa +118%

GROWTH OF THE FIVE LARGEST

(In millions of persons)

NEW YORK

CHICAGO   PHILADELPHIA

DETROIT

LOS ANGELES

1920   1930   1940   1950   1960

1. Next to the fastest and next to the slowest cities in growth among the following since 1950 are:

(A) Chicago and El Paso
(B) San Diego and New York
(C) Tampa and Philadelphia
(D) Detroit and Phoenix
(E) Tulsa and Dallas

2. Cities that did not decrease in population rank since 1950 are:

(A) Los Angeles, Houston, St. Paul, Detroit
(B) Norfolk, Fort Worth, New Orleans, Seattle
(C) Milwaukee, Dallas, Cincinnati, Denver
(D) Omaha, Memphis, San Diego, San Antonio
(E) El Paso, Phoenix, Indianapolis, Washington

3. Among the five largest cities, a significant population decline occurred:

(A) 1920-1930
(B) 1930-1940
(C) 1940-1950
(D) 1950-1960
(E) at no time

4. The smallest percent of decrease since 1950 has taken place in:

(A) Jersey City
(B) Los Angeles
(C) Boston
(D) Minneapolis
(E) New York

5. The greatest percent of increase between 1950 and 1960 has occurred in:

(A) Omaha
(B) Miami
(C) Phoenix
(D) Louisville
(E) San Antonio

6. The city that will probably show a population increase in 1970, according to the general pattern, is:

(A) Philadelphia
(B) New York
(C) Detroit
(D) Los Angeles
(E) Chicago

7. Three cities west of Chicago that make up about a million people in the aggregate are:

(A) Tulsa, Phoenix, Oklahoma City
(B) Phoenix, Los Angeles, El Paso
(C) San Diego, Oklahoma City, Dallas
(D) Omaha, Tampa, Phoenix
(E) San Antonio, Houston, San Diego

ANSWER KEY

1. C
2. B
3. D
4. E

5. C
6. D
7. A

EXPLANATORY ANSWERS

1. **(C)** From the chart "Rate of Change," we see that the fastest growing cities are those depicted by a circle—the larger the circle, the faster the growth. Phoenix has the largest circle and the next to largest is either Tampa or El Paso. Of these last two, Tampa is the next to fastest growing city with a rate of change of 118%. Similarly, for the slowest growing city we look for the largest black square (which represents negative rates of change) and that is for Detroit. The next to largest square is for Philadelphia, and that makes Philadelphia the next to the slowest growing city. The answer is then Tampa and Philadelphia.

2. **(B)** We have to check each answer in turn trying to find an answer in which all the cities increased their ranking in population. That is, they moved up in rank and their rank number decreased. Doing this, we find that (B) is the correct answer because it has no city that decreases in population rank.

3. **(D)** Looking at the chart for the "Growth of the Five Largest" cities, we find that four of them experienced a significant decline from 1950 to 1960.

4. **(E)** To find the city with the smallest percent decrease since 1950, we look for a city with the present population very nearly equal to but still slightly smaller now than in 1950. Looking at the table of the "Fifty Largest Now," we note that New York comes closest to this criterion, largely because its population is so large.

5. **(C)** From the chart on the "Rate of Change," we find that the largest circle represents the fastest rate of growth, and the fastest rate of growth is for the city with the largest percentage increase in population for the given time period. That city is Phoenix, with a 320% increase in population and the largest circle on the chart.

6. **(D)** Looking at the answers, we find that each city is one of the five largest, so we only have to look at the "Growth of the Five Largest" cities to find that Los Angeles is the only city in that group that increased in population from 1950 to 1960 and probably can be expected to show an increase in population for 1970.

7. **(A)** Note that the largest city west of Chicago is Los Angeles, and that has a population of 2.448 million people. Then any answer with Los Angeles in it cannot have an aggregate population of only a million people. Also, any answer with the city of Houston can also be eliminated (unless the other cities in that answer are very small) since Houston has slightly under a million people. In this way we can eliminate answers (B) and (E). Also, since Tampa is east of Chicago, answer (D) can be eliminated. Checking the remaining two answers, we get:
$258 + 430 + 317 = 1,005$ thousand (A)
$547 + 317 + 672 = 1,536$ thousand (C)
So the correct answer is (A).

TEST 3

DIRECTIONS: The following questions are to test your ability to read and interpret graphs and tables. Answer each question based on your reading of the graphs or tables provided. Circle the letter preceding your answer.

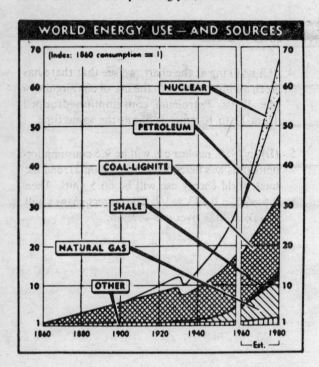

1. From 1920 to 1960, petroleum increased in use:

   (A) 2 times
   (B) 6 times
   (C) 12 times
   (D) 20 times
   (E) 25 times

2. Nuclear use will have approximately how many consumption units in 1980?

   (A) 10
   (B) 15
   (C) 3
   (D) 1
   (E) none of the above

3. By 1980, coal-lignite is expected to have how many more consumption units than nuclear material will have?

   (A) 2
   (B) 10
   (C) 20
   (D) 30
   (E) 40

4. The graph shows that there has been—or there is expected to be—an interruption in the increase in the use of coal-lignite and

   (A) natural gas
   (B) shale
   (C) petroleum
   (D) nuclear material
   (E) "other" material

5. The estimated use of nuclear materials in 1980 is what part of all other combined sources of world energy estimated for 1980?

   (A) a little over one-half
   (B) a little over one-quarter
   (C) a little over three-quarters
   (D) a little over one-seventh
   (E) about equal

ANSWER KEY

1. B
2. A
3. B

4. C
5. D

EXPLANATORY ANSWERS

1. **(B)** Petroleum use is depicted by the white portion of the chart. In 1920, it was about $10 - 8$, or 2 consumption units. In 1960, it was $29 - 18$, or 11 consumption units. This represents an increase of about 6 times.

2. **(A)** In 1980, nuclear use (represented by the dotted portion of the chart) will be $66.5 - 57$, or 9.5 consumption units.

3. **(B)** In 1980, coal-lignite use will be $32.5 - 13.5$, or 19 consumption units, and nuclear use will be 9.5 units (determined in question 2). Coal-lignite use will be about $19 - 9.5$, or 9.5 units more than nuclear use. This is close to 10 units.

4. **(C)** Looking at the chart, we see that there has been an interruption in the use of coal-lignite in the 1930s. Petroleum consumption dropped from 12 to 10 units at about the same time.

5. **(D)** In 1980, nuclear use will be 9.5 consumption units (this was determined in question 2), and the total world energy use will be 66.5 units. Then $9.5/66.5 = 0.143 = 1/7$. The correct answer will be (D), a little over one-seventh.

DATA SUFFICIENCY

TEST 1

DIRECTIONS: Each question below is followed by two numbered facts. You are to determine whether the data given in the statements is sufficient for answering the question. Use the data given, plus your knowledge of math and everyday facts, to choose between the five possible answers.

(A) if statement 1 alone is sufficient to answer the question, but statement 2 alone is not sufficient.
(B) if statement 2 alone is sufficient to answer the question, but statement 1 alone is not sufficient.
(C) if both statements together are needed to answer the question, but neither statement alone is sufficient.
(D) if either statement by itself is sufficient to answer the question asked.
(E) if not enough facts are given to answer the question.

Write in the correct letter next to each question number.

1. What is the value of x?

    (1) $x^2 + x = 2$
    (2) $x^2 + 2x - 3 = 0$

2. Is AB parallel to CD?

    (1) Angle a + angle b = 180°
    (2) Angle a + angle c + angle d + angle e = 360°

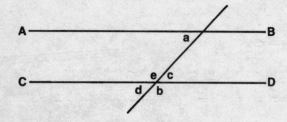

3. A,B, and C are three consecutive even integers (not necessarily in order). Which has the greatest value?

    (1) A + B = C
    (2) C is a positive number.

4. If x and y are equal whole numbers greater than zero, what is the value of y?

    (1) x + y = 2
    (2) y − x = 4

5. Which has a greater area, circle O, or square ABCD?

    (1) The radius of circle O is $\pi/2$.
    (2) One side of square ABCD is π.

6. Is John a policeman?

    (1) All of Sam's friends are policemen.
    (2) John is not Sam's friend.

7. How many red marbles are there in a bag containing 12 marbles, including red, green, and blue ones?

    (1) There are more red marbles than there are blue and green combined.
    (2) There are twice as many blue marbles as there are green ones.

8. Does John have a sister?

    (1) John's only brother Bill has no children, and yet John has two nephews.
    (2) The sisters of John's wife have no children.

9. A school has three teams: football, baseball, and basketball. Alan, Bob and Carl are each on two teams. How many of the three are on the football team?

    (1) No team has all three boys on it.
    (2) Bob plays basketball, while Carl and Alan play baseball.

10. Is m evenly divisible by 2?

    (1) $(m^2 + 2m - 9)$ is even
    (2) $m + \dfrac{1}{m} = 2$

11. A figure is composed of ten 1-inch cubes. What is its weight?

    (1) The cubes are arranged in five rows of two each.
    (2) The cubes have an average weight of 1 ounce each.

12. What month is it?

    (1) I do not attend school in July or August.
    (2) This month begins with a "J."

13. How many quarts of water does tank A hold?

    (1) Tank B holds twice as much as tank A.
    (2) Tanks A and B together hold nine gallons.

14. How many pennies does Fred have?

    (1) He has 73¢
    (2) He has 6 coins.

15. A man has twelve 3-lb. weights, ten 5-lb. weights, and seven 10-lb. weights. He places eight of these weights on a scale. How many 5-lb. weights are used?

    (1) The scale registers 47 lbs.
    (2) The number of 10-lb weights used is one less than the number of 3-lb. weights used.

16. How many degrees in angle s?

    (1) BCDE is a parallelogram.
    (2) The area of △ ABE = the areas of △ ACB and △ ADE combined.

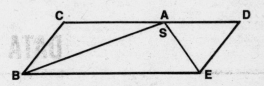

17. How many hours does it take Bill to do a certain job?

    (1) Working together, Bill and Jim can complete it in eight hours.
    (2) Jim can do the job in twelve hours.

18. If x and y are non-negative, is (x + y) greater than xy?

    (1) $x = y$
    (2) $x + y$ is greater than $x^2 + y^2$

19. How heavy is one brick?

    (1) Two bricks weigh as much as three 6-lb. weights.
    (2) Three bricks weigh as much as one brick plus 18 lbs.

20. In the diagram, find the length of AB.

    (1) ABCD is a rectangle.
    (2) AC − AE = AB + BE

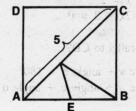

ANSWER KEY

1. C	6. E	11. B	16. E
2. A	7. C	12. E	17. C
3. C	8. E	13. C	18. C
4. A	9. A	14. C	19. D
5. C	10. D	15. A	20. B

EXPLANATORY ANSWERS

1. **(C)** From equation (1), x may be either 1 or -2. From equation (2), x may be 1 or -3. Thus, if both are true, $x=1$.

2. **(A)** Angle b= angle e, a+e=$180°$, which means AB is parallel to CD. Equation (2) shows us only that a=b, which makes the two lines parallel only where a=b=$90°$.

3. **(C)** There are three possible combinations fulfilling (1): $-2+(-4)=(-6); -2+2=0;$ and $2+4=6$. Of these, only the last satisfies property (2).

4. **(A)** Since x and y are whole numbers greater than zero, and x+y=2, the only possibility is that x=y=1. For y-x=4, there are no possible solutions.

5. **(C)** The area of circle O is $\pi(\pi/2)^2$. The area of ABCD is π^2. Therefore, the square is larger.

6. **(E)** It is not necessary that every policeman be Sam's friend.

7. **(C)** Because of (1), there must be at least 7 red marbles, so the blue and green ones cannot total more than 5. By (2), there is only one possible combination: 1 green, 2 blue, 9 red. If there were 2 green, there would be 4 blue, and only 6 red, which is not more than the combined blue and green.

8. **(E)** Since Bill has no children, either John has a sister, or he is married, and his wife's brother has two nephews. Either of these cases may be true, so we cannot tell from the given information whether or not John has a sister.

9. **(A)** Since no team has all three boys on it, there must be two of the three on each team.

10. **(D)** From (1), m^2+2m-9 is even, so $(m^2+2m+1)-10$ is even, and (m^2+2m+1) is also even. This is $(m+1)^2$, so m+1 is even, and m is odd. From (2) m=1, and therefore is odd.

11. **(B)** The arrangement is immaterial, and only the weight is important.

12. **(E)** The fact that I do not attend school in July or August is totally irrelevant, since this does not mean I am not attending school now.

13. **(C)** Tank B holds 6 gallons, tank A holds 3 gallons.

14. **(C)** He must have three pennies. Otherwise, the two conditions would not be fulfilled.

15. **(A)** For the last digit of the total weight to be a 7, there must be either four 3's or nine 3's, or more. Nine or more are impossible, so there must be four 3's. This leaves four weights chosen from the 5's and 10's to make up 35 lbs. The only possible way to do this is by using three tens and one 5.

16. **(E)** Assuming (1) and (2) to be true, there is still no indication about the size of angle s, since (2) is true for all parallelograms.

17. **(C)** Jim does $1/12$ of the job in 1 hour. Together, Jim and Bill do $1/8$ of the job in 1 hour. Bill alone, therefore, does $1/8-1/12$ of the job in 1 hour $= 1/24$. Accordingly, it will take Bill 24 hours to do the entire job by himself.

18. **(C)** Since x=y,
    2x > 2x² or
    $2x > 2x^2$ or
    $1 > x$.
    Thus $x+y > xy$.

19. **(D)** One brick weighs nine pounds.

20. **(B)** Taking equation (2) and adding AE to both sides, we have: AC=AB+BE+AE. Since BE+AE=AB, AC=2AB, so AB=2½.

TEST 2

DIRECTIONS: Each question below is followed by two numbered facts. You are to determine whether the data given in the statements is sufficient for answering the question. Use the data given, plus your knowledge of math and everyday facts, to choose between the five possible answers.

(A) if statement 1 alone is sufficient to answer the question, but statement 2 alone is not sufficient.
(B) if statement 2 alone is sufficient to answer the question, but statement 1 alone is not sufficient.
(C) if both statements together are needed to answer the question, but neither statement alone is sufficient.
(D) if either statement by itself is sufficient to answer the question asked.
(E) if not enough facts are given to answer the question.

Write in the correct letter next to each question number.

1. What is the value of $x^2 + y^2$?

   (1) $x - y = 4$
   (2) $xy = 4$

2. John is a member of the Fine Fellows. Is Tim also a member?

   (1) If a member's brother wants to join, he may become a member.
   (2) Tim is John's sister's brother.

3. Is ABCD a rhombus (all four sides equal)?

   (1) ABCD is a square.
   (2) AB is parallel to and equal to CD.

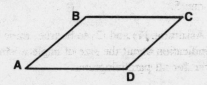

4. If *x* and *y* are whole numbers, both greater than 3, what is the value of *x*?

   (1) $xy = 49$
   (2) $x^2 - y = 12$

5. Which has a greater length: AB or CD?

   (1) AB is the diameter of a circle with an area of 4 square inches.
   (2) CD is the diagonal of a square of side AB.

6. Is Sam a policeman?

   (1) A man is a policeman only if he has passed the necessary test.
   (2) Sam has passed the policeman's test.

7. How long does it take John to run one mile?

   (1) Charlie takes five minutes to run a mile.
   (2) John finishes a one-mile race five hundred feet ahead of Charlie.

8. At what time did Jerry arrive at the theater?

   (1) He left his house at 6:30 P.M.
   (2) He arrived five minutes late for the play which took three hours altogether.

9. Is ABCD a rectangle?

   (1) Angle ABD + angle BDC= 108°
   (2) BD=½(AB+AD)

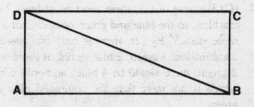

10. In the diagram on the following page, find the number of degrees in angle x.

    (1) AO=OB
    (2) AB=OC

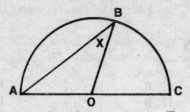

11. What is the area of circle *O?*

    (1) ABC is a right triangle
    (2) AB=10 inches.

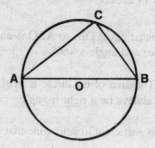

12. What day of the month is it?

    (1) Last Thursday was September 30.
    (2) In three days it will be October 7.

13. A man wants to cover his floor with one foot
square tiles. All the tiles will be green except
those on the outside border of the room. If the
room is rectangular, how many green tiles must
he use?

    (1) The room measures 8′×14′.
    (2) There are 38 border tiles.

14. How many boys are there in this class?

    (1) There are eight girls in the class.
    (2) The number of boys in the class is equal to
twice the number of girls minus three times
the number of boys.

15. A boy can swim two miles per hour in still water.
What is his speed relative to the shore, in a river?

    (1) The river's current flows at 3 miles per hour.

    (2) The boy swims "with" (in the same direction as) the current.

16. What is the value of *p?*

    (1) $p=4q$
    (2) $q=4p$

17. Is ABCD a square?

    (1) AB is parallel to CD.
    (2) BCD is an equilateral triangle.

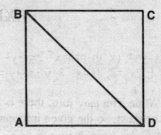

18. If it snows today, will I go to the movies?

    (1) If I don't go to the movies, then it is not
snowing.
    (2) Whenever I go to the movies, it snows.

19. What is the value of x, if $x=4A+3B+C$? (A, B,
and C are whole numbers.)

    (1) $A=2+C-3B$
    (2) $B=1-\dfrac{4A+C}{3}$

20. Find the length of line AB.

    (1) DE is parallel to AB
    (2) BE=DC and AD= CE

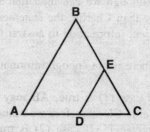

ANSWER KEY

1. C	6. E	11. B	16. C
2. E	7. E	12. B	17. B
3. A	8. E	13. A	18. A
4. A	9. B	14. C	19. B
5. B	10. B	15. C	20. E

EXPLANATORY ANSWERS

1. **(C)** $x-y=4$; $(x-y)^2=16=x^2-2xy+y^2$
   $xy=4$; $2xy=8$; $16=x^2-8+y^2$; $x^2+y^2=24$

2. **(E)** While Tim *may* join, there is no implication that he must, so the given information is insufficient.

3. **(A)** Since all squares have four equal sides, (1) is sufficient. (2) provides only that ABCD be a parallelogram.

4. **(A)** If $xy=49$, and both x and y are greater than 3, the only possibility is $x=y=7$.

5. **(B)** The diagonal of a square is always longer than one side.

6. **(E)** *Only* here changes the entire sense of (1). If *only* were omitted, the correct answer would be C, but as the question stands, Sam might have passed the test and then decided to become a doctor instead.

7. **(E)** Although we can infer that John is a faster runner than Charlie, the statements do not give sufficient information to answer the question.

8. **(E)** There is not enough information given.

9. **(B)** If case (1) is true, AB may or may not be parallel to CD, therefore we cannot tell if ABCD is a rectangle. If case (2) is true, BD will be shorter than AB or AD, since it is the average of the two, so A cannot be a right angle.

10. **(B)** If AB=OC, since AO, BO, and CO are radii,

AO *must* equal OB, so ABO is an equilateral triangle, and angle $x=60°$.

11. **(B)** The area of the circle is $\frac{1}{4}\pi(10)^2$, but ABC will always be a right triangle.

12. **(B)** is sufficient to determine that it is October 4.

13. **(A)** If the room measures $8'\times14'$, then there will be 6×12, or 72.

14. **(C)** This can be solved by elementary algebra, $x=$ number of boys, $x=2\times8-3x$. There are four boys.

15. **(C)** It is important that the boy's direction be given, as in (2). His speed relative to the shore is five miles per hour.

16. **(C)** These two can be true only if $p=q=0$.

17. **(B)** (2) makes it impossible for ABCD to be a square.

18. **(A)** Reason as follows: "If I don't go to the movies, then it is not snowing . . . but it is snowing, so therefore I will go to the movies."

19. **(B)** Multiply equation (2) by 3, and it resolves to $x=3$.

20. **(E)** It is impossible to find the length of any line when we have no basis for comparison—the picture may be increased proportionally without contradicting either stipulation.

Part Five

Final Practice Examination

FINAL PRACTICE EXAMINATION

This is your Final ARCO Practice Examination, similar to the Graduate Management Admission Test you are going to take in structure, length, and level of difficulty. The question-types and examination sections approximate those of the actual GMAT.

Take this examination after: (1) taking all the other Practice Examinations, (2) reviewing your performance, and (3) studying the review sections. Take this examination as if you were taking the real test. Follow all instructions and observe the time limits indicated. Remember to mark all your answers on the Answer Sheet provided, which is similar to the one you will find on the actual examination.

An Answer Key and Explanatory Answers for every question in the Final Practice Examination are provided at the end of the exam. Check your answers; your score on this exam will give you an approximate idea of how well you will do on the actual GMAT.

The total time allowed for this test is 3 hours.

ANALYSIS AND TIMETABLE: FINAL EXAMINATION

Subject Tested	Time Allowed
READING RECALL	30 minutes
DATA INTERPRETATION	25 minutes
DATA SUFFICIENCY	30 minutes
PRACTICAL BUSINESS JUDGMENT	20 minutes
ENGLISH USAGE	20 minutes
PRACTICAL BUSINESS JUDGMENT	20 minutes
VALIDITY OF CONCLUSION	35 minutes

ANSWER SHEET
FINAL PRACTICE EXAMINATION

SECTION I: READING RECALL

1 Ⓐ Ⓑ Ⓒ Ⓓ Ⓔ	6 Ⓐ Ⓑ Ⓒ Ⓓ Ⓔ	11 Ⓐ Ⓑ Ⓒ Ⓓ Ⓔ	16 Ⓐ Ⓑ Ⓒ Ⓓ Ⓔ	21 Ⓐ Ⓑ Ⓒ Ⓓ Ⓔ
2 Ⓐ Ⓑ Ⓒ Ⓓ Ⓔ	7 Ⓐ Ⓑ Ⓒ Ⓓ Ⓔ	12 Ⓐ Ⓑ Ⓒ Ⓓ Ⓔ	17 Ⓐ Ⓑ Ⓒ Ⓓ Ⓔ	22 Ⓐ Ⓑ Ⓒ Ⓓ Ⓔ
3 Ⓐ Ⓑ Ⓒ Ⓓ Ⓔ	8 Ⓐ Ⓑ Ⓒ Ⓓ Ⓔ	13 Ⓐ Ⓑ Ⓒ Ⓓ Ⓔ	18 Ⓐ Ⓑ Ⓒ Ⓓ Ⓔ	23 Ⓐ Ⓑ Ⓒ Ⓓ Ⓔ
4 Ⓐ Ⓑ Ⓒ Ⓓ Ⓔ	9 Ⓐ Ⓑ Ⓒ Ⓓ Ⓔ	14 Ⓐ Ⓑ Ⓒ Ⓓ Ⓔ	19 Ⓐ Ⓑ Ⓒ Ⓓ Ⓔ	24 Ⓐ Ⓑ Ⓒ Ⓓ Ⓔ
5 Ⓐ Ⓑ Ⓒ Ⓓ Ⓔ	10 Ⓐ Ⓑ Ⓒ Ⓓ Ⓔ	15 Ⓐ Ⓑ Ⓒ Ⓓ Ⓔ	20 Ⓐ Ⓑ Ⓒ Ⓓ Ⓔ	25 Ⓐ Ⓑ Ⓒ Ⓓ Ⓔ

SECTION II: DATA INTERPRETATION

1 Ⓐ Ⓑ Ⓒ Ⓓ Ⓔ	6 Ⓐ Ⓑ Ⓒ Ⓓ Ⓔ	11 Ⓐ Ⓑ Ⓒ Ⓓ Ⓔ	16 Ⓐ Ⓑ Ⓒ Ⓓ Ⓔ	21 Ⓐ Ⓑ Ⓒ Ⓓ Ⓔ
2 Ⓐ Ⓑ Ⓒ Ⓓ Ⓔ	7 Ⓐ Ⓑ Ⓒ Ⓓ Ⓔ	12 Ⓐ Ⓑ Ⓒ Ⓓ Ⓔ	17 Ⓐ Ⓑ Ⓒ Ⓓ Ⓔ	22 Ⓐ Ⓑ Ⓒ Ⓓ Ⓔ
3 Ⓐ Ⓑ Ⓒ Ⓓ Ⓔ	8 Ⓐ Ⓑ Ⓒ Ⓓ Ⓔ	13 Ⓐ Ⓑ Ⓒ Ⓓ Ⓔ	18 Ⓐ Ⓑ Ⓒ Ⓓ Ⓔ	23 Ⓐ Ⓑ Ⓒ Ⓓ Ⓔ
4 Ⓐ Ⓑ Ⓒ Ⓓ Ⓔ	9 Ⓐ Ⓑ Ⓒ Ⓓ Ⓔ	14 Ⓐ Ⓑ Ⓒ Ⓓ Ⓔ	19 Ⓐ Ⓑ Ⓒ Ⓓ Ⓔ	24 Ⓐ Ⓑ Ⓒ Ⓓ Ⓔ
5 Ⓐ Ⓑ Ⓒ Ⓓ Ⓔ	10 Ⓐ Ⓑ Ⓒ Ⓓ Ⓔ	15 Ⓐ Ⓑ Ⓒ Ⓓ Ⓔ	20 Ⓐ Ⓑ Ⓒ Ⓓ Ⓔ	25 Ⓐ Ⓑ Ⓒ Ⓓ Ⓔ

SECTION III: PRACTICAL BUSINESS JUDGMENT

1 Ⓐ Ⓑ Ⓒ Ⓓ Ⓔ	5 Ⓐ Ⓑ Ⓒ Ⓓ Ⓔ	9 Ⓐ Ⓑ Ⓒ Ⓓ Ⓔ	13 Ⓐ Ⓑ Ⓒ Ⓓ Ⓔ	17 Ⓐ Ⓑ Ⓒ Ⓓ Ⓔ
2 Ⓐ Ⓑ Ⓒ Ⓓ Ⓔ	6 Ⓐ Ⓑ Ⓒ Ⓓ Ⓔ	10 Ⓐ Ⓑ Ⓒ Ⓓ Ⓔ	14 Ⓐ Ⓑ Ⓒ Ⓓ Ⓔ	18 Ⓐ Ⓑ Ⓒ Ⓓ Ⓔ
3 Ⓐ Ⓑ Ⓒ Ⓓ Ⓔ	7 Ⓐ Ⓑ Ⓒ Ⓓ Ⓔ	11 Ⓐ Ⓑ Ⓒ Ⓓ Ⓔ	15 Ⓐ Ⓑ Ⓒ Ⓓ Ⓔ	19 Ⓐ Ⓑ Ⓒ Ⓓ Ⓔ
4 Ⓐ Ⓑ Ⓒ Ⓓ Ⓔ	8 Ⓐ Ⓑ Ⓒ Ⓓ Ⓔ	12 Ⓐ Ⓑ Ⓒ Ⓓ Ⓔ	16 Ⓐ Ⓑ Ⓒ Ⓓ Ⓔ	20 Ⓐ Ⓑ Ⓒ Ⓓ Ⓔ

SECTION IV: DATA SUFFICIENCY

1 Ⓐ Ⓑ Ⓒ Ⓓ Ⓔ	6 Ⓐ Ⓑ Ⓒ Ⓓ Ⓔ	11 Ⓐ Ⓑ Ⓒ Ⓓ Ⓔ	16 Ⓐ Ⓑ Ⓒ Ⓓ Ⓔ	21 Ⓐ Ⓑ Ⓒ Ⓓ Ⓔ
2 Ⓐ Ⓑ Ⓒ Ⓓ Ⓔ	7 Ⓐ Ⓑ Ⓒ Ⓓ Ⓔ	12 Ⓐ Ⓑ Ⓒ Ⓓ Ⓔ	17 Ⓐ Ⓑ Ⓒ Ⓓ Ⓔ	22 Ⓐ Ⓑ Ⓒ Ⓓ Ⓔ
3 Ⓐ Ⓑ Ⓒ Ⓓ Ⓔ	8 Ⓐ Ⓑ Ⓒ Ⓓ Ⓔ	13 Ⓐ Ⓑ Ⓒ Ⓓ Ⓔ	18 Ⓐ Ⓑ Ⓒ Ⓓ Ⓔ	23 Ⓐ Ⓑ Ⓒ Ⓓ Ⓔ
4 Ⓐ Ⓑ Ⓒ Ⓓ Ⓔ	9 Ⓐ Ⓑ Ⓒ Ⓓ Ⓔ	14 Ⓐ Ⓑ Ⓒ Ⓓ Ⓔ	19 Ⓐ Ⓑ Ⓒ Ⓓ Ⓔ	24 Ⓐ Ⓑ Ⓒ Ⓓ Ⓔ
5 Ⓐ Ⓑ Ⓒ Ⓓ Ⓔ	10 Ⓐ Ⓑ Ⓒ Ⓓ Ⓔ	15 Ⓐ Ⓑ Ⓒ Ⓓ Ⓔ	20 Ⓐ Ⓑ Ⓒ Ⓓ Ⓔ	25 Ⓐ Ⓑ Ⓒ Ⓓ Ⓔ

SECTION V: ENGLISH USAGE

1 Ⓐ Ⓑ Ⓒ Ⓓ Ⓔ	7 Ⓐ Ⓑ Ⓒ Ⓓ Ⓔ	13 Ⓐ Ⓑ Ⓒ Ⓓ Ⓔ	19 Ⓐ Ⓑ Ⓒ Ⓓ Ⓔ	25 Ⓐ Ⓑ Ⓒ Ⓓ Ⓔ
2 Ⓐ Ⓑ Ⓒ Ⓓ Ⓔ	8 Ⓐ Ⓑ Ⓒ Ⓓ Ⓔ	14 Ⓐ Ⓑ Ⓒ Ⓓ Ⓔ	20 Ⓐ Ⓑ Ⓒ Ⓓ Ⓔ	26 Ⓐ Ⓑ Ⓒ Ⓓ Ⓔ
3 Ⓐ Ⓑ Ⓒ Ⓓ Ⓔ	9 Ⓐ Ⓑ Ⓒ Ⓓ Ⓔ	15 Ⓐ Ⓑ Ⓒ Ⓓ Ⓔ	21 Ⓐ Ⓑ Ⓒ Ⓓ Ⓔ	27 Ⓐ Ⓑ Ⓒ Ⓓ Ⓔ
4 Ⓐ Ⓑ Ⓒ Ⓓ Ⓔ	10 Ⓐ Ⓑ Ⓒ Ⓓ Ⓔ	16 Ⓐ Ⓑ Ⓒ Ⓓ Ⓔ	22 Ⓐ Ⓑ Ⓒ Ⓓ Ⓔ	28 Ⓐ Ⓑ Ⓒ Ⓓ Ⓔ
5 Ⓐ Ⓑ Ⓒ Ⓓ Ⓔ	11 Ⓐ Ⓑ Ⓒ Ⓓ Ⓔ	17 Ⓐ Ⓑ Ⓒ Ⓓ Ⓔ	23 Ⓐ Ⓑ Ⓒ Ⓓ Ⓔ	29 Ⓐ Ⓑ Ⓒ Ⓓ Ⓔ
6 Ⓐ Ⓑ Ⓒ Ⓓ Ⓔ	12 Ⓐ Ⓑ Ⓒ Ⓓ Ⓔ	18 Ⓐ Ⓑ Ⓒ Ⓓ Ⓔ	24 Ⓐ Ⓑ Ⓒ Ⓓ Ⓔ	30 Ⓐ Ⓑ Ⓒ Ⓓ Ⓔ

SECTION VI: PRACTICAL BUSINESS JUDGMENT

1 Ⓐ Ⓑ Ⓒ Ⓓ Ⓔ	5 Ⓐ Ⓑ Ⓒ Ⓓ Ⓔ	9 Ⓐ Ⓑ Ⓒ Ⓓ Ⓔ	13 Ⓐ Ⓑ Ⓒ Ⓓ Ⓔ	17 Ⓐ Ⓑ Ⓒ Ⓓ Ⓔ
2 Ⓐ Ⓑ Ⓒ Ⓓ Ⓔ	6 Ⓐ Ⓑ Ⓒ Ⓓ Ⓔ	10 Ⓐ Ⓑ Ⓒ Ⓓ Ⓔ	14 Ⓐ Ⓑ Ⓒ Ⓓ Ⓔ	18 Ⓐ Ⓑ Ⓒ Ⓓ Ⓔ
3 Ⓐ Ⓑ Ⓒ Ⓓ Ⓔ	7 Ⓐ Ⓑ Ⓒ Ⓓ Ⓔ	11 Ⓐ Ⓑ Ⓒ Ⓓ Ⓔ	15 Ⓐ Ⓑ Ⓒ Ⓓ Ⓔ	19 Ⓐ Ⓑ Ⓒ Ⓓ Ⓔ
4 Ⓐ Ⓑ Ⓒ Ⓓ Ⓔ	8 Ⓐ Ⓑ Ⓒ Ⓓ Ⓔ	12 Ⓐ Ⓑ Ⓒ Ⓓ Ⓔ	16 Ⓐ Ⓑ Ⓒ Ⓓ Ⓔ	20 Ⓐ Ⓑ Ⓒ Ⓓ Ⓔ

SECTION VII: VALIDITY OF CONCLUSION

1 Ⓐ Ⓑ Ⓒ Ⓓ Ⓔ	8 Ⓐ Ⓑ Ⓒ Ⓓ Ⓔ	15 Ⓐ Ⓑ Ⓒ Ⓓ Ⓔ	22 Ⓐ Ⓑ Ⓒ Ⓓ Ⓔ	29 Ⓐ Ⓑ Ⓒ Ⓓ Ⓔ	36 Ⓐ Ⓑ Ⓒ Ⓓ Ⓔ
2 Ⓐ Ⓑ Ⓒ Ⓓ Ⓔ	9 Ⓐ Ⓑ Ⓒ Ⓓ Ⓔ	16 Ⓐ Ⓑ Ⓒ Ⓓ Ⓔ	23 Ⓐ Ⓑ Ⓒ Ⓓ Ⓔ	30 Ⓐ Ⓑ Ⓒ Ⓓ Ⓔ	37 Ⓐ Ⓑ Ⓒ Ⓓ Ⓔ
3 Ⓐ Ⓑ Ⓒ Ⓓ Ⓔ	10 Ⓐ Ⓑ Ⓒ Ⓓ Ⓔ	17 Ⓐ Ⓑ Ⓒ Ⓓ Ⓔ	24 Ⓐ Ⓑ Ⓒ Ⓓ Ⓔ	31 Ⓐ Ⓑ Ⓒ Ⓓ Ⓔ	38 Ⓐ Ⓑ Ⓒ Ⓓ Ⓔ
4 Ⓐ Ⓑ Ⓒ Ⓓ Ⓔ	11 Ⓐ Ⓑ Ⓒ Ⓓ Ⓔ	18 Ⓐ Ⓑ Ⓒ Ⓓ Ⓔ	25 Ⓐ Ⓑ Ⓒ Ⓓ Ⓔ	32 Ⓐ Ⓑ Ⓒ Ⓓ Ⓔ	39 Ⓐ Ⓑ Ⓒ Ⓓ Ⓔ
5 Ⓐ Ⓑ Ⓒ Ⓓ Ⓔ	12 Ⓐ Ⓑ Ⓒ Ⓓ Ⓔ	19 Ⓐ Ⓑ Ⓒ Ⓓ Ⓔ	26 Ⓐ Ⓑ Ⓒ Ⓓ Ⓔ	33 Ⓐ Ⓑ Ⓒ Ⓓ Ⓔ	
6 Ⓐ Ⓑ Ⓒ Ⓓ Ⓔ	13 Ⓐ Ⓑ Ⓒ Ⓓ Ⓔ	20 Ⓐ Ⓑ Ⓒ Ⓓ Ⓔ	27 Ⓐ Ⓑ Ⓒ Ⓓ Ⓔ	34 Ⓐ Ⓑ Ⓒ Ⓓ Ⓔ	
7 Ⓐ Ⓑ Ⓒ Ⓓ Ⓔ	14 Ⓐ Ⓑ Ⓒ Ⓓ Ⓔ	21 Ⓐ Ⓑ Ⓒ Ⓓ Ⓔ	28 Ⓐ Ⓑ Ⓒ Ⓓ Ⓔ	35 Ⓐ Ⓑ Ⓒ Ⓓ Ⓔ	

SECTION I: READING RECALL

30 Minutes

25 Questions

DIRECTIONS: You are allowed 15 minutes to closely read the following passages. Afterwards you will be asked to recall certain ideas and facts about the passages. You are not allowed to refer back to the passages.

Passage 1

A Polish proverb claims that fish, to taste right, should swim three times—in water, in butter and in wine. The early efforts of the basic scientists in the food industry were directed at improving the preparation, preservation, and distribution of safe and nutritious food. Our memories of certain foodstuffs eaten during the Second World War suggest that, although these might have been safe and nutritious, they certainly did not taste right nor were they particularly appetizing in appearance or smell. This neglect of the sensory appeal of foods is happily becoming a thing of the past. Indeed, in 1957 the University of California considered the subject of sufficient importance to warrant the setting-up of a course in the analysis of foods by sensory methods. The book, *Principles of Sensory Evaluation of Food,* grew out of this course. The authors hope that it will be useful to food technologists in industry and also to others engaged in research into the problem of sensory evaluation of foods.

The scope of the book is well illustrated by the chapter headings: "The Sense of Taste"; "Olfaction"; "Visual, Auditory, Tactile, and Other Senses"; and "Factors Influencing Sensory Measurements." There are further chapters on panel testing, difference and directional difference tests, quantity-quality evaluation, consumer studies, statistical procedures (including design of experiments), and physical and chemical tests. An attempt has clearly been made to collect every possible piece of information which might be useful, more than one thousand five hundred references being quoted. As a result, the

book seems at first sight to be an exhaustive and critically useful review of the literature. This it certainly is, but this is by no means its only achievement, for there are many suggestions for further lines of research, and the discursive passages are crisply provocative of new ideas and new ways of looking at established findings.

Of particular interest is the weight given to the psychological aspects of perception, both objectively and subjectively. The relation between stimuli and perception is well covered, and includes a valuable discussion of the uses and disadvantages of the Weber fraction in the evaluation of differences. It is interesting to find that in spite of many attempts to separate and define the modalities of taste, nothing better has been achieved than the familiar classification into sweet, sour, salty and bitter. Nor is there as yet any clear-cut evidence of the physiological nature of the taste stimulus. With regard to smell, systems of classification are of little value because of the extraordinary sensitivity of the nose and because the response to the stimulus is so subjective. The authors suggest that a classification based on the size, shape and electronic status of the molecule involved merits further investigation, as does the theoretical proposition that weak physical binding of the stimulant molecule to the receptor site is a necessary part of the mechanism of stimulation.

Apart from taste and smell, there are many other components of perception of the sensations from food in the mouth. The basic modalities of pain, cold, warmth and touch, together with vibration sense, discrimination and localization may all play a part, as, of course, does auditory reception of bone-conducted vibratory stimuli from the teeth when eating crisp or crunchy foods. In this connection the authors rightly point out that this type of stimulus requires much more investigation, suggesting that a start might be made by using subjects afflicted with various forms of deafness. It is, of course, well known that extraneous noise may alter discrimination, and the attention of the authors is directed to the work of Prof. H. J. Eysenck on the ''stimulus hunger'' of extroverts and the ''stimulus avoidance'' of introverts. (It is perhaps unfair to speculate, not that the authors do, that certain breakfast cereals rely on sound volume to drown any deficiencies in flavor, or that the noisier types are mainly eaten by extroverts.)

Passage 2

The future of the American project to drill a hole through the mantle of the Earth now seems in doubt. Recently, the Committee on Science and Astronautics of the U.S. House of Representatives jibed at approving the new estimate of 28 million dollars for the cost of completing the Mohole. It remains to be seen whether the corresponding Senate committee will take the same view, but the prospects are not encouraging. For even if the Senate should consider that present costs are justifiable, the difference between the House and the Senate would somehow have to be reconciled before work could go ahead. Nobody will be surprised that those most closely associated with the Mohole project have been cast down by this latest twist in the long tortuous history of this project.

Two separate questions arise. The wisdom of the House Committee's decision is, for example, open to question, chiefly because the Mohole project is now so far advanced. A technique for drilling deep holes in the ocean floor has been developed, and orders for the drilling barges have been placed. By canceling now, Congress will save only a proportion of the total cost of the Mohole. It is capricious, to say the least of it, for the politicians to pull hard on the purse-strings at this late stage. It would have been much more to the point if they had taken a hard skeptical look at the project four years ago, for there was then good reason for believing that the drilling program was being pushed ahead too quickly, and with too little preliminary study. A more deliberate program might have been easier to contain within the bounds of a public budget, and might have been more rewarding as well. But Congress cannot put the clock back to the beginning by a crude cancellation.

The second issue is even more alarming. Hitherto, Congress has not exercised to any important extent its constitutional right to arbitrate on the fine details of scientific programs financed by public money. It is true that plans for building—and siting—big particle accelerators have usually been examined in detail by Congressional committees, and the National Institutes of Health have occasionally been showered with more money than they could usefully spend, but the great public agencies have usually been allowed to manage their own affairs within the framework of a budget agreed by Congress. Though the details of the programs of the National Science Foundation have been examined by Congress in the process of accounting for the spending of public money, Congress has usually trusted the judgment of its scientific public servants on the disposition of these funds. On the face of it, the Mohole decision looks like a departure from this practice. It could be a dangerous precedent.

Passage 3

Hong Kong's size and association with Britain, and its position in relation to its neighbours in the Pacific, particularly China, determine the course of conduct it has to pursue. Hong Kong is no more than a molecule in the great substance of China. It was part of the large province of Kwangtung, which came under Chinese sovereignty about 200 B.C., in the period of the Han Dynasty. In size, China exceeds 3¾ million square miles, and it has a population estimated to be greater than 700 million. Its very immensity has contributed to its survival over a great period of time. Without probing into the origins of its remarkable civilization, we can mark that it has a continuous history of more than 4,000 years. And, through the centuries, it has always been able to defend itself in depth, trading space for time.

In this setting Hong Kong is minute. Its area is a mere 398 square miles, about one two-hundredth part of the province of which it was previously part, Kwangtung. Fortunately, however, we cannot dispose of Hong Kong as simply as this. There are components in its complex and unique existence which affect its character and, out of all physical proportion, increase its significance.

Amongst these, the most potent are its people, their impressive achievements in partnership with British administration and enterprise, and the rule of law which protects personal freedom in the British tradition.

What is Hong Kong, and what is it trying to do? In 1841 Britain acquired outright, by treaty, the Island of Hong Kong, to use as a base for trade with China, and, in 1860, the Kowloon Peninsula, lying immediately to the north, to complete the perimeter of the superb harbour, which has determined Hong Kong's history and character. In 1898 Britain leased for 99 years a hinterland on the mainland of China to a depth of less than 25 miles, much of it very hilly. Hong Kong prospered as a centre of trade with China, expanding steadily until it fell to the Japanese in 1941. Although the rigors of a severe occupation set everything back, the Liberation in 1945 was the herald of an immediate and spectacular recovery in trade. People poured into the Colony, and this flow became a flood during 1949–50, when the Chinese National Government met defeat at the hands of the Communists. Three-quarters of a million people entered the Colony at that stage, bringing the total population to 2⅓ million. Today the population is more than 3¾ million.

Very soon two things affected commercial expansion. First, the Chinese Government restricted Hong Kong's exports to China, because she feared unsettled internal conditions, mounting inflation and a weakness in her exchange position. Secondly, during the Korean War, the United Nations imposed an embargo on imports into China, the main source of Hong Kong's livelihood. This was a crisis for Hong Kong; its China trade went overnight, and, by this time, it had over one million refugees on its hands. But something dramatic happened. Simply stated, it was this: Hong Kong switched from trading to manufacture. It did it so quickly that few people, even in Hong Kong, were aware at the time of what exactly was happening, and the rest of the world was not quickly convinced of Hong Kong's transformation into a centre of manufactures. Its limited industry began to expand rapidly and, although more slowly, to diversify, and it owed not a little to the immigrants from Shanghai, who brought their capital, their experience and expertise with them. Today Hong Kong must be unique amongst so-called developing countries in the dependence of its economy on industrialization. No less than 40 percent of the labor force is engaged in the manufacturing industries; and of the products from these Hong Kong exports 90 percent, and it does this despite the fact that its industry is exposed to the full competition of the industrially mature nations. The variety of its goods now ranges widely from the products of shipbuilding and ship-breaking, through textiles and plastics, to airconditioners, transistor radios and cameras.

More than 70 percent of its exports are either manufactured or partly manufactured in Hong Kong, and the value of its domestic exports in 1964 was about 750 million dollars. In recent years these figures have been increasing at about 15 percent a year. America is the largest market, taking 25 percent of the value of Hong Kong's exports; then follows the United Kingdom, Malaysia, West Germany, Japan, Canada and Australia; but all countries come within the scope of its marketing.

Passage 4

Do students learn from programmed instruction? The research leaves us in no doubt of this. They do, indeed, learn. They learn from linear programs, from branching programs built on the Skinnerian model, from scrambled books of the Crowder type, from Pressey review tests with immediate knowledge of results, from programs on machines or programs in texts. Many kinds of students learn—college, high school, secondary, primary, preschool, adult, professional, skilled labor, clerical employees, military, deaf, retarded, imprisoned—every kind of student that programs have been tried on. Using programs, these students are able to learn mathematics and science at different levels, foreign languages, English language correctness, the details of the U.S. Constitution, spelling, electronics, computer science, psychology, statistics, business skills, reading skills, instrument flying rules, and many other subjects. The limits of the topics which can be studied efficiently by means of programs are not yet known.

For each of the kinds of subject matter and the kinds of student mentioned above, experiments have demonstrated that a considerable amount of learning can be derived from programs; this learning has been measured either by comparing pre– and post-tests or the time and trials needed to reach a set criterion of performance. But the question, how well do students learn from programs as compared to how well they learn from other kinds of instruction, we cannot answer quite so confidently.

Experimental psychologists typically do not take very seriously the evaluative experiments in which learning from programs is compared with learning from conventional teaching. Such experiments are doubtless useful, they say, for school administrators or teachers to prove to themselves (or their boards of education) that programs work. But whereas one can describe fairly well the characteristics of a program, can one describe the characteristics of a classroom teaching situation so that the result of the comparison will have any generality? What kind of teacher is being compared to what kind of program? Furthermore, these early evaluative experiments with programs are likely to suffer from the Hawthorne effect: that is to say, students are in the spotlight when testing something new, and are challenged to do well. It is very hard to make allowance for this effect. Therefore, the evaluative tests may be useful administratively, say many of the experimenters, but do not contribute much to science, and should properly be kept for private use.

These objections are well taken. And yet, do they justify us in ignoring the evaluative studies? The great strength of a program is that it permits the student to learn efficiently by himself. Is it not therefore important to know how much and what kind of skills, concepts, insights, or attitudes he can learn by himself from a program as compared to what he can learn from a teacher? Admittedly, this is a very difficult and complex research problem, but that should not keep us from trying to solve it.

QUESTIONS

DIRECTIONS: You have 15 minutes to answer the following questions based upon the preceding passages. You are not to refer back to the passages.

Passage 1

1. The reviewer uses a Polish proverb at the beginning of the article in order to

   (A) introduce, in an interesting manner, the discussion of food
   (B) show the connection between food and nationality
   (C) indicate that there are various ways to prepare food
   (D) bring out the difference between American and Polish cooking
   (E) impress upon the reader the food value of fish

2. The reviewer's appraisal of *Principles of Sensory Evaluation of Food* is one of

   (A) mixed feelings
   (B) indifference
   (C) derogation
   (D) high praise
   (E) faint praise

3. The article points out that

   (A) many people suffered from food poisoning during World War II
   (B) at least one institution of higher learning has conducted a course in how to enjoy food
   (C) what is one man's poison is another man's meat

   (D) you must have a good sense of smell to enjoy good food
   (E) in the forties, food, in many cases, was unappetizing

4. The Weber fraction was originated by

   (A) Max Weber (1881–1961), an American painter
   (B) Ernest Heinrich Weber (1795–1878), German physiologist
   (C) Baron Karl Maria Friedrich Ernest von Weber (1786–1826), German composer
   (D) Max Weber (1864–1920), German political economist and sociologist
   (E) George Weber (1808–1888), a German historian

5. The writer of the article does *not* express the view, either directly or by implication, that

   (A) more sharply defined classifications of taste are needed than those which are used at present
   (B) more research should be done regarding the molecular constituency of food
   (C) food values are objectively determined by an expert "smeller"
   (D) psychological considerations would play an important part in food evaluation
   (E) temperature is an important factor in the appraisal of food

6. The authors of the book suggest the use of deaf subjects because

   (A) deaf people are generally introversive
   (B) all types of subjects should be used to insure the validity of an experiment

(C) they are more objective in their attitude than normal subjects would be when it comes to food experimentation

(D) the auditory sense is an important factor in food evaluation

(E) they are more fastidious in their choice of foods

7. The chapter headings listed for *Principles of Sensory Evaluation of Food* make no specific reference to the sense of

(A) smell
(B) sight
(C) touch
(D) hearing
(E) muscular movement

Passage 2

8. The mantle of the Earth is

(A) the Earth's crust
(B) close to the Earth's center
(C) approximately halfway between the surface of the Earth and its center
(D) about fifteen miles from the Earth's surface
(E) none of the above can be determined from the passage

9. It is true that

(A) the total appropriation for the Mohole project was between twenty-five and thirty million dollars
(B) the Committee on Science and Astronautics is in favor of continuing the Mohole project
(C) both houses of Congress see eye-to-eye on the completion of the Mohole project
(D) before resumption of the Mohole project, it will be necessary to start ordering drilling equipment
(E) Congressmen demonstrated indelicacy in their Mohole decision-making

10. The article implies that

(A) the Senate favors scientific research more than the House of Representatives
(B) the National Science Foundation is a Congressional Committee
(C) the legislators are far from frugal in their allotment for the Mohole project

(D) the federal lawmakers have been manifesting an undemocratic attitude
(E) the House of Representatives has employed a watchdog attitude toward scientific expenditures whereas the Senate has been permissive.

11. The reader may infer that

(A) the project was started about two years ago
(B) the project has been discontinued because of the dangers involved
(C) the decision to continue the project is the responsibility of the lower House—not the upper House of Congress
(D) there is·a question of unconstitutionality in disbanding the project
(E) the project was poorly planned at the start

12. The word "siting" used in the passage

(A) is a misspelling
(B) is a variant spelling
(C) means locating
(D) means setting
(E) means sorting

13. "Mohole" is likely derived from

(A) an Indian tribe
(B) more hole
(C) Mohorovicic, Yugoslavian geologist
(D) a follower of Mohammed
(E) Bohenjo-Daro, an ancient civilization

Passage 3

14. The article gives the impression that

(A) English rule constituted an important factor in Hong Kong economy
(B) refugees from China were a liability to the financial status of Hong Kong
(C) Hong Kong has taken a developmental course comparable to that of the new African nations
(D) British forces used their military might imperialistically to acquire Hong Kong
(E) there is a serious dearth of skilled workers in Hong Kong

15. The economic stability of Hong Kong is mostly attributable to

(A) its shipbuilding activity
(B) businessmen and workers from Shanghai who settled in Hong Kong
(C) its political separation from China
(D) its exports to China
(E) a change in the area of business concentration

16. Hong Kong's commerce was adversely affected by

(A) the Han Dynasty
(B) Japanese occupation
(C) British administration
(D) the defeat of the Chinese National Government
(E) the conversion from manufacturing to trading

17. Hong Kong's population is about _____ that of China.

(A) 1/50
(B) 1/100
(C) 1/200
(D) 1/500
(E) 1/1000

18. The author states or implies that

(A) the United States imports more goods from Hong Kong than all the other nations combined
(B) about three-quarters of its exports are made exclusively in Hong Kong
(C) Malaysia, Canada, and West Germany provide excellent markets for Hong Kong goods
(D) approximately one-half of the Hong Kong workers are involved with manufacturing
(E) the United Nations has consistently cooperated to improve the economy of Hong Kong

19. Hong Kong first came under Chinese rule approximately

(A) a century ago
(B) eight centuries ago
(C) fourteen centuries ago
(D) twenty-one centuries ago
(E) forty centuries ago

Passage 4

20. The word Skinnerian refers to

(A) a linguistic phenomenon
(B) a nineteenth century textbook
(C) a psychologist
(D) a television program
(E) a culinary device

21. The article implies that programmed instruction

(A) is inferior to other instruction
(B) is superior to other instruction
(C) is beneficial regardless of the type of programming used
(D) is best for certain educational levels
(E) is probably of temporary duration

22. Psychologists view the results of program experiments

(A) lightly
(B) enthusiastically
(C) with distaste
(D) with complete acceptance
(E) with risibility

23. The article indicates that, with programmed instruction, the teacher

(A) may be dispensed with
(B) may prove of negative value
(C) and principal must work together
(D) must be superior to get results
(E) remains an important factor

24. Programmed learning

(A) is a recent educational innovation
(B) has been used in our schools for many years
(C) is confined to teaching machines
(D) refers to a student's school program
(E) is always in linear form

25. The expression "scrambled books" refers to a program type in which the student

(A) eats while he learns
(B) learns in a disorganized manner
(C) learns by the Hawthorne effect
(D) is directed to different pages not in consecutive order
(E) must do complex research

Stop

END OF SECTION I. IF YOU HAVE ANY TIME LEFT, GO OVER YOUR WORK IN THIS SECTION ONLY. DO NOT WORK IN ANY OTHER SECTION OF THE TEST. WHEN YOUR TIME IS UP, GO ON TO THE NEXT SECTION.

SECTION II: DATA INTERPRETATION

25 Minutes

25 Questions

DIRECTIONS: The following questions are to test your ability to read and interpret graphs and tables. Answer each question based on your reading of the graphs or tables provided.

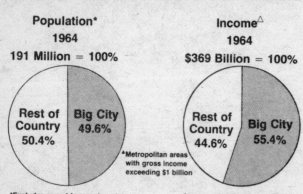

Big City△ Share of:

Population*
1964
191 Million = 100%

Income△
1964
$369 Billion = 100%

Rest of Country 50.4% | Big City 49.6%

Rest of Country 44.6% | Big City 55.4%

△Metropolitan areas with gross income exceeding $1 billion

*Excludes armed forces abroad

△Based on gross income reported on federal individual income tax

Questions 1–5

1. On a per capita basis, the average income of a big-city resident was approximately
   (A) $2,000
   (B) $2,150
   (C) $2,400
   (D) $2,700
   (E) $2,950

2. On a per capita basis, the average income for people living in the rest of the country was approximately
   (A) $1,000
   (B) $1,200
   (C) $1,400
   (D) $1,700
   (E) $2,000

3. The per capita income of big-city residents was what percent greater than the per capita income of people living in the rest of the country?

   (A) 2.5
   (B) 35.0
   (C) 8.4
   (Γ) 31.3
   (E) 26.5

4. Approximately how many degrees are there in the central angle of the sector of the Income circle for Big City Income?
   (A) 185
   (B) 190
   (C) 195
   (D) 200
   (E) 205

5. What is the approximate ratio of Big City Income to Income in the Rest of the Country?
   (A) 5:4
   (B) 7:5
   (C) 4:3
   (D) 3:2
   (E) 8:5

Questions 6–9

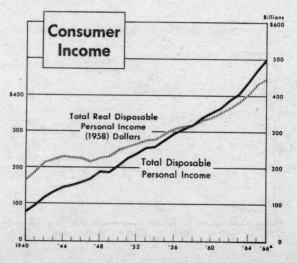

Consumer Income

Billions $600

500

$400 / 400

Total Real Disposable Personal Income (1958) Dollars

300 / 300

200 / 200

Total Disposable Personal Income

100 / 100

0
1940   '44   '48   '52   '56   '60   '64 '66△

356

6. In 1958, what was the total disposable personal income, in billions of dollars? (approx.)

   (A) 300
   (B) 325
   (C) 350
   (D) 370
   (E) 395

7. What was the percent increase in total disposable personal income from 1940 to 1966?

   (A) 500
   (B) 510
   (C) 525
   (D) 590
   (E) 610

8. What was the percent increase in total *real* disposable personal income from 1940 to 1966?

   (A) 110
   (B) 135
   (C) 150
   (D) 180
   (E) 210

9. If the population in 1966 was 200 million, what was the average per capita disposable personal income in 1966 dollars?

   (A) 2000
   (B) 2100
   (C) 2200
   (D) 2350
   (E) 2500

Questions 10–16 are based on the graph below.

U.S. GROSS NATIONAL PRODUCT 1935–1963

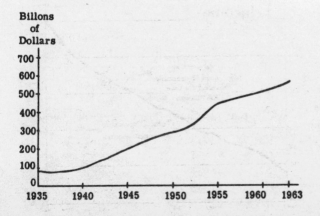

10. What is the approximate ratio of the Gross National Product in 1960 to that in 1940?

    (A) 5:1
    (B) 5:2
    (C) 6:1
    (D) 7:1
    (E) 7:2

11. The *least* increase in Gross National Product occurred in the five-year period commencing

    (A) 1955
    (B) 1950
    (C) 1945
    (D) 1940
    (E) 1935

12. The *greatest* increase in Gross National Product occurred in the five-year period commencing

    (A) 1955
    (B) 1950
    (C) 1945
    (D) 1940
    (E) 1935

13. What is the approximate percentage increase in GNP from 1940 to 1963?

    (A) 5.85
    (B) 4.85
    (C) 3.85
    (D) 485
    (E) 58.5

14. What is the approximate percentage increase in GNP from 1960 to 1963?

    (A) 30
    (B) 40
    (C) 65
    (D) 85
    (E) 17

15. If the GNP gains at the same rate from 1963 to 1966 as it did from 1960 to 1963, what is it in 1966? (approx.)

    (A) 600
    (B) 620
    (C) 640
    (D) 685
    (E) 700

16. The ratio of the GNP in 1945 to that in 1940 is approximately

    (A) 2:1
    (B) 3:1
    (C) 3:2
    (D) 4:3
    (E) 5:3

Answer Questions 17–19 with reference to the graph below.

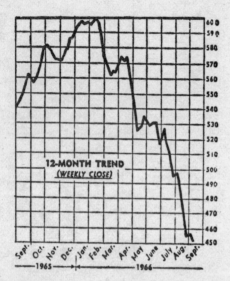

The graph shows the *New York Times* Industrial Stock Averages over a 12-month period.

17. In what month was the stock average highest?

    (A) December
    (B) January
    (C) February
    (D) October
    (E) April

18. In what month was the average lowest?

    (A) November
    (B) March
    (C) April
    (D) July
    (E) September

19. What is the approximate ratio of the highest stock average to lowest?

    (A) 4:3
    (B) 5:3
    (C) 2:1
    (D) 3:2

(E) 5:2

Questions 20–25 are to be answered with reference to the graph below.

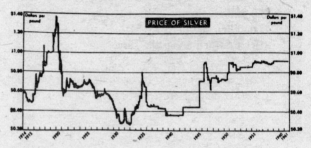

20. The decade in which there was the greatest variation in the price of silver is

    (A) 1920–30
    (B) 1930–40
    (C) 1940–50
    (D) 1950–60
    (E) not the kind of information given

21. The price of silver in 1934 was about what fraction of the price in 1931?

    (A) 1/2
    (B) 3/4
    (C) 1/1
    (D) 2/1
    (E) 4/3

22. Which of the following is *false,* according to the chart?

    (A) The price of silver was higher in 1947 than in 1937.
    (B) There was a sharp drop in the price of silver between 1920 and 1921.
    (C) Silver prices between 1943 and 1945 averaged $0.45 per pound.
    (D) The price of silver in 1960 was higher than that in any year from 1921 through 1931.
    (E) The three years with the three highest silver prices were 1920, 1935, 1946.

23. The price was most steady during the period

    (A) 1915–1917
    (B) 1929–1931
    (C) 1935–1937
    (D) 1943–1945
    (E) 1954–1956

24. The graph indicates that the price of silver, since 1940, has

    (A) risen slightly
    (B) risen sharply
    (C) fallen slightly
    (D) fallen sharply
    (E) remained about the same

25. A year during which the price was approximately the same as the year immediately preceding was

    (A) 1919
    (B) 1929
    (C) 1935
    (D) 1944
    (E) 1951

Stop

END OF SECTION II. IF YOU HAVE ANY TIME LEFT, GO OVER YOUR WORK IN THIS SECTION ONLY. DO NOT WORK IN ANY OTHER SECTION OF THE TEST. WHEN YOUR TIME IS UP, GO ON TO THE NEXT SECTION.

SECTION III: PRACTICAL BUSINESS JUDGMENT

20 Minutes
20 Questions

DIRECTIONS: This section consists of a reading selection which details a business situation followed by two sets of questions, data evaluation and data application. In the first set, data evaluation, you will be asked to classify certain of the facts presented in the passage on the basis of their importance. The second set, data application, will test your grasp of specific details of the situation.

Handborn, Inc. is a major publisher that specializes in scientific textbooks and magazines. A management consulting firm questions whether Handborn can make money from its trade book division. Cogent arguments are given for disbanding the division, based chiefly on its unprofitability and Handborn's lack of experience in this field. Peter Handborn believes there are valid arguments for its continued existence. He considers both sides of the question.

At the suggestion of the Board of Directors, Prudence, Inc., a management consulting firm, is called in to examine the structure of the entire company. After eight months of exhaustive study, it submits the following recommendations:

(1) Handborn, Inc. should divest itself of certain technical magazines. These are no longer profitable since they are aimed at trades and crafts declining due to technological advance.

(2) Handborn, Inc. has bought two companies within the last five years. They specialize in the home-study market. This is a rapidly growing area of the book field, and one that is likely to continue expanding. Many people find home-study courses desirable for polishing job skills and for keeping abreast of new developments. Prudence recommends that Handborn, Inc. seek further acquisitions in this segment of publishing.

(3) Handborn, Inc. has a substantial base in the college text market. However, it is weak in providing special materials for the two-year community colleges which are cropping up everywhere. Prudence, the management consulting firm, suggests that a separate division be created for books for these schools. Again, this represents an opportunity for expansion.

(4) Handborn, Inc. has been a major publisher in the elementary-high school field for only ten years. It has acquired several companies which operate independently. One division produces and sells textbooks, another audio-visual materials, a third scientific equipment, and another reading and skill tests. For the sake of efficiency, Prudence recommends that these divisions be merged. This would help to drive down costs, an important point, since these divisions have yielded little profit.

(5) Finally, and most important, it is urged that the trade division be discontinued, and that its books be sold to other companies. Prudence points out that trade books represent the most hazardous area of book publishing. Handborn, Inc. has neither sufficient skill nor knowledge to exploit the field successfully.

Peter Handborn considers the recommendations. He concurs that unprofitable technical magazines should be discontinued.

He also agrees that acquiring additional home-study companies would be desirable. The same holds true for "spinning off" a two-year college division out of the present college division.

He is more hesitant when it comes to the idea of combining the various divisions serving the elementary-high school field. He feels that the consultants have ignored some very important facts. Not all school products are sold in the same way, nor are they always purchased by the same customers. Textbooks are reached by contacting teachers and supervisors, and Handborn, Inc. maintains a large sales staff for just this purpose. On the other hand, audio-visual materials are usually sold by free-lance equipment dealers who work on a commission basis. They generally deal with audio-visual directors. Handborn decides this suggestion needs more study.

Handborn is most disturbed by the recommendation to sell the trade book division. He recognizes the validity of the argument that this publishing activity is off the Handborn trail. Nonetheless, he feels that a solid trade book division is one of the best ways to build up a good public image. And the reputation gained via trade books pays off in the sales of textbooks and technical magazines.

The trade book division is relatively new in the history of the company. Although it still has to realize a profit, it hasn't had a fair chance in his opinion. More time is needed.

There is one more consideration that the consultants overlooked. Handborn trade books written for children and teen-agers have been most successful. Several of them have won awards and more than fifty percent have been in existence for at least five years—an excellent record in trade books. It is the only profitable part of the trade book division.

Perhaps the adult trade books could be sold to another company. But Peter Handborn doubts that any other publisher would want the adult books alone. Handborn, Inc. would probably have to sell all the trade books—juvenile as well as adult—and the Board of Directors would not stand for this.

Decision. Peter Handborn will oppose the sale or dissolution of the trade book division. He will study further the feasibility of merging the elementary-high school divisions. He will recommend adoption of the other Prudence suggestions at the next board meeting.

DATA EVALUATION

DIRECTIONS: Based on your analysis of the business situation, classify each of the following elements in one of five categories. Mark:

(A) if the element is a MAJOR OBJECTIVE in making the decision; that is, the outcome or result sought by the decision maker.

(B) if the element is a MAJOR FACTOR in arriving at the decision; that is, a consideration explicitly mentioned in the passage that is basic in determining the decision.

(C) if the element is a MINOR FACTOR in making the decision; that is, a secondary consideration in determining the decision.

(D) if the element is a MAJOR ASSUMPTION made in deliberating; that is, a supposition or projection made by the decision maker before weighing the variables.

(E) if the element is an UNIMPORTANT ISSUE in getting to the point; that is, a factor that is insignificant or not immediately relevant to the situation.

1. Retaining the trade book division will be an assured benefit to the company.

2. Trade books can help create a good public image.

3. The trade book division has yet to realize a profit.

4. The consulting firm has recommended that the trade book division be discontinued.

5. A reputation gained through trade books helps to sell textbooks.

6. Trade books are an uncertain source of revenue.

7. Handborn's books for juveniles have won awards.

8. The Handborn company lacks experience in marketing trade books.

9. The trade book division is a relatively new division of Handborn.

10. Books for juveniles are the only profitable part of the trade book division.

DATA APPLICATION

DIRECTIONS: Based on your understanding of the business situation, answer the following questions testing your comprehension of the information supplied in the passage. For each question, select the choice which best answers the question or completes the statement.

11. The recommendations regarding the trade book division originated with

   (A) Peter Handborn
   (B) the Board of Directors
   (C) executives of Handborn, Inc.
   (D) a Senate committee which is investigating monopoly
   (E) Prudence, Inc.

12. Prudence, Inc. sees a great potential in the home-study field because

   (A) textbooks are easily acquired in this field
   (B) no other company provides adequate texts
   (C) the federal government provides funds to

ghetto youth to take job-training home-study courses

(D) many people wish to up-date their job skills

(E) fewer and fewer high school graduates go on to college

13. The management consulting team sees potential growth in which one of the following?

(A) texts for community colleges

(B) technical magazines for trades and crafts

(C) adult trade books

(D) juvenile trade books

(E) elementary-high school textbooks

14. Which of the following is one of the five recommendations made by Prudence, Inc.?

(A) The juvenile trade book line should be retained while the adult trade book line should be sold.

(B) Handborn, Inc. should sell some of its elementary-high school divisions.

(C) New magazines should be started.

(D) The elementary-high school divisions should be merged.

(E) The college division should be dissolved.

15. Peter Handborn's view of the recommendations is that

(A) none of them should be adopted

(B) all of them should be put into action immediately

(C) there are good suggestions concerning two-year colleges, magazines, and home-study courses

(D) at least two divisions should be sold as quickly as possible

(E) it doesn't matter if the trade book division makes a profit or not

16. The problem in merging the elementary-high school division is

(A) there would be a foolish mixing of profitable and unprofitable divisions

(B) the various Handborn divisions in this market do not sell in the same way

(C) Handborn, Inc. should really get out of this field altogether

(D) Handborn, Inc. is not the sole owner of some of the divisions

(E) the divisions are located in different parts of the country

17. The main factor in Peter Handborn's deliberation over selling the trade book division is his belief that

(A) a solid trade book division is a creator of good public relations

(B) there is an enormous profit to be made in adult trade books

(C) the Magnerson-Milton affair has shown that Handborn, Inc. knows little about trade books

(D) the adult trade books should be separated from juveniles so the adult books would show a profit

(E) the trade book division has had ample time to show a profit

18. Regarding the recommendations of Prudence, Inc., Peter Handborn is most dubious about their suggestions concerning

(A) certain technical magazines

(B) the home-study market

(C) the college text market

(D) the adult trade book division

(E) the elementary-high school divisions

19. It can be inferred from the passage that Handborn, Inc. is a company that

(A) is much too hesitant about entering new and promising fields

(B) is well-diversified in the field of publishing

(C) is known primarily in the field of elementary texts

(D) sells most of its books by mail

(E) is well-established in the two-year community college field

20. Within the last five years, Handborn, Inc. has acquired two companies that specialize in

(A) trade books

(B) technical magazines

(C) elementary-high school materials

(D) materials for two-year community colleges

(E) materials for home-study and self-improvement

Stop

END OF SECTION III. IF YOU HAVE ANY TIME LEFT, GO OVER YOUR WORK IN THIS SECTION ONLY. DO NOT WORK IN ANY OTHER SECTION OF THE TEST. WHEN YOUR TIME IS UP, GO ON TO THE NEXT SECTION.

SECTION IV: DATA SUFFICIENCY

30 Minutes
25 Questions

DIRECTIONS: Each question below is followed by two numbered facts. You are to determine whether the data given in the statements is sufficient for answering the question. Use the data given, plus your knowledge of math and everyday facts, to choose between the five possible answers.

(A) if statement 1 alone is sufficient to answer the question, but statement 2 alone is not sufficient.
(B) if statement 2 alone is sufficient to answer the question, but statement 1 alone is not sufficient.
(C) if both statements together are needed to answer the question, but neither statement alone is sufficient.
(D) if either statement by itself is sufficient to answer the question asked.
(E) if not enough facts are given to answer the question.

1. What is the area of the parallelogram ABCD?

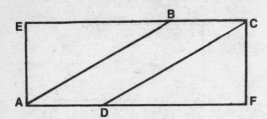

   (1) AECF is a rectangle with an area of 18 square inches
   (2) BC=CF

2. What month is it?

   (1) Next Friday will be the 29th.
   (2) This is leap year.

3. A man wants to cover a rectangular room with a carpet. How much will it cost him?

   (1) The service charge is $10, and each square yard costs $15.
   (2) If the room were half as large, it would cost him $165 less.

4. What is the value of x^3+1?

   (1) $x^2-x+1=0$
   (2) $x^3-1=(x-1)(x^2+x+1)$

5. Alice, Betsy, and Chris are three sisters. What is the order of their ages?

   (1) The sum of Alice's age and Betsy's age is equal to twice Chris' age.
   (2) Five years ago, Betsy was twice as old as Chris.

6. Find the number of degrees in angle C.

   (1) AD is parallel to BC
   (2) Angle A=45°

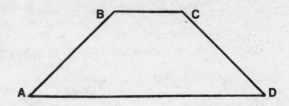

7. How many men are marching in the Odd Fellows' parade?

   (1) They can arrange themselves in three, five, or seven equal rows.
   (2) There is an even number of men marching.

8. Is F greater than G?

   (1) $F=(a-1)(a^2+a+1)$ and $G=(a+1)(a^2-a+1)$
   (2) $F=2G$

9. John studies Chinese in high school. Which school does he attend?

   (1) All students at Jefferson High School take French.
   (2) Maysville High School offers only Chinese.

10. Find the length of one side of the square ABCD.

    (1) BE=3 inches
    (2) The area of the shaded semicircle is ¼ the area of the large circle.

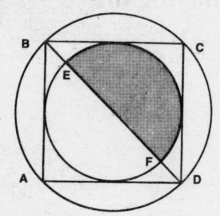

11. George and Sam go on a 300-mile trip by car. They take turns driving, each driving for 8 hours. What is the average rate of each?

    (1) George drove 48 miles more than Sam.
    (2) George averaged 6 miles an hour faster than Sam.

12. There are 30 boys in a club. How many are both boy scouts and junior high school graduates?

    (1) 10 are boy scouts.
    (2) 20 are junior high school graduates.

13. What is the value of x?

    (1) x + y = 5
    (2) x − y = 1

14. How many pennies does a boy have?

    (1) He has 37 cents in coins.
    (2) One of the coins is a nickel.

15. In triangle RST, angle S is 90° and SR=ST. Find the area of triangle RST.

    (1) RS=7
    (2) RT=$7\sqrt{2}$

16. $3x-6y=5$. What is the value of y?

    (1) x−2y=⅝
    (2) x=3

17. In △ ABC, what is the length of side AC?

    (1) AB=10 inches
    (2) BC=12 inches

18. Find three consecutive odd numbers.

    (1) The sum of the numbers is 63.
    (2) The largest number is 4 more than the smallest.

19. What is the ratio of x to y?

    (1) x=²/₇y
    (2) 7x−y=y

20. What is the total cost of linoleum needed for a room 9 feet by 12 feet?

    (1) Linoleum tiles are 6 inches square.
    (2) Linoleum tiles cost 52¢ per square foot.

21. What is the value of x/y?

    (1) x = y − 4
    (2) 3x = 2y

22. In the figure below, what is the perimeter of ABCD?

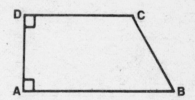

    (1) AD = 3, CB = 5
    (2) AB = 10

23. Pamela's weight is a whole number. What is Pamela's weight?

    (1) If Pamela gains 6 pounds, she will weigh less than 130 pounds.
    (2) If Pamela gains 8 pounds, she will weigh more than 130 pounds.

24. In the figure on the next page, line segment MN contains the centers of three overlapping circles. What is the length of PQ (P is the center of circle I and Q is the center of circle III)?

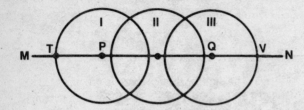

(1) The radii of circles I, II, and III are 10, 6 and 8 respectively.
(2) The length of the segment from T to V is 40.

$$
\begin{array}{r}
{}^{*}\ \triangle\ {}^{*} \\
+\ \triangle\ {}^{*}\ \triangle \\
\hline
1\ 3\ 3\ 2
\end{array}
$$

25. In the sum of the three-digit numbers above, * and △ are different positive integers less than 10. What is the integer *?

   (1) △ = 7
   (2) * + 2 = △

Stop

END OF SECTION IV. IF YOU HAVE ANY TIME LEFT, GO OVER YOUR WORK IN THIS SECTION ONLY. DO NOT WORK IN ANY OTHER SECTION OF THE TEST. WHEN YOUR TIME IS UP, GO ON TO THE NEXT SECTION.

SECTION V: ENGLISH USAGE

20 Minutes
30 Questions

DIRECTIONS: In each of the sentences below, four words or phrases have been underlined. Select the underlined part which contains an error in usage, grammar, or punctuation. If there is no error, mark answer space E.

1. Many themes considered <u>sacrilegious</u> in the nine-
   <u>A</u>   <u>B</u>
   <u>teen</u>th century are treated <u>casually</u> on <u>today's</u>
   C   C   D
   stage. <u>No error.</u>
          E

2. The color of <u>his</u> eyes <u>are</u> <u>brown.</u> <u>No error.</u>
   A   B   C   D   E

3. All of my experience as a reporter of sports

   events <u>indicate</u> that the <u>San Francisco Giants</u> can-
          A   B
   not <u>possibly</u> <u>lose</u> the pennant. <u>No error.</u>
       C   D   E

4. We <u>need</u> <u>further</u> information before we can <u>accede</u>
      A   B   C
   to your <u>request.</u> <u>No error.</u>
           D   E

5. Just between <u>you</u> and <u>I</u>, these theories <u>won't</u>
   A   B   C   D
   work. <u>No error.</u>
         E

6. If you <u>would have gone</u> <u>into the hall,</u> you <u>would</u>
   A   B   C   D
   have met your friends. <u>No error.</u>
                          E

7. The <u>Confederate Army</u> retreated during the <u>win-</u>
       A   B
   <u>ter in order</u> to conserve <u>their</u> strength. <u>No error.</u>
       C   D   E

8. Let's keep this <u>strictly</u> between <u>you</u> and <u>me.</u> <u>No</u>
   A   B   C   D   E
   <u>error.</u>

9. In <u>this</u> type of problem, the <u>total</u> of all the <u>items</u>
      A   B   C
   <u>are</u> always a positive number. <u>No error.</u>
   D   E

10. I <u>never have</u> and <u>never intend</u> <u>to visit</u> foreign
       A   B   C
    <u>countries.</u> <u>No error.</u>
    D   E

11. His <u>clothing</u> <u>laid</u> on the floor <u>until</u> his mother
        A   B   C
    <u>picked</u> it up. <u>No error.</u>
    D   E

12. When the <u>coach</u> makes the decision <u>as to which</u>
            A   B
    of the two boys will play, you may be sure that

    he will <u>choose</u> the <u>best</u> one. <u>No error.</u>
            C   D   E

13. He <u>would have been</u> more successful if <u>he would</u>
       A   B
    have had the <u>training</u> all of us <u>received.</u> <u>No error.</u>
                 C   D   E

367

14. Mr. Martin, together with all the members of his
    A
    family, are having a good time in Europe. No
    B   C   D   E
    error.

15. This technique may be usable in your business if
    A   B
    you can adopt it to your particular situation. No
    C   D   E
    error.

16. If the manager would have planned more care-
    A   B
    fully, bankruptcy might have been avoided. No
    C   D   E
    error.

17. The prisoners were accused of robbery, assault,
    A   B
    embezzlement and forging. No error.
    C   D   E

18. Since there was no evidence to indicate who's
    A
    ring it was, the presiding magistrate dismissed
    B   C   D
    the case. No error.
    E

19. Offer the nomination to whoever commands the
    A   B
    respect of the people. No error.
    C   D   E

20. Two astronauts were disappointed because they
    A
    had hoped to have made the first trip to the
    B   C   D
    moon. No error.
    E

21. If you want me to express my opinion, I think
    A   B
    that Report A is equally as good as Report B. No
    C   D   E
    error.

22. "Frank's dog is still in the yard," my father
    A
    said, "perhaps he had better stay there until we
    B   C   D
    have finished our dinner." No error.
    E

23. He had a chance to invest wisely, establish his
    A   B
    position, and displaying his ability as an execu-
    C   D
    tive. No error.
    E

24. The snow fell during the night so that it was lay-
    A   B
    ing in big drifts on the highway the next morn-
    C   D
    ing. No error.
    E

25. The coach with his entire team are traveling by
    A   B   C   D
    plane. No error.
    E

26. By his perseverance, he succeeded in overcom-
    A   B
    ing the apathy of his pupils. No error.
    C   D   E

27. This is one of those tricky questions that has two
    A   B   C   D
    answers. No error.
    E

28. She did the work very well, however, she showed
    A   B
    no interest in anything beyond her assignment.
    C   D
    No error.
    E

29. Roberts, a man whom we trusted with the most
    A   B   C
    difficult task of all proved loyal to his country.
    D
    No error.
    E

30. It was hard to believe that conscientious pupils
    A   B
    could misspell so many words in their quizzes.
    C   D
    No error.
    E

Stop

END OF SECTION V. IF YOU HAVE ANY TIME LEFT, GO OVER YOUR WORK IN THIS SECTION ONLY. DO NOT WORK IN ANY OTHER SECTION OF THE TEST. WHEN YOUR TIME IS UP, GO ON TO THE NEXT SECTION.

SECTION VI: PRACTICAL BUSINESS JUDGMENT

20 Minutes
20 Questions

DIRECTIONS: This section consists of a reading selection which details a business situation followed by two sets of questions, data evaluation and data application. In the first set, data evaluation, you will be asked to classify certain of the facts presented in the passage on the basis of their importance. The second set, data application, will test your grasp of specific details of the situation.

Mary Beth Talbot is one of the most successful people in the cosmetics industry. The 48-year-old woman was a minor motion picture star in the late 1940s. When her acting career faltered, she used her carefully saved money to start a cosmetics line called YoungLook. The wide line of lipsticks, eye shadow, lotions, and other items is sold on a commission basis by women who make house calls.

The company showed a profit from the very beginning. But Miss Talbot did not let this initial success mar her shrewd business judgment. She resisted the temptation to expand too quickly beyond the company's financial means, so that YoungLook grew slowly and steadily. Last year, sales revenue reached a record high of 32 million dollars. Her California-based company has six branch offices throughout the U.S. and two in Europe, with slightly more than 9,000 part-time sales representatives.

Surprisingly, YoungLook is still a privately held corporation. Andrew Dauphin, a member of her board of directors and her financial advisor since the company's inception, tells Mary Beth Talbot that it is time for her to diversify. He believes she should enter the health-salon field. These franchised salons would emphasize weight reduction and would sell natural foods as a sideline.

Dauphin feels that this new enterprise would require a public offering of 20 million dollars. With YoungLook's excellent record of price-earnings ratio for many years, there would be no trouble in selling this public offering.

Miss Talbot has some reservations, the principal one being her lack of knowledge of franchises and of health salons.

But she also weighs the advantages. Health salons and natural foods are businesses growing by leaps and bounds. She does not believe that they are fads, but represent increasing concern with personal appearance. As such, they would make a perfect combination for YoungLook. Also, with the cosmetics field becoming more and more competitive, Miss Talbot sees a limit to YoungLook's sales revenue.

Decision. She overcomes her conservativism and misgivings and tells Dauphin to begin work on a public offering.

DATA EVALUATION

DIRECTIONS: Based on your analysis of the business situation, classify each of the following elements in one of five categories. Mark:

(A) if the element is a MAJOR OBJECTIVE in making the decision; that is, the outcome or result sought by the decision maker.

(B) if the element is a MAJOR FACTOR in arriving at the decision; that is, a consideration explicitly mentioned in the passage that is basic in determining the decision.

(C) if the element is a MINOR FACTOR in making the decision; that is, a secondary consideration in determining the decision.

(D) if the element is a MAJOR ASSUMPTION made in deliberating; that is, a supposition or projection made by the decision maker before weighing the variables.

(E) if the element is an UNIMPORTANT ISSUE in getting to the point; that is, a factor that is insignificant or not immediately relevant to the situation.

1. High competition in the cosmetics industry.

2. The possibility of raising 20 million dollars for the new enterprise through a public offering.

3. YoungLook's branch offices in Europe.

4. Ease of selling a public offering.

5. YoungLook and health salons as a natural combination.

6. Record sales revenue of 32 million dollars.

7. Development of increased sales revenue for the YoungLook company.

8. YoungLook's price-earnings ratios.

9. Country-wide reputation of YoungLook.

10. National concern with personal appearance.

DATA APPLICATION

DIRECTIONS: Based on your understanding of the business situation, answer the following questions testing your comprehension of the information supplied in the passage. For each question, select the choice which best answers the question or completes the statement.

11. Miss Talbot's general attitude toward business can be characterized as

    (A) fearful
    (B) cautious and conservative
    (C) daring and reckless
    (D) unwilling to take chances
    (E) uninformed

12. YoungLook's products are sold

    (A) by commissioned saleswomen
    (B) through department stores
    (C) in beauty parlors
    (D) in health salons
    (E) by direct mail

13. YoungLook's growth has been

    (A) meteoric
    (B) characterized by sharp declines and even sharper recoveries
    (C) minuscule
    (D) slow and steady
    (E) nonexistent

14. The number of people who comprise Young-Look's sales staff is about

    (A) 1,000

(B) 4,000
(C) 9,000
(D) 14,000
(E) 19,000

15. Andrew Dauphin recommends that YoungLook

    (A) start a chain of natural-food stores
    (B) publish books on grooming
    (C) remain a privately held firm
    (D) expand its European market
    (E) establish health salons

16. Which of the following will be included in YoungLook's new venture?

    I. natural foods
    II. weight reduction
    III. franchises
    (A) I only
    (B) II only
    (C) I and II only
    (D) II and III only
    (E) I, II and III

17. YoungLook would have to finance its new venture

    (A) by bank loans
    (B) out of present profits
    (C) from investment by a mutual fund organization
    (D) by a public stock offering
    (E) out of Miss Talbot's personal funds

18. Which of the following reasons explains Miss Talbot's caution towards Dauphin's proposal?

    I. She wants her firm to remain privately held.
    II. She lacks knowledge about franchises.
    III. She feels that health salons are fads.
    (A) I only
    (B) II only
    (C) I and II only
    (D) II and III only
    (E) I, II and III

19. A public offering should be well subscribed because

    (A) of YoungLook's excellent price-earnings ratios
    (B) Miss Talbot and her products are household words

(C) there is a great deal of interest in natural foods

(D) the company has had successful public offerings before

(E) the price per share would be low

20. Which of the following is NOT a factor that influences Miss Talbot's ultimate decision?

(A) Competition in the cosmetics field.

(B) Health salons are a natural extension of YoungLook.

(C) The need to hire more sales people.

(D) The company's steady past growth.

(E) The company's record of price-earnings ratio.

Stop

END OF SECTION VI. IF YOU HAVE ANY TIME LEFT, GO OVER YOUR WORK IN THIS SECTION ONLY. DO NOT WORK IN ANY OTHER SECTION OF THE TEST. WHEN YOUR TIME IS UP, GO ON TO THE NEXT SECTION.

SECTION VII: VALIDITY OF CONCLUSION

35 Minutes
39 Questions

DIRECTIONS: Each of the following 4 sets consists of a reading passage followed by a conclusion drawn from the passage. Each conclusion is followed by statements which have a possible bearing on the conclusion. For each statement, you are to choose from the following the option which best expresses the relationship between the statement and the conclusion:

(A) The statement proves the conclusion.
(B) The statement supports the conclusion but does not prove it.
(C) The statement disproves the conclusion.
(D) The statement weakens the conclusion.
(E) The statement is irrelevant to the conclusion.

SET 1

Monty Maxim had failed to show up for Monday morning batting practice. Once again the Rebels' team manager, Willie Marlin, was furious with Maxim and called him into his office. The other baseball players could hear a heated argument, with threats and obscenities on both sides. Finally, shortly after 12 noon, Monty strode out of the office, slammed the door behind him, and left the clubhouse. The other players were uncertain about what had transpired. Had Monty quit the team? Had he been suspended? Knowing the tempers of the two men they decided to let the matter rest. Finally at 4 P.M. one of the coaches entered Marlin's office. He was dead. An open bottle of tranquilizers and a typed suicide note were on his desk. In his note Marlin cited his depression about the team's losing season and how nothing seemed to be working out for the team. The police were reluctant to accept Marlin's death as a suicide.

CONCLUSION. The police concluded that Maxim had killed Marlin.

1. One of the coaches testified that Marlin was enthusiastic about his job and was encouraged about some recent team improvements.

2. It was learned that Marlin never used a typewriter, but always wrote things out.

3. Marlin's office showed signs of a struggle.

4. Several players had heard Maxim, a former convict, say that he would not hesitate to kill Marlin if provoked.

5. Marlin had been seeing a therapist who testified that Marlin had talked of taking his own life on several occasions.

6. The police estimated the time of death at 3 P.M.

7. The police estimated the time of death at noon.

8. A newspaper reporter claimed to have had a telephone interview with Marlin at 1 P.M.

9. Marlin had been using tranquilizers to help him sleep.

10. Several players testified that despite frequent verbal flare ups with his manager, Maxim actually had had a great deal of respect and admiration for Marlin.

SET 2

Bill Jones, following his usual Sunday morning routine, arrived at the Edgewater Swimming and Exercise Club in order to begin swimming shortly after the club opened at 8 A.M. Bill noticed that hardly anyone was around except for a few workers in the concession area and a cleaning crew. After dressing in the locker room, he used an entrance to the pool that he and other members often used as a shortcut. It was through the door, two long strides, and then a jump into the pool. But this time, to Bill's horror, there was only an empty concrete floor awaiting his perfect dive.

CONCLUSION: In awarding Jones his half-million dollar suit the court concluded that Edgewater Swimming and Exercise Club was culpably responsible for Jones' multiple fractures and his broken arm.

11. The club had closed for two weeks of cleaning and repairs and Jones had failed to notice the public notices of the closing.

12. Jones had failed to realize that he had arrived at 7 A.M., an hour before the pool was open to the public. There were, however, no signs indicating whether the pool was open or closed.

13. The refill pump had unexpectedly broken and in their concern to fill the pool the club's personnel did not post any precautions.

14. The lifeguard was not yet on duty and the club rules clearly indicate that no one is allowed in the pool if there is no lifeguard on duty.

15. In entering the swimming area Jones had gone through a door marked "Lifeguard Personnel Only."

16. The club manager on hearing about an unscheduled visit from the Health Commissioner ordered the pool closed for cleaning. The "Swim Area Closed for Cleaning" sign was posted twenty minutes after the pool area was scheduled to open.

17. Jones had not realized that he had arrived twenty minutes early and the pool doors, usually closed at that time, had been mistakenly left open by the cleaning crew.

18. The club lawyer pointed out that Jones was in violation of the rule "Dive into pool only at designated diving boards." This rule is frequently violated and never enforced.

19. Because most of its members are usually traveling on weekends the club is much less crowded at that time.

SET 3

Nineteen-year-old Barbara Reynolds was found dead at 4 A.M. near the city's recycling center, her face and throat bruised. It was determined that she had been dead for three hours. According to two girlfriends who had seen her at midnight, she was on her way to a meeting with her former boyfriend, twenty-year-old Fred Haney, with whom she had not spoken for over a month. Haney was picked up for questioning about the death.

CONCLUSION: Authorities concluded that Haney was not instrumental in his former girlfriend's death and released him.

20. A nightwatchman at the recycling center saw Haney speeding away in his car about 1 A.M. on the day of Reynolds' death.

21. On the evening of Barbara's death Haney told friends that he would kill his former girlfriend if she refused to go back with him.

22. After he had broken up with Miss Reynolds, Haney had little interest in dating other women.

23. According to Barbara's mother, it had been Haney who wanted to end the relationship and he had only reluctantly agreed to meet her on the evening of her death.

24. On his way to meet Miss Reynolds, Haney was involved in an automobile accident which kept him at the scene of the accident until 2 A.M.

25. Witnesses saw Miss Reynolds struggling with a man in his fifties or sixties shortly before 1 A.M.

26. A coroner's report indicates that death was due to an overdose of sleeping pills.

27. When Haney was picked up by the police he was very calm and very cooperative.

28. Barbara had telephoned a friend from the recycling center after Haney had driven off.

29. At 2 A.M. Haney, enraged, asked a friend for a gun. He swore he would see Barbara again that night and kill her.

SET 4

Johnson Ice Cream Co. operates a number of ice cream trucks throughout the city. On one of its daily runs near City Hall one of the Johnson trucks was mysteriously blown up. The explosion at 11:15 A.M. left several people dead. A local terrorist group calling itself the Green Gang, thought to be based near City Hall, was known to have been responsible for several bombings that had occurred in the area.

CONCLUSION: The chief of police concluded that the explosion was the work of the Green Gang.

30. Shattered fragments of two spare gasoline cans were found in the back of the truck and scattered throughout the debris.

31. A Green Gang leader, whose phone had been tapped, had made several references to a Johnson Ice Cream truck several days before the explosion.

32. A member of the gang was one of those killed by the explosion.

33. In twenty-five years of business this was Johnson's third such explosion and all three explosions had occurred in the past year in trucks experimenting with a new and powerful cooling system.

34. After considerable coverage of the explosion by the media the Green Gang claimed responsibility for what had happened.

35. An inside informant reported that the surprised gang called off their plans to sabotage a Johnson truck when they learned of the explosion.

36. On the day of the explosion a member of the gang had told his wife to make certain that no one in the family go near City Hall.

37. Prior to the explosion the chief of police received a certified letter from the Green Gang correctly specifying the day and the time of the subsequent explosion.

38. Johnson had recently received some sensational publicity over the artificiality and the impurity of their products.

39. A survey indicated that Johnson Ice Cream was the least preferred by the supermarket shopper.

Stop

END OF EXAMINATION

END OF SECTION VII. IF YOU HAVE ANY TIME LEFT, GO OVER YOUR WORK IN THIS SECTION ONLY. DO NOT WORK IN ANY OTHER SECTION OF THE TEST. WHEN YOUR TIME IS UP, CHECK YOUR ANSWERS WITH THE ANSWER KEY AND EXPLANATORY ANSWERS PROVIDED ON THE FOLLOWING PAGES.

ANSWER KEY

SECTION I

1. A	6. D	11. E	16. B	21. C
2. D	7. E	12. C	17. C	22. A
3. E	8. E	13. C	18. C	23. E
4. B	9. E	14. A	19. D	24. A
5. C	10. D	15. E	20. C	25. D

SECTION II

1. B	6. B	11. E	16. A	21. E
2. D	7. C	12. B	17. C	22. E
3. E	8. D	13. D	18. E	23. D
4. D	9. E	14. E	19. A	24. B
5. A	10. A	15. D	20. A	25. D

SECTION III

1. A	6. B	11. E	16. B
2. B	7. C	12. D	17. A
3. B	8. B	13. A	18. D
4. B	9. C	14. D	19. B
5. B	10. C	15. C	20. E

SECTION IV

1. E	6. E	11. D	16. B	21. B
2. E	7. E	12. E	17. E	22. C
3. C	8. A	13. C	18. A	23. C
4. A	9. E	14. E	19. D	24. C
5. C	10. A	15. D	20. B	25. D

SECTION V

1. E	7. D	13. B	19. E	25. C
2. C	8. E	14. B	20. C	26. E
3. A	9. D	15. C	21. D	27. D
4. E	10. A	16. A	22. B	28. B
5. C	11. B	17. D	23. C	29. D
6. B	12. D	18. A	24. B	30. E

SECTION VI

1. B	6. E	11. B	16. E
2. B	7. A	12. A	17. D
3. E	8. C	13. D	18. B
4. D	9. C	14. C	19. A
5. B	10. C	15. E	20. C

SECTION VII

1. B	11. C	21. D	31. B
2. B	12. D	22. E	32. E
3. B	13. A	23. B	33. D
4. B	14. C	24. A	34. B
5. D	15. D	25. A	35. C
6. C	16. A	26. A	36. B
7. A	17. B	27. E	37. A
8. C	18. D	28. A	38. E
9. E	19. E	29. B	39. E
10. D	20. D	30. D	

EXPLANATORY ANSWERS

SECTION I

1. **(A)** This is the only logical choice. The passage does not deal with the differences between the foods of different nations (B and D). Nor does it deal principally with various ways of preparing food (C) or the food value of fish (E).

2. **(D)** The reviewer praises the book's scope, the exhaustiveness of its material, and the intelligence of its innovative suggestions.

3. **(E)** The article states: "Our memories of certain foodstuffs eaten during the Second World War suggest that, although these might have been safe and nutritious, they certainly did not taste right nor were they particularly appetizing in appearance or smell."

4. **(B)** It requires no specific knowledge to deduce from the context of the article that the Weber fraction was originated by the physiologist Ernest Heinrich Weber. The article tells us that the Weber fraction is involved with the relation between stimuli and perception. This is a matter which clearly falls into the domain of physiology and choice (B) is the only physiologist mentioned.

5. **(C)** This is the only view not stated in the article.

6. **(D)** The article states: ". . . a start might be made by using subjects afflicted with various forms of deafness. It is, of course, well known that extraneous noise may alter discrimination (i.e., between tastes)."

7. **(E)** This is the only choice not mentioned. Olfaction is the sense of smell and the word tactile refers to the sense of touch. All of the other senses are plainly mentioned. Also, muscular movement is not, properly speaking, one of the senses.

8. **(E)** The structure and location of the earth's mantle is not discussed in the passage.

9. **(E)** Choice (E) can be clearly inferred from the criticism leveled at Congress in the passage.

10. **(D)** This is implied in the last paragraph.

11. **(E)** The author states that, at the start of the project, there was "good reason for believing that the drilling program was being pushed ahead too quickly, and with too little preliminary study."

12. **(C)** This is implied in the last paragraph when the author states that "plans for building—and siting—big particle accelerators have usually been examined in detail by Congressional committees. . . ."

13. **(C)** Given the tendency for important scientific projects to be named after the founder or developer, or the scientist most associated with the project, choice (C) seems the most plausible.

14. **(A)** This is the best answer. The passage tells us that the British were instrumental in developing Hong Kong's trade economy.

15. **(E)** This passage tells us that Hong Kong survived the crisis caused by the United Nations' embargo on imports into China by changing from a trade economy to a manufacturing economy.

16. **(B)** The passage states that the economy suffered a setback under the Japanese occupation. Choice (E) would be the exact opposite. Choices (C) and (D) also would imply an economic growth. Choice (A) could not be determined by the reading.

17. **(C)** The passage tells us that the population of China is over 700 million. It later states that Hong Kong's population is over 3¾ million. From these figures we can calculate that 3¾ is roughly 1/200 of 700.

18. **(C)** This is the best answer. These are among the nations listed by the author as leading importers of goods from Hong Kong.

19. **(D)** The passage clearly states that Hong Kong first came under Chinese sovereignty in about 200 B.C.

20. **(C)** None of the other choices make sense within the context of the passage. Skinnerian refers to the noted behavioral scientist B.F. Skinner.

21. **(C)** The author stresses that students benefit from all types of programmed learning.

22. **(A)** This is plainly stated in the third paragraph.

23. **(E)** The passage indicates that not enough has been determined about programmed instruction and that the teacher must remain an important factor in an instructional situation.

24. **(A)** Choices (B) through (E) make no sense. Choice (A) is clearly implied by the experimental nature of programmed learning.

25. **(D)** Only (D) makes any sense among the choices offered.

SECTION II

1. **(B)** From the income graph, the big city residents had an income of $.554 \times (369 \text{ Billion}) = \$204.426$ Billion. From the population graph, there were $(.496) \times (191 \text{ million}) = 94.736$ million big-city residents.
   Hence, the per capita income
   $$= \frac{\$204.426 \times 10^9}{94.736 \times 10^6} = \$2,150 \text{ approx.}$$

2. **(D)** Income (rest of country)
   $$= (.446) (369 \text{ billion})$$
   $$= 164.574 \text{ billion dollars}$$
   Rest of country residents
   $$= (.504) (191 \text{ million})$$
   $$= 96.264 \text{ million}$$
   Per Capita Income =
   $$\frac{\$164.574 \times 10^9}{96.264 \times 10^6} = \$1,700$$

3. **(E)** The big-city resident has an income which is $450 more on the average.
   Hence $\frac{450}{1700} \times 100 = 26.47\%$

4. **(D)** $(.554) (360°) = 200°$ (approx)

5. **(A)** Ratio $= \dfrac{55.4}{44.6} = \dfrac{5}{4}$

6. **(B)** In 1958, the two lines cross where the personal income is about \$325 billion.

7. **(C)** Increase $= 500 - 80 = 420$

   Percent Increase $= \dfrac{420}{80} \times 100 = 525\%$

8. **(D)** Increase $= 450 - 160 = 290$

   Percent Increase $= \dfrac{290}{160} \times 100 = 180\%$

9. **(E)** $\dfrac{500 \text{ billion}}{200 \text{ million}} = \dfrac{500 \times 10^9}{200 \times 10^6}$

   $= 2.5 \,(10^3) = \$2500$

10. **(A)**

year	GNP
1960	500
1940	100

    Ratio $= \dfrac{500}{100} = 5{:}1$

11. **(E)** The flattest part of the curve shows the least increase. That occurs in the period commencing 1935.

12. **(B)** The steepest part of the curve shows the greatest increase. This occurs in period commencing 1950.

13. **(D)** Increase is from 100 to 585, or an increase of 485.

    Thus, % increase $= {}^{485}/_{100} = 4.85 \times 100\% = 485\%$

14. **(E)** Increase is from 500 to 585, or an increase of 85.

    Increase $= {}^{85}/_{500} \times 100 = 17\%$.

15. **(D)** There will be another 17% increase on 585. Hence, in 1966, GNP $=$

    $585 + \left(585 \times \dfrac{17}{100}\right) = 684.45$

16. **(A)** ${}^{200}/_{100} = 2{:}1$

17. **(C)** Highest point of curve occurred in February, when it reached 600.

18. **(E)** Lowest point of curve was reached in September 1966.

19. **(A)** Highest was 600.
    Lowest was about 450.

    Ratio $= \dfrac{600}{450} = \dfrac{4}{3}$

20. **(A)** In 1920, the price was almost \$1.40 per pound, while in 1930, the price was only about \$0.30.

21. **(E)** In 1934, the price was about 40¢ per pound and in 1931 it was about 30¢. 40¢ is 4/3 of 30¢. Do not be fooled by the appearance of the graph, which suggests that the answer should be 2/1. This effect is produced by making the first level \$0.20, instead of \$0.00.

22. **(E)** 1920 was the highest year, but it is obvious that silver prices were higher in 1919 than in 1935 or 1946.

23. **(D)** In the 1943–45 period, the price of silver was almost constant.

24. **(B)** The graph clearly indicates the sharp rise from 1940.

25. **(D)** In 1943, and also in 1944, the price was about \$0.45.

SECTION III

1. **(A)** The decision of whether or not to retain the trade book division is based on the assumption that the trade book division will benefit the company, either directly through sales or indirectly through the enhancement of the company's image which will stimulate sales of texts.

2. **(B)** A major factor in deciding whether or not to retain the trade book division is the favorable image that the trade book line can create.

3. **(B)** A major consideration is the lack of profit from the trade book division.

4. **(B)** A major consideration mentioned in the passage is the recommendation of the consulting

firm that the trade book division be discontinued.

5. **(B)** That the reputation gained through trade books may help sell texts is a consideration that Peter Handborn makes in his decision to retain the trade book division.

6. **(B)** One of the reasons Prudence, Inc. gives in its recommendation that the trade book line be discontinued is that trade books represent the most hazardous area of book publishing.

7. **(C)** The fact that Handborn's books for juveniles have won awards is a consideration that relates to the favorable image created by the trade book line.

8. **(B)** That Handborn, Inc. lacks experience in the trade book field is a major consideration pointed out by Prudence, Inc.

9. **(C)** That the trade book division is relatively new is related to Handborn, Inc.'s lack of experience in this field; hence the lack of profit in this area.

10. **(C)** The fact that the juvenile trade books are successful is incorporated in major considerations of profit and reputation to be gained through the trade book division.

11. **(E)** The Board of Directors did not make the recommendations, but suggested that the consulting firm be hired. Peter Handborn is reacting to the consultants' report.

12. **(D)** Perhaps home study is the cheapest and best way to learn, but this is not mentioned, nor is any special federal program. The number of high school graduates going to college has no bearing upon home studies.

13. **(A)** Prudence, Inc. believes that the technical magazines, published for declining crafts, should be eliminated. The consulting team did not mention the growth potential of trade books, juvenile trade books, or elementary-high school textbooks.

14. **(D)** The merger of the separate elementary-high school divisions is recommended on the grounds of efficiency and economy. The management consultants believe that the entire trade book line should be sold. The management consultants realize that the college division is solidly based. The only change they would make would be to add a community college division. Peter Handborn is thinking about starting new magazines, but this idea did not come from the management consultants nor did the management consultants suggest selling any of the elementary-high school divisions.

15. **(C)** If you marked (E), you were fairly close, but it would not be fair to say that he does not care whether the trade book division becomes profitable or not. He only wishes that it would be given more time to get into the black. Choice C is the best answer.

16. **(B)** There are some grounds for merging the elementary-high school divisions, and Peter Handborn does not turn the idea down completely. However, he is aware that the various divisions have different customers within the school-product market. A merger would probably decrease costs and increase efficiency. The mixing of profitable and unprofitable divisions did not come into his thinking at all, nor has there been any suggestion that Handborn, Inc. should divest itself of its elementary-high school lines.

17. **(A)** Peter Handborn is keenly aware that trade books enhance a company's public image. He does not reflect on whether or not enormous profits can be attained in the adult trade book field, nor would he probably agree with the contention that Handborn, Inc. knows little about trade books. (D) is wrong because the juvenile trade books are making money. Peter Handborn does not believe that the trade book division has had time enough to show a profit.

18. **(D)** Peter Handborn does not believe that another publisher will buy the unprofitable adult trade books without the profitable juvenile trade books.

19. **(B)** Handborn, Inc. is well-diversified as far as the publishing industry is concerned. It certainly does not show too much hesitation when it sees new opportunities; yet its posture is cautious and it does not enter new fields rashly. (D) and (E) are completely false.

20. **(E)** The two companies Handborn, Inc. has purchased specialize in the home-study market.

SECTION IV

1. **(E)** If we let CF grow larger and decrease EC correspondingly, we can change the area of ABCD without contradicting either statement.

2. **(E)** Just because the 29th is mentioned, there is no reason to believe it is February. It might be any month.

3. **(C)** The charge without service would be ($165 × 2) = $330, so the total charge is $330 + $10 = $340.

4. **(A)** Since (2) is always true, it makes no difference. $x^3 + 1 = (x + 1)(x^2 - x + 1) = 0$

5. **(C)** (1) tells us that Chris is in the middle, since her age is the average of the other two. (2) tells us that Betsy is older than Chris, so Betsy is the oldest, Chris is next, and Alice is the youngest.

6. **(E)** Not enough information is given.

7. **(E)** The number may be any even multiple of 210.

8. **(A)** $F = a^3 - 1$ and $G = a^3 + 1$, so G is greater.

9. **(E)** Statement 1 simply eliminates Jefferson H.S. Statement 2 tells us that John *may* attend Maysville H.S. However, other high schools may offer Chinese.

10. **(A)** In any case (2) is true. Since the proportions remain constant, once BE is given, the side of the square can be calculated as $6(\sqrt{2} + 1)$.

11. **(D)** From Statement 1, George drove $x + 48$ if Sam drove x. $x + 48 + x = 300$. $x = 126$ which is the distance George drove in 8 hours. We can now find his average rate. From Statement 2, we merely subtract 6 miles from George's average rate to get Sam's average rate.

12. **(E)** Statements 1 and 2 together tell us that the number of boy scouts is 10 and the number of junior high school graduates is 20. But a boy scout may also be a junior high school graduate. More information is needed to solve the question.

13. **(C)** Add Statements 1 and 2 to get $2x = 6$ or $x = 3$. We can easily determine the value of y now.

14. **(E)** Neither of the statements supplies us with the necessary information concerning pennies.

15. **(D)** The area of the triangle $= \frac{1}{2} \times 7 \times 7 = 24\frac{1}{2}$. That was from Statement 1. Now, Statement 2 will give us this information: $(7\sqrt{2})^2 = (RS)^2 + (ST)^2$. Since RS = ST, $49 \times 2 = 2(RS)^2$. Therefore, RS = 7. From this point, we are able to find the area of the triangle.

16. **(B)** With Statement 2, we know that $3 \times 3 - 6y = 5$. Therefore, it is easy to find the value of y. The information given in Statement 1 is of no help.

17. **(E)** Neither Statement gives us sufficient information. The size of one of the angles would help us.

18. **(A)** Let the first odd number = x. Then, $x + (x + 2) + (x + 4) = 63$. The equation can easily be solved. The information in Statement 2 is not sufficient.

19. **(D)** From Statement 1, we find that $\frac{x}{y} = \frac{2}{7}$

The ratio is, accordingly, established. From Statement 2: $7x = 2y$. Again, we establish the ratio asked for.

20. **(B)** Since Statement 1 does not give us the cost of the tiles, it is an insufficient statement. Statement 2, on the other hand, gives us the information required—namely, the cost of the tiles. The linoleum will cost $108 \times \frac{52}{100} = \$56.16$.

21. **(B)** By statement (2)
$3x = 2y$
$\frac{x}{y} = \frac{2}{3}$

22. **(C)** Use both statements to find the side CD.

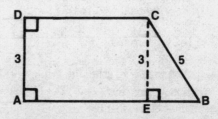

Draw CE ⊥ AB, CE = AD = 3. △ CEB is now a 3, 4, 5 rt. △. EB = 4. Therefore, AE = 6 = CD. The perimeter of ABCD can now be found: 3+6+5+10=24.

23. **(C)** Let x = Pamela's weight.
Statement (1) x + 6 < 130
          x < 124
Statement (2) x + 8 > 130
          x > 122
If 122 < x < 124, x = 123.

24. **(C)** Using statement (1) the diameter of circles I and III are 20 and 16 respectively. By statement (2) the distance from T to V is 40, hence the distance from circle I to circle II is 40 − 36 or 4. To find the length of PQ, 10 + 4 + 8 = 22.

25. **(D)** By statement (1) if △ = 7, then * could only be 5 to obtain the sum indicated. By statement (2) 7 and 5 are the only two digits whose difference is 2 that would obtain the same sum.

SECTION V

1. **(E)** There are no errors in this sentence.

2. **(C)** . . . color . . . *is* . . . .

3. **(A)** All . . . *indicates* . . .

4. **(E)** There are no errors this sentence.

5. **(C)** Between you and *me*, . . . "Me" is the object of the preposition "between"; therefore the objective form is required.

6. **(B)** If you *had* gone . . . This is a conditional sentence.

7. **(D)** *Its* strength, not theirs.

8. **(E)** There are no errors in this sentence.

9. **(D)** . . ., the total . . . *is* . . . .

10. **(A)** I never have *intended*.

11. **(B)** Clothing *lay*. To lie: lie, lying, lay, lain. To lay: lay, laying, laid, laid. The former is to recline, the latter is to place.

12. **(D)** . . . he will choose the *better* one. (The better of two, the best of three.)

13. **(B)** . . . if he *had* had the training. This is a conditional sentence.

14. **(B)** Mr. Martin *is*.

15. **(C)** *Adapt*, not adopt.

16. **(A)** If the manager *had* . . . This is a conditional sentence.

17. **(D)** *Forgery*, not forging. The latter means to work metal.

18. **(A)** *Whose*, not who's. The latter means who is.

19. **(E)** There are no errors in this sentence.

20. **(C)** . . . they had hoped *to make*. . . .

21. **(D)** Take out "equally"; it is not needed: "Report A is as good as Report B."

22. **(B)** . . . my father said. "Perhaps . . . . A new sentence has been started.

23. **(C)** . . . and *display*, not displaying. Parallel verb forms require the infinitive form of the verb "to display" to agree with "invest" and "establish."

24. **(B)** The snow . . . was lying in big drifts. . . . To lay means to place; to lie means to recline.

25. **(C)** The coach . . . is . . . .

26. **(E)** There are no errors in this sentence.

27. **(D)** . . . one of those questions that *have* . . . . . "That" refers to "questions," not "one".

28. **(B)** . . . very well, *but* she showed . . . . "However" should not be used in place of "but."

29. **(D)** . . . , a man whom we trusted with the most difficult task of *all*, . . . is an appositive and must be set off by commas.

30. **(E)** There are no errors in this sentence.

SECTION VI

1. **(B)** It is the heavy competition in the cosmetics field that makes Miss Talbot think there is a limit to her sales revenues. Therefore, she welcomes an opportunity to diversify.

2. **(B)** The raising of money through a public offering is certainly a major factor in arriving at a decision.

3. **(E)** The European offices have absolutely no bearing in Miss Talbot's calculations.

4. **(D)** That the total offering will be sold is an assumption, although it is a pretty sure one.

5. **(B)** The combination of YoungLook and health salons does seem a good marriage to Miss Talbot.

6. **(E)** Last year's sales revenues are not pertinent to the considerations leading to the decision.

7. **(A)** The growth of YoungLook in the future is a major objective.

8. **(C)** The excellent price-earnings ratios throughout the years is a minor factor leading to the major one of a public offering.

9. **(C)** YoungLook's reputation is a minor factor that makes success in the new enterprise a possibility.

10. **(C)** A minor factor influencing a major factor. National concern with personal appearance leads to Miss Talbot's thought that health salons and YoungLook comprise a natural combination.

11. **(B)** Miss Talbot certainly is not daring or reckless, as the slow and steady growth of the company shows. She is not fearful because she does take advantage of opportunities when they present themselves. But she looks before she leaps and informs herself as much as she can about the new venture.

12. **(A)** So stated.

13. **(D)** So stated.

14. **(C)** So stated.

15. **(E)** So stated.

16. **(E)** YoungLook will franchise health salons which will emphasize weight reduction and will sell natural foods.

17. **(D)** So stated. For a firm of this sales volume, a public offering for 20 million dollars seems the wisest course.

18. **(B)** It is never stated that Miss Talbot is in the least concerned about YoungLook becoming a publicly held firm. She does not believe health salons are fads.

19. **(A)** It is probably true that Miss Talbot and YoungLook are household words and that there is great interest in natural foods. But the earnings record over the years would count most with potential investors.

20. **(C)** It is stated that Miss Talbot is concerned about cosmetics competition and that she sees health salons as a perfect combination for YoungLook. But it is never stated that she needs new saleswomen.

SECTION VII

1. **(B)** This throws doubt on the authenticity of the suicide note and supports the only other alternative, viz., that Marlin had been killed by Maxim.

2. **(B)** For the same reason as 1.

3. **(B)** The struggle could have led to Marlin's murder by Maxim. Of course, there could have been a struggle that did not lead to murder.

4. **(B)** This would indicate that Maxim was prepared to go to the extreme of killing.

5. **(D)** This would support but not establish the alternative hypothesis of suicide.

6. **(C)** This eliminates Maxim as the killer since he left the scene at 12 noon.

384 / Final Practice Examination

7. **(A)** This would establish Maxim as the killer since he left Marlin after the time of death.

8. **(C)** This would eliminate Maxim as the killer since Marlin would still have been alive after Maxim left him.

9. **(E)** This accounts for the presence of the pills, but the fact has no bearing on Maxim's alleged guilt.

10. **(D)** If the testimony is true it makes it difficult to explain what could have provoked Maxim to murder. Still it is possible that Maxim was provoked, especially since both men were known for their tempers.

11. **(C)** The club could argue that, since it was officially closed and had announced that closing, they could not be held responsible for Jones' ignorance and subsequent accident.

12. **(D)** Since Jones was using the club before it was officially open, this weakens the conclusion but since the club could have done more to indicate that it was closed there remains some basis for arguing the club's liability.

13. **(A)** This would prove the conclusion since the pool management was aware of the unusual situation and did nothing to warn members.

14. **(C)** The club could argue that since the rules make it clear that Jones was not to be in the swimming area, they cannot be held responsible for what happened to him while in the swimming area.

15. **(D)** Since Jones had used an unauthorized entrance to the pool there is a basis for arguing against the conclusion. However, as made clear in the case description, this door was in fact often used by non-lifeguard personnel and the pool management would have been aware of this practice.

16. **(A)** This would prove the conclusion since the pool management failed to give an appropriate warning to anyone intending to use the pool during the first twenty minutes.

17. **(B)** Since the doors were open there would be some reason for thinking the pool to be open and thus some reason for holding the pool management responsible for misleading Jones. However, their responsibility is not conclusively established since the actual time was prior to their stated opening.

18. **(D)** Because of the rule violation the club would have a basis for arguing against the conclusion. However, as in question 5, a case could be made for saying that the club must be held responsible for common rule violations of which the club is aware.

19. **(E)** This fact about attendance habits of club members is irrelevant to the question of the club's responsibility.

20. **(D)** This weakens the conclusion since it puts Haney at the scene of the crime at the time of death. Still it does not in itself establish that he was instrumental in her death.

21. **(D)** This weakens the conclusion since it establishes that Haney had a strong motive for murdering the woman he was about to see. The possibility remains open that he did not carry out his threat.

22. **(E)** Though this might indicate an interest in resuming his relationship with Miss Reynolds, the information in no way helps us determine if Haney was involved in Miss Reynold's death.

23. **(B)** This information makes Haney a somewhat less likely suspect since it makes it unlikely that he would have acted out of violent feelings of rejection. Still there are other possible motives that could have been open to him.

24. **(A)** This proves the conclusion by establishing that Haney was at a different location at the time of Miss Reynolds' death.

25. **(A)** This proves the conclusion by ruling out the twenty-year-old Haney as Miss Reynolds' assailant.

26. **(A)** Though Haney may have been responsible for the face and throat bruises these were not instrumental in her death. He cannot be held responsible for a lethal overdose taken earlier in the evening.

27. **(E)** Haney's mental state at the time of questioning is not a reliable indicator of guilt or innocence.

28. **(A)** This would indicate that Barbara was still alive after she saw Haney.

29. **(B)** If Haney's behavior is genuine this indicates that he left Barbara alive and could not have been responsible for her death at 1 A.M. There remains the possibility that his behavior was not genuine.

30. **(D)** This would indicate that the explosion could have been the result of the gasoline can being ignited accidentally. Still there is the possibility that it was not an accident.

31. **(B)** The references to the Johnson truck before the explosion by a terrorist group known to be active in the area could hardly be a coincidence. Still we do not have conclusive evidence of their actually causing the explosion.

32. **(E)** We have no indication that the gang member was an innocent bystander or whether he was a casualty of his own terrorist activity.

33. **(D)** The third such explosion in a year in one of the experimental trucks would seem to be a conclusive reason for suspecting the experimental cooling system. However, we cannot be certain that this truck was equipped with an experimental cooling system.

34. **(B)** The gang's claims of responsibility would seem to prove the conclusion, but given terrorist groups' tendencies to claim responsibility for violent acts they haven't committed, the claim in and of itself is not conclusive.

35. **(C)** The unexpected explosion making the planned sabotage unnecessary conclusively establishes the noninvolvement of the gang in the explosion.

36. **(B)** This is strong indication that the gang was aware of and had something to do with the subsequent disaster.

37. **(A)** The exact prediction would be a conclusive reason for holding the gang responsible.

38. **(E)** Though the controversy might indicate that the Johnson Ice Cream Co. could possibly be the object of attack from an outraged consumer, we really have no indication of such an action.

39. **(E)** We are given no information relevant to the cause of the explosion.

Appendix I

GMAT
Graduate School List

GMAT GRADUATE SCHOOL LIST

The following schools require GMAT scores for admission to their graduate business programs.

Adelphi University
School of Business Administration
Garden City, NY 11530

The American University
School of Business Administration
Washington, DC 20016

Angelo State University
Business Administration Department
San Angelo, TX 76901

Appalachian State University
Department of Business Administration
Boone, NC 28608

Aquinas College
Department of Business Administration
Grand Rapids, MI 49506

Arizona State University
College of Business Administration
Tempe, AZ 85281

Armstrong College
Berkeley, CA 94704

Armstrong State College
Savannah, GA 30314

Atlanta University
School of Business Administration
Atlanta, GA 30314

Auburn University
School of Business
Auburn, AL 36830

Augusta College
Department of Business Administration
Augusta, GA 30904

Babson College
Babson Park, MA 02157

Baldwin-Wallace College
Berea, OH 44017

Ball State University
College of Business
Muncie, IN 47306

Barry College
Miami, FL 33161

Baylor University
Hankamer School of Business
Waco, TX 76706

Bellarmine College
Louisville, KY 40205

Belmont College
Nashville, TN 37203

Bentley College
Waltham, MA 02154

Berry College
Department of Business Administration
Mount Berry, GA 30149

Bloomsburg State College
Bloomsburg, PA 17815

Boise State College
School of Business
1910 Campus Drive
Boise, ID 83725

Boston College
School of Management
Chestnut Hill, MA 02167

Boston University
College of Business Administration
685 Commonwealth Avenue
Boston, MA 02215

Bowling Green State University
College of Business Administration
Bowling Green, OH 43403

Bradley University
College of Business Administration
Peoria, IL 61606

Brigham Young University
College of Business
Provo, UT 84601

Bryant College
Smithfield, RI 02917

Bucknell University
College of Business Administration
Lewisburg, PA 17837

Butler University
College of Business Administration
Indianapolis, IN 46208

California Lutheran College
Thousand Oaks, CA 91360

California State College, Bakersfield
School of Business and Public Administration
9001 Stockdale Highway
Bakersfield, CA 93309

California State College, Dominquez Hills
Business Administration
Carson, CA 90747

California State College, San Bernardino
Department of Administration
550 State College Parkway
San Bernardino CA 92407

California State College, Stanislaus
Division of Business Administration
Turlock, CA 95380

California Polytechnic State University
School of Business and Social Sciences
San Luis Obispo, CA 93401

California State Polytechnic University, Pomona
School of Business Administration
Pomona, CA 91768

California State University, Chico
School of Business
Chico, CA 95926

California State University, Fresno
School of Business
Fresno, CA 93710

California State University, Fullerton
School of Business Administration and Economics
Fullerton, CA 92634

California State University, Hayward
School of Business and Economics
Hayward, CA 94542

California State University, Humboldt
School of Business and Economics
Arcata, CA 95521

California State University, Long Beach
School of Business Administration
Long Beach, CA 90840

California State University, Los Angeles
School of Business and Economics
Los Angeles, CA 90032

California State University, Northridge
School of Business Administration and Economics
Northridge, CA 91324

California State University, Sacramento
School of Business Administration
6000 Jay Street
Sacramento, CA 95819

California State University, San Diego
School of Business Administration
San Diego, CA 92115

California State University, San Francisco
School of Business
1600 Holloway Avenue
San Francisco, CA 94132

California State University, San Jose
School of Business
San Jose, CA 95192

California State University, Sonoma
Department of Business Administration
Sonoma, CA 94928

California State University, San Luis Obline
Department of Business Administration
San Luis Obline, CA 93407

Canisius College
School of Business Administration
Buffalo, NY 14208

Capital University
Department of Business Administration and
    Economics
Columbus, OH 43209

Carnegie-Mellon University Graduate School of
    Industrial Administration
Pittsburgh, PA 15213

Case Western Reserve University
School of Management
Cleveland, OH 41106

Centenary College
Shreveport, LA 71104

Central Michigan University
School of Business Administration
Mount Pleasant, MI 48858

Central Missouri State University
School of Business and Economics
Warrensburg, MO 64096

Central State University
School of Business
Edmond, OK 73034

Chaminade-University of Honolulu
Honolulu, HI 96816

Chapman College
Department of Business Administration
Orange, CA 92666

The Citadel
Charleston, SC 29409

City University of New York
The Bernard M. Baruch College

School of Business and Public Administration
17 Lexington Avenue
New York, NY 10010

Claremount Graduate School
Department of Business Administration
Claremount, CA 91711

Clarion State College
Division of Business Administration
Clarion, PA 16214

Clark University
Division of Business Administration
Worcester, MA 01610

Clarkson College of Technology
Potsdam, NY 13676

Clemson University
College of Industrial Management and Textile
    Science
Clemson, SC 29631

Cleveland State University
The James J. Nance College of Business
    Administration
Cleveland, OH 44115

College of Insurance
New York, NY 10038

College of Notre Dame
Belmont, CA 94002

College of Saint Rose
Albany, NY 12203

College of Saint Thomas
St. Paul, MN 55105

College of William and Mary
School of Business Administration
Williamsburg, VA 23185

Colorado State University
College of Business
Fort Collins, CO 80521

Columbia University
Graduate School of Business
New York, NY 10027

Columbus College
Department of Business Administration
Columbus, GA 31907

Cornell University
Graduate School of Business and Public
  Administration
Ithaca, NY 14850

Creighton University
College of Business Administration
Omaha, NE 68178

Dartmouth College
The Amos Tuck School of Business Administration
Hanover, NH 03755

DePaul University
College of Commerce
Chicago, IL 60604

Delta State University
Department of Business Administration
Cleveland, MS 38732

Dowling College
Oakdale, NY 11769

Drake University
College of Business Administration
25th and University
Des Moines, IA 50311

Drexel University
College of Business and Administration
Philadelphia, PA 19104

Drury College
Breech School of Business Administration
Springfield, MO 65802

Duke University
School of Business Administration
Durham, NC 27706

Duquesne University
Graduate School of Business and Administration
Pittsburgh, PA 15219

East Carolina University
School of Business
Greenville, NC 27834

East Tennessee State University
College of Business Administration and Economics
Johnson City, TN 37601

East Texas State University
College of Business Administration
Commerce, TX 75428

East Illinois University
School of Business
Charleston, IL 61920

Eastern Kentucky University
College of Business
Richmond, KY 40475

Eastern Michigan University
College of Business
Ypsilanti, MI 48197

Eastern New Mexico University
Portales, NM 88130

Eastern Washington State College
School of Business and Administration
Cheney, WA 99004

Emory University
Graduate School of Business Administration
Atlanta, GA 30322

Emporia State University
Emporia, KA 66801

Fairleigh Dickinson University
College of Business Administration
Teaneck, NJ 07666

Florida Atlantic University
College of Business Administration
Boca Raton, FL 33432

Florida International University
College of Business Administration
Miami, FL 33199

Florida State University
School of Business
Tallahassee, FL 32306

Florida Technological University
College of Business Administration
Orlando, FL 32916

Fordham University
College of Business Administration
Bronx, NY 10458

Furman University
Department of Economics and Business
  Administration
Greenville, SC 29613

Gannon College
Division of Business Administration
Erie, PA 16501

George Mason University
Department of Business Administration
Fairfax, VA 22030

George Washington University
School of Government and Business Administration
Washington, DC 20006

Georgetown University
College of Business Administration
Washington, DC 20007

Georgia College
School of Business Administration
Milledgeville, GA 31061

Georgia Institute of Technology
College of Industrial Management
225 North Avenue, NW
Atlanta, GA 30332

Georgia Southern College
School of Business
Statesboro, GA 30458

Georgia State University
School of Business Administration
33 Gilmer Street, SE
Atlanta, GA 30303

Gonzaga University
School of Business Administration
Spokane, WA 99202

Governors State University
College of Business and Public Service
Park Forest South, IL 60466

Grand Valley State College
School of Business and Economics
Allendale, MI 49401

Hartford Graduate Center
Department of Management
Hartford, CT 06120

Harvard University
Graduate School of Business Administration
Soldiers Field
Boston, MA 02163

Hofstra University
School of Business
1000 Fulton Avenue
Hempstead, NY 11550

Houston Baptist University
Department of Business Administration
Houston, TX 77036

Howard University
School of Business and Public Administration
Washington, DC 20001

Idaho State University
College of Business
Pocatello, ID 83201

Illinois Benedictine College
Lisle, IL 60532

Illinois Insitute of Technology
Stuart School of Management and Finance
Chicago, IL 60616

Illinois State University
School of Business
Normal, IL 61761

Indiana Central University
Department of Business Administration
Indianapolis, IN 46227

Indiana University
The Graduate School of Business
Bloomington, IN 47401

Indiana University
School of Business
Fort Wayne, IN 46805

Indiana University
School of Business
Gary, IN 46408

Indiana University
School of Business
South Bend, IN 46615

Indiana University of Pennsylvania
School of Business
Indiana, PA 15701

Indiana University-Purdue
School of Business Administration
Fort Wayne, IN 46805

Iona College
School of Business Administration
New Rochelle, NY 10801

Jackson State College
Jackson, MS 39217

Jacksonville State University
Jacksonville, AL 36265

James Madison University
Harrisonburg, VA 22801

John Carroll University
School of Business
Cleveland, OH 44118

Kansas State University
College of Business Administration
Manhattan, KS 66506

Kent State University
College of Business Administration
Kent, OH 44242

LaSalle College
School of Business
Philadelphia, PA 19141

Lehigh University
College of Business and Economics
Bethlehem, PA 18015

Lewis University
Lockport, IL 60441

Lincoln University
School of Business
San Francisco, CA 94118

Lincoln University
Jefferson City, MO 65101

Lindenwood College
St. Charles, MO 63301

Long Island University
Brooklyn Center
School of Business Administration
Brooklyn, NY 11201

Long Island University
C.W. Post Center
School of Business Administration
Greenvale, NY 11548

Louisiana State University
College of Business Administration
Baton Rouge, LA 70803

Louisiana Tech University
College of Administration and Business
Box 5796, Tech Station
Ruston, LA 71270

Loyola College
Department of Accounting and Business
    Administration
Baltimore, MD 21210

Loyola University
School of Business Administration
Lewis Towers
820 North Michigan Avenue
Chicago, IL 60611

Loyola University
College of Business Administration
New Orleans, LA 70118

Loyola Marymount University
Los Angeles, CA 90045

Lynchburg University
School of Business
Lynchburg, VA 24505

Manhattan College
Riverdale, NY 10471

Mankato State College
School of Business
Mankato, MN 56001

Marist College
Poughkeepsie, NY 12601

Marquette University
The Robert A. Johnston College of Business
Administration
Milwaukee, WI 53233

Marshall University
School of Business
Huntington, WV 25701

Marywood College
Department of Business
Scranton, PA 18509

Massachusetts Institute of Technology
Alfred P. Sloan School of Management
Cambridge, MA 02139

McNeese State University
School of Business
Lake Charles, LA 70601

Memphis State University
College of Business Administration
Memphis, TN 38152

Miami University
School of Business Administration
Oxford, OH 45056

Michigan State University
The Graduate School of Business Administration
East Lansing, MI 48823

Michigan Technological University
School of Business and Engineering Administration
Houghton, MI 49931

Middle Tennessee State University
School of Business and Economics
Murfreesboro, TN 37130

Mississippi College
Division of Business and Economics
Clinton, MS 39058

Mississippi State University
College of Business and Industry
Mississippi State, MS 39762

Monmouth College
Department of Business Administration
West Long Branch, NJ 07764

Moorhead State College
Division of Business
Moorhead, MN 56560

Morgan State College
Department of Economics and Business
Baltimore, MD 21239

Mount Saint Mary's College
Hooksett, NH 03106

Murray State University
School of Business
Murray, KY 42071

New Hampshire College
Department of Business Administration
Manchester, NH 03104

New Mexico State University
College of Business Administration and Economics
Las Cruces, NM 88003

New York Institute of Technology
Division of Business and Management
888 Seventh Avenue
New York, NY 10019

New York University
College of Business and Public Administration
Washington Square
New York, NY 10003

Nicholls State University
College of Business Administration
Thibodaux, LA 70301

North Texas State University
College of Business Administration
Denton, TX 76203

Northeast Louisiana University
College of Business Administration
Monroe, LA 71201

Northeast Missouri State University
School of Business
Kirksville, MO 63501

Northeastern University
College of Business Administration
Boston, MA 02115

Northern Arizona University
College of Business Administration
Flagstaff, AZ 86001

Northern Illinois University
College of Business
De Kalb, IL 60115

Northeast Michigan University
Department of Business Administration
Marquette, MI 49855

Northrop University
School of Business
Inglewood, CA 90306

Northwest Missouri State University
Department of Business and Economics
Maryville, MO 64468

Northwestern State University of Louisiana
College of Business
Natchitoches, LA 71457

Northwestern University
Graduate School of Management
Leverone Hall
2001 Sheridan Rd.
Evanston, IL 60201

Nova University
Fort Lauderdale, FL 33314

Oakland University
School of Economics and Management
Rochester, MI 48063

Ohio State University
College of Administrative Science
Columbus, OH 43210

Ohio University
College of Business Administration
Athens, OH 45701

Oklahoma City University
School of Business
Oklahoma City, OK 73106

Oklahoma State University
College of Business Administration
Stillwater, OK 74074

Old Dominion University
School of Business Administration
Norfolk, VA 23508

Oral Roberts University
School of Business Administration
Tulsa, OK 74102

Oregon State University
School of Business and Technology
Corvallis, OR 97331

Pace University
Lubin School of Business Administration
New York, NY 10038

Pace University
School of Business
Pleasantville, NY 10570

Pacific Lutheran University
School of Business Administration
Tacoma, WA 98447

The Pennsylvania State University
College of Business Administration
120 Boucke Building
University Park, PA 16802

Pennsylvania State University, Capitol Campus
Administration and Business Graduate and Under-
　graduate Programs
Middletown, PA 17057

Pepperdine University
School of Business and Management
Los Angeles, CA 90044

Philadelphia College of Textiles and Sciences
Marketing and Management
Philadelphia, PA 19144

Polytechnic Institute of New York
Department of Business Management
Brooklyn, NY 11201

Portland State University
School of Business Administration
P.O. Box 751
Portland, OR 97207

Prairie View Agricultural and Mechanical University
Prairie View, TX 77445

Providence College
Department of Business Administration
Providence, RI 02918

Purdue University
Krannert Graduate School of Industrial
    Administration
West Lafayette, IN 47907

Rensselaer Polytechnic Institute
Troy, NY 12180

Rice University
School of Business Administration
Houston, TX 77001

Rider College
School of Business Administration
Trenton, NJ 08602

Robert Morris College
Pittsburgh, PA 15219

Rochester Institute of Technology
College of Business
Rochester, NY 14623

Rockhurst College
Kansas City, MO 64108

Rollins College
Roy E. Crummer School of Finance and Business
    Administration
Winter Park, FL 32789

Roosevelt University
Walter E. Heller College of Business Administration
430 South Michigan Avenue
Chicago, IL 60605

Rosary College
River Forest, IL 60305

Rutgers University
Graduate School of Business Administration
Newark, NJ 07102

Rutgers University, Camden
Department of Business and Economics
Camden, NJ 08102

Sacred Heart University
School of Business
Bridgeport, CT 06604

Saginaw Valley State College
Department of Business Administration
University Center, MI 48710

Saint Ambrose College
Davenport, IA 52830

Saint Bonaventure University
School of Business
St. Bonaventure, NY 14778

Saint Cloud State College
School of Business
Saint Cloud, MN 56301

St. John's University
College of Business Administration
Utopia and Grand Central Parkways
Jamaica, NY 11432

St. John's University
College of Business Administration
Staten Island, NY 10301

Saint Joseph's College
Philadelphia, PA 19131

Saint Louis University
School of Business and Administration
St. Louis, MO 63108

St. Mary's University
School of Business Administration
2700 Cincinnati Avenue
San Antonio, TX 78284

Samford University
School of Business
Birmingham, AL 35209

Sangamon State University
Springfield, IL 62708

Savannah State College
Department of Business Administration
Savannah, GA 31740

Seattle University
School of Business
Seattle, WA 98122

Seton Hall University
School of Business Administration
South Orange, NJ 07079

Shippensburg State College
Department of Business Administration
Shippensburg, PA 17257

Simmons College
Department of Business Administration
Boston, MA 02115

Southeastern Massachusetts University
School of Business Administration
North Dartmouth, MA 02747

Southeastern University
Department of Business Administration
Washington, DC 20024

Southern Illinois University at Carbondale
School of Business
Carbondale, IL 62901

Southern Illinois University at Edwardsville
Division of Business
Edwardsville, IL 62025

Southern Methodist University
School of Business Administration
Dallas, TX 75222

Southern Oregon State University
Ashland, OR 97520

Stanford University
Graduate School of Business
Stanford, CA 94305

State University of New York at Albany
School of Business
Albany, NY 12222

State University of New York at Binghamton
School of Management
Binghamton, NY 13901

Stephen F. Austin State University
School of Business
Nacogdoches, TX 75961

Stevens Institute of Technology
Department of Management Sciences
Hoboken, NJ 07030

Suffolk University
College of Business Administration
Boston, MA 02114

Sul Ross State University
Department of Business Administration
Alpine, TX 79830

Syracuse University
School of Management
116 College Place
Syracuse, NY 13210

Temple University
School of Business Administration
Philadelphia, PA 19122

Tennessee Technological University
School of Business Administration
Cookeville, TN 38501

Texas Christian University
M.J. Neeley School of Business
Fort Worth, TX 76129

Texas Tech University
Lubbock, TX 79409

Thomas College
Department of Business Administration
Waterville, ME 04901

Trinity College
Washington, DC 20017

Troy State University
Department of Business Administration
Troy, AL 36801

Tulane University
Graduate School of Business Administration
New Orleans, LA 70118

Union College and University
Schenectady, NY 12308

United States International University
School of Business Administration
San Diego, CA 92131

University of Akron
College of Business Administration
Akron, OH 44304

University of Alabama
College of Commerce and Business Administration
Graduate School of Business
University, AL 35486

University of Alabama in Birmingham
School of Business
Birmingham, AL 34294

University of Alaska
School of Business
Anchorage, AL 99514

University of Alaska
School of Business
Fairbanks, AL 99701

University of Arizona
College of Business and Public Administration
Tucson, AZ 85721

University of Arkansas
College of Business Administration
Little Rock, AR 72204

University of Arkansas
College of Business Administration
Fayetteville, AR 72701

University of Baltimore
School of Business
Baltimore, MD 21201

University of Bridgeport
College of Business Administration
Bridgeport, CT 06602

University of California
Graduate School of Business Administration
Berkeley, CA 94720

University of California, Los Angeles
Graduate School of Management
Los Angeles, CA 90024

University of Chicago
The Graduate School of Business
Chicago, IL 60637

University of Cincinnati
College of Business Administration
Cincinnati, OH 45221

University of Colorado
Graduate School of Business Administration
Boulder, CO 80302

University of Connecticut
Department of Business Administration
Storrs, CT 06268

University of Dallas
University of Dallas Station, TX 75061

University of Dayton
School of Business Administration
Dayton, OH 45409

University of Delaware
College of Business and Economics
Newark, DE 19711

University of Denver
College of Business Administration
University Park
Denver, CO 80210

University of Detroit
College of Business and Administration
Graduate School
McNichols Road at Livernois
Detroit, MI 48221

University of Evansville
School of Business Administration
Evansville, IN 47701

University of Georgia
College of Business Administration
Athens, GA 30602

University of Hawaii
College of Business Administration
2404 Maile Way
Honolulu, HI 96822

University of Houston
College of Business Administration
3801 Cullen Boulevard
Houston, TX 77004

University of Idaho
College of Business and Economics
Moscow, ID 83843

University of Illinois
College of Commerce and Business Administration
Urbana, IL 61801

University of Illinois at Chicago Circle
College of Business Administration
Box 4348
Chicago, IL 60680

University of Iowa
College of Business Administration
Iowa City, IA 52242

University of Kansas
School of Business
Lawrence, KS 66044

University of Kentucky
College of Business and Economics
Lexington, KY 40506

University of Louisville
School of Business
Louisville, KY 40208

University of Lowell
Lowell, MA 01854

University of Maine
College of Business Administration
Orono, ME 04473

University of Maryland
College of Business and Management
College Park, MD 20742

University of Massachusetts
School of Business Administration
Amherst, MA 01002

University of Miami
School of Business Administration
Coral Gables, FL 33124

The University of Michigan
Graduate School of Business Administration
Ann Arbor, MI 48104

University of Minnesota
School of Business Administration
Duluth, MN 55812

University of Minnesota
School of Business
Minneapolis, MN 55455

University of Mississippi
School of Business Administration
University, MS 38677

University of Missouri, Columbia
College of Administration and Public Affairs
Columbia, MO 65201

University of Missouri, Kansas City
School of Administration
5100 Rockhill Road
Kansas City, MO 64110

University of Missouri, St. Louis
School of Business Administration
8001 Natural Bridge Road
St. Louis, MO 63121

University of Montana
School of Business Administration
Missoula, MT 59801

University of Nebraska, Lincoln
College of Business Administration
Lincoln, NE 68508

University of Nebraska, Omaha
College of Business Administration
Omaha, NE 68101

University of Nevada, Las Vegas
College of Business and Economics
Las Vegas, NV 89154

University of Nevada, Reno
College of Business Administration
Reno, NV 89507

University of New Hampshire
Whittemore School of Business and Economics
Durham, NH 03824

The University of New Mexico
School of Business and Administrative Sciences
Albuquerque, NM 87131

University of New Orleans
College of Business Administration
New Orleans, LA 70122

University of North Alabama
Florence, AL 35630

University of North Carolina, Chapel Hill
Graduate School of Business Administration
Chapel Hill, NC 27514

The University of North Carolina, Charlotte
College of Business Administration
Charlotte, NC 28213

University of North Carolina, Greensboro
School of Business and Economics
Greensboro, NC 27412

University of North Dakota
College of Business and Public Administration
Grand Forks, ND 58201

University of Northern Iowa
Department of Business
Cedar Falls, IA 50613

University of Notre Dame
College of Business Administration
Notre Dame, IN 46556

University of Oklahoma
College of Business Administration
Norman, OK 73069

University of Oregon
Graduate School of Management and Business
Eugene, OR 97403

University of Pennsylvania
The Wharton School
3620 Locust Walk
Philadelphia, PA 19174

University of Pittsburgh
Graduate School of Business
Pittsburgh, PA 15213

University of Portland
School of Business Administration
Portland, OR 97203

University of Puget Sound
School of Business and Public Administration
Tacoma, WA 98416

University of Rhode Island
College of Business Administration
302 Ballentine Hall
Kingston, RI 02881

University of Richmond
School of Business
Richmond, VA 23173

University of Rochester
The Graduate School of Management
Rochester, NY 14627

University of San Diego
Department of Business Administration
San Diego, CA 92110

University of San Francisco
College of Business Administration
San Francisco, CA 94117

University of Santa Clara
Graduate School of Business and Administration
Santa Clara, CA 95053

University of South Alabama
Mobile, AL 36688

University of South Carolina
Graduate School of Business
Columbia, SC 29208

University of South Dakota
School of Business
Vermillion, SD 57069

University of South Florida
College of Business Administration
Tampa, FL 33630

University of Southern California
Graduate School of Business Administration
University Park
Los Angeles, CA 90007

University of Southern Mississippi
School of Business Administration
Hattiesburg, MS 39401

University of Tennessee
College of Business Administration
Knoxville, TN 37916

University of Tennessee
College of Business Administration
Nashville, TN 37388

University of Tennessee, Chattanooga
Department of Economics and Business
  Administration
Chattanooga, TN 37401

The University of Tennessee, Martin
School of Business Administration
Martin, TN 38237

The University of Texas, Arlington
College of Business Administration
Arlington, TX 76010

University of Texas, San Antonio
College of Business
San Antonio, TX 78284

University of Texas
School of Business
Dallas, TX 75230

University of Toledo
College of Business Administration
Toledo, OH 43606

University of Tulsa
College of Business Administration
Tulsa, OK 74104

University of Utah
College of Business
Salt Lake City, UT 84112

University of Vermont
Burlington, VT 05401

University of Virginia
The Colgate Darden Graduate School of Business
  Administration
Charlottesville, VA 22906

University of Washington
Graduate School of Business Administration
Seattle, WA 98195

University of West Los Angeles
Culver City, CA 90230

University of Wisconsin, La Crosse
School of Business Administration
La Crosse, WI 54601

University of Wisconsin, Madison
Graduate School of Business
Madison, WI 53706

University of Wisconsin, Milwaukee
School of Business Administration
Milwaukee, WI 53201

University of Wisconsin, Oshkosh
School of Business Administration
Oshkosh, WI 54901

University of Wisconsin, Whitewater
College of Business and Economics
Whitewater, WI 53190

University of Wyoming
College of Commerce and Industry
Laramie, WY 82070

Utah State University
College of Business
Logan, UT 84321

Valdosta State College
Department of Business Administration
Valdosta, GA 31601

Vanderbilt University
Graduate School of Management
Nashville, TN 37203

Virginia Commonwealth University
School of Business
Richmond, VA 23220

Virginia Polytechnic Institute
College of Business
Blacksburg, VA 24061

Wake Forest University
Charles H. Babcock School of Business
   Administration
Winston-Salem, NC 27109

Washington State University
College of Economics and Business
Pullman, WA 99163

Washington University
The Graduate School of Business Administration
St. Louis, MO 63130

Wayne State University
School of Business Administration
Detroit, MI 48202

West Georgia College
School of Business
Carrollton, GA 30117

West Texas State University
School of Business
Canyon, TX 79016

West Virginia College of Graduate Studies
Institute, WV 25112

West Virginia University
College of Business and Economics
Morgantown, WV 26506

Western Carolina University
School of Business
Cullowhee, NC 28723

Western Connecticut State College
Danbury, CT 06810

Western Illinois University
Macomb, IL 61455

Western Kentucky University
College of Business and Public Affairs
Bowling Green, KY 42101

Western Michigan University
College of Business
Kalamazoo, MI 49001

Wichita State University
College of Business Administration
Wichita, KS 67208

Widener College
Department of Business Administration
Chester, PA 19013

Williamette University
College of Business Administration
Salem, OR 97301

Wright State University
College of Business and Administration
Dayton, OH 45431

Xavier University
College of Business Administration
Cincinnati, OH 45207

Yale University
School of Business Administration
New Haven, CT 06520

York College of Pennsylvania
Department of Business Administration
York, PA 17405

Youngstown State University
School of Business Administration
Youngstown, OH 44503

NOTES

NOTES

NOTES

NOTES